A
People
and a
Nation

A History of the United States

BRIEF EDITION ▪ VOLUME A: TO 1877 ▪ FIFTH EDITION

Mary Beth Norton
Cornell University

David M. Katzman
University of Kansas

Paul D. Escott
Wake Forest University

Howard P. Chudacoff
Brown University

Thomas G. Paterson
University of Connecticut

William M. Tuttle, Jr.
University of Kansas
and

William J. Brophy
Stephen F. Austin State University

Houghton Mifflin Company   Boston   New York

P9-APB-076

Associate Sponsoring Editor: Colleen Shanley Kyle
Senior Project Editor: Carol Newman
Senior Production/Design Coordinator: Carol Merrigan
Senior Manufacturing Coordinator: Marie Barnes
Senior Marketing Manager: Sandra McGuire

Cover designer: Jon Valk

Cover image: *Indiana Yearly Meeting of Friends*, 1844. Marcus Mote, Earlham College.

Text photographs researched by Pembroke Herbert and
Sandi Rygiel/Picture Research Consultants.

Copyright © 1999 by Houghton Mifflin Company.
All Rights Reserved.

No part of this work may be reproduced or transmitted
in any form or by any means, electronic or mechanical,
including photocopying and recording, or by any
information storage or retrieval system without the
prior written permission of Houghton Mifflin Company
unless such copying is expressly permitted by federal
copyright law. Address inquiries to College Permissions,
Houghton Mifflin Company, 222 Berkeley Street,
Boston, MA 02116-3764.

Printed in the U.S.A.

Library of Congress Catalog Card Number: 98-72223

ISBN: 0-395-92132-5

4 5 6 7 8 9-VH-02 01 00

Brief Contents

Contents

1

Three Old Worlds Create a New, 1492–1600 *3*

2

Europeans Colonize North America, 1600–1640 *25*

3

American Society Takes Shape, 1640–1720 *44*

4

Growth and Diversity, 1720–1770 *65*

5

Severing the Bonds of Empire, 1754–1774 *83*

Maps

Charts

Preface to the Brief Fifth Edition

This text is a condensation and updating of the highly successful Fifth Edition of *A People and a Nation*. As with earlier brief editions, the authors have preserved the strengths of their full-length work—its readability, scholarship, comprehensiveness, and, most important, its dynamic blend of social, cultural, political, foreign relations, and economic history. This treatment of the whole story of United States history is especially suited for short courses or courses in which additional readings are assigned.

In preparing this brief edition, the authors have ensured that it reflects the changes in content and organization incorporated into the full-length Fifth Edition (see the Preface to the full-length edition, which follows). William J. Brophy, who prepared the condensation, collaborated closely with the six authors of the full-length edition to revise with great care; every line was scrutinized. We thus avoided deleting entire sections and attained our objective by paring down detail. Where two examples were used in the full-length edition, we deleted one; where many statistics were presented, we used a few. Although we abridged or deleted some excerpts from diaries and letters, we have retained many quotations and accounts of everyday life.

Creation of the Brief Edition

The brief edition is available in both one-volume and two-volume formats. The two-volume format divides as follows: Volume A contains Chapters 1 through 16, beginning with a discussion of three cultures—American, African, and European—that intersected during the exploration and colonization of the New World and ending with a discussion of the Reconstruction era. Volume B contains Chapters 16 through 33, beginning its coverage at Reconstruction and extending the history of the American people to the present. The chapter on Reconstruction appears in both volumes

to provide greater flexibility in matching a volume to the historical span covered by a specific course.

While the following Preface to the full-length Fifth Edition elaborates on specific content changes, in brief, the authors paid increased attention to the following: the interaction of the private sphere of everyday life with the public sphere of politics and government; grassroots movements; religion; the emerging cultural globalism of American foreign relations; the development of the American West; and the relationship of the people to the land, including conflict over access to natural resources. These new emphases, as well as the up-to-date scholarship on which they are based, are retained in the Brief Fifth Edition.

Changes in This Edition

While each author feels answerable for the whole of *A People and a Nation*, we take primary responsibility for particular chapters: Mary Beth Norton, Chapters 1 through 8; David M. Katzman, Chapters 9, 10, 12, and 13; Paul D. Escott, Chapters 11, 14, 15, and 16; Howard P. Chudacoff, Chapters 17 through 21 and 24; Thomas G. Paterson, Chapters 22, 23, 26, 29, and 30; William J. Tuttle, Jr., Chapters 25, 27, 28, and 31 through 33.

A number of useful learning and teaching aids accompany the Fifth Edition of *A People and a Nation*, Brief Edition. They are designed to help instructors and students achieve their teaching and learning goals. *@history: an interactive American history source* is a multimedia teaching/learning package that combines a variety of material on a cross-platformed CD-ROM—primary sources (text and graphic), video, and audio—with activities that can be used to analyze, interpret, and discuss primary sources; to enhance collaborative learning; and to create multimedia lecture presentations. *@history* also has an

Study and Teaching Aids

accompanying website, located at *www.hmco.com/college/*, where additional primary sources, on-line resources for *A People and a Nation*, and links to relevant sites can be found.

The two-volume *Study Guide*, prepared by George Warren and Cynthia Ricketson of Central Piedmont Community College, includes an introductory chapter on studying history that focuses on interpreting historical facts, test-taking hints, and critical analysis. The guide also includes learning objectives, a thematic guide, lists of terms, multiple-choice and essay questions for each chapter, as well as map exercises and sections on organizing information of some chapters. An answer key alerts students to the correct response and also explains why the other choices are wrong.

A new *Instructor's Resource Manual with Test Items*, prepared by Donald Frazier of Texas Christian University, contains ten chronological resource units in addition to teaching ideas for each chapter of the text. Each chronological resource unit includes sections on geography, technology, physical and material culture, historical sites, documentary films, popular films, and music. The manual also includes for each text chapter an overview of material in the chapter, a brief list of learning objectives, a chapter outline, ideas for classroom activities, discussion questions, and ideas for paper topics. There are also more than 1,000 new multiple-choice questions, identification terms, and essay questions.

A *Computerized Test Item File* is available to adopters for both Windows and Macintosh computers. This program allows professors to create customized tests by editing and adding questions.

There is also a set of over one hundred fifty full-color *American History Map Transparencies*, available in two volume sets upon adoption.

A variety of *videos*, documentaries and docudramas by major film producers, is available for use with *A People and a Nation*.

Please contact your local Houghton Mifflin representative for more information about the ancillary items or to obtain desk copies.

Acknowledgments

Author teams rely on review panels to help create and execute successful revision plans. Many historians advised us on the revision of this fifth edition, and the book is better because of their thoughtful insights and recommendations. We heartily thank:

James H. O'Donnell III, *Marietta College*

Linda Madson Papageorge, *Kennesaw State University*

William D. Young, *Johnson County Community College*

Monica Maria Tetzlaff, *Indiana University South Bend*

Ann DeJesús Riley, *Hartnell College*

Richard M. Ugland, *Ohio State University*

Regina Lee Blaszczyk, *Boston University*

Richard M. Chapman, *Concordia College*

Patrick J. Kelly, *University of Texas at San Antonio*

Finally, we want to thank the many people who have contributed their thoughts and labors to this work, including the talented staff at Houghton Mifflin.

For the authors, WILLIAM J. BROPHY

Preface to the Full-Length Fifth Edition

Some twenty years ago, when we first embarked on this textbook-writing adventure, most survey texts adequately covered American politics and diplomacy, important historical events, and the famous people at the top of the hierarchy of power, but something was missing: the stories of ordinary Americans. Our experience as teachers told us that, although a rich scholarship in social history had emerged, it was not yet being incorporated into survey texts. We set out to weave this significant dimension of American history into the traditional fabric of party politics, congressional legislation, wars, economic patterns, and local and state government. The response to our approach proved exceptionally gratifying.

As we wrote subsequent editions, always challenged by enriching scholarship, the task changed from "inserting" social history to integrating it fully into the historical narrative and treating social history not only as the study of the private lives of Americans but also as power relationships among competing groups that looked to the public sphere of politics and government to mediate their differences. In this new edition we especially worked to accomplish this new task. After all, like other teachers and students, we are always recreating our past, restructuring our memory, rediscovering the personalities and events that have shaped us, inspired us, and bedeviled us. This book represents our rediscovery of America's history—its diverse people and the nation they created and have sustained. As this book demonstrates, there are many different Americans and many different memories. We have sought to present all of them, in both triumph and tragedy, in both division and unity.

After meeting in frank and searching planning sessions, critiquing one another's work, and reading numerous evaluations of the fourth edition of *A People and a Nation*, we developed a plan for this edition. Guided by up-to-date scholarship, we

New Thematic Emphases

decided to place new emphasis on several themes and subjects that we had discussed in previous editions but believed needed more attention: the interaction of the private sphere of everyday life with the public sphere of politics and government; grass-roots movements; religion; the emerging cultural globalism of American foreign relations; the development of the American West; and the relationship of people to the land, including conflict over access to natural resources. By reexamining every sentence, editing every paragraph, and condensing, reconfiguring, and reconceptualizing chapters (see below), we accomplished a thorough revision (reducing the book by one chapter) while including a considerable amount of fresh material for new emphases, examples, and interpretations.

As before, we challenge students to think about the meaning of American history, not just to memorize facts. Through a readable narrative about all of the American people, we invite students to take themselves back in time to experience what it was like to live in—and to make life's choices in—a different era. Chapter-opening vignettes that dramatically recount stories of people contending with their times help define the key questions of a chapter (two-thirds of the vignettes are new to this edition). Succinct, focused introductions and conclusions frame each chapter. Illustrations, graphs, tables, and maps tied closely to text encourage visual and statistical explorations. We do not detail historiographical debates, but we acknowledge interpretations different from our own, and in the "Suggestions for Further Reading" sections at the end of each chapter we cite works with varying points of view to demonstrate that the writing of history is very much infused with debate.

Especially successful in the fourth edition, and strengthened here, is the "How Do Historians

Know?" feature, which explains how historians go about using evidence to arrive at conclusions. In this

"How Do Historians Know?"

highlighted section, our discussion—coupled with illustrations—explores how historians can draw conclusions from a variety of sources: crafts, political cartoons, maps, medical records, diaries, tape recordings, postcards, census data, telegrams, popular art, photographs, and more. This feature also helps students to understand how scholars can claim knowledge about historical events and trends. More than half of these discussions are new to this edition.

A People and a Nation is comprehensive in its treatment of the many ways in which Americans have defined themselves—by gender, race, class, region, ethnicity, religion, sexual orientation—and of the

How We Study the Past

many subjects that have reflected Americans' multidimensional experiences: social, political, economic, diplomatic, military, environmental, intellectual, cultural, and more. We highlight the remarkably diverse everyday life of the American people—in cities and on farms and ranches, in factories and in corporate headquarters, in neighborhood meetings and in powerful political chambers, in love relationships and in hate groups, in recreation and in the workplace, in the classroom and in military uniform, in secret national security conferences and in public foreign relations debates, in church and in prison, in polluted environments and in conservation areas. We pay particular attention to lifestyles, diet and dress, family life and structure, labor conditions, gender roles, and childbearing and child rearing. By discussing music, sports, theater, print media, film, radio, television, graphic arts, and literature—in both "high" culture and "low" culture—we explore how Americans have entertained and informed themselves.

The private sphere of everyday life always interacts with the public sphere of politics and government. To understand how Americans have sought to protect their different ways of life and to work out solutions to thorny problems, we emphasize their expectations of government at the local, state, and federal levels; government's role in providing answers; the lobbying of interest groups; the campaigns and outcomes of elections; and the hierarchy of power in any period. Because the United States has long been a major participant in world affairs, we explore America's descent into wars, interventions in other nations, empire building, immigration patterns, images of foreign peoples, cross-national cultural ties, and international economic trends.

Mary Beth Norton, who had primary responsibility for Chapters 1 through 8, further developed her comparative focus in Chapters 1 and

Major Changes in This Edition

2, explaining the growth of contrasting American, African, and European societies in the colonial world, giving new attention to the Spanish borderlands. Chapter 3 includes new discussion of the introduction of slavery into English mainland colonies and comparisons with New France and the Spanish borderlands. Chapter 4 has been recast with new emphasis on intercultural interactions among Indians and Europeans and comparisons of families in New France, the Spanish borderlands, and the English colonies (including Indian and mixed-race families). Chapter 7 includes new material on economic/fiscal issues in the Confederation period.

David M. Katzman, who had primary responsibility for Chapters 9, 10, 12, and 13, rewrote to emphasize the role of the federal government and debates over centralized political authority. New emphases are found in his discussion of the conquering of the West (including a new vignette featuring Lewis and Clark in Chapter 9) and the growth of a Mexican-American culture in the Southwest (Chapter 12). He also widened his presentation of ethnic diversity, mental health reform, family and marriage (including divorce laws and women's property legislation), and manifest destiny.

Paul D. Escott, who had primary responsibility for Chapters 11, 14, 15, and 16, introduced new material on the westward movement of slaveholders and slaves and attitudes toward centralized government, African-American soldiers during the Civil

War, and Confederate relations with Indians in the West. A new chart details the unprecedented losses of the Civil War, and several new and rarely seen photographs capture the drama of the Civil War period on many levels.

Howard P. Chudacoff, who had primary responsibility for Chapters 17 through 21 and 24, added new material on and gave new thematic emphasis to land (and water) control, conflict over access to natural resources, and environmental management in a newly titled Chapter 17, "The Development of the West and South, 1877–1892." Multiracial composition and racial tensions in the West are highlighted in Chapters 17 and 19, and new material is also presented on home life—indoor and family amusements and the impact of engineers and technology on household life—in Chapter 19. Chudacoff also reworked the section on agrarian protest and Populism, especially in the Rockies and Far West, and reconceptualized Gilded Age politics, adding the religio-cultural dimension (Chapter 20). To his discussion of Progressive reform (Chapter 21), he added coverage of women's clubs, the National Consumer's League, and federal policy on resource conservation. In his new account of the 1920s (Chapter 24), he emphasized the clash between "tried-and-true" and "modern" values and added new references to lobbying as a major influence in political decision making.

Thomas G. Paterson, who had primary responsibility for Chapters 22, 23, 26, 29, and 30, gave added emphasis to the theme of cultural relations and the conditioning of the foreign relations decision-making environment by ideology and images of foreign peoples. For Chapter 22, he included new material on relations with Africa, Canada, China, Chile, and Hawai'i and on international environmental agreements. In Chapter 23, on the First World War, the role of women in the peace movement, African-American attitudes toward the war, the economic impact of the war, and treatment of the war dead also received added attention. In Chapter 26, newly titled "Peaceseekers and Warmakers: United States Foreign Relations, 1920–1941," Paterson integrated new material on the role of nongovernmental organizations such

as the Rockefeller Foundation and the Americanization of Europe. As part of the restructuring of the post-1945 chapters in the text, Chapters 29 and 30 carry the foreign relations story to the present. These chapters, well cross-referenced, especially reflect the post–Cold War declassification of documents from foreign sources (Russian, Chinese, and German, for example). Here the reader will discover new examinations of the origins of the Korean War, the Cuban missile crisis, Japan's "economic miracle," covert activities of the Central Intelligence Agency, human rights, United States Information Agency propaganda, the Middle East peace process, Haiti, and the debate over foreign aid. In lengthy coverage of the Vietnam War, Paterson included new material on Ho Chi Minh's relationship with Americans in 1945, the Tonkin Gulf crisis, and the My Lai massacre.

William M. Tuttle, Jr., had primary responsibility for Chapters 25 and 27, and the post-1945 Chapters 28 and 31 through 33. In Chapter 25, he added new material on Social Security and the end of the New Deal. In Chapter 27 on the Second World War, readers will find new discussions of race and ethnic relations, women and children, and the decision to drop the atomic bomb. Tuttle substantially rewrote and reorganized the material on post-1945 domestic history, reducing the number of chapters covering this period by one. In a new Chapter 28 he interweaves the political, economic, social, and cultural history from 1945 to 1961, adding fresh material on Cold War politics, civil rights, and the baby boom. Chapter 31 takes the story from 1961 to 1974, shedding new light on the Equal Rights Amendment, women in the civil rights movement, *Roe v. Wade*, and Richard Nixon and the Watergate tapes. The next chapter incorporates recent studies on economic woes, the new immigration from Latin America and Asia, social polarization, and the rise of political and cultural conservatism in the 1970s and 1980s. Chapter 33, which concludes the book, is a new history of the 1990s, focusing on Americans' political disaffection and on their hopes and fears as they approach the twenty-first century.

The multidimensional Appendix, prepared by Thomas G. Paterson, includes a new, extensive table on the "Fifty States, the District of Columbia, and Puerto Rico." Here students will discover essential information on dates of admission with rank, capital cities, population with rank, racial/ethnic distribution, per capita personal income with rank, and total area in square miles. Once again, the Appendix begins with a guide to reference works on key subjects in American history. Students may wish to use this updated and enlarged list of encyclopedias, atlases, chronologies, and other books when they start to explore topics for research papers, when they seek precise definitions or dates, when they need biographical profiles, or when they chart territorial or demographic changes. The table of statistics on key features of the American people and nation also have been updated and expanded, as have the tables on presidential elections, the cabinet members of all administrations, party strength in Congress, and the justices of the Supreme Court.

Many instructors and students who have used this book in their courses have found its many learning and teaching aids very useful. The most

Study and Teaching Aids

exciting addition to our ancillary lineup is *@history: an interactive American history source.* This multimedia teaching/learning package combines a variety of material—primary sources (text and graphic), videos, audio, and links to Web sites—with activities that can be used to analyze, interpret, and discuss primary sources; to enhance collaborative learning; and to create multimedia presentations. *@history* provides instructors with an interactive multimedia tool that can improve the analytical skills of students and introduce them to historical sources.

The *Study Guide*, prepared by George Warren and Cynthia Ricketson of Central Piedmont Community College, includes an introductory chapter on studying history that focuses on interpreting historical facts, test-taking hints, and critical analysis. The guide also includes learning objectives, a thematic guide, lists of terms, multiple-choice and essay questions for each chapter, as well as map exercises and sections on organizing information for some chapters. An answer key alerts students to the correct response and also explains why the other choices are wrong.

A *Computerized Study Guide* is also available for students. It provides approximately 15 multiple-choice questions for each chapter and functions as a tutorial that gives students information on incorrect as well as correct answers. The computerized guide is available in Macintosh, IBM, and IBM-compatible formats.

"A new *Instructor's Resource Manual*, prepared by Donald Frazier, Marvin Schultz, and Bruce Winders of Texas Christian University and Robert Pace of Longwood College, contains ten chronological resource units in addition to teaching ideas for each chapter of the textbook. Each chronological resource unit includes sections on geography, technology, physical and material culture (artifacts), historical sites, documentary films, popular films, and music. The manual also includes for each textbook chapter a content overview, a brief list of learning objectives, a comprehensive chapter outline, ideas for classroom activities, discussion questions, and ideas for paper topics.

A *Test Items* file, also prepared by George Warren, provides approximately 1,700 new multiple-choice questions, more than 1,000 identification terms, and approximately 500 essay questions.

A *Computerized Test Items File* for IBM and Macintosh computers is available to adopters. This computerized version of the printed *Test Items* file allows professors to create customized tests by editing and adding questions.

A set of full-color map transparencies is also available to instructors on adoption. A variety of videos—documentaries and docudramas by major film producers—is available for use with *A People and a Nation.*

At each stage of this project, historians read drafts of our chapters. Their suggestions, corrections, and pleas helped guide us through our revisions. We could not include

Acknowledgments

all of their recommendations, but the book is better for our having heeded most of their advice.

We heartily thank

Diane Allen, *Columbia Gorge Community College*
David E. Conrad, *Southern Illinois University*
Paige Cubbison, *Miami Dade Community College, Kendall*
Joseph A. Devine, Jr., *Stephen F. Austin State University*
Shirley M. Eoff, *Angelo State University*
Maurine Greenwald, *University of Pittsburgh*
Melanie Gustafson, *University of Vermont*
D. Harland Hagler, *University of North Texas*
Craig Hendricks, *Long Beach City College*
Robert Kenzer, *University of Richmond*
Timothy Koerner, *Oakland Community College*
Lisa M. Lane, *Miracosta College*
Larry MacLestch, *Mendocino College*
Jeff Ostler, *University of Oregon*
William Robbins, *Oregon State University*
Athan Theoharis, *Marquette University*
Lynn Weiner, *Roosevelt University*
Marianne S. Wokeck, *Indiana University–Purdue University of Indianapolis*
Gerald Wolff, *University of South Dakota*

Once again we thank the extraordinary Houghton Mifflin team who designed, edited, produced, and nourished this book. Their high standards and careful attention to both general structure and fine detail are unmatched in publishing. Many thanks to Jean Woy, editor-in-chief; Pat Coryell, senior sponsoring editor; Ann West, basic book editor; Jeffrey Greene, senior associate editor, Keith Mahoney, assistant editor; Carol Newman, senior project editor; Carol Merrigan, senior production/design coordinator; Charlotte Miller, art editor; and Florence Cadran, manufacturing manager.

For helping us in many essential ways, we also extend our thanks to Michael Donoghue, Jan D. Emerson, Steven Jacobson, Andrea Katzman, Eric Katzman, Sharyn Brooks Katzman, Walter D. Kamphoefner, G. Stanley Lemons, Pam Levitt, Shane J. Maddock, Jill Norgren, Aaron M. Paterson, Norman G. Radford, Zil-e-Rehman, Paul L. Silver, Peter Solonysznyi, Julee Stephens, Luci Tapahonso, Kathryn Nemeth Tuttle, Samuel Watkins Tuttle, and Daniel H. Usner, Jr. Some of these individuals sent us suggestions for improving *A People and a Nation*, and we took their recommendations seriously. We welcome comments from professors and students about this new edition, too.

For the authors, THOMAS G. PATERSON

A
People
and a
Nation

BRIEF EDITION

CHAPTER

1

Three Old Worlds
Create a New
1492–1600

At birth, she was called Malinalli. The Spaniards christened her
Doña Marina. History knows her as Malinche, a name formed by
adding the Aztec suffix *che*, a term of respect, to her original
name. She has been celebrated as the symbolic mother of the modern
Mexican people and maligned as a traitor to Mexico's ancient residents.

Born sometime between 1502 and 1505, Malinalli was the daughter
of a village chief within the Aztec Empire. Her father died while she was
young, and her mother soon remarried. To protect the inheritance of the
son born to that second marriage, the mother sold her daughter into
slavery. Eventually, Malinalli came to live with Mayan-speaking people.

In 1519, she was presented as a gift to the Spanish conquistador
Hernán Cortés. Cortés, who first arrived in the Spanish West Indies in
1504, embarked for the mainland in search of wealthy cities rumored to
exist there. Little did he know that Doña Marina would be one of the
keys to his conquest of Mexico. She spoke the languages of both the
Aztecs and the Mayas, learned Spanish, and became Cortés's translator
and mistress. Accompanying Cortés on his travels in Mexico, Doña Marina did more than simply interpret words for him: she explained the
meanings that lay behind the language, opening the Aztec world to the
Spaniards.

The Aztecs and subsequent Mexican historians have blamed Malinche for betraying her own people. But who were her people? The

Aztecs, in whose empire she had been born and who had sold her as a slave? The Mayas, among whom she was raised? Or the Europeans, who relied on her translations?

Malinche's life history, and her dual image as betrayer of ancient Mexico and symbolic mother of the modern mixed-race nation, encapsulate many of the ambiguities of the first encounter between Europeans and Americans. Sold into slavery by her Aztec-connected family, she owed that people little loyalty. The Spaniards gave her respect, yet she did not become Spanish: Cortés never married her. Malinche was caught between two worlds, part of both and of neither, alternately praised and blamed for her actions. Many people from both sides of the Atlantic were to meet the same fate as they attempted to cope with the rapidly changing world of the fifteenth and sixteenth centuries.

As European explorers and colonizers sought to exploit the resources of the rest of the globe, peoples from different races and cultural traditions came into regular contact for the first time. All were profoundly changed by the resulting interaction. By the time Cortés and his troops invaded Mexico in 1519, the age of European expansion and colonization was already well under way. Over the next 350 years, Europeans would spread their influence across the globe. The history of the tiny colonies in North America that became the first components of the United States must be seen in this broad context of European exploration and exploitation.

When the Europeans arrived, the Americas were already populated by skillful plant breeders who had developed vegetable crops more nutritious and productive than those grown in Europe, Asia, or Africa. They had also invented systems of writing and mathematics and had created calendars fully as accurate as those used on the other side of the Atlantic. In the Americas, as in Europe, states rose and fell as leaders succeeded or failed at the goal of expanding their political and economic power. The Europeans' arrival in their world immeasurably altered the Americans' struggles with each other.

After 1400, European nations tried to improve their positions relative to neighboring countries

not only by waging wars on their own continent but also by acquiring valuable colonies and trading posts elsewhere in the world. In response, nations in Asia, Africa, and the Americas attempted to use the alien intruders to their own advantage or, failing that, to adapt successfully to the Europeans' presence in their midst. All the participants in the resulting interaction of divergent cultures were indelibly affected by the process. The contest among Europeans for control of the Americas and Africa changed the course of history on four continents. Although in the end Europeans emerged politically dominant, they did not control many aspects of the interactions.

 ## American Societies

Human beings probably originated on the continent of Africa, where humanlike remains about 3 million years old have been found in what is now Ethiopia. Over many millennia, the growing human population slowly dispersed to the other continents. About 30,000 years ago, a land bridge that scholars have called Beringia linked the Asian and North American continents at the site of the Bering Strait. Some of the peoples participating in the vast worldwide migration crossed this now-submerged land bridge.

Those forerunners of the American population are known as Paleo-Indians. The earliest confirmed evidence of their presence in the Americas dates to approximately 28,000 years ago. The Paleo-Indians were nomadic hunters of game and gatherers of wild plants. Spreading throughout North and South America, they probably moved as extended families, or *bands*. By about 11,500 years ago, the Paleo-Indians were making fine stone projectile points, which they attached to wooden spears and used to kill and butcher the large mammals then living in the Americas. But as the Ice Age ended and the human population increased, all the large American mammals except the bison (buffalo) disappeared. Scholars cannot agree whether overhunting or the change in climate caused their

Paleo-Indians

• *Important Events* •

30,000–10,000 B.C.E.	Paleo-Indians began migrating from Asia to North America across the Beringia land bridge	1494	Treaty of Tordesillas divides land claims between Spain and Portugal in Africa, India, and South America
7000 B.C.E.	Cultivation of food crops begins in America	1496	Last of the Canary Islands falls to Spanish attack
c. 1000 B.C.E.	Olmec civilization appears	1497	John Cabot reaches North American coast
c. 300–600 C.E.	Height of influence of Teotihuacán		
c. 600–900 C.E.	Classic Mayan civilization	1513	Ponce de León explores Florida
1000 C.E.	Anasazi settlements in modern states of Arizona and New Mexico flourish as trading centers	1518–30	Smallpox epidemic devastates Indian population of West Indies and Central and South America
1001	Norse establish settlement in "Vineland" (Newfoundland)	1519	Hernán Cortés invades Mexico
1050–1250	Height of influence of Cahokia; prevalence of Mississippian culture in midwestern and southeastern United States	1521	Tenochtitlán surrenders to Cortés; Aztec Empire falls to Spaniards
		1534–35	Jacques Cartier explores St. Lawrence River
14th century	Aztec rise to power	1539–42	Hernando de Soto explores southeastern United States
1450s–80s	Portuguese explore and colonize islands in the Mediterranean Atlantic and São Tomé in Gulf of Guinea	1540–42	Francisco Vásquez de Coronado explores southwestern United States
1477	Publication of Marco Polo's *Travels*, describing China	1587–90	Sir Walter Raleigh's Roanoke colony vanishes
1492	Christopher Columbus reaches Bahama Islands	1588	Thomas Harriot publishes *A Briefe and True Report of the New Found Land of Virginia*

demise. In either case, the Paleo-Indians, deprived of their primary source of meat, had to find new ways of survival.

Consequently, by approximately 9,000 years ago, the residents of what is now central Mexico began to cultivate food crops, especially maize (corn), squash, beans, and peppers. In the Andes Mountains of South America, people started to grow potatoes. As knowledge of agricultural techniques improved and spread through the

Importance of Agriculture

Americas, vegetables and maize proved a more reliable source of food than hunting and gathering. Except for those living in the harshest climates, most Americans started to adopt a more sedentary style of life so they could tend fields regularly. Some established permanent settlements; others moved several times a year among fixed sites. All the American cultures emphasized producing sufficient food to support themselves. Although they traded goods, no society ever became dependent on another group for items vital to its survival.

Wherever agriculture dominated the economy, complex civilizations flourished. Such societies were able to accumulate wealth, produce ornamental objects, and create elaborate rituals and ceremonies. In North America, the successful cultivation of nutritious crops seems to have led to the growth and development of all the major civilizations: first the large city-states of Mesoamerica (modern Mexico and Guatemala), then the urban clusters known collectively as the Mississippian culture and located in the present-day United States. Each society reached its height only after achieving success in agriculture. Each later declined and collapsed after reaching the limits of its food supply. Even the powerful Aztec Empire that the Spaniards encountered in 1519 is thought to have been approaching the point at which it could no longer sustain its population.

The Aztecs were the heirs of a series of Mesoamerican civilizations, the history of which stretched back to the Olmecs, who about 3,000 years ago lived near the Gulf of Mexico in large cities dominated by temple pyramids.

Mesoamerican Civilizations

More than 1,000 years later, the Mayan civilization developed on the Yucatán Peninsula. The Mayas built large urban centers containing tall pyramids and temples. They studied astronomy, created the first writing system in the Americas, and developed a richly symbolic religious life. By the fifth century C.E. (Common Era), or about 1,500 years ago, the kings of the Mayan city-states started to war with each other, attempting conquest on a grand scale. Eventually, the constant fighting combined with overpopulation and resulting environmental stress to cause the collapse of the most powerful cities ending the classic era of Mayan civilization by 900 C.E.

The largest Mesoamerican metropolis was contemporary with, and a major trading partner of, the Mayas. Teotihuacán, founded about 300 B.C.E. (Before the Common Era)—some 2,300 years ago—in the Valley of Mexico, was one of the largest cities in the world in the fifth century C.E., with a population of over 100,000. The rulers of Teotihuacán gained their position chiefly through

commerce; their trading network extended hundreds of miles in all directions. Teotihuacán also served as a religious center; pilgrims must have come long distances to visit the impressive Pyramid of the Sun and Pyramid of the Moon and the great temple of Quetzalcoatl—the feathered serpent, the primary god of central Mexico.

Teotihuacán's influence was felt so widely in Mesoamerica before its decline in the eighth century C.E. that some scholars have argued that this Mexican city-state also influenced societies farther north, in what is now the United States. The Moundbuilders of the Ohio River region, who flourished about two thousand years ago, just as Teotihuacán rose to prominence, constructed earthen mounds. But the Ohioan mounds were used as burial sites, not as bases for temple pyramids. Also, the Moundbuilders' economy, which was based on hunting and gathering, bore little resemblance to that of Mesoamerica. Trade goods from as far away as the Great Lakes and the Gulf of Mexico have been found in the mounds, but direct evidence of contact with Teotihuacán is lacking.

Moundbuilders, Anasazi, and Mississippians

The same is true for sites inhabited by the Anasazi peoples in the modern states of Arizona and New Mexico. Pueblo Bonito in Chaco Canyon, a city that by 1000 C.E. consisted of many large adobe buildings constructed along the sides of the canyon, served as a major regional trading center. The Anasazi cultivated maize and other Mesoamerican crops, but they did not construct temple pyramids, nor did their towns resemble those built by their contemporaries in what is now Mexico. Accordingly, scholars have concluded that their contact with Mesoamerica was slight.

More likely, Teotihuacán and later Mesoamerican empires like that of the Aztecs had an impact on the development of the Mississippian culture, which flourished around 1000 C.E. in what is now the midwestern and southeastern United States. This civilization, like those to the south, was based on the cultivation of maize, beans, and squash. Not until about 700 to 900 C.E. were these crops grown successfully in the present-day United

Pueblo Bonito in Chaco Canyon in what is now the state of New Mexico. More than six hundred buildings were present on the well-defended site. The circular structures were kivas, used for food storage and for religious rituals. David Muench photography.

States; soon after their introduction, large cities with plazas and earthen pyramids first appeared in the region. With a population of at least 15,000, the largest of the cities was Cahokia, near modern St. Louis. Until about 1250 C.E., Cahokia was a religious and trading center. Its main pyramid, today called the Monk's Mound, was in 1492 the third largest structure in the Western Hemisphere. Spanish explorers encountered other Mississippian peoples in present-day South Carolina, Alabama, and Georgia in the mid-sixteenth century. The Natchez, a society characterized by temple mounds and autocratic priestly rulers, survived in the lower Mississippi River valley until the 1720s.

The Aztecs' histories tell of the long migration of their people (who called themselves Mexica) into the Valley of Mexico during the twelfth century. The uninhabited ruins of Teotihuacán, which by then had been deserted for at least two hundred years, awed

Aztecs

and mystified the migrants. The Aztecs' primary god, Huitzilopochtli, was a god of war represented by an eagle. Aztec chronicles record that Huitzilopochtli directed the Aztecs to establish their capital at the spot on an island where they saw an eagle eating a serpent (thus symbolizing Huitzilopochtli's triumph over the traditional deity, Quetzalcoatl). That island city became Tenochtitlán, the center of a rigidly stratified society composed of hereditary classes of warriors, merchants, priests, common folk, and slaves.

The Aztecs conquered their neighbors and forced them to pay tribute in luxury items, raw materials, and human beings who could be sacrificed to Huitzilopochtli. The war god's taste for blood was not easily quenched. In the Aztec year Ten Rabbit (1502) at the coronation of Motecuhzoma II (Montezuma, to the Spanish), five thousand people are thought to have been sacrificed by having their still-beating hearts torn from their bodies.

How do historians know that the ruins of Teotihuacán "awed and mystified" the Aztecs when they arrived in the Valley of Mexico at least two hundred years after that city had been abandoned by its inhabitants? One striking indication of the Aztecs' attitude toward the earlier civilization is this beautiful greenstone mask with polished obsidian eyes, which was created at Teotihuacán. Archaeologists found it not there but rather in the ruins of the Aztecs' Templo Mayor, constructed in Tenochtitlán (the site of modern Mexico City) about a thousand years after the mask was sculpted. The temple had two sides, one dedicated to the war god Huitzilopochtli, the other to the rain god Tlaloc.

The place where the two sides met was at the heart of the Aztecs' most sacred site. There they buried this mask, which they must have found at Teotihuacán, about 20 miles from Tenochtitlán. Although we cannot know for certain what the Aztecs intended to accomplish by this gesture, it seems reasonable to conclude that they hoped to draw on the mysterious powers that the mask (and the civilization it represented) symbolized for them. Had they not been awed by it, they never would have buried the mask where they did. Michel Zabe-Thiriat.

The Aztecs believed that they lived in the age of the Fifth Sun. Four times previously, they wrote, the earth and all the people who lived on it had been destroyed. They predicted that their own world would end in earthquakes and hunger. In the Aztec year Thirteen Flint, volcanoes erupted, sickness and hunger spread, wild beasts attacked the Aztecs' children, and an eclipse of the sun darkened the sky. Did some priest wonder whether the Fifth Sun was approaching its end? Eventually, the Aztecs learned that their year Thirteen Flint was called 1492 by the Europeans.

North America in 1492

Over the centuries, the Americans who lived north of Mexico had adapted their once-similar ways of life to very different geographical settings, thus creating the diverse cultures that the Europeans encountered when they first arrived (see map).

Bands that lived in environments not well suited to agriculture because of inadequate rainfall or poor soil, for example, followed a nomadic lifestyle. Within the area of the present-day United States, these groups included the Paiutes and Shoshones, who inhabited the Great Basin (now Nevada and Utah). Because of the difficulty of finding sufficient food for more than a few people, such hunter-gatherer bands were small. Where large game was more plentiful and food supplies therefore more certain, as in present-day Canada and the Great Plains, bands of hunters were somewhat larger.

In more favorable environments, larger groups combined agriculture with gathering, hunting, and fishing. Those who lived near the seacoasts, like the Chinooks of present-day Washington and Oregon, consumed fish and shellfish in addition to growing crops and gathering seeds and berries. Residents of the interior (for example, the Arikaras of the Missouri River valley) hunted large animals

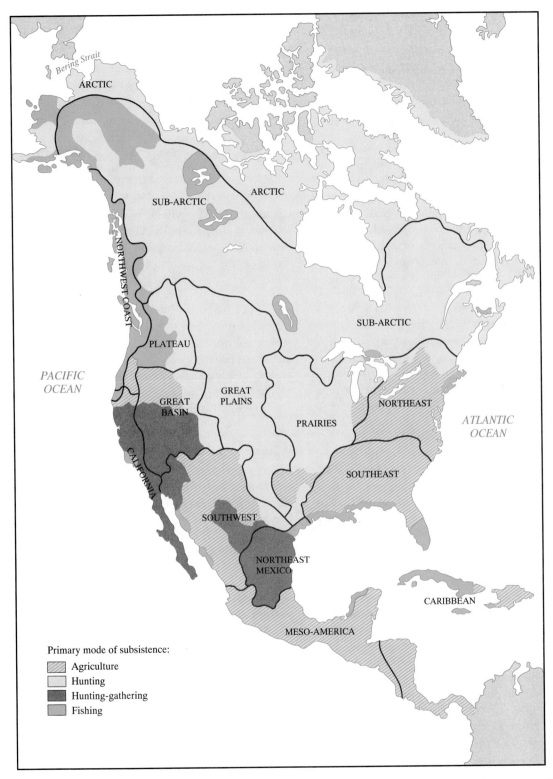

Bering Strait

ARCTIC

ARCTIC

SUB-ARCTIC

NORTHWEST COAST

SUB-ARCTIC

PACIFIC
OCEAN

PLATEAU

GREAT
PLAINS

NORTHEAST

ATLANTIC
OCEAN

GREAT
BASIN

PRAIRIES

CALIFORNIA

SOUTHEAST

SOUTHWEST

NORTHEAST
MEXICO

CARIBBEAN

MESO-AMERICA

Primary mode of subsistence:

Agriculture

Hunting

Hunting-gathering

Fishing

Native Cultures of North America *The natives of the North American continent used the resources of the regions in which they lived. Coastal groups relied on fishing, residents of fertile areas engaged in agriculture, and other peoples employed hunting (often combined with gathering) as a primary mode of subsistence.*

while also cultivating maize, squash, and beans. The Algonkian-speaking peoples of what is now eastern Canada and the northeastern United States also combined hunting and agriculture.

Societies that relied primarily on hunting large animals assigned that task to men and allotted food processing, clothing production, and child rearing to women. Be-

Sexual Division of Labor in North America

fore such nomadic bands acquired horses from the Spaniards, women—occasionally assisted by dogs—also carried the family's belongings whenever the band relocated. Such a sexual division of labor was universal among hunting peoples. Agricultural societies, by contrast, differed in their assignments of work to the sexes. In what is now the southwestern United States, the Pueblo peoples defined agricultural labor as men's work. In the East, Algonkian, Iroquoian, and Muskogean peoples allocated most agricultural chores to women, although men cleared the land. In all the farming societies, women gathered wild foods, prepared food for consumption or storage, and cared for children, while men were responsible for hunting.

The southwestern and eastern agricultural peoples had similar social organizations. They lived in villages, sometimes sizable ones with a thousand or more inhabitants. The Pueblos, descendants of the Anasazi, lived in large, multistory buildings constructed on terraces along the sides of cliffs or other easily defended sites. Northern Iroquois villages (in modern New York State) were composed of large, rectangular, bark-covered structures, or long houses. In the present-day southeastern United States, Muskogeans and southern Algonkians lived in large houses made of thatch. Most eastern villages were surrounded by wood palisades and ditches to aid in fending off attackers. The defensive design of such villages and of the western pueblos discloses the significance of warfare in pre-Columbian America.

In all these agricultural societies, each dwelling housed an extended family defined *matrilineally* (through a female line of descent). Mothers, their married daughters, and their daughters' husbands and children all lived together. Matrilineal descent did not imply *matriarchy*, or the wielding

of power by women, but rather served as a means of reckoning kinship. Extended families were linked into *clans*, also defined by matrilineal ties. The nomadic bands of the Great Plains, by contrast, were most often related *patrilineally* (through the male line).

American leaders governed largely through consensus, but political structures in the various groups differed considerably. Among Pueblo

Native American Politics and Religion

and Muskogean peoples, the village council was the highest political authority; no government structure connected the villages. The Iroquois, by contrast, had an elaborate political hierarchy incorporating villages into nations and nations into a widespread confederation. In all the North American cultures, political power was divided between civil and war leaders, who, unlike Europe's autocratic rulers, wielded authority only so long as they retained the confidence of the people.

The political position of women varied. Women were more likely to assume leadership roles among agricultural peoples than among nomadic hunters. Squaw sachems (female rulers) led Algonkian villages in what is now Massachusetts, but women were never chosen as heads of hunting bands of the Great Plains. Iroquois women did not become chiefs, yet clan matrons exercised political power. Probably the most powerful female chiefs were found in what is now the southeastern United States. In the mid-sixteenth century a female ruler known as the Lady of Cofitachequi governed a large group of villages in present-day western South Carolina.

Americans' religious beliefs varied, but all the peoples were *polytheistic*, worshiping a multitude of gods. One common thread was their integration with nature. Thus each group's most important beliefs and rituals were closely tied to its economy. The major deities of agricultural peoples were associated with cultivation, and their chief festivals centered on planting and harvest. The most important gods of hunters were associated with animals, and their major festivals were related to hunting. A band's economy and women's role in it helped to determine women's potential as religious leaders.

Women held the most prominent positions in those agricultural societies (like the Iroquois) in which they were also the chief food producers.

A wide variety of cultures, comprising more than 5 million people, thus inhabited mainland North America when Europeans arrived. The diverse inhabitants of North America spoke well over one thousand different languages. For obvious reasons, they did not consider themselves one people, nor did they—for the most part—think of uniting to repel the European invaders.

African Societies

Fifteenth-century Africa also housed a variety of cultures adapted to different geographical settings (see map). In the north, along the Mediterranean Sea, lived the Berbers, a Muslim people. (Muslims are adherents of Islam, founded by the prophet Mohammed in the seventh century C.E.) On the east coast of Africa, Muslim city-states engaged in extensive trade with India, the Moluccas (part of modern Indonesia), and China. Through the East African city-states passed a considerable share of the trade between the eastern Mediterranean and the Far East; the rest followed the long land route across Central Asia known as the Silk Road.

In the African interior, south of the Mediterranean coast, lie the great Sahara and Libyan deserts. Below the deserts, much of the continent is divided between tropical rain forests (along the coasts) and grassy plains (in the interior). People speaking a variety of languages and pursuing different economic strategies lived in a wide belt south of the deserts.

Most of the enslaved people carried to North America came from West Africa. The Europeans called this land of tropical forests and small-scale farming Guinea. The northern region of West Africa, or Upper Guinea, was heavily influenced by Islamic culture. As early as the eleventh century C.E., many of the region's inhabitants had become Muslims. Trade between Upper Guinea and the Muslim Mediterranean was sub-Saharan Africa's major connection to Europe and the Middle East.

West Africa (Guinea)

In return for salt, dates, silk, and cotton cloth, Africans exchanged ivory, gold, and slaves with northern merchants.

The people of the so-called Rice Coast of upper Guinea (present-day Gambia, Sénégal, and Guinea) fished and cultivated rice. The Grain Coast, the next region to the south, was thinly populated. Its people concentrated on farming and raising livestock. Both the Rice and the Grain Coasts—especially the former—supplied slaves destined for sale in the Americas, but even more enslaved people came from Lower Guinea.

In West Africa, land was not owned by individuals, but people could be; and the possession of slaves allowed the accumulation of wealth. Slaves—mostly debtors, wartime captives, criminals, or their descendants—were therefore essential components of the African economy. The first slave voyages diverted some of the thriving internal traffic in slaves to Europe or the Americas.

Many of the first slaves destined for sale across the Atlantic came from the Gold Coast, comprising thirty little kingdoms known as the Akan States. By the eighteenth century, though, it was the area farther east, the modern nations of Togo and Benin, that supplied most of the slaves sold in the English colonies. While seeking to enhance their positions by acquiring European trade goods, the Adja kings of the region, which became known as the Slave Coast, encouraged the founding of slave-trading posts and served as middlemen in the trade. Initially, those sent to the Americas came from the ranks of the already enslaved. By the early eighteenth century, however, after the demand for bondspeople in the American colonies had increased dramatically, African rulers appear to have warred on other groups primarily to obtain slaves for sale.

The societies of West Africa, like those of the Americas, assigned different tasks to men and women. In general, the sexes shared agricultural duties. Men also hunted, managed livestock, and did most of the fishing. Women were responsible for childcare, food preparation, and cloth manufacture. Everywhere in West Africa, women were the primary local traders.

Sexual Division of Labor in West Africa

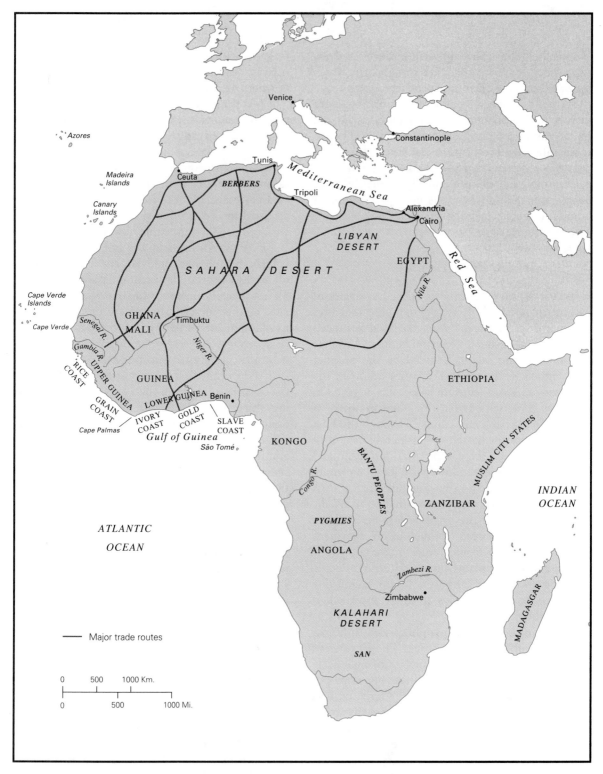

Africa and Its Peoples, c. 1400 *Even before Europeans began to explore Africa's coastlines, its northern regions were linked to the Mediterranean (and thus to Europe) by a network of trade routes.*

Despite different economies and the rivalries among states, the peoples of Lower Guinea had similar social systems. In Lower Guinea, each sex handled its own affairs: just as male political and religious leaders governed men, so females ruled women. In the Dahomean kingdom, for example, every male official had his female counterpart; in the Akan States, chiefs inherited their status through the female line, and each male chief had a female assistant who supervised other women.

Throughout Lower Guinea, religious beliefs likewise stressed complementary male and female roles. Both women and men served as heads of the cults and secret societies that directed the spiritual life of the villages. Young women were initiated into the Sandé cult, young men into Poro. Although West African women (unlike some of their Native American contemporaries) rarely held formal power over men, female religious leaders did govern other members of their sex within the Sandé cult.

West African Religion

The West Africans brought to the Americas, then, were agricultural peoples, skilled at tending livestock, hunting, fishing, and manufacturing cloth from plant fibers and animal skins. Both men and women were accustomed to working communally, alongside other members of their own sex. They were also accustomed to a relatively egalitarian relationship between the sexes, especially within the context of religion. In the New World, they entered societies that had little respect for their cultural traditions.

 ## European Societies

In the fifteenth century, Europeans, too, were agricultural peoples. The daily lives of Europe's rural people had changed little for several hundred years. Split into numerous small, warring countries, Europe was divided linguistically, politically, and economically, yet in social terms Europeans' lives were more similar than different. European societies were hierarchical: a few families wielded arbitrary power over the majority of the people. Europe's kingdoms accordingly resembled those of Africa or Mesoamerica but differed greatly from the more egalitarian, consensus-based societies then established in America north of Mexico.

Most Europeans, like most Africans and Native Americans, lived in small villages. European farmers, who were called *peasants*, owned or leased separate landholdings, but they worked the fields communally. Because fields had to lie fallow (unplanted) every second or third year to regain fertility, families could ensure food supplies only if all the villagers shared the work and the annual crop. Men did most of the fieldwork; women helped out chiefly at planting and harvest. Women's duties consisted primarily of childcare and household tasks, including preserving food, milking cows, and caring for poultry. If a woman's husband was an artisan or a storekeeper in a city, she might assist him in business. Since Europeans kept domesticated animals (pigs, goats, sheep, and cattle) for meat, hunting had little economic importance in their cultures.

Sexual Division of Labor in Europe

Unlike African and Native American societies, men dominated all areas of life in Europe. A few women—notably Queen Elizabeth I of England—achieved status or power, but the vast majority were excluded from positions of political authority. In the Roman Catholic Church and later in the new Protestant denominations, leadership roles were reserved for men. In short, European women generally held inferior social, economic, and political positions.

When the fifteenth century began, European nations were slowly beginning to recover from the devastating epidemic of plague known as the Black Death. Bubonic plague, spread by rats and fleas as well as by human contact, arrived in Europe from China, traveling with long-distance traders along the Silk Road. During the 1360s and 1370s, an estimated one-third of Europe's people died. That led to a precipitous economic decline and to severe social, political, and religious disruption because of the deaths of clergymen and other leading figures.

Black Death

As plague ravaged the population, England and France waged the Hundred Years War

(1337–1453), initiated because the English monarchy claimed the French throne. The war interrupted overland trade routes through France that connected northern Europe to the Italian city-states and thence to Central Asia. Merchants in the eastern Mediterranean thus had to find new ways of reaching their northern markets. They solved that dilemma by forging a regular maritime link with the north to replace the overland route. The use of a triangular, or lateen, sail (rather than the then-standard square rigging) improved the maneuverability of ships. The perfection of navigational instruments like the astrolabe and the quadrant also allowed oceangoing sailors to estimate their position (latitude) by measuring the relationship of sun, moon, or stars to the horizon.

Political, Economic, and Technological Change

In the aftermath of the Hundred Years War, European monarchs relied on nationalistic feelings to consolidate their previously diffuse political power and to raise new revenues through increased taxation of an already hard-pressed peasantry. In England, Henry VII in 1485 founded the Tudor dynasty and began uniting a previously divided land. In France, the successors of Charles VII unified the kingdom. Most successful of all were Ferdinand of Aragón and Isabella of Castile. In 1469 they married and combined their kingdoms, thereby creating the foundation of a strongly Catholic Spain. In 1492, they defeated the Muslims, who had lived in Spain and Portugal for centuries, therefter expelling all Jews and Muslims from their domain.

The fifteenth century also brought technological change to Europe. Movable type and the printing press, invented in Germany in the 1450s, made information more accessible than ever before. Printing stimulated the Europeans' curiosity about fabled lands across the seas, lands they could now read about in books. The most important such work, Marco Polo's *Travels*, printed in 1477, noted that China was bordered on the east by an ocean. Polo's account led many Europeans to believe that they could trade directly with China in oceangoing vessels instead of relying on the Silk Road or the trade route through East Africa.

The European explorations of the fifteenth and sixteenth centuries were made possible by technological advances and by the growing strength of newly powerful national rulers. The primary motivation for exploratory voyages was each country's craving for easy access to desirable African and Asian goods—spices like pepper, cloves, cinnamon, and nutmeg (to season the bland European diet); silk; dyes; perfumes; jewels; and gold. A secondary motive was to spread Christianity around the world. The linking of materialist and spiritual goals might seem contradictory today, but fifteenth-century Europeans saw no conflict.

Motives for Exploration

Early European Explorations and the Columbus Voyages

Before European mariners could discover new lands, they had to discover the oceans. To reach Asia, seafarers needed not just the maneuverable vessels and navigational aids increasingly used in the fourteenth century, but also knowledge of the sea, its currents, and especially its winds. How did the winds run? Where would Atlantic breezes carry their ships?

Europeans learned the answers to these questions in the Mediterranean Atlantic, the expanse of the Atlantic that is south and west of Spain and is bounded by the island groups of the Azores (on the west) and the Canaries (on the south), with the Madeiras in their midst (see map). Europeans reached all three sets of islands during the fourteenth century. The Canaries proved a popular destination for mariners from Iberia (the peninsula that includes Spain and Portugal). Sailing to the Canaries from Europe was easy, because strong winds known as the Northeast Trades blow southward along the Iberian and African coastlines. The problem was getting back. The very winds that had brought the Iberian sailor so quickly to the Canaries now blew directly at him.

Sailing in the Mediterranean Atlantic

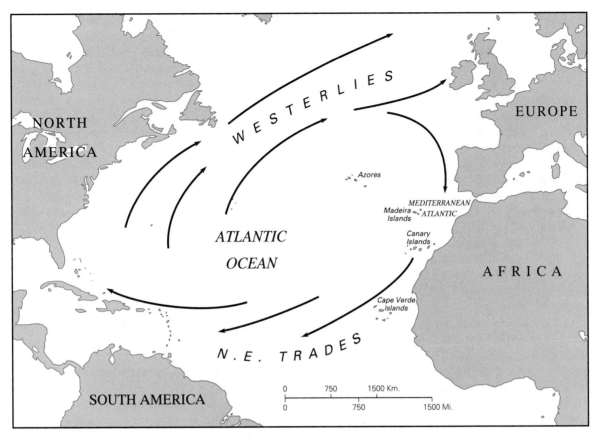

Atlantic Winds and Islands *European mariners had to explore the oceans before they could find new lands. The first realm they investigated was the Atlantic winds and islands.*

What could be done? Some unknown seafarer figured out the answer: sailing "around the wind." If a mariner could not sail against the trade winds, he had to sail as close as possible to the direction from which the wind was coming without being forced to tack. In the Mediterranean Atlantic, that meant pointing his vessel northwest into the open ocean, away from land, until—weeks later—he reached the winds that would carry him home, the so-called Westerlies. Those winds blow northward along the coast of North America before heading east toward Europe.

This solution proved to be the key to successful exploration of both the Atlantic and the Pacific Oceans. Once a sailor understood the winds and their allied currents, he no longer feared leaving Europe without being able to return. Faced with a contrary wind, all he had to do was sail around it until he found a wind to carry him in the proper direction.

During the fifteenth century, armed with knowledge of the winds and currents of the Mediterranean Atlantic, Iberian seamen regularly visited its islands, all of which they could reach in two weeks or less. By the 1450s Portuguese colonists were employing slaves (probably Jews and Muslims brought from Iberia) to grow large quantities of sugar on Madeira, which developed into the world's first colonial plantation economy.

Islands of the Mediterranean Atlantic

After the Spaniards conquered the Guanche people in the Canaries in 1496, they devoted the land to sugar cultivation. Collectively, the Canaries and Madeira became known as the Wine Islands because much of their sugar production was employed to make sweet wines.

For Portugal's Prince Henry the Navigator, however, the islands were steppingstones to Africa. He knew that vast wealth awaited the first European nation to tap the riches of Africa and Asia directly. Each year he dispatched ships southward along the African coast, attempting to discover an oceanic route to Asia. But not until after Prince Henry's death did Bartholomew Dias round the southern tip of Africa (1488) and Vasco da Gama finally reach India (1498).

Portuguese Trading Posts in Africa

Long before these voyages, West African states allowed the Portuguese to establish trading posts along their coasts. Charging the traders rent and levying duties on the goods they imported, the African kingdoms set the terms of exchange and benefited considerably from their new, easier access to European manufactures. The Portuguese gained too, for they no longer had to rely on the long trans-Saharan trade route. They earned immense profits by swiftly transporting African gold to Europe. Another valuable cargo was slaves. When they carried previously enslaved Africans back to the Iberian Peninsula, the Portuguese introduced black slavery into Europe.

An island off the African coast, previously uninhabited, proved critical to Portuguese success. São Tomé, located in the Gulf of Guinea (see map, page 12) was colonized in the 1480s. The soil of São Tomé proved ideal for raising sugar, and plantation agriculture there expanded rapidly. Large numbers of slaves were imported from the mainland to work in the cane fields, thus creating the first colonial economy based primarily on the bondage of black Africans.

By the 1490s, even before Christopher Columbus set sail to the west, Europeans had learned three key lessons of colonization from their experiences in the islands of the Mediterranean Atlantic and the African coast. First, they knew that they could transplant their crops and livestock successfully to exotic locations. Second, they learned that the native peoples of unknown lands could be either conquered or exploited to European advantage. Third, they successfully developed a model of plantation slavery and a system for supplying nearly unlimited quantities of bound workers. The stage was set for a critical moment in world history, and the man of the hour was a sailor named Christopher Columbus.

Lessons of Early Colonization

Columbus was well schooled in the lessons of the Mediterranean Atlantic. Born in 1451 in the Italian city-state of Genoa, Columbus was by the 1490s an experienced sailor and mapmaker. Like many mariners of the day, he was drawn to Portugal and its islands, especially Madeira, where he commanded a merchant vessel. At least once he voyaged to the Portuguese colony on the Gold Coast. There he acquired an obsession with gold; and there he came to understand the economic potential of the slave trade.

Christopher Columbus

Like all accomplished seafarers, Columbus knew the world was round. But he differed from other cartographers in his estimate of the earth's size: he thought that Japan lay only 3,000 miles from the southern European coast. Thus, he argued, it would be easier to reach Asia by sailing west than by making a difficult voyage around the southern tip of Africa. Experts scoffed at this crackpot notion, accurately predicting that the two continents lay 12,000 miles apart. When Columbus in 1484 asked the Portuguese authorities to back his plan to sail west to Asia, they rejected the proposal.

Ferdinand and Isabella of Spain, ruling a newly united kingdom and jealous of Portugal's successes in Africa, were more receptive to Columbus's ideas. Urged on by some Spanish noblemen and a group of Italian merchants residing in Castile, the monarchs agreed to finance the risky voyage. And so, on August 3, 1492, in command of three ships—the *Pinta*, the *Niña*, and the *Santa Maria*—Columbus set sail from the southern Spanish port of Palos.

On October 12, he and his men landed on an island in the Bahamas, which he named San Salvador. (Because Columbus's sketchy description of his landfall can be variously interpreted, two different places—Watling Island and Samana Cay—are today proposed as possible landing sites.) Later he went on to explore the islands now known as Cuba and Hispaniola, which their residents, the Taíno people, called Colba and Bohío. Because he thought he had reached the Indies, Columbus referred to the inhabitants of the region as *Indians*.

Three themes predominate in Columbus's log, the major source of information on this first encounter. First, he insistently asked the Taínos

Columbus's Observations

where he could find gold, pearls, and valuable spices. Each time, his informants replied (largely via signs) that such products could be obtained on other islands, on the mainland, or in cities in the interior.

Second, Columbus wrote repeatedly of the strange and beautiful plants and animals. Yet Columbus's interest was not only aesthetic. "I believe that there are many plants and trees here that could be worth a lot in Spain for use as dyes, spices, and medicines," he observed, adding that he was carrying home to Europe "a sample of everything I can," so that experts could examine them.

Third, Columbus also described the islands' human residents, and he seized some to take back to Spain. The Taínos were, he said, very hand-

The Taíno People

some, gentle, and friendly. Columbus believed the Taínos to be likely converts to Catholicism. But he also thought that the islanders "ought to make good and skilled servants."

Thus the very first encounter between Europeans and America and its residents revealed a theme that would be of enormous significance for centuries to come: the Europeans' desire to extract profits from North and South America by exploiting their natural resources, including plants, animals, and peoples alike.

Christopher Columbus made three more voyages to the west, exploring most of the major Caribbean islands and sailing along the coasts of Central and South America.

Naming of America

Until the day he died in 1506, Columbus believed that he had reached Asia. Even before his death, others knew better. Because the Florentine Amerigo Vespucci, who explored the South American coast in 1499, was the first to publish the idea that a new continent had been discovered, Martin Waldseemüller in 1507 labeled the land "America." By then, Spain, Portugal, and Pope Alexander VI had signed the Treaty of Tordesillas (1494), confirming Portugal's dominance in Africa and Brazil in exchange for Spanish preeminence in the rest of the New World.

The first mariners to explore the region of North America that was to become the United States and Canada followed a very different route.

Northern Voyages

Some historians argue that European sailors may have found the rich Newfoundland fishing grounds in the 1480s but kept their discoveries a secret so that they alone could exploit the sea's bounty. Whether or not fishermen had crossed the entire width of the Atlantic, they had thoroughly explored its northern reaches. In the same way the Portuguese traveled the Mediterranean Atlantic, fifteenth-century English seafarers and others voyaged among the European continent, England, Ireland, and Iceland.

Five hundred years before Columbus, in the year 1001, the Norseman Leif Ericsson and other explorers from Greenland briefly established a settlement at a western site they named Vineland (now L'anse aux Meadows, Newfoundland) before attacks by local residents forced them to depart hurriedly. Therefore, the European generally credited with "discovering" North America is John Cabot. More precisely, it might be said that Cabot brought to Europe the first formal knowledge of the northern coastline of the continent.

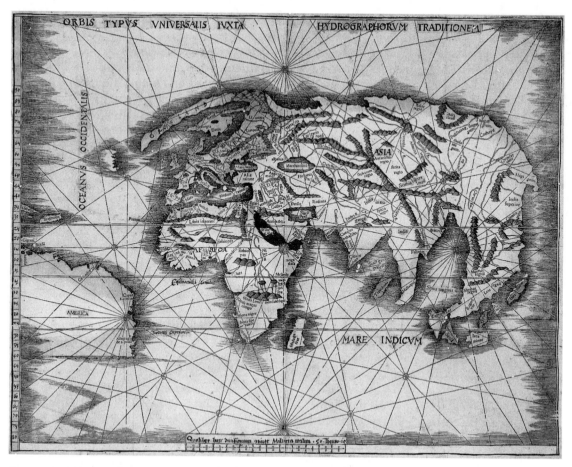

In 1507 Martin Waldseemüller, a German mapmaker, was the first person to designate the newly discovered southern continent as "America." He named the continent after Amerigo Vespucci, the Italian explorer who realized that he had reached a "new world" rather than islands off the coast of Asia.   John Carter Brown Library at Brown University.

Cabot was a master mariner from the Italian city-state of Genoa who was in Spain when Columbus returned from his first trip to America. Calculating that England—

John Cabot's Explorations

which traded with Asia only through a long series of middlemen stretching from Belgium to Venice to the Muslim world—would be eager to sponsor exploratory voyages, Cabot sought and won the support of King Henry VII. He set sail from Bristol in late May 1497, reaching his destination on June 24. Scholars disagree about the location of his landfall (some say it was Cape Breton Island, others New-

foundland), but all recognize the importance of his month-long exploration of the coast.

The voyages of Columbus, Cabot, and their successors finally brought the Eastern and Western Hemispheres together. The Portuguese explorer Pedro Alvares Cabral reached Brazil in 1500; John Cabot's son Sebastian followed his father to North America in 1507; France financed Giovanni da Verrazzano in 1524 and Jacques Cartier in 1534; and in 1609 and 1610 Henry Hudson explored the North American coast for the Dutch West India Company (see map). Although these men were primarily searching for the legendary, nonexistent "Northwest Passage" through the Americas, what

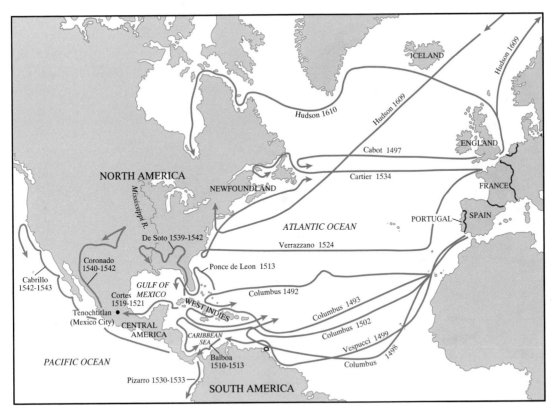

European Explorations in America   *In the century following Columbus's voyages, European adventurers explored the coasts and parts of the interior of North and South America.*

they learned interested European nations in exploring North and South America.

Spanish Colonization and the Exchange of Diseases, Plants, and Animals

The Europeans' greatest impact on the Americas was unintended. Diseases carried from Europe and Africa by the alien invaders killed millions of Indians, who had no immunity to germs that had infested the other continents for centuries. The statistics are staggering. When Columbus landed on Hispaniola in 1492, more than 1 million

Smallpox and Other Diseases

people probably resided there. Fifty years later, only 500 were still alive. The greatest killer was smallpox. In 1518 a smallpox epidemic began in Hispaniola. When Cortés and his men carried the epidemic to the mainland, its impact on Tenochtitlán, the Aztec capital he besieged, was devastating. As an old Aztec man recalled, "Some quite covered [with pustules] on all parts—their faces, their heads, their breasts. . . . There was great havoc. Very many died of it." In the Aztec year Three House, on the day One Serpent (August 1521), Tenochtitlán surrendered. On the site of the Aztec capital, the Spaniards built what is now Mexico City.

Far to the north, where smaller American populations encountered only a few Europeans, disease also ravaged the countryside. A great epidemic, most likely chickenpox, swept through the villages along the coast north of Cape Cod from 1616 to 1618. The mortality rate may have been as high as

The Codex Florentino, *which has the fullest Aztec account of the Spaniards' conquest of Mexico, contains this image of an Indian afflicted with the smallpox that ravaged Tenochtitlán during the Spanish siege of the city.*   Biblioteca Medicea Laurenziana, Florence.

90 percent. Because of this dramatic depopulation of the area, just a few years later English colonists were able to establish settlements virtually unopposed.

The Americans, though, took a revenge of sorts. They gave the Europeans syphilis, a virulent venereal disease. The first recorded case of the new disease in Europe occurred in Barcelona, Spain, in 1493, shortly after Columbus's return from the Caribbean. Carried by soldiers, sailors, and prostitutes, it spread quickly through Europe and Asia, reaching as far as China by 1505.

The exchange of diseases was only part of a broader mutual transfer of plants and animals that resulted directly from European voyages. Many large mammals like cattle and horses were native to the connected continents of Europe, Asia, and Africa, but the Americas contained no domesticated beasts larger than dogs

Exchange of Plants and Animals

and llamas. However, the vegetable crops of the New World—particularly corn, beans, squash, cassava, and potatoes—were more nutritious and produced higher yields than those of the Old World, like wheat and rye. In time, the Native Americans learned to raise and consume European livestock, and the Europeans and Africans became accustomed to planting and eating American crops. As a result, the diets of all three peoples were vastly enriched.

The exchange of two other commodities significantly influenced European and American civilizations. In America, Europeans encountered tobacco, which was at first believed to have beneficial medicinal effects. Smoking and chewing the "Indian weed" became a fad in the Old World after it was planted in Turkey in the sixteenth century.

Also important was the impact of the horse on some Indian cultures. Horses brought to America by the Spaniards inevitably fell into the hands of Native Americans. Traded northward, descendants of these horses became essential to the life of the nomadic buffalo hunters of the Great Plains, who used horses for transportation and hunting. They also calculated their wealth in the number of horses owned and waged wars primarily from horseback. Women no longer had to carry the bands' belongings on their backs. Through the acquisition of horses, then, a mode of subsistence that had been based on hunting several different animals, in combination with gathering and agriculture, became one focused almost wholly on hunting buffalo.

The European and African invasion of the Americas therefore had a significant biological component, for the invaders carried plants and animals with them. Some creatures, such as livestock, they brought deliberately. Others, including rats, weeds, and diseases, arrived unexpectedly. And the same process occurred in reverse. When the Europeans returned home, they deliberately took back such crops as corn, potatoes, and tobacco, along with that unanticipated hitchhiker, syphilis.

Only in the areas that Spain explored and claimed did formal colonization begin immediately. On his second voyage in 1493, Columbus brought to Hispaniola seventeen ships loaded with twelve hundred men, seeds, plants, livestock, chickens, and dogs. The settlement named Isabela (in the modern Dominican Republic) and its successors became the staging area for the Spanish invasion of America.

Spanish Colonization

At first, Spanish explorers fanned out around the Caribbean basin. In 1513, Juan Ponce de León reached Florida and Vasco Núñez de Balboa crossed the Isthmus of Panama to the Pacific Ocean. Eight years later, the Spaniards' dreams of wealth were realized when Cortés conquered the Aztec Empire, seizing a fabulous treasure of gold and silver. Venturing northward, conquistadors like Juan Rodriguez Cabrillo (who sailed along the California coast), Hernando de Soto (who journeyed to the Mississippi River), and Francisco Vásquez de Coronado (who explored the southwestern portion of what is now the United States)

found few of the products the Spanish coveted. By contrast, Francisco Pizarro, who explored the western coast of South America, acquired the richest silver mines in the world by conquering and enslaving the Incas in 1535. By 1550, Spain controlled the richest, most extensive empire Europe had known since ancient Rome.

Spain established a three-element model of colonization that other countries later attempted to imitate. First, the Crown maintained tight control over the colonies, establishing a hierarchical government that allowed little autonomy to New World jurisdictions. Second, most of the colonists sent from Spain were male. They married Indian—and later African—women, thereby creating the racially mixed population that characterizes much of Latin America to the present day. Third, the colonies' wealth was based on the exploitation of both the native population and slaves imported from Africa. The *encomienda* system, which granted tribute from Indian villages to individual conquistadors as a reward for their services to the Crown, in effect legalized Indian slavery. Yet in 1542 a new code of laws reformed the system, forbidding Spaniards from enslaving Indians. In response, the conquerors, familiar with slavery in Spain, began to import Africans in order to increase the labor force under their direct control.

Spanish wealth derived from American suffering. The Spaniards deliberately leveled American cities, building cathedrals and monasteries on sites once occupied by Aztec, Incan, and Mayan temples. Some conquistadors sought to erase all vestiges of the great Indian cultures by burning the written records they found. With traditional ways of life in disarray, devastated by disease, and compelled to labor for their conquerors, many demoralized residents of Mesoamerica accepted the Christian religion brought to New Spain by friars of the Franciscan and Dominican orders.

The friars devoted their energies to persuading Mesoamerican people to move into new towns and to build Roman Catholic churches. In such

Christianity in New Spain

towns, they were exposed to European customs and to religious rituals newly elaborated in an attempt to assimilate Christianity and pagan beliefs.

For example, the friars deliberately juxtaposed the cult of the Virgin Mary with that of the corn goddess. These conversion efforts met with remarkable success as thousands of Indians residing in Spanish territory embraced Catholicism.

European Traders, Fishermen, and Early Settlements

Northern Europeans, denied access to the wealth of Mesoamerica by the Spanish and beaten to South America by the Portuguese (who founded a colony in Brazil in 1532), were initially more interested in exploiting North America's abundant natural resources than in the difficult task of establishing colonies on the mainland. Following John Cabot's report of a plentiful supply of fish along the North American coastline, European fishermen sailed into the area. By the 1570s, more than 350 ships were exploiting the bounty of the Newfoundland Banks each year, bringing back to their homelands a much desired and inexpensive source of nourishment.

European fishermen soon learned that they could supplement their profits by exchanging cloth and metal goods like pots and knives for the Native Americans' beaver pelts. At first the Europeans conducted their trading from ships sailing along the coast,

Northern Traders

but later they established permanent outposts on the mainland to centralize and control the traffic in furs.

The Europeans' insatiable demand for furs, especially beaver, was matched by the Native Americans' desire for European goods that could make their lives easier and establish their superiority over their neighbors. Some bands began to concentrate so completely on trapping for the European market that they abandoned their traditional economies. The intensive trade in pelts also had serious ecological consequences. In some regions, beavers were completely wiped out. The disappearance of their dams led to soil erosion, especially when combined with the extensive clearing of forests by later European settlers.

Although their nation reaped handsome profits from fishing, English merchants and political leaders watched enviously as Spain's American possessions enriched Spain immeasurably. In the mid-sixteenth century, English "sea dogs" like John Hawkins and Sir Francis Drake began to raid Spanish treasure fleets sailing home from the West Indies. Their actions helped to foment a war that in 1588 culminated in the defeat of a huge invasion force—the Spanish Armada—off the English coast. As a part of the contest with Spain, English leaders started to think about planting colonies in the Western Hemisphere, thereby gaining better access to valuable trade goods and simultaneously preventing their enemy from dominating the Americas.

The first English colonial planners hoped to reproduce Spanish successes by dispatching to America men who would similarly exploit the native peoples for their own and their nation's benefit. In the 1580s, a group that included Sir Humphrey Gilbert and his younger half-brother Sir Walter Raleigh promoted a scheme to establish outposts that could trade with the Indians and provide bases for attacks on New Spain. Approving the idea, Queen Elizabeth I authorized Raleigh and Gilbert to colonize North America.

Sir Walter Raleigh's Roanoke Colony

Gilbert failed to plant a colony in Newfoundland, and Raleigh was only briefly more successful. In 1587 he sent 117 colonists to the territory he named Virginia, after Elizabeth, the "Virgin Queen." They established a settlement on Roanoke Island, in what is now North Carolina, but in 1590 a resupply ship could not find them. The colonists had vanished, leaving only the name of a nearby island carved on a tree.

Thus England's first attempt to plant a permanent settlement on the North American coast failed, as had earlier efforts by Portugal on Cape Breton Island (early 1520s) and France in northern Florida (mid-1560s). All three enterprises collapsed for the same reasons: inability to be self-sustaining with respect to food and hostile neighbors.

The explanation for such failings becomes clear in Thomas Harriot's *A Briefe and True Report of the*

New Found Land of Virginia, published in 1588 to publicize Raleigh's colony. Harriot, a noted scientist who

Thomas Harriot's *Briefe and True Report*

sailed on an exploratory voyage to Roanoke, was charged with describing the animals, plants, and people of the region for an English readership. His account revealed that although the explorers were almost wholly dependent on nearby villagers for food, they needlessly antagonized their neighbors by killing some of them for what Harriot himself admitted were unjustifiable reasons.

Harriot's *Briefe and True Report* depicted a bountiful land full of opportunities for a quick profit. The people already residing there would, he thought, "in a short time be brought to civilitie" through conversion to Christianity, admiration for European superiority, or conquest—if they did not die from disease, the ravages of which he witnessed. Harriot's prediction was far off the mark. European dominance of North America was to be difficult to achieve.

 Conclusion

The process of initial contact between Europeans and Americans that ended near the close of the sixteenth century had begun approximately 250 years earlier when Portuguese sailors first sailed into the Mediterranean Atlantic. That region of the Atlantic so close to European and African shores nurtured the mariners who, like Christopher Columbus, ventured into previously unknown waters. When Columbus first reached the Americas, he thought he had found Asia, his intended destination. Later explorers knew better but, except for the Spanish, regarded the Americas primarily as a barrier that prevented them from reaching their long-sought goal of an oceanic route to the riches of China and the Moluccas. Ordinary European fishermen were the first to realize that the northern coasts had valuable products to offer: fish and furs, both much in demand in their homelands.

The wealth of the north could not compare to that of Mesoamerica. The Aztec Empire dazzled the conquistadors with the magnificence of its buildings and its seemingly unlimited wealth. Nonetheless, the Spaniards destroyed the great temples and used their stones (and Indian laborers) to construct cathedrals honoring their God, rather than Huitzilopochtli. The conquerors employed first American and later enslaved African workers to till the fields, mine the precious metals, and herd the livestock that earned immense profits for themselves and their mother country.

The initial impact of Europeans on the Americas proved devastating. Flourishing civilizations were, if not entirely destroyed, markedly altered in just a few short decades. By the end of the sixteenth century, many fewer people resided on the continent than had lived there before Columbus's arrival, even taking into account the arrival of many Europeans and Africans. And the people who did live there—Indian, African, and European—resided in a world that was literally new—a world engaged in the unprecedented process of combining foods, religions, economies, styles of life, and political systems that had developed separately for millennia. Conflict and dissension permeated that process.

Suggestions for Further Reading

General

Alfred W. Crosby, *The Columbian Exchange: Biological and Cultural Consequences of 1492* (1972); Alfred W. Crosby, *Ecological Imperialism: The Biological Expansion of Europe, 800–1900* (1986); D. W. Meinig, *Atlantic America, 1492–1800* (1986); Herman Viola and Carolyn Margolis, eds., *Seeds of Change: Five Hundred Years Since Columbus* (1991).

Mesoamerican Civilizations

Brian Fagan, *Kingdoms of Gold, Kingdoms of Jade: The Americas Before Columbus* (1991); Eduardo Matos Moctezuma and David Carrasco, *Moctezuma's Mexico: Visions of the Aztec World* (1992); Linda Schele and David Friedel, *A Forest of Kings* [on the Mayas] (1990).

North American Indians

Brian Fagan, *Ancient North America: The Archaeology of a Continent* (1991); Francis Jennings, *The Founders of America: From the Earliest Migrations to the Present* (1993); Alvin Josephy, Jr., ed., *America in 1492* (1992); Lynda N. Shaffer, *Native Americans Before 1492: The Moundbuilding Centers of the Eastern*

Woodlands (1992); Colin F. Taylor, ed., *The Native Americans: The Indigenous People of North America* (1992).

Africa

Jacob Ade Ajayi and Michael Crowder, *History of West Africa* (1985); Paul Bohannon and Philip Curtin, *Africa and Africans* (1988); John Thornton, *Africa and Africans in the Making of the Atlantic World, 1400–1680* (1992).

Exploration and Discovery

Emerson Baker et al., eds., *American Beginnings: Exploration, Culture, and Cartography in the Land of Norumbega* (1994); Felipe Fernández-Armesto, *Before Columbus: Exploration and Colonization from the Mediterranean to the Atlantic, 1229–1492* (1987); Felipe Fernández-Armesto, *Columbus* (1991); Jerald T. Milanich and Susan Milbrath, eds., *First Encounters: Spanish Explorations in the Caribbean and the United States, 1492–1570* (1989); Samuel Eliot Morison, *The European Discovery of America: The Northern Voyages, A.D. 1500–1600* (1971); Samuel Eliot Morison, *The European Discovery of America: The Southern Voyages, A.D. 1492–1616* (1974); J. H. Parry, *The Age of Reconnaissance* (1963); J. H. Parry, *The Discovery of the Sea* (1974); William and Carla Phillips, *The Worlds of Christopher Columbus* (1992); David B. Quinn, *North America from Earliest Discovery to First Settlements* (1977); Paolo Emilio Taviani, *Columbus: The Great Adventure* (1991).

The Conquest of Mexico

Ross Hassig, *Mexico and the Spanish Conquest* (1994); Miguel León-Portilla, ed., *The Broken Spears: The Aztec Account of the Conquest of Mexico* (1992); Hugh Thomas, *Conquest: Montezuma, Cortés, and the Fall of Old Mexico* (1993).

Early European Settlements

Kenneth Andrews, *Trade, Plunder and Settlement: Maritime Enterprise and the Genesis of the British Empire, 1480–1630* (1984); Charles Gibson, *Spain in America* (1966); Karen O. Kupperman, *Roanoke, the Abandoned Colony* (1984); David J. Weber, *The Spanish Frontier in North America* (1992).

2

Europeans Colonize
North America
1600 – 1640

In August 1630, Fray Alonso de Benavides brought thrilling news to Madrid. Franciscan friars in the remote territory called New Mexico had successfully converted to Roman Catholicism at least eighty thousand heathens. In village after village, Indians had embraced baptism and built beautiful churches and schools with their own hands.

Fray Alonso supervised the New Mexico missions from 1626 to 1629. His account of the Franciscans' successes created a sensation in Europe. Alonso's *Memorial* not only was immediately published in Spanish but also was quickly translated into Latin, French, Dutch, and German. Fray Alonso undertook the arduous and successful journey to Spain to convince the king to increase his financial and administrative support of the Franciscan missions.

Yet de Benavides's report contained a troubling undercurrent. The colonial capital at Santa Fe, he noted, was inhabited by only about 250 Spaniards (along with another 750 Pueblos and mestizos). The soldiers were "few and poorly equipped," and the church had been "a miserable hut" before Fray Alonso ordered the construction of a new one. Furthermore, not all the local Indians had been receptive to the friars' message. The residents of Picurís pueblo, for one, had tried to murder the priests stationed there.

So, while praising the Spaniards' stunning successes in New Mexico, Fray Alonso revealed their equally striking weaknesses: more than a few

Native Americans staunchly combated their missionizing; both priests and soldiers lacked adequate financial resources; and the one tiny, impoverished European settlement was surrounded by tens of thousands of potentially troublesome Pueblos, Apaches, and Navajos. And there was an additional problem he did not describe: royal governors often clashed with the Franciscans in a struggle for primacy in the region.

By the time Fray Alonso arrived in Madrid in 1630, England, France, and the Netherlands had also founded permanent colonies in North America. No longer were the Spaniards the only Europeans on that vast continent. Just as Franciscans played a major role in the Spanish settlements, so too Jesuit priests were active in New France. The French and Dutch colonies, like the Spanish outposts, were peopled largely by European men. Like the conquistadors, French and Dutch merchants and planters hoped to make a quick profit and then perhaps return to their homelands.

In contrast to other Europeans, most of the English settlers came to America intending to stay. Especially in the area that came to be known as New England, they arrived in family groups. They recreated European society and family life to an extent not possible in the other colonies, where migrant men had to find their sexual partners within the Native American or African populations. Among the English colonies, those in the Chesapeake region and on the Caribbean islands most closely resembled colonies founded by other nations. Their economies, like those of Hispaniola or Brazil, soon came to be based on large-scale production for the international market by a labor force composed of bonded servants and slaves.

Wherever they settled, the English, like other Europeans, prospered only after they learned to adapt to the alien environment. The first permanent English colonies survived only because nearby Indians assisted the newcomers. The settlers had to learn to grow unfamiliar American crops. They also had to develop extensive trading relationships with Native Americans and with colonies established by other European countries. In need of laborers for their fields, they first used English indentured servants, then later began to import African slaves. Thus the early history of the region that became the United States and the English Caribbean can best be understood as a series of complex interactions among a variety of European, African, and American peoples and environments rather than as a simple story of English colonization.

 ## New Spain, New France, New Netherland, and the Caribbean

Spaniards were the first Europeans to establish a permanent settlement within the boundaries of the modern United States, but they were not the first to attempt that feat.

Florida

Twice in the 1560s groups of French Protestants (Huguenots) sought to escape from persecution in their homeland by planting colonies on the south Atlantic coast. The first colony, in present-day South Carolina, collapsed when its starving inhabitants had to be rescued by a passing ship. The second, near modern Jacksonville, Florida, was destroyed in 1565 by a Spanish expedition under the command of Pedro Menéndez de Avilés. To ensure Spanish domination of the strategically important region (located near sea lanes used by Spanish treasure ships bound for Europe), Menéndez set up a small fortified outpost, which he named St. Augustine—now the oldest continuously inhabited European settlement in the United States. By the end of the sixteenth century a chain of Franciscan missions stretched across northern Florida.

More than thirty years passed after the founding of St. Augustine before conquistadors ventured anew into the present-day United States. In 1598, drawn northward by rumors of rich cities, Juan de Oñate, a Mexican-born adventurer, led a group of about five hundred soldiers and settlers to New Mexico. At first, the Pueblos greeted the interlopers cordially. When the Spaniards began to torture, murder, and rape the villagers to extort food and clothing,

New Mexico

• *Important Events* •

1533	Henry VIII divorces Catherine of Aragon; English Reformation begins	**1620**	Plymouth colony founded, first permanent English settlement in New England
1558	Elizabeth I becomes queen	**1622**	Powhatan Confederacy attacks Virginia colony
1565	Founding of St. Augustine (Florida), oldest permanent European settlement in present-day United States	**1624**	Dutch settle on Manhattan Island (New Amsterdam)
1598	Juan de Oñate conquers Pueblos in New Mexico for Spain		English colonize St. Christopher, first island in Lesser Antilles to be settled by Europeans
1603	James I becomes king		James I proclaims Virginia a royal colony
1607	Jamestown founded, first permanent English settlement in North America	**1625**	Charles I becomes king
1608	Quebec founded by the French	**1629**	Massachusetts Bay colony founded
1609	Henry Hudson explores Hudson River for the Dutch	**1634**	Maryland founded
1610	Founding of Santa Fe, New Mexico	**1635**	Roger Williams expelled from Massachusetts Bay; founds Providence, Rhode Island
1611	First Virginia tobacco crop	**1636**	Connecticut founded
1614	Fort Orange (Albany) founded by the Dutch	**1637**	Pequot War in New England
1619	First Africans arrive in Virginia	**1638**	Anne Hutchinson expelled from Massachusetts Bay colony, goes to Rhode Island
	Virginia House of Burgesses established, first representative assembly in the English colonies	**c. 1640**	Sugar cultivation begins on Barbados
		1642	Montréal founded by the French

however, the residents of Acoma pueblo killed several soldiers. The invaders responded ferociously, killing more than eight hundred people. Not surprisingly, the other Pueblo villages surrendered.

Finding little wealth in New Mexico and learning that it was too far from the Pacific coast to assist in protecting Spanish sea lanes, many of the Spanish officials considered abandoning the isolated colony. Instead, in 1609, the authorities decided to maintain a small military outpost and a few Christian missions in the area, with the capital at Santa Fe (founded 1610). This was the constricted world in which Fray Alonso de Benavides arrived in 1626.

After Spain's destruction of France's Florida settlement in 1565, the French turned their attention northward. In 1608 Samuel de Champlain founded a trading post at an interior site that he named

New France

Quebec. He had chosen well: Quebec was the most easily defended spot in the entire St. Lawrence River valley, a stronghold that controlled access to the heartland of the continent. In 1642, the French established a second post, Montréal, at the falls of the St. Lawrence (and thus at the end of navigation by oceangoing vessels).

Before the founding of Quebec and Montréal, French fishermen served as the major conduits through which North American beaver pelts reached France, but the two new posts quickly took over control of the lucrative trade in furs. In

The Founding of Permanent European Colonies in North America, 1565–1640

Colony	Founder(s)	Date	Basis of Economy
Florida	Pedro Menéndez de Avilés	1565	Farming
New Mexico	Juan de Oñate	1598	Livestock
Virginia	Virginia Company	1607	Tobacco
New France	France	1608	Fur trading
New Netherland	Dutch West India Company	1614	Fur trading
Plymouth	Pilgrims	1620	Farming, fishing
Maine	Sir Ferdinando Gorges	1622	Fishing
St. Kitts, Barbados, et al.	European migrants	1624	Sugar
Massachusetts Bay	Massachusetts Bay Company	1630	Farming, fishing, fur trading
Maryland	Cecilius Calvert	1634	Tobacco
Rhode Island	Roger Williams	1635	Farming
Connecticut	Thomas Hooker	1636	Farming, fur trading
New Haven	Massachusetts migrants	1638	Farming
New Hampshire	Massachusetts migrants	1638	Farming, fishing

an attempt to attract settlers, the colony's leaders offered land grants along the river to prospective settlers, including wealthy seigneurs (nobles) who were expected to import tenants to work their farms. Even so, more than twenty-five years after Quebec's founding, it had just sixty-four resident families, along with traders and soldiers.

One other important group was part of the population of New France: missionaries of the Society of Jesus (Jesuits), a Roman Catholic order dedicated to converting nonbelievers to Christianity. First arriving in the colony in 1625, the Jesuits, whom the Indians called Black Robes, initially tried to persuade indigenous peoples to live near French settlements and to adopt European agricultural methods as well as the Europeans' religion. When that effort failed, the Jesuits learned native languages and traveled to remote regions of the interior, where they lived in twos and threes among hundreds of potential converts.

Jesuit Missions in New France

Using a variety of strategies, Jesuits sought to undermine the authority of village shamans (the traditional religious leaders) and to gain the confidence of leaders who could influence others. Trained in rhetoric, they won admirers by their eloquence. Immune to smallpox (for all had survived the disease already), they explained epidemics among the Indians as God's punishment for sin. Perhaps most important, they amazed the villagers by communicating with each other over long distances and periods of time by employing marks on paper. The Native Americans' desire to learn how to harness the extraordinary power of literacy was one of the most critical factors in making them receptive to the missionaries' message.

Although the process took many years, the Jesuits slowly gained thousands of converts. The converts replaced their own culture's traditional equal treatment of men and women with notions more congenial to the Europeans' insistence on male dominance and female subordination. Further, they altered their practice of allowing premarital sexual relationships and easy divorce because Catholic doctrine prohibited both customs.

Jesuit missionaries faced little competition from other Europeans for Native Americans' souls, but French fur traders had to confront a direct challenge. In 1614, only five years after Henry Hudson sailed up the river that now bears his name, his sponsor, the Dutch West India Company, established an outpost (Fort Orange) on that river at the site of present-day Albany, New York. Like the French, the Dutch sought beaver pelts, and their presence so close to Quebec posed a threat to French domination of the region. The Netherlands, at the time the world's dominant commercial power, was interested primarily in trade rather than colonization, and New Netherland, like New France, therefore remained small. The colony's southern anchor was New Amsterdam, a town founded in 1624 on Manhattan Island.

As the Dutch West India Company's colony in North America, New Netherland was a relatively unimportant part of a vast commercial empire.

New Netherland

Autocratic directors-general ruled the colony for the company; with no elected assembly, settlers felt little loyalty to their nominal leaders. Migration was sparse. Even a company policy of 1629 that offered a large land grant, or patroonship, to anyone who would bring fifty settlers to the province failed to attract takers. As late as the mid-1660s, New Netherland had only about five thousand inhabitants.

Despite their geographical proximity and their trading rivalry, New France and New Netherland did not come into armed conflict with each other. Yet their Indian allies did. In the 1640s, the Iroquois, who traded chiefly with the Dutch and lived in modern upstate New York, went to war against their northern neighbors the Hurons, who traded primarily with the French and lived in present-day Ontario (see map, page 30). Using guns supplied by the Dutch, the Iroquois largely exterminated the Hurons. The Iroquois thus established themselves as a major force in the region, one that Europeans could ignore only at their peril.

It was in the Caribbean, though, that France, the Netherlands, and England clashed most openly in the first half of the seventeenth century.

The Caribbean

The Spanish concentrated their colonization efforts on the Greater Antilles—Cuba, Hispaniola, Jamaica, and Puerto Rico. They left many smaller islands alone, partly because the mainland offered greater wealth for less effort. But other European powers coveted the tiny islands as bases from which to attack Spanish vessels loaded with American gold and silver. They also viewed them as sources of valuable tropical products, such as spices, dyes, and fruits.

England was the first northern European nation to establish a permanent foothold in the smaller West Indian islands (the Lesser Antilles). English people settled on St. Christopher (St. Kitts) in 1624, then later on other islands such as Barbados (1627). France was able to colonize Guadeloupe and Martinique, and the Dutch gained control of St. Eustatius (strategically located near St. Kitts). As a result of conflict among the European powers, most of the islands were attacked at least once during the course of the century, and some changed hands.

Why did other Europeans devote so much energy to gaining control of these tiny bits of land neglected by Spain? The primary answer to that question was sugar, one of the most important components of the post-Columbian exchange of plants and animals. First domesticated in the East Indies, it was being grown in North Africa and southern Spain by 1000 C.E. Canary Island sugar canes were among the plants Columbus carried to Hispaniola on his 1493 voyage.

Satisfying Europe's Sweet Tooth

At the end of the sixteenth century, most American sugar was being produced in Brazil, part of which the Dutch controlled between 1630 and 1654. There the Dutch learned how to grow and process sugar cane, skills they then taught to the English on Barbados. In return, the Dutch expected to sell African slaves to West Indian planters and to carry to Europe barrels of molasses and rum, which was distilled from sugar. The

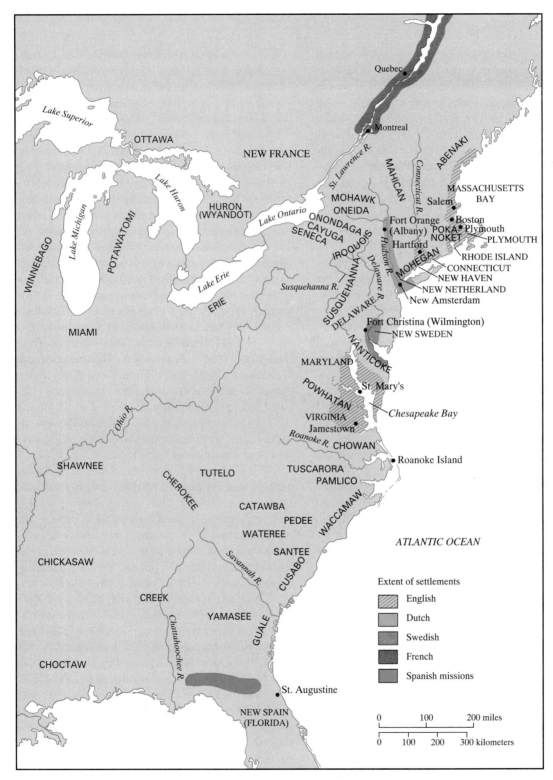

European Settlements and Indians in Eastern North America, 1650 *Note the widely scattered European settlements along the ocean and riverbanks, while America's native inhabitants controlled the vast interior.*

results must have exceeded their wildest dreams. The Barbados sugar boom in the 1640s was both explosive and lucrative. Planters, slave traders, and Dutch shipping interests alike earned immense profits. Indeed, for a hundred years sugar was the most important American commodity. In the eighteenth century, sugar grown by slaves in British Jamaica and French St. Domingue dominated the world market. Yet, in the long run, the future economic importance of the Europeans' American colonies lay on the mainland rather than in the Caribbean.

England Colonizes Mainland North America

The failure of Raleigh's attempt to colonize Virginia ended English efforts to settle in North America for nearly two decades. When the English decided in 1606 to try once more, they again planned colonies that imitated the Spanish model. Success came only when they abandoned that model and sent large numbers of men and women to set up agriculturally based colonies on the mainland. Two major developments prompted approximately 200,000 ordinary English men and women to move to North America in the seventeenth century and led their government to encourage that migration.

The first major development that led English folk to move to North America was the onset of dramatic social and economic change caused by the doubling of the English population in the 150-year period after 1530, largely as a result of the introduction of nutritious American crops into Europe. All those additional people needed food, clothing, and other goods. The competition for goods led to high inflation, coupled with a fall in real wages as the number of workers increased. Those with sizable landholdings benefited from the increased demand for food and clothing fibers, but landless laborers and those with very small amounts of land fell into unremitting poverty.

Social Change in England

Well-to-do English people reacted with alarm to what they saw as the disappearance of traditional ways of life. Steady streams of the landless and homeless filled the streets and highways. Obsessed with the problem of maintaining order, officials came to believe that England was overcrowded. They concluded that colonies established in North America could siphon off England's "surplus population," thus easing social strains at home. For similar reasons, many English people decided that they could improve their circumstances by migrating from a small, land-scarce, apparently overpopulated island to a large, land-rich continent. Such economic considerations were rendered even more significant in light of the second development, a major change in English religious practice.

The sixteenth century witnessed a religious transformation that eventually led large numbers of English dissenters to leave their homeland. In 1533, Henry VIII, wanting a male heir and infatuated with Anne Boleyn, sought to annul his marriage to his Spanish-born queen, Catherine of Aragon. When the pope refused to approve the annulment, Henry left the Roman Catholic Church. He founded the Church of England and—with Parliament's concurrence—proclaimed himself its head. The English people welcomed the schism. At first the reformed Church of England differed little from Catholicism in its practices, but under Henry's daughter Elizabeth I, new currents of religious belief that had originated on the European continent early in the sixteenth century dramatically affected the English church.

English Reformation

The leaders of the continental Protestant Reformation were Martin Luther, a German monk, and John Calvin, a French cleric and lawyer. Combating the Catholic doctrine that priests must serve as intermediaries between laypeople and God, Luther and Calvin insisted that each person could interpret the Bible for himself or herself. Both Luther and Calvin rejected Catholic rituals and denied the need for an elaborate church hierarchy. They also asserted that salvation came through faith alone, rather than—as Catholic teaching had it—through a combination of faith and good works. Calvin, though, went further than Luther in stressing God's absolute omnipotence and emphasizing the need for people to submit totally to God's will.

Elizabeth I tolerated religious diversity among her subjects as long as they generally acknowledged her authority as head of the Church of England. Accordingly, during her long reign (1558–1603) Calvin's ideas gained influence within the English church. By the late sixteenth century, many English Calvinists—those who came to be called Puritans because they wanted to purify the Church of England—believed that the English Reformation had not gone far enough. Henry had simplified the church hierarchy; they wanted to abolish it altogether. Henry had subordinated the church to the interests of the state; they wanted a church free from political interference. And, unlike the inclusive Church of England, the Puritans believed that only the "saved" should be church members.

Puritans

Elizabeth I's Stuart successors, her cousin James I (1603–1625) and his son Charles I (1625–1649), were less tolerant of Puritans than she had been. As Scots, they also had little respect for the traditions of representative government that had developed in England. As adherents to the theory of the *divine right of kings*, the Stuarts insisted that a monarch's power came directly from God and that his subjects had a duty to obey him. A king's authority was absolute, they argued.

The First Stuart Monarchs

Both James I and Charles I believed that their authority included the power to enforce religious conformity among their subjects. Because Puritans were challenging many of the most important precepts of the English church, the monarchs authorized the removal of Puritan clergymen from their pulpits. In the 1620s and 1630s a number of English Puritans accordingly decided to move to America, where they hoped to put their religious beliefs into practice unmolested by the Stuarts or the church hierarchy.

However, the initial impetus for the establishment of what was to become England's first permanent colony in the Western Hemisphere came not from the Puritans but from a group of merchants and wealthy gentry. In 1606, envisioning the possibility of earning great profits by finding precious metals and opening new trade routes, the men established a joint-stock company, the Virginia Company, to plant colonies in America.

Joint-stock companies had been developed in England during the sixteenth century as a mechanism for pooling the resources of many small investors, primarily to finance trading voyages. For that purpose they worked well: no one risked too much money, and investors usually received quick returns. Joint-stock companies turned out to be a poor way to finance colonies, because the early settlements required enormous amounts of capital and, with rare exceptions, failed to return much immediate profit. Colonies founded by joint-stock companies consequently suffered from a chronic lack of capital.

Joint-Stock Companies

The Virginia Company was no exception to this rule. Chartered by James I in 1606, the company tried but failed to start a colony in Maine and barely succeeded in planting one in Virginia. In May 1607, the company dispatched 104 men and boys who established a settlement called Jamestown on a swampy peninsula in a river they also named for their monarch.

Founding of Virginia

The colonists were ill equipped for survival in the unfamiliar environment, and the settlement was afflicted by dissension and disease. Many were gentlemen unaccustomed to working with their hands; others were artisans with irrelevant skills like glassmaking. Having come to Virginia expecting to make easy fortunes, most could not adjust to the conditions they encountered. They resisted living "like savages," retaining English dress and casual work habits despite their desperate circumstances. Such attitudes, combined with the effects of chronic malnutrition and epidemic disease, took a terrible toll. Only when Captain John Smith, one of the colony's founders, imposed military discipline on the colonists in 1608 was Jamestown saved from collapse. But after Smith's departure the settlement experienced a severe "starving time" (the winter of 1609–1610). Although more settlers (including a few women and children) arrived in 1608 and 1609 and living conditions slowly improved, as late as 1624 only 1,300 of approximately 8,000 English migrants to Virginia remained alive.

That Jamestown survived was a tribute not to the English but rather to the Native Americans within whose territories they settled, a group of six Algonkian tribes known as the Powhatan Confederacy (see map, page 30). A shrewd and powerful leader, Powhatan was aggressively consolidating his authority over some twenty-five other small tribes when the Europeans arrived. Fortunately for the colonists, Powhatan at first viewed them as potential allies. He found the English colony a reliable source of items such as steel knives and guns, which gave him a technological advantage over his Indian neighbors. In return, Powhatan's tribes traded their excess corn and other foodstuffs to the starving settlers. The initially cordial relationship soon deteriorated, however. The English colonists kidnapped Powhatan's daughter, Pocahontas, holding her as a hostage in retaliation for Powhatan's seizure of several settlers. In captivity, she agreed in 1614 to marry a colonist, John Rolfe.

Powhatan Confederacy

The relationship between the Jamestown colony and the coastal tribes was uneasy. English and Algonkian peoples had much in common: deep religious beliefs, a lifestyle oriented around agriculture, clear political and social hierarchies, and sharply defined gender roles. Yet the English and the Powhatans themselves usually focused on their cultural differences. English men thought that Algonkian men were lazy because they did not work in the fields, and that the women were oppressed because they did heavy fieldwork. Algonkian men, however, thought English men effeminate because they did "women's work" of cultivation.

Other differences between the two cultures caused serious misunderstandings. Although both societies were hierarchical, the nature of the hier-

Theodor de Bry's America *depicted crucial events in the continent's history. This illustration is de Bry's version of the kidnapping of Pocahontas, Powhatan's daughter, in 1612. In the foreground, two other Native Americans are enticing Pocahontas to join the English; at right center, she is being led onto a ship; in the background, English raiders are burning the villages of Powhatan's people.* Library of Congress.

Algonkian and English Cultural Differences

archies differed considerably. Among the East Coast Algonkian tribes, people were not born to positions of leadership, nor were political power and social status necessarily inherited through the male line. Members of the English gentry inherited their position from their fathers, and English political and military leaders tended to rule autocratically. By contrast, the authority of Algonkian leaders rested on consensus. Accustomed to the European concept of powerful kings, the English sought such figures within the tribes. Often (for example, when negotiating treaties) they willfully overestimated the ability of chiefs to make independent decisions for their people.

Furthermore, the Algonkians and the English had very different notions of property ownership. In most Algonkian villages, land was held communally by the entire group. Rights to use the land might be transferred, but the land could not be bought or sold. English people, in contrast, were accustomed to individual farms and to buying and selling land. In addition, the English refused to accept the validity of Indians' claims to traditional hunting territories, insisting that only land intensively cultivated could be regarded as owned or occupied.

Above all, the English settlers believed unwaveringly in the superiority of their civilization. They expected Native Americans to adopt English customs and to convert to Christianity. They showed little respect for traditional Indian ways of life, especially when they believed their own interests were at stake. That attitude was clearly revealed in the Virginia colony's treatment of the Powhatan Confederacy in subsequent years.

The spread of tobacco cultivation upset the balance of power in early Virginia. In tobacco the settlers and the Virginia Company found the salable commodity for which they had been searching. John Rolfe planted the first crop in 1611. By 1630, Virginians were exporting 1.5 million pounds of cured leaves. The great tobacco boom had begun, fueled by high prices and substantial profits for planters. Although the price fluctuated wildly from year to year, tobacco became the foundation of Virginia's prosperity. The colony developed from a small outpost peopled exclusively by males into an agricultural settlement inhabited by both men and women.

Tobacco: The Basis of Virginia's Success

Successful tobacco cultivation required abundant land, since the crop quickly drained soil of nutrients. Planters soon learned that a field could produce only about three satisfactory crops before it had to lie fallow for several years to regain its fertility. Soon eager planters applied to the Virginia Company for large land grants on both sides of the James River and its tributary streams.

Opechancanough, Powhatan's brother and successor, watched the English colonists steadily encroaching on the confederacy's lands and attempting to convert its members to Christianity. Recognizing the danger, the war leader launched coordinated attacks all along the river on March

Indian Uprising

22, 1622. By the end of the day, 347 colonists (about one-quarter of the total) lay dead, and only a timely warning from two Christian converts saved Jamestown itself from destruction. The colony survived this war and the one waged by Openchancanough in 1644. His defeat in the latter ended the Powhatan Confederacy's efforts to resist the spread of English settlement.

Life in the Chesapeake: Virginia and Maryland

In 1624 James I made Virginia a *royal colony*—a colony ruled by the king through appointed officials. The king also allowed the Virginia Company's "headright" system to continue. Under this system (adopted in 1617), every new arrival paying his or her own way was promised a land grant of 50 acres; those who financed the passage of others received similar headrights for each person. To ordinary English farmers, many of whom owned little or no land, the headright system offered a powerful incentive to migrate to Virginia. To wealthy gentry, it promised even more: the prospect of vast agricultural enterprises worked by large numbers of laborers.

Headrights

In 1619, the company had introduced a second policy that James was more reluctant to retain: it had authorized the landowning men of the major Virginia settlements to elect representatives to an assembly called the House of Burgesses. James at first abolished the assembly, but Virginians protested so vigorously that by 1629 the House of Burgesses was functioning once again. Only two decades after the first permanent English settlement was planted in North America, the colonists successfully insisted on governing themselves at the local level. Thus the political structure of England's American possessions came to differ from that of New Spain, New France, and New Netherland, all of which were ruled autocratically.

The House of Burgesses

By the 1630s, tobacco was firmly established in Virginia as the staple crop and chief source of revenue. It quickly became just as important in the second English colony planted on Chesapeake Bay: Maryland, settled in 1634 and given by Charles I to the Calvert family as a personal possession, a *proprietorship*. The Calverts intended the colony to serve as a haven for their fellow Roman Catholics, who were being persecuted in England. Cecilius Calvert, second Lord Baltimore, became the first colonizer to offer freedom of religion to all Christian settlers; he understood that protecting the Protestant majority was the only way to ensure Catholics' rights.

Founding of Maryland

In everything but religion the two Chesapeake colonies resembled each other. In both colonies, planters spread out along the region's deep, wide rivers, which served as the means of transporting imported and exported goods. With little need for commercial centers and with a dispersed population, few towns existed in the Chesapeake.

Because the tasks associated with tobacco culture were labor intensive, planters faced the problem of finding increasing numbers of workers. Nearby Indians, their numbers reduced by war and disease, could not supply them. Nor could Dutch traders; although they did carry a few Africans to the Chesapeake beginning in 1619, they could more easily and profitably sell slaves in the West Indies. In the first half of the seventeenth century, therefore, only a few Africans, some of them free, arrived in the Chesapeake. By 1650 only about three hundred blacks lived in Virginia.

Need for Laborers

Chesapeake tobacco planters thus looked primarily to England to supply their labor needs. Because of the headright system (which Maryland also adopted in 1640), a prospective tobacco planter anywhere in the Chesapeake could simultaneously obtain both land and labor by importing workers from England. Through good management, a planter could use his profits to pay for the passage of more workers and thereby gain title to more land.

Because prevailing gender roles dictated that field laborers should be men, most migrants were male. They came as *indentured servants*—in return for their passage, they contracted to work for planters for periods ranging from four to seven years. Indentured servants accounted for 75 to 85 percent of the approximately 130,000 English migrants to Virginia and Maryland during the seventeenth century. Roughly three-quarters of the servant migrants were males between the ages of fifteen and twenty-four; only one in five or six was female. Most of the men had been farmers and laborers and were what their contemporaries called the "common sort."

English Migrants

For such people the Chesapeake appeared to offer good prospects. After fulfilling the terms of their indentures, servants were promised "freedom dues" consisting of clothes, tools, livestock, casks of corn and tobacco, and sometimes even land. Yet the migrants' lives were difficult. Servants typically worked six days a week, ten to fourteen hours a day. Their masters could discipline or sell them, and they faced severe penalties for running away. Even so, the laws did offer them some protection. For example, their masters were supposed to supply them with sufficient food, clothing, and shelter. Servants who were especially cruelly treated turned to the courts for assistance.

Conditions of Servitude

Servants and planters alike had to contend with epidemic disease. Migrants first had to survive the process the colonists called "seasoning"—a bout with disease (probably malaria) that usually occurred during their first Chesapeake summer. They then had to endure recurrences of malaria, along with dysentery, typhoid fever, and other diseases. As a result, approximately 40 percent of male servants did not survive long enough to become freedmen.

For those who survived the term of their indentures, however, the opportunities for advancement were real. Until the last decades of the seventeenth century, former servants were usually able to become independent planters ("freeholders") and to live a modest but comfortable existence. Some even assumed positions of political prominence. But after 1670, tobacco prices fell, good land grew scarce and expensive, and Maryland

How do historians know what seventeenth-century settlements looked like? Recent excavations at St. Mary's City, Maryland, founded as the capital and sole town of Calvert's colony in 1634, demonstrate the importance of cooperation between historians and archaeologists. St. Mary's City is one of only two major seventeenth-century English settlements in America not now buried under modern cities. (The other, Jamestown, was located in 1996, although for many years historians believed that it had been eroded into the James River.) The site of St. Mary's City was abandoned in 1696 when the colonial capital was moved to Annapolis; later the area was incorporated into a tobacco plantation. Working from written documents like deeds and wills, historians created hypotheses about the layout of the town. But when archaeologists began digging into the soil, they discovered what the documents had not revealed: the town plan was based on triangles intersecting at the town's central square. A modern artist's reconstruction of the town as it might have looked in 1685 shows portions of those triangles. At far right, top, is the Jesuit chapel, the first Catholic church in Anglo-America. At center is the square, with the large Country's House, the building once used as the capitol, on the left. (The new state house constructed in 1676 is off this map to the far left, at the point of a triangle at the same distance from the square as the chapel.) The artist needed both archival and archaeological data to produce this drawing. Historic St. Mary's City Commission.

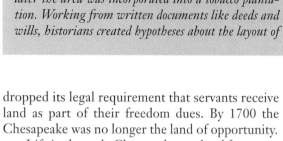

dropped its legal requirement that servants receive land as part of their freedom dues. By 1700 the Chesapeake was no longer the land of opportunity.

Life in the early Chesapeake was hard for everyone. Farmers (and sometimes their wives) toiled in the fields alongside servants. Most people rose and went to bed with the sun, consumed a diet based on pork and corn, and lived in ramshackle dwellings with just one or two rooms. As a rule, planters devoted their income to improving their

Standard of Living

farms, buying livestock, and purchasing more laborers rather than to improving their standard of living.

The predominance of males, the incidence of servitude, and the high mortality rates combined to produce unusual patterns of family life. Female servants normally were not allowed to marry during their terms of indenture because masters did not want pregnancies to deprive them of workers. Many male ex-servants could not marry at all because there were relatively few women. In con-

Chesapeake Families

trast, nearly every adult free woman in the Chesapeake married, and widows usually remarried within a few months of a husband's death. Yet because their marriages were delayed by servitude or broken by death, Chesapeake women bore only one to three children, in contrast to English women, who normally had at least five.

This low rate of natural increase meant that migrants would make up a majority of the Chesapeake population throughout the seventeenth century, with important implications for politics in Maryland and Virginia. Migrants composed the vast majority of the membership of Virginia's House of Burgesses and Maryland's House of Delegates (established in 1635). So, too, in each colony they dominated the governor's council, which was simultaneously the colony's highest court, part of the legislature, and executive adviser to the governor.

Chesapeake Politics

English-born colonists naturally tended to look to England for solutions to their problems, and they often relied on English allies to advance their cause. Because of the low birth rates and high mortality, no cohesive native-born ruling elite emerged until the early eighteenth century. Before that, the Chesapeake colonies' immigrant leaders engaged in bitter and prolonged struggles for power, which thwarted the ability of the Virginia and Maryland governments to function effectively. Thus the existence of representative assemblies failed to create political stability. Indeed, instability may have been the price of the region's demographic patterns.

The Founding of New England

The economic motives that prompted English people to move to the Chesapeake colonies also drew men and women to New England. But two factors combined to make New England different from the Chesapeake. First, the northern climate and landscape were more conducive to diversified small farms than to large production units yielding staple crops. Second, Puritans organized the New England colonies, and their church became the region's most important institution. Neither the Church of England nor Roman Catholicism held that significance in the Chesapeake.

Religion was a constant presence in the lives of pious Puritans. They believed that God predestined souls to heaven or hell before birth and that Christians could do nothing to change their ultimate fate. One of their primary duties as Christians, though, was to assess the state of their own souls. They devoted themselves to self-examination and Bible study, and families prayed together each day under the guidance of the husband and father. Yet even the most pious could never be absolutely certain they were numbered among the saved (or elect). Consequently, devout Puritans were filled with anxiety about their spiritual state.

Puritan Beliefs

Some Puritans (called Congregationalists) wanted to reform the Church of England rather than abandon it. Another group, known as Separatists, believed the Church of England to be so corrupt that it could not be salvaged. The only way to purify it, they believed, was to start anew, establishing their own religious bodies, with membership restricted to the saved, as nearly as they could be identified.

In 1620, some Separatists, many of whom had earlier migrated to Holland in quest of the right to practice their religion freely, received permission to settle in part of the territory controlled by the Virginia Company. Later that year, more than one hundred people, only thirty of them Separatists, set sail from England on the old and crowded *Mayflower*. Two months later, in November, they landed in America, but farther north than they had intended. Still, given the lateness of the season, they decided to stay where they were. They established their colony on a fine harbor, and they named their settlement Plymouth.

Founding of Plymouth

Even before they landed, the Pilgrims had to surmount their first challenge—from the "strangers," or non-Puritans, who had sailed with them to America. Because they landed outside the jurisdiction of the Virginia Company, some of the strangers questioned the authority of the colony's leaders. In response, the Mayflower Compact, signed in November 1620 while everyone was still on board the *Mayflower*, established a "Civil Body Politic" and a rudimentary legal authority for the colony. The settlers elected a governor and at first made all decisions for the colony at town meetings. Later, after more towns had been founded, Plymouth, like Virginia and Maryland, created an assembly to which the landowning male settlers elected representatives.

A second challenge facing the Pilgrims was survival. Like the Jamestown settlers before them, they were poorly prepared to subsist in the new environment. Their difficulties were compounded by the season of their arrival, for winter quickly descended on them. Only half of the *Mayflower*'s passengers were still alive by spring. But, again like the Virginians, the Pilgrims benefited from the political circumstances of their Native American neighbors.

The Pokanokets (a branch of the Wampanoags) controlled the area in which the Pilgrims had settled. To protect themselves from the powerful Narragansetts of the

Pokanokets

southern New England coast, the Pokanokets decided to ally themselves with the newcomers. In the spring of 1621, their leader, Massasoit, signed a treaty with the Pilgrims, and during the colony's first difficult years the Pokanokets supplied the English with essential foodstuffs. The settlers were also assisted by Squanto, a Pokanoket who in the early 1610s had been captured by fishermen and taken to England, where he learned to speak English. Squanto became the Pilgrims' interpreter and a major source of information about the unfamiliar environment.

Before the 1620s ended, another group of Puritans—this time Congregationalists—launched the colonial enterprise that would come to dominate New England. The event

Massachusetts Bay Company

that stimulated their interest in North America was Charles I's accession to the throne in 1625. Charles was more hostile to Puritan beliefs than his father had been. Because of Charles's actions, some non-Separatists began to think about settling in America. A group

of Congregationalist merchants sent out a body of colonists to Cape Ann, north of Cape Cod, in 1628. The following year the merchants obtained a royal charter as a new joint-stock company, constituting themselves as the Massachusetts Bay Company.

The company quickly attracted Puritans of the "middling sort" who increasingly feared they no longer would be able to practice their religion freely in England. They remained committed to the goal of reforming the Church of England but concluded that they could better pursue that aim in America. In a dramatic move, the Congregationalist merchants boldly decided to transfer the company's headquarters to New England. The settlers would then be answerable to no one in the mother country and would be able to handle their affairs as they pleased.

The most important recruit to the new venture was John Winthrop, a member of the lesser English gentry. In October 1629, the Massachusetts Bay Company elected Winthrop as its governor. It

Governor John Winthrop

fell to Winthrop to organize the initial segment of the great Puritan migration to America. In 1630 more than one thousand English men and women moved to Massachusetts—most of them to Boston, which soon became the largest town in British North America. By 1643 nearly twenty thousand compatriots had followed them.

Winthrop's was a transcendent vision. The society Winthrop foresaw in Puritan America was a true *commonwealth*, a community in which each person put the good of the whole ahead of his or her private concerns. It was also to be a society whose members all lived according to the precepts of Christian love. Although the ideal was beyond human reach, it long prevailed as a Puritan goal.

The Puritans expressed their communal ideal chiefly in the doctrine of the covenant. They believed God had made a covenant—that is,

Ideal of the Covenant

an agreement or contract— with them when they were chosen for the special mission to America. In turn they covenanted with each other, promising to work together toward their goals.

The founders of churches and towns in the new land often drafted formal documents setting forth the principles on which such institutions would be based. The same was true of the colonial governments of New England.

The leaders of Massachusetts Bay likewise transformed their original joint-stock company charter into the basis for a covenanted community based on mutual consent. Under pressure from landowning male settlers, they gradually changed the General Court—officially the company's small governing body—into a colonial legislature. They also granted the status of freeman, or voting member of the company, to all property-owning adult male church members residing in Massachusetts. Less than two decades after the first large group of Puritans had arrived in Massachusetts Bay, the colony had a functioning system of self-government composed of a governor and a two-house legislature. The General Court also established a judicial system modeled on England's.

The colony's method of distributing land helped to further the communal ideal. Groups of families—often from the same region of England—applied together to the General Court for grants of land on which to establish towns. The men who received the original town grant had the sole authority to determine how the land would be distributed. First they laid out town lots for houses and a church. Then they gave each family parcels of land scattered around the town center: pasture here, a woodlot there, an arable field elsewhere. They reserved the best and largest plots for the most distinguished among them (including the minister).

New England Towns

When migrants began to move beyond the territorial limits of the Massachusetts Bay colony into Connecticut (1636), New Haven (1638), and New Hampshire (1638), the same pattern of town land grants was maintained. Only Maine, with coastal regions thinly populated by fishermen and their families, deviated from the standard practice.

Thus New England settlements initially tended to be more compact than those of the Chesapeake. Town centers grew up quickly, developing in three distinctly different ways. Some, chiefly isolated agricultural settlements in the interior, tried to sustain Winthrop's vision of harmonious community life based on diversified family farms. A second group, the coastal towns like Boston and Salem, became bustling seaports. The third category, commercialized agricultural towns, grew up in the Connecticut River valley, where easy water transportation enabled farmers to sell surplus goods readily.

The migration to the Connecticut valley ended the Puritans' relative freedom from clashes with their Native American neighbors. The first English settlers in the valley moved there from Newtown (Cambridge, Massachusetts), under the direction of their minister, Thomas Hooker. Connecticut was fertile, and the wide river promised ready access to the ocean. The site had just one problem: it fell within the territory controlled by the powerful Pequots.

The Pequots' dominance was based on their role as primary middlemen in the trade between New England Indians and the Dutch in New Netherland. The arrival of English settlers signaled the end of the Pequots' power over the regional trading networks, for their tributary bands could now trade directly with Europeans. Clashes between Pequots and English colonists began even before the Connecticut valley settlements were established, but their founding tipped the balance toward war. After two English traders were killed (probably not by Pequots), the English raided a Pequot village. In return, the Pequots attacked the new town of Wethersfield in April 1637, killing nine and capturing two of the colonists. To retaliate, a Massachusetts Bay expedition the following month attacked and burned the main Pequot town on the Mystic River. At least four hundred Pequots, mostly women and children, were slaughtered.

Pequot War

For the next thirty years, the New England Indians tried to accommodate themselves to the spread of European settlement. They traded with the newcomers and sometimes worked for them, but they resisted acculturation or incorporation into English society. The Native Americans clung to their traditional farming methods. Indeed, the only European agricultural practice they adopted was keeping livestock; in the absence of game, domesticated animals provided excellent sources of meat.

Although the official seal of the Massachusetts Bay colony showed an Indian crying "Come over and help us," most colonists showed little interest in converting the New England Algonkians to Christianity. Only a few Massachusetts clerics, most notably John Eliot, seriously undertook missionary activities. Eliot insisted that converts should reside in towns, farm the land in English fashion, assume English names, wear European-style clothing and shoes, cut their hair, and stop observing a wide range of their own customs. He understandably met with little success. At the peak of Eliot's efforts, only eleven hundred Native Americans lived in the fourteen "Praying Towns" he had established.

John Eliot and the Praying Towns

The Jesuits' successful missions in New France contrasted sharply with the Puritans failure to win many converts. Initially, Catholicism had several advantages over Puritanism. The Catholic Church employed attractive rituals, instructed converts that through good works they could help to earn their own salvation, and offered Indian women an inspiring role model—the Virgin Mary. In Montréal and Quebec, communities of nuns taught Indian women and children and ministered to their needs. Furthermore, the few French colonists on the St. Lawrence did not alienate potential converts by encroaching steadily on their lands (as did New Englanders). Perhaps most important, the Jesuits understood that Christian beliefs were to some extent compatible with Native American culture. Unlike Puritans, Jesuits were willing to accept converts who did not wholly adopt European styles of life.

Puritan and Jesuit Missions Compared

Life in New England

New England's colonizers adopted lifestyles that differed considerably from those of both their Indian neighbors and their European counterparts in the Chesapeake. Unlike the Algonkian bands, who usually moved four or five times each year to take full advantage of their environment, English people lived year-round in the same location. And unlike residents of the Chesapeake, New Englanders constructed sturdy dwellings intended to last. They used the same fields again and again, believing it was less arduous to employ manure as fertilizer than to clear new fields every few years. Furthermore, they had to fence their croplands to prevent them from being overrun by their cattle, sheep, and hogs. When New Englanders began to spread out over the countryside, the reason was not so much human crowding as it was animal crowding.

Because Puritans commonly moved to America in family groups, the age range in early New England was wide; and because many more women went to New England than to the tobacco colonies, the population could immediately begin to reproduce itself. Moreover, New England was much healthier than the Chesapeake. New England was even healthier than the mother country. Although adult male migrants to the Chesapeake lost about ten years from their English life expectancy of fifty to fifty-five years, their Massachusetts counterparts gained five or more years. Consequently, while Chesapeake population patterns gave rise to families that were few in number, small in size, and transitory, the demographic characteristics of New England made families there numerous, large, and long-lived. If seventeenth-century Chesapeake women could expect to rear one to three healthy children, New England women could anticipate raising five to seven.

New England Families

The nature of the population had other major implications for family life. New England in effect created grandparents, since in England people rarely lived long enough to know their children's children. And whereas early southern parents commonly died before their children married, northern parents exercised a good deal of control over their adult children. Young men could not marry without acreage to cultivate, and because of the communal land-grant system they were dependent on their fathers to supply them with that land. Daughters, too, needed the dowry of household goods that their parents would give them when they married. Yet parents needed their children's labor and often were reluctant to see them marry and start their own households. Generational conflict existed, but children had few alternatives and thus obeyed their parents' wishes.

Another important difference lay in the influence of religion on New Englanders' lives. Puritans controlled their governments. With the exception of Rhode Island, Congregationalism was the only officially recognized religion; members of other sects had no freedom of worship.

Impact of Religion

Some non-Puritans voted in town meetings, but in Massachusetts Bay and New Haven, church membership was a prerequisite for voting in colony elections. All households were taxed to build meetinghouses and pay ministers' salaries. Massachusetts's first legal codes (1641 and 1648) incorporated regulations drawn from Old Testament scriptures into the laws of the colony; those codes were later copied by New Haven, Plymouth, New Hampshire, and Connecticut.

In addition, the Puritan colonies attempted to enforce strict codes of moral conduct. Colonists there were frequently tried for drunkenness, cardplaying, even idleness. Couples who had sex during their engagement—as revealed by the birth of a baby less than nine months after their wedding— were fined and publicly humiliated. (Maryland, by contrast, did not penalize premarital pregnancy, only bastardy.) More harshly treated in both regions were men—and a handful of women—who engaged in behaviors that today would be called homosexual. (The term did not then exist.)

In New England, church and state were thus intertwined. Puritans objected to secular interference in religious affairs but at the same time expected the church to influence the conduct of politics and the affairs of society. They also believed that the state had an obligation to support and protect the one true church—theirs. As a result, though they came to America seeking freedom to worship as they wished, they saw no contradiction in their refusal to grant that freedom to others. Indeed, the two most significant divisions in early Massachusetts were caused by religious disputes and by Massachusetts Bay's unwillingness to tolerate dissent.

Roger Williams, a Separatist, migrated to Massachusetts Bay in 1631. He soon began to express some eccentric ideas: that the king of England had no right to give away land already occupied by Native Americans, that church and state should be kept entirely separate, and

Roger Williams

that Puritans should not impose their religious beliefs on others. Banished from Massachusetts in late 1635, Williams founded the town of Providence on Narragansett Bay. Because of Williams's beliefs, Providence and other towns in what became the colony of Rhode Island adopted a policy of tolerance toward all religions, including Judaism.

The other dissenter, and an even greater challenge to Massachusetts Bay orthodoxy, was Anne Marbury Hutchinson. A skilled medical practitioner popular with the women of Boston, she was a follower of John Cotton, a minister who stressed the *covenant of grace*, or God's free

Anne Hutchinson

gift of salvation to unworthy human beings. By contrast, most Massachusetts clerics emphasized the need for Puritans to engage in good works, study, and reflection in preparation for receiving God's grace. After teaching her ideas during childbed discussions (when no men were present), Hutchinson began holding women's meetings in her home to discuss Cotton's sermons. She emphasized the covenant of grace more than did Cotton himself, and she even adopted the belief that the elect could be assured of salvation and communicate directly with God. Such ideas had an immense appeal for Puritans. Anne Hutchinson offered them certainty of salvation instead of a state of constant anxiety.

Hutchinson's ideas were a dangerous threat to Puritan orthodoxy. So in November 1637, the leaders of the General Court charged her with having maligned the colony's ministers by accusing them of preaching the covenant of works, the idea that people could earn their own salvation.

For two days she defended herself cleverly against her accusers. But then Hutchinson triumphantly and boldly declared that God had spoken to her "by an immediate revelation," telling her that he would curse the Puritans' descendants for generations if they harmed her. That assertion assured her banishment to Rhode Island.

The authorities in Massachusetts Bay perceived Anne Hutchinson as doubly dangerous, for she threatened not only religious orthodoxy but also traditional gender roles. Puritans believed in the equality before God of all souls, but they considered actual women (as distinct from their spiritual selves) inferior to men. Christians had long followed Saint Paul's dictum that women should keep silent in church and be submissive to their husbands. Hutchinson did neither. A minister at her church trial told her bluntly: "You have stept out of your place, you have rather bine a Husband than a Wife and a preacher than a Hearer."

The New England authorities' reaction to Hutchinson reveals the depth of their adherence to European gender-role concepts. To them, an orderly society required the submission of wives to husbands as well as the obedience of subjects to rulers. English colonists intended to change many aspects of their lives, but not the sexual division of labor or the assumption of male superiority.

 ## Conclusion

By the middle of the seventeenth century, Europeans had unquestionably come to North America to stay, a fact that signaled major changes for the peoples of both hemispheres. Europeans killed Indians with their weapons and diseases and had but limited success in converting them to European religions. Contacts with the Native Americans taught Europeans to eat new foods, speak new languages, and recognize the persistence of other cultural patterns. The prosperity and even survival of many of the European colonies depended heavily on the cultivation of American crops (maize and tobacco), thus attesting to the importance of post-Columbian ecological change.

In America, Spaniards reaped the benefits of their South and Central American gold and silver mines, while French people earned their primary profits from Indian trade (in Canada) and cultivating sugar cane (in the Caribbean). Sugar also enriched the Portuguese. The Dutch concentrated on commerce—trading in furs and sugar as well as carrying human cargoes of enslaved Africans to South America and the Caribbean. Of these nations, only France and Spain went beyond the economic relationships they established with native peoples to attempt to Christianize them.

Although the English colonies at first sought to rely on trade, they quickly took another form altogether when so many English people of the "middling sort" decided to migrate to North America. To a greater extent than their European counterparts, the English transferred the society of their homeland to a new environment. Although New England and the Chesapeake differed in many ways, both were English in origin, and in the years to come both regions would be drawn into the increasingly fierce rivalries besetting the European powers. Those rivalries would continue to affect Americans of all races until after France and England had fought the greatest war yet known in the mid-eighteenth century and the Anglo-American colonies had won their independence.

Suggestions for Further Reading

General

David Hackett Fischer, *Albion's Seed: Four British Folkways in America* (1989); D. W. Meinig, *Atlantic America, 1492–1800* (1986); Gary B. Nash, *Red, White, and Black: The Peoples of Early America*, 2d ed. (1982); Mary Beth Norton, *Founding Mothers & Fathers: Gendered Power and the Forming of American Society* (1996); Paula Treckel, *To Comfort the Heart: Women in Seventeenth-Century America* (1996); Alden T. Vaughan, *Roots of American Racism* (1994).

New Spain, New Netherland, New France, and the Caribbean

Karen Anderson, *Chain Her by One Foot: The Subjugation of Native Women in Seventeenth-Century New France* (1991); Denys Delâge, *Bitter Feast: Amerindians and Europeans in Northeastern North America, 1600–64* (1993); Richard S. Dunn, *Sugar and Slaves: The Rise of the Planter Class in the English West Indies, 1624–1713* (1972); William J. Eccles, *France in America*, rev. ed. (1990); Donna Merwick, *Possessing Albany, 1630–1710* (1990); Sidney Mintz, *Sweetness and Power: The Place of Sugar in Modern*

History (1985); Marc Simmons, *The Last Conquistador: Juan de Oñate and the Settling of the Far Southwest* (1991); David J. Weber, *The Spanish Frontier in North America* (1992).

England

Susan Dwyer Amussen, *An Ordered Society: Gender and Class in Early Modern England* (1988); Peter Laslett, *The World We Have Lost*, 3d ed. (1984); Keith Wrightson, *English Society, 1580–1680* (1982).

Early Contact Between Europeans and Indians

James Axtell, *The Invasion Within: The Contest of Cultures in Colonial North America* (1985); Philip Barbour, *Pocahontas and Her World* (1970); William Cronon, *Changes in the Land: Indians, Colonists, and the Ecology of New England* (1983); Francis Jennings, *The Invasion of America: Indians, Colonialism, and the Cant of Conquest* (1975); Karen O. Kupperman, *Settling with the Indians: The Meeting of English and Indian Cultures in America, 1580–1640* (1980); Neal Salisbury, *Manitou and Providence: Indians, Europeans, and the Making of New England, 1500–1643* (1982); Timothy Silver, *A New Face on the Countryside: Indians, Colonists, and Slaves in South Atlantic Forests, 1500–1800* (1990); Peter Wood et al., eds., *Powhatan's Mantle: Indians in the Colonial Southeast* (1989).

Chesapeake Society and Politics

Lois Green Carr et al., *Robert Cole's World: Agriculture and Society in Early Maryland* (1991); David Galenson, *White Servitude in Colonial America: An Economic Analysis* (1981); James Horn, *Adapting to a New World: English Society in the Seventeenth-Century Chesapeake* (1994); Ivor Noël Hume, *The Virginia Adventure: Roanoke to James Towne* (1994); Gloria L. Main, *Tobacco Colony: Life in Early Maryland, 1650–1720* (1983); Edmund S. Morgan, *American Slavery, American Freedom: The Ordeal of Colonial Virginia* (1975); Alden T. Vaughan, *American Genesis: Captain John Smith and the Founding of Virginia* (1975).

New England Communities, Politics, and Religion

David D. Hall, *Worlds of Wonder, Days of Judgment: Popular Religious Belief in Early New England* (1989); Stephen Innes, *Creating the Commonwealth: The Economic Culture of Puritan New England* (1995); Stephen Innes, *Labor in a New Land: Economy and Society in 17th-Century Springfield* (1983); Sydney V. James, *Colonial Rhode Island* (1975); George Langdon, *Pilgrim Colony: A History of New Plymouth, 1620–1691* (1966); John Frederick Martin, *Profits in the Wilderness: Entrepreneurship and the Founding of New England Towns in the 17th Century* (1991); Edmund S. Morgan, *The Puritan Dilemma: The Story of John Winthrop* (1958); Darrett Rutman, *Winthrop's Boston* (1965).

New England Women and Family Life

David Cressy, *Coming Over: Migration and Communication Between England and New England in the Seventeenth Century* (1987); John Demos, *A Little Commonwealth: Family Life in Plymouth Colony* (1970); Lyle Koehler, *A Search for Power: The "Weaker Sex" in Seventeenth-Century New England* (1980); Edmund S. Morgan, *The Puritan Family*, rev. ed. (1966); Roger Thompson, *Sex in Middlesex: Popular Mores in a Massachusetts County, 1649–1699* (1986).

3

American Society
Takes Shape
1640–1720

The hangman tightened the noose around the condemned man's neck and shoved him off the ladder. The rope broke, and the notorious pirate Captain William Kidd lay on the ground, dazed. The hangman repeated the procedure with a new rope. This time it held. The event happened on May 23, 1701, near the London docks. As a warning to others, Kidd's body was left dangling from a gibbet on the bank of the Thames.

William Kidd, born in Scotland, had made his home in New York, the port once known as New Amsterdam. The merchants there, being none too choosy about the source of their profits, eagerly provisioned pirates' ships and purchased goods pirated from ships plying the expanded trade routes. In the 1690s, Manhattan's economy depended on this illegal trade. For years Kidd and other pirates could count on New York's governors to ignore their activities in exchange for shares of the bounty.

Why was Captain Kidd condemned to die? His fatal enterprise began in London in early 1696, when he gained financial backing from several powerful and prominent English investors for a voyage to the Indian Ocean. After more than a year of buccaneering, Kidd returned to New York by way of the Caribbean, hoping to avoid prosecution for piracy by paying off his investors in full and by bribing colonial officials. Unfortunately for Kidd, one of his financial backers, the earl of Bellomont, had become governor of New York. Bellomont was waging a vigorous campaign against piracy and could not afford to protect Kidd. In addition, as governor he could claim one-third of any confiscated illegal cargo. Kidd's fate was sealed when Bellomont ordered his arrest and shipped him back to England for trial.

The saga of William Kidd illustrates above all the involvement of the English mainland colonies in a growing network of trade and international contacts. North America, like England itself, was becoming increasingly embedded in a worldwide matrix of exchange and warfare. The web woven by oceangoing vessels now crisscrossed the globe, carrying West Indian sugar to Europe, Africans to America, cloth and spices from the East Indies to Africa, and New England fish and wood products to the Caribbean. Formerly tiny outposts, the North American colonies had expanded their territorial claims and embarked on a deliberate course of economic development. In response, the English government for the first time began to adopt policies to systematize colonial administration, passing laws that regulated trade and reshaped the American governments.

Three developments shaped life in the mainland colonies between 1640 and 1720: the introduction of a system of chattel slavery, especially in the south Atlantic coastal regions; changes in the colonies' relationship with their mother country; and increasing conflicts with their North American neighbors, both European and Native American.

The explosive growth of the slave trade was of critical significance in the colonial economy. For slave trader and planter alike, slaves meant huge profits. The arrival of large numbers of West African peoples dramatically reshaped colonial society and fueled the international trading system. Moreover, the burgeoning North American economy attracted new attention from officials in London who attempted to supervise the American settlements more effectively and thus ensure that England benefited from their economic growth.

Neither English colonists nor London administrators could ignore other peoples living on the North American continent. As the English settlements expanded, they came into violent conflict not only with the powerful Indians of the interior but also with the Dutch, the Spanish, and especially the French. By 1720, war had become an all-too-frequent feature of American life.

The English Civil War, the Stuart Restoration, and the American Colonies

In 1642, England erupted into civil war. Disputes over taxation, religion, and other issues led to armed conflict between supporters of the Puritan-dominated Parliament and King Charles I. After four years of warfare, Parliament triumphed. Charles I was executed in 1649, and the parliamentary army's leader, Oliver Cromwell, assumed control of the government. Yet after Cromwell's death in 1658 Parliament decided to restore the monarchy if Charles I's son and heir would agree to restrictions on his authority. In 1660, Charles II ascended the throne, having promised to support the Church of England and to seek Parliament's consent for any new taxes. Thus ended the Interregnum (Latin for "between reigns") or Commonwealth period.

The Civil War, the Interregnum, and the reign of Charles II (1660–1685) had far-reaching significance for the Anglo-American colonies. During the Civil War and the Commonwealth period when Puritans controlled the English government, the migration to New England largely ceased. During the subsequent reign of Charles II, six of the thirteen colonies that eventually would form the American nation were either founded or came under English rule: New York, New Jersey, Pennsylvania (including Delaware), and North and South Carolina. All were proprietorships granted in their entirety to one man or to a group of men who held title to the soil and controlled the government. Charles II gave these vast American holdings as rewards to men who had supported him during the Civil War. Collectively, these became known as the Restoration colonies, because they were created by the restored Stuart monarchy.

One of the first to benefit was Charles's younger brother James, the duke of York. In 1664, Charles II gave James the region between the

New Netherland Becomes New York

Connecticut and Delaware Rivers, including the Hudson valley and Long Island. James immediately organized an invasion fleet. In late August the vessels anchored off Manhattan Island and demanded New

The Founding of English Colonies in North America, 1664–1732

Colony	Founder(s)	Date	Basis of Economy
New York (formerly New Netherland)	James, duke of York	1664	Farming, fur trading
New Jersey	Sir George Carteret, John Lord Berkeley	1664	Farming
North Carolina	Carolina proprietors	1665	Tobacco, forest products
South Carolina	Carolina proprietors	1670	Rice, indigo
Pennsylvania	William Penn	1681	Farming
Georgia	James Oglethorpe	1732	Rice, forest products

Netherland's surrender. The colony complied without resistance.

Thus England acquired a tiny but heterogeneous possession. In 1664, an appreciable minority of English people already lived in the colony. New York, as it was now called, also included sizable numbers of Indians, Germans, and Scandinavians, as well as a smattering of other European peoples. Because the Dutch had actively imported slaves into the colony, almost one-fifth of Manhattan's approximately fifteen hundred inhabitants were of African descent.

Recognizing the population's diversity, the duke of York's representatives moved cautiously in their efforts to establish English authority. The Duke's Laws, a legal code proclaimed in 1665, at first applied solely to the English settlements on Long Island, only later being extended to the rest of the colony. Dutch forms of local government were maintained, Dutch land titles confirmed, and Dutch residents allowed to maintain customary legal practices. Religious toleration was guaranteed by allowing each town to decide which church to support with its tax revenues. Much to the dismay of English residents of the colony, the Duke's Laws made no provision for a representative assembly. Like other Stuarts, James was suspicious of legislative bodies, and not until 1683 did he agree to the colonists' requests for an elected legislature.

The English takeover thus had little immediate effect on the colony. Its population grew slowly, barely reaching eighteen thousand by the time of the first English census in 1698. One of the chief reasons the English conquest brought so little change to New York was that the duke of York in 1664 regranted the land between the Hudson and Delaware Rivers—East and West Jersey—to his friends Sir George Carteret and John Lord Berkeley. That grant deprived his own colony of much fertile land and hindered its economic growth. Meanwhile, the Jersey proprietors acted rapidly to attract settlers, promising generous land grants, limited freedom of religion, and—without authorization from the Crown—a representative assembly. New Jersey grew quickly; in 1726, it had 32,500 inhabitants, only 8,000 fewer than New York.

Founding of New Jersey

Within twenty years, Berkeley and Carteret sold their interests in the Jerseys to separate groups of investors. The purchasers of all of Carteret's share (West Jersey) and portions of Berkeley's (East Jersey) were members of the Society of Friends, seeking a refuge from persecution in England. The Society of Friends, also called Quakers, denied the need for intermediaries between individuals and God. They believed that anyone could receive the "inner light" and be saved and that all were equal in God's sight. They had no formally trained clergy; any Quaker, male or female, could speak in meetings or become a "public friend" and travel from meeting to meet-

• *Important Events* •

1642–46	English Civil War; end of first New England economic system based on furs and migrants		**1681**	Pennsylvania chartered
1649	Charles I executed		**1685**	James II becomes king
1651	First Navigation Act passed to regulate colonial trade		**1686–89**	Dominion of New England established, superseding all charters of colonies from Maine to New Jersey
1660	Stuarts restored to throne; Charles II becomes king		**1688–89**	James II deposed in Glorious Revolution; William and Mary ascend throne
1662	Halfway Covenant drafted in New England, creating category of partial membership in Congregational churches		**1689–97**	King William's War fought on northern New England frontier
1663	Carolina chartered		**1692**	Witchcraft oubreak in Salem Village; nineteen executions result
1664	English conquer New Netherland; New York founded New Jersey established		**1696**	Board of Trade and Plantations established to coordinate English colonial administration
1670s	Jacques Marquette, Louis Jolliet, and Robert Cavelier de La Salle explore the Great Lakes and Mississippi valley for France		**1701**	Iroquois adopt neutrality policy toward France and England
			1702–13	Queen Anne's War fought by French and English
1675–76	King Philip's (Metacom's) War devastates New England		**1711–13**	Tuscarora War (North Carolina) leads to capture or migration of most Tuscaroras
1676	Bacon's Rebellion disrupts Virginia government; Jamestown destroyed		**1715**	Yamasee War nearly destroys South Carolina
1680–92	Pueblo revolt temporarily drives Spaniards from New Mexico		**1718**	New Orleans founded in French Louisiana
			1732	Georgia chartered

ing to discuss God's word. The Quaker message of radical egalitarianism was not welcome in either England or Puritan New England.

The Quakers obtained their own colony in 1681, when Charles II granted the region between Maryland and New York to his close, personal friend William Penn, a prominent member of the sect. Although Penn held the colony as a personal proprietorship, he saw his province as a haven for his persecuted coreligionists. He offered land to all comers on liberal terms, promised toleration of all religions (though only Christians were given the vote), guaranteed Eng-

Pennsylvania: A Quaker Haven

lish liberties such as trial by jury, and pledged to establish a representative assembly. He also publicized throughout Europe the ready availability of land in Pennsylvania.

Penn's activities and the attraction of his lands for Quakers gave rise to a migration whose magnitude was equaled only by the Puritan exodus to New England in the 1630s. By 1689 Pennsylvania's population had reached twelve thousand—among them Welsh, Irish, Dutch, and Germans. Philadelphia, carefully planned to be the major city in the province, drew merchants and artisans from throughout the English-speaking world. From mainland and West Indian colonies alike came Quakers seeking religious freedom. Pennsylvania's lands were both plentiful and fertile, and the colony soon began exporting flour and other foodstuffs to the West Indies. Practically overnight Philadelphia acquired more than two thousand citizens and began to challenge Boston's commercial dominance.

A pacifist with egalitarian principles, Penn attempted to treat Native Americans fairly. Before selling land to European settlers, he purchased it from the Delawares (or Lenapes). He also established strict regulations for trade and forbade the sale of alcohol to Indians.

William Penn's Indian Policy

Penn's policies attracted Indians who moved to Pennsylvania near the end of the seventeenth century to escape repeated clashes with English colonists in Maryland, Virginia, and North Carolina. Most important were the Tuscaroras. Shawnees and Miamis moved eastward from the Ohio valley. By a supreme irony, however, the same toleration that attracted Indians also brought non-Quaker Europeans who showed little respect for Indian claims to the soil. In effect, Penn's policy was so successful that it caused its own downfall. The Scots-Irish, Palatine Germans, and Swiss who settled in Pennsylvania clashed repeatedly over land with groups of Indians who had also recently migrated to the colony.

The other proprietary colony, granted by Charles II in 1663, encompassed a huge tract of land stretching from the southern boundary of Virginia to Spanish Florida. The area had great strategic importance; a successful English settlement there would prevent Spaniards from pushing farther north. The proprietors named their new province Carolina in honor of Charles, whose Latin name was *Carolus*. The Fundamental Constitutions of Carolina, which they asked the political philosopher John Locke to draft for them, set forth an elaborate plan for a colony governed by a hierarchy of landholding aristocrats. But Carolina failed to follow the course the proprietors laid out. Instead, it quickly developed two distinct population centers, which in 1729 permanently split into two separate colonies.

Founding of Carolina

The Albemarle region that became North Carolina was settled by Virginia planters. They established a society much like their own, with an economy based on tobacco cultivation and the export of such forest products as pitch, tar, and timber. Because North Carolina lacked a satisfactory harbor, its planters continued to rely on Virginia's ports and merchants to conduct their trade. Although North Carolina planters held some slaves, they never became as dependent on slave labor as did the other population center in Carolina.

Charleston, South Carolina, was founded in 1670 by a group of settlers from the island of Barbados. The English migrants from Barbados brought with them the slaves who had worked on their sugar plantations and the legal codes that had governed those laborers, thereby shaping the future of South Carolina and the subsequent history of the United States.

The North American Slave Trade and the Enslavement of Africans

Since England had no tradition of slavery, why did English settlers begin to enslave Africans around the middle of the seventeenth century? The answer to that question lies in a combination of the settlers' need for labor and the experience of other Europeans.

Although the English had not previously practiced slavery, other Europeans had. Both the Spanish and Portuguese had imported enslaved Africans as laborers into the islands of the Mediterranean Atlantic during the fifteenth century. They then extended that practice to their American possessions. No free people of any description were willing to toil for wages in the difficult and dangerous conditions of South American mines or Caribbean sugar plantations. To produce the profitable goods they had come to America to seek, Europeans needed bound laborers—people who, by law or contract, could be forced to work. Dutch, French, and English Caribbean planters eagerly purchased slaves from the 1640s on. Twenty years later, in the 1660s, when the supply of English indentured servants began to dry up, Chesapeake planters also turned to Africans.

In the early mainland English settlements, the few residents of African descent varied in status: some were free, some indentured, some enslaved.

Atlantic Creoles

All came from a population that historian Ira Berlin recently termed "Atlantic creoles"—people who participated in the new international system of trade and piracy. Often of mixed race, they were already familiar with Europeans and fitted easily into established niches in the many-faceted hierarchical social structures of the early colonies. Slave status was not clearly defined in law, and individuals moved back and forth across boundaries of freedom, indenture, and enslavement.

Before the 1660s, none of the English mainland colonies systematically categorized Africans as slaves. But after Chesapeake planters began to

Systematic Enslavement of Africans

import already enslaved Africans from Caribbean sugar islands and then to purchase slaves directly from Africa, that situation changed decisively. As increasing numbers of slaves arrived each year beginning in the 1670s, the enslaved population changed from acculturated creole to newly imported African, and most of the English colonies adopted codes to govern slaves' behavior. By the end of the century, African slavery was firmly established as the basis of the economy in the Chesapeake.

One of the most remarkable aspects of the adoption of the slave system was that the English enslavers never seem to have questioned—or even felt the need to justify with racist rationalizations—the decision to hold Africans and their descendants in perpetual bondage. That fact suggests the importance both of prior Spanish and Portuguese practice and of economic motives in leading to this momentous development. The English did not contend that Africans were inferior to other peoples. Accepting Africans' already enslaved status, English planters wanted to employ the bound laborers to their own advantage.

Between 1492 and 1770 more Africans than Europeans came to the Americas. The vast major-

ity of them went to Brazil or the Caribbean: of at least 10 million enslaved people brought to the Americas during the existence of slavery, only about 260,000 had been imported by 1775 into the region that later became the United States. The magnitude of the slave trade raises three related questions. What was its impact on West Africa and Europe? How was the trade organized and conducted? What was its effect on the people it carried and on the region to which they were taken?

West Africa was one of the most fertile and densely inhabited regions of the continent, so the trade in human beings did not seriously depopulate the area. Even so, because

West Africa and the Slave Trade

American planters preferred to purchase male slaves, the trade significantly affected the sex ratio of the remaining population. The relative lack of men increased the work demands on women and simultaneously encouraged *polygyny*.

In Guinea, the primary consequences of the trade were political and economic. Coastal rulers served as middlemen, allowing the establishment of permanent slave-trading posts in their territories and supplying resident Europeans with slaves to fill ships that stopped regularly at the coastal forts. Such rulers controlled both European traders' access to slaves and inland peoples' access to desirable European goods. The centralizing tendencies of the slave trade helped to create such powerful eighteenth-century kingdoms as Dahomey and Asante.

Europeans, however, were the chief beneficiaries of this traffic in slaves. The expanding network of trade between Europe and its colonies

Europe and the Slave Trade

in the seventeenth and eighteenth centuries was fueled by the sale and transportation of slaves, the exchange of commodities produced by slave labor, and the need to feed and clothe so many bound laborers. The sugar planters of the Caribbean and Brazil, along with the tobacco and rice planters of North America, eagerly purchased slaves from Africa, dispatched shiploads of valuable staple crops to Europe, and bought large quantities of cheap food, much of it from elsewhere in the Americas.

The European economy, previously oriented toward the Mediterranean and Asia, shifted its emphasis to the Atlantic Ocean. By the late seventeenth century commerce in slaves and the products of slave labor constituted the basis of the European economic system. The irony of Columbus's discoveries was thus complete: seeking the wealth of Asia, Columbus found instead the lands that ultimately replaced Asia as the source of European prosperity.

European nations fought bitterly to control the slave trade. The Portuguese had at first dominated the trade, but they were supplanted by the Dutch in the 1630s. The Dutch in turn lost out to the English, who controlled the trade through the Royal African Company, a joint-stock company chartered by Charles II in 1672. Holding a monopoly on all English trade with sub-Saharan Africa, the company transported more than 120,000 slaves to England's colonies in the Caribbean and on the mainland. Yet even before the company's monopoly expired in 1712, many individual English traders had illegally entered the market for slaves. By the early eighteenth century, independent traders were carrying most of the Africans imported into the colonies and earning huge profits.

The experience of the Middle Passage (thus named because it was the middle section of the so-called triangular trade among England, Africa, and the Americas; see page 58) was always traumatic and sometimes fatal. An average of 10 to 20 percent of slaves died en route. On voyages that were unusually long or plagued by epidemic diseases, mortality rates were much higher. In addition, some slaves died either before the ships left Africa or shortly after their arrival in the Americas. Their European captors also died at high rates, chiefly through exposure to diseases endemic to Africa. Once again, the exchange of diseases caused unanticipated death and destruction.

The Middle Passage

One of the most vivid accounts of the Middle Passage was written by Olaudah Equiano, who was eleven years old in 1756 when African raiders kidnapped him. Terrified by the light complexions, long hair, and strange language of the sailors, he was afraid that "I had gotten into a world of bad spirits." After a long voyage during which many Africans died of disease brought on by the cramped, unsanitary conditions and poor food, the ship arrived at Barbados. Equiano and his shipmates feared that "these ugly men" were cannibals, but experienced slaves came on board to assure them that they would not be eaten and that many Africans like themselves lived on the island. "This report eased us much," Equiano recalled, "and sure enough soon after we landed there came to us Africans of all languages." He was not purchased in the West Indies but was instead carried to Virginia, where he was soon sold and put to work on a tobacco plantation before being resold to a visiting ship captain.

The voyage Equiano described was typical, for most slave ships landed in the Caribbean before heading north to Virginia. So many Africans were imported so rapidly that by 1710 one-fifth of the Chesapeake population was of African descent. Slaves usually cost about two-and-a-half times as much as indentured servants, but they repaid the greater investment with a lifetime of service.

Slavery in the Chesapeake

Although planters with enough money could acquire slaves and accumulate greater wealth, the less affluent could not even buy indentured servants, whose price was driven up by scarcity. As time passed, Anglo-American society in the Chesapeake became more and more stratified—that is, the gap between rich and poor steadily widened.

Cultural values were also affected by the involuntary arrival of Africans. Without realizing it, Anglo-Americans in the Chesapeake adopted African modes of thought about the use of time and the nature of work. Africans were more accustomed than European migrants to life in a hot climate. Anglo-Americans soon learned the benefits of African patterns of time usage—working early and late, taking a long rest in the midday heat. And unlike New England's Puritans who scorned all

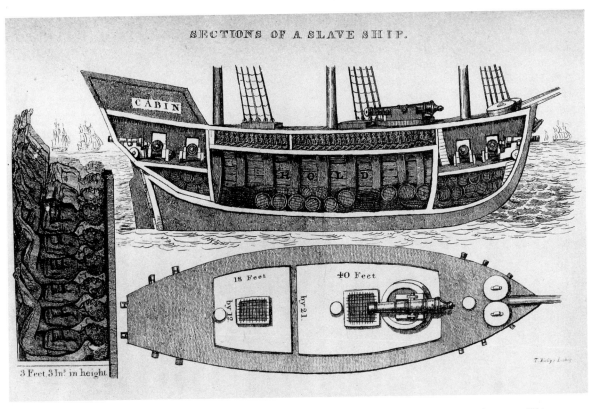

Slave traders tightly packed their human cargoes, attempting to carry as many people as possible on each voyage. This cutaway view of a typical vessel gives the ship's dimensions and shows the way slaves were transported in cramped quarters, with only small openings providing light and air. British Library.

leisure-time activities, Chesapeake dwellers came to recognize the importance of recreation.

Since Africans were included among the first colonists to come to South Carolina from Barbados in 1670, they composed one-quarter to one-third of the early population. The Barbadian slaveowners quickly discovered that Africans had a variety of skills well suited to the semitropical environment of South Carolina. African-style dugout canoes became the chief means of transportation in the colony, which was crisscrossed by rivers, and Africans' skill at killing crocodiles equipped them to handle alligators. Finally, Africans also adapted their traditional techniques of cattle herding for use in America.

African-Americans in South Carolina

Since meat and hides—not the exotic products originally envisioned—were the colony's chief exports in its earliest years, Africans contributed significantly to South Carolina's prosperity.

The similarity of South Carolina's environment to West Africa's, coupled with the large proportion of Africans in the population, ensured that more aspects of West African culture survived in that colony than elsewhere on the North American mainland. Only in South Carolina did enslaved parents continue to give their children African names; only there did a dialect develop that combined English words with African terms. (Known as Gullah, it still survives in isolated areas.) African skills remained useful, so techniques that in other regions were lost when the migrant generation died were instead passed down to the

How do historians know that en-slaved Africans were able to preserve at least some as-pects of their cultural heritage in colonial North America? Although most enslaved people were illiter-ate and therefore did not leave written records of their cultural beliefs or practices, African-Americans did create objects that showed their connections to their homeland even more vividly than could words on a page. Many such objects have been found in the United States. The drum on the left was constructed on the Gold Coast of Africa in the nineteenth century, that on the right in Virginia sometime before the middle of the eighteenth century. The similarities of style and decoration suggest strong cultural affinities between the two drum builders, although they were separated by three thousand miles of ocean and at least one hundred years. Photo: Trustees of The British Museum; Smithsonian Institution, Washington, D.C.

migrants' children. And in South Carolina, as in Guinea, African women were the primary traders.

Significantly, the importation of large num-bers of Africans near the end of the seventeenth century coincided with the successful introduction of rice as a staple crop in South Carolina. English people knew

Rice and Indigo

little about the techniques of growing and processing rice, but people from Africa's Rice Coast (see Chapter 1, page 12) had spent their lives working with the crop. It seems likely that the Africans' expertise enabled their English masters to cultivate the crop profitably. After rice had become South Carolina's

major export, 43 percent of the Africans imported into the colony came from rice-producing regions.

South Carolina later developed a second sta-ple crop, and it, too, made use of slaves' special skills. The crop was indigo, much prized in Eu-rope as a source of blue dye for clothing. In the early 1740s, Eliza Lucas, a young woman who was managing her father's plantations, began to exper-iment with indigo cultivation. Drawing on the knowledge of slaves and overseers from the West Indies, she developed the planting and processing techniques later adopted throughout the colony. Indigo was grown on high ground, and rice was planted in low-lying swampy areas; rice and indigo also had different growing seasons. Thus the two crops complemented each other perfectly.

After 1700, southern planters were irrevocably committed to slavery as their chief source of labor but northerners were not. Lacking large-scale agricultural enterprises, the rural North did not demand many bound laborers. In northern urban areas, though, European domestic servants were hard to find and slaves were often used. Slaves accounted for more than 10 percent of the population in some northern colonial cities (notably Newport, Rhode Island, and New York City).

Slavery in the North

The introduction of large-scale slavery in the South, coupled with its near absence in the rural North, accentuated regional differences that already had begun to develop in England's American colonies. To the distinction between diversified agriculture and staple-crop production was now added a crucial difference in the status of most laborers.

Relations Between Europeans and Indians

Everywhere in North America, European colonizers depended heavily on the labor of native peoples. In the Northeast, France, England, and the Netherlands competed for the pelts supplied by Indian trappers. In the Southeast, England, Spain, and later France each tried to control a thriving trade with the Indians in deerskins and Indian slaves. In the Southwest, Spain attempted to exploit the agricultural and artisan skills of the Pueblo peoples (see map).

After Fray Alonzo de Benavides departed for Madrid in 1629 (see Chapter 2), Franciscan friars continued their conversion efforts, with mixed success. The Pueblo peoples were willing to add Christianity to their own religious beliefs but not to give up their indigenous rituals. Friars and secular colonists who held *encomiendas* also placed heavy demands on the Indians. As the decades passed, Franciscans adopted brutal tactics in an at-

Popé and the Pueblo Revolt

tempt to wipe out all traces of the native religion. Finally, in 1680 the Pueblos revolted under the leadership of Popé, a respected shaman, and drove the Spaniards out of New Mexico. After Spanish authority was restored in 1692, Spanish governors stressed cooperation with the Pueblos, rather than confrontation, and no longer attempted to reduce them to bondage or to violate their cultural integrity. The Pueblo revolt was the most successful and longest-sustained Indian resistance movement in colonial North America.

When the Spanish expanded their territorial claims to the east and north, they followed the same strategy they had used in New Mexico, establishing their presence through military outposts and Franciscan missions. The army's role was to maintain order among the subject peoples and to guard the boundaries of the Spanish Empire from possible incursions, especially by the French. By the late eighteenth century, Spain claimed a vast territory that stretched from California (first colonized in 1769) through Texas (settled after 1700) to the Gulf Coast.

Spain's North American Possessions

Europeans along the eastern seaboard valued Indians as hunters rather than as agricultural workers, but they were no less dependent on Indian labor than were Spaniards in the Southwest. To obtain pelts and deerskins from indigenous peoples, Europeans had to supply trade goods the Indians wanted. Such commodities included ammunition, clothing, and alcohol (usually rum distilled from West Indian molasses). The demand for alcohol (a commodity introduced by the traders) made rum a key component of colonial commerce, and alcohol abuse hastened the deterioration of villages already devastated by disease and dislocation.

Also destructive of tribal communities was traffic in Indian slaves. Carolina Indians, especially the Creeks, profited from selling their captive enemies to the English, who either kept them as slaves or exported them to other mainland settlements or to the West Indies. There are no reliable statistics on the extent of the trade in

Indian Slave Trade in the Southeast

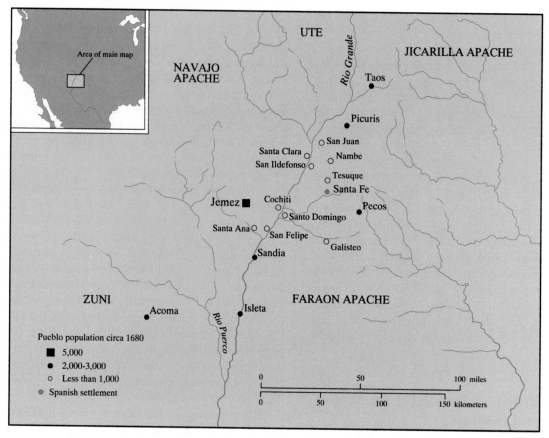

New Mexico, ca. 1680   *In 1680, the lone Spanish settlement at Santa Fe was surrounded and vastly outnumbered by the many pueblos nearby.*   Source: Adapted from *Apache, Navaho, and Spaniard*, by Jack D. Forbes. Copyright ©1960 by the University of Oklahoma Press. Used by permission.

Indian slaves, but in 1708 they composed 14 percent of the South Carolina population.

Bitter conflicts between the Carolina settlers and indigenous peoples also produced mass migrations. In 1711 the Tuscaroras, an Iroquoian peo-

Tuscarora and Yamasee Wars

ple, attacked a Swiss-German settlement at New Bern, which had expropriated their lands without payment. The Tuscaroras were slave traders who often sold captured Algonkian enemies into slavery. Therefore the Algonkians joined the English colonists to defeat their enemy in a bloody two-year war. In the end, more than a thousand Tuscaroras were themselves sold into slavery, and the remnants of the group drifted northward, where they joined the Five Nations Iroquois in New York.

The slave trade's abuses led to yet another Indian war in Carolina. Colonial traders were notorious for cheating Native Americans, physically abusing them (including raping women), and selling friendly peoples into slavery. In the spring and summer of 1715, the Yamasees, aided by Creeks and others, retaliated by attacking English settlements. Refugees by the hundreds streamed into Charleston; the Creek-Yamasee offensive came close to driving the intruders from the mainland altogether. But colonial reinforcements arrived from the north, and Cherokees joined English settlers to fight the Creeks, their ancient enemies.

The war pointed up both the difficulty of achieving unity among the Indians and their critical dependence on European weapons. When the Creeks and Yamasees ran out of ammunition and could not repair their broken guns, their cause was lost. The Yamasees moved south to Florida, and the Creeks retreated to villages in the west.

That the Yamasees could escape by migrating southward exposed the one remaining gap in the line of English coastal settlements, the area between South Carolina's southern border and Spanish Florida. The gap was plugged in 1732 with the chartering of Georgia, the last of the colonies that would become part of the United States. Intended as a haven for English debtors by its founder James Oglethorpe, Georgia was specifically designed as a garrison province. Since all its landholders were expected to serve as militiamen to defend English settlements, the charter prohibited women from inheriting or purchasing land in the colony. The charter also prohibited slavery and the use of alcoholic beverages. Such provisions reveal the founders' intention that Georgia should be peopled by sturdy, sober yeoman farmers who could take up their weapons at a moment's notice against Indians or Spaniards. None of the original conditions of the charter were enforced, however, and all of them had been abandoned by 1752, when Georgia became a royal colony.

Founding of Georgia

In the Northeast, relationships were complicated by the number of European and Indian nations involved in the fur trade. The key players were the Iroquois, not one tribe but five—the Mohawks, Oneidas, Onondagas, Cayugas, and Senecas. (In 1722, the Tuscaroras became the sixth.) Under the terms of a defensive alliance forged early in the sixteenth century, decisions of war and peace for the entire Iroquois Confederacy were made by a council of tribal representatives. Each nation retained some autonomy, and none could be forced to comply with a council directive against its will.

Iroquois Confederacy

The Iroquois were unique among Native Americans, not only because of the strength and persistence of their alliance but also because of the role played by their clan matrons. The older women of each village chose its chief and could either start wars (by calling for the capture of prisoners to replace dead relatives) or stop them (by refusing to supply warriors with necessary foodstuffs).

Before the arrival of Europeans, the Iroquois waged wars primarily to acquire captives to replenish their population. The Europeans' coming created an economic motive for warfare: the desire to control the fur trade and gain unimpeded access to European goods. The war with the Hurons in the 1640s (see page 29) was but the first of a series of conflicts with other tribes known as the Beaver Wars, in which the Iroquois fought desperately to maintain a dominant position in the trade.

In the mid-1670s, just when they were achieving their goal, the French stepped in; an Iroquois triumph would have destroyed France's plans to trade directly with the Indians of the Great Lakes and Mississippi valley. Over the next twenty years the French launched repeated attacks on Iroquois villages. The English offered little assistance other than weapons to their trading partners. Their people and resources depleted by constant warfare, the Iroquois in 1701 negotiated neutrality treaties with France, England, and their Indian neighbors. For the next half-century they maintained their power through trade and skillful diplomacy rather than warfare.

The wars against the Iroquois Confederacy were crucial components of French Canada's plan to penetrate the heartland of North America. The plan included the explorations of Father Jacques Marquette, Louis Jolliet, and Robert Cavelier de La Salle in the Great Lakes and Mississippi valley regions in the 1670s. French officials hoped a trade route to Mexico would be found; La Salle sought to monopolize the fur trade by establishing trading posts along the Mississippi River.

French Expansion

Unlike Spaniards, French adventurers did not attempt to subjugate the Native Americans they encountered or even to claim the territory formally for France. Still, when France decided to strengthen its presence near the Gulf of Mexico by founding New Orleans in 1718—to counter both the westward thrust of the English colonies and the eastward moves of the Spanish—the Mississippi posts became the glue of empire (see map).

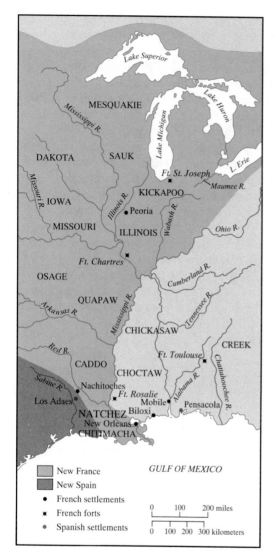

Louisiana, ca. 1720 *By 1720, French forts and settlements dotted the Mississippi River and its tributaries in the interior of North America. Two isolated Spanish outposts were situated near the Gulf of Mexico.* Source: Adapted from *France in America*, by William J. Eccles. Copyright ©1972 by William J. Eccles. Reprinted by permission of Harper-Collins Publishers Inc.

Most of the posts consisted of a small military garrison and a priest, surrounded by powerful Indian nations. The Indians permitted French soldiers and traders to remain among them because they wanted easy access to valuable European goods. The French, for their part, sought political as well as economic ends, attempting to prevent the English from encroaching too far into the interior. Their goals were limited; they neither engaged in systematic efforts to convert nearby Native American peoples to Christianity nor coveted substantial amounts of their land for agricultural purposes.

Matters were very different in the English colonies, where white colonists had an avid interest in acquiring more land. By the early 1670s, some Virginians were eagerly eyeing rich lands north of the York River that early treaties had reserved for Native Americans. Using as a pretext the July 1675 killing of an English servant by some Doeg Indians, the settlers attacked not only the Doegs but also the powerful Susquehannocks. In retaliation, Susquehannock bands raided frontier plantations in the winter of 1676. The land-hungry Anglo-Americans rallied behind the leadership of Nathaniel Bacon, a recently arrived planter, who wanted "to ruine and extirpate all Indians in general." Governor William Berkeley, however, hoped to avoid setting off a major war.

Bacon's Rebellion

Berkeley and Bacon soon clashed. After Bacon forced the House of Burgesses to authorize him to attack the Indians, Berkeley declared Bacon and his men to be in rebellion. As the chaotic summer of 1676 wore on, Bacon alternately pursued Indians and battled with the governor's supporters. In September Bacon marched on Jamestown itself and burned the capital to the ground. But when Bacon died of dysentery the following month, the rebellion collapsed. Even so, a new treaty signed in 1677 opened much of the disputed territory to English settlement.

More than coincidentally, New England—also colonized more than fifty years earlier—was wracked by conflict with Native Americans at precisely the same time. In each area, the colonists' original accommodation with the Indians no longer satisfied both parties.

In the half-century since the founding of New England, colonial settlement had spread far into the interior. In the process, the colonists had completely surrounded the ancestral lands of the Pokanokets (Wampanoags) on Narragansett Bay. Their chief, Metacom (known to the English as King Philip), was troubled by encroachments on Pokanoket lands and equally concerned about the impact European culture and Christianity were having on his people. Metacom led his warriors in attacks on nearby communities in June 1675.

King Philip's War

The Nipmucks and the Narragansetts soon joined Metacom's forces. In the fall, the three tribes jointly attacked settlements in the northern Connecticut River valley. In early 1676, they devastated well-established villages and even attacked Plymouth and Providence. Altogether, the alliance totally destroyed twelve of the ninety Puritan towns and attacked forty others.

New England's very survival seemed at stake. But the tide turned in the summer of 1676, as the Indian coalition ran short of food and ammunition. After Metacom was killed in an ambush in August, the alliance crumbled. Many surviving Pokanokets, Nipmucks, and Narragansetts were captured and sold into slavery in the West Indies. The power of New England's coastal tribes had been broken. Thereafter they lived in small clusters, subordinated to the colonists and often working as servants or sailors.

New England and the Web of Imperial Trade

From the early years of colonization to the close of the seventeenth century, New England changed in three major ways. The population grew dramatically; the residents' relationship to Puritanism altered; and the economy developed in unanticipated ways.

By 1700, New England's population had quadrupled to reach approximately 100,000. Such an increase placed great pressure on available land, and many third- and fourth-generation New Englanders had to migrate—north to New Hampshire or Maine, south to New York, west beyond the Connecticut River—to find sufficient farmland for themselves and their children. Others abandoned agriculture and learned skills like blacksmithing or carpentry.

Population Pressures

The passage of time also brought changes in Puritanism, for two of the Puritans' fundamental beliefs came inevitably into conflict. Puritans practiced infant baptism, yet at the same time they insisted that only the saved could be members of their churches. No one foresaw the problem that confronted congregations in the 1660s: young people baptized as children married and had babies before undergoing the searching examination of their faith required to join a church. Could the offspring of such couples be baptized? The need to answer that question led in 1662 to the adoption of the so-called Halfway Covenant, which established a category of "halfway" membership in Puritan congregations. If previously baptized adults acknowledged the church's authority over them, the ministers declared, they could have their children baptized.

By the 1660s, women were far more likely than men to become either full or halfway members of Puritan congregations. This phenomenon prompted Cotton Mather, the most prominent member of a family of distinguished ministers, to deliver sermons outlining women's proper role in church and society—the first formal examination of that theme in American history. Mather advised American women to be submissive to their husbands, watchful of their children, and attentive to religious duty.

Women, Men, and Puritan Churches

But why had New England's men become more reluctant to acknowledge the church's authority over them? One historian hypothesizes that the connection between church membership and political obligation was critical. Believing that unchurched men were unlikely to be elected to office, male New Englanders may well have failed to join congregations because they wanted to avoid having to serve as constables or militia officers. Such jobs not only took them away from their farms and families but also could cause dissension in their neighborhoods. Others hypothesize that men in seaport towns like Boston and Salem became more worldly and less interested in religion as the economy of the New England colonies changed.

Initially, New England's economy rested on two foundations: the fur trade and the constant flow of migrants. Together, those had allowed New Englanders to acquire the manufactured goods they needed. The fur trade gave them valuable pelts to sell in England, and the migrants were always willing to exchange clothing and other items for the earlier settlers' surplus seed, grains, and livestock. But New England's supply of furs was quickly exhausted by excessive trapping, and the migrants stopped coming after the English Civil War began. Thus in the early 1640s that first economic system collapsed.

New England's First Economy

The Puritans then began a search for new markets and salable crops. They found the trade goods in fish, grain, and wood products. By 1643 they had also found the markets: the Wine Islands and the English colonies in the Caribbean, which lacked precisely the goods that New England could produce in abundance: cheap food (corn and salted fish) to feed to slaves and wood for barrels to hold wine and molasses (the form in which sugar was shipped).

Thus developed the series of transactions that has become known, inaccurately, as the triangular trade. The northern colonists sold their goods in the West Indies and elsewhere to earn the money with which to purchase English imports. There soon grew up in New England's ports a cadre of merchants who acquired—usually through barter—cargoes of timber and foodstuffs, which they then dispatched to the West Indies for sale. In the Caribbean, the ships sailed from island to island, exchanging fish, barrel staves, and grains

Atlantic Trading System

for molasses, fruit, spices, and slaves. Once they had a full load, the ships returned to Boston, Newport, or New Haven to dispose of their cargoes.

Most important, northerners distilled West Indian molasses into rum, a key component of the only part of the trade that could be termed triangular. Rhode Islanders took rum to Africa and traded it for slaves, whom they carried to the West Indies to exchange for more molasses to produce still more rum. With that exception, the trading pattern was not a triangle but a shifting set of two-way voyages (see map, page 59).

The New Englanders who ventured into commerce were soon differentiated from their rural counterparts by their ties to a wider transatlantic world and their preoccupation with material endeavors. As time passed, increasing numbers of Puritans became involved in trade. Small investors who owned shares of voyages soon dominated the field numerically if not monetarily.

The gulf between commercial and farming interests widened after 1660, when, with Stuart Restoration, merchants who were members of the Church of England (Anglicans) began to migrate to New England. Such men had little stake in the survival of Massachusetts Bay and Connecticut in their original forms, and some were openly antagonistic to Puritan traditions. As non-Congregationalists they were denied the vote, but they were still taxed to support the church. Further, Anglicans were forbidden to practice their own religion freely. They resented their exclusion from the governing elite, believing that their wealth and social status entitled them to political power. Congregationalist clergymen returned their hostility, preaching sermons lamenting New England's new commercial orientation. But the ministers spoke for the past, because by the 1670s colonial America, including New England, was part of an international trading network upon which Anglo-America's prosperity depended.

English officials seeking a new source of revenue after the disruptions of the Civil War realized that the colonies could make important contributions to England's economic well-being. Additional tax revenues could put England back on a sound fi-

Mercantilism

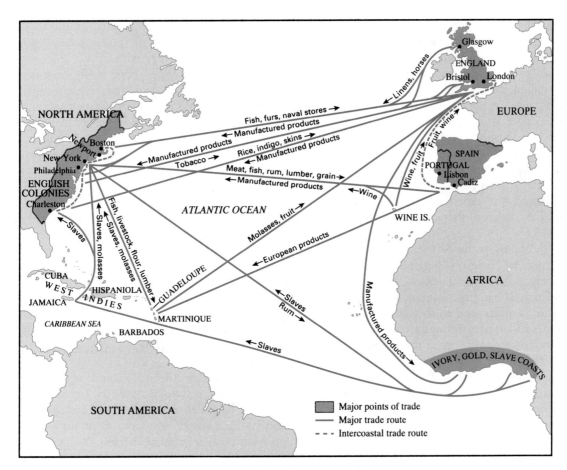

Atlantic Trade Routes   *By the late seventeenth century, the countries and colonies bordering the Atlantic Ocean were linked by an elaborate trade network. The most valuable commodities exchanged were enslaved people and the products of slave labor.*

nancial footing, and English merchants wanted to ensure that they—not their Dutch rivals—reaped the benefits of trading with the English colonies. Parliament and the restored Stuart monarchs accordingly began to draft laws designed to confine the profits of colonial trade primarily to the mother country.

England based its commercial policy on a series of assumptions about the operations of the world's economic system. Collectively, these assumptions are usually called *mercantilism,* though the term and the theory were formulated only a century later. The economic world was seen as a collection of national states, whose governments actively competed for shares of a finite amount of wealth. Each nation's goal was to become as economically self-sufficient as possible while maintaining a favorable balance of trade with other countries by exporting more than it imported. Under the system, colonies could supply the mother country with valuable raw materials and serve as markets for the mother country's manufactured goods.

Parliament applied mercantilist thinking to the American colonies in laws known as the Navigation Acts. The major acts—passed between 1651 and 1673—established three main principles. First, **Navigation Acts** only English or colonial merchants and ships could engage in trade in the colonies. Second, certain valuable American products could be sold only in the mother country or in other English colonies. At first, these "enumerated" goods were wool, sugar, tobacco, indigo, ginger, and dyes; later acts added rice, naval stores (masts, spars, pitch, tar, and turpentine), copper, and furs to the list. Third, all foreign goods destined for sale in the colonies had to be shipped by way of England and were subject to English import duties. Some years later, a new series of laws established a fourth principle: the colonies could not export items (such as wool clothing, hats, or iron) that competed with English products.

The intention of the Navigation Acts was to center American trade on England. The mother country was to benefit from colonial imports and exports. England had first claim on the most valuable colonial exports, and all foreign imports into the colonies had to pass through England first, enriching its customs revenues in the process. Some colonies, like those in the West Indies and the Chesapeake, were adversely affected by the laws because they could not seek new markets for their staple crops. In others, the impact was less severe. The northern and middle colonies, for example, produced such nonenumerated goods as fish, flour, and barrel staves that could be traded directly to foreign purchasers as long as they were carried in English or American ships.

The English authorities soon learned that it was easier to write mercantilist legislation than to enforce it. The many harbors of the American coast provided ready havens for smugglers, and colonial officials often ignored the sale of illegally imported goods. Consequently, Parliament in 1696 enacted another Navigation Act. This law established in America a number of vice-admiralty courts, which operated without juries. Because American juries had already demonstrated a tendency to favor local smugglers over customs officers, Parliament decided to remove Navigation Act cases from the regular colonial courts.

England took another major step in colonial administration in 1696 by creating the fifteen-member Board of Trade and Plantations, which

Board of Trade and Plantations

thereafter served as the chief organ of government concerned with the American colonies. (Previously, no single body had that responsibility.) It gathered information, reviewed Crown appointments in America, scrutinized legislation passed by colonial assemblies, supervised trade policies, and advised successive ministries on colonial issues. Still, the Board of Trade did not have any direct powers of enforcement. It also shared jurisdiction over American affairs with the customs service, the navy, and the secretary of state for the southern department, the member of the ministry responsible for the colonies. In short, supervision of the American provinces remained decentralized and haphazard.

 ## Colonial Political Development and Imperial Reorganization

English officials in the 1670s and 1680s confronted not only resistance to the Navigation Acts but also a bewildering array of colonial governments. Massachusetts Bay and Plymouth functioned under their original charters. Neighboring Connecticut (including the formerly independent New Haven) and Rhode Island had been granted charters by Charles II in 1662 and 1663, respectively. Virginia was a royal colony, and New York also became one when its proprietor ascended the throne in 1685 as James II. All the other mainland settlements were proprietorships.

Still, in political structure the colonies shared certain characteristics. Most were ruled by a governor and a two-house legislature. In New England, the governors were elected by property-holding men or by the legislature; in the Chesapeake and the middle colonies, they were appointed by the king or the proprietor. A council, either elected or appointed, advised the governor on matters of policy and sometimes served as the colony's highest court. The councils also served as upper houses of colo-

Colonial Political Structures

nial legislatures. At first, councilors and elected representatives met jointly to debate and adopt laws affecting the colony. But as time passed, the fundamental differences between the two legislative groups' purposes and constituencies led them to separate. Thus developed the two-house legislature still used in almost all of the states.

Meanwhile, local political institutions were taking shape. In New England, elected selectmen initially governed the towns, but by the end of the century town meetings—held at least annually and attended by most free adult male residents—handled matters of local concern. In the Chesapeake colonies and both of the Carolinas, appointed justices of the peace ran local governments. At first the same was true in Pennsylvania, but by the early eighteenth century elected county officials began to take over some government functions. And in New York, local elections were the rule even before the establishment of the colonial assembly in 1683.

Thus by the late seventeenth century, Anglo-American colonists everywhere were accustomed to a considerable degree of local political autonomy. Those who owned property expected to have a voice in how they were governed—and especially how they were taxed. These expectations clashed with those of the crown. James II and his successors sought to bring order to the apparently chaotic state of colonial administration by tightening the reins of government and reducing the colonies' political autonomy. They began to chip away at the privileges granted in colonial charters and to reclaim proprietorships for the Crown. New Hampshire (1679), its parent colony Massachusetts (1691), New Jersey (1702), and the Carolinas (1729) all became royal colonies. The charters of Rhode Island, Connecticut, Maryland, and Pennsylvania were temporarily suspended but ultimately were restored to their original status.

The most drastic reordering of colonial administration targeted Puritan New England, which English officials believed was a hotbed of smuggling. Moreover, Puritans refused to allow freedom of religion to non-Congregationalists and insisted on maintaining laws that ran

Dominion of New England

counter to English practice. New England thus seemed an appropriate place to exert English authority with greater vigor. The charters of all the colonies from New Jersey to Maine (then part of Massachusetts) were revoked, and a Dominion of New England was established in 1686. Sir Edmund Andros, the governor, was given immense power: all the assemblies were dissolved, and he needed only the consent of an appointed council to make laws and levy taxes.

New Englanders endured Andros's autocratic rule for more than two years. Then came the dramatic news that James II had been overthrown in a bloodless coup known as the Glorious Revolution and had been replaced on the throne by his daughter Mary and her husband, the Dutch prince William of Orange. James II had levied taxes without parliamentary approval. He also had announced his conversion to Roman Catholicism. Through the Glorious Revolution, Parliament affirmed its supremacy and that of Protestantism. Meanwhile, New Englanders jailed Andros, proclaimed their loyalty to William and Mary, and wrote to England for instructions about the form of government they should adopt.

Glorious Revolution in America

In other American colonies, too, the Glorious Revolution was a signal for revolt. In Maryland the Protestant Association overturned the government of the Catholic proprietor, and in New York a militia officer of German origin, Jacob Leisler, assumed control of the government. Like the New Englanders, the Maryland and New York rebels saw themselves as carrying out the colonial phase of the English revolt against Stuart absolutism.

William and Mary, however, like James II, believed that England should exercise tighter control over its unruly American possessions. Consequently, the only American rebellion that received royal sanction was that in Maryland, primarily because of its anti-Catholic thrust. In New York, Jacob Leisler was hanged for treason, and Massachusetts (including the formerly independent jurisdiction of Plymouth) became a royal colony with an appointed governor. The province was allowed to retain its town meeting system of local government and to elect its council, but the new charter issued in 1691 eliminated the traditional religious test for voting and officeholding. An Anglican parish was set up in the heart of Boston.

Compounding New England's difficulties in a time of political upheaval and economic uncertainty was a war with the French and their Native American allies. King Louis XIV of France allied himself with the deposed James II, and England declared war on France in 1689. The conflict, which lasted until 1697, was known in Europe as the War of the League of Augsburg, but the colonists called it King William's War. The American war was fought chiefly on the northern frontiers of New England and New York.

In this period of extreme stress an outbreak of witchcraft accusations occurred in Salem Village (now Danvers), Massachusetts. Like their contemporaries elsewhere, seventeenth-century New Englanders believed in the existence of witches. Before 1689, 103 New Englanders, most of them middle-aged women, had been charged with practicing witchcraft, chiefly by neighbors who attributed their misfortunes to the suspected witch. Only a few of the accused were convicted, and fewer still were executed.

Witchcraft in Salem Village

The crisis began in early 1692 when a group of girls and young women accused some older female neighbors of having bewitched them. Before the hysteria spent itself ten months later, nineteen people (including several men, most of them related to convicted female witches) were hanged, one was pressed to death with heavy stones, and more than one hundred persons were jailed. The events at Salem Village can best be understood when seen in the context of political and legal disorder, Indian war, and religious and economic crises. These factors undermined the sense of security Puritan New Englanders had about their future.

Nowhere was that more true than in Salem Village, a farming town torn between old and new styles of life because of its position on the edge of the bustling port of Salem. And no residents of the village had more reason to feel insecure than those who issued the first accusations. Many had been orphaned in recent Indian attacks on Maine and

No seventeenth-century New Englander ever drew a picture of a witchcraft trial or execution, but an artist did record the hanging of several witches in England around 1650. The multiple executions of Salem witches in the summer of 1692 probably resembled this gallows scene. Folger Shakespeare Library.

were living in Salem Village as domestic servants. Their involvement with witchcraft began as an experiment with fortunetelling as a means of foreseeing their futures, in particular the identities of their eventual husbands. As the most powerless people in a town apparently powerless to direct its fate, they offered a compelling explanation for the seemingly endless chain of troubles afflicting their province: it was under direct attack from the Devil and his legion of witches. Accordingly, it is not so much the number of witchcraft prosecutions that seems surprising but rather their abrupt cessation in the fall of 1692.

There were three reasons for the rapid end to the crisis. First, the accusers grew too bold. When they began to charge some of the colony's most distinguished and respected residents with being in league with the Devil, members of the ruling elite began to doubt their veracity. Second, the colony's ministers formally expressed strong reservations about the validity of the spectral evidence used against most of the accused. Third, the implementation of the new royal charter ended the worst period of political uncertainty, eliminating a major source of stress.

Over the course of the next three decades, Massachusetts and the rest of the English colonies in America accommodated themselves to the new imperial order. While resenting the officials sent to implement English policies, most colonists adjusted to the trade restrictions imposed by the Navigation Acts. They fought another imperial war—the War of the Spanish Succession, or Queen Anne's War—from 1702 to 1713, without enduring the stresses of the first. Colonists who allied themselves with royal government received patronage in the form of offices and land grants and composed "court parties" that supported English officials. Others, who were either less fortunate in their friends or more principled in defense of colonial autonomy, made up the opposition, or "country" interest. By the end of the first quarter of the eighteenth century, most men in both groups had been born in America and were members of elite families.

 Conclusion

The eighty years from 1640 to 1720 established the basic economic and political patterns that were to structure all subsequent changes in mainland colonial society. In 1640 there were just two isolated centers of English population, New England and the Chesapeake. In 1720, nearly the entire east coast of North America was in English hands, and Indian power east of the Appalachian Mountains had been broken. What had been a migrant population was now mostly American-born; economies originally based on the fur trade had become far more complex and more closely linked with the mother country; and a wide variety of political structures had been reshaped into a more uniform pattern. Yet at the same time the introduction of large-scale slavery into the Chesapeake and the Carolinas irrevocably differentiated their societies from those of the colonies to the north.

Meanwhile, the Spanish had expanded from the small outpost in Sante Fe, New Mexico, to Texas and California. As for the French, they dominated the length of the Mississippi River and the Great Lakes region. The extensive Spanish and French presence to the south and west of the English settlements meant that future conflicts among the European powers in North America were nearly inevitable.

By 1720, the essential elements of the imperial administrative structure that would govern the English colonies until 1775 were firmly in place. The regional economic systems originating in the late seventeenth and early eighteenth centuries also continued to dominate North American life for another century—until after independence had been won. And Anglo-Americans had developed the commitment to autonomous local government that later would lead them into conflict with Parliament and the king.

Suggestions for Further Reading

General

Wesley Frank Craven, *The Colonies in Transition, 1660–1713* (1968); W. J. Eccles, *France in America*, rev. ed. (1990); Jack P. Greene and J. R. Pole, eds., *Colonial British America* (1984).

New Netherland and the Restoration Colonies

Edwin Bronner, *William Penn's "Holy Experiment": The Founding of Pennsylvania, 1681–1701* (1962); Wesley Frank Craven, *New Jersey and the English Colonization of North America* (1964); Joyce Goodfriend, *Before the Melting Pot: Society and Culture in Colonial New York City, 1664–1730* (1992); Oliver Rink, *Holland on the Hudson: An Economic and Social History of Dutch New York* (1986); Robert C. Ritchie, *The Duke's Province: A Study of Politics and Society in Colonial New York, 1660–1691* (1977); Robert M. Weir, *Colonial South Carolina: A History* (1983).

Africa and the Slave Trade

Jay Coughtry, *The Notorious Triangle: Rhode Island and the African Slave Trade, 1700–1807* (1981); Joseph Inikori and Stanley Engerman, eds., *The Atlantic Slave Trade* (1992); Robin Law, *The Slave Coast of West Africa, 1550–1750: The Impact of the Atlantic Slave Trade on an African Society* (1991); Daniel C. Littlefield, *Rice and Slaves: Ethnicity and the Slave Trade in Colonial South Carolina* (1981); James Rawley, *The Transatlantic Slave Trade: A History* (1981); Barbara Solow, ed., *Slavery and the Rise of the Atlantic System* (1991).

Africans in Anglo-America

Douglas Deal, *Race and Class in Colonial Virginia: Indians, Englishmen, and Africans on the Eastern Shore During the Seventeenth Century* (1993); Allan Kulikoff, *Tobacco and Slaves: The Development of Southern Cultures in the Chesapeake, 1680–1800* (1986); Edgar J. McManus, *Black Bondage in the North* (1973); Peter H. Wood, *Black Majority: Negroes in Colonial South Carolina from 1670 Through the Stono Rebellion* (1974).

European–Native American Relations in the North

Russell Bourne, *The Red King's Rebellion: Racial Politics in New England, 1675–1678* (1991); John Demos, *The Unredeemed Captive: A Family Story from Early America* (1994); Matthew Dennis, *Cultivating a Landscape of Peace: Iroquois-European Encounter in Seventeenth-Century America* (1993); Michael Puglisi, *Puritans Beseiged: The Legacies of King Philip's War in the Massachusetts Bay Colony* (1991); Daniel Richter, *The Ordeal of the Longhouse: The Peoples of the Iroquois League in the Era of European Colonization* (1992); Richard White, *The Middle Ground: Indians, Empires, and Republics in the Great Lakes Region, 1650–1815* (1991).

European–Native American Relations in the South and West

Verner W. Crane, *The Southern Frontier, 1660–1732* (1929); Elizabeth A. H. John, *Storms Brewed in Other Men's Worlds: The Confrontation of Indians, Spanish, and French in the Southwest, 1540–1795* (1975); Andrew Knaut, *The Pueblo Revolt of 1680* (1995); James Merrell, *The Indians' New World: Catawbas and Their Neighbors from European Contact through the Era of Removal* (1989); Daniel H. Usner, Jr., *Indians, Settlers, and Slaves in a Frontier Exchange Economy: The Lower Mississippi Valley before 1783* (1992).

New England

Bernard Bailyn, *The New England Merchants in the Seventeenth Century* (1955); Christine Heyrman, *Commerce and Culture: The Maritime Communities of Colonial Massachusetts, 1690–1750* (1984); Richard Melvoin, *New England Outpost: War and Society in Colonial Deerfield* (1990); Amanda Porterfield, *Female Piety in Puritan New England* (1991); Laurel Thatcher Ulrich, *Good Wives: Image and Reality in the Lives of Women in Northern New England, 1650–1750* (1982).

New England Witchcraft

Paul Boyer and Stephen Nissenbaum, *Salem Possessed: The Social Origins of Witchcraft* (1974); Elaine Breslaw, *Tituba, Reluctant Witch of Salem: Devilish Indians and Puritan Fantasies* (1996); John Demos, *Entertaining Satan: Witchcraft and the Culture of Early New England* (1982); Peter Hoffer, *The Devil's Disciples: Makers of the Salem Witchcraft Trials* (1996); Carol Karlsen, *The Devil in the Shape of a Woman: Witchcraft in Early New England* (1987); Bernard Rosenthal, *Salem Story: Reading the Witch Trials of 1692* (1993).

Imperial and Colonial Politics

Robert M. Bliss, *Revolution and Empire: English Politics and the American Colonies in the Seventeenth Century* (1991); Lawrence W. Harper, *The English Navigation Laws: A Seventeenth-Century Experiment in Social Engineering* (1939); Richard P. Johnson, *Adjustment to Empire: The New England Colonies, 1675–1715* (1981); David S. Lovejoy, *The Glorious Revolution in America* (1972); Robert C. Ritchie, *Captain Kidd and the War Against the Pirates* (1986); I. K. Steele, *Politics of Colonial Policy: The Board of Trade in Colonial Administration* (1968); Stephen Saunders Webb, *Lord Churchill's Coup: The Anglo-American Empire and the Glorious Revolution Reconsidered* (1995); Stephen Saunders Webb, *1676: The End of American Independence* (1984); Stephen Saunders Webb, *The Governors-General: The English Army and the Definition of the Empire, 1569–1681* (1979).

4

Growth and Diversity
1720–1770

Maturina, a free black resident of New Orleans, awoke with a start at 3 A.M. on June 2, 1782, to the shouts of her neighbor, a slave woman named Louisa. "Maturina, someone has stolen your hens!" Louisa yelled. Leaping from her bed, Maturina ran to investigate. She knew where to look for missing chickens. At dawn, Maturina went with her son and her brother Nicolas to the city market on the levee (river bank), where they soon encountered a man carrying her three fowls. By threatening him with prosecution, they learned that he had purchased the hens from a French grocer named La Rochelle. So the three confronted La Rochelle at his hut. Under questioning, the grocer reluctantly admitted that "it was a negro who had brought them to him to sell." Suspicious, Maturina searched La Rochelle's own hut, rousting out the thief, who was hiding within. He tried to escape, but Nicolas pursued and captured him. Brought before the authorities, the thief proved to be Juan, a runaway slave from the countryside.

That much of this action took place on the Mississippi River levee is not surprising. In the mid-eighteenth century, the crude market centered there was a focal point of New Orleans. To the levee came Indian traders, French and German farmers, free and enslaved Africans—all intent on buying and selling.

The lively markets in New Orleans and Anglo-American cities such as Boston and Philadelphia illuminate several key themes of colonial development in the mid-eighteenth century: population growth, ethnic diversity, the increasing importance of colonial urban centers, the creation of an urban elite that purchased food and clothing from other colonists, rising levels of consumption for all social ranks, and the new significance of internal markets. In the French and English mainland colonies, exports continued to dominate the economy. Yet expanding local populations demanded greater quantities and types of goods, and Europe could not supply all those needs. As a result, colonists came increasingly to depend on exploiting and consuming their own resources.

Ethnic diversity was especially pronounced in the small colonial cities, but even the countryside attracted settlers from a wide range of nations. Only the Spanish Borderlands and rural New England had few resident newcomers. The middle and southern Anglo-American colonies attracted by far the largest number of immigrants, both free and enslaved. Their arrival swelled the total population, altered political balances, and affected the religious climate by introducing new sects.

The ruling elites in the colonies paid little heed to the newcomers. In New France and New Spain, ordinary settlers were already denied any voice in their government, but even in Anglo-America elected and appointed leaders often refused to allow recent migrants from Europe adequate representation and government services. A series of violent clashes ensued after midcentury. By that time, native-born elites dominated the English colonies and contended with governors and other officials born in the mother country for control of the government machinery.

Intermarried webs of wealthy families developed in each of Europe's American possessions by the 1760s. Such well-off, educated colonists participated in transatlantic intellectual communities, whereas many colonists of the "lesser sort" could neither read nor write. The elites lived comfortably, while most colonists, whether free or enslaved, struggled just to survive. Such divisions were most pronounced in British America, where by 1750 the social and economic distance among different ranks of Anglo-Americans had widened noticeably.

Wealthy Anglo-Americans in particular were heavily influenced by the Enlightenment, the prevailing European intellectual movement of the day. The Enlightenment stressed reason and empirical knowledge, deliberately discarding superstition and instinct as guides to human behavior. Enlightened thinkers saw God as a distant presence who had ordered the world, setting forth natural laws that humans could discover through careful investigation and logical thought. Thus the religious revival known as the Great Awakening, which erupted in the English colonies in the 1740s, aroused much opposition from elites because that revival drew primarily on the Calvinist concept of a God that people could never fully comprehend.

In 1720, much of the North American continent still fell under Indian control. By 1770, settlements of Europeans and Africans ruled by Great Britain filled almost all of the region between the Appalachian Mountains and the Atlantic Ocean; and the British, thanks to their victory over France in the Seven Years War (see pages 86–88), dominated the extensive system of rivers and lakes running through the heart of the continent. Spanish missions extended in a great arc from present-day northern California to the Gulf Coast. Such geographic, economic, and social changes transformed the character of Europe's North American possessions.

 ## Population Growth and Ethnic Diversity

One of the most striking characteristics of the English mainland colonies in the eighteenth century was their rapid population growth. Only about 250,000 European- and African-Americans resided in the colonies in 1700; by 1775, 2.5 million lived there. Such rapid expansion appears even more remarkable when compared to the modest changes that occurred in Louisiana, New Mexico, California, and Texas. By the last quarter of the eighteenth century, Texas had only about 2,500 Spanish residents and California even fewer; the largest Spanish colony, New Mexico, included just 20,000 or so. The total European population of New France was about 70,000 in the 1760s, but only between Quebec and Montréal and in New Orleans were there significant concentrations of French settlers.

• *Important Events* •

1691	Locke's *Two Treatises of Government* published, applying Enlightenment thought to the realm of politics
1739	Stono Rebellion (South Carolina) leads to increased white fears of slave revolts
	George Whitefield arrives in America; Great Awakening broadens
1739–48	King George's War disrupts American economy
1740	Black population of Chesapeake begins to grow by natural increase, contributing to rise of large plantations
1741	New York City "conspiracy" reflects whites' continuing fears of slave revolts
1760s	Baptist congregations take root in Virginia
1760–75	Peak of eighteenth-century European and African migration to English colonies
1765–66	Hudson River land riots pit tenants and squatters against large landlords
1767–69	Regulator movement (South Carolina) tries to establish order in back country
1771	North Carolina Regulators defeated by eastern militia at Battle of Alamance

Although migration accounted for a considerable share of the growth in English America, most of the growth resulted from natural increase. Once the difficult early decades of settlement had passed, the American population doubled approximately every twenty-five years. Such a rate of growth was then unparalleled in human history. Among its causes were women's youthful age at the onset of childbearing. Since married women became pregnant every two or three years, women normally bore five to ten children. Because the colonies were healthful places to live (especially north of Virginia), a large proportion of children who survived infancy reached maturity and began families of their own. As a result, about half of the American population was under sixteen years old in 1775. (By contrast, only about one-third of the American population was under sixteen in 1990.)

Africans (about 278,000) constituted the largest racial or ethnic group that came to the mainland English colonies during the eighteenth century.

Newcomers from Africa and Europe

In the slaveholding societies of South America and the Caribbean, a surplus of males over females and appallingly high mortality rates meant that only a large, continuing flow of enslaved Africans could maintain the captive work force at constant levels. South Carolina, where rice cultivation was difficult and unhealthy, bore some resemblance to such colonies. But in the Chesapeake the number of black residents grew especially rapidly, because the new African workers were added to a population that began to sustain itself through natural increase after 1740.

The offspring of slaves were also slaves, whereas the children of servants were free. The consequences of this important difference between enslaved and indentured labor were not clear until after 1720. It then became evident that a planter who owned adult female slaves could watch the size of his labor force increase steadily—through the births of their children. Not coincidentally, the first truly large Chesapeake plantations appeared in the 1740s.

In addition to the new group of Africans, about 585,000 Europeans moved to North America during the eighteenth century, most of them after 1730 (see maps). Because some of these migrants (for example, convicts sentenced to exile by English courts) and all the slaves did not freely choose to come to the colonies, approximately one-third of the newcomers moved to America against their will.

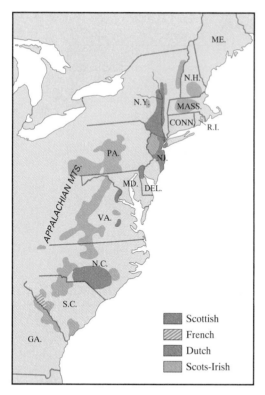
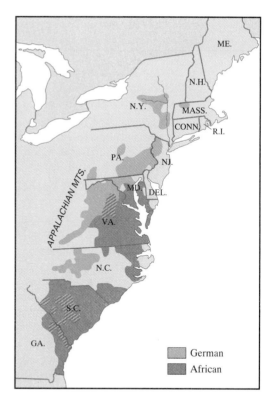

Non-English Ethnic Groups in the British Colonies, c. 1775 *Non-African immigrants arriving in the years after 1720 were pushed to the peripheries of settlement, as is shown by these maps. Scottish, Scots-Irish, French, and German newcomers had to move to the frontiers. The Dutch remained where they had originally settled in the seventeenth century. Africans were concentrated in coastal plantation regions.*

One of the largest groups of immigrants—nearly 150,000—came from Ireland or Scotland. About 66,000 were Scots-Irish, descended from Presbyterian Scots who had settled in the north of Ireland during the seventeenth century. Some 35,000 people came directly to America from Scotland. Another 43,000 migrated from southern Ireland. Fleeing economic distress and religious discrimination, they were also lured by hopes of obtaining land. Scots, Irish, and Scots-Irish immigrants often arrived in Philadelphia. They moved west and south, settling chiefly in Pennsylvania, Maryland, Virginia, and the Caroli-

Scots-Irish, Germans, and Scots

nas. Frequently unable to afford any acreage, they squatted on land belonging to Indians, land speculators, or colonial governments.

Migrants from Germany numbered about 85,000. Most emigrated from the Rhineland between 1730 and 1755, also usually arriving in Philadelphia. By the late 1700s, they and their descendants accounted for one-third of Pennsylvania's residents. But many other Germans moved west and then south along the eastern slope of the Appalachian Mountains, eventually finding homes in western Maryland and Virginia. Others sailed first to Charleston or Savannah and settled in the interior of South Carolina or Georgia. The Germans belonged to a wide variety of Protestant sects and therefore added to the already substantial religious diversity of the middle colonies.

The most concentrated period of immigration to the colonies fell between 1760 and 1775. Tough times in Germany and the British Isles led many to decide to seek a better life in America; simultaneously, the slave trade burgeoned. In those fifteen years alone arrived more than 220,000 persons—or nearly 10 percent of the entire population of British North America in 1775. Late-arriving free immigrants had little choice but to remain in the cities or move to the edges of settlement; land elsewhere was fully occupied.

Because of these migration patterns and the concentration of slaveholding in the South, half of the colonial population south of New England was of non-English origin by 1775. Whether the migrants assimilated readily into Anglo-American culture depended on patterns of settlement, the size of the group, and the strength of the migrants' ties to their common culture. For example, the Huguenots—French Protestants who fled religious persecution in their homeland after 1685—settled in tiny enclaves in American cities but were unable to sustain either their language or their religious practices. Within two generations they were almost wholly absorbed into Anglo-American culture. By contrast, the equally small group of colonial Jews maintained a distinct identity. In a few cities—notably New York and Newport, Rhode Island—they established synagogues and worked actively to preserve their culture. Members of the larger groups of migrants (Germans, Irish, and Scots) found it easier to sustain Old World ways. Countless localities were settled almost exclusively by one group or another.

Effects of Ethnic Diversity

Recognizing the benefits of keeping other racial and ethnic groups divided, the English elites on occasion deliberately fostered antagonisms. When the targets of their policies were European migrants, the goal was the maintenance of political and economic power. When the targets were Indians and Africans, as they were in South Carolina, the stakes were considerably higher. South Carolinians of English origin, a minority of the population, wanted to prevent Indians and Africans from making common cause against them. To foster antagonism, Anglo-Americans employed Indians to catch runaway slaves and used slaves as soldiers in Indian wars.

The elites probably would have preferred to ignore the English colonies' growing racial and ethnic diversity, but they could not do so for long and still maintain their power. When such men decided to lead a revolution in the 1770s, they recognized that they needed the support of non-English Americans. Quite deliberately, they then began to speak of "the rights of man," rather than "English liberties," when they sought recruits for their cause.

 ## Economic Growth and Development

The dramatic increase in the population of Anglo-America served as a source of stability for the colonial economy and provided a firm basis for further growth. Again, a comparison to French and Spanish America reveals significant differences. The population and economy of New Spain's Borderlands stagnated. The isolated settlements produced few items for export (notably, hides and skins); residents were more likely to exchange goods illegally with their French and English neighbors than with the distant centers of Spanish Mexico or the Caribbean. French Canada exported large quantities of furs and fish, but monopolistic trade practices ensured that most of the profits ended up in the home country. The Louisiana colony required substantial government subsidies to survive, despite its active internal trade and some agricultural exports such as tobacco and rice. Of France's American possessions, only the Caribbean islands flourished economically.

British, French, and Spanish Colonies Compared

In British North America, by contrast, each year the rising population generated ever-greater demands for goods and services, which led to the development of small-scale colonial manufacturing and a complex network of internal trade. As the area of settlement expanded, roads, bridges, mills, and stores were built to serve the new communities. A lively coastal trade developed; by the late 1760s, 54 percent of the vessels leaving Boston harbor were sailing to other mainland colonies rather than to foreign ports. Such ships not only collected goods for export and distributed imports but also sold items made in America. The colonies thus began to move away from their earlier pattern of near total dependence on Europe for manufactured goods. For the first time, the American population was generating sufficient demand to encourage manufacturing enterprises. The largest indigenous industry was iron making; by 1775, American furnaces and forges were producing more iron than was England itself.

The major energizing, yet destabilizing, influence on the colonial economy nevertheless remained foreign trade. Colonial prosperity still depended heavily on overseas demand for American products like tobacco, rice, indigo, fish, and barrel staves; the sale of such items earned the colonists the credit they needed to purchase English and European imports. If demand for American exports slowed, the colonists' income dropped and so did their ability to buy imported goods.

Despite fluctuations, the economy grew slowly during the eighteenth century. That growth produced better standards of living for all property-owning Americans. In the first two decades of the century, households began to acquire amenities such as chairs and earthenware dishes. Diet also improved as trading networks brought access to more varied foodstuffs. Thus the colonists became *consumers*, in the sense that for the first time they could make choices among a wide variety of products and also could afford to buy items not absolutely essential for survival and subsistence.

Growth of Consumption

Yet the benefits of economic growth were not evenly distributed: wealthy Americans improved their position relative to other colonists. The native-born elite families who dominated American political, economic, and social life by 1750 were those who had begun the century with sufficient capital to take advantage of the changes caused by population growth. They were urban merchants, large landowners, slave traders, and the owners of rum distilleries. Their rise helped to make the social and economic structure of mid–eighteenth-century America more stratified than before.

Despite the increased stratification, there seems to have been relatively little severe poverty among free settlers in rural areas, where 90 percent of the colonists lived. But in the cities, families of urban laborers lived on the edge of destitution. In Philadelphia, for instance, a male laborer's average annual earnings fell short of the amount needed to supply his family with the bare necessities. Even in a good year, his wife or children had to do wage work; in a bad year, the family could be reduced to beggary. By the 1760s public urban poor-relief systems were overwhelmed with applicants for assistance, and some cities began to build workhouses or almshouses to shelter the growing number of poor people.

Urban Poverty

Within this overall picture, it is important to distinguish among the various regions: New England, the middle colonies, the Chesapeake, and the Lower South (the Carolinas and Georgia). Each region of the colonies had its own economic rhythm derived from the nature of its export trade.

In New England, three elements combined to influence economic development: the nature of the landscape, New England's leadership in colonial shipping, and the impact of imperial wars. New England's poor soil did not produce salable surpluses other than livestock, so wood products constituted a major cash crop. Farms were worked primarily by family members; the region had relatively few hired laborers. It also had the lowest average wealth per freeholder in the colonies. But New England had many wealthy men: merchants and professionals whose income was drawn from trade with the West Indies.

New England and King George's War

Boston, by the 1730s a major shipbuilding center, soon felt the effects when warfare resumed in 1739. British vessels clashed with Spanish ships in the Caribbean, setting off a conflict that became

How do historians know that the residents of colonial North America began to purchase luxury items in the eighteenth century and that those goods came from wide-ranging trade networks? Probate inventories—written records of what people possessed at the time of their deaths—are a useful documentary source. But perhaps even more revealing are the results of archaeological excavations at the sites of colonial settlements. The shards shown on the left were found at one of the first French outposts in Louisiana—Old Mobile, established in 1702 on Mobile Bay, in what is now Alabama. The pots, of which only these small pieces remain (see the complete example), represent the final stage in a long trade route originating in China. The Chinese sold ceramics to traders in the Philippines, which Spain controlled, in exchange for Mexican silver. Spanish ships then carried the porcelain across the Pacific to Mexico, where it was purchased at annual fairs in Acapulco, carried by mule train across Mexico to Vera Cruz, then shipped to Caribbean ports and to Spain itself. The three hundred or so residents of Old Mobile bought such items from the Spanish settlement at Pensacola in nearby Florida. A brief description in an inventory could not convey so much information nearly as vividly as do these small bits of pottery. Fragments: The Magazine Antiques. Pot: The Metropolitan Museum of Art.

known in America as King George's War. Nominally the war was fought to determine who would sit on the Austrian throne (in Europe it was called the War of the Austrian Succession), but one of its causes was European commercial rivalries over the lucrative West Indian trade. The war's first impact on Boston's economy was positive. Area seamen were used by the British as privateers to seize enemy shipping and merchants profited from military supply contracts.

But Boston suffered heavy losses of manpower. Massachusetts's most costly and successful expedition was its 1745 capture of the French fortress of Louisbourg (in modern Nova Scotia), which guarded the sea lanes leading to New France. Afterward, though, Massachusetts had to levy heavy taxes on its residents to pay for the expensive effort. For decades Boston's economy felt the continuing effects of King George's War. Widows and children were put on the relief rolls, taxes remained high, and the shipbuilding boom ceased with the war's end. As a final blow to the colony, Britain gave Louisbourg back to France in the Treaty of Aix-la-Chapelle (1748).

The middle colonies were more positively affected by King George's War and its aftermath because of the greater fertility of the soil in New York and Pennsylvania, where commercial farming was the norm. With the outbreak of hostilities, the middle colonies were able to profit from the wartime demand for grain and meat. After the war poor grain harvests in Europe

Prosperity of the Middle Colonies

caused flour prices to rise rapidly. Philadelphia and New York became agricultural export centers, but Boston, lacking a fertile hinterland, found its economy stagnating.

Increased European demand for grain had a significant impact on the Chesapeake as well. After 1745, some Chesapeake planters began to con-

Change in the Chesapeake

vert tobacco fields to wheat and corn. By diversifying their crops, they could avoid dependency on one product for their income. Tobacco still ruled the region and remained the largest single export from the mainland colonies. Yet the conversion to grain cultivation brought about the first significant change in Chesapeake settlement patterns by encouraging the development of port towns (like Baltimore) to house the merchants who marketed the new products.

Like the Chesapeake, the Lower South depended on staple crops and an enslaved labor force. But in contrast to tobacco prices, which rose slowly

Trade and the Lower South

through the middle decades of the century, rice prices doubled by the late 1730s. Because Parliament removed rice from the list of enumerated products (see pages 56–60) in 1730, South Carolinians were able to do what colonial tobacco planters never could: trade directly with continental Europe. Dependence on European sales had its drawbacks, however. When the outbreak of King George's War disrupted trade with Europe, rice prices plummeted, and South Carolina entered a depression. Still, prosperity returned by the 1760s. Indeed, the Lower South experienced more rapid economic growth in that period than did the other regions of the colonies. Partly as a result, it had the highest average wealth per freeholder in Anglo-America by the time of the American Revolution.

The varying economic results of King George's War and its aftermath on the English mainland colonies point up a crucial fact: they did not compose a unified whole. They were linked economically into regions, but they had few political or social ties beyond or even within those regions. Despite the growing coastal trade, the individual colonies' economic fortunes depended not on their

neighbors in America but rather on the shifting markets of Europe and the West Indies.

 Colonial Cultures

A seventeenth-century resident of England's American possessions miraculously transported to 1750 would have been surprised by what the historian Richard Bushman has termed

Genteel Culture

"the refinement of America." Wealthy colonists spent their money ostentatiously. Most notably, they built large houses containing rooms specifically designed for such forms of socializing as dancing, cardplaying, or drinking tea. Sufficiently well-off to enjoy "leisure" time, they attended the theater, gambled at horse-races, and played games. They also cultivated polite manners, adopting stylized forms of address and paying attention to "proper" ways of behaving. Elite families in New Mexico, Louisiana, and Quebec also set themselves off from the "lesser sort."

Affluent men prided themselves not only on their possessions and their positions in the colonial political, social, and economic hierarchy, but also on their level of education

Education and the Enlightenment

and their intellectual connections to Europe. Many had been tutored by private teachers; some even attended college in Europe or America. (Harvard, the first colonial college, was founded in 1636.) In the seventeenth century, studies focused heavily on ancient languages and theology. But by the mid-eighteenth century, colleges broadened their curricula to include courses on mathematics, the natural sciences, law, and medicine. Accordingly, young men from elite or upwardly mobile families enrolled in college to study for careers other than the ministry. Colonial women, however, except for some in Canada and Louisiana who joined convents, were uniformly excluded from advanced education.

The learned clergymen who headed colonial colleges in the eighteenth century were deeply affected by the intellectual current known as the Enlightenment. About the middle of the previous century, some European thinkers began to analyze nature in an effort to determine the laws that govern the universe. They employed experimentation and abstract reasoning to discover general principles behind phenomena such as the motions of planets and stars, the behavior of falling objects, and the characteristics of light and sound. Above all, Enlightenment philosophers emphasized acquiring knowledge through reason.

The Enlightenment had an enormous impact on educated, well-to-do people in Europe and America. It supplied them with a common vocabulary and a unified view of the world through which they endeavored to make sense of God's orderly creation. Thus American naturalists like John and William Bartram supplied European scientists with information about New World plants and animals so that they could be included in newly formulated universal classification systems.

Enlightenment rationalism also affected politics. John Locke's *Two Treatises of Government* (1691) challenged previous concepts of a divinely sanctioned political order. Governments, declared Locke, were created by men and so could be altered by them. If a ruler broke his contract with the people and did not protect their rights, he could legitimately be ousted from power by peaceful—or even violent—means. The aim of government was the good of the people, Enlightenment theorists proclaimed. A proper political order could prevent the rise of tyrants; even the power of monarchs was subject to God's natural laws.

Yet the world in which such ideas were discussed was that of the few, not the many. Most residents of North America did not know how to read or write. Books were scarce and expensive, public schools supported by tax levies were few and far between. European youngsters who learned to read were usually taught by their parents or older siblings. A few months at a private "dame school" run by a literate local widow might complete their education by teaching them the basics of writing and simple arithmetic. Enslaved African-American children were denied even that level of learning; teaching slaves to read and write was forbidden as too subversive of the social order. And only the most zeal-

Oral Cultures

ous Indian converts were taught Europeans' literacy skills.

Thus the cultures of colonial North America were primarily oral, communal, and—at least through the first half of the eighteenth century—intensely local. The major means of communication was face-to-face conversation. Information tended to travel slowly and within relatively confined regions. Different locales developed divergent cultural traditions, and racial and ethnic variations heightened those differences. Public rituals served as the chief means through which the colonists forged their cultural identities.

Attendance at church was perhaps the most important such ritual. In Congregational (Puritan) churches, seating was assigned by church leaders to reflect standing in the community. In early New England, men and women sat on opposite sides of a central aisle, arranged in ranks according to age, wealth, and church membership. By the mid-eighteenth century, wealthy men and their wives sat in privately owned pews; their children, servants, and the less fortunate were still seated in sex-segregated fashion at the rear or sides of the church. In eighteenth-century Virginia, seating in Anglican parishes also conformed to the local status hierarchy. In the city of Quebec, Catholic feast days were celebrated by formal processions of men into the parish church; each participant's rank determined his placement in the procession. By contrast, Quaker meetinghouses used an egalitarian but sex-segregated seating system.

Religious Rituals

Communal culture centered on the civic sphere as well. In New England, colonial governments proclaimed official days of thanksgiving and days of fasting and prayer. Everyone was expected to participate in the public rituals held in churches on such occasions. Monthly militia musters also brought the community together, since all able-bodied men between the ages of sixteen and sixty were members of the militia.

Civic Rituals

In the Chesapeake, important cultural rituals occurred on court and election days. When the county court was in session, men would come from miles around to file suits, appear as witnesses, serve as jurors, or simply observe the goings-on. Attendance at court functioned as a method of civic education; from watching the proceedings men learned what behavior their neighbors expected of them. Elections served the same purpose, for freeholders voted in public. An election official, often flanked by the candidates for the office in question, would call each man forward to declare his preference. The voter would then be thanked politely by the gentleman for whom he had cast his oral ballot.

Everywhere in colonial North America, the public punishment of criminals served not just to humiliate the offender but also to remind the community of proper standards of behavior. Public hangings and whippings expressed the community's outrage about crimes and restored harmony to its ranks. Judges often assigned penalties that shamed miscreants in especially appropriate ways. In New Mexico, for example, a man who had assaulted his father-in-law was directed not merely to pay medical expenses but also to kneel before him and to beg his forgiveness publicly, in front of the entire community.

The wide availability of consumer goods after the early years of the eighteenth century fostered new rituals centered on consumption. The rituals

Rituals of Consumption

began with the acquisition of desirable and often nonessential items in specialty shops. By 1750 New York, Boston, Philadelphia, and New Orleans had many such stores. Even small and medium-size towns had one or two retail establishments by then. A colonist with money to spend would set aside time to "go shopping," a novel and pleasurable activity. The purchase of a desired object—for example, a ceramic bowl or a mirror—marked only the beginning of consumption rituals. Consumers would then deploy their purchases in an appropriate manner: hanging the mirror prominently on a wall of the house or displaying the bowl on a table or sideboard. Individual colonists clearly took personal pleasure in owning lovely objects, but they also could take pride in displaying their acquisitions (and thus their wealth and good taste) publicly to kin and neighbors.

Tea drinking played an especially important role in Anglo-American consumption rituals. From early in the eighteenth century, households with aspirations to genteel status sought to acquire the items necessary for the proper consumption of tea, including strainers, sugar tongs, bowls, and even special tables. And because of its cost, tea served as a crucial marker of status. Although poor households also consumed tea, they could not afford the fancy equipment used by their better-off neighbors.

Rituals also allowed the disparate cultures of colonial North America to interact with one another. Particularly important were the rituals that developed on what the historian Richard White has termed "the middle ground"—that is, the psychological and geographical space in which Indians and Europeans encountered each other.

When Europeans sought to trade with Indians, they came into contact with an indigenous system of exchange that stressed gift giving rather than formalized buying and

Intercultural Rituals

selling. Although French and English traders complained constantly about the need to present gifts prior to negotiating for furs and skins, such a step was essential to successful bargaining. Over time, an appropriate ritual developed. A European trader arriving at a village would give gifts (cloth, rum, gunpowder, and other items) to Indian hunters. Eventually, those gifts would be reciprocated. To the detriment of Indian societies, rum became a crucial component of these intercultural trading rituals. With some reason, traders came to believe that drunken Indians would sell their furs more cheaply.

Rituals surrounding murders were also critical points of cultural interaction. Indians and Europeans both believed that murders required a compensatory act, but the two groups differed on what that act should be. Europeans sought primarily to identify the murderer and to punish, perhaps to kill, that person. Such "eye for an eye" revenge was for Indians only one of many possible responses. Compensation could also be accomplished by capturing someone who could take the dead person's place or—most important for maintaining peace on the frontiers— by "covering the dead," or providing the family of the deceased with goods that could compensate for the loss. Among the French and the Algonkians a ritual evolved in which frontier murders were investigated and murderers identified, but by mutual agreement deaths were usually "covered" by trade goods rather than by blood revenge.

Throughout colonial North America, therefore, rituals both cemented ties and established rank within communities. They also allowed those communities to interact peacefully with one another.

 ## Colonial Families

As Europeans consolidated their hold on the North American continent during the first three quarters of the eighteenth century, Native Americans were

Indian and Mixed-Race Families

forced to adapt to novel circumstances. Bands reduced in numbers by disease and warfare recombined into new units; for example, the group later known as the Catawbas emerged in the 1730s in the western Carolinas from the fragmentary remains of several earlier Indian nations. Likewise, Indian family forms were reshaped under pressure from European secular and religious authorities. Whereas many Indian societies had permitted easy divorce, English, French, and Spanish missionaries frowned on such practices; and those societies that had allowed polygynous marriages (including New England Algonkians) redefined such relationships, designating one wife as "legitimate" and others as "concubines."

Continued high mortality rates in traditional societies gave new importance to extended kin who could assume responsibility for surviving children. Family forms also were affected by European dominance and the accompanying changes in traditional modes of subsistence in an occupied region. In New England, for instance, many Algonkian husbands and wives were unable to live together because they were supporting themselves by working separately for Anglo-Americans (perhaps wives as domestic servants, husbands as sailors). And in New Mexico, detribalized Navajos, Pueblos, and Apaches employed as servants by Spanish settlers clustered in the small towns of the Borderlands. Known collectively as *genizaros*, they lost contact with Indian cultures and instead lived on the fringes of Hispanic society.

Wherever there were relatively few European women in the population, sexual liaisons occurred among European men and Indian women. The resulting mixed-race population of mestizos and métis worked as a familial "middle ground" to ease other cultural interactions. In New France and the Anglo-American backcountry, such families frequently resided in Indian villages and were enmeshed in trading networks; often, children of these unions became prominent leaders of Native American societies. By contrast, in the Spanish Borderlands the offspring of Europeans and genizaros were treated as degraded individuals.

Family life among the many European migrants to North America was far more stable than that among Indian and mestizo peoples. Families (rather than individuals)

European-American Families

constituted the basic units of colonial society. Headed by European men or their widows, households were the chief mechanisms of production and consumption. Their members—bound by ties of blood or servitude—worked together to produce goods for consumption or sale. The head of the household represented it to the outside world, managing the finances and holding legal authority over the rest of the family—his wife, his children, and his servants or slaves. (At the time, *family* meant everyone who occupied one house, whether or not they were blood kin.) Such households were considerably larger than American families today. Most of those large families were nuclear—that is, they did not include extended kin like aunts, uncles, or grandparents.

In English, French, and Spanish America alike, the vast majority of European families supported themselves through agriculture. The scale and nature of the work varied: the production of tobacco in the Chesapeake required different sorts of labor from subsistence farming in New England or cattle ranching in New Mexico and Texas. As in the European, African, and Native American societies, household tasks were allocated by sex, discussed in Chapter 1.

The mistress was responsible for what Anglo-Americans called "indoor affairs." She and her female helpers prepared food, cleaned the house, did laundry, and often made clothing. These basic chores were complex and time-consuming. Preparing food, for instance, involved planting and cultivating a garden, harvesting and preserving vegetables, salting and smoking meat, drying apples and pressing cider, milking cows and making butter and cheese, not to mention cooking and baking. The head of the household and his male helpers, responsible for "outdoor affairs," also had heavy workloads. They had to plant and cultivate the fields, build fences, chop wood for the fireplace, harvest and market crops, care for livestock, and butcher cattle and hogs to provide the household with meat.

A European-American man's household could include African-American families as well as his own kin. More than 95 percent of colonial African-Americans were held in perpetual bondage. Although many of them lived on farms with only one or two other slaves, most lived and worked in a largely black setting. In South Carolina and Louisiana, a majority of the population was of African origin; in Georgia, about half; and in the Chesapeake, 40 percent.

Large plantations enabled the specialization of labor. Each had its own enslaved male blacksmiths, carpenters, and shoemakers, along with slave women who worked as seamstresses, cooks, dairymaids, and midwives. These skilled slaves—between 10 and 20 percent of the African-American population—were essential to the smooth functioning of the plantation. But most slaves, male or female, worked in the fields.

African-American Families

Because all the colonies legally permitted slavery, African-Americans had few potential refuges from bondage. Some recently arrived Africans stole boats to try to return home or ran off in groups to frontier regions to join the Indians. Some slaves from South Carolina and Georgia managed to reach Spanish Florida, where they were allowed to establish a free community on the outskirts of St. Augustine. Violent resistance had even less to recommend it than running away because European-American colonists, although in the minority in some areas, controlled the guns and ammunition.

Lack of rebellion, however, did not imply an absence of resistance to enslavement. Family ties often provided a key means for such resistance. Even though slaves were not allowed to marry legally, they established strong family structures in which youngsters usually carried their parents' and grandparents' names. Extended-kin groups protested excessive punishment of relatives and asked to live in the same quarters. The links that developed among African-American families who had lived on the same plantation for several generations served as insurance against the uncertainties of existence under slavery. If a nuclear family was broken up by sale, other relatives could help with child rearing and similar tasks. Among African-Americans, just as among Indians, the extended family served a more important function than it did among European-Americans.

Most slave families managed to carve out a small measure of autonomy, especially in their working and spiritual lives. Enslaved Muslims often clung to their Islamic faith. Other Africans converted to Christianity, finding comfort in the assurances that all people would be free and equal in heaven. On many plantations, slaves were allowed or required to plant their own gardens, hunt, or fish to supplement the minimal diet their masters supplied. In some regions, most notably South Carolina and Louisiana, enslaved people were allowed to accumulate personal property by working for themselves once they had finished their assigned tasks. Late in the century, some Chesapeake planters with a surplus of laborers began to hire out slaves to others, often allowing the workers to keep a small part of their earnings. Such accumulated property could buy desired goods or serve as a legacy for children.

Month the Earth begins to bring forth Fruits. The 2d

April called after Aperie, because in this

Month of the Roman martial Year.

Farmer Abraham's Almanac, published in Philadelphia in 1759, contained this crude woodcut showing women engaged in chores associated with dairying: at right, milking a cow; at left, churning butter. American Antiquarian Society.

Just as African- and European-Americans lived together on plantations, so, too, were both groups found in cities. Yet the few colonial cities were nothing but large towns by today's standards. In 1750 the largest, Boston, had just seventeen thousand inhabitants. Still, city life differed considerably from rural life. City dwellers everywhere, purchased foodstuffs and wood at markets and cloth in shops, instead of laboriously producing such items themselves.

Life in the Cities

City people also had much more contact with the world beyond their own homes than did their rural counterparts. By the 1750s, most major cities had at least one weekly newspaper that printed the latest "advices from London," news from other English colonies, and local reports. Newspapers were available at taverns and inns, so people who could not afford to buy them could catch up on the news. Even illiterates could do so, since literate customers often read the papers aloud. Contact with the outside world also had drawbacks: sailors sometimes brought exotic and deadly diseases into port.

 ## Politics and Religion: Stability and Crisis in British America

In the first decades of the eighteenth century, Anglo-American political life exhibited a new stability. Despite substantial migration from overseas, most residents of the mainland had been born in America. Men from genteel families dominated the political structures in each province, for voters (free male property holders) tended to defer to their well-educated "betters" on election days.

Throughout the Anglo-American colonies, political leaders sought to increase the powers of elected assemblies relative to the powers of the governors and other appointed officials. Assemblies began to claim privileges associated with the British House of Commons, such as the rights to initiate all tax legislation and to control the militia. The assemblies also developed effective ways of influencing British appointees, especially threats of withholding salaries. In some colonies (Virginia and South Carolina, for example), elite members of the assemblies usually presented a united front to royal officials; in others (like New York), they fought bitterly with each other. New York took the first steps on the road to modern American democracy. In an attempt to win hotly contested elections, the province's genteel leaders began to appeal to "the people," competing openly for the votes of ordinary freeholders. Yet in 1733 that same New York government imprisoned a newspaper editor, John Peter Zenger, who had too vigorously criticized its actions. Defending Zenger against the charge of "seditious libel," his lawyer argued that the truth could not be defamatory, thus helping to establish a free-press principle now found in American law.

Rise of the Assemblies

Eighteenth-century assemblies bore little resemblance to twentieth-century state legislatures. Only on rare occasions did they formulate new policies or pass laws of real importance. Members of the assemblies believed their primary function was to stop the governors or councils from enacting oppressive taxes, rather than to pass laws that would actively benefit their constituents.

By midcentury, politically aware colonists commonly drew analogies between their own governments and Great Britain's balance of king, lords, and commons—a combination that had been thought to produce a stable polity. Although the analogy was not exact, political leaders equated their governors with the monarch, their councils with the aristocracy, and their assemblies with the House of Commons. All three were thought essential to good government, but Americans viewed the appointed governors and councils as potential threats to colonial freedoms and customary ways of life. By contrast, colonists saw the assemblies as the people's protectors. And the assemblies in turn regarded themselves as representatives of the people.

Such beliefs should not, however, be equated with modern practice. The assemblies, firmly controlled by dominant families whose members were reelected year after year, rarely responded to the concerns of their poorer constituents. Although settlement continually spread westward, assemblies failed to reapportion themselves to provide adequate representation for newer communities—a lack of action that led to serious grievances among frontier dwellers. Thus it is important to distinguish between the colonial ideal of protecting the people's liberties and the reality of protecting wealth and privilege.

At midcentury, the political structures were confronted with a series of crises. None affected all the mainland provinces, but no colony escaped wholly untouched. The crises exposed the internal tensions building in the pluralistic American society, foreshadowing the greater disorder of the revolutionary era. Most important, they demonstrated that the political accommodations arrived at in the aftermath of the Glorious Revolution were no longer adequate to govern Britain's American empire.

One of the first and greatest crises occurred in South Carolina in 1739. Early one September morning, about twenty South Carolina slaves gathered near the Stono River south of Charleston. Seizing guns and ammunition from a store, they killed the storekeepers and some nearby planter families. Then, joined by other local slaves, they headed south toward Florida in hopes of finding refuge. By that afternoon, a troop of militia attacked the fugitives, who then numbered about a hundred, killing some and dispersing the rest. More than a week later, most of the remaining conspirators were captured. Those not killed on the spot were later executed.

Stono Rebellion

The Stono Rebellion shocked slaveholding South Carolinians and residents of other colonies as well, and British America stiffened its laws governing the behavior of African-Americans. The most immediate response came in New York City, which had suffered a slave revolt in 1712. There the news from the South, coupled with fears of Spain generated by the outbreak of King George's War, set off a reign of terror in the summer of 1741. Hysterical whites interpreted a biracial gang of thieves as malevolent conspirators who wanted to foment a slave uprising under the guidance of a supposed priest in the pay of Spain. By summer's end, thirty-one blacks and four whites had been executed for participating in the "plot." The Stono Rebellion and the New York conspiracy exposed Anglo-Americans' deepest fears about the dangers of slaveholding and revealed the assemblies' inability to prevent serious internal disorder. Events of the next two decades confirmed that pattern.

By midcentury, most of the fertile land east of the Appalachians had been purchased or occupied. As a result, conflicts over land titles and conditions of landholding grew in number and frequency as colonists competed for control of land good for farming. In 1746, for example, some New Jersey farmers clashed violently with agents of the East Jersey proprietors. The proprietors claimed the farmers' land as theirs and demanded annual payments, called quitrents, for the use of the property.

Land Riots in New Jersey and New York

The most serious land riots of the period took place along the Hudson River in 1765 and 1766. Late in the seventeenth century, several huge tracts in the lower Hudson valley had been granted to prominent colonial families. The proprietors in turn divided these estates into small farms, which they rented chiefly to poor Dutch and German migrants. After 1740, though, increasing migration from New England brought conflict to the great New York estates. The New Englanders squatted on vacant portions of the manors and resisted all attempts at eviction. In the mid-1760s the Philipse family sued the New Englanders, some of whom had lived on Philipse land for twenty or thirty years. New York courts upheld the Philipse claim and ordered squatters to make

way for tenants with valid leases. Instead of complying, the farmers organized a rebellion against the proprietors. For nearly a year insurgent farmers terrorized proprietors and loyal tenants. The rebellion was put down only after British troops dispatched from New York City captured its leaders.

Violent conflicts of a different sort erupted just a few years later in the Carolinas. The Regulator movements of the late 1760s (South Carolina) and early 1770s (North Carolina) pitted backcountry farmers against wealthy eastern planters who controlled the provincial governments. Frontier dwellers, most of whom were Scots-Irish, protested their lack of an adequate voice in colonial political affairs. South Carolinians for months policed the countryside in vigilante bands, contending that law enforcement in the region was too lax and biased against them. North Carolinians, whose primary grievance was heavy taxation, fought and lost a battle with eastern militiamen at Alamance in 1771.

Regulators in the Carolinas

The most widespread crisis, however, was religious. From the late 1730s through the 1760s, waves of religious revivalism—today known collectively as the Great Awakening—swept over various parts of the colonies, primarily New England (1735–1745) and Virginia (1750s and 1760s). Orthodox Calvinists were eager to combat Enlightenment rationalism, which denied innate human depravity. In addition, many recent immigrants and residents of the backcountry had no prior religious affiliation, thus presenting evangelists with a potential source of converts.

First Great Awakening

The first signs of the Great Awakening appeared during 1734 and 1735 in western Massachusetts, in the Northampton Congregational Church. There the Reverend Jonathan Edwards, a noted preacher and theologian, taught that individuals could attain salvation only through recognition of their own depraved natures and the need to surrender completely to God's will. Such surrender, Edwards noticed, brought to members of his congregation an intensely emotional release from sin, which came to be seen as a single identifiable moment of conversion.

The effects of such conversions remained isolated until 1739, when George Whitefield, an English Anglican cleric, arrived in America. For

George Whitefield

fifteen months he toured the British colonies, preaching to large audiences from Georgia to New England. A gripping orator, Whitefield was the chief generating force behind the Great Awakening. Thousands turned out to listen—and to experience conversion. At first, regular clerics welcomed Whitefield and the American-born itinerant evangelist preachers who sprang up to imitate him. Soon, however, many clergymen began to realize that although "revived" religion filled their churches, it ran counter to their own approach to doctrine and matters of faith.

Opposition to the Awakening heightened rapidly, causing large numbers of congregations to splinter. "Old Lights"—traditional clerics and their followers—engaged in bitter disputes with the "New Light" evangelicals. Already characterized by numerous sects, American Protestantism became further divided as the major denominations split into Old Light and New Light factions and as new evangelical sects—Methodists and Baptists—gained adherents. Paradoxically, the angry fights and the rapid rise in the number of distinct denominations eventually led to an American willingness to tolerate religious diversity.

The most important effect of the Awakening was its impact on American modes of thought. The revivalists' message directly challenged the colonial tradition of deference.

Impact of the Awakening

Itinerant preachers, only a few of whom were ordained clergymen, claimed they understood the will of God better than did orthodox clerics. The Awakening's emphasis on emotion rather than learning undermined the validity of received wisdom, and New Lights questioned not only religious but also social and political orthodoxy.

Nowhere was this trend more evident than in Virginia. By the 1760s Baptists had gained a se-

Built in the late eighteenth century and still standing in Fairfax County, Virginia, the Frying Pan Meetinghouse was one of the Baptist churches with a racially integrated congregation from its earliest years. The existence of such egalitarian religious bodies directly challenged the colony's hierarchical society. Virginia Department of Historic Resources, VA.

cure foothold in Virginia; their beliefs and behavior were openly at odds with

Virginia Baptists

the way most genteel families lived. They rejected as sinful the horseracing, gambling, and dancing that occupied much of the gentry's leisure time. They addressed each other as "brother" and "sister" regardless of social status, and they elected the leaders of their congregations.

Strikingly, almost all the Virginia Baptist congregations included both black and white members. Church rules applied equally to all members; interracial sexual relationships, divorce, and adultery were forbidden to everyone. In addition, masters were directed not to break up slave marriages through sale. Biracial committees investigated complaints about church members' misbehavior. Churches also excommunicated masters for physically abusing their slaves. Some other Baptists decided that owning slaves was "unrighteous" and freed their bondspeople.

 ## Conclusion

The Great Awakening thus injected an egalitarian strain into Anglo-American life at midcentury and further disrupted traditional structures of existence. Although primarily a religious movement, the Awakening also had important social and political consequences, calling into question habitual modes of behavior in the secular as well as the religious realm. In short, the Great Awakening helped to break Anglo-Americans' ties to their limited seventeenth-century origins.

Also important were the changes in the economy that enmeshed the colonies in an international network of trade, drawing them into European wars and creating the wealthy class of merchants and landowners who dominated colonial life.

By 1750 the colonies mixed diverse European, American, and African traditions into a novel cultural blend that owed much to Europe and North America. Colonists continued to identify themselves as French, Spanish, or British rather than as Americans. That did not change in Canada, Louisiana, or the Spanish Borderlands, but in the 1760s some Anglo-Americans began to realize that their interests were not necessarily identical to those of Great Britain or its monarch.

Suggestions for Further Reading

General

Jack P. Greene, *Pursuits of Happiness: The Social Development of the Early Modern British Colonies and the Formation of American*

Culture (1988); Peter C. Mancall, *Deadly Medicine: Indians and Alcohol in Early America* (1995); Stephanie G. Wolf, *As Various as Their Land: The Everyday Lives of 18th Century Americans* (1992).

New France and New Spain

Ramón Gutiérrez, *When Jesus Came, the Corn Mothers Went Away: Marriage, Sexuality, and Power in New Mexico, 1500–1846* (1991); Gwendolyn Midlo Hall, *Africans in Colonial Louisiana: The Development of Afro-Creole Culture in the Eighteenth Century* (1992); Dale Miquelon, *New France, 1701–1744* (1987); G. F. G. Stanley, *New France, 1744–1760* (1968); Daniel H. Usner, Jr., *Indians, Settlers, and Slaves in a Frontier Exchange Economy: The Lower Mississippi Valley Before 1783* (1992).

Anglo-American Society

T. H. Breen, *Tobacco Culture* (1985); Lois Green Carr et al., eds., *Colonial Chesapeake Society* (1988); Rhys Isaac, *The Transformation of Virginia, 1740–1790* (1982); Christopher Jedrey, *The World of John Cleaveland: Family and Community in Eighteenth-Century New England* (1979); Sung Bok Kim, *Landlord and Tenant in Colonial New York: Manorial Society, 1664–1775* (1978); Peter C. Mancall, *Valley of Opportunity: Economic Culture Along the Upper Susquehanna, 1700–1800* (1991); Gary B. Nash, *The Urban Crucible: Social Change, Political Consciousness, and the Origins of the American Revolution* (1979); Michael Zuckerman, *Peaceable Kingdoms: New England Towns in the Eighteenth Century* (1970).

Anglo-American Economics and Politics

Bernard Bailyn, *The Origins of American Politics* (1968); Patricia U. Bonomi, *A Factious People: Politics and Society in Colonial New York* (1971); Richard Bushman, *King and People in Provincial Massachusetts* (1985); Richard Bushman, *The Refinement of America: Persons, Houses, Cities* (1992); Cary Carson et al., eds., *Of Consuming Interests: The Style of Life in the Eighteenth Century* (1994); Stephen Innes, ed., *Work and Labor in Early America* (1988); John J. McCusker and Russell R. Menard, *The Economy of British America, 1607–1789* (1985).

Immigration to British America

Bernard Bailyn, *The Peopling of British North America* (1986); Bernard Bailyn, *Voyagers to the West* (1986); Bernard Bailyn and Philip Morgan, eds., *Strangers Within the Realm* (1991); R. J. Dickson, *Ulster Immigration to Colonial America, 1718–1775* (1966); David Dobson, *Scottish Immigration to Colonial America, 1607–1785* (1994); A. Roger Ekirch, *Bound for America: The Transportation of British Convicts to the Colonies, 1718–1775* (1987); Ned Landsman, *Scotland and Its First American Colony* (1985); A. G. Roeber, *Palatines, Liberty, and Property: German Lutherans in Colonial British America* (1993).

African-Americans

Thomas J. Davis, *A Rumor of Revolt: The "Great Negro Plot" in Colonial New York* (1985); Marvin L. Michael Kay and Lorin Lee Cary, *Slavery in North Carolina, 1748–1775* (1995); Allan Kulikoff, *Tobacco and Slaves: The Development of Southern Cultures in the Chesapeake, 1680–1800* (1986); Michael Mullin, *Africa in America: Slave Acculturation and Resistance in the American South and the British Caribbean, 1736–1834* (1992); William Pierson, *Black Yankees: The Development of an Afro-American Subculture in Eighteenth-Century New England* (1988); Mechal Sobel, *The World They Made Together: Black and White Values in Eighteenth-Century Virginia* (1987).

Anglo-American Women and Families

Cornelia Hughes Dayton, *Women Before the Bar: Gender, Law, and Society in Connecticut, 1639–1789* (1995); Joan Gundersen, *To Be Useful to the World: Women in Eighteenth-Century America* (1996); Barry J. Levy, *Quakers and the American Family* (1988); Marylynn Salmon, *Women and the Law of Property in Early America* (1986); Daniel Blake Smith, *Inside the Great House: Planter Family Life in Eighteenth-Century Chesapeake Society* (1980).

Anglo-American Education, Science, and the Enlightenment

Patricia Cline Cohen, *A Calculating People: The Spread of Numeracy in Early America* (1982); Lawrence A. Cremin, *American Education: The Colonial Experience, 1607–1783* (1970); Richard Beale Davis, *Intellectual Life in the Colonial South, 1585–1763* (1978); Henry F. May, *The Enlightenment in America* (1976); William Sloan and Julie Williams, *The Early American Press, 1690–1783* (1994); Raymond P. Stearns, *Science in the British Colonies of America* (1970).

Religion and the Great Awakening

Patricia U. Bonomi, *Under the Cope of Heaven: Religion, Society, and Politics in Colonial America* (1986); J. M. Bumstead and John E. Van de Wetering, *What Must I Do to Be Saved? The Great Awakening in Colonial America* (1976); Jon Butler, *Awash in a Sea of Faith: Christianizing the American People* (1990); Harry S. Stout, *The Divine Dramatist: George Whitefield and the Rise of Modern Evangelicalism* (1991); Patricia Tracy, *Jonathan Edwards, Pastor* (1980).

CHAPTER

5

Severing the Bonds
of Empire
1754–1774

The two men must have found the occasion remarkable. The artist customarily painted portraits of the wealthy and high born, not of artisans. Moreover, the political sympathies of the painter, John Singleton Copley, lay primarily with Boston's conservatives, whereas the sitter, the silversmith Paul Revere, was a noted leader of resistance to British policies. Yet some time in 1768 Revere commissioned Copley to paint his portrait, and the result is one the greatest works of American art.

Copley portrayed Revere surrounded by the tools of his trade and contemplating a teapot he was crafting. Revere's pose and apparel convey an impression of thoughtfulness, virtuous labor, and solidity. The teapot, too, carries a message, especially in the year 1768. Simultaneously a reflection of a craftsman's skills and a prominent emblem of the new "empire of goods" in British America, it resonated with symbolism because, as shall be seen later in this chapter, tea boycotts were an important component of colonial resistance to Great Britain.

In retrospect, John Adams identified the years between 1760 and 1775 as the era of the true American Revolution. The Revolution, Adams declared, was completed before the fighting started, for it was "in the Minds of the people," involving not the actual winning of independence but a fundamental shift of allegiance from Britain to America. Not all historians would agree with Adams's interpretation, but none would

John Singleton Copley's portrait of Paul Revere is generally regarded as one of his masterpieces. Copley captured Revere's character as a hard-working, respectable artisan—a man unafraid of displaying his humble origins to the world.   Museum of Fine Arts, Boston. Gift of John W., William B., and Edward H. R. Revere.

deny the importance of the events of those crucial years.

The story of the 1760s and early 1770s describes an ever-widening split between Great Britain and Anglo-America. In the long history of British settlement in the Western Hemisphere, considerable tension had at times marred the relationship between individual provinces and the mother country. Still, that tension rarely had been sustained for long, nor had it been widespread, except during the crisis following the Glorious Revolution in 1689. In the 1750s, however, a series of events caused colonists to begin to examine their relations with Great Britain. It all started with the Seven Years War.

Britain's overwhelming victory in that war, confirmed by treaty in 1763, forever altered the balance of power in North America. France was ousted from the continent and Spain from Florida, events with major consequences for both the indigenous peoples of the interior and the residents of the British colonies. Indians could no longer play off European powers against one another and so lost one of their major diplomatic tools. Anglo-Americans, for their part, no longer had to fear the French threat on their northern and western borders or the Spanish in the Southeast.

The British victory in 1763, then, constituted a major turning point in American history because of its direct effect on all the residents of North America. It also had a significant impact on Great Britain. To win the war, Britain went heavily into debt. To reduce the debt, Parliament for the first time imposed on the colonies revenue-raising taxes in addition to the customs duties that had long regulated trade. That decision exposed differences in the political thinking of Americans and Britons.

During the 1760s and early 1770s a broad coalition of Anglo-Americans resisted new tax levies and attempts by British officials to tighten controls over provincial governments. The colonies' elected leaders became ever more suspicious of Britain's motives as the years passed. They laid aside old antagonisms to coordinate their response to the new measures, and they slowly began to reorient their political thinking. As late as the summer of 1774, though, few harbored thoughts of independence.

 ## Renewed Warfare Among Europeans and Indians

The English colonies along the Atlantic seaboard were surrounded by hostile, or potentially hostile, neighbors: Indians everywhere, the Spanish in Florida and along the coast of the Gulf of Mexico, the French along the great inland system of rivers and lakes that stretched from the St. Lawrence to the Mississippi. The Spanish outposts posed little direct threat, for Spain's days as a major power had passed. The French were another matter. Their long chain of forts and settlements dominated the North American interior, facilitating trading partnerships and alliances with the Indians. In none of the three wars fought between 1689 and 1748 was

• *Important Events* •

1754	Albany Congress meets to try to forge colonial unity Fighting breaks out with Washington's defeat at Fort Necessity	**1766**	Stamp Act repealed Declaratory Act insists that Parliament can tax the colonies
1756	Britain declares war on France; Seven Years War officially begins	**1767**	Townshend Acts lay duties on trade within the empire, send new officials and judges to America
1759	British forces take Quebec	**1768–70**	Resistance to Townshend duties takes form of boycotts and public demonstrations but divides merchants and urban artisans
1760	American phase of war ends with fall of Montréal to British troops George III becomes king		
1763	Treaty of Paris ends Seven Years War Pontiac's allies attack British forts in West Proclamation of 1763 attempts to close land west of Appalachians to English settlement	**1770**	Lord North becomes prime minister Townshend duties repealed, except for tea tax Boston Massacre kills five colonial rioters
		1772	Boston Committee of Correspondence formed
1764	Sugar Act lays new duties on molasses, tightens customs regulations Currency Act outlaws paper money issued by the colonies	**1773**	Tea Act aids East India Company Boston Tea Party protests the Tea Act
1765	Stamp Act requires stamps on all printed materials in colonies Sons of Liberty formed	**1774**	Coercive Acts punish Boston and the colony of Massachusetts as a whole Quebec Act reforms government of Quebec

England able to shake France's hold on the American frontier. Under the Peace of Utrecht, which ended Queen Anne's War in 1713, the English won control of such peripheral northern areas as Newfoundland, Hudson's Bay, and Nova Scotia (Acadia). But Britain made no territorial gains in King George's War.

During both Queen Anne's War and King George's War, the Iroquois Confederacy pursued a policy of neutrality and skillfully played the Europeans off against each other.

Iroquois Neutrality

When the Iroquois went to war, it was against their traditional southern enemies, the Catawbas. Since France repeatedly urged them to attack the Catawbas, who were allied with Britain, the Iroquois achieved desirable goals. They kept the French happy and si-

multaneously consolidated their control over the entire interior region north of Virginia. The campaign against a common enemy also enabled the confederacy to cement its alliance with the Shawnees and Delawares.

But even careful Iroquois diplomats could not prevent the region inhabited by the Shawnees and Delawares (now western Pennsylvania and eastern Ohio) from providing the spark that set off a major war. That conflict spread from America to Europe, proving decisive in the contest for North America. Trouble began in 1752 when Anglo-American fur traders ventured into the area known as the Ohio country (see map, page 87). The French could not permit their rivals to gain a foothold in the region: a permanent British presence in the Ohio country could challenge France's control of the western fur trade and even threaten its prominence in the

The Colonial Wars, 1689–1763

American Name	European Name	Dates	Participants	American Sites	Dispute
King William's War	War of the League of Augsburg	1689–97	England, Holland versus France, Spain	New England, New York, Canada	French power
Queen Anne's War	War of Spanish Succession	1702–13	England, Holland, Austria versus France, Spain	Florida, New England	Throne of Spain
King George's War	War of Austrian Succession	1739–48	England, Holland, Austria versus France, Spain, Prussia	West Indies, New England, Canada	Throne of Austria
French and Indian War	Seven Years War	1756–63	England versus France, Spain	Ohio country, Canada	Possession of Ohio country

Mississippi valley. Accordingly, in 1753 the French pushed southward from Lake Erie, building fortified outposts at strategic points.

In response to the French threat to their western frontiers, delegates from seven northern and middle colonies gathered in Albany, New York, in June 1754. With the backing of administrators in London, they sought two goals: to persuade the Iroquois to abandon their traditional neutrality and to coordinate the defenses of the colonies. They succeeded in neither. The Iroquois saw no reason to change a policy that had served them well for half a century. And although the Albany Congress delegates adopted a Plan of Union (which would have established an elected intercolonial legislature with the power to tax), their provincial governments uniformly rejected the plan—primarily because those governments feared a loss of autonomy.

Albany Congress

While the Albany Congress delegates deliberated, the war they sought to prepare for was already beginning. Virginia claimed ownership of the Ohio country, and its governor sent a small force westward to counter the French. But the Virginia militiamen arrived too late. The French had already taken possession of the strategic point—

now Pittsburgh—where the Allegheny and Monongahela Rivers meet to form the Ohio, and they were busily engaged in constructing Fort Duquesne. The inexperienced young officer who commanded the Virginians attacked a French detachment and then allowed himself to be trapped in his crudely built Fort Necessity at Great Meadows, Pennsylvania. After a day-long battle (on July 3, 1754), twenty-two-year-old George Washington surrendered. He and his men were allowed to return to Virginia.

Washington had blundered grievously, setting off a war that eventually would encompass nearly the entire world. He also ensured that the Ohio valley Indians would for the most part support France in the conflict. The Indians took Washington's mistakes as an indication of Britain's inability to win the war, and nothing that occurred in the next four years made them change their minds. In July 1755, a few miles south of Fort Duquesne, a combined force of French and Indians ambushed British and colonial troops led by General Edward Braddock. Braddock was killed, and his men were demoralized by a devastating defeat. After news of the debacle reached London, Britain declared war

Seven Years War

Lake Superior

CHIPPEWA

NEW FRANCE

Quebec

• Montreal

Ft. Western
(Augusta)

MAINE
(Part of Mass.)

• Falmouth
(Portland)

N.H.

• Portsmouth

CHIPPEWA

Lake Huron

Lake Ontario

Ft. Niagara

St. Lawrence R.

MOHAWK

ONEIDA
TUSCARORA
ONONDAGA
CAYUGA

Ft. Stanwix

Albany

Boston

MASS.

OTTAWA

SENECA

NEW
YORK

Hartford

Providence

Lake Michigan

Ft. Detroit

Lake Erie

CONN.

R.I.

POTAWATOMI

Allegheny R.

1720–1760

New York

MIAMI

PENNSYLVANIA

WYANDOT

DELAWARE

Ft. Duquesne
(Pitt)

Philadelphia

N.J.

OHIO COUNTRY

Monongahela R.

New Castle

WEA

Ft.
Necessity

Baltimore

M.D.

DEL.

SHAWNEE

Tuscarora Migration

Richmond

Ohio R.

VIRGINIA

Williamsburg

ILLINOIS CONFEDERATION

Proclamation Line of 1763

Hillsboro

Salem

NORTH CAROLINA

New Bern

Mississippi R.

CHEROKEE

CATAWBA

Wilmington

Camden

ATLANTIC OCEAN

SOUTH CAROLINA

CHICKASAW

Ft. Augusta
(Augusta)

GEORGIA

Charleston

Total population of
English colonies: c. 1.5 million

Extent of settlement

CREEK

Savannah

CHOCTAW

NEW SPAIN

St. Augustine

| 0 | 100 | 200 miles |

| 0 | 100 | 200 | 300 kilometers |

European Settlements and Native Americans, 1750 *By 1750, Europeans had expanded the*
limits of the English colonies to the eastern slopes of the Appalachian Mountains.

on France in 1756, thus formally beginning the conflict known as the Seven Years War.

For three more years one disaster followed another for Great Britain. The tide began to change in 1757 when William Pitt was named secretary of state. Under his leadership the British mounted the effort that won them the war in North America. By agreeing to reimburse the colonies for their military expenditures and placing troop recruitment wholly in local hands, Pitt gained wholehearted American support for the war effort. Earlier in the war, British officers had usually tried to coerce the colonies into supplying men and materiel to the army. In July 1758, British forces recaptured the fortress at Louisbourg. Then, in a surprise night attack in September 1759, General James Wolfe's soldiers defeated the French on the Plains of Abraham and took Quebec. Sensing a British victory, the Iroquois abandoned their policy of neutrality and allied themselves with Britain. A year later the British captured Montréal and the American phase of the war ended.

In the Treaty of Paris (1763), France ceded its major North American holdings to Britain. Spain, an ally of France toward the end of the war, gave Florida to the victors. Britain, fearing the presence of France on its western borders, forced the French to cede Louisiana to Spain. The British thus gained control of the fur trade of the entire continent. And no longer would the English seacoast colonies have to worry about the threat to their existence posed by France's extensive North American territories.

Because most of the fighting had occurred in the Northeast, the war had especially pronounced effects on New Englanders. Wartime service left a lasting impression on the New Englanders who served in the provincial army. For the first time, ordinary Americans came into extended contact with Britons—and they did not like what they saw. The provincials regarded the British troops as haughty, profane Sabbath-breakers who arbitrarily imposed overly harsh punishments on anyone who broke the rules.

American Soldiers

The New England soldiers also learned that British troops did not share their adherence to

principles of contract and consensus—the values that had governed their lives at home. Colonial regiments mutinied or rebelled en masse if they believed they were being treated unfairly, as happened, for example, when they were not allowed to leave at the end of their formal enlistments. One private in these circumstances grumbled in his journal in 1759, "Although we be Englishmen born, we are debarred Englishmen's liberty." Such men would later recall their personal experience of British "tyranny" when they decided to support the Revolution.

The overwhelming British triumph stimulated some Americans to think expansively about the colonies' future. People like the Philadelphia printer Benjamin Franklin, who had long touted the colonies' wealth and potential, predicted a glorious new future for British North America. Such men uniformly opposed any laws that would retard America's growth and after 1763 persistently supported steps to increase Americans' control over their own destiny.

 ## 1763: A Turning Point

The great victory over France had an irreversible impact on North America, felt first by the indigenous peoples of the interior. With France excluded from the continent altogether and Spanish territory now confined to the area west of the Mississippi, the diplomatic strategy that had served the Indians well for so long could no longer be employed. The consequences were immediate and devastating.

Even before the Treaty of Paris, southern Indians had to adjust to the new circumstances. After Britain gained the upper hand in the American war in 1758, Creeks and Cherokees lost their ability to force concessions by threatening to turn instead to France or Spain. In desperation, and in retaliation for British atrocities, Cherokees attacked the Carolina and Virginia frontiers in 1760. Though initially victorious, the Indians were defeated the following year by a force of British regulars and colonial militia. Late in 1761 the two sides concluded a treaty under which the Cherokees allowed the construction of British forts in tribal territories and opened a large tract of land to European settlement.

In the Ohio country the Ottawas, Chippewas, and Potawatomis reacted angrily when Great Britain raised the price of trade goods and ended traditional gift-giving practices. Britain also allowed settlers to move into the Monongahela and Susquehanna valleys, onto Delaware and Iroquois lands.

Pontiac, the war chief of an Ottawa village near Detroit, understood that only unity among the western tribes could prevent total dependence on and subordination to the victorious British. Using his considerable powers of persuasion, in the spring of 1763 he forged an unprecedented alliance among Hurons, Chippewas, Potawatomis, Delawares, Shawnees, and even some Mingoes (Pennsylvania Iroquois). Pontiac then laid siege to Fort Detroit while war parties attacked other British outposts in the Great Lakes region. Detroit withstood the siege, but by late June all the other forts west of Niagara and north of Fort Pitt (old Fort Duquesne) had fallen to the Indian alliance. But the alliance could not take the strongholds of Niagara, Fort Pitt, or Detroit. In early August, colonial militiamen soundly defeated a combined Indian force at Bushy Run, Pennsylvania. Conflict ceased when Pontiac broke off the siege of Detroit in late October. A treaty ending the war was finally negotiated three years later.

Pontiac's Uprising

Pontiac's uprising showed Great Britain that the huge territory it had just acquired from France would not be easy to govern. In October, in a futile attempt to assert control over the interior, the British ministry issued the Proclamation of 1763, which declared the headwaters of rivers flowing into the Atlantic from the Appalachian Mountains to be the temporary western boundary for colonial settlement (see map, page 87). The proclamation was intended to prevent clashes between Indians and colonists by forbidding whites to move onto Indian lands until tribes had given up their land by treaty. But many whites had already established farms or purchased property

Proclamation of 1763

west of the proclamation line, and from the outset the policy was doomed to failure.

Other decisions made in London in 1763 and thereafter had a wider impact in British North America. The hard-won victory created both problems and opportunities for the British government. The most pressing problem, Britain's immense war debt, had to be solved by King George III and his new prime minister, George Grenville.

George III had assumed the British throne in 1760. The twenty-two-year-old king was a man of mediocre intellect and an erratic judge of character. During the crucial years between 1763 and 1770, when the rift with the colonies was growing ever wider, he replaced ministries with bewildering rapidity. Moreover, the king often substituted stubbornness for intelligence, and he regarded adherence to the status quo as the hallmark of patriotism.

George III

The man he selected as prime minister in 1763, George Grenville, confronted a financial crisis: England's burden of indebtedness had nearly doubled since 1754. Grenville's ministry had to find new sources of funds, and the British people themselves were already heavily taxed. Since the colonists had benefited greatly from the wartime expenditures, Grenville concluded that Anglo-Americans should be asked to pay a greater share of the cost of running the empire.

Grenville did not question Great Britain's right to levy taxes on the colonies. Like all his countrymen, he believed that the government's legitimacy derived ultimately from the consent of the people, but he defined consent far more loosely than did the colonists. Americans had come to believe that they could be represented only by men for whom they or their property-holding neighbors actually voted. Grenville and his English contemporaries, however, believed that Parliament—king, lords, and commons acting together—by definition represented all British subjects, even colonists who could not vote.

Theories of Representation

According to this theory of government, called *virtual representation*, the colonists were seen as virtually, if not actually, represented in Parliament. Thus their consent to acts of Parliament could be presumed. By contrast, in the colonies members of the lower houses of the assemblies were viewed as specifically representing the voters who had elected them.

Events in the 1760s threw into sharp relief Americans' attitudes toward political power. The colonists had become accustomed to a central government that wielded only limited authority over them and affected their daily lives very little. In consequence, they believed that a good government was one that largely left them alone, a view in keeping with the theories of a group of British writers known as the Real Whigs. These writers stressed the dangers inherent in a powerful government, particularly one headed by a monarch. Real Whigs warned that political power was always to be feared, that rulers would try to corrupt and oppress the people, and that only the perpetual vigilance of people and their elected representatives could preserve their fragile yet precious liberty, which was closely linked to their right to hold private property.

Britain's attempts to tighten the reins of government and raise revenues from the colonies in the 1760s and early 1770s convinced many Americans that the Real Whigs' reasoning applied to their circumstances, especially because of the link between liberty and property rights. Excessive and unjust taxation, they believed, could destroy their freedoms. They began to interpret British measures in light of the Real Whigs' warnings and to see oppressive designs behind the actions of Grenville and his successors. In the mid-1760s, however, colonial leaders did not immediately accuse Grenville of an intent to oppress them. They at first simply questioned the wisdom of the laws he proposed.

Parliament passed the first such measures, the Sugar and Currency Acts, in 1764. The Sugar Act revised existing customs regulations and laid new duties on some foreign imports into the colonies. It also established a vice-admiralty court at Halifax, Nova Scotia, and included provisions aimed at stopping the widespread smuggling of molasses,

Sugar and Currency Acts

one of the chief commodities in American trade. Although the Sugar Act appeared to resemble the Navigation Acts, which the colonies had long accepted as legitimate, it broke with tradition because it was explicitly designed to raise revenue, not to channel American trade through Britain. The Currency Act effectively outlawed colonial issues of paper money. (British merchants had complained that Americans were paying their debts in inflated local currencies.) Americans could accumulate little sterling, since they imported more than they exported; thus the act seemed to the colonists to deprive them of a useful medium of exchange.

Because the Sugar and Currency Acts were imposed on an economy already in the midst of a postwar depression, it is not surprising that some Americans objected to them. But lacking any precedent for a united campaign against acts of Parliament, Americans in 1764 took only hesitant and uncoordinated steps. Eight colonial legislatures sent separate petitions to Parliament requesting the Sugar Act's repeal. They argued that its commercial restrictions would hurt Britain as well as the colonies and that they had not consented to its passage. The protests had no effect. The law remained in force, and Grenville proceeded with another revenue plan.

 ## The Stamp Act Crisis

The Stamp Act (1765), Grenville's most important proposal, was modeled on a law that had been in effect in Great Britain for almost a century. It touched nearly every colonist by requiring tax stamps on most printed materials. The heaviest burden fell on merchants and other members of the colonial elite, who used printed matter more frequently than did ordinary folk. Anyone who, for example, purchased a newspaper or pamphlet, made a will, transferred land, bought dice or playing cards, or borrowed money would have to pay the tax. Never before had a revenue measure of such scope been proposed for the colonies. The act also required that tax stamps be paid for with sterling, which was scarce, and that violators be tried in vice-admiralty courts, which operated without juries. Finally, such a law would break decisively with the colonial tradition of self-imposed taxation.

The most important colonial pamphlet protesting the Sugar Act and the proposed Stamp Act was *The Rights of the British Colonies Asserted and Proved*, by James Otis, Jr., a brilliant young Massachusetts

James Otis's
Rights of the
British Colonies

attorney. Otis starkly exposed the ideological dilemma that was to confound the colonists for the next decade. How could they justify their opposition to certain acts of Parliament without questioning Parliament's authority over them? On the one hand, Otis asserted, Americans were "entitled to all the natural, essential, inherent, and inseparable rights" of Britons, including the right not to be taxed without their consent. On the other hand, Otis was forced to admit that under the British system, "the power of parliament is uncontrollable but by themselves, and we must obey."

Otis's first contention implied that Parliament could not constitutionally tax the colonies because Americans were not represented in its ranks. Yet his second point both acknowledged political reality and accepted the prevailing theory that Parliament was the sole, supreme authority in the empire. Even unconstitutional laws enacted by Parliament had to be obeyed until Parliament decided to repeal them. Otis tried to find a middle ground by proposing colonial representation in Parliament, but his idea was never taken seriously on either side of the Atlantic. The British believed that colonists were already virtually represented in Parliament, and Anglo-Americans quickly realized that a handful of colonial delegates to London would simply be outvoted.

Otis published his pamphlet before the Stamp Act was passed. When Americans first learned of the act's adoption in the spring of 1765, they were uncertain how to react. Few colonists publicly favored the law, but colonial petitions had already failed to prevent its adoption and further lobbying appeared futile. Perhaps Otis was right that the only course open to Americans was to pay the stamp tax, reluctantly but loyally.

Not all the colonists shared his views. One of them was a twenty-nine-year-old lawyer serving his first term in the Virginia House of Burgesses. Patrick Henry later recalled that he was appalled by his fellow

Patrick Henry
and the
Virginia Stamp
Act Resolves

legislators' unwillingness to oppose the Stamp Act. Henry decided to act. "Alone, unadvised, and unassisted," he wrote the Virginia Stamp Act Resolves.

Patrick Henry introduced his seven proposals near the end of the legislative session, when many burgesses had already departed for home. Henry's fiery speech led the Speaker of the House to accuse him of treason. (Henry denied the charge.) The few burgesses remaining in Williamsburg adopted five of Henry's resolutions by a bare majority. Although they repealed the most radical of the five the next day, their action had far-reaching effects.

The four propositions adopted by the burgesses repeated Otis's arguments, asserting that the colonists had never forfeited the rights of British subjects, among which was consent to taxation. The three rejected resolutions had gone much further. The one that was repealed claimed for the burgesses "the only exclusive right" to tax Virginians. The final two (those never considered) asserted that residents of Virginia need not obey tax laws passed by other legislative bodies (namely Parliament).

The burgesses' decision to accept only the first four of Henry's resolutions anticipated the position most Americans would adopt the following decade. Though willing to contend for their rights,

Continuing
Loyalty
to Britain

the colonists did not seek independence. They rather wanted some measure of self-government. Accordingly, they backed away from the assertions that they owed Parliament no obedience and that only their own assemblies could tax them.

Over the next ten years, America's political leaders searched for a formula that would enable them to control their internal affairs, especially taxation, but remain under British rule. The chief difficulty lay in British officials' inability to compromise on the issue of parliamentary power. The notion that Parliament could exercise absolute authority over all colonial possessions was basic to the British theory of government. In effect, the Americans wanted British leaders to revise their fundamental understanding of the workings of their government. But that was simply too much to expect.

The ultimate effectiveness of Americans' resistance to the Stamp Act came not from ideological arguments but from the decisive and inventive actions of some colonists. In August 1765, the Loyal Nine, a Boston social club of printers, distillers, and other artisans, organized a demonstration against the Stamp Act. Hoping to show that people of all ranks opposed the act, they approached the leaders of the city's rival laborers' associations, based in Boston's North End and South End neighborhoods. The Loyal Nine convinced them to lay aside their differences to participate in the demonstration.

Loyal Nine

Early on August 14, the demonstrators hung an effigy of Andrew Oliver, the province's stamp distributor, from a tree on Boston Common. That night a large crowd led by a group of about fifty well-dressed tradesmen paraded the effigy around the city and threw stones at officials who tried to disperse them. In the midst of the melée, the North End and South End leaders drank a toast to their successful union. The Loyal Nine achieved success when Oliver publicly promised not to fulfill the duties of his office. Twelve days later, a mob reportedly led by the South End leader Ebenezer MacIntosh attacked the homes of several customs officers. This time the violence drew no praise from Boston's respectable citizens; the mob completely destroyed Lieutenant Governor Thomas Hutchinson's townhouse.

The differences between the two Boston mobs of August 1765 exposed divisions that would continue to characterize subsequent colonial protests. The skilled craftsmen who composed the Loyal Nine, and the merchants, lawyers, and other members of the educated elite preferred orderly demonstrations confined to political issues. For the city's laborers, by contrast,

Americans' Divergent Interests

economic grievances may have been paramount. Certainly, the wrecking of Hutchinson's house suggests a resentment against his ostentatious display of wealth.

Colonists, like Britons, had a long tradition of crowd action in which disfranchised people took to the streets to redress deeply felt local grievances. But the Stamp Act controversy drew ordinary urban folk into the vortex of transatlantic politics for the first time. Matters that previously had been of concern only to the gentry or to members of colonial legislatures were now discussed on every street corner.

The entry of unskilled workers, slaves, and women into the realm of imperial politics both threatened and afforded an opportunity to the elite men who wanted to mount effective opposition to British measures. The elite realized that crowd action could have a stunning impact. Anti–Stamp Act demonstrations occurred from Nova Scotia to the Caribbean island of Antigua. They were so successful that by November 1, when the law was scheduled to take effect, not one stamp distributor was willing to carry out his official duties. Thus the act could not be enforced. But wealthy men also recognized that mobs composed of the formerly powerless could endanger their own dominance of society. What would happen, they wondered, if the crowd turned against them?

They therefore attempted to channel resistance into acceptable forms by creating an intercolonial association, the Sons of Liberty. The first such group was created in New York in early November, and branches spread rapidly through the coastal cities. Composed of merchants, lawyers, prosperous tradesmen, and others, the Sons of Liberty by early 1766 linked protest leaders from Charleston, South Carolina, to Portsmouth, New Hampshire.

Sons of Liberty

The Sons of Liberty could influence events but not control them. In Charleston in October 1765, an informally organized crowd forced the resignation of the South Carolina stamp distributor. But the new Charleston chapter of the Sons of Liberty was horrified when in January 1766 local slaves paraded through the streets crying "Liberty." That was not the sort of liberty elite slave-owners had in mind. And in Philadelphia, resistance leaders were dismayed when an angry mob threatened to attack Benjamin Franklin's house. The city's laborers believed Franklin to be partly responsible for the Stamp Act, since he had obtained the post of stamp distributor for a close friend. But Philadelphia's artisans—the backbone of the opposition movement there and elsewhere—were fiercely loyal to Franklin. They protected his home and family from the crowd, but the resulting split between the better-off tradesmen and the common laborers prevented the establishment of a successful workingmen's alliance like that of Boston.

During the fall and winter of 1765–1766, opposition to the Stamp Act proceeded on three separate fronts. Colonial legislatures petitioned Parliament to repeal the hated law and in October sent delegates to an intercolonial congress. The Stamp Act Congress met in New York to draft a unified but conservative statement of protest. At the same time, the Sons of Liberty held mass meetings, attempting to rally public support for the resistance movement. Finally, American merchants organized nonimportation associations to pressure British exporters. By the 1760s, one-quarter of all British exports were being sent to the colonies, and American merchants reasoned that London merchants whose sales suffered severely would lobby for repeal. Since times were bad, American merchants also believed that nonimportation would reduce their bloated inventories.

In March 1766, Parliament repealed the Stamp Act. The nonimportation agreements had had the anticipated effect. But boycotts, formal protests, and crowd actions were less important in winning

Repeal of the Stamp Act

repeal than was the appointment of a new prime minister. Lord Rockingham, who replaced Grenville in the summer of 1765, had opposed the Stamp Act, not because he believed Parliament lacked power to tax the colonies but because he thought the law unwise and divisive. Thus, although Rockingham proposed repeal, he linked it to passage of the Declaratory Act, which asserted Parliament's ability to tax and legislate for Britain's American possessions "in all cases whatsoever." As they celebrated the Stamp Act's repeal, few colonists saw the ominous implications of the Declaratory Act.

Resistance to the Townshend Acts

The colonists had accomplished their immediate aim, but the long-term prospects were unclear. In the summer of 1766, another change in the ministry in London revealed how fragile their victory had been. The new prime minister, William Pitt, was ill much of the time, and another minister, Charles Townshend, became the dominant force in the ministry. An ally of Grenville, Townshend decided to renew the attempt to obtain additional funds from Britain's American possessions.

The taxes Townshend proposed in 1767 were to be levied on trade goods like paper, glass, and tea, and thus seemed to be nothing more than extensions of the existing Navigation Acts. But the Townshend duties differed from previous customs duties in two ways. First, they were levied on items imported into the colonies from Britain, not from foreign countries. Thus they were at odds with mercantilist theory (see page 59). Second, they were designed to raise money to pay the salaries of some royal officials in the colonies. That posed a direct challenge to the colonial assemblies, which derived considerable power from threatening to withhold officials' salaries. In addition, Townshend's scheme provided for the creation of an American Board of Customs Commissioners and of vice-admiralty courts at Boston, Philadelphia, and Charleston. Both moves angered merchants, whose profits would be threatened by more vigorous enforcement of the Navigation Acts.

The passage of the Townshend Acts drew a quick response. One series of essays in particular, *Letters from a Farmer in Pennsylvania* by the prominent lawyer John Dickinson, expressed a broad consensus. Dickinson contended that Parliament could regulate colonial trade but could not exercise that power to raise

John Dickinson's Farmer's Letters

revenue. By drawing a distinction between trade regulation and unacceptable commercial taxation, Dickinson avoided the sticky issue of consent and how it affected colonial subordination to Parliament. But his argument in effect obligated the colonies to assess Parliament's motives in passing any law pertaining to trade before deciding whether to obey it—an unworkable position in the long run.

The Massachusetts assembly responded to the Townshend Acts by drafting a letter to be circulated among the other colonial legislatures, calling

Massachusetts Assembly Dissolved

for unity and suggesting a joint petition of protest. Not the letter itself but the ministry's reaction to it united the colonies. When Lord Hillsborough, the first secretary of state for America, learned of the circular letter, he ordered Governor Francis Bernard of Massachusetts to insist that the assembly recall it. He also directed other governors to prevent their assemblies from discussing the letter. Hillsborough's order gave colonial assemblies the incentive they needed to join forces to oppose this new threat to their prerogatives. In late 1768 the Massachusetts legislature met, debated, and resoundingly rejected recall. Bernard immediately dissolved the assembly, and other governors followed suit when their legislatures debated the circular letter.

During the subsequent campaign against the Townshend duties, the Sons of Liberty and other American leaders made a deliberate effort to involve ordinary folk in the resistance movement. Most important, they urged colonists not to purchase or consume British products. The new consumerism that previously had linked colonists economically now linked them politically as well, supplying them with a ready method of displaying their allegiance.

As the primary purchasers of textiles and household goods, women played a central role in the nonconsumption movement. In Boston, more than three hundred matrons

Daughters of Liberty

publicly promised not to buy or drink tea. The women of Wilmington, North Carolina, burned their tea after walking

A Society of Patriotic Ladies *(1775), attributed to Philip Dawes, an English printmaker. This grotesque caricature of female patriots shows the women emptying their tea into a chamber pot (at left) and flirting with their male counterparts (at center), while a neglected child sits below the table. The cartoon bears no resemblance to the actual event, the signing of an anti-British petition by female residents of Edenton, North Carolina.* Library of Congress.

through town in a solemn procession. The best known of the protests (because it was satirized in a British cartoon reproduced here), the so-called Edenton Ladies Tea Party, actually had little to do with tea. It was a meeting of prominent North Carolina women who pledged formally to work for the public good and to support resistance to British measures.

Women also encouraged home manufacturing. In many towns, young women calling themselves Daughters of Liberty met to spin in public in an effort to persuade other women to make homespun and thus end the colonies' dependence on British cloth. The young ladies from well-to-do families who sat publicly at spinning wheels all day, eating only American food and drinking local herbal tea were serving as political instructors. Many women took great satisfaction in their new-found role.

Even so, the colonists were by no means united in support of nonimportation and nonconsumption. If the Stamp Act protests had occasionally revealed a division between artisans and merchants on the one side and common laborers on the other, resistance to the Townshend Acts exposed a rift between urban artisans and merchants. The split was caused by changed economic conditions.

Divided Opinion over Boycotts

The Stamp Act boycotts had helped to revive a depressed economy by creating a demand for local products and reducing merchants' inventories. But in 1768 and 1769, merchants were enjoying boom times. They had no financial incentive to support a boycott, and they signed the agreements only reluctantly. In contrast, artisans supported nonimportation enthusiastically, recognizing that the absence of British goods would create a ready market for their own manufactures. They also used coercion to enforce nonimportation.

Such tactics were effective: colonial imports from England dropped dramatically in 1769. But the tactics also aroused heated opposition. Some Americans who supported resistance to British measures began to question the use of violence to force others to join the boycott. In addition, wealthier and more conservative colonists were frightened by the threat to private property inherent in the campaign. Moreover, political activism by ordinary colonists challenged the ruling elite's domination.

Americans were relieved when news arrived in April 1770 that the Townshend duties had been repealed, with the exception of the tea tax. A new prime minister, Lord North, had persuaded Parliament that duties on trade within the empire were bad policy. Although some colonial leaders argued that nonimportation should continue until the tea tax was repealed, merchants

Repeal of the Townshend Duties

quickly resumed importing. The rest of the Townshend Acts remained in force, but repeal of the taxes made the other laws appear less objectionable.

 ## Growing Rifts

On the very day Lord North proposed repeal of the Townshend duties, however, a clash between civilians and soldiers in Boston led to the death of five Americans. The origins of the event that patriots called the Boston Massacre lay in repeated clashes between customs officers and the people of Massachusetts. The decision to base the American Board of Customs Commissioners in Boston was the source of the problem.

From the day of their arrival in November 1767, the customs commissioners were frequent targets of mob action. During a 1768 riot sparked by the seizure of John Hancock's sloop *Liberty* on suspicion of smuggling, customs officers' property was destroyed. The British responded by assigning troops to maintain order in the city. For Bostonians, the redcoats were a constant reminder of the oppressive potential of British power.

Bostonians found themselves hemmed in at every turn. Guards on Boston Neck, the entrance to the city, checked all travelers and their goods. Redcoat patrols roamed the city day and night, questioning and sometimes harassing passersby. But the greatest potential for violence lay in the uneasy relationship between the soldiers and Boston laborers. Many redcoats sought employment in their off-duty hours, competing for unskilled jobs with the city's ordinary workingmen.

Violence erupted early on the evening of March 5, 1770, when a crowd of laborers began throwing hard-packed snowballs at soldiers guarding the Customs House. Goaded beyond endurance, the sentries acted against express orders and fired on the crowd, killing four and wounding eight, one of whom died a few days later. Resistance leaders idealized the dead rioters as martyrs for the cause of liberty, holding a solemn funeral and later commemorating March 5 annually with patriotic orations. Paul Revere's engraving of the

Boston Massacre

massacre was part of the propaganda campaign. (See How Do Historians Know? on page 97.)

Leading patriots wanted to ensure that the soldiers did not become martyrs as well. Thus when the soldiers were tried for the killings in November, they were defended by John Adams and Josiah Quincy, Jr., both unwavering patriots. All but two of the accused men were acquitted, and those convicted were released after being branded on the thumb. Undoubtedly the favorable outcome of the trials prevented London officials from taking further steps against the city.

For the next two years, a superficial calm descended on the colonies, but questions remained. The most outspoken colonial newspapers accused Great Britain of a deliberate plan to oppress the colonies.

A British Plot? After the Stamp Act's repeal, the patriots had praised Parliament; following repeal of the Townshend duties, they warned of impending tyranny. The apparent isolated mistake—a single ill-chosen stamp tax—now appeared to be part of a plot against American liberties. Essayists pointed to the stationing of troops in Boston and the growing number of vice-admiralty courts as evidence of plans to enslave the colonists. Indeed, patriot writers played repeatedly on the word *enslavement.* Most white colonists had direct knowledge of slavery, and the threat of enslavement by Britain must have hit them with peculiar force.

Still, no one yet advocated complete independence from the mother country. Though the patriots were becoming increasingly convinced that they should seek freedom from parliamentary authority, they continued to acknowledge their British identity and their allegiance to George III. They began, therefore, to envision a system that would enable them to be ruled by their own elected legislatures while remaining loyal to the king. But any such scheme was alien to Britons' conception that Parliament held sole undivided sovereignty over the empire.

Although most of the duties had been repealed, the remainder of the Townshend Acts were still in force, and in the fall of 1772, the North ministry began to implement the section that provided for governors and judges to be paid from customs revenues. In early November, voters at a Boston town meeting established a Committee of Correspondence to publicize the decision by exchanging letters with other Massachusetts towns. Heading the committee was the man who had proposed its formation, Samuel Adams.

Samuel Adams Samuel Adams was fifty-one in 1772, a decade the senior of most other leaders of American resistance. He had been a member of the Massachusetts assembly, an ally of the Loyal Nine, and a member of the Sons of Liberty. An experienced political organizer, Adams continually stressed the necessity of prudent collective action. His Committee of Correspondence thus undertook the task of creating an informed consensus among all the residents of Massachusetts.

Such committees, which were eventually established throughout the colonies, represented the next logical step in the organization of American resistance.

Boston Committee of Correspondence Until 1772, the protest movement was largely confined to the seacoast and primarily to major cities and towns. Adams realized that the time had come to widen the movement by involving the residents of the interior in the struggle. Accordingly, the Boston town meeting directed the Committee of Correspondence "to state the Rights of the Colonists and of this Province in particular," to list "the Infringements and Violations thereof that have been, or from time to time may be made," and to send copies to the other towns in the province.

The committee's statement declared that Americans had absolute rights to life, liberty, and property. The idea that "a British house of commons, should have a right, at pleasure, to give and grant the property of the colonists" was "irreconcileable" with "the first principles of natural law and Justice . . . and of the British Constitution in particular." The list of grievances complained of taxation without representation, the presence of unnecessary troops and customs officers on American soil, the use of imperial revenues to pay colonial officials, the expanded jurisdiction of vice-admiralty courts, and even the nature of the

How do historians know whether ordinary people were familiar with the ideas propounded by the leaders of the American Revolution? This is a difficult question to answer, because most of the evidence about the patriots' ideology comes from pamphlets and newspapers aimed at the well educated. People who could read at only a basic level might not have been able to understand the sophisticated criticisms of British policies advanced in such writings. But because an engraver made his point visually rather than verbally, anyone, even illiterate folk, could interpret an image like Paul Revere's masterful portrayal of the Boston Massacre. The label "Butcher's Hall" on the Customs House merely reinforces the patriot view of the incident on March 5, 1770. The British soldiers are shown firing on an unresisting crowd (not the aggressive, angry mob described at the soldiers' trial), and a gun with smoke drifting up from its barrel emerges from a window above the redcoats, suggesting the complicity of civilian officials in what the patriots interpreted as an outrageous act.   Photo: Library of Congress.

instructions given to American governors by their superiors in London. No mention was made of obedience to Parliament. Patriots—at least in Boston—had placed American rights first, loyalty to Great Britain a distant second.

In their responses, most towns aligned themselves with the city. From Braintree came the assertion that "all civil officers are or ought to be Servants to the people and dependent upon them for their official Support, and every instance to the Contrary from the Governor downwards tends to crush and destroy civil liberty." The citizens of Petersham commented that resistance to tyranny was "the first and highest social Duty of this people." Beliefs like these made the next crisis in Anglo-American affairs the final one.

 ### The Boston Tea Party

The only Townshend duty still in effect by 1773 was the tax on tea. Although a continuing tea boycott was less than fully effective, tea retained its explosive symbolic character. In May 1773, Parliament passed an act designed to save the East India Company from bankruptcy. The company, which held a legal monopoly on British trade with the East Indies, was of critical importance to the British economy (and to the financial well-being of many prominent British politicians). Under the Tea Act, certain duties paid on tea were to be returned to the company. Only designated agents were to sell tea, which would enable the East India Company to avoid colonial middlemen and undersell any competitors, even smugglers.

Tea Act

The net result of bypassing the middlemen would be cheaper tea for American consumers. Resistance leaders, however, interpreted the new measure as a pernicious device to make them admit Parliament's right to tax them, for the less-expensive tea would still be taxed under the Townshend law. Others saw the Tea Act as the first step in the establishment of an East India Company monopoly of all colonial trade. Residents of the four cities designated to receive the first shipments of tea ac-

cordingly prepared to respond to what they perceived as a new threat to their freedom.

In New York City, the tea ships failed to arrive on schedule. In Philadelphia, the governor of Pennsylvania persuaded the captain to sail back to Britain. In Charleston, the tea was unloaded, stored under the direction of local tradesmen, and later destroyed. The only confrontation occurred in Boston, where the town meeting on one side and Governor Thomas Hutchinson on the other rejected compromise.

The first of three tea ships entered Boston harbor on November 28. The customs laws required cargo to be landed and the appropriate duty paid by its owners within twenty days of a ship's arrival; otherwise, the cargo would be seized by customs officers and sold at auction. After a series of mass meetings, Bostonians voted to post guards on the wharf to prevent the tea from being unloaded. Hutchinson, for his part, refused to permit the vessels to leave the harbor.

On December 16, one day before the cargo would have been confiscated, more than five thousand people (nearly a third of the city's population) crowded into Old South Church. The meeting, chaired by Samuel Adams, made a final attempt to persuade Hutchinson to send the tea back to England. But the governor remained adamant. In the early evening Adams reportedly announced "that he could think of nothing further to be done—that they had now done all they could for the Salvation of their Country." Cries then rang out from the back of the crowd: "Boston harbor a tea-pot tonight! The Mohawks are come!" Within a few minutes, about sixty men crudely disguised as Indians, including Paul Revere and other artisans, assembled at the wharf, boarded the three ships, and dumped the cargo (342 chests of tea) into the harbor.

While supporters of the resistance movement rejoiced over the tea party, the North administration reacted with considerably less enthusiasm. In March 1774, Parliament adopted the first of four laws that became known as the Coercive, or Intolerable, Acts. It ordered the port of Boston closed until the tea was paid for, prohibiting all but

Coercive and Quebec Acts

coastal trade in food and firewood. Later in the spring, Parliament passed three other punitive measures. The Massachusetts Government Act altered the province's charter, substituting an appointed council for the elected one, increasing the governor's powers, and forbidding most town meetings. The Justice Act provided that a person accused of committing murder in the course of suppressing a riot or enforcing the laws could be tried outside the colony where the incident had occurred. Finally, the Quartering Act gave broad authority to military commanders seeking to house their troops in private dwellings. Thus the Coercive Acts punished not only Boston but also Massachusetts as a whole, alerting other colonies that their residents, too, could be subject to retaliation if they opposed British authority.

After passing the last of the Coercive Acts, Parliament turned its attention to much-needed reforms in the government of Quebec. The Quebec Act thereby became linked with the Coercive Acts in the minds of the patriots. Intended to ease strained relations with the former French colony, the Quebec Act granted greater religious freedom to Catholics—alarming Protestant colonists, who equated Roman Catholicism with religious and political despotism. It also reinstated French civil law and established an appointed council as the governing body of the colony. Finally, in an attempt to provide northern Indians with some protection against Anglo-American settlement, the act annexed to Quebec the area east of the Mississippi River and north of the Ohio River. That region, parts of which were claimed by individual seacoast colonies, was thus removed from their jurisdiction.

Members of Parliament who voted for the punitive legislation believed that the acts would be obeyed. To patriots, the Coercive Acts and the

Implications of the Coercive Acts Quebec Act revealed Great Britain's deliberate plan to oppress Americans by denying them their rights and liberties. If the port of Boston could be closed, why not the ports of Philadelphia or New York? If the royal charter of Massachusetts could be changed, why not the charter of South Carolina? If certain people could be removed from their home colonies for trial,

why not all violators of all laws? If troops could be forcibly quartered in private houses, did not that action pave the way for the occupation of all of America? If the Roman Catholic Church could receive favored status in Quebec, why not everywhere?

The Boston Committee of Correspondence urged all the colonies to join in an immediate renewed boycott of British goods. But the other provinces were not yet ready to take such a drastic step. They suggested that another intercolonial congress be convened to consider an appropriate response. Few people wanted to take hasty action; even the most ardent patriots remained loyal to Britain and hoped for reconciliation with its leaders. So the colonies agreed to send delegates to Philadelphia in September to attend a Continental Congress.

 Conclusion

During the preceding decade, momentous changes had occurred in the ways colonists thought about themselves and their allegiance. Once linked unquestioningly to Great Britain, they had begun to develop a sense of their own identity as Americans. They had started to realize that their concept of the political process differed from that held by people in the mother country. They also had come to understand that their economic interests did not necessarily coincide with those of Great Britain. Colonial political leaders reached such conclusions only after a long train of events, some of them violent, had altered their understanding of their relationship with the mother country.

In the late summer of 1774, the Americans were committed to resistance but not to independence. Even so, they had started to sever the bonds of empire.

Suggestions for Further Reading

General

Ian R. Christie and Benjamin W. Labaree, *Empire or Independence, 1760–1776: A British-American Dialogue on the Coming of the American Revolution* (1976); Marc Egnal, *A Mighty*

Empire: The Origins of the American Revolution (1988); Ronald Hoffman and Peter Albert, eds., *The Transforming Hand of Revolution: Reconsidering the American Revolution as a Social Movement* (1995); Merrill Jensen, *The Founding of a Nation: A History of the American Revolution, 1763–1776* (1968); Robert W. Tucker and David C. Hendrickson, *The Fall of the First British Empire: Origins of the War of American Independence* (1982).

Colonial Warfare and the British Empire

Fred Anderson, *A People's Army: Massachusetts Soldiers and Society in the Seven Years' War* (1984); Douglas Leach, *Roots of Conflict: British Armed Forces and Colonial Americans, 1677–1763* (1986); Robert C. Newbold, *The Albany Congress and Plan of Union of 1754* (1955); Alan Rogers, *Empire and Liberty: American Resistance to British Authority, 1755–1763* (1974); John Shy, *Toward Lexington: The Role of the British Army in the Coming of the American Revolution* (1965); James Titus, *The Old Dominion at War: Society, Politics, and Warfare in Late Colonial Virginia* (1991).

British Politics and Policy

James E. Bradley, *Popular Politics and the American Revolution in England* (1986); John Brooke, *King George III* (1972); Michael Kammen, *A Rope of Sand: The Colonial Agents, British Politics, and the American Revolution* (1968); Nancy F. Koehn, *The Power of Commerce: Economy and Governance in the First British Empire* (1994); P. D. G. Thomas, *Tea Party to Independence* (1991); P. D. G. Thomas, *The Townshend Duties Crisis* (1987); P. D. G. Thomas, *British Politics and the Stamp Act Crisis* (1975).

Native Americans and the West

Gregory Dowd, *A Spirited Resistance: The North American Indian Struggle for Unity, 1745–1815* (1992); Francis Jennings, *Empire of Fortune: Crowns, Colonies and Tribes in the Seven Years' War in America* (1988); Howard H. Peckham, *Pontiac and the Indian Uprising* (1947); Richard White, *The Middle Ground: Indians, Empires and Republics in the Great Lakes Region, 1650–1815* (1991).

Political and Economic Thought

Bernard Bailyn, *The Ideological Origins of the American Revolution* (1967); J. C. D. Clark, *The Language of Liberty, 1660–1832: Political Discourse and Social Dynamics in the Anglo-American World* (1994); J. E. Crowley, *This Sheba, Self: The Conceptualization of Economic Life in Eighteenth-Century America* (1974); Jay Fliegelman, *Prodigals and Pilgrims: The American Revolution Against Patriarchal Authority, 1750–1800* (1982).

American Resistance

David Ammerman, *In the Common Cause: American Response to the Coercive Acts of 1774* (1974); Richard D. Brown, *Revolutionary Politics in Massachusetts: The Boston Committee of Correspondence and the Towns, 1772–1774* (1970); Benjamin W. Labaree, *The Boston Tea Party* (1964); Pauline R. Maier, *The Old Revolutionaries: Political Lives in the Age of Samuel Adams* (1980); Pauline R. Maier, *From Resistance to Revolution: Colonial Radicals and the Development of American Opposition to Britain, 1765–1776* (1972); Edmund S. Morgan and Helen M. Morgan, *The Stamp Act Crisis: Prologue to Revolution* (1953); Bruce A. Ragsdale, *A Planters' Republic: The Search for Economic Independence in Revolutionary Virginia* (1996); Richard Ryerson, *The Revolution Has Now Begun: The Radical Committees of Philadelphia, 1765–1776* (1978); John W. Tyler, *Smugglers and Patriots: Boston Merchants and the Advent of the American Revolution* (1986); Richard Walsh, *Charleston's Sons of Liberty: A Study of the Artisans, 1763–1789* (1959); Hiller B. Zobel, *The Boston Massacre* (1970).

CHAPTER

6

A Revolution, Indeed
1774–1783

W hen John Provey and Richard Weaver appeared before the loyalist claims commissioners in London at the end of the Revolution, the commissioners were not impressed with their descriptions of losses and loyal service to the king. Such men had "no right to ask or expect any thing from Government," the commissioners declared. So Provey and Weaver were denied any assistance from the funds allocated by Parliament to compensate loyalists for the damages they had incurred by opposing the Revolution. Why were Weaver and Provey treated thus? They were African-Americans.

Provey, a former slave from North Carolina, had served in a black corps of the British army during the war; the freeborn Weaver had left Philadelphia with the British troops when they evacuated that city in 1778. Because they were denied the help they sought, they and their families, along with hundreds of other African-Americans, became dependent on charity.

Seeing no future for themselves in London, they both agreed to emigrate to West Africa, to the new colony of Sierra Leone. Provey died on shipboard, but Weaver made it to Sierra Leone and was elected the first governor of the tiny colony, composed largely of exiled African-American loyalists. Conflicts with a nearby ruler and with slavers who established a post near the settlement almost destroyed it. But in 1792 the future of the colony was assured by the arrival of an additional twelve hundred African-American refugees.

The little-known tale of the black loyalists who returned to the homeland of their ancestors is but one dramatic example of the disruptive effects of the American Revolution. The Revolution uprooted thousands of families, disrupted the economy, reshaped society by forcing many colonists into permanent exile, led Americans to develop new conceptions of politics, and created a nation from thirteen separate colonies.

The struggle for independence required revolutionary leaders to accomplish three tasks. The first was political and ideological: transforming a consensus favoring loyal resistance into a coalition supporting independence. Various means, including coercion, were used to enlist all European-Americans in the patriot cause. Fearing that Indians and blacks would side with Britain, the colonies' elected leaders hoped at least to ensure those groups' neutrality in the impending conflict. The second task involved foreign relations. To win independence, patriot leaders knew they needed international recognition and aid, particularly from France. Thus they dispatched to Paris the most experienced American diplomat, Benjamin Franklin, who skillfully negotiated the Franco-American alliance of 1778, which was to prove crucial to winning independence.

Only the third task directly involved the British. George Washington, commander-in-chief of the American army, soon recognized that his primary goal should be not to win battles but to avoid losing them decisively. The outcome of any one battle was less important than ensuring that his army survived to fight another day. Consequently, the story of the Revolutionary War reveals British action and American reaction, British attacks and American defenses. The American war effort was aided by Britain's focus on winning battles rather than on the primary goal of retaining the colonies' allegiance.

 ## Government by Congress and Committee

When the fifty-five delegates to the First Continental Congress convened in Philadelphia in September 1774, they knew that many Americans would support any measures they adopted. That summer, open meetings held throughout the colonies had endorsed the idea of another nonimportation pact.

Committees of correspondence publicized these meetings so effectively that Americans everywhere knew about them. Since governors had forbidden regular assemblies to conduct formal elections, most congressional delegates were selected by extralegal local gatherings. Thus the very act of designating delegates to attend the Congress involved Americans in open defiance of British authority.

The colonies' leading political figures—most of them lawyers, merchants, and planters—attended the Philadelphia Congress. The Massachusetts delegation included both Samuel Adams and his younger cousin John, an ambitious lawyer. Among others, New York sent John Jay, a talented young attorney. From Pennsylvania came the conservative Joseph Galloway and his long-time rival, John Dickinson. Virginia elected Richard Henry Lee and Patrick Henry, both noted for their patriotic zeal, as well as George Washington.

First Continental Congress

The congressmen faced three tasks when they convened on September 5, 1774. The first two were explicit: defining American grievances and developing a plan for resistance. The third—outlining a theory of their constitutional relationship with Great Britain—proved troublesome. Radical congressmen, like Lee of Virginia, argued that colonists owed allegiance only to George III and that Parliament was nothing more than a local legislature for Great Britain, with no authority over the colonies. The conservatives—Joseph Galloway and his allies—proposed a formal plan of union that would have required Parliament and a new American legislature to consent jointly to all laws pertaining to the colonies. The delegates, who narrowly rejected Galloway's plan, also refused to accept the radicals' position.

Finally, they accepted a compromise position worked out by John Adams. The crucial clause that Adams drafted in the Congress's Declaration of Rights and Grievances read in part: "From the necessity of the case, and a regard to the mutual interest of both countries, we cheerfully consent to the operation of such acts of

Declaration of Rights and Grievances

• *Important Events* •

1774	First Continental Congress meets in Philadelphia, adopts Declaration of Rights and Grievances
	Continental Association implements economic boycott of Britain; committees of observation established to oversee boycott
1774–75	Provincial conventions replace collapsing colonial governments
1775	Battles of Lexington and Concord; first shots of war fired
	Second Continental Congress begins
	Lord Dunmore's proclamation offers freedom to patriots' slaves if they join British forces
1776	Thomas Paine publishes *Common Sense*, advocating independence
	British evacuate Boston
	Declaration of Independence adopted
	New York City falls to British
1777	British take Philadelphia
	Burgoyne surrenders at Saratoga
1778	French alliance brings vital assistance to the United States
1779	Sullivan expedition destroys Iroquois villages
1780	British take Charleston
1781	Cornwallis surrenders at Yorktown
1782	Peace negotiations begin
1783	Treaty of Paris signed, granting independence to the United States

the British parliament, as are bona fide, restrained to the regulation of our external commerce." Notice the key phrases. "From the necessity of the case" declared that Americans would obey Parliament only because they thought that doing so was in the best interest of both countries. "Bona fide, restrained to the regulation of our external commerce" made it clear to Lord North that they would continue to resist taxes in disguise, like the Townshend duties. Most striking of all was that such language—which only a few years before would have been regarded as irredeemably radical—could be presented and accepted as a compromise in the fall of 1774.

With the constitutional issue resolved, the delegates readily agreed on the laws they wanted repealed (notably the Coercive Acts) and decided to implement an economic boycott while petitioning the king for relief. They adopted the Continental Association, which called for nonimportation of British goods (effective December 1, 1774), nonconsumption of British products (effective March 1, 1775), and nonexportation of American goods to Britain and the British West Indies (effective

September 10, 1775, so that southern planters could market their 1774 tobacco crop).

To enforce the Continental Association, Congress recommended the election of committees of observation and inspection in every American locality. By specifying that committee members be chosen by all persons qualified to vote for members of the lower house of the colonial legislatures, Congress guaranteed the committees a broad popular base. The seven to eight thousand committeemen became the local leaders of American resistance.

Committees of Observation

Though created to oversee the boycott's implementation, the committees soon became de facto governments. They examined merchants' records and published the names of those who continued to import British goods. They also promoted home manufactures, encouraging Americans to adopt simple modes of dress and behavior to symbolize their commitment to liberty and virtuous behavior. Since expensive leisure-time activities were believed to reflect vice and corruption, Congress urged Americans to forgo dancing, gambling, horseracing, cockfighting, and other forms of "extravagance and dissipation." By enforcing these injunctions, the committees gradually extended their authority over many aspects of American life.

The committees also attempted to identify opponents of American resistance, developing elaborate spy networks, circulating copies of the Continental Association for signatures, and investigating reports of dissident remarks and activities. Suspected dissenters were first urged to support the colonial cause; if they failed to do so, the committees had them watched, restricted their movements, or tried to force them to leave the area. People engaging in casual political exchanges with friends one day could find themselves charged with "treasonable conversation" the next.

By early 1775, the regular colonial governments were collapsing. Only in Connecticut, Rhode Island, Delaware, and Pennsylvania did

Provincial Conventions

legislatures continue to meet without encountering patriot challenges to their authority. In every other colony, popularly elected provincial conventions took over the task of running the government. In late 1774 and early 1775, these conventions approved the Continental Association, elected delegates to the Second Continental Congress (scheduled for May), organized militia units, and gathered arms and ammunition. Unable to stem the tide of resistance, the British-appointed governors and councils watched helplessly as their authority crumbled.

Royal officials throughout the colonies became politically impotent. Courts were prevented from holding sessions; taxes were paid to the conventions' agents rather than to provincial tax collectors; sheriffs' powers were challenged; and militiamen would muster only when committees ordered. In short, during the six months preceding the battles at Lexington and Concord, independence was being won at the local level. Not many Americans fully realized what was happening. The vast majority still proclaimed their loyalty to Great Britain and denied that they sought to leave the empire. Among the few who recog-

nized the trend toward independence were those who opposed it.

 ## Choosing Sides: Loyalists, African-Americans, and Indians

The first protests against British measures had won the support of most colonists, but in the late 1760s and early 1770s, many Americans began to question the aims and tactics of the resistance movement. By 1774 and 1775 such people found themselves in a difficult position. Most of them objected to parliamentary policies, favoring some kind of constitutional reform. Nevertheless, if forced to a choice, these colonists sympathized with Great Britain rather than with an independent America. Their objections to violent protest, their desire to uphold the legally constituted colonial governments, and their fears of anarchy combined to make them especially sensitive to the dangers of resistance.

Some conservatives began in 1774 and 1775 to publish essays and pamphlets critical of the Congress and its allied committees. In Pennsylvania, Joseph Galloway published a tract attacking the Continental Congress for rejecting his plan of union. In Massachusetts, the young attorney Daniel Leonard, writing under the pseudonym Massachusettensis, engaged in a prolonged newspaper debate with Novanglus (John Adams). Leonard realized that the dispute was becoming less about American subordination to Parliament and more about whether the colonies would remain linked to Great Britain at all.

Some colonists heeded the conservative pamphleteers' warnings. About one-fifth of the Anglo-American population remained loyal to

Loyalists, Patriots, and Neutrals

Great Britain, actively opposing independence. With notable exceptions, most people of the following descriptions remained loyal to the Crown: British-appointed government officials; merchants whose trade depended on imperial connections; Anglican clergy everywhere and lay Anglicans in the North; former officers and enlisted men from the British army, many of whom had settled in America after 1763; non-English ethnic minorities, especially Scots; tenant farmers, particularly those whose landlords sided with the patriots; members of persecuted religious sects; and many of the backcountry southerners who had rebelled against eastern rule in the 1760s and early 1770s. All these people had one thing in common: patriot leaders were their long-standing opponents. Local and provincial disputes thus helped determine which side people would choose in the imperial conflict.

Active patriots, who accounted for about two-fifths of the population, came chiefly from the groups that had dominated colonial society, either numerically or politically. Among them were yeoman farmers, members of dominant Protestant sects, Chesapeake gentry, merchants dealing mainly in American commodities, city artisans, elected officeholders, and people of English descent. Wives usually but not always adopted their husbands' political beliefs. Although all these patriots supported the Revolution, they pursued divergent goals within the broader coalition. Some sought limited political reform, others extensive political change, and still others social and economic reforms.

About two-fifths of the white population fell somewhere between the loyalists and the active patriots. Some of those who tried to avoid taking sides were sincere pacifists, such as Quakers. Others opportunistically shifted their allegiance to whatever side happened to be winning at the time. Still others simply wanted to be left alone. The latter group made up an especially large proportion of the population in the southern backcountry, where Scots-Irish settlers had little love for either the patriot gentry or the English authorities.

To American patriots, those who were not for them were against them. By the winter of 1775–1776, the Second Continental Congress was recommending that all "disaffected" persons be disarmed and arrested. State legislatures passed laws prescribing severe penalties for suspected loyalists. Loyalists who were banished often had their property confiscated and the funds from its sale used for the war efforts. Perhaps as many as 100,000 Americans preferred to leave their homeland rather than live in a nation independent of British rule. And patriots worried not only about loyalists but also about the reactions of Indians and slaves.

Bondspeople faced their own dilemma: how could they best pursue their goal of escaping slavery? Should they fight with or against their masters? No correct choice was immediately apparent. Some African-Americans joined the revolutionaries, but to most an alliance with Great Britain appeared more promising. Thus news of slave conspiracies surfaced in different parts of the colonies in late 1774 and early 1775. All shared a common element: a plan to assist the British in return for freedom. The most serious incident occurred in 1775 in Charleston, where Thomas Jeremiah, a free black harbor pilot, was brutally executed after being convicted of attempting to foment a slave revolt.

African-Americans' Dilemma

Fear of such acts made sugar planters in the British West Indian colonies more cautious in their opposition to parliamentary policies than were their counterparts on the mainland. On most of the Caribbean islands, slaves outnumbered their masters by six or seven to one. With the ever-present threat of slave revolt or foreign attack hanging over their heads, planters could not afford to risk opposing Britain, their chief protector.

Slavery affected politics in the continental colonies as well. In the North, with few resident slaves, revolutionary fervor was at its height. In Virginia and Maryland, where free people also constituted a safe majority, there was occasional alarm over potential slave revolts but no disabling fear. But South Carolina and Georgia, where slaves composed more than half of the population, were noticeably less enthusiastic about resistance. Georgia sent no delegates to the First Continental Congress and reminded its representatives at the second one to

Slavery and Patriotic Fervor

consider its circumstances, "with our blacks and tories [loyalists] within us," when voting on the question of independence.

The slaveowners' worst fears were realized in November 1775, when Lord Dunmore, the governor of Virginia, offered to free any slaves and indentured servants who would leave their patriot masters to join the British forces. Dunmore hoped to use African-Americans in his fight against the revolutionaries and to disrupt the economy by depriving planters of their labor force. But at most only two thousand African-Americans rallied to the British standard. Even so, Dunmore's proclamation led Congress in January 1776 to modify an earlier policy that had prohibited the enlistment of African-Americans in the regular American army.

Although slaves did not pose a serious threat to the revolutionary cause in its early years, the patriots turned rumors of slave uprisings to their own advantage. In South Carolina, resistance leaders argued that unity under the Continental Association would protect masters from their slaves at a time when royal government was unable to muster adequate defense forces. This strategy undoubtedly kept many fearful whites in the patriot camp.

Similarly, the threat of Indian attacks helped persuade some reluctant westerners to support the struggle against Great Britain. In the years since the Proclamation of 1763, British officials had won the trust of the interior tribes by attempting to protect them from land-hungry European-Americans. British-appointed superintendents of Indian affairs, John Stuart in the South and Sir William Johnson in the North, lived among and understood the Indians. In 1768, Stuart and Johnson negotiated separate agreements modifying the proclamation line and attempting to draw realistic, defensible boundaries between tribal holdings and European-American settlements. The treaties supposedly established permanent western borders for the colonies. But just a few years later, the British pushed the southern boundary even farther west to accommodate the demands of settlers in western Georgia and Kentucky.

By 1775, many Indian groups were impatient with European-Americans' aggressive pressure on their lands. Such pressure, when combined with their confidence in Stuart and Johnson, predisposed most Indians toward an alliance with Great Britain. Even so, the latter hesitated to make full and immediate use of these potential allies because Indian war aims and tactics were not compatible with those of the British. Accordingly, they sought from the tribes only a promise of neutrality.

Indians' Grievances

Recognizing that their standing with the tribes was poor, the patriots also sought the Indians' neutrality. In 1775 the Second Continental Congress sent a general message to the tribes describing the war as "a family quarrel between us and Old England" and requesting that they "not join on either side" since "you Indians are not concerned in it." A group of Cherokees led by Chief Dragging Canoe nevertheless decided that the "family quarrel" would allow them to settle some old scores. They attacked settlements along the western borders of the Carolinas and Virginia in the summer of 1776. But a militia campaign destroyed many of their towns. Dragging Canoe and his diehard followers fled to the west, establishing new outposts; the rest of the Cherokees agreed to a treaty that ceded still more of their land.

The fate of the Cherokees foreshadowed the history of Indian involvement in the Revolution. The British victory over France in 1763 had removed the Indians' strongest weapon: their ability to play the European powers off against one another. Successful strategies were difficult to envision under these new circumstances, and even if the interests of several neighboring tribes coincided, old enmities kept them from forming alliances. Consequently, during the Revolution many Indian nations avoided active involvement in the war.

Native Americans' Diverse Interests

Thus, although patriots could never completely ignore the threats posed by loyalists, neutrals, slaves, and Indians, only rarely did fear of these groups seriously hamper the revolutionary movement. The reality was that the practical impossibility of a large-scale slave revolt, coupled with tribal feuds and the patriots' successful campaign to disarm and neutralize loyalists, ensured that the revolutionaries would remain firmly in control as they fought for independence.

 ## War Begins

On January 27, 1775, Lord Dartmouth, secretary of state for America, addressed a fateful letter to General Thomas Gage in Boston. Expressing his belief that American resistance was nothing more than the response of a "rude rabble without plan," Dartmouth urged Gage to take a decisive step.

Dartmouth's letter did not reach Gage until April 14. He responded by sending an expedition to confiscate provincial military supplies stockpiled at Concord. Bostonians dispatched two messengers, William Dawes and Paul Revere (later joined by Dr. Samuel Prescott), to rouse the countryside. So when the British vanguard of several hundred men approached Lexington at dawn on April 19, they found a ragtag group of seventy militiamen drawn up before them on the common. The Americans' commander ordered his men to withdraw, realizing they could not halt the redcoats' advance. But as they began to disperse, a shot rang out; the British soldiers then fired several volleys. When they stopped, eight Americans lay dead and another ten had been wounded. The British moved on to Concord, 5 miles away.

Battles of Lexington and Concord

There the contingents of militia were larger, Concord residents having been joined by groups of men from nearby towns. An exchange of gunfire at the North Bridge spilled the first British blood of the Revolution: three men were killed and nine wounded. Thousands of militiamen then fired from houses and from behind trees and bushes at the British forces as they retreated to Boston. By the end of the day, the redcoats had suffered 272 casualties, including 70 deaths. The patriots had suffered just 93 casualties.

By the evening of April 20, approximately twenty thousand American militiamen had gathered around Boston. Many soon returned home for spring planting, but those who remained dug in along siege lines encircling the city. For nearly a year the two armies sat and stared at each other across those lines. The redcoats attacked their besiegers only once, on June 17, when they drove the Americans from trenches atop Breed's Hill in Charlestown. In that misnamed Battle of Bunker Hill, the British incurred their greatest losses of the entire war: over 800 wounded and 228 killed. The Americans, though forced to abandon their position, lost less than half that number.

First Year of War

During the same eleven-month period, patriots captured Fort Ticonderoga, a British fort on Lake Champlain, acquiring much-needed cannon. Trying to bring Canada into the war on the American side, they also mounted an uncoordinated northern campaign that ended in disaster at Quebec in early 1776. Most significant, the lull in the fighting at Boston gave both sides a chance to regroup, organize, and plan their strategies.

Lord North and his new American secretary, Lord George Germain, made three central assumptions about the war they faced. First, they concluded that patriot forces could not withstand the assaults of trained British regulars. Accordingly, they dispatched to America the largest force Great Britain had ever assembled anywhere: 370 transport ships carrying 32,000 troops and tons of supplies, accompanied by 73 naval vessels and 13,000 sailors. Such an extraordinary effort, they thought, would ensure a quick victory.

British Strategy

Second, British officials and army officers treated this war as comparable to wars they had fought successfully in Europe. They adopted a conventional strategy of capturing major American cities and defeating the rebel army decisively without suffering serious casualties themselves. Third, they assumed that a clear-cut military victory would automatically bring about their goal of retaining the colonies' allegiance.

All these assumptions proved false. North and Germain vastly underestimated Americans' commitment to armed resistance. Battlefield defeats did not lead patriots to abandon their political aims and sue for peace. The ministers in London also failed to recognize the significance of the American population's dispersal over an area 1,500 miles long. Although Great Britain would control each of the most important American ports at one time or another during the war, less than 5 percent of the population lived in those cities. Furthermore, the coast offered so many excellent harbors that essential commerce was easily rerouted. In other words, the loss of cities did little to damage the American cause.

Most of all, British officials failed at first to understand that military triumph would not necessarily lead to political victory. Securing the colonies permanently would require hundreds of thousands of Americans to return to their original allegiance. The British thus needed to both overpower and convert the patriots. After 1778, the ministry adopted a strategy designed to achieve that goal through the expanded use of loyalist forces and the restoration of civilian authority in occupied areas. But the new policy came too late. Britain's leaders never fully realized that they were fighting not a conventional European war but rather an entirely new kind of conflict: the first modern war of national liberation.

Great Britain at least had a bureaucracy ready to supervise the war effort. The Americans had only the Second Continental Congress, originally planned as a brief gathering to consider the ministry's response to the Continental Association. Instead, the delegates who convened in Philadelphia on May 10, 1775, found that they had to assume the mantle of intercolonial government. As the summer passed, Congress authorized the printing of money with which to purchase necessary goods, established a committee to supervise relations with foreign countries, and took steps to strengthen the militia. Most important, it created the Continental Army and appointed its generals.

Second Continental Congress

Until Congress met, the Massachusetts provincial congress had taken responsibility for organizing the militiamen encamped at Boston. Because the cost of maintaining that army was a burden, Massachusetts asked the Continental Congress to assume the task of directing the army. As a first step, Congress had to choose a commander-in-chief. Since the war had thus far been a wholly northern affair, many delegates recognized the importance of naming someone who was not a New Englander. There seemed only one obvious candidate: they unanimously selected their fellow delegate, the Virginian George Washington.

Washington was no fiery radical, nor had he played a prominent role in the prerevolutionary agitation. But his devotion to the American cause was unquestioned. He was dignified, conservative, and respectable—a man of unimpeachable integrity. Though unmistakably an aristocrat, he was unswervingly committed to representative government. His stamina was remarkable, and he both looked and acted like a leader.

George Washington: A Portrait of Leadership

Washington needed all the coolness and caution he could muster when he took command of the army outside Boston in July 1775. It took him months to impose hierarchy and discipline on the unruly troops and to bring order to the supply system. But by March 1776, when the arrival of cannon from Ticonderoga finally enabled him to put direct pressure on the redcoats in the city, the army was prepared to act. As it happened, an assault on Boston proved unnecessary. Sir William Howe, who had replaced Gage, had for some time planned to transfer his troops to New York City. The patriots' new cannon decided the matter. On March 17, the British and more than a thousand of their loyalist allies abandoned Boston forever.

British Evacuate Boston

That spring of 1776, as the British fleet left Boston for the temporary haven of Halifax, Nova Scotia, the colonies were moving inexorably toward the unthinkable—a declaration of independence. Even months after fighting began, American leaders still denied seeking a break with

Thomas Paine, the English radical who wrote Common Sense. *James Watson prepared this 1783 engraving from a portrait by Charles Willson Peale, who depicted his subject accompanied by the tools of the writer's trade—several sheets of paper and a quill pen.* National Portrait Gallery, Smithsonian Institution, Washington, D.C.

Great Britain. But in January 1776 there appeared a pamphlet by a man who both thought and advocated the unthinkable.

Thomas Paine's *Common Sense* exploded on the American scene like a bombshell. Within three months of publication, it sold 120,000 copies.

Thomas Paine's *Common Sense*

The author, a radical English printer who had lived in America only since 1774, called stridently and stirringly for independence. More than that: Paine rejected the notion that a balance of monarchy, aristocracy, and democracy was necessary to preserve freedom. Instead, he advocated the establishment of a *republic*, a government by the people with no king or nobility. Paine also denied the benefits of links to the mother country, insisting that

Britain had exploited the colonies unmercifully. In place of the frequently heard assertion that an independent America would be weak and divided, he substituted an unlimited confidence in America's strength when freed from European control.

There is no way of knowing how many people were converted to the cause of independence by reading *Common Sense*. But by late spring in 1776 independence had become inevitable. On May 10, the Second Continental Congress formally recommended that individual colonies "adopt such governments as shall, in the opinion of the representatives of the people, best conduce to the happiness and safety of their constituents in particular, and America in general." From that source stemmed the first state constitutions.

June 7 brought confirmation of the movement toward independence. Richard Henry Lee of Virginia, seconded by John Adams of Massachusetts, introduced the crucial resolution: "that these United Colonies are, and of right ought to be, free and independent States, that they are absolved of all allegiance to the British Crown, and that all political connection between them and the State of Great Britain is, and ought to be, totally dissolved." Congress debated Lee's resolution and directed Thomas Jefferson, John Adams, and Benjamin Franklin to draft a declaration of independence. The committee assigned primary responsibility for writing the declaration to Jefferson.

Thomas Jefferson was at the time thirty-four years old, a Virginia lawyer educated at the College of William and Mary. A member of the House of Burgesses, he had read widely in history and political theory. His broad knowledge was evident not only in the declaration but also in his draft of the Virginia state constitution.

Thomas Jefferson and the Declaration of Independence

The draft of the declaration was laid before Congress on June 28, 1776. The delegates officially voted for independence four days later, then debated the wording of the declaration for two more days, adopting it with some changes on July 4. Since Americans had long ago ceased to see themselves as legitimate subjects of Parliament, the Declaration of Independence concentrated on George III (see the Appendix). That focus also provided an identifiable villain. The document accused the king of attempting to destroy representative government in the colonies and of oppressing Americans through the unjustified use of excessive force.

The declaration's chief long-term importance, however, lay not in its lengthy catalog of grievances against George III but in its ringing statements of principle that have served ever since as the ideal to which Americans aspire: "We hold these truths to be self-evident: That all men are created equal; that they are endowed by their Creator with certain unalienable rights; that among these are life, liberty and the pursuit of happiness; that, to secure these rights, governments are instituted among men, deriving their just powers from the consent of the governed; that whenever any form of government becomes destructive of these ends, it is the right of the people to alter or to abolish it, and to institute new government." These phrases have echoed down through American history like no others.

When the delegates in Philadelphia adopted the declaration, they risked their necks: they were committing treason. Thus when they concluded the declaration with the assertion that they "mutually pledge[d] to each other our lives, our fortunes, and our sacred honor," they spoke no less than the truth.

The Long Struggle in the North

In late June 1776, the first ships carrying Sir William Howe's troops from Halifax appeared off the coast of New York (see map). On July 2, the day Congress voted for independence, redcoats landed on Staten Island. Howe, though, waited until mid-August, after the arrival of more troops from England, to begin his attack on the city. The delay gave Washington sufficient time to march his army of seventeen thousand south to meet the threat. But both he and his men, still inexperienced in

Loss of New York City

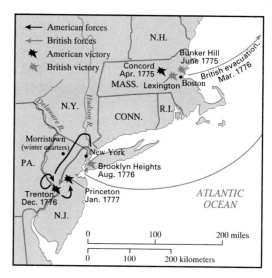

The War in the North, 1775–1777 *The early phase of the Revolutionary War, as shown in this map, was dominated by British troop movements in the Boston area, the redcoats' evacuation to Nova Scotia in the spring of 1776, and the subsequent British invasion of New York and New Jersey.*

fighting and maneuvering, made major mistakes, losing battles at Brooklyn Heights and on Manhattan Island. The city fell to the British, who captured nearly three thousand American soldiers.

During the autumn months, Washington retreated across New Jersey, with Howe in leisurely pursuit. The British took control of most of the state, and hundreds of New Jerseyites and Pennsylvanians accepted pardons for their "treasonous" activities. Occupying troops met little opposition, and the revolutionary cause appeared to be in disarray.

Campaign in New Jersey

The British let their advantage slip away as redcoats stationed in New Jersey went on a rampage of rape and plunder. Because loyalists and patriots were indistinguishable to British and Hessian troops, families on both sides suffered nearly equally. The troops seized crops, looted houses, and desecrated churches and public buildings. Yet nothing was better calculated to rally doubtful

Americans to the cause than the murder of innocent civilians and the rape of women.

The soldiers' marauding alienated potentially loyal New Jerseyites and Pennsylvanians whose allegiance the British could ill afford to lose. It also spurred Washington's determination to strike back. Moving quickly, he attacked a Hessian encampment at Trenton early in the morning of December 26, while the redcoats were still reeling from their Christmas celebration. A few days later, Washington attacked again at Princeton. Having gained command of the field and buoyed American spirits with the two swift victories, Washington set up winter quarters at Morristown, New Jersey.

The 1776 campaign established patterns that persisted throughout much of the war, despite changes in British leadership and strategy. The British forces were usually more numerous and often better led than the Americans. But their ponderous style of maneuvering, lack of familiarity with the terrain, and inability to live off the land without antagonizing the populace partially offset those advantages. Furthermore, although Washington always seemed to lack regular troops—the Continental Army never numbered more than 18,500 men—he could usually count on the militia to join him at crucial times. American militiamen did not like to sign up for long terms of service or to fight far from home; but when their homes were threatened, they rallied to the cause.

As the war dragged on, the Continental Army and the militia took on decidedly different

At the Battle of Princeton in early 1777, American forces under George Washington cemented the victory they had won a few days earlier at Trenton. This view was painted in 1787 by James Peale, who fought in the battle. Princeton University Library.

characters. State governments, responsible for filling military quotas, discovered

The American Army

that most men willing to enlist for long periods in the regular army were young, single, and footloose. Farmers with families tended to prefer short-term militia duty. As the supply of men willing to sign up with the Continentals dwindled, recruiters in northern states turned increasingly to African-Americans, both slave and free. Perhaps as many as five thousand blacks eventually served in the army, and most of them won their freedom as a result. Also attached to the American forces were a number of wives and widows of poor soldiers. Such camp followers worked as cooks, nurses, and launderers in return for rations and low wages. The American army was unwieldy and difficult to manage, yet its shapelessness provided an almost unlimited reservoir of manpower and woman-power.

In 1777, the chief British effort was planned by Howe's subordinate, "Gentleman Johnny" Burgoyne, a playboy general who had gained the ear of Lord George

Planning the 1777 Campaign

Germain. Burgoyne convinced Germain that he could lead an invading force of redcoats and Indians down the Hudson River from Canada, cutting off New England from the rest of the states. He proposed to rendezvous near Albany with a similar force that would move east along the Mohawk River valley. The combined forces would then presumably link up with Sir William Howe's troops in New York City.

That Burgoyne's scheme would give "Gentleman Johnny" all the glory did not escape Sir William's notice. While Burgoyne was plotting in London, Howe was laying his own plans to take Philadelphia. Just as Burgoyne left Howe out of his plans, Howe left Burgoyne out of his. Thus the two major British armies in America would operate independently in 1777, and the result would be a disaster.

Howe captured Philadelphia, but he did so in inexplicable fashion, taking six weeks to transport his troops by sea instead of marching them over-

Howe Takes Philadelphia

land. That maneuver cost him at least a month, debilitated his men, depleted his supplies, and placed him only 40 miles closer to Philadelphia than when he started. By the time Howe was ready to move on Philadelphia, Washington had had time to prepare its defenses. Twice, at Brandywine Creek and again at Germantown, the two armies clashed near the patriot capital. Although the British won both engagements, the Americans handled themselves well. The redcoats took Philadelphia in late September, but to little effect. The campaign season was nearly over, and far to the north, Burgoyne was going down to defeat.

Burgoyne and his men set out from Montréal in mid-June 1777, floating down Lake Champlain into New York. They easily took Fort Ticonderoga, but they started having

Burgoyne's Campaign in New York

trouble when Burgoyne began an overland march. Because his clumsy artillery carriages and baggage wagons foundered in the heavy forests and ravines, Burgoyne's troops took twenty-four days to travel 23 miles. In August, the campaign suffered two sharp blows—first, when a force of redcoats and Indians turned back after a battle at Oriskany, New York; second, when in a clash near Bennington, Vermont, American militiamen nearly wiped out eight hundred of Burgoyne's German mercenaries. Yet the general continued to dawdle, giving the Americans more than enough time to prepare for his coming. After several skirmishes with an American army commanded by General Horatio Gates, Burgoyne was surrounded near Saratoga, New York. On October 17, 1777, he surrendered his entire force of more than six thousand men.

The August 1777 battle at Oriskany was also important because it revealed a division in the Iroquois Confederacy (see page 55). In 1776 the

Split of the Iroquois Confederacy

Six Nations had formally pledged to remain neutral in the Anglo-American struggle. But two influential Mohawk leaders, Joseph and Mary Brant, worked tirelessly to persuade the Iroquois to join the British. Mary Brant, a powerful tribal matron, was also the widow of the Indian superintendent Sir William Johnson. Her younger brother Joseph, a renowned warrior, was convinced that the Six Nations should ally themselves with the British in order to prevent American encroachment on their lands. The Brants won over to the British the Senecas, Cayugas, and Mohawks. But the Oneidas preferred the American side and brought the Tuscaroras with them. The Onondagas split into three factions, one on each side and one supporting neutrality. At Oriskany, the three-hundred-year league of friendship was torn apart as confederation warriors fought on both sides.

The collapse of Iroquois unity and the confederacy's abandonment of neutrality had significant consequences. In 1778, Iroquois warriors allied with the British raided frontier villages in Pennsylvania and New York. Americans under General John Sullivan retaliated by so thoroughly destroying Iroquois crops and settlements that many bands had to abandon their ancestral homeland. A large number of Iroquois people never returned to New York but settled in British Canada.

Burgoyne's surrender at Saratoga so discouraged the British that Lord North authorized a peace commission to offer the Americans what they had requested in 1774—in effect, a return to the imperial system of 1763. It was, of course, far too late for that: the patriots rejected the overture.

Most important of all, the American victory at Saratoga drew France formally into the conflict. Ever since 1763, the French had sought to avenge their defeat in the Seven Years' War, and the American Revolution gave them that opportunity. Even before Benjamin Franklin arrived in Paris in late 1776, France was covertly supplying the revolutionaries with military necessities.

Franklin worked tirelessly to strengthen ties between the two nations. By presenting himself as a representative of American simplicity, he played on the French image of Americans as virtuous yeomen. Franklin's efforts culminated in 1778 when the countries signed two treaties. In the Treaty of Amity and Commerce, France recognized American independence and established trade ties

Franco-American Alliance of 1778

with the new nation. In the Treaty of Alliance, France and the United States promised—assuming that France would go to war with Britain, which it soon did—that neither would negotiate peace with the enemy without consulting the other. France also abandoned all its claims to Canada and to North American territory east of the Mississippi River.

The French alliance had two major benefits for the patriot cause. First, France began to aid the Americans openly, sending troops and naval vessels in addition to arms, ammunition, clothing, and blankets. Second, Great Britain could no longer focus solely on the American mainland, for it had to fight France in the Caribbean and elsewhere. Spain's entry into the war in 1779 as an ally of France (but not of the United States) further magnified Britain's problems, for the Revolution then became a global war.

 ## The Long Struggle in the South

In the aftermath of the Saratoga disaster, the British reassessed their strategy and decided that they might attain success by shifting the field of battle southward. Howe's replacement, Sir Henry Clinton, became convinced that a southern strategy would succeed. In late 1779 he sailed down the coast from New York to attack Charleston, the most important city in the South (see map, page 115).

The Americans worked hard to bolster Charleston's defenses, but the city fell to the British on May 12, 1780. General Benjamin Lincoln surrendered the entire southern army—5,500 men—to the invaders. In the weeks that followed, the redcoats spread through South Carolina, established garrisons at key points in the interior, and organized loyalist regiments.

Fall of Charleston

Yet the British triumph was less complete than it appeared. The success of the southern campaign depended on British control of the seas, for only by sea could the widely dispersed British armies coordinate their efforts. For the moment, the Royal Navy safely dominated the American coastline, but

French naval power posed a threat to the entire southern enterprise. Moreover, patriot bands continued to operate freely in the state and thus denied loyalists the guaranteed protection they desired. Last but not least, the fall of Charleston did not dishearten the patriots; instead, it spurred them to greater exertions.

Nevertheless, the war in South Carolina went badly for the patriots throughout most of 1780. In August, a reorganized southern army under Horatio Gates was crushingly defeated at Camden by the forces of Lord Cornwallis, the new British commander in the South. The redcoats were joined wherever they went by enslaved African-Americans seeking freedom on the basis of Lord Dunmore's proclamation. They ran away from their patriot masters in such numbers that they seriously disrupted planting and harvesting in 1780 and 1781. More than fifty-five thousand slaves were lost to their owners as a result of the war. Not all of them joined the British or won their freedom if they did, but their flight had exactly the effect Dunmore wanted.

After the defeat at Camden, Washington appointed General Nathanael Greene of Rhode Island to command the southern campaign. Greene adopted a conciliatory policy toward loyalists and neutrals,

Greene Rallies South Carolina

persuading the governor of South Carolina to offer pardons to those who had fought for the British if they would join the patriot militia. He also ordered his troops to treat captives fairly and not to loot loyalist property. Greene recognized that the patriots could win only by convincing the populace that they could bring stability to the region.

Greene also took a conciliatory approach to the southern Indians. With his desperate need for soldiers, he could not afford to have frontier militia companies occupied in defending their homes against Indian attacks. Greene's diplomatic efforts with the southern Indians worked and by war's end only the Creeks remained allied with Great Britain.

Even before Greene took command of the southern army in December 1780, the tide had begun to turn. In October, at King's Mountain, a force from the settlements west of the Appalachians defeated a large party of redcoats and loyalists. Then in January 1781 Greene's trusted aide Brigadier General Daniel Morgan brilliantly defeated the crack British regiment Tarleton's Legion at Cowpens. Greene himself confronted the main body of British troops under Lord Cornwallis at Guilford Court House, North Carolina, in March. Although Cornwallis controlled the field at the end of the day, most of his army had been destroyed. He had to retreat to the coast, to receive supplies and fresh troops from New York by sea.

Cornwallis had already ignored explicit orders not to leave South Carolina unless the state was safely in British hands. He headed north into Virginia, where he joined forces with a detachment of redcoats

Surrender at Yorktown

commanded by the American traitor Benedict Arnold. Instead of acting decisively with his new army of 7,200 men, Cornwallis withdrew to the peninsula between the York and James Rivers, where he fortified Yorktown and waited for supplies and reinforcements. Seizing the opportunity, Washington quickly moved more than 7,000 troops south from New York City. When a French fleet defeated the Royal Navy vessels sent to relieve Cornwallis, the British general was trapped (see map, page 115). On October 19, 1781, Cornwallis surrendered to the combined American and French forces.

When news of the surrender reached London, Lord North's ministry fell. Parliament voted to cease offensive operations in America and authorized peace negotiations. But guerrilla warfare between patriots and loyalists continued to ravage the Carolinas and Georgia for more than a year, and in the North vicious raids by both sides kept the frontier aflame. The persistence of conflict among guerrillas, frontiersmen, and Indians after the Battle of Yorktown serves to underscore the significance of the internal conflict that accompanied the war's more famous battles.

The costs of winning independence were heavy. More than twenty-five thousand American men died in the war, only about one-quarter of them from wounds suffered in battle. The rest were declared missing in action or died of disease

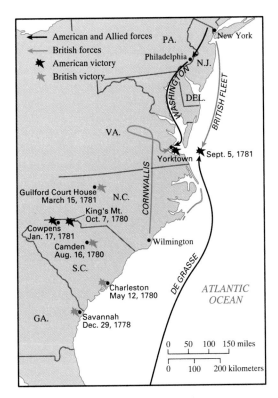

American and Allied forces
British forces
★ American victory
✦ British victory

PA.
New York
Philadelphia
N.J.
WASHINGTON
DEL.
BRITISH FLEET
VA.
Yorktown — Sept. 5, 1781
CORNWALLIS
Guilford Court House
March 15, 1781
N.C.
King's Mt.
Oct. 7, 1780
Cowpens
Jan. 17, 1781
Camden
Aug. 16, 1780
S.C.
Wilmington
DE GRASSE
ATLANTIC
OCEAN
Charleston
May 12, 1780
GA.
Savannah
Dec. 29, 1778

0   50   100   150 miles
0   100   200 kilometers

The War in the South *The southern war—after the British invasion of Georgia in late 1778—was characterized by a series of British thrusts into the interior, leading to battles with American defenders in both North and South Carolina. Finally, after promising beginnings, Cornwallis's foray into Virginia ended with disaster at Yorktown in October 1781.*

or as prisoners of war. In the South, years of guerrilla warfare and the loss of thousands of runaway slaves shattered the economy. Indebtedness soared, and local governments were crippled for lack of funds, since few people could afford to pay their taxes.

Americans rejoiced when they learned of the signing of a preliminary peace treaty at Paris in November 1782. The American diplomats—Benjamin Franklin, John Jay, and John Adams—ignored their instructions from Congress to be guided by France and instead negotiated directly with Great Britain. Their instincts were sound: the

Treaty of Paris

French government was more an enemy to Britain than a friend to the United States. In fact, French ministers worked secretly behind the scenes to try to prevent the establishment of a strong and unified government in America. But the American delegates proved adept at playing the game of power politics, and the new British ministry, headed by Lord Shelburne was weary of war and made numerous concessions.

The treaty, signed formally on September 3, 1783, granted the Americans unconditional independence. The boundaries of the new nation were generous: to the north, approximately the present-day boundary with Canada; to the south, the 31st parallel (about the modern northern border of Florida); to the west, the Mississippi River. Florida, which Britain had acquired in 1763, was returned to Spain. The Americans also gained unlimited fishing rights off Newfoundland. In ceding so much land to the United States, Great Britain ignored the territorial rights of its Indian allies, sacrificing their interests to the demands of European politics. Loyalists and British merchants were also poorly served by British diplomats. The treaty's ambiguously worded clauses pertaining to the payment of prewar debts and the postwar treatment of loyalists caused trouble for years to come and proved impossible to enforce.

 Conclusion

The victorious Americans could look back on their achievement with satisfaction and awe. They had taken on the world's greatest military power and won. The Americans won few victories, but their army survived its defeats and ultimately wore down the enemy. In winning the war, the Americans abandoned the British identity that once was so important to them and began the process of creating loyalty to a new nation. They also established a claim to most of the territory east of the Mississippi River and south of the Great Lakes, thereby greatly expanding the land potentially open to their settlements.

In achieving independence, Americans surmounted formidable challenges. But in the future they would face perhaps even greater ones:

How do historians know that Americans had only incomplete knowledge of the boundaries of their new nation? They know from consulting written documents and from looking at early maps like this one, "A New and Correct Map of the United States of North America," produced in 1784. New it certainly was, but correct it was not. A comparison with a standard map of the United States and Canada today shows many errors of scale, proportion, and placement of natural features. To point out just a few: the Ohio River is shown much too far south; the northern part of the Mississippi River is misplaced to the west; Lake Superior is too small, and its islands are too large; and the Nova Scotia peninsula is misshapen. What links all these features is that they were on the periphery of the new nation and thus on the margins of Americans' knowledge. But even so well known a waterway as Chesapeake Bay is inaccurately drawn, suggesting that residents of the United States still had much to learn about the geography of their country.   Photo: New Jersey Historical Society.

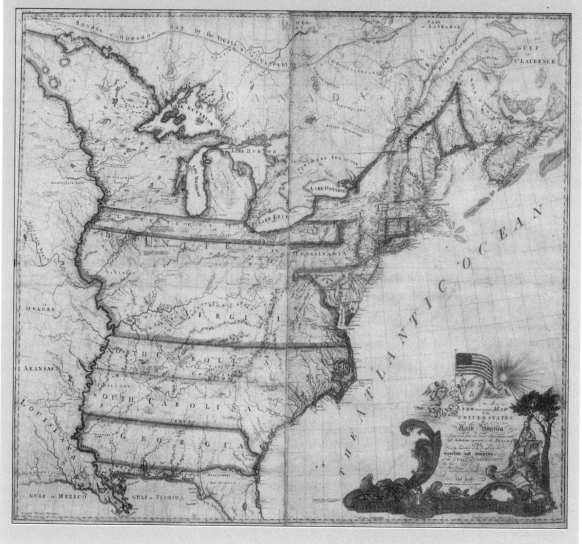

establishing stable republican governments at the state and national levels and ensuring their government's continued existence in a world of bitter rivalries among the major powers—Britain, France, and Spain. Those European rivalries soon posed significant threats to the survival of the new nation.

Suggestions for Further Reading

General

Colin Bonwick, *The American Revolution* (1991); Edward Countryman, *The American Revolution* (1985); Theodore Draper, *A Struggle for Power: The American Revolution* (1996); Robert Middlekauff, *The Glorious Cause: The American Revolution, 1763–1783* (1982); Harry M. Ward, *The American Revolution: Nationhood Achieved, 1763–1788* (1995); Alfred F. Young, ed., *Beyond the American Revolution* (1993).

Military Affairs

E. Wayne Carp, *To Starve the Army at Pleasure: Continental Army Administration and American Political Culture, 1775–1783* (1984); Stephen Conway, *The War of American Independence 1775–1783* (1995); John C. Dann, ed., *The Revolution Remembered: Eyewitness Accounts of the War for Independence* (1980); Don Higginbotham, *The War of American Independence: Military Attitudes, Policies, and Practice, 1763–1789* (1971); Piers Mackesy, *The War for America, 1775–1783* (1964); Charles Royster, *A Revolutionary People at War: The Continental Army and American Character, 1775–1783* (1980).

Local and Regional Studies

Richard Buel, *Dear Liberty: Connecticut's Mobilization for the Revolutionary War* (1980); Edward Countryman, *A People in Revolution: The American Revolution and Political Society in New York, 1760–1790* (1981); Jeffrey Crow and Larry Tise, eds., *The Southern Experience in the American Revolution* (1978); David Hackett Fischer, *Paul Revere's Ride* (1994); Robert A. Gross, *The Minutemen and Their World* (1976); Ronald Hoffman, *A Spirit of Dissension: Economics, Politics, and the Revolution in Maryland* (1973); Ronald Hoffman, Thad W. Tate, and Peter Albert, eds., *An Uncivil War: The Southern Backcountry During the American Revolution* (1985); Jean B. Lee, *The Price of*

Nationhood: The American Revolution in Charles County (1994); John Selby, *The Revolution in Virginia, 1775–1783* (1988).

Indians and African-Americans

Colin Calloway, *The American Revolution in Indian Country: Crisis and Diversity in Native American Communities* (1995); Sylvia Frey, *Water from the Rock: Black Resistance in a Revolutionary Age* (1991); Barbara Graymont, *The Iroquois in the American Revolution* (1972); James H. O'Donnell III, *Southern Indians in the American Revolution* (1973).

Loyalists

Bernard Bailyn, *The Ordeal of Thomas Hutchinson* (1974); Robert McCluer Calhoon, *The Loyalists in Revolutionary America, 1760–1781* (1973); Mary Beth Norton, *The British-Americans: The Loyalist Exiles in England, 1774–1789* (1972); James W. St. G. Walker, *The Black Loyalists: The Search for a Promised Land in Nova Scotia and Sierra Leone, 1783–1870* (1976).

Women

Richard Buel and Joy Buel, *The Way of Duty: A Woman and Her Family in Revolutionary America* (1984); Ronald Hoffman and Peter Albert, eds., *Women in the Age of the American Revolution* (1989); Linda K. Kerber, *Women of the Republic: Intellect and Ideology in Revolutionary America* (1980); Mary Beth Norton, *Liberty's Daughters: The Revolutionary Experience of American Women, 1750–1800* (1980).

Foreign Policy

Jonathan Dull, *A Diplomatic History of the American Revolution* (1985); Ronald Hoffman and Peter Albert, eds., *Peace and the Peacemakers: The Treaty of 1783* (1986); Ronald Hoffman and Peter Albert, eds., *Diplomacy and Revolution: The Franco-American Alliance of 1778* (1981); Jan Willem Schulte Nordholt, *The Dutch Republic and American Independence* (1982).

Patriot Leaders

Fawn M. Brodie, *Thomas Jefferson: An Intimate History* (1974); Richard Brookhiser, *Founding Father: Rediscovering George Washington* (1996); Eric Foner, *Tom Paine and Revolutionary America* (1976); Norman Risjord, *Thomas Jefferson* (1994); Charles Royster, *Light-Horse Harry Lee and the Legacy of the American Revolution* (1981); Sheila Skemp, *Benjamin and William Franklin: Father and Son, Patriot and Loyalist* (1994); Esmond Wright, *Franklin of Philadelphia* (1986).

CHAPTER

7

Forging a National Republic
1776–1789

On January 25, 1787, an army of fifteen hundred farmers from western Massachusetts advanced on the Springfield federal armory. Inside the arsenal, General William Shepard prepared his group of one thousand militiamen to resist the assault. First, though, he dispatched two aides to warn the farmers that they would soon draw the fire of men who had been their officers during the Revolutionary War. "That is all we want, by God!" replied one of the rebels. The farmers moved toward the armory, urged on by the commands of Daniel Shays, one of their leaders. Shepard fired two cannon over the heads of the farmers, and then—when that did not frighten them—ordered his men to shoot directly at the straggling ranks. Four men died, twenty were wounded, and the rebels withdrew.

What caused this violent clash between former comrades in arms? Massachusetts farmers were angered by high taxes and the scarcity of money. Since the preceding summer, they had organized committees and crowd actions—the tactics used so successfully in the 1760s and early 1770s—to halt state efforts to seize property for nonpayment of taxes. Many of the insurgents were respected war veterans. Clearly the episode could not be dismissed as the work of an unruly rabble. What did the uprising mean for the republic's future?

The protesters explained their position in an address to the Massachusetts government. They proclaimed their loyalty to the nation but objected to the state's fiscal policies, which, they said, prevented them from providing adequately for their families. Referring to their experience as revolutionary soldiers, they asserted that they "esteem[ed] one moment of Liberty to be worth an eternity of Bondage." The Massachusetts gov-

A woodcut of Daniel Shays and one of his chief officers, Job Shattuck, in 1787. National Portrait Gallery, Smithsonian Institution, Washington, D.C.

ernment was "tyrannical," Shays asserted, and, like that of Great Britain, deserved to be overthrown.

To the state's elected leaders, the most ominous aspect of the uprising was the farmers' attempt to link their rebellion with the earlier struggle for independence. The state legislature insisted that "in a republican government the majority must govern. If the minor part governs it becomes aristocracy; if every one opposed at his pleasure, it is no government, it is anarchy and confusion." In short, the crowd actions that once had been a justifiable response to British tyranny were no longer legitimate. In a republic, reform had to come through the ballot box rather than by force.

The confrontation at the Springfield armory symbolized for many Americans the trials facing the new nation. To American political leaders, Shays's Rebellion suggested the first signs of disintegration of the republic.

Republicanism—the idea that governments should be based wholly on the consent of the people—originated with political theorists in ancient Greece and Rome. Republics, such writers declared, were desirable yet fragile forms of government. Unless their citizens were especially virtuous—that is, sober, moral, and industrious—and largely in agreement on key issues, republics were doomed to failure. When Americans left the British Empire, they committed themselves to republicanism. Now they faced the task of creating a stable republic based upon a popular consensus.

America's political and intellectual leaders worked hard to inculcate virtue in their fellow countrymen and countrywomen. After 1776, American literature, theater, art, architecture, and education all pursued explicitly moral goals. The education of women was considered particularly important, for as the mothers of the republic's children, they were primarily responsible for ensuring the nation's future. On such matters Americans could agree, but they disagreed on many other critical issues. Almost all white men concurred that women, Indians, and African-Americans should be excluded from formal participation in politics, but they found it difficult to reach a consensus on how many of their own number should be included, how often elections should be held, or how their new governments should be structured.

Republican citizens had to make many other decisions as well. Should a republic conduct its dealings with Indian nations and foreign countries any differently than other types of governments did? Were republics, in other words, obliged to negotiate fairly and honestly at all times? And how could republicans who proclaimed that "all men are created equal" justify holding African-Americans in perpetual bondage? Some answered that question by freeing their slaves or by voting for state laws that abolished slavery. Others denied blacks were "men" in the same sense as whites.

The most important task facing Americans in these years was the construction of a genuinely national government. Before 1765, the British mainland colonies had rarely cooperated on common endeavors, but fighting the Revolutionary War had fostered a new nationalistic spirit in which Americans began the process of replacing loyalties to state and region with loyalties to the nation.

Still, forging a national republic was neither easy nor simple. America's first such government, under the Articles of Confederation, proved to be inadequate. But some of the nation's political leaders learned from their experiences and tried another approach when they drafted the Constitution in 1787. Though some historians have argued that the Constitution represents an "aristocratic" counterrevolution against the "democratic" Articles, the two documents are more accurately viewed as successive attempts to solve the same problems.

 ## Creating a Virtuous Republic

When the colonies declared their independence from Great Britain, John Dickinson recalled many years later, "there was no question concerning forms of Government, no enquiry whether a Republic or a limited Monarchy was best. . . . We knew that the people of this country must unite themselves under some form of Government and that this could be no other than the republican form." But how should that goal be implemented?

Three different definitions of *republicanism* emerged in the new United States. The first, held chiefly by members of the educated elite, was based directly on ancient history and political theory. The histories of popular governments in Greece and Rome seemed to prove that republics could succeed only if they were small in size and homogeneous in population. Unless a republic's citizens were willing to sacrifice their own private interests for the good of the whole, the government would collapse. In return for sacrifices, though, a republic offered its citizens equality of opportunity. Under such a government, society would be governed by members of a "natural aristocracy" of men whose rank would be based on merit rather than inherited wealth and status.

Varieties of Republicanism

A second definition, advanced by other members of the elite but also by some skilled craftsmen, drew more on economic theory than on political thought. Instead of perceiving the nation as an organic whole composed of people nobly sacrificing for the common good, this version of republicanism followed the Scottish theorist Adam Smith in emphasizing individuals' pursuit of rational self-interest. When republican men sought to improve their own economic and social circumstances, the entire nation would benefit. Republican virtue would be achieved through the pursuit of private interests, rather than through subordination to some communal ideal.

The third notion of republicanism was more egalitarian than the other two. This view was less influential because many of its proponents were illiterate or barely literate and thus wrote little to promote their beliefs. Men who advanced the third version of republicanism called for widening men's participation in the political process. They also wanted government to respond directly to the needs of ordinary folk, rejecting any notion that the "lesser sort" should automatically defer to

• *Important Events* •

1776	Second Continental Congress directs states to draft constitutions		Constitutional Convention drafts new form of government
1777	Articles of Confederation sent to states for ratification	**1788**	Hamilton, Jay, and Madison write *The Federalist* to urge ratification of the Constitution by New York
1781	Articles of Confederation ratified		Constitution ratified
1786	Annapolis Convention meets, discusses reforming government	**1794**	Defeat of Miami Confederacy at Fallen Timbers
1786–87	Shays's Rebellion in western Massachusetts raises questions about future of the republic	**1795**	Treaty of Greenville opens Ohio to white settlement
1787	Northwest Ordinance organizes territory north of Ohio River and east of Mississippi River	**1800**	Mason Locke Weems publishes his *Life of Washington*

their "betters." They were, indeed, democrats in more or less the modern sense.

Despite the differences, the three strands of republicanism shared many of the same assumptions. All three contrasted a virtuous, industrious America to the corruption of Britain and Europe. In the first version, that virtue manifested itself in frugality and self-sacrifice; in the second, it would prevent self-interest from becoming vice; in the third, it was the justification for including even propertyless free men in the ranks of voters.

As citizens of the United States set out to construct their republic, they believed they were embarking on an unprecedented enterprise. With great pride in their new nation, they expected to replace the vices of monarchical Europe with the sober virtues of republican America. They wanted to embody republican principles not only in their governments but also in their society and culture. They looked to painting, literature, drama, and architecture to convey messages of nationalism and virtue to the public.

Americans faced a crucial contradiction at the very outset of their efforts. To some republicans, the fine arts themselves were manifestations of

Virtue and the Arts

vice. What need did a frugal yeoman have for a painting, a novel, or a play? The first American artists, playwrights, and authors thus confronted an impossible dilemma. They wanted to produce works embodying virtue, but those very works were viewed by many as corrupting.

Still, they tried. William Hill Brown's *The Power of Sympathy* (1789), the first novel written in the United States, was a lurid tale of seduction intended as a warning to young women, who made up a large proportion of America's fiction readers. In Royall Tyler's *The Contrast* (1787), the first successful American play, the virtuous conduct of Colonel Manly was contrasted (hence the title) with the reprehensible behavior of the fop Billy Dimple. The most popular book of the era, Mason Locke Weems's *Life of Washington*, published in 1800 shortly after George Washington's death, was intended by its author to "hold up his great Virtues . . . to the imitation of Our Youth."

Painting and architecture, too, were expected to embody high moral standards. Two of the most prominent artists of the period, Gilbert Stuart and Charles Willson Peale, painted innumerable portraits of upstanding republican citizens. John Trumbull's vast canvases depicted milestones of American history, such as the Battle of Bunker

Hill and Cornwallis's capitulation at Yorktown. Such works were intended to instill patriotic sentiments in their viewers.

Architects likewise hoped to convey in their buildings a sense of the young republic's ideals. When the Virginia government asked Thomas Jefferson for advice on the design of the state capitol in Richmond, Jefferson unhesitatingly recommended copying a Roman building. Jefferson set forth ideals that would guide American architecture for a generation to come: simplicity of line, harmonious proportions, a feeling of grandeur. Nowhere were these rational goals of republican art manifested more clearly than in Benjamin H. Latrobe's plans for the majestic domed United States Capitol in Washington, D.C., built in the early 1800s.

Despite the artists' efforts (or, some would have said, because of them), some Americans were beginning to detect signs of luxury and corruption by the mid-1780s. The resumption of European trade after the war brought a return to fashionable clothing and abandonment of the homespun garments patriots had once worn with pride. Elite families again attended balls and concerts. Parties no longer seemed complete without gambling and cardplaying. Especially alarming to fervent republicans was the establishment in 1783 of the Society of the Cincinnati, a hereditary organization of Revolutionary War officers and their descendants. Many feared that the group would become the nucleus of a native-born aristocracy. All these developments directly challenged the United States's self-image as a virtuous republic.

Americans' deep-seated concern for the future of the infant republic focused their attention on their children, the "rising generation." Throughout the history of the colonies, education had been seen chiefly as a private means to personal advancement, of concern only to individual families. Now, though, education would serve a public purpose. If young people were to resist the temptations of vice, they would have to learn the lessons of virtue at home and at school. In fact, the very survival of the nation depended on it. The early republican

Educational Reform

period was thus a time of major educational reform.

The 1780s and 1790s brought two significant changes in American educational practice. First, in contrast to the colonies, where nearly all education had been privately financed, some northern states began to use tax money to support public elementary schools. In 1789, Massachusetts became one of the first states to require towns to offer their citizens free public elementary education.

Second, schooling for girls was improved. Americans' recognition of the importance of the rising generation led to the realization that mothers would have to be properly educated if they were to instruct their children adequately. Therefore Massachusetts insisted in its 1789 law that town elementary schools be open to girls as well as boys. Throughout the United States, private academies were founded to give teenage girls from well-to-do families an opportunity for advanced schooling. No one yet proposed opening colleges to women, but a few fortunate girls could study history, geography, rhetoric, and mathematics.

The chief theorist of women's education in the early republic was Judith Sargent Murray of Gloucester, Massachusetts. In a series of essays published in the 1780s and 1790s, Murray argued that women and men had equal intellectual capacities, that boys and girls should have equivalent scholastic training, and that girls should be taught to support themselves by their own efforts.

Judith Sargent Murray and Women's Education

Murray's educational theories were part of a general rethinking of women's position that occurred as a result of the Revolution. Male patriots who enlisted in the army or served in Congress were away from home for long periods of time. In their absence their wives, who previously had handled only the "indoor affairs" of the household, shouldered the responsibility for "outdoor affairs" as well. The shift in responsibilities caused subtle but significant change. Like other women, for example, Abigail Adams (the wife of John Adams) stopped calling their farm "yours" in letters to her husband and began referring to it as "ours." Both men and women realized that female patriots had made vital and important contributions to winning the war and that notions of proper gender roles had to be rethought. Americans began to develop new ideas about the role women should play in a republican society.

The best-known example of those new ideas is a letter Abigail Adams addressed to her husband in March 1776. "In the new Code of Laws which I

Abigail Adams: "Remember the Ladies"

suppose it will be necessary for you to make I desire you would Remember the Ladies," she wrote. "If perticuliar care and attention is not paid to the Laidies we are determined to foment a Rebelion, and will not hold ourselves bound by any Laws in which we have no voice, or Representation." With these words, Abigail Adams took a step that was soon to be duplicated by other disfranchised Americans. She deliberately applied the ideology developed to combat parliamentary supremacy to purposes revolutionary leaders had never intended.

Abigail Adams did not ask that women be allowed to vote, but others claimed that right. The men who drafted the New Jersey state constitution in 1776 defined voters carelessly as "all free inhabitants" who met certain property qualifications. They thereby unintentionally gave the vote to property-holding white spinsters and widows, as well as to free blacks. Qualified women and African-Americans regularly voted in New Jersey's local and congressional elections until 1807, when they were disfranchised by the state legislature. Yet the fact that women voted at all was evidence of their altered perception of their place in political life of the country.

Such dramatic episodes were unusual. After the war, European-Americans still viewed women in traditional terms, continuing to believe that

Women's Role in the Republic

women's primary function was to be good wives, mothers, and mistresses of households. They perceived significant differences between male and female characters. That distinction eventually enabled Americans to resolve the conflict between

the two most influential strands of republican thought. Because wives could not own property or participate directly in economic life, women in general came to be seen as the embodiment of self-sacrificing, disinterested republicanism. Through new female-run charitable associations founded after the war, better-off women assumed public responsibilities, in particular through caring for poor widows and orphaned children. Thus men were freed from the naggings of conscience as they pursued their economic self-interest (that other republican virtue), secure in the knowledge that their wives and daughters were fulfilling the family's obligation to the common good. The ideal republican man, therefore, was an individualist, seeking advancement for himself and his family. The ideal republican woman, by contrast, always put the well-being of others ahead of her own.

Together white men and women established the context for the creation of a virtuous republic. But nearly 20 percent of the American population was black. How did approximately 700,000 African-Americans fit into the developing national plan?

Emancipation and the Growth of Racism

Revolutionary ideology exposed one of the primary contradictions in American society. Both blacks and whites saw the irony in slaveholding Americans' claims that one of their aims in taking up arms was to prevent Britain from "enslaving" them. In 1773 Dr. Benjamin Rush called slavery "a vice which degrades human nature," and he warned that liberty "cannot thrive long in the neighborhood of slavery."

African-Americans did not need ideology to tell them that slavery was wrong, but they quickly took advantage of that revolutionary ideology. In 1779 a group of slaves from Portsmouth, New Hampshire, asked the state legislature "from what authority [our masters] assume to dispose of our lives, freedom and property." The same year several bondspeople in Fairfield, Connecticut, petitioned the legislature for their freedom, characterizing slavery as a "dreadful Evil" and "flagrant Injustice."

Both legislatures responded negatively, but the postwar years did witness the gradual abolition of slavery in the North. Vermont abolished slavery

Gradual Emancipation

in its 1777 constitution. Massachusetts courts decided in the 1780s that a clause in the state constitution prohibited slavery. Pennsylvania passed an abolition law in 1780; four years later Rhode Island and Connecticut provided for gradual emancipation, followed by New York (1799) and New Jersey (1804).

No southern state adopted similar general emancipation laws, but the legislatures of Virginia (1782), Delaware (1787), and Maryland (1790 and 1796) altered laws that previously had restricted slaveowners' ability to free their bondspeople. South Carolina and Georgia never considered adopting such acts, and North Carolina insisted that all manumissions (emancipations of individual slaves) be approved by county courts.

Revolutionary ideology thus had limited impact on the well-entrenched economic interests of large slaveholders. Only in the North, where slaves were relatively rare and where little money was invested in human capital, could state legislatures easily vote to abolish slavery. Even there, legislators' concern for property rights led them to favor gradual emancipation over immediate abolition. Most states provided only for the freeing of children born after passage of the law. And even those children were to remain slaves until reaching adulthood. Still, by 1840 in only one northern state— New Jersey—were African-Americans legally held in bondage.

Despite the slow progress of abolition, the number of free people of African descent in the United States grew dramatically in the first years

Growth of Free Black Population

after the Revolution. Before the war there had been few free blacks in America. But wartime disruptions radically changed the size of the freed population. Slaves who had escaped from plantations during the war, others who had served

in the American army, and still others who had been emancipated by their owners or by state laws were now free. By 1790 there were nearly 60,000 free people of color in the United States; ten years later they numbered more than 108,000, nearly 11 percent of the total African-American population.

In the 1780s and thereafter, freed people often made their way to northern port cities. Boston and Philadelphia, where slavery was abolished sooner

Migration to Northern Cities

than in New York City, were popular destinations. Women outnumbered men among the migrants by a margin of three to two. Black women found more opportunities for employment, particularly as domestic servants, in the cities than in the countryside. Some freedmen also worked in domestic service, but larger numbers were employed as unskilled laborers and seamen. A few of the women and a sizable proportion of men (nearly one-third of those in Philadelphia in 1795) were skilled workers or retailers. As soon as possible these freed people established independent two-parent nuclear families instead of continuing to live in their employers' households. They also began to occupy distinct neighborhoods, probably as the combined result of discrimination and a desire for racial solidarity.

Emancipation did not bring equality. Even whites who recognized African-Americans' right to freedom were unwilling to accept them as equals. Laws discriminated against emancipated blacks as they had against slaves. South Carolina, for example, did not permit free blacks to testify against whites in court. Public schools often refused to educate their children. Freedmen found it difficult to purchase property and find good jobs. And whites rarely allowed African-Americans an equal voice in church affairs.

Gradually, freed people developed their own institutions. In Charleston, they formed the Brown Fellowship Society, which provided insur-

Freed People's Churches and Associations

ance coverage for its members, financed a school, and helped to support orphans. In 1794, blacks in Philadelphia and Baltimore founded societies that

How do historians know that the 1780s and 1790s marked a key turning point in the history of slavery and racism in the United States? The emancipation and manumission laws adopted by state legislatures, coupled with debates in pamphlets and newspapers, are important indications of a shift in Americans' thinking. But a painting such as the one reproduced here, Liberty Displaying the Arts and Sciences, *offers a unique visual perspective on the same developments. In 1792, the Library Company of Philadelphia, a private lending library founded in the mid-eighteenth century, commissioned the artist Samuel Jennings to produce a depiction of slavery and abolitionism showing the "figure of Lib-* erty (with her Cap and proper Insignia) displaying the arts." *The library's directors reportedly were well pleased with the results. The painting, probably the first to celebrate emancipation, shows the blonde goddess presenting books (symbolizing knowledge and freedom) to several suppliant and grateful blacks, while in the background a group of former slaves dances joyfully around a liberty pole. Although the theme is abolition and the African-Americans in the foreground have realistic features, the portrayal of blacks in passive roles and diminutive sizes portends future stereotypical images. Thus the picture simultaneously linked emancipation and the growth of racism.*   The Library Company of Philadelphia.

eventually became the African Methodist Episcopal (AME) denomination. AME churches later sponsored schools in a number of cities and, along with African Baptist, African Episcopal, and African Presbyterian churches, became cultural centers of the free black community.

Such endeavors were all the more necessary because the postrevolutionary years witnessed the development of a coherent racist theory in the United States. Whites had long regarded their slaves as inferior, but the most influential writers on race attributed that inferiority to environmental rather than hereditary factors. In the Revolution's aftermath, though, white southerners needed to defend their enslavement of other human beings against the notion that "all men are created equal." Consequently, they began to argue that blacks were less than fully human and that the principles of republican equality applied only to whites.

Development of Racist Theory

This racism had several intertwined elements. First was the assertion that, as Thomas Jefferson suggested in 1781, blacks were "inferior to the whites in the endowments both of body and mind." Then came the belief that blacks were congenitally lazy, dishonest, and uncivilized (or uncivilizable). Third, and of crucial importance, was the notion that all blacks were sexually promiscuous and that black men lusted after white women. The specter of sexual intercourse between black men and white women haunted early American racist thought. Significantly, the more common sexual exploitation of enslaved black women by their white masters aroused little comment.

African-Americans did not allow these developing racist notions to go unchallenged. Benjamin Banneker, a free black surveyor, astronomer, and mathematical genius, directly disputed Thomas Jefferson's belief in blacks' intellectual inferiority. In 1791 Banneker sent Jefferson a copy of his latest almanac (which included his astronomical calculations) as an example of blacks' mental powers. Jefferson's response admitted Banneker's capability but indicated that he regarded Banneker as an exception.

At its birth, then, the republic was defined by its leaders as an exclusively white enterprise. Indeed, some historians have argued that the subjugation of blacks was a necessary precondition for equality among whites. They have pointed out that identifying a common racial antagonist helped to create white solidarity and to lessen the threat to gentry power posed by the enfranchisement of poorer whites. Some have asserted that it was less dangerous to allow whites with little property to participate formally in politics than to open the possibility that they might join with former slaves to question the rule of the "better sort." That was perhaps one reason why after the Revolution the division of American society between slave and free was transformed into a division between blacks—some of whom were free—and whites. The wielders of power ensured their continued dominance in part by substituting race for enslavement as the primary determinant of African-Americans' status.

A Republic for Whites Only

Designing Republican Governments

In May 1776 the Second Continental Congress directed states to devise new republican governments to replace the provincial congresses and committees that had met since 1774. Thus Americans initially concentrated on drafting state constitutions and devoted little attention to their national government.

They first faced the problem of defining just what a constitution is. The British Constitution could not serve as a model because it was a mixture of law and custom; Americans wanted tangible documents specifying the fundamental structures of government. Several years passed before states concluded that their constitutions could not be drafted by regular legislative bodies. Following the lead established by Vermont in 1777 and Massachusetts in 1780, they began to call conventions for the sole purpose

Drafting of State Constitutions

of drafting constitutions. Thus states sought direct authorization from the people—the theoretical sovereigns in a republic—before establishing new governments. After preparing new constitutions, delegates submitted them to voters for ratification.

The framers of state constitutions concerned themselves primarily with outlining the distribution of and limitations on government power. Because of their experiences under British rule, Americans had learned to fear the power of the governor—usually, the appointed agent of king or proprietor—and to see the legislature as their defender. Accordingly, the first state constitutions typically provided for the governor to be elected annually (commonly by the legislature), limited the number of terms he could serve, and gave him little independent authority. Simultaneously, the constitutions expanded the legislature's powers. Every state except Pennsylvania and Vermont retained a two-house structure, with members of the upper house having longer terms and being required to meet higher property-holding standards than members of the lower house. But they also redrew electoral districts to reflect population patterns more accurately, and they increased the number of members in both houses. Finally, most states lowered property qualifications for voting. Thus the revolutionary era witnessed the first deliberate attempt to broaden the base of American government.

The constitutions also contained provisions, including explicit limitations on government power, to protect the people from those who would misuse power. Seven of the con-

Limits on State Governments

stitutions contained formal bills of rights, and the others had similar clauses. Most guaranteed citizens freedom of the press and of religion, the right to a fair trial, the right of consent to taxation, and protection against general search warrants. An independent judiciary was charged with upholding such rights.

In sum, the constitution makers put far greater emphasis on preventing state governments from becoming tyrannical than on making them effective wielders of political authority. Their approach to shaping governments was understandable, given the American experience with Great Britain. But establishing such weak political units, especially in wartime, practically ensured that the constitutions soon would need revision.

When Americans realized that legislative supremacy did not in itself guarantee good government, they attempted to achieve that goal by balancing the powers of the legislative, executive, and judicial branches against one another.

The constitutional theories that Americans applied at the state level did not at first influence their conception of national government. Since American political leaders had little time to devote to legitimizing their de facto government while organizing the military struggle against Britain, the powers and structure of the Continental Congress evolved by default early in the war. Not until late 1777 did Congress send the Articles of Confederation to the states for ratification.

The chief organ of national government was a unicameral (one-house) legislature in which each state had one vote. Its powers included conduct-

Articles of Confederation

ing foreign relations, settling disputes between states, controlling maritime affairs, regulating Indian trade, and valuing state and national coinage. The Articles did not give the national government the ability to raise revenue effectively or to enforce a uniform commercial policy. The United States of America was described as "a firm league of friendship" in which each state "retains its sovereignty, freedom and independence, and every Power, Jurisdiction and right, which is not by this confederation expressly delegated to the United States, in Congress assembled."

The Articles required the unanimous consent of the state legislatures for ratification or amendment, and a clause concerning western lands proved troublesome. The draft accepted by Congress allowed states to retain all land claims derived from their original colonial charters. Because Maryland feared being overpowered by states that would grow in size and power through western land claims, it refused to accept the Articles until 1781, when Virginia finally promised to surrender its western holdings to national jurisdiction. Other states followed suit, establishing the principle that unorganized lands would be held by the nation as a whole.

The capacity of a single state to delay ratification for three years was a portent of the fate of American government under the Articles of Confederation. The Articles' authors had not given adequate thought to the distribution of power within the national government or to the relationship between the Confederation and the states. The Congress they created was simultaneously a legislative body and a collective executive, but it had no independent income and no authority to compel the states to accept its rulings. What is surprising is not how poorly the Confederation functioned but rather how much the government was able to accomplish.

Trials of the Confederation

The most persistent problem faced by the American governments, state and national, was finance. Because of a reluctance to levy taxes, both Con-

Financial Problems

gress and the states tried to finance the war by printing currency. Even though the money was backed by nothing but good faith, it circulated freely and without excessive depreciation during 1775 and most of 1776. But in late 1776, as the American army suffered reverses in New York and New Jersey, prices began to rise and inflation set in. The currency's value rested on Americans' faith in their government, a faith that was sorely tested in the years that followed. By early 1780 it took forty paper dollars to purchase one silver dollar. Soon, Continental currency was worthless.

In 1781, faced with total collapse of the monetary system, the congressmen undertook ambitious reforms. After establishing a department of finance under the wealthy Philadelphia merchant Robert Morris, they asked the states to amend the Articles of Confederation to allow Congress to levy a duty of 5 percent on imported goods. Morris put national finances on a solid footing, but the customs duty was never adopted. First Rhode Island and then New York refused to agree to the

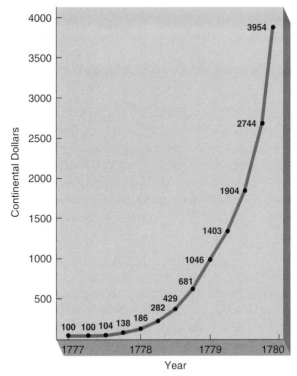

Depreciation of Continental Currency, 1777–1780

Depreciation of Continental Currency, 1777–1780 *The depreciation of Continental currency accelerated in 1778, as is shown in this graph measuring its value against one hundred silver dollars. Thereafter, its value dropped almost daily.* Source: Data from John J. McCusker, "How Much Is That in Real Money? A Historical Price Index for Use as a Deflator of Money Values in the Economy of the United States," *Proceedings of the American Antiquarian Society,* Vol. 101, Pt. 2 (1991), Table C-1.

tax. The states' resistance reflected fear of a too-powerful central government.

Congress also faced major diplomatic problems at the close of the war. Chief among them were issues involving the peace treaty itself. Article 4, which promised the repayment of prewar debts (most

Weakness in Foreign Affairs and Commerce

of them owed by Americans to British merchants), and Article 5, which recommended that states allow loyalists to recover their confiscated property, aroused considerable opposition. States passed laws denying British subjects the right to sue for recovery of debts or property in American courts. Since most purchasers of confiscated loyalist property had been prominent patriots, states had no desire to enforce Article 5.

The refusal of state and local governments to comply with Articles 4 and 5 gave Britain an excuse to maintain military posts on the Great Lakes long after its troops were supposed to have withdrawn. Furthermore, Congress's inability to convince states to implement the treaty pointed up its lack of power. Concerned nationalists argued publicly that enforcement of the treaty, however unpopular, was a crucial test for the republic. "Will foreign nations be willing to undertake anything with us or for us," asked Alexander Hamilton, "when they find that the nature of our governments will allow no dependence to be placed on our engagements?"

Congress's weakness was especially evident in the realm of trade because the Articles of Confederation denied it the power to establish a national commercial policy. Immediately after the war, Britain, France, and Spain all restricted American trade with their colonies. Americans watched helplessly as British manufactured goods flooded the United States while American produce could no longer be sold in the British West Indies. Although Americans reopened commerce with other European countries and started a profitable trade with China in 1784, neither substituted for access to closer and larger markets.

Congress also had difficulty dealing with the threat posed by Spain's presence on the nation's southern and western borders. Determined to prevent the republic's expansion, Spain in 1784 closed the Mississippi River to American navigation. It thus deprived the growing settlements west of the Appalachians of their major access route to the rest of the nation and the world. Congress opened negotiations with Spain in 1785, but even John Jay, one of the nation's most experienced diplomats, could not win the necessary concessions on navigation. The talks collapsed the fol-

Failed Negotiations with Spain

lowing year after Congress divided sharply on the question of whether agreement should be sought on other issues. Southerners, voting as a bloc, insisted on navigation rights on the Mississippi; northerners were willing to abandon that claim in order to win commercial concessions.

Diplomatic problems of another sort confronted congressmen when they considered the status of land beyond the Appalachians. Although tribal claims were not discussed by British and American diplomats, the United States assumed that the Treaty of Paris (1783) cleared its title to all land east of the Mississippi except the area still held by Spain. But recognizing that some sort of land cession should be obtained from the most powerful tribes, Congress initiated negotiations with both northern and southern Indians (see map, page 130). At Fort Stanwix, New York, in 1784, and at Hopewell, South Carolina, in late 1785 and early 1786, American diplomats signed separate treaties with chiefs purporting to represent the Iroquois and with emissaries from the Choctaw, Chickasaw, and Cherokee nations. Later, all four groups denied that the men who agreed to the treaties had been authorized to speak for them. But the United States still took the treaties as confirmation of its sovereignty over the territories in question. European-Americans soon poured over the southern Appalachians, provoking the Creeks—who had not agreed to the Hopewell treaties—to defend their territory by declaring war. Only in 1790 did they come to terms with the United States.

Encroachment on Indian Lands

In 1786 the Iroquois Confederacy repudiated the Fort Stanwix treaty and threatened new attacks on frontier settlements, but everyone knew the threat was empty. The flawed treaty stood by default. By 1790 the once-dominant confederacy was confined to a few scattered reservations.

Led by a remarkable prophet, Handsome Lake, the Iroquois sought to adapt to their new circumstances by embracing the traditional values of their culture and renouncing drinking alcohol, gambling, and other destructive European customs. Yet simultaneously,

Handsome Lake's Reforms

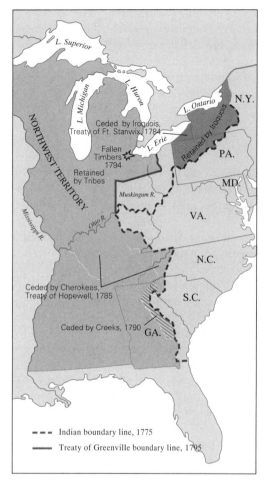

Cession of Tribal Lands to the United States,
1775–1790 *The land claims of the United States*
meant little as long as Indian nations still controlled vast
territories within the new country's formal boundaries.
A series of treaties in the 1780s and 1790s opened some
lands to white settlement.   Source: From Lester J. Cappon
et al., eds., *Atlas of Early American History: The Revolutionary Era,*
1760–1790. Copyright ©1976 by Princeton University Press,
Reprinted by permission of Princeton University Press.

with Handsome Lake's approval, Quaker missionaries taught the Iroquois Anglo-American styles of
agricultural subsistence. Men were now to be cultivators rather than hunters—since their hunting
territories were lost—and women to be house-
keepers rather than cultivators. Paradoxically, only
by adopting a sexual division of labor that had

originated in Europe could the Iroquois maintain
a semblance of their culture.

Western nations such as the Shawnees, Chippewas, Ottawas, and Potawatomis formed a new
confederacy, hoping to present a united front
and avoid the piecemeal sur-
render of land by individual
tribes. They demanded direct
negotiations with the United
States, but Congress ignored
them. Congress then began to organize the
Northwest Territory, bounded by the Mississippi
River, the Great Lakes, and the Ohio River (see
map). Ordinances passed in 1784, 1785, and 1787
outlined the process through which the land could
be sold to settlers and formal governments could
be organized.

**Northwest
Ordinances**

To ensure orderly development, Congress in
1785 directed that the land be surveyed into town-
ships 6 miles square, each divided into thirty-six
sections of 640 acres (1 square mile). Revenue
from the sale of the sixteenth section of each township was to be reserved for the support of public
schools—the first instance of federal aid to education in American history. The minimum price per
acre was set at one dollar, and the minimum sale
was one section. The minimum outlay of $640 was
beyond the reach of ordinary Americans. Proceeds
from land sales were the first independent revenues available to the national government.

The most important ordinance was the third,
passed in 1787. The Northwest Ordinance contained a bill of rights guaranteeing settlers freedom of religion and the right to a jury trial,
forbidding cruel and unusual punishments, and
nominally prohibiting slavery. The prohibition
had little immediate effect. Some residents of the
territory already held slaves, and Congress did not
intend to deprive them of their property. Moreover, the ordinance also contained a provision allowing slaveowners to "lawfully reclaim" runaway
bondspeople who took refuge in the territory—
the first national fugitive slave law. Still, the ordinance prevented slavery from taking deep root by
discouraging slaveholders from moving into the
territory with their human chattel, but not until
1848 was enslavement abolished throughout the
region, now known as the Old Northwest.

The ordinance also specified the process by which residents of the territory could organize state governments and seek admission to the Union "on an equal footing with the original States." Early in the nation's history, therefore, Congress laid down a policy of admitting new states on the same basis as the old and assuring residents of the territories the same rights held by citizens of the original states.

In a sense, the Northwest Ordinance was purely theoretical at the time it was passed. The Miamis, Shawnees, and Delawares refused to acknowledge American sovereignty. In 1788 the Ohio Company, to which Congress had sold a large tract of land at reduced rates, established the town of Marietta at the juncture of the Ohio and Muskingum Rivers. But Indians prevented the company from extending settlement very far into the interior. After General Arthur St. Clair, the Northwest Territory's first governor, failed to negotiate a meaningful treaty with the tribes in early 1789, it was apparent that the United States would clash with the Miami-led western confederacy.

Little Turtle, the able war chief of the Miami Confederacy, defeated first General Josiah Harmar (1790) and then St. Clair himself (1791) in major battles near the present border between Indiana and Ohio. More than six hundred of St. Clair's men were killed and scores more wounded; it was the whites' worst defeat in the entire history of the American frontier. In 1793 the Miami Confederacy declared that peace could be achieved only if the United States recognized the Ohio River as its northwestern boundary. But the national government refused to relinquish its claim in the region. A new army under the command of General Anthony Wayne, a Revolutionary War hero, attacked and defeated the confederacy in August 1794 at the Battle of Fallen Timbers. Peace negotiations began after the victory.

War in the Old Northwest

The Treaty of Greenville (1795) gave each side a portion of what it wanted. The United States gained the right to settle much of what was to become the state of Ohio, the tribes retaining only the northwest corner of the region. Indians,

though, received the acknowledgment they had long sought: American recognition of their rights to the soil. At Greenville, the United States formally accepted the principle of Indian sovereignty, by virtue of residence, over all lands the tribes had not ceded. Never again would the United States government claim that it had acquired Indian territory solely through negotiation with a European or North American country.

The problems the United States encountered in ensuring safe settlement of the Northwest Territory pointed up the basic weakness of the Confederation government. Not until after the Articles of Confederation were replaced with a new constitution could the United States muster sufficient force to implement the Northwest Ordinance.

From Crisis to the Constitution

The most obvious inadequacies of the Articles of Confederation concerned finance, overseas trade, and foreign affairs. Congress could not levy taxes, nor could it impose its will on the states to establish a uniform commercial policy or to ensure the enforcement of treaties. The problems involving trade were particularly serious. Less than a year after the war's end, the American economy slid into a depression. The postwar restrictions that European powers imposed on American commerce hurt exporters of such staple crops as rice and tobacco. Although some of the restrictions were eased and recovery began by 1786, the war's effects proved impossible to erase entirely.

The war had permanently changed the American economy. The near total cessation of foreign commerce in nonmilitary items during the war years stimulated domestic manufacturing. Consequently, despite the influx of European goods after 1783, the postwar period witnessed the stirrings of American industrial development. For example, the first American textile mill began production in Pawtucket, Rhode Island, in 1793. Moreover, foreign trade patterns shifted from Europe and toward the West Indies. Foodstuffs shipped to the

Economic Change

French and Dutch Caribbean islands became America's largest single export.

Recognizing the Confederation Congress's inability to deal with commercial matters, Virginia invited the other states to a convention at Annapolis, Maryland, to discuss trade policy. Although eight states named representatives to the meeting in September 1786, only five delegations attended. Those present realized that they were too few in number to have any real impact on the political system. They issued a call for another convention, to be held in Philadelphia nine months later, "to devise such further provisions as shall . . . appear necessary to render the constitution of the federal government adequate to the exigencies of the Union." The other states did not respond immediately, but then Shays's Rebellion occurred.

Annapolis Convention

The reaction to the rebellion hastened the movement toward comprehensive revision of the Articles. After most of the states had already appointed delegates, the Confederation Congress belatedly endorsed the convention. In mid-May 1787, fifty-five men, representing all the states but Rhode Island, assembled in Philadelphia to begin their deliberations.

The vast majority of delegates to the Constitutional Convention were men of property and substance. Among their number were merchants, planters, physicians, generals, governors, and especially lawyers. Most had been born in America. In an era when only a tiny proportion of the population had any advanced education, more than half of the delegates had attended college. A few had been educated in Britain, but most were graduates of American institutions. The youngest delegate was twenty-six, the oldest—Benjamin Franklin—eighty-one. Like George Washington, whom they elected their presiding officer, most were in their vigorous middle years. A dozen men did the bulk of the convention's work. Of these, James Madison of Virginia was by far the most important; he truly deserves the title "Father of the Constitution."

Constitutional Convention in Philadelphia

Madison was unique among the delegates in his systematic preparation for the Philadelphia meeting. He bought more than two hundred books on history and government, carefully analyzing their accounts of past confederacies and republics. A month before the Constitutional Convention began, he summed up the results of his research in a lengthy paper entitled "Vices of the Political System of the United States." In this paper, Madison set forth the principle of checks and balances. The government, he believed, had to be constructed in such a way that it could not become tyrannical or fall wholly under the influence of a particular interest group. He regarded the large size of a potential national republic as an advantage in that respect. Rejecting the common assertion that republics had to be small, Madison argued that a large, diverse republic should be preferred. Because the nation would include many different interest groups, no one of them would be able to control the government. Political stability would result from compromises among the contending parties.

James Madison: Father of the Constitution

Madison's conception of national government was embodied in the so-called Virginia Plan, introduced on May 29 by his fellow Virginian Edmund Randolph. The plan provided for a two-house legislature, the lower house elected directly by the people and the upper house selected by the lower; proportional representation in both houses; an executive elected by Congress; a national judiciary; and congressional veto over state laws. The Virginia Plan gave Congress the broad power to legislate "in all cases to which the separate states are incompetent." Had it been adopted intact, it would have created a government in which national authority reigned unchallenged and state power was greatly diminished. Proportional representation in both houses would also have given large states a dominant voice in the national government.

Virginia and New Jersey Plans

The convention included many delegates who recognized the need for change but believed the

Virginians had gone too far in the direction of national consolidation. The disaffected delegates united under the leadership of William Paterson of New Jersey, who presented an alternative scheme—the New Jersey Plan, calling for modifying the Articles rather than completely overhauling the government. Paterson proposed retaining a unicameral congress but giving it new powers of taxation and trade regulation. Although the convention initially rejected Paterson's position, he and his allies won a number of victories in the months that followed.

The delegates began their work by discussing the structure and functions of Congress. They readily agreed that the new national government should have a two-house (bicameral) legislature. But they proposed different answers to three key questions: Should representation in both houses of Congress be proportional to population? How was representation in either or both houses to be apportioned among the states? And, finally, how were the members of the two houses to be elected?

The Debates: Houses of Congress

The last issue was the easiest to resolve. To quote John Dickinson, the delegates thought it "essential" that members of the lower branch of Congress be elected directly by the people and "expedient" that members of the upper house be chosen by state legislatures. Since legislatures had selected delegates to the Confederation Congress, they would expect a similar privilege in the new government.

Considerably more difficult was the matter of proportional representation in the Senate. The delegates accepted without much debate the principle of proportional representation in the lower house. But small states argued for equal representation in the Senate, while large states supported a proportional plan for the upper house. For weeks the convention deadlocked on the issue. A committee appointed to work out a compromise recommended equal representation in the Senate, coupled with a proviso that all appropriation bills originate in the lower house. But not until the convention accepted a suggestion that a state's two

senators vote as individuals rather than as a unit was a breakdown averted.

One critical question remained: how was representation in the lower house to be apportioned among states? Delegates from states with large numbers of slaves wanted African and European inhabitants to be counted equally; delegates from states with few slaves wanted only free people to be counted. Delegates resolved the dispute by using a formula developed by the Confederation Congress in 1783 to allocate financial assessments among states: three-fifths of slaves would be included in population totals. (The formula reflected delegates' judgment that slaves were less efficient producers of wealth than free people, not that they were 60 percent human and 40 percent property.) The three-fifths compromise on representation won unanimous approval.

The Debates: Slavery and Representation

Although the words *slave* and *slavery* do not appear in the Constitution (the framers used euphemisms such as *other persons*), direct and indirect protections for slavery were deeply embedded in the document. The three-fifths clause, for example, assured white southern voters not only congressional representation out of proportion to their numbers but also a disproportionate influence on the selection of the president, since the number of each state's electoral votes was determined by the size of its congressional delegation. Congress was prevented from outlawing the slave trade for at least twenty years. By guaranteeing that the national government would aid any states threatened with "domestic violence," the Constitution promised aid in putting down future slave revolts.

Constitutional Protections for Slavery

Once agreement was reached on the problems of slavery and representation, the delegates readily achieved consensus on the other issues confronting them. All agreed that the national government needed the authority to tax and to regulate commerce. And while the delegates enumerated congressional powers, they then provided for flexibility by granting all authority "necessary and proper" to carry out those powers. Foreign policy was placed in the hands of the executive, who was also made commander-in-chief of the armed forces. Moreover, the Constitution plus national laws and treaties would constitute "the supreme law of the land; and the judges in every state shall be bound thereby." As another means of circumscribing state powers, the delegates drafted a long list of actions forbidden to the states—such as "impair[ing] the obligation of contracts." Finally, the delegates established the electoral college and a four-year term for the chief executive, who could seek reelection.

Separation of Powers

The key to the Constitution was the distribution of political authority—separation of powers among executive, legislative, and judicial branches of the national government, and division of powers between states and nation. The system of checks and balances would make it difficult for the government to become tyrannical. At the same time, though, the elaborate system would sometimes prevent the government from acting quickly and decisively. Furthermore, the line between state and national powers was ambiguously and vaguely drawn.

The convention held its last session on September 17, 1787. Of the forty-two delegates present, only three refused to sign the Constitution. (Two of the three declined in part because of the lack of a bill of rights.) Though the delegates had accepted the Constitution, another question remained: would the states ratify it?

Opposition and Ratification

The ratification clause provided for the new system to take effect once it was approved by special conventions in at least nine states, with delegates being elected by qualified voters. Thus the national Constitution, unlike the Articles of Confederation, would rest directly on popular authority.

As states began to elect delegates to the special conventions, discussion of the proposed government grew more heated. Federalists (sup-

THE FEDERAL ALMANACK.

FEDERAL HALL.

LET Trumpets found, and fwift wing'd Fame,
Thefe glorious tidings far proclaim ;
On Virtue's bafe, by Wifdom plann'd ;
And rear'd by Union's facred hand ;
The FEDERAL DOME, is rais'd fublime :
Its PILLARS folid, ftrong as time ;
Rife ! Commerce ! rife ! unfurl the fail,
Rich Golden harvefts blefs the vale :
Arts & Science ! Genius ! fpring to light ;
And Freedom burft on realms of Night

The Federal Almanack for 1789 trumpeted the virtues of the new Constitution. Not all Americans were so certain that the national government, here symbolized as an edifice supported by thirteen pillars, was as "solid, strong as time" as the printer proclaimed. American Antiquarian Society.

porters of the Constitution) and Antifederalists (its opponents) published newspaper essays and pamphlets vigorously defending or attacking the convention's decisions. The extent of the debate was unprecedented, and it quickly became apparent that the disputes within the Constitutional

Convention had been mild compared with divisions of opinion within the populace as a whole.

Federalists claimed that the nation did not need to fear centralized authority when good men were in charge and that the carefully structured

Federalists

government would preclude the possibility of tyranny. A republic could be large, they declared, if the government was designed to prevent any one group from controlling it. The separation of powers among legislative, executive, and judicial branches, and the division of powers between states and nation, would accomplish that goal. Thus people did not need to be protected from the powers of the new government in a formal way.

Antifederalists feared a too-powerful central government, although they recognized the need for a national source of revenue. They saw the

Antifederalists

states as the chief protectors of individual rights; consequently, their weakening could bring the onset of arbitrary power. Antifederalist arguments against the Constitution often consisted of lists of potential abuses of government authority.

Heirs of the Real Whig ideology of the late 1760s and early 1770s, Antifederalists stressed the need for constant popular vigilance to avert oppression. Indeed, some of the Antifederalists were the very men who originally promulgated those ideas—Samuel Adams, Patrick Henry, and Richard Henry Lee were leaders of the opposition to the Constitution. The Antifederalist ranks were also peopled by small farmers, who were preoccupied with guarding their property against excessive taxation, and by ambitious, upwardly mobile men who would gain more from an economic and political system less tightly controlled than the one the Constitution promised to establish.

As public debate continued, Antifederalists focused on the Constitution's lack of a bill of rights. Even if states were weakened by the new system,

Importance of a Bill of Rights

they believed, people could still be protected from tyranny if their rights were specifically guaranteed. *Letters of a Federal Farmer,* perhaps the most

widely read Antifederalist pamphlet, listed the rights that should be protected: freedom of the press and of religion, the right to trial by jury, and guarantees against unreasonable search warrants. America's minister to France, Thomas Jefferson, was also concerned over "the omission of a bill of rights."

As state conventions met to consider ratification, the lack of a bill of rights loomed ever larger as a flaw in the proposed government. Four of the

Ratification of the Constitution

first five states to ratify did so unanimously, but serious disagreements then surfaced. Massachusetts, in which Antifederalist forces had been bolstered by a backlash against the state government's heavy-handed treatment of the Shays rebels, ratified by a majority of only 19 votes out of 355 cast. In June 1788, when New Hampshire ratified, the requirement of nine states was satisfied. But New York and Virginia had not yet voted, and everyone realized the new Constitution could not succeed unless those key states accepted it.

Despite a valiant effort by the Antifederalist Patrick Henry, pro-Constitution forces won by 10 votes in the Virginia convention. In New York, James Madison, John Jay, and Alexander Hamilton campaigned for ratification by publishing *The Federalist,* a political tract that explained the theory behind the Constitution and masterfully answered its critics. Their reasoned arguments, coupled with Federalists' promise to add a bill of rights to the Constitution, helped win the battle. On July 26, 1788, New York ratified the Constitution by the slim margin of 3 votes. Although the last state (Rhode Island) did not formally join the Union until 1790, the new government was a reality.

 Conclusion

During the 1770s and 1780s the nation took shape as a political union. It began to develop an economy independent of the British Empire, and it designed a foreign policy that attempted to chart its own course in the world in order to protect the national interests. An integral part of the formation of the Union was the systematic formulation of American racist thought. Emphasizing race as a determinant of African-Americans' standing in the nation allowed white men to define republicanism to exclude all people but themselves and thus ensure their control of the country.

The experience of fighting a war and of struggling for survival as an independent nation altered the political context of American life in the 1780s. At the outset of the war, most politically aware Americans believed that "that government which governs best governs least," but by the late 1780s many had changed their minds. These were the drafters and supporters of the Constitution.

Suggestions for Further Reading

General

Richard Beeman et al., eds., *Beyond Confederation: Origins of the Constitution and American National Identity* (1987); Joseph M. Ellis, *After the Revolution: Profiles of Early American Culture* (1979); Ronald Hoffman et al., eds., *The Economy of Early America: The Revolutionary Period, 1763–1790* (1988); Cathy Matson and Peter S. Onuf, *A Union of Interests: Political and Economic Thought in Revolutionary America* (1990); Kenneth Silverman, *A Cultural History of the American Revolution* (1976); Gordon S. Wood, *The Radicalism of the American Revolution* (1992); Gordon S. Wood, *The Creation of the American Republic, 1776–1787* (1969); Alfred F. Young et al, eds., *We the People: Voices and Images of the New Nation* (1993).

Continental Congress and Articles of Confederation

E. James Ferguson, *The Power of the Purse: A History of American Public Finance, 1776–1790* (1961); H. James Henderson, *Party Politics in the Continental Congress* (1974); Merrill Jensen, *The New Nation: A History of the United States During the Confederation, 1781–1789* (1950); Richard B. Morris, *The Forging of the Union, 1781–1789* (1987); Peter S. Onuf, *Statehood and Union: A History of the Northwest Ordinance* (1987); Jack N. Rakove, *The Beginnings of National Politics: An Interpretive History of the Continental Congress* (1979).

State Politics

Willi Paul Adams, *The First American Constitutions: Republican Ideology and the Making of the State Constitutions in the Revolutionary Era* (1980); Robert Gross, ed., *In Debt to Shays* (1992); Ronald Hoffman and Peter Albert, eds., *Sovereign States in an Age of Uncertainty* (1981); Jackson Turner Main, *The Sovereign States, 1775–1783* (1973); David P. Szatmary, *Shays' Rebellion: The Making of an Agrarian Insurrection* (1980).

The Constitution

Thornton Anderson, *Creating the Constitution: The Convention of 1787 and the First Congress* (1993); Lance Banning, *The Sacred Fire of Liberty: James Madison and the Founding of the Federal Republic* (1995); Roger H. Brown, *Redeeming the Republic: Federalists, Taxation, and the Origins of the Constitution* (1993); Christopher Duncan, *The Anti-Federalists and Early American Political Thought* (1995); Frederick W. Marks III, *Independence on Trial: Foreign Affairs and the Making of the Constitution* (1973); Jack N. Rakove, *Original Meanings: Politics and Ideas in the Making of the Constitution* (1996); Robert A. Rutland, *The Ordeal of the Constitution: The Antifederalists and the Ratification Struggle of 1787–88* (1966); Abraham Sofaer, *War, Foreign Affairs, and Constitutional Power,* vol. 1, *The Origins* (1976).

Women

Edith Gelles, *Portia: The World of Abigail Adams* (1992); Susan Juster, *Disorderly Women: Sexual Politics and Evangelicalism in Revolutionary New England* (1994); Linda K. Kerber, *Women of the Republic: Intellect and Ideology in Revolutionary America* (1980); Mary Beth Norton, *Liberty's Daughters: The Revolutionary Experience of American Women, 1750–1800* (1980); Rosemarie Zagarri, *A Woman's Dilemma: Mercy Otis Warren and the American Revolution* (1995).

African-Americans and Slavery

Ira Berlin and Ronald Hoffman, eds., *Slavery and Freedom in the Age of the American Revolution* (1983); David Brion Davis, *The Problem of Slavery in the Age of Revolution, 1770–1823* (1975); Paul Finkelman, *Slavery and the Founders: Race and Liberty in the Age of Jefferson* (1996); Duncan J. Macleod, *Slavery, Race, and the American Revolution* (1974); Gary Nash, *Forging Freedom: The Formation of Philadelphia's Black Community, 1720–1840* (1988); Donald L. Robinson, *Slavery in the Structure of American Politics, 1765–1820* (1971); Shane White, *Somewhat More Independent: The End of Slavery in New York City, 1770–1810* (1991); Arthur Zilversmit, *The First Emancipation: The Abolition of Slavery in the North* (1967).

Indians

Harvey L. Carter, *The Life and Times of Little Turtle* (1987); Gregory E. Dowd, *A Spirited Resistance: The North American Indian Struggle for Unity, 1745–1815* (1992); Francis Paul Prucha, *American Indian Policy in the Formative Years: The Indian Trade and Intercourse Acts, 1790–1834* (1962); Wiley Sword, *President Washington's Indian War: The Struggle for the Old Northwest, 1790–1795* (1985); Anthony F. C. Wallace, *The Death and Rebirth of the Seneca* (1969).

8

Politics and Society
in the Early Republic
1789 – 1800

"$\mathbf{S}$hall I commence my journal, my dear Elizabeth, with a description of the pain I felt at taking leave of all my friends, or shall I leave you to imagine?" wrote Margaret Dwight as she began a chronicle of her arduous journey from New Haven, Connecticut, to Warren, Ohio. An orphan at age twenty, Margaret was traveling west to live with relatives. She filled her pages with comments on poor roads, dirty taverns, profane wagoneers, troublesome fellow travelers, and brawling "dutchmen" (Germans), whose failure to observe the Sabbath disgusted her. Margaret also noticed differences in English usage: "The people here talk curiously, they all reckon instead of expect—Youns is a word I have heard used several times, but what it means I don't know."

Many people she encountered assumed that Margaret was moving west to find a husband. But Margaret resisted, writing that she was "determin'd not to oblige myself to spend my days there, by marrying should I even have an opport[unit]y." At the end of her trip Margaret found Warren "pleasanter than I expected." About a year later, she married William Bell, a local merchant who soon relocated to Pittsburgh. Eventually, she gave birth to eight children in the West she had disdained.

Margaret Dwight was just one of the many thousand people who moved west in the decades following the Revolution. Their mobility signaled the beginnings of a new age, as large numbers of European-Americans and African-Americans poured through the Appalachian

Mountains for the first time. North of the Ohio River (Margaret's destination), the strength of the Miami Confederacy blocked westward expansion until after the Treaty of Greenville in 1795. South of the river, western settlements appeared as early as the 1770s, but they were isolated from the Atlantic coast by the long chain of mountains.

The dispersal of the population was accompanied by political fragmentation and economic difficulties. The United States economy still depended on the export trade. When warfare between England and France resumed in 1793, Americans found their commerce disrupted yet again. And the fight over the Constitution presaged an even wider division over the major political, economic, and diplomatic questions confronting the young republic.

Believing that the Constitution would resolve the problems that had arisen during the Confederation period, Americans did not anticipate the political disagreements that would characterize the 1790s. Moreover, they could not understand or fully accept the division of America's political leaders into two factions—not yet political parties—known as Federalists and Republicans, because in republics factions were seen as signs of decay and corruption. As the decade closed with the first fully partisan presidential election, Americans still had not come to terms with the implications of partisan politics.

Building a Workable Government

Americans in many cities celebrated the ratification of the Constitution with a series of parades on July 4, 1788. The processions were carefully

Celebrating Ratification

planned to symbolize the unity of the new nation. Like prerevolutionary protest meetings, the parades served as political lessons for literate and illiterate Americans alike. Men and women who could not read were thereby educated about the significance of the new Constitution for the nation.

They also were instructed about political leaders' hopes for industry and frugality on the part of a virtuous American public.

The nationalistic spirit expressed in the ratification processions carried over to the first session of Congress. Only a few Antifederalists ran for office in the congressional elec-

Nationalism in the First Congress

tions held late in 1788, and even fewer were elected. Thus the First Congress consisted chiefly of men who supported a strong national government. The drafters of the Constitution had deliberately left many key issues undecided, so the nationalists' domination of Congress meant that their views on those points quickly prevailed.

Congress faced four immediate tasks when it convened in April 1789: raising revenue to support the new government, responding to state ratification conventions' call for a bill of rights, setting up executive departments, and organizing the federal judiciary. The last task was especially important. The Constitution established a Supreme Court but left it to Congress to decide whether to have other federal courts as well.

James Madison, who had been elected to the House of Representatives, soon became as influential in Congress as he had been at the Constitutional Convention. A few months into the first session, he persuaded Congress to adopt the Revenue Act of 1789, imposing a 5 percent tariff on certain imports. Thus the First Congress quickly achieved what the Confederation Congress never had: an effective national tax law. The new government would have problems in its first years, but lack of revenue was not one of them.

Madison also took the lead on the issue of constitutional amendments. He placed nineteen proposed amendments before the House. Eventu-

Bill of Rights

ally, the states ratified ten, which officially became part of the Constitution on December 15, 1791 (see the Appendix for the Constitution and all amendments). Their adoption defused Antifederalist opposition and rallied support for the new government. The First Amendment specifically prohibited Congress

• *Important Events* •

1789	George Washington inaugurated as first president
	Judiciary Act of 1789 organizes federal court system
	French Revolution begins
1790	Alexander Hamilton's *Report on Public Credit* proposes assumption of state debts
1791	First ten amendments (Bill of Rights) ratified
1793	France declares war on Britain, Spain, and Holland
	Washington's neutrality proclamation keeps the United States out of the war
	Democratic-Republican societies founded, the first grassroots political organizations
1794	Whiskey Rebellion in western Pennsylvania protests taxation
1795	Jay Treaty with England
1796	First contested presidential election: John Adams elected president, Thomas Jefferson vice president
1798	XYZ affair arouses American opinion against France
	Alien and Sedition Acts punish political dissenters
	Virginia and Kentucky resolutions protest suppression of dissent
1798–99	Quasi-War with France
1800	Franco-American Convention ends the Quasi-War
	Jefferson elected president, Aaron Burr vice president
	Gabriel's Rebellion threatens slaveholders
1801	Second Great Awakening sweeps through Kentucky

from passing any law restricting the right to freedom of religion, speech, press, peaceable assembly, or petition. The next two amendments arose directly from the former colonists' fear of standing armies as a threat to freedom. The Second Amendment guaranteed people's right "to keep and bear arms" because of the need for a "well-regulated Militia." Thus the constitutional right to bear arms was based on the expectation that most able-bodied men would serve the nation as citizen soldiers and there would be little need for a standing army. The Third Amendment defined the circumstances in which troops could be quartered in private homes.

The Fourth Amendment prohibited "unreasonable searches and seizures." The Fifth and Sixth established the rights of accused persons. The Seventh specified the conditions for jury trials in civil (as opposed to criminal) cases, and the Eighth forbade "cruel and unusual punishments."

The Ninth and Tenth Amendments reserved to the people and the states other unspecified rights and powers. In short, the amendments' authors made clear that, in listing some rights, they did not mean to preclude the exercise of others.

While debating proposed amendments, Congress also considered the organization of the executive branch. It readily agreed to continue the three administrative departments established under the Articles of Confederation: War, Foreign Affairs (renamed State), and Treasury. Congress instituted two lesser posts: the attorney general—the nation's official lawyer—and the postmaster general. Congress also established the principle that the heads of executive departments are responsible to the president when it agreed that the president alone could dismiss officials he had originally appointed with the consent of the Senate.

Executive Branch

Aside from constitutional amendments, the most far-reaching piece of legislation enacted by the First Congress was the Judiciary Act of 1789, which defined the jurisdiction of the federal judiciary

Judiciary Act of 1789

and established a six-member Supreme Court, thirteen district courts, and three circuit courts of appeal. Its most important provision, Section 25, allowed appeals from state courts to federal courts when cases raised certain types of constitutional issues. Section 25 thus implemented Article VI of the Constitution, which stated that federal laws and treaties were to be considered "the supreme Law of the Land."

During its first decade, the Supreme Court handled few cases of any importance. But in a significant 1796 decision, *Ware* v. *Hylton*, the Court for the first time declared a state law unconstitu-

The Early Supreme Court

tional. The same year it also reviewed the constitutionality of an act of Congress, upholding its validity in the case of *Hylton* v. *U.S.* The most important case of the decade, *Chisholm* v. *Georgia* (1793), established that states could be sued in federal courts by citizens of other states. This decision, unpopular with state governments, was overruled five years later by the Eleventh Amendment to the Constitution.

John Trumbull, known primarily for his larger-than-life portraits of patriot leaders, painted this miniature of George Washington, who posed for it during his presidency (c. 1792–1794). Division of Political History, Smithsonian Institution, Washington, D.C.

 ## Domestic Policy Under Washington and Hamilton

In 1783 George Washington returned to Mount Vernon with thoughts of peaceful life as a planter. Within a few years, however, his countrymen would again seek his service.

Election of the First President

Once the Constitution was ratified, Americans concurred that only George Washington had sufficient stature to serve as the republic's first president. The unanimous vote of the electoral college was just a formality, and he was inaugurated in 1789.

Washington acted cautiously during his first months in office, knowing that whatever he did would set precedents for the future. When the title by which he should be addressed aroused controversy

Washington's First Steps

(Vice President John Adams favored "His Highness, the President of the United States of America, and Protector of their Liberties"), Washington said nothing. The accepted title soon became a plain "Mr. President." By using the heads of the executive departments collectively as his chief advisers, he created the cabinet. Washington also concluded that he should exercise his veto power over congressional legislation very sparingly—only, indeed, if he was convinced a bill was unconstitutional.

Washington's first major task as president was to choose the heads of the executive departments. For the War Department he selected an old comrade-in-arms, Henry Knox. His choice for the State Department was his fellow Virginian Thomas Jefferson, who had just returned to the United States from his post as minister to France. And for the crucial position of secretary of the treasury, the president chose the brilliant, intensely ambitious Alexander Hamilton.

Two traits distinguished Hamilton from most of his contemporaries. First, he displayed an undivided loyalty to the nation as a whole. As a West Indian who had lived on the mainland only briefly before the war, Hamilton had no ties to a particular state. He showed little sympathy for, or understanding of, demands for local autonomy. Thus the aim of his fiscal policies was always to consolidate power at the national level. Further, he never feared the exercise of centralized executive authority, as did older counterparts who had clashed repeatedly with colonial governors, nor was he afraid of maintaining close political and economic ties with Britain.

Alexander Hamilton

Second, he regarded his fellow human beings with unvarnished cynicism. Perhaps because of his difficult early life (he was the illegitimate child of an aristocrat and had lived in poverty) and his own overriding ambition, Hamilton believed people to be motivated primarily by self-interest. Unlike some other Americans, he foresaw no rosy future in which public-spirited citizens would pursue the common good rather than their own private advantage.

In 1789, Congress ordered the new secretary of the treasury to assess the public debt and to submit recommendations for supporting the government's credit. Hamilton found that the country's remaining war debts fell into three categories: those owed by the nation to foreign governments and investors, mostly to France (about $11 million); those owed by the national government to merchants, former soldiers, holders of revolutionary bonds, and the like (about $27 million); and, finally, similar debts owed by state governments (roughly $25 million). With respect to the national debt, there was little disagreement: politi-

National and State Debts

cally aware Americans recognized that if their new government was to succeed it would have to repay its indebtedness at full face value.

The state debts were another matter. Some states—notably Virginia, Maryland, North Carolina, and Georgia—already had paid off most of their war debts. They would oppose the national government's assumption of responsibility for other states' debts, since their citizens would be taxed to pay such obligations. Massachusetts, Connecticut, and South Carolina, by contrast, still had sizable unpaid debts and would welcome a system of national assumption. The possible assumption of state debts also had political implications. Consolidating the debt in the hands of the national government would help to concentrate economic and political power at the national level. A contrary policy would reserve greater independence of action for the states.

Hamilton's first *Report on Public Credit*, sent to Congress in January 1790, reflected both his national loyalty and his cynicism. He proposed that Congress assume outstanding state debts, combine them with national obligations, and issue new securities covering both the principal and the accumulated unpaid interest. Current holders of state or national debt certificates would have the option of taking a portion of their payment in western lands. Hamilton's aims were clear: he wanted to expand the financial reach of the United States government, simultaneously reducing the states' economic power. He also wanted to ensure that holders of public securities—many of them wealthy merchants and speculators—would have a significant financial stake in the survival of the national government.

Hamilton's Financial Plan

Hamilton's plan stimulated lively debate in Congress. The opposition coalesced around his former ally James Madison. Well aware that speculators had purchased large quantities of debt certificates at a small fraction of their face value, Madison proposed that the original holders of the debt also be compensated by the government. Madison's plan, though fairer than Hamilton's, would have been difficult, if not impossible, to administer. The House of Representatives rejected it.

At first, the House also rejected the assumption of state debts. The Senate, however, adopted Hamilton's plan largely intact, and a series of compromises followed. Hamilton agreed to changes in the assumption plan that would benefit Virginia (Madison's home state) in particular. The assumption bill also became linked to the other controversial issue of that congressional session: the location of the permanent national capital. Both northerners and southerners wanted the capital in their region. The legend that Hamilton and Madison agreed over Jefferson's dinner table to exchange assumption of state debts for a southern site is not supported by the surviving evidence, but a political deal was undoubtedly struck. The Potomac River was designated as the site for the capital, and the first part of Hamilton's financial program became law in August 1790.

Four months later Hamilton submitted to Congress a second report on public credit, recommending the chartering of a national bank. The

First Bank of the United States

Bank of the United States was to be capitalized at $10 million, of which only $2 million would come from public funds. Private investors would supply the rest. The bank's charter would run for twenty years, and the government would name one-fifth of the directors. The bank's notes would circulate as the nation's currency. The bank would also act as collecting and disbursing agent for the Treasury and would lend money to the government. Most political leaders recognized that such an institution would be beneficial, especially because it would solve the problem of America's perpetual shortage of an acceptable medium of exchange. But another issue loomed large: did the Constitution give Congress the power to establish such a bank?

James Madison answered that question with a resounding no. He pointed out that Constitutional Convention delegates had specifically rejected a clause authorizing Congress to issue corporate charters. Consequently, he argued, that power could not be inferred from other parts of the Constitution.

Madison's contention disturbed Washington, who decided to request other opinions before

signing the bill into law. Thomas Jefferson, the secretary of state, agreed with

Strict and Broad Constructions of the Constitution

Madison that the bank was unconstitutional. Jefferson referred to Article I, Section 8, of the Constitution, which gave Congress the power "to make all Laws which shall be necessary and proper for carrying into Execution the foregoing Powers." The key word, Jefferson argued, was *necessary*: Congress could do what was needed, but could not do what was merely desirable. Thus Jefferson formulated the strict-constructionist interpretation of the Constitution.

Washington asked Hamilton to reply to the negative assessments of his proposal. Hamilton's *Defense of the Constitutionality of the Bank*, presented to the president in February 1791, was a brilliant exposition of what has become known as the broad-constructionist view of the Constitution. Hamilton argued forcefully that Congress could choose any means not specifically prohibited by the Constitution to achieve a constitutional end. If the end was constitutional and the means was not unconstitutional, then the means was also constitutional. Washington was convinced and signed the bill.

In December 1791, Hamilton presented to Congress his *Report on Manufactures*, the last of his prescriptions for the American economy. In it he outlined an ambitious plan for encouraging and protecting the United States's infant industries, like shoemaking and textile manufacturing. Hamilton argued that the nation could never be truly independent as long as it relied heavily on Europe for manufactured goods. He thus urged Congress to promote the immigration of technicians and laborers and to support industrial development through a limited use of protective tariffs. Many of Hamilton's ideas were implemented in later decades, but in 1791 most congressmen believed that America's future lay in agriculture and that the mainstay of the republic was the virtuous yeoman farmer. They therefore rejected the report.

That same year Congress accepted another feature of Hamilton's financial program, an excise tax on whiskey. The tax was needed to pay the cost

Whiskey Rebellion

of funding the state debts. An excise tax on whiskey was attractive because it affected relatively few farmers—those in the West who sold their grain in the form of distilled spirits as a means of avoiding the high cost of transportation—and because it might reduce consumption of whiskey. Moreover, Hamilton knew that those western farmers were Jefferson's supporters, and he saw the benefits of taxing them rather than the merchants who supported his own policies.

News of the excise law set off protests in frontier areas of Pennsylvania. For two years unrest persisted on the frontiers not only of Pennsylvania but also of Maryland and Virginia. President Washington responded with restraint until violence erupted in July 1794, when western Pennsylvania farmers resisted a federal marshal and a tax collector trying to enforce the law. Three rioters were killed and several militiamen wounded. About seven thousand rebels convened on August 1 to plot the destruction of Pittsburgh but decided not to face the heavy guns of the fort guarding the town. Washington then took decisive action to prevent a crisis reminiscent of Shays's Rebellion. On August 7, he called on the insurgents to disperse and summoned nearly thirteen thousand militia from Pennsylvania and neighboring states. By the time federal forces marched westward in October and November, the disturbances had ended.

The chief importance of the Whiskey Rebellion was the forceful message Washington's response conveyed to the American public: he had demonstrated that the national government would not allow violent resistance to its laws. In the republic, change would be effected peacefully, by legal means.

Republicans and Federalists

By 1794, a group of Americans was already beginning to seek change systematically through electoral politics, even though traditional political theory regarded organized opposition—especially in a republic—as illegitimate. The controversy grew out of the belief by opposition leaders Thomas Jefferson and James Madison that Hamilton's policies of favoring wealthy commercial interests at the expense of agriculture would impose a corrupt, aristocratic government on the United States. They contended that they were the true heirs of the Revolution and that Hamilton was plotting to subvert republican principles. To dramatize their point, Jefferson, Madison, and their followers in Congress began calling themselves *Republicans.*

Hamilton in turn accused Jefferson and Madison of the same crime: attempting to destroy the republic. Hamilton and his supporters began calling themselves *Federalists*, to legitimize their claims and link themselves with the Constitution. In short, each group accused the other of being an illicit faction working to destroy the republican principles of the Revolution. (By traditional definition, a faction was a group opposed to the public good.)

At first, President Washington tried to remain aloof from the political dispute that divided Hamilton and Jefferson, his chief advisers. Even so, the controversy helped persuade him to seek a second term of office in 1792 in hopes of promoting political unity. But in 1793 and thereafter, developments in foreign affairs magnified the disagreements.

Partisan Politics and Foreign Policy

The initial years under the Constitution were blessed by international peace. Soon, however, the French Revolution, which began in 1789, brought about the resumption of hostilities between France, America's wartime ally, and Great Britain, America's most important trading partner.

At first Americans welcomed the news that France was turning toward republicanism, but by the early 1790s the reports from France were disquieting. Outbreaks of violence continued; ministries succeeded each other with bewildering rapidity; executions were commonplace. The king himself was beheaded in early 1793. Although many Americans, including Jefferson

The French Revolution

and Madison, retained their sympathy for the revolutionaries, others including Hamilton, began to view France as a prime example of the perversion of republicanism.

When France declared war on Britain, Spain, and Holland in 1793, the Americans faced a dilemma. The 1778 Treaty of Alliance with France bound them to that nation "forever," and a mutual commitment to republicanism created ideological bonds. Yet the United States was connected to Great Britain through a shared history and language, and through an economic partnership. Americans purchased most of their manufactured goods from Great Britain. Indeed, since the financial system of the United States depended heavily on import tariffs as a source of revenue, the nation's economic health in effect required uninterrupted trade with Britain.

The political and diplomatic climate was further complicated in April 1793, when Citizen Edmond Genêt, a representative of the French government, landed in Charleston.

Citizen Genêt

As Genêt made his way northward to New York City, he recruited Americans for expeditions against British and Spanish colonies in the Western Hemisphere, and he distributed privateering commissions with a generous hand. Genêt's arrival raised a series of troubling questions for President Washington. Should he receive Genêt, thus officially recognizing the French revolutionary government? Should he acknowledge an obligation to aid France under the terms of the 1778 Treaty of Alliance? Or should he proclaim American neutrality?

For once, Hamilton and Jefferson saw eye to eye. Both told Washington that the United States could not afford to ally itself with either side. Washington agreed. He received Genêt but also issued a proclamation informing the world that the United States would adopt "a conduct friendly and impartial toward the belligerent powers."

Genêt himself was removed from politics when his faction fell from power in Paris, but his disappearance from the diplomatic scene did not lessen the impact of the French Revolution in America. The domestic divisions Genêt helped to widen

were perpetuated by clubs called Democratic-Republican societies, formed by Americans sympathetic to the French Revolution and worried about the policies of the Washington administration.

More than forty Democratic-Republican societies were organized between 1793 and 1800. Their members saw themselves as heirs of the Sons of Liberty, seeking the protection of people's liberties against encroachments by corrupt and self-serving rulers. They criticized the Washington administration's fiscal and foreign policies and repeatedly proclaimed their belief in the rights to free speech, free press, and assembly. Like the Sons of Liberty, the Democratic-Republican societies were composed chiefly of artisans and craftsmen, although professionals, farmers, and merchants also joined.

Democratic-Republican Societies

The rapid growth of such groups deeply disturbed Hamilton and eventually Washington himself. Some newspapers charged that the societies were subversive agents of a foreign power. The climax of the counterattack came in the fall of 1794, when Washington accused the societies of having fomented the Whiskey Rebellion.

In retrospect, Washington and Hamilton's reaction to the Democratic-Republican societies seems disproportionately hostile. But it must be recalled that factional disputes were believed to endanger the survival of republics. As the first organized political dissenters in the United States, the Democratic-Republican societies alarmed elected officials, who had not yet accepted the idea that one component of a free government was an organized loyal opposition.

Also in 1794 George Washington dispatched Chief Justice John Jay to London to negotiate four unresolved questions affecting Anglo-American affairs. The first point at issue was recent British seizures of American merchant ships trading in the French West Indies. The United States wanted to establish the principle of freedom of the seas and to assert its right, as a neutral nation, to trade freely with both combatants. Second, in violation of the 1783 peace treaty, Great Britain had not yet evacuated its

Jay Treaty

posts in the American Northwest. The Americans also hoped for a commercial treaty and sought compensation for the slaves who had left with the British army at the end of the war.

The negotiations in London proved difficult, since Jay had little to offer in exchange for the concessions he sought. Britain did agree to evacuate the western forts and ease restrictions on American trade to England and the West Indies. No compensation for slaves was agreed to, but the treaty established two arbitration commissions—one to deal with prewar debts Americans owed to British creditors and the other to hear claims for captured American merchant ships. Under the circumstances, Jay did remarkably well: the treaty averted war with England. Nevertheless, most Americans, including the president, were dissatisfied.

At first, potential opposition was blunted because the Senate debated and ratified the treaty in secret. Not until after it was approved by a vote of 20 to 10 in June 1795 was the public informed of its provisions. The Democratic-Republican societies led protests against the treaty. Once President Washington had signed the treaty, though, there seemed to be little the Republicans could do to prevent it from taking effect. Just one opportunity remained: Congress had to appropriate funds to carry out the treaty provisions.

When the House debated the issue in March 1796, members opposing the treaty tried to prevent approval of the appropriations. To that end, they asked Washington to submit to the House all documents pertinent to the negotiations. In successfully resisting the House's request, Washington established the doctrine of *executive privilege*—the power of the president to withhold information from Congress if he believes circumstances warrant doing so.

The treaty's opponents initially appeared to be in the majority. Frontier residents, however, were eager to have the British posts evacuated, and merchants wanted to reap benefits from expanded trade. Furthermore, Thomas Pinckney of South Carolina had negotiated a treaty with Spain giving the United States navigation privileges on the Mississippi, which would be an economic boost to the West and South. The popularity of Pinckney's Treaty helped to overcome opposition to the Jay

Treaty. For all these reasons, the House voted the necessary funds by the narrow margin of 51 to 48.

Analysis of the vote reveals both the regional nature of the division and the growing cohesion of the Republican and Federalist factions in Congress. Voting for the appropriations were 44 Federalists and 7 Republicans; voting against were 45 Republicans and 3 Federalists. The final tally was also split by region. Southerners cast the vast majority of votes against the bill, and almost all proponents came from New England and the middle states.

Partisan Divisions in Congress

The small number of defectors on both sides reveals a new force at work in American politics: partisanship. Voting statistics from the first four Congresses show the ever-increasing tendency of members of the House of Representatives to vote as cohesive groups, rather than as individuals. The growing division cannot be accurately explained in the terms used by Jefferson and Madison (aristocrats versus the people) or by Hamilton and Washington (true patriots versus subversive rabble). Simple economic differences between agrarian and commercial interests do not provide the answer either.

Bases of Partisanship

Yet certain distinctions can be made. Republicans, who were especially prominent in the southern and middle states, tended to be self-assured, confident, and optimistic about both politics and the economy. Southern planters, firmly in control of their region, foresaw a prosperous future based partly on continued westward expansion, which they expected to dominate. Republicans employed democratic rhetoric to win the allegiance of small farmers south of New England. Members of non-English ethnic groups—especially Irish, Scots, and Germans—found Republicans' words attractive. Republicans of all descriptions emphasized developing America's own resources and were less concerned than the Federalists about the nation's position in the world. Republicans also remained sympathetic to France in international affairs.

By contrast, Federalists, concentrated in New England, came mostly from English stock. They

How do historians know that *Americans were intensely patriotic in the early years of the republic? One piece of evidence is supplied by the many items incorporating patriotic motifs that decorated the homes of American citizens. The artisans of the new nation (and of England as well) quickly recognized that "patriotism sold," so they created a wide variety of objects to satisfy Americans' demand for furniture, wallpaper, curtains, and pottery goods displaying such themes. Only middling and well-to-do Amreicans could afford to buy such items, but a less-well-off American woman could produce some of these goods for herself. We do not know who made this eagle hooked rug, but a poor woman with just a few moments to spare each day could well have labored for months to display her allegiance to the new nation in this fashion.* New York State Historical Association, Cooperstown.

drew considerable support from commercial interests and were insecure, uncertain of the future. They stressed the need for order, authority, and regularity in the political world. Federalists had no grassroots political organization and put little emphasis on involving ordinary people in government. Many were farmers who, prevented from expanding agricultural production because of New England's poor soil, gravitated toward the more conservative party. Federalists, like Republicans, assumed that southern interests would dominate the land west of the mountains, so they had little incentive to work actively to develop that potentially rich territory. In Federalist eyes, the nation was perpetually threatened by potential enemies, both internal and external, and was best protected by a continuing alliance with Great Britain.

The presence of the two organized groups—not yet parties in the modern sense—made the presidential election of 1796 the first that was seri-

Washington's Farewell Address

ously contested. Tired of the criticism to which he had been subjected, George Washington decided to retire from office. In September he published his Farewell Address. In it Washington outlined two principles that would guide American foreign policy at least until the late 1940s: to maintain commercial but not political ties to other nations and to enter no permanent alliances. In doing so, Washington stressed the need for unilateralism (independent action in foreign affairs). He also lamented the existence of factional divisions among his countrymen, and he attacked the legitimacy of the Republican opposition.

To succeed Washington, the Federalists in Congress put forward Vice President John Adams, with the diplomat Thomas Pinckney as his running mate. Congressional Re-

Election of 1796

publicans caucused and chose Thomas Jefferson as their presidential candidate; the lawyer, Revolutionary War veteran, and active Republican politician Aaron Burr of New York agreed to run for vice president.

That the election was contested did not mean that its outcome was decided by the people. Voters could cast their ballots only for electors, not for the candidates themselves. More than 40 percent of the members of the electoral college were chosen by state legislatures rather than by popular vote. Moreover, the method of voting in the electoral college did not take into account the possibility of party slates. The Constitution's drafters had not foreseen the development of competing national political organizations, so the Constitution provided no way to express support for one person for president and another for vice president. The electors simply voted for two people. The man with the highest total became president; the second highest, vice president. Thus Adams, the Federalist, with 71 votes became the president, and Jefferson, the Republican, with 68 votes became the vice president.

John Adams and Political Dissent

John Adams took over the presidency peculiarly blind to the partisan developments of the previous four years. As president he never abandoned an outdated notion that the president should be above politics, an independent and dignified figure who did not seek petty factional advantage. Thus Adams kept Washington's cabinet intact, despite its key members' allegiance to his chief rival, Alexander Hamilton. Adams often adopted a passive posture, letting others (usually Hamilton) take the lead when

he should have acted decisively. As a result, his administration gained a reputation for inconsistency. When Adams's term ended, the Federalists were severely divided, and the Republicans had won the presidency. But Adams's detachment from Hamilton's maneuverings did enable him to weather the greatest international crisis the republic had yet faced: the so-called Quasi-War with France.

The Jay Treaty improved America's relationship with Great Britain, but it provoked retaliation by France. Angry that the United States had reached agreement with its enemy, the French government ordered its vessels to seize American ships carrying British goods. In response, Adams appointed three commissioners to try to reach a settlement with France. Simultaneously, Congress increased military spending.

For months, the American commissioners sought negotiations with Talleyrand, the French foreign minister, but Talleyrand's agents demanded

XYZ Affair

a bribe of $250,000 before talks could begin. The Americans retorted, "No, no; not a sixpence," and reported the incident in dispatches that President Adams received in early March 1798. Adams informed Congress of the impasse and recommended increased appropriations for defense.

Convinced that Adams had deliberately sabotaged the negotiations, congressional Republicans insisted that the dispatches be turned over to Congress. Adams complied, aware that releasing the reports would work to his advantage. He withheld only the names of the French agents, referring to them as *X*, *Y*, and *Z*. The revelation that the Americans had been treated with contempt stimulated a wave of anti-French sentiment in the United States. Cries for war filled the air. Congress formally abrogated the Treaty of Alliance and authorized American ships to seize French vessels.

Thus began an undeclared war with France. The so-called Quasi-War was fought in the West Indies, between warships of the United States Navy and French privateers

Quasi-War with France

seeking to capture American merchant vessels. Initial American losses of merchant shipping were heavy. By early

This cartoon drawn during the XYZ affair depicts the United States as a maiden being victimized by the five leaders of the French government's directorate. In the background, John Bull (England) watches from on high, while other European nations discuss the situation.   The Lilly Library, Indiana University, Bloomington, Indiana.

1799, however, the United States Navy had established its superiority in Caribbean waters, easing the threat to America's vital West Indian trade.

The Republicans, who opposed war and continued to sympathize with France, could do little to stem the tide of anti-French feelings. The Federalists saw this climate of opinion as an opportunity to deal a death blow to their Republican opponents. Now that the country seemed to see the truth of what they had been saying ever since the Whiskey Rebellion in 1794—that Republicans were subversive foreign agents—Federalists sought to codify that belief into law. In 1798, the Federalist-controlled Congress adopted a set of four laws known as the Alien and Sedition Acts, intended to suppress dissent and to prevent further growth of the Republican party.

Alien and Sedition Acts

Three of the acts were aimed at immigrants, whom Federalists accurately suspected of being Republican in their sympathies. The Naturalization Act lengthened the residency period required for citizenship and ordered all resident aliens to register with the federal government. The two Alien Acts provided for the detention of enemy aliens in time of war and gave the president authority to deport any alien he deemed dangerous to the nation's security. Neither act was implemented during the Adams administration, however.

The fourth act, the Sedition Act, sought to control both citizens and aliens. It outlawed conspiracies to prevent the enforcement of federal laws and set the maximum punishment for such offenses at five years in prison and a $5,000 fine. The act also tried to control speech. Writing, printing, or uttering "false, scandalous and malicious" statements against the government or the president "with intent to defame . . . or to bring them or either of them, into contempt or disrepute" became a crime punishable by as much as two years' imprisonment and a fine of $2,000.

The Sedition Act led to fifteen indictments and ten convictions. Most of the accused were outspoken Republican newspaper editors. But the first victim—whose story may serve as an example of the rest—was a hot-tempered Republican congressman from Vermont, Matthew Lyon. The Irish-born Lyon was convicted, fined $1,000, and sent to prison for four months for declaring in print that John Adams had displayed "a continual grasp for power" and "an unbounded thirst for ridiculous pomp, foolish adulation, and selfish avarice." While in jail, Lyon ran a successful reelection campaign.

Faced with prosecutions of their supporters, Jefferson and Madison sought an effective means of combating the acts. They turned to constitutional theory and the state legislatures. Carefully concealing their own role—it would not have been desirable for the vice president to be indicted for sedition—Jefferson and Madison each drafted a set of resolutions. Introduced into the Kentucky and Virginia legislatures, respectively, in the fall of 1798, the resolutions differed somewhat but had the same import. Since the Constitution was created by a compact among the states, they contended, people speaking through their states had a legitimate right to judge the constitutionality of actions taken by the federal government. Both sets of resolutions pronounced the Alien and Sedition Acts null and void and asked other states to join in the protest.

Virginia and Kentucky Resolutions

Although no other state endorsed them, the Virginia and Kentucky resolutions were nevertheless influential. First, they were superb political propaganda, rallying Republican opinion and placing the party squarely in the revolutionary tradition of resistance to tyrannical authority. Second, the theory of union they proposed inspired southern states' rights advocates in the 1830s and thereafter. Jefferson and Madison had identified a key constitutional issue: how far could states go in opposing the national government? How could a conflict between the two be resolved?

Meanwhile, the Federalists split over the course of action the United States should take toward France. Hamilton and his supporters still called for a declaration legitimizing the undeclared naval war. But Adams received a number of private signals that the French government regretted its treatment of the American commissioners. Acting on these assurances, he dispatched the envoy William Vans Murray to Paris. The United States asked for two things: compensation for ships the French had seized since 1793 and abrogation of the treaty of 1778. The Convention of 1800, which ended the Quasi-War, provided for the latter but not the former. The results of the negotiations were not known in the United States until after the presidential election of 1800. By then, the split in the Federalist camp had already cost Adams the election.

Convention of 1800

The Republicans entered the 1800 presidential race firmly united behind Jefferson and Burr. Although they would win the election, their lack of foresight almost cost them dearly. The problem was the system of voting in the electoral college. All Republican electors voted for both Jefferson and Burr, giving each 73 votes (Adams had 65). Because neither Republican had a plurality, the Constitution required that the contest be decided in the House of Representatives, with each state's representatives voting as a unit. Because the new House, dominated by Republicans, would not take office for some months, Federalist representatives decided the election by selecting Jefferson—to them, a lesser evil than Burr—on the thirty-fifth ballot. In response to the tangle, the Twelfth Amendment to the Constitution (1804) changed the method of voting in the electoral college to allow for a party ticket.

Election of 1800

Westward Expansion, Social Change, and Religious Ferment

The United States experienced a dramatic increase in internal migration in the postrevolutionary years. As much as 5 to 10 percent of the population moved each year, approximately half relocating to another state. The major population shifts were from east to west (see map): from New England to upstate New York and Ohio, from New Jersey to western Pennsylvania, from the Chesapeake to the new states of Kentucky and Tennessee. Very few people moved north or south.

The first permanent white settlements beyond the Appalachian Mountains were established in western North Carolina in 1771. But not until af-

Settlement in the West

ter the defeat of the Shawnees in 1774 and the Cherokees in 1776 was the way cleared for a more general migration. By 1790, more than 100,000 people lived in the future states of Kentucky and Tennessee. Settlements grew more slowly north of the Ohio River because of the strength of the Miami Confederacy. But once the Treaty of Greenville was signed in 1795, the Ohio country also grew rapidly.

The transplanted New Englanders in particular did their best to re-create the societies they had left behind, laying out farms and towns in neat checkerboard patterns and founding libraries and Congregational churches. Early arrivals' enthusiastic letters describing Ohio's rich soil and potential for growth recruited others to join them, setting off a phenomenon known in New England as "Ohio Fever."

The westward migration of slaveholders, first to Kentucky and Tennessee and then later into the rich lands of western Georgia and eventually

African-Americans in the West

the Gulf Coast, had an adverse impact on African-Americans. The web of family connections built up over several generations of residence in the Chesapeake was torn apart by the population movement. Even those few large planters who moved their entire slave force west rarely owned all the members of every family on their plantations. Most commonly the migrants were either younger sons of eastern slaveholders, whose inheritance included only a portion of the family's slaves, or small farmers with just one or two bondspeople. In the early years of American settlement in the West, the population was widely

dispersed; accordingly, African-Americans raised among large numbers of kin in the Chesapeake had to adapt to lonely lives on isolated farms. Many of them also had to build new families to replace those unwillingly left behind in the East.

The mobility of the population created a volatile mix in southern frontier areas. Since most of the migrants were young, single men just starting to lead inde-

Second Great Awakening

pendent lives, western society was at first unstable. Like the seventeenth-century Chesapeake, the late–eighteenth-century American West was a society in which single women like Margaret Dwight married quickly. The few women among the migrants lamented their lack of congenial female friends. Isolated, far from familiar surroundings, women and men strove to create new communities to replace those left behind.

Among the migrants to Kentucky and Tennessee were clergymen and committed lay members of the evangelical sects that had arisen in America after the First Great Awakening: Baptists, Presbyterians, and Methodists. That First Awakening had flourished in the southern backcountry well into the 1760s, and the Second Great Awakening, which began around 1800 in the West and continued into the 1840s, was an extension of the earlier revival.

At protracted camp meetings, sometimes attended by thousands of people, clergymen exhorted their audiences to repent their sins. Many declared that salvation was open to all, rejecting the Calvinistic doctrine of predestination. Stressing the emotional nature of the conversion experience and downplaying the need for Bible study, such preachers were in effect democratizing American religion, making it available to all rather than to a preselected and educated elite.

The most famous camp meeting took place in August 1801 at Cane Ridge, Kentucky. At a time when the largest settlement in the state had no more than two thousand inhabitants, about ten thousand people came to Cane Ridge. One witness saw "sinners dropping down on every hand, shrieking, groaning, crying for mercy." Such scenes were to be repeated many times in the decades that fol-

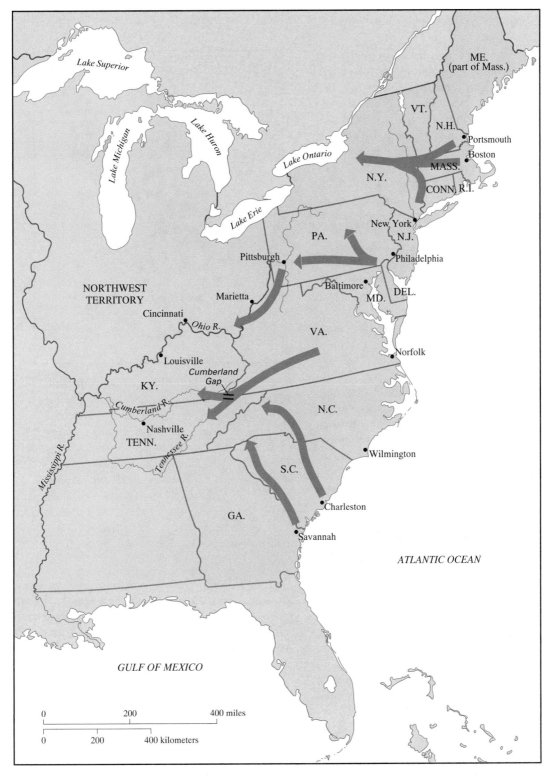

Western Expansion, 1785–1805 *After the Revolutionary War, large numbers of white and black Americans ventured west of the Appalachian Mountains for the first time.*

lowed. Revivals swept across different regions of the country, leaving an indelible legacy of evangelism to many American Protestant churches.

The established churches of the colonial era—supported, like the Congregationalists in Massachusetts or the Anglicans in Virginia, by tax revenues—came under vigorous attack from dissenters who used revolutionary ideology to great advantage. Consequently, many states dissolved their ties to churches during or immediately after the war, and others vastly reduced state support for established denominations. Without state support, churches had to generate new sources of revenue. Revivals, which were genuine outpourings of religious sentiment, also proved a convenient means of increasing church membership and contributions.

Attacks on Established Churches

An analysis of secular society can help to explain the conversion patterns of the Second Awakening. Unlike the First Great Awakening, when converts were evenly divided by sex, more women than men—particularly young women—answered the call of Christianity during the Second Awakening. The increase in female converts seems to have been directly related to fundamental changes in women's circumstances in the late eighteenth century. In some areas of the country, especially New England, women outnumbered men after 1790 (see map). Thus eastern girls could no longer count on finding marital partners. The uncertainty of their social and familial position seems to have led them to seek spiritual certainty in the church. In the churches, they created hundreds of associations to aid widows and orphans, collect money for foreign missions, and improve the quality of maternal care. Thus American women collectively assumed the role of keepers of the nation's conscience, taking the lead in charitable enterprises and freeing men from concern for such moral issues.

Women and the Second Awakening

The religious ferment in frontier regions of the Upper South contributed to racial ferment as well, for people of both races attended the

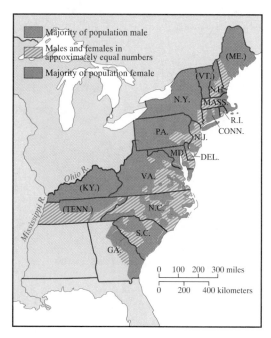

Sex Ratio of White Population, 1790 *The first census revealed that the sex ratio varied dramatically in different parts of the country. In many older, coastal areas, women predominated; on the frontier, men were in the majority. The variations had important implications for life in those regions, as the text points out.* Source: From Lester J. Cappon et al., eds., *Atlas of Early American History: The Revolutionary Era, 1760–1790.* Copyright ©1976 by Princeton University Press. Reprinted by permission of Princeton University Press.

Unrest Among African-Americans

camp meetings to hear black and white preachers. When revivals spread eastward into more heavily slave-holding areas, planters became fearful of the egalitarianism implied in the evangelical message of universal salvation and harmony. Their fear was heightened by events in the West Indies. In 1793, in the French colony of Saint Domingue (Haiti), mulattos and blacks under the leadership of Toussaint L'Ouverture overthrew European rule in a bloody revolt. News of the successful rebellion traveled rapidly among slaves and slaveowners in the South.

The West Indies revolt coincided with the single most massive inflow of Africans into North America since the beginnings of the slave trade. The two sources of the new demand for bondspeople were the expansion of cotton production after the invention of the cotton gin in 1793 and the beginnings of the large-scale westward migration of settlers. Before the legal trade was halted in 1808, more than ninety thousand new Africans had been imported into the United States. Their mere presence increased slaveholders' anxieties about the possibilities for revolt. Moreover, like their white compatriots, African-Americans (both slave and free) had become familiar with notions of liberty and equality. The circumstances were thus ripe for an explosion.

At this juncture in Virginia, Gabriel, an enslaved Richmond blacksmith who argued that African-Americans should fight for their freedom, planned a large-scale revolt.

Gabriel's Rebellion

Identifying his targets not as all whites but rather as those "merchants" who oppressed artisans of both races, Gabriel first recruited to his cause other skilled African-Americans who like himself lived in semifreedom under minimal supervision. Next he enlisted rural slaves. The conspirators planned to attack Richmond on the night of August 30, 1800, setting fire to the city, seizing the state capitol, and capturing the governor. At that point, Gabriel believed, other slaves and sympathetic poor whites would join in.

The plan showed considerable political sophistication, but heavy rain forced a postponement. Several planters then learned of the plan from their slaves and spread the alarm. Gabriel avoided capture for some weeks, but most of the other leaders of the rebellion were quickly arrested and interrogated. Twenty-six conspirators, including Gabriel himself, were hanged, but that outcome did not put an end to unrest among Virginia's slaves.

At his trial, one of Gabriel's followers had made explicit the links that so frightened Chesapeake slaveholders. He told his judges that, like George Washington, "I have adventured my life in endeavouring to obtain the liberty of my countrymen, and am a willing sacrifice in their cause."

Southern state legislature responded to such claims by increasing the severity of the laws regulating slavery. Before long, all talk of emancipation (gradual or otherwise) ceased, and slavery became even more firmly entrenched as an economic instituion and way of life.

 ## Conclusion

As the nineteenth century began, inhabitants of the United States were moving toward an accommodation to their changed lives in the new republic. Native American peoples east of the Mississippi found that they had to give up some parts of their traditional culture to preserve others. African-Americans and European-Americans tried to create new lives for themselves in the West and to adjust to changed economic circumstances in the East. Building on successful negotiations with both Britain and France, the United States developed its diplomatic independence, striving to avoid entanglement with the European powers. The 1790s spawned vigorous debates over foreign and domestic policy and saw the beginnings of a system of political parties. Religious revivals swept portions of the countryside and contributed to social unrest.

At the end of the 1790s, after years of struggle, the Jeffersonian interpretation of republicanism finally prevailed over Hamilton's approach. In the years to come the country would be characterized by a decentralized economy, minimal government (especially at the national level), and maximum freedom of action and mobility for individual white men. Jeffersonian Republicans, like other white men before them, failed to extend to white women, Indian peoples, and African-Americans the freedom and individuality they recognized as essential for themselves.

Suggestions for Further Reading

National Government and Administration

Ralph Adams Brown, *The Presidency of John Adams* (1975); William R. Casto, *The Supreme Court in the Early Republic: The Chief Justiceships of John Jay and Oliver Ellsworth* (1995); Stanley

Elkins and Eric McKitrick, *The Age of Federalism, 1788–1800* (1993); Morton Frisch, *Alexander Hamilton and the Political Order* (1991); Forrest McDonald, *The Presidency of George Washington* (1974); John R. Nelson, Jr., *Liberty and Property: Political Economy and Policymaking in the New Nation, 1789–1812* (1987); James R. Sharp, *American Politics in the Early Republic: The New Nation in Crisis* (1993); Garry Wills, *Cincinnatus: George Washington and the Enlightenment* (1984).

Partisan Politics

Joyce Appleby, *Capitalism and a New Social Order: The Republican Vision of the 1790s* (1984); Lance Banning, *The Jeffersonian Persuasion: Evolution of a Party Ideology* (1978); Richard Buel, *Securing the Revolution: Ideology in American Politics, 1789–1815* (1972); Joseph Charles, *The Origins of the American Party System* (1956); Richard Hofstadter, *The Idea of a Party System: The Rise of Legitimate Opposition in the United States, 1780–1840* (1970); John Zvesper, *Political Philosophy and Rhetoric: A Study of the Origins of American Party Politics* (1977).

Foreign Policy

Harry Ammon, *The Genêt Mission* (1973); Jerald A. Combs, *The Jay Treaty* (1970); Alexander DeConde, *The Quasi-War: Politics and Diplomacy of the Undeclared War with France, 1797–1801* (1966); Felix Gilbert, *To the Farewell Address: Ideas of Early American Foreign Policy* (1961); Reginald Horsman, *The Diplomacy of the New Republic, 1776–1815* (1985); Bradford Perkins, *The First Rapprochement: England and the United States,* *1795–1805* (1967); William Stinchcombe, *The XYZ Affair* (1981).

Civil Liberties

Leonard W. Levy, *Emergence of a Free Press* (1985); Leonard W. Levy, *Origins of the Fifth Amendment* (1968); Robert A. Rutland, *The Birth of the Bill of Rights, 1776–1791*, rev. ed. (1983); James Morton Smith, *Freedom's Fetters: The Alien and Sedition Laws and American Civil Liberties* (1956).

Social Change and Westward Expansion

Andrew Cayton, *The Frontier Republic: Ideology and Politics in the Ohio Country, 1789–1812* (1986); Douglas Egerton, *Gabriel's Rebellion: The Virginia Slave Conspiracies of 1800 and 1802* (1993); John Mack Faragher, *Daniel Boone: The Life and Legend of an American Pioneer* (1992); Allen Kulikoff, *The Agrarian Origins of American Capitalism* (1992); Malcolm Rohrbough, *The Trans-Appalachian Frontier: Peoples, Societies, and Institutions, 1775–1850* (1979); Thomas Slaughter, *The Whiskey Rebellion* (1986).

Religion

Catharine Albanese, *Sons of the Fathers: The Civil Religion of the American Revolution* (1976); Ruth Bloch, *Visionary Republic: Millennial Themes in American Thought* (1985); Paul Conkin, *Cane Ridge: America's Pentecost* (1990); Nathan O. Hatch, *The Democratization of American Christianity* (1990); Ronald Hoffman and Peter J. Albert, eds., *Religion in a Revolutionary Age* (1994).

CHAPTER

9

The Empire of Liberty
1801 – 1824

Nez Perce villagers on the western slope of the Rockies were fearful of the group of bearded strangers who descended upon them in September 1805. The strangers, a scouting party headed by William Clark, were invited into the village by an old man who used signs to communicate. The Nez Perce fed Clark and his group pieces of buffalo, dried salmon, and camas bread. Clark's party then traveled to the next Nez Perce village, where the people also welcomed them. A Nez Perce chief mapped out the terrain for them, indicating that in another camp was an important leader, Twisted Hair. Clark then sent a message to his partner Meriwether Lewis and the majority of the exploring group, saying he and his companions would meet them at Twisted Hair's settlement.

According to the Nez Perce's oral tradition, their cautious but friendly welcome of Lewis and Clark was due in part to the efforts of Watkuweis, an elderly woman whose experience with white people had been positive, although she had once been a slave of a white trader. The Nez Perce also welcomed Lewis and Clark because they wanted guns and ammunition, which the expedition was carrying. In the spring of 1805 men from a Nez Perce band had traded with other Indians for six guns and had heard about the Lewis and Clark expedition. Lewis and Clark gave the chiefs the usual gifts—tobacco, clothing, flags, and medals—but Nez Perce self-interest, not trading goods, was responsible for the good relations.

Prior to crossing the Rockies, Shoshones had warned Lewis and Clark that the trail was treacherous and that little game was to be had. But they also told Lewis and Clark that the Nez Perce traversed it frequently, and the American explorers believed that if the Indians could make the climb, so could they. Only thirty members of the fifty-man party survived to reach the Nez Perce villages. From there they went on to the Pacific Ocean and then spent another year on the return journey.

President Thomas Jefferson had commissioned Lewis and Clark in 1803 to explore the newly purchased Lousiana Territory. Their mission had both scientific and political importance. They gathered information on the natural history of the areas they passed through, but they had political goals as well: to counter British advances to the Indians and to map the territory so that it could be opened to settlement and exploitation.

The Lewis and Clark expedition (1804–1806) proved successful. The explorers reached the Pacific, and their good relations with the Indians and the fame of their travels led to the opening of the territory to settlement and prevented British advances. Their collection of information about natural specimens and artifacts from the area was thorough. Along the way they had been aided by trappers and Native Americans.

The Lewis and Clark expedition was part of American expansion. Like the purchase of the Louisiana Territory from France in 1803 it extended, in Jefferson's phrase, the American "empire of liberty." Lewis and Clark were harbingers of the future, of the expansion and settlement of the United States.

Americans passed a political test at home when President Jefferson succeeded President Adams peacefully in 1800, despite the bitterness of the election and political intrigue. Presidential succession by ballot rather than arms helped secure constitutional government.

The transfer of power to the Republicans from the Federalists intensified political conflict. In the tradition of the Revolution, Republican presidents would seek to restrain the national government, believing that limited government would foster republican virtue. The Federalists would advocate a strong national government with centralized authority to promote economic development. As both factions competed for popular support, they laid the basis for the evolution of democratic politics. But factionalism, personal animosities, and partisanship within each group prevented the development of cohesive political parties, and the Federalists, unable to build a strong base of popular support, slowly faded away.

Events abroad and in the West encouraged and threatened Americans. Seizing one opportunity, the United States purchased the Louisiana Territory, pushing its border to the Pacific Ocean. But then from the high seas came war. Caught between the warring British and French, the United States found its ships seized and its sailors impressed, in violation of its rights as a neutral and independent nation. When the humiliation and threat to United States interests became too great, Americans took up arms in the War of 1812 both to defend their rights as a nation and to expand farther to the west and north.

The War of 1812 unleashed a wave of nationalism and self-confidence. War needs promoted domestic manufacturing and internal improvements. With peace, the federal government championed business and the construction of roads and canals. The new spirit encouraged economic growth and western expansion at home, trade abroad, and assertiveness throughout the Western Hemisphere. By the 1820s, the United States was no longer an experiment; a new nation had emerged.

Economic growth and territorial expansion, however, generated new problems. In 1819 a financial panic brought hardship and conflict that sowed the seeds for the Jacksonian movement in the 1820s and 1830s. More ominously, sectional differences and the presence of slavery created divisions that would widen in the wake of further westward expansion during the 1840s and 1850s.

 ## Jefferson in Power

Thomas Jefferson viewed the election of 1800 as a revolution that restored government to its limited role. He stressed republican virtues of independ-

• *Important Events* •

1801	John Marshall becomes Chief Justice of the United States
	Thomas Jefferson inaugurated as first Republican president
1801–05	United States defeats Barbary pirates in Tripoli War
1803	*Marbury* v. *Madison* establishes judicial review
	United States purchases Louisiana Territory from France
1804	Burr kills Hamilton in a duel
	Jefferson reelected
1804–06	Lewis and Clark explore Louisiana Territory
1805	Prophet emerges as Shawnee leader
1807	*Chesapeake* affair almost leads to war with Great Britain
	Embargo Act halts foreign trade
1808	Congress bans importation of slaves to the United States
	James Madison elected president
1808–13	Prophet and Tecumseh organize Native American tribal resistance
1812–15	United States and Great Britain fight the War of 1812
1813	Death of Tecumseh ends effective pan-Indian resistance

1814	Andrew Jackson's defeat of Creeks at Battle of Horseshoe Bend gives rise to process of Indian removal from the South
	Treaty of Ghent ends the War of 1812
1814–15	Hartford Convention undermines Federalists
1815	Battle of New Orleans makes Jackson a national hero
1816	Second Bank of the United States chartered
	James Monroe elected president
1817	Rush-Bagot Treaty limits British and American naval forces on Lake Champlain and the Great Lakes
1819	*McCulloch* v. *Maryland* establishes supremacy of federal over state law
	Adams-Onís Treaty with Spain gives Florida to United States and defines Louisiana territorial border
1819–23	Financial panic and depression: hard times for Americans
1820	Missouri Compromise creates a formula for admitting slave and free states
	Monroe reelected
1823	Monroe Doctrine closes Western Hemisphere to European intervention

ence, self-reliance, and equality. He believed in a limited and frugal government. He cut federal operations, and with his Republican successors (James Madison and James Monroe) invigorated the federal government. Jefferson did not hesitate to use federal power, even when questionable, as in the purchase of Louisiana. Although he stressed the importance of domestic issues, during his term of office foreign crises, in particular, strengthened federal institutions.

In his inaugural address Jefferson sought unity by declaring, "We are all Republicans, we are all Federalists." Still, the Federalists and Republicans continued to distrust each other. Republicans considered Federalists antidemocratic. Federalists accused Republicans of favoring egalitarianism, which they believed had recently led to anarchy in France. By doing away with Federalist social pomp and excessive government, Jefferson intended to restore the simplicity and civic virtue that had fueled the American Revolution.

Jefferson aggressively extended the Republicans' grasp on the national government. Virtually all officials appointed during the administrations

This portrait of President Thomas Jefferson was painted by Rembrandt Peale in 1805. Charles Willson Peale (Rembrandt's father) and his five sons helped establish the reputation of American art in the new nation. Rembrandt Peale was most famous for his presidential portraits; here he captured Jefferson in a noble pose without the usual symbols of office or power, befitting the Republican age.   New-York Historical Society.

Republican Appointments

of Washington and Adams were loyal Federalists. To bring into his administration men who shared his vision of an agrarian republic and individual liberty, Jefferson refused to recognize appointments that Adams had made in the last days of his presidency, and he dismissed Federalist customs collectors from New England ports and awarded vacant treasury and judicial offices to Republicans. By July 1803 Federalists still held only 130 of 316 presidentially controlled offices. Jefferson adroitly used patronage to build a party organization.

The Republican Congress proceeded to affirm its belief in limited government. Albert Gallatin, secretary of the treasury, and Representative John Randolph of Virginia put the federal govern-

ment on a diet. Congress repealed all internal taxes, including the whiskey tax. Gallatin cut the army budget in half and reduced the 1802 navy budget by two-thirds. Gallatin moved to reduce the national debt—which Alexander Hamilton viewed as the engine of economic growth—from $83 million to $57 million, as part of a plan to retire it altogether by 1817.

More than frugality, however, distinguished Republicans from Federalists. Opposition to the Alien and Sedition Acts of 1798 had helped unite Republicans. Jefferson now declined to use the acts against his opponents, and Congress let them expire in 1801 and 1802. Congress also repealed the Naturalization Act of 1798, which had required fourteen years of residency for citizenship. The 1802 act that replaced it required only five years of residency.

The Republicans turned next to the judiciary, the last stronghold of Federalist power. During the 1790s not a single Republican had occupied the federal bench. The Judiciary Act of 1801, passed in the final days of the Adams administration, created fifteen new judgeships, which Adams filled by signing midnight appointments until his term was just hours away from expiring. The act also reduced by attrition the number of justices on the Supreme Court from six to five. Since that reduction would have denied Jefferson a Supreme Court appointment until two vacancies had occurred, the new Republican-dominated Congress repealed the 1801 act.

The Republicans also targeted opposition judges for removal. Federalist judges had refused to review the Sedition Act under which Federalists

Attacks on the Judiciary

had prosecuted critics of the Adams administration. At Jefferson's prompting, the House impeached (indicted) Federal District Judge John Pickering of New Hampshire, an emotionally disturbed alcoholic, and in 1804 the Senate removed him from office.

The day Pickering was convicted, the House impeached Supreme Court Justice Samuel Chase for judicial misconduct. Chase had repeatedly denounced Jefferson's administration from the bench. The Republicans, however, failed to muster the two-thirds majority of senators necessary to convict him. Their failure to remove Chase preserved the Court's independence and established the precedent that criminal actions, not political disagreements, were the only proper grounds for impeachment. Time soon cured the Republicans' grievances; in his tenure as president, Jefferson appointed three new Supreme Court justices. Nonetheless, the Court remained a Federalist stronghold under Chief Justice of the United States John Marshall.

Marshall, a Virginia Federalist, was an astute lawyer with keen political sense. Under his domination, the Supreme Court retained a Federalist outlook even after Republican justices achieved a majority in

John Marshall

1811. Throughout his tenure (from 1801 until 1835), the Court consistently upheld federal supremacy over the states and protected the interests of commerce and capital.

Marshall made the Court an equal branch of government in practice as well as theory. He unified the Court, influencing the justices to issue joint majority opinions rather than a host of individual concurring judgments. Marshall himself became the voice of the majority: from 1801 through 1810 he wrote 85 percent of the Court's opinions, including every important decision.

Marshall also increased the Court's power, notably in the landmark case *Marbury* v. *Madison* (1803). William Marbury, one of Adams's midnight appointees, had been named a justice of the peace in

Marbury v. *Madison*

the District of Columbia. James Madison, Jefferson's new secretary of state, declined to certify Marbury's appointment so that the president could appoint a Republican. Marbury sued, requesting a writ of mandamus (a court order forcing the president to appoint him). The case presented a political dilemma. If the Supreme Court ruled in favor of Marbury and issued a writ of mandamus, the president probably would not comply with it, and the Supreme Court had no way to force him to do so. But if the Federalist-dominated Court refused to issue the writ, it would be handing the Republicans a victory.

Marshall avoided both pitfalls. Speaking for the Court, he ruled that Marbury had a right to his appointment but that the Court could not compel Madison to honor the appointment because the Constitution did not grant the Court power to issue a writ of mandamus. In the absence of any specific mention in the Constitution, Marshall ruled, the section of the Judiciary Act of 1789 that authorized the Court to issue such writs was unconstitutional. In *Marbury* v. *Madison*, the Supreme Court denied itself the power to issue writs of mandamus but established its great power to judge the constitutionality of laws passed by Congress.

In succeeding years Marshall fashioned the theory of *judicial review*, the power of the Court to decide the constitutionality of legislation. Since the Constitution was the supreme law, he reasoned, any federal or state act contrary to the Constitution must be null and void. The Supreme Court, whose duty it was to uphold the law, would decide whether or not a legislative act contradicted the Constitution. The power of judicial review established with *Marbury* v. *Madison* permanently enhanced the independence of the judiciary.

While Marshall was enlarging the power of the Court, President Jefferson had his eye on enlarging the borders of the nation. Jefferson shared with other Americans the belief that the United States was

Louisiana Purchase

destined to expand its "empire of liberty." By 1800 hundreds of thousands of Americans in search of land had settled in the rich Mississippi and Ohio valleys. These settlers floated their farm goods down the Mississippi and Ohio Rivers to New Orleans for export. Whoever controlled the port of New Orleans thus had a hand on the throat of the American economy. Spain had owned Louisiana since 1763, but rumors of a transfer back to France persisted.

The rumors proved true. The United States learned of the transfer in 1802, when Napoleon threatened to rebuild a French empire in the New World. "Every eye in the United States is now focused on the affairs of Louisiana," Jefferson wrote to Robert R. Livingston, the American minister in Paris. Then, on the eve of ceding control to the

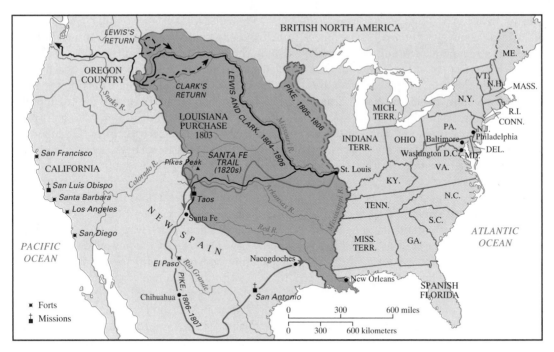

Louisiana Purchase   *The Louisiana Purchase (1803) doubled the area of the United States and opened the trans-Mississippi West for American settlement.*

French, Spain violated Pinckney's Treaty by denying Americans the privilege of storing their products at New Orleans prior to transshipment to foreign markets. Western farmers and eastern merchants thought a devious Napoleon had closed the port; they grumbled and talked war.

To relieve the pressure for war and to win western farm support, Jefferson prepared for war while sending James Monroe to join Robert Livingston in France to try to buy the port of New Orleans. Meanwhile, Congress authorized the call-up of eighty thousand militiamen in case war became necessary. Arriving in Paris in April, Monroe was astonished to learn that France already had offered to sell all 827,000 square miles of Louisiana to the United States for a mere $15 million. On April 30 Monroe and Livingston signed the Louisiana treaty to purchase the vast territory, whose borders were undefined and whose land was uncharted (see map).

The Louisiana Purchase doubled the size of the nation and promised fulfillment of Jefferson's dream of a continental nation reaching to the Pacific. But was this most popular move of his presidency legal? The Constitution did not authorize the president to acquire new territory and incorporate it into the nation. Jefferson considered proposing a constitutional amendment to allow the purchase but decided not to. His justification for authorizing the purchase was that he was exercising the president's implied powers to protect the nation. The people signaled their approval of Jefferson's decision on election day in 1804.

Americans eager to expand the nation sought information and routes westward. Lieutenant Zebulon Pike followed Lewis and Clark in 1805 and 1806 in search of the source of the Mississippi and a navigable water route to the Far West. The vast lands were not uninhabited, as Lewis and Clark had demonstrated. When Pike and his men wandered into Spanish territory to the south, the Spanish held them captive for several months in Mexico. After his release, Pike wrote an account of his experiences that set commercial minds spin-

Exploration of the West

ning. Over the next few decades, as Americans avidly read accounts of western exploration, expansion seized their imagination. The vision of a road to the Southwest became a reality with the opening of the Santa Fe Trail in the 1820s.

Tejas—Texas—was a buffer province between Spain's Mexican colonies and the Louisiana Territory. Texas officials welcomed Americans, some of whom migrated and fought with Indians and Mexican rebels in a twelve-year war with Spain that ended in 1821 with Mexican independence. The establishment of an independent Mexico stirred dreams of an independent Texas nation. Many Americans, however, did not want to include Mexicans—a mix of European, Indian, and African peoples—in the "empire of liberty."

 ## Republicans Versus Federalists

Prior to the Republican victory in 1800, most Federalists, unlike their Republican opponents, had disdained popular campaigning. They believed in government by the "best" people—those whose education, wealth, and experience qualified them to be leaders. For candidates to debate their own merits in front of their inferiors—the voters—seemed demeaning.

After the resounding Federalist defeat in 1800, however, a younger generation of Federalists began to imitate the Republicans. Led by

Political Campaigning

men like Josiah Quincy, a Massachusetts congressman, the Younger Federalists campaigned for popular support. Quincy cleverly presented the Federalists as the people's party, attacking Republicans as autocratic planters. In attacking frugal government, the Younger Federalists played on fears of a weakened army and navy. Eastern merchants depended on a strong navy to protect ocean trade; westerners looked to the army for support as they encroached on the territory of Native Americans.

In states where both factions organized and ran candidates, people became more involved in politics. In some states about 90 percent of the eligible voters—nearly all of whom were white

males—cast ballots between 1804 and 1816. As popular interest and participation in elections increased, states expanded suffrage. But the popular base remained restricted: property qualifications for voting and holding office persisted.

Yet political competition and a vigorous, partisan press prompted grassroots campaigning. Political barbecues symbolized the new style of campaign. At these barbecues, people ate, drank beer, and listened to candidates deliver lengthy speeches in which they often made wild accusations about their opponents. Given the slow speed of communications, the accusations might go unanswered until after the election.

Both factions held political barbecues, but the Federalists never fully mastered the art of wooing voters. Older Federalists still opposed blatant campaigning. And though strong in Connecticut, Delaware, and a few other states, the Federalists never offered the Republicans sustained competition. Moreover, the extremism of some Older Federalists discredited them all. A case in point was Timothy Pickering, a Massachusetts congressman and former secretary of state. Pickering opposed the Louisiana Purchase, feared Jefferson's reelection, and urged the secession of New England in 1803 and 1804. He won some support, but most Federalists opposed his plan for secession. Ever the opportunist, Vice President Aaron Burr flirted with Pickering, fantasizing about leading New York into secession, with other states following. But when Burr lost his bid to become governor of New York in 1804, his and Pickering's dream of a northern confederacy evaporated.

Both Republicans and Federalists suffered from divisiveness and personal animosities. Aaron Burr and Alexander Hamilton, for instance, had

Hamilton–Burr Duel

long despised each other. Hamilton always seemed to block Burr's path. He thwarted Burr's attempt to steal the election of 1800 from Jefferson, and in the 1804 New York gubernatorial race Burr lost to a rival Republican faction backed by the Federalist Hamilton. The embittered Burr challenged Hamilton to a duel, which Hamilton, though he found dueling repugnant, accepted.

How do historians know that popular interest in elections was increasing early in the nineteenth century? Election data are not available, but paintings like John Lewis Krimmel's Election Day in Philadelphia *(1815) convey that interest. Only white males could vote at the time, and the crowd is composed mostly of white men, although at least one African-American and some women and children are present. The artist depicts a festive occasion. Citizens riding on a float in the background carry their own flag; they have created a parade. A holiday spirit seems to prevail as men cluster in groups talking, arguing, sharing jokes, and generally appearing to have a good time. Perhaps there is a hint of overindulgence as well. The man sitting in front of an overturned chair (left foreground), with his hat on* the ground behind him, seems to have fallen, perhaps from too much drink—a common affliction in the party atmosphere of election day. Among the spectators are two women (center foreground), one of whom is holding the hand of a little girl. They suggest a restraining force on the raucous scene. The woman dressed in white and her friend offer a common female image of the time: the woman as an emblem of republican virtue. The space between the female and male figures suggests that the women stand apart not only as nonvoters but also as symbols of virtue and seriousness absent in the male world. Overall, the painting depicts a popular event, mixing a party atmosphere with civic duty. From a sober exercise of democratic responsibility, voting had become a popular, festive occasion.   Photo: Winterthur Museum.*

The duel took place in New Jersey. (New York had banned dueling.) Hamilton did not fire a shot and was killed; Burr was indicted for murder.

His political career in ruins, Burr plotted to create in the Southwest a new empire carved out of the Louisiana Territory. With the collusion of General James Wilkinson, the United States com-mander in the Mississippi valley, Burr planned to raise a private army to grab land from the United States or from Spain (his exact plans remain uncertain). Wilkinson switched sides and informed President Jefferson of Burr's intention. In 1807 Burr was acquitted on the charge of treason. He then fled to Europe to avoid further prosecution.

Campaigning for reelection in 1804, Jefferson claimed credit for western expansion and the restoration of republican values. Republicans bragged of ending the Federalist threat to liberty by repealing the Alien and Sedition and Judiciary Acts. They also had reduced the size of government by cutting spending. Despite his opponents' charges, Jefferson had demonstrated that Republicans supported commerce and promoted free trade. American trade with Europe was flourishing.

Jefferson's Reelection

Jefferson's opponent was Charles Cotesworth Pinckney, a wealthy South Carolina lawyer and former Revolutionary War aide to George Washington. As Adams's vice-presidential running mate in 1800, Pinckney had inherited the Federalist leadership. Jefferson easily won reelection. His victory was a personal and an organizational triumph. The political dissenters of the 1790s had fashioned the Democratic-Republican societies into successful political organizations. More than anything else, opposition to the Federalists had given them cohesion. Indeed, in areas where the Federalists were strongest—in commercial New York and Pennsylvania in the 1790s and in New England in the 1800s—the Republicans had organized most effectively.

Although this period is commonly called the era of the first party system, parties as such were not fully developed. Competition at the polls encouraged rudimentary party organization, but personal ambition, personality clashes, and local, state, and regional loyalties undermined it. Increasingly, too, external events overpowered party ties.

 ## Preserving American Neutrality in a World at War

"Peace, commerce, and honest friendship with all nations, entangling alliance with none," President Jefferson had proclaimed in his first inaugural address. Jefferson's efforts to stand aloof from European conflict were successful until 1805. Indeed, American commerce initially benefited from the May 1803 renewal of the Napoleonic wars. As the world's largest neutral carrier, the United States became the chief supplier of food to Europe. American merchants also gained control of most of the West Indian trade.

Meanwhile, the United States victory in the Tripoli War on the north coast of Africa (against the Barbary states) provided Jefferson with his one clear success in protecting American trading rights. In 1801 the sultan of Tripoli had demanded payment not to prey on American vessels and sailors in the Mediterranean. Jefferson refused to pay and instead sent a naval squadron to protect American merchant ships from the Barbary pirates. The United States signed a peace treaty with Tripoli in 1805 but continued to pay tribute to other Barbary states until 1815. That year the navy, again under the command of Stephen Decatur, forced Algiers and Tunis to renounce attacks against Americans. The Tripoli War and its aftermath made clear that the United States would protect its commerce anywhere.

American merchants grew increasingly concerned about Anglo-French interference with trade. In October 1805 Britain tightened its control of the high seas by defeating the French and Spanish fleets at the Battle of Trafalgar. Two months later Napoleon defeated the Russian and Austrian armies at Austerlitz. Stalemated, France and Britain launched a commercial war, blockading each other's trade. As a trading partner of both countries, the United States paid a high price.

Britain was suffering a severe shortage of sailors. Few men were enlisting, and those in service frequently deserted, demoralized by poor shipboard conditions. The Royal Navy resorted to stopping American ships and seizing British deserters, British-born naturalized American seamen, and other unlucky sailors suspected of being British. Perhaps six to eight thousand Americans were impressed (forcibly drafted) in this way between 1803 and 1812.

Impressment of American Sailors

In February 1806 the Senate denounced British impressment. In protest, Congress passed the Non-Importation Act, prohibiting importation from Great Britain of cloth and metal articles. In November Jefferson suspended the act temporarily while William Pinckney, a Baltimore lawyer, joined James Monroe in London to negotiate a settlement. But the treaty Monroe and Pinckney carried home violated their instructions—it did not mention impressment—and Jefferson never submitted it to the Senate for ratification.

Less than a year later, the *Chesapeake* affair exposed American military weakness. In June 1807 the forty-gun frigate U.S.S. *Chesapeake* left Norfolk, Virginia, and while still inside American territorial wa-

Chesapeake Affair

ters, it met the fifty-gun British frigate *Leopard*. When the *Chesapeake* refused to be searched for deserters, the *Leopard* repeatedly fired its guns broadside into the American ship. Three Americans were killed and eighteen wounded, including the ship's captain. The British seized four deserters from the Royal Navy—three of them American citizens.

Had the United States been better prepared militarily, the ensuing howl of public indignation might have brought about a declaration of war.

Embargo Act

But the United States was no match for the British navy. With Congress in recess, Jefferson was able to avoid hostilities. In July, the president closed American waters to British warships to prevent similar incidents, and soon thereafter he increased military and naval expenditures. In December Jefferson again invoked the Non-Importation Act, followed eight days later by a new restriction, the Embargo Act. Jefferson thought of the embargo as a short-term measure intended to avoid war. The embargo forbade virtually all exports from the United States to any country. Foreign ships delivering goods left American ports with empty holds. Smuggling blossomed overnight.

Few American policies were as well intentioned or as unpopular and unsuccessful as Jefferson's embargo. Mercantile New England, the heart of Federalist opposition to Jefferson, felt the brunt of the resulting economic depression. Shipping collapsed as exports fell by 80 percent between 1807 and 1808. In the winter of 1808–1809, talk of secession spread through New England port cities. Great Britain, meanwhile, was only mildly affected by the embargo, and France used the policy as an excuse to set privateers against American ships that had escaped the embargo. The French cynically claimed that such vessels were British ships in disguise, because the embargo prevented American vessels from sailing.

In the election of 1808, the Republicans faced not only the Federalists but also dissatisfaction with the embargo and factional dissent. Jefferson

Election of 1808

followed Washington's lead in renouncing a third term. He supported James Madison, his secretary of state, as the Republican standard-bearer. Madison won the endorsement of the Republican congressional caucus, and with his running mate, Vice President George Clinton, defeated the Federalist ticket.

Under the pressure of domestic opposition, the embargo eventually collapsed. In his last days in office Jefferson had tried to lighten the burden

Non-Intercourse Act

through the Non-Intercourse Act of 1809. This act reopened trade with all nations except Britain and France, and it authorized the president to resume trade with Britain or France if either of them ceased to violate neutral rights. But the new act solved only the problems created by the embargo; it did not prevent further British and French interference with American commerce.

When the Non-Intercourse Act expired in 1810, Congress substituted a variant, Macon's Bill Number 2. The bill reopened trade with both Great Britain and France but provided that when either nation stopped violating American commercial rights, the president could suspend American commerce with the other. Madison, eager to avoid war, was tricked at his own game. When Napoleon accepted the offer, Madison declared nonintercourse with Great Britain in 1811. Napoleon, however, did not keep his word. The French continued to seize American ships, and nonintercourse failed a second time. But because the Royal Navy dominated the seas, Britain, not France, became the main target of American hostility.

Angry American leaders tended to blame problems in the West on British agitation, ignoring the Indians' legitimate protests against treaty violations. In the early 1800s two Shawnee brothers, Prophet and Tecumseh, attempted to build a pan-Indian federation. Prophet's early experiences typified the experiences of the Indians of the Old Northwest. Born in 1775, a few months after his father's death in battle, Prophet, called Lalawethika ("Noisemaker") as a young man, was expelled to Ohio along with other Shawnees under the 1795 Treaty of Greenville (see page 131), and he later moved to Indiana. Within the shrunken territory granted the Shawnees, game soon became scarce. Encroachment by whites and the periodic ravages of disease brought further misery to the Shawnees.

Shawnee Resistance

In 1804, Lalawethika became a tribal medicine man. The next year, after a bout with an illness, he assumed the name Tenskwatawa or "the Prophet." Claiming to have died and been resurrected, he traveled widely in the Ohio River valley as a religious leader, attacking the decline of moral values among Native Americans, warning of damnation for those who drank whiskey, condemning intertribal battles, and stressing harmony and respect for elders. He urged Indians to return to the old ways and abandon white customs. Prophet's message was well received by the Shawnees and other western groups. As the message spread, settlers and the federal government became alarmed.

By 1808, Prophet and his older brother Tecumseh were talking less about spiritual renewal and more about resisting American aggression. Their refusal to leave lands claimed by the government was encouraged by the British. In repudiating land cessions to the government under the Treaty of Fort Wayne (1809), Tecumseh told Indiana's governor William Henry Harrison at Vincennes in 1810 that "the only way to check and stop this evil is, for all the red men to unite in claiming a common and equal right in the land, as it was at first, and should be yet; for it . . . belongs to all, for the use of each. . . . No part has a right to sell, even to each other, much less to strangers." Tecumseh, who had overshadowed his brother as

The Prophet and Tecumseh

the Shawnee leader, then warned Harrison that they would resist white occupation of the 2.5 million acres on the Wabash River that they had ceded in the Treaty of Fort Wayne.

 ## The War of 1812

Conflict over Native American loyalties in the West and over impressment on the seas strained relations between Britain and the United States. Having exhausted all efforts to alter British policy, the United States in 1811 and early 1812 drifted toward war with Great Britain until Republican "War Hawks" elected to Congress in 1810 led the charge to war. Meanwhile, in June 1812, Britain reopened the seas to American shipping. Hard times had hit the British Isles: the Anglo-French conflict had blocked much of British commerce with the European continent, and exports to the United States had fallen 80 percent. But two days after the change in British policy, before word of it had crossed the Atlantic, Congress declared war.

The War of 1812 was the logical outcome of United States policy after the renewal of warfare in Europe in 1803. The grievances President Madison enumerated in his message to Congress on June 1, 1812, were old ones: impressment, interference with neutral commerce, and British alliances with the western tribes. Not mentioned was the resolve to defend American independence and honor and American expansionists' thirst for British Canada.

The Vote for War

The war Congress was a partisan one. Much of the war fever came from the War Hawks, land-hungry southerners and westerners, all Republicans, led by John C. Calhoun of South Carolina and House Speaker Henry Clay of Kentucky. Most representatives from the coastal states opposed war, because armed conflict with the great naval power would interrupt American shipping. In June, when the votes were tallied in the House and the Senate, not a single Federalist voted for war.

Though unprepared for war in 1812, the nation could not avoid it. The United States had tried economic pressure, but had failed to protect

American ships and sailors. The United States Army and Navy and the state militias were not fully prepared to wage war against the British.

After six months of preparation, American forces were still not ready for war. The United States Navy had a corps of experienced officers,

Recruiting an Army

but compared with the Royal Navy the American navy was minuscule. And the United States Army had neither an able staff nor an adequate force of enlisted men. By 1812 the United States Military Academy at West Point, founded in 1802, had produced only eighty-nine regular officers. The American army thus turned to political leaders and the state militias to recruit volunteers, and not all states cooperated. The government courted enlistees with a sign-up bonus of $16, monthly pay of $5, a full set of clothes, and a promise of three months' pay and 160 acres of western land upon discharge.

Canada offered the United States the only readily available battlefront on which to confront Great Britain and conquer land. The mighty Royal Navy could not reach

Invasion of Canada

the Great Lakes separating the United States and Canada, because there was no river access to them from the Atlantic.

Begun with high hopes, the invasion of Canada ended in disaster. The American strategy concentrated on the West, aiming to split Canadian forces and isolate the Indians who were supporting the British. Tecumseh joined the British when the war began in return for the promise of an Indian nation in the Great Lakes region. United States General William Hull, governor of the Michigan Territory, marched his troops into Upper Canada, near Detroit. Despite superior numbers, Hull waged a timid campaign, retreating more than he attacked. His abandonment of Mackinac Island and Fort Dearborn in Chicago and his surrender of Fort Detroit left the entire Midwest exposed to the enemy. The only bright spot was the September 1812 defense of Fort Harrison in Indiana Territory by Captain Zachary Taylor, who provided the Americans with their first land victory. By the winter of

1812–1813, the British controlled about half of the Old Northwest.

The United States had no greater success on the Niagara front, where New York borders Canada. At the Battle of Queenstown, north of Niagara, the United States Army met defeat because the New York militia refused to leave New York. This scenario was repeated near Lake Champlain, where American plans to attack Montréal were foiled when the New York militia again declined to cross the border into Canada.

The navy provided the only bright ray in the first year of the war: the U.S.S. *Constitution*, the U.S.S. *Wasp*, and the U.S.S. *United States* all bested British warships on the Atlantic. In victory, the Americans lost 20 percent of their ships. In defeat, however, the British lost just 1 percent of their naval strength. The British admiralty simply shifted its fleet away from the American ships, and by 1813 the Royal Navy again commanded the seas.

The Royal Navy blockaded the Chesapeake and Delaware Bays in December 1812, and by 1814 the blockade covered nearly all American ports along the Atlantic and Gulf coasts. Since 1811, American trade overseas had declined nearly 90 percent, and the decline in revenues from customs duties threatened to bankrupt the federal government.

The contest for control of the Great Lakes, the key to the war in the Northwest, was largely a shipbuilding race. Under Master Commandant Oliver Hazard Perry and

Great Lakes Campaign

shipbuilder Noah Brown, the United States outbuilt the British on Lake Erie and defeated them at the bloody Battle of Put-in-Bay on September 10, 1813. With this costly victory, the Americans gained control of Lake Erie.

General William Henry Harrison then began the march that proved to be among the United States's most successful moments in the war. Harrison's force of forty-five hundred men attacked and took Detroit and then entered Canada. They pursued the British, Shawnee, and Chippewa forces, defeating them on October 5 at the Battle of the Thames. This victory permitted the United

States to retain control of the Old Northwest. Tecumseh died in the battle, and with his death expired Native American unity. After the Battle of the Thames, the Americans razed York (now Toronto), the Canadian capital.

After defeating Napoleon in April 1814, the British stepped up the land campaign against the United States, concentrating on the Chesapeake Bay region. In retaliation for the burning of York—and to divert American troops from Lake Champlain, where the British planned a new offensive—royal troops occupied Washington, D.C., in August and set it ablaze. The attack on the capital, however, was only a diversion. The major battle occurred at Baltimore, where the Americans held firm. Francis Scott Key, witnessing the British fleet's bombardment of Fort McHenry in Baltimore harbor, was inspired to write the verses of "The Star-Spangled Banner" (which became the national anthem in 1931). Although the British inflicted heavy damage, they achieved little militarily. Equally unsuccessful was their offensive at Lake Champlain. That offensive was discontinued, and the war was essentially a stalemate.

The last campaigns of the war were waged in the South, along the Gulf of Mexico against the Creeks and against the British around New Orleans. The Creeks had

Campaign Against the Creeks

responded to Tecumseh and Prophet's calls to resist United States expansion.In December 1812 General Andrew Jackson raised his Tennessee militia to fight the Creeks. By late 1813 his anti-Creek campaign was stalled by lack of supplies, and his men, who had signed up for a year, were talking about going home. Jackson refused to discharge them. In March 1814 Jackson executed John Woods, a militiaman, for disobedience and mutiny. This act broke the opposition within the ranks, and Jackson's men defeated the Creek nation at the Battle of Horseshoe Bend in Mississippi Territory in March 1814. As a result, the Creeks ceded two-thirds of their land and withdrew to southern and western Alabama. Jackson continued south toward the Gulf of Mexico. To forestall a British invasion at Pensacola Bay, which guarded an overland route

to New Orleans, Jackson seized Pensacola—in Spanish Florida—in November 1814. Then, after securing Mobile, he marched on to New Orleans.

The Battle of New Orleans was the last campaign of the war. Early in December the British fleet landed fifteen hundred men east of the city,

Battle of New Orleans

hoping to control the Mississippi River and thus strangle the lifeline of the American West. They faced American regular army troops, Tennessee and Kentucky volunteers, and two companies of free African-Americans from New Orleans. For three weeks the British and the Americans played cat-and-mouse. Finally, on January 8, 1815, the two forces met head-on. In fortified positions, Jackson's poorly trained army held its ground against two frontal assaults from a British contingent of six thousand. At day's end, more than two thousand British soldiers lay dead or wounded; the Americans suffered only twenty-one casualties. Andrew Jackson emerged a national hero. Unknown to the participants, a peace treaty had been signed at Ghent, Belgium, two weeks before the battle.

The Ghent treaty made no mention of the issues that had led to war. The United States received no satisfaction on impressment, blockades, or other maritime rights for neutrals. British demands for

Treaty of Ghent

an independent Indian nation in the Northwest and territorial cessions from Maine to Minnesota were not satisfied. Essentially, the Treaty of Ghent restored the prewar status quo. It provided for an end to hostilities with the British and with Native Americans, release of prisoners, restoration of conquered territory, and arbitration of boundary disputes.

Why did the negotiators settle for so little? Events in Europe had made these terms acceptable. Napoleon's fall from power and the subsequent peace in Europe made impressment and interference with American trade moot questions. And Britain—its treasury nearly depleted—stopped pressing for a military victory.

The War of 1812 affirmed the independence of the American republic. Although conflict with

Great Britain continued, it never again led to war.

Consequences of the War of 1812

The experience strengthened America's resolve to steer clear of European politics, for it had been the British-French conflict that had drawn the United States into war. For the rest of the century, the United States would shun involvement in European political issues and wars. The war also convinced the government in Washington, D.C., to maintain a standing army of ten thousand men—triple the number from Jefferson's time.

The war had disastrous results for most Native Americans. Although they were not a party to the Treaty of Ghent, the ninth article of the treaty pledged the United States to end hostilities and to restore "all the possessions, rights, and privileges" that Indians had enjoyed before the war. More than a dozen treaties were signed with midwestern Indian leaders in 1815, but they had little meaning. With the death of Tecumseh in 1813, the Indians had lost their most powerful political and military leader; with the withdrawal of the British, they had lost their strongest ally. The Shawnees, Potawatomis, Chippewas, and others had lost the means to resist American expansion.

Perhaps most important of all, the war stimulated economic growth. The embargo, the Non-Importation and Non-Intercourse Acts, and the war itself spurred the production of manufactured goods: New England capitalists began to invest in home manufactures. The effects of these changes were to be far-reaching. Finally, the war sealed the fate of the Federalists.

That party's presidential candidate, DeWitt Clinton, lost to President Madison in 1812, despite increases in the number of Federalists in Congress and despite the vigorous campaign waged by the Younger Federalists. Once more, extremism had hurt the party. During the war Federalists had revived talk of secession. With the war stalemated, delegates from New England met in Hartford, Connecticut, for three weeks in the winter of 1814–1815 to discuss revising the national compact or pulling out of the republic.

Hartford Convention

Moderates prevented a resolution of secession, but convention members condemned the war and the embargo and endorsed radical changes in the Constitution. They wanted to restrict the presidency to one term and require a two-thirds congressional vote to admit new states to the Union. They proposed forbidding naturalized citizens from holding office. The proceedings were a fruitless attempt to preserve New England Federalist political power as electoral strength shifted to the South and West and immigrants became politically active.

The timing of the Hartford Convention proved lethal. The victory at New Orleans and news of the peace treaty made the convention look ridiculous if not treasonous. Rather than harassing a beleaguered wartime administration, the Federalists found themselves in retreat before a rising tide of nationalism. Though Federalism survived in a handful of states until the 1820s, the Federalist faction began to dissolve.

 ## Postwar Nationalism and Diplomacy

With peace came a new surge of American nationalism. Self-confident, the nation asserted itself at home and abroad as Republicans borrowed a page from Federalists' agenda and encouraged commerce and economic development. In his message to Congress in December 1815, President Madison embraced Federalist doctrine by recommending military expansion and a program of economic growth. Wartime experiences, he said, had demonstrated the need for a national bank (the charter of the first Bank of the United States had expired) and the need for better transportation. To raise government revenues and perpetuate the wartime growth of manufacturing, Madison called for a protective tariff—a tax on imported goods designed to protect American manufactures. Though he strayed from Jeffersonian Republicanism, Madison did so within limits. Only a constitutional amendment, he argued, could give the federal government the authority to build roads and canals that were less than national in scope.

The congressional leadership pushed Madison's nationalist program energetically in the belief that it would unify the country. Republican Congressman John C. Calhoun of South Carolina and Speaker of the House Henry Clay of Kentucky believed the tariff would stimulate industry. The agricultural South and West would sell cotton to the new mills and sell food to the millworkers. New roads would make possible the flow of produce and goods, and tariff revenues would provide the money to build them. A national bank would facilitate all these transactions.

Nationalist Program

In 1816, Congress enacted much of the nationalistic program. The Second Bank of the United States was chartered. Like its predecessor, the bank was a blend of public and private ownership, and had one-fifth of its directors appointed by the government. To aid America's young industries, Congress also passed the nation's first substantial protective tariff—the Tariff of 1816. The act levied taxes on imported woolens and cottons (especially inexpensive ones) and on iron, leather, hats, paper, and sugar, in effect raising their cost. Some New England members of Congress viewed the tariff as interference in free trade, and southern members (except Calhoun and a few others) opposed it because it raised the cost of imported goods to southern families. But the western and Middle Atlantic states backed it.

Congress did not share Madison's scruples about the constitutionality of using federal funds to build local roads. "Let us, then, bind the republic together," Calhoun declared, "with a perfect system of roads and canals." Madison, insisting that internal improvements were the province of the states and private enterprise, vetoed Calhoun's internal improvements bill. He did, however, approve funds for the extension of the National Road, which began in western Maryland, to Ohio, on the grounds that the road was a military necessity.

James Monroe, Madison's successor as president, continued Madison's domestic program, supporting the national bank and tariffs and vetoing internal improvements on constitutional grounds. In 1816, after defeating the last Federalist candidate, Monroe declared that "discord does not belong to our system." The American people were, he said, "one great family with a common interest." A Boston newspaper dubbed the one-party period the "Era of Good Feelings."

Led by Federalist chief justice John Marshall, the Supreme Court became the bulwark of a nationalist point of view. In *McCulloch* v. *Maryland* (1819), the Court struck down a Maryland law taxing a branch of the federally chartered Second Bank of the United States. Maryland had imposed the tax in an effort to destroy the bank's Baltimore branch. The issue was thus one of state versus federal jurisdiction. Speaking for a unanimous Court, Marshall asserted the supremacy of the federal government over the states.

McCulloch v. Maryland

The Court went on to consider whether Congress could issue a bank charter. The Constitution did not spell out such power, but Marshall noted that Congress had the authority to pass "all laws which shall be necessary and proper for carrying into execution" the enumerated powers of the government. Echoing Alexander Hamilton's notion of implied powers, Marshall ruled that Congress could legally exercise "those great powers on which the welfare of the nation essentially depends." If the ends were legitimate and the means were not prohibited, Marshall ruled, a law was constitutional. The bank charter was declared legal.

McCulloch v. *Maryland* thus combined Federalist nationalism with Federalist economic views. By asserting federal supremacy, Marshall was protecting the commercial and industrial interests that favored a national bank. The decision was only one in a series. In *Fletcher* v. *Peck* (1810), the Court had voided a Georgia law that violated individuals' rights to make contracts. In *Dartmouth College* v. *Woodward* (1819), the Court nullified a New Hampshire act altering the charter of Dartmouth College. Marshall ruled that the charter was a contract, and in protecting such contracts he thwarted state interference in commerce and business.

Monroe's secretary of state, John Quincy Adams, matched the self-confident Marshall Court in assertiveness and nationalism. From 1817 to

John Quincy Adams as Secretary of State

1825 he brilliantly managed the nation's foreign policy, stubbornly pushing for expansion, fishing rights for Americans in Atlantic waters, political distance from the Old World, and peace. An ardent expansionist, he nonetheless placed conditions on expansion, believing that it must come about through negotiations, not war, and that newly acquired territories must bar slavery.

An Anglophobe, Adams nonetheless worked to strengthen the peace with Great Britain. In 1817 the two nations agreed in the Rush-Bagot Treaty to limit their naval forces to one ship each on Lake Champlain and Lake Ontario and to two ships each on the four other Great Lakes. This first disarmament treaty of modern times led to the demilitarization of the border between the United States and Canada. Adams then pushed for the Convention of 1818, which fixed the United States–Canadian border from Lake of the Woods in Minnesota westward to the Rockies along the 49th parallel (see map, page 173). When agreement could not be reached on the territory west of the Rockies, Britain and the United States settled on joint occupation of Oregon for ten years (renewed indefinitely in 1827).

Adams next moved to settle long-term disputes with Spain. During the War of 1812 the United States had seized Mobile and the remainder of West Florida. After the war Adams took advantage of Spain's preoccupation with domestic and colonial troubles to negotiate for the purchase of East Florida. During the talks, which took place in 1818, General Andrew Jackson took it on himself to occupy much of present-day Florida on the pretext of suppressing Seminole raids against American settlements across the border. Adams was furious with Jackson but defended his brazen act.

The following year, Don Luís de Onís, the Spanish minister to the United States, agreed to cede Florida to the United States without payment. The Adams-Onís, or Transcontinental, Treaty also defined the southwestern boundary of the Louisiana Purchase. In return, the United States government assumed $5 million worth of claims by American citizens against Spain and gave up its dubious claim to northern Mexico (Texas). Expansion was thus achieved at little cost and without war.

Adams-Onís Treaty

When the Spanish flag was last raised over Florida, its residents differed in the welcome they gave to the United States. Some planter-slaveholders and traders were pleased to be living under the American flag, but Creeks and Seminoles, free blacks, runaway slaves who had escaped to Florida, smugglers who worked the coast, and Spanish-speaking town dwellers, were not pleased.

Conflict between the United States and European nations was temporarily resolved by the Rush-Bagot Treaty of 1817, the Convention of 1818, and the Adams-Onís Treaty, but events to the south still threatened American interests. John Quincy Adams's desire to insulate the United States and the Western Hemisphere from European conflict brought about his greatest achievement: the Monroe Doctrine.

The immediate issue was the recognition of new governments in Latin America. Between 1808 and 1822, the United Provinces of the Río de la Plata (present-day northern Argentina, Paraguay, and Uruguay), Chile, Peru, Colombia, and Mexico all broke free from Spain. Although many Americans favored recognizing their independence, Monroe and Adams moved cautiously. They sought to avoid conflict with Spain and to be assured of the stability of the new regimes. Then in 1822, shortly after the Adams-Onís Treaty was signed and ratified, the United States became the first nation outside Latin America to recognize the new states.

Soon events in Europe again threatened the stability of the New World. Spain suffered a domestic revolt, and France, in an attempt to bolster the weak Spanish monarchy against the rebels, occupied Spain. The United States feared that France would return the new Latin American states to colonial rule. Great Britain, similarly distrustful of France, proposed a joint United States–British declaration against European intervention in the Western Hemisphere and a joint disavowal of territorial ambitions in the region. Adams rejected the British overture. In accordance with George Washington's admonition to avoid foreign entanglements, he insisted that the United States act independently.

The result was the Monroe Doctrine, a unilateral declaration against European interference in the New World. President Monroe presented the American position to Congress in December 1823. His message called for *noncolonization* of the Western Hemisphere by European nations, a principle that addressed American anxiety not only about Latin America but also about Russian expansion on the West Coast. (Russia held Alaska and had built settlements and forts as far south as California.) He also demanded *nonintervention* by Europe in the affairs of independent New World nations, and he pledged *noninterference* by the United States in European affairs, including those of Europe's existing New World colonies.

Monroe Doctrine

Monroe's words, however, carried no force. Indeed, the policy could not have succeeded without the support of the British, who already were committed to keeping other European nations out of the hemisphere to protect their dominance in the Atlantic trade. Europeans ignored the Monroe Doctrine; it was the Royal Navy they respected, not American policy.

The Panic of 1819 and Renewed Sectionalism

Monroe's domestic record did not match the diplomatic successes of his administration. In 1819, financial panic subverted postwar confidence and revived sectional loyalties. Neither panic nor the resurgence of sectionalism hurt Monroe politically; without a rival political party to rally opposition, he won a second term in 1820 unopposed.

But hard economic times spread. The postwar expansion has been built on easy credit; state banks had printed notes too freely, fueling speculative buying of western land. When manufacturing fell in 1818, prices spiraled downward. The Second Bank of the

Hard Times

United States cut back on loans, thus further contracting the economy. Distressed urban workers became politically involved by demonstrating for easy credit and internal improvements. Farmers clamored for lower tariffs on imported manufactured goods. Hurt by a sharp decline in the price of cotton, southern planters railed at the protective Tariff of 1816, which had raised prices on all imported goods. Manufacturers, by contrast, demanded greater tariff protection and eventually got it in the Tariff of 1824.

Western farmers suffered, too. Those who had purchased public land on credit could not repay their loans. To avoid mass bankruptcy, Congress delayed the deadlines for repayment, and western state legislatures passed "stay laws" restricting mortgage foreclosures. Many westerners blamed the panic on the Second Bank of the United States for tightening the money supply. As state banks folded, westerners bitterly accused the Second Bank of saving itself while the nation went to ruin.

Far more divisive was the question of slavery. Ever since the drafting of the Constitution, political leaders had tried to avoid the issue. The one exception was an act ending the foreign slave trade after January 1, 1808, which passed without much opposition. In 1819, however, slavery crept onto the political agenda when Missouri residents petitioned Congress for admission to the Union as a slave state. For the next two-and-a-half years the issue dominated all congressional action.

The Slavery Question

The debate transcended slavery in Missouri. At stake were the compromises that had kept the issue under wraps since the Constitutional Convention. Five new states had joined the Union since 1812: Louisiana (1812), Indiana (1816), Mississippi (1817), Illinois (1818), and Alabama (1819). Of these, Louisiana, Mississippi, and Alabama permitted slavery. Because Missouri was on the same latitude as free Illinois, Indiana, and Ohio (a state since 1803), its admission as a slave state would thrust slavery farther northward. It would also tilt the uneasy political balance in the Senate toward the slave states. In 1819 the Union consisted of eleven slave and eleven free states. If

Missouri joined, slave states would have a two-vote edge in the Senate.

The moral issues made slavery an explosive question. The settlers of Missouri were mostly Kentuckians and Tennesseeans who had grown up with slavery. But many northerners had concluded that it was evil. When Representative James Tallmadge, Jr., of New York proposed gradual emancipation in Missouri, a passionate and sometimes violent debate ensued. The House, which had a northern majority, passed the Tallmadge amendment, but the Senate rejected it. The two sides were deadlocked.

A compromise emerged in 1820 under pressure from House Speaker Henry Clay: the admission of free Maine, carved out of Massachusetts, was linked with the admission of slave Missouri. In the rest of the Louisiana Territory north of latitude 36°30′ (Missouri's southern boundary), slavery was prohibited forever (see map). The compromise carried, but the agreement almost came apart in November when Missouri submitted a constitution that barred free blacks from entering the state. Congressional arguments over Missouri's constitution were resolved when Clay produced a second compromise: Missouri guaranteed that none of its laws would discriminate against citizens of other states.

**Missouri
Compromise**

Although political leaders succeeded in removing slavery from the congressional agenda, sectional issues undermined Republican unity. The Republican party came apart in 1824 as presidential candidates from different sections of the country scrambled for support. Sectionalism and the question of slavery ultimately would threaten the Union itself.

 Conclusion

The first decades of the nineteenth century were a time of self-definition and growth for the young republic. Political parties broadened white male involvement in politics and quieted factional divisions. A tradition of peaceful transition of power

through presidential elections was established. And the United States expanded continuously, from the acquisition of Louisiana to the purchase of Florida.

The Revolution still cast a shadow over the new nation. Federalists harked back to British precedents. Republicans sought to maintain the ideals and virtues associated with the Revolution and the founding of a republic in which citizens would place civic virtue above individual gain. A second war with Britain—the War of 1812—reaffirmed American independence and thwarted Indian opposition to United States expansion.

The War of 1812 and diplomatic assertiveness brought a sense of national identity and self-confidence. After the war, all branches of the government pursued a vigorous national policy. The Supreme Court promoted national unity by extending federal power over the states and encouraging commerce and economic growth. In spite of Jefferson's vision of an agrarian society, the country was gradually shifting to a market economy in which people produced goods to sell to others. Developments in transportation further stimulated the economy and expansion. Under the guidance of John Quincy Adams, the United States pursued its interests through diplomacy, not direct intervention. The Monroe Doctrine was among his finest achievements.

Sectionalism accompanied nationalism and geographic expansion. War, tariffs, economic hard times, and slavery brought out sectional discord. Politicians kept the question of slavery off the national agenda as long as possible and worked out the Missouri Compromise as a stopgap measure. But territorial acquisitions and further westward expansion in the 1840s and 1850s would collide with a rising tide of reform to make the question of slavery unavoidable.

Over the next two decades, the way Americans lived and worked changed at a quickening pace. When Americans celebrated the fiftieth anniversary of the signing of the Declaration of Independence in 1826, they recognized that their future would be very different from the world of the founders. Economic development, rising population, the spread of settlement, and the growth of

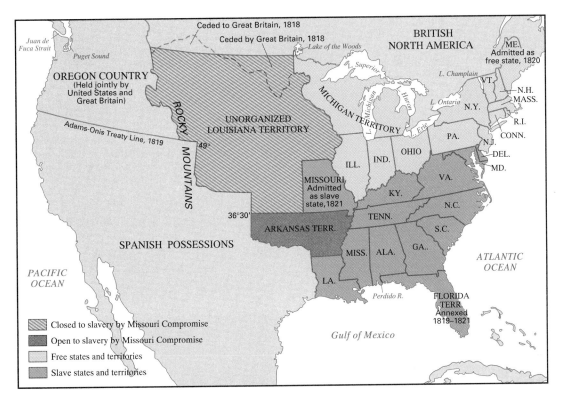

Juan de
Fuca Strait

Puget Sound

OREGON COUNTRY
(Held jointly by
United States and
Great Britain)

Ceded to Great Britain, 1818
Ceded by Great Britain, 1818
Lake of the Woods

BRITISH
NORTH AMERICA

ME.
Admitted as
free state, 1820

L. Superior

Adams-Onis Treaty Line, 1819

ROCKY MOUNTAINS

UNORGANIZED
LOUISIANA TERRITORY

MICHIGAN TERRITORY

L. Michigan

Huron

L. Ontario

L. Champlain

VT.

N.H.
MASS.

N.Y.

R.I.
CONN.

Erie

PA.

N.J.

DEL.

49°

OHIO

MD.

ILL.

IND.

MISSOURI
Admitted
as slave
state,1821

VA.

KY.

N.C.

36°30'

TENN.

ARKANSAS TERR.

S.C.

SPANISH POSSESSIONS

MISS.

ALA.

GA..

ATLANTIC
OCEAN

LA.

PACIFIC
OCEAN

Perdido R.

FLORIDA
TERR.
Annexed
1819–1821

Gulf of Mexico

Closed to slavery by Missouri Compromise

Open to slavery by Missouri Compromise

Free states and territories

Slave states and territories

Missouri Compromise and the State of the Union, 1820   *The compromise worked out by House Speaker Henry Clay established a formula that avoided debate over whether new states would allow or prohibit slavery. In the process, it divided the United States into northern and southern regions.*

cities were transforming people, their lives, and their communities.

Suggestions for Further Reading

General

Noble E. Cunningham, Jr., *The United States in 1800: Henry Adams Revisited* (1988); George Dangerfield, *The Awakening of American Nationalism, 1815–1828* (1965); George Dangerfield, *The Era of Good Feelings* (1952); Jean V. Matthews, *Toward a New Society: American Thought and Culture, 1800–1830* (1991); John Mayfield, *The New Nation, 1800–1845* (1981).

Party Politics

James M. Banner, *To the Hartford Convention: The Federalists and the Origins of Party Politics in the Early Republic, 1789–1815* (1967); Noble E. Cunningham, Jr., *The Jeffersonian Republicans in Power: Party Operations, 1801–1809* (1963); David Hackett Fischer, *The Revolution of American Conservatism: The Federalist*

Party in the Era of Jeffersonian Democracy (1965); Linda K. Kerber, *Federalists in Dissent* (1970); Milton Lomask, *Aaron Burr*, 2 vols. (1979, 1983); Richard P. McCormick, *The Presidential Game: The Origins of American Presidential Politics* (1982); Drew McCoy, *The Elusive Republic* (1980); James Sterling Young, *The Washington Community, 1800–1828* (1966).

The Virginia Presidents

Harry Ammon, *James Monroe: The Quest for National Identity* (1971); Noble E. Cunningham, Jr., *In Pursuit of Reason: The Life of Thomas Jefferson* (1987); Ralph Ketcham, *Presidents Above Party: The First American Presidency, 1789–1829* (1984); Drew R. McCoy, *The Last of the Fathers: James Madison and the Republican Legacy* (1989); Norman K. Risjord, *Thomas Jefferson* (1994); Robert W. Tucker and David C. Hendrickson, *Empire of Liberty: The Statecraft of Thomas Jefferson* (1990).

The Supreme Court and the Law

Leonard Baker, *John Marshall: A Life in Law* (1974); Robert Lowry Clinton, *Marbury v. Madison and Judicial Review* (1989); Richard E. Ellis, *The Jeffersonian Crisis: Courts and Politics in the*

Young Republic (1971); Morton J. Horowitz, *The Transformation of American Law, 1780–1860* (1977); R. Kent Newmyer, *The Supreme Court Under Marshall and Taney* (1968).

Expansionism, the War of 1812, and Diplomacy

Alexander De Conde, *This Affair of Louisiana* (1976); R. David Edmunds, *Tecumseh and the Quest for Indian Leadership* (1984); Clifford L. Egan, *Neither Peace nor War: Franco-American Relations, 1803–1812* (1983); Donald R. Hickey, *The War of 1812* (1989); Bradford Perkins, *The Creation of a Republican Empire, 1776–1865* (1993); James P. Ronda, *Lewis and Clark Among the Indians* (1984); J. C. A. Stagg, *Mr. Madison's War:*

Politics, Diplomacy, and Warfare in the Early Republic, 1783–1830 (1983); Anders Stephanson, *Manifest Destiny: American Expansionism and the Empire of Right* (1995); Steve Watts, *The Republic Reborn: War and the Making of a Liberal America, 1790–1820* (1987); David J. Weber, *The Spanish Frontier in North America* (1992).

The Monroe Doctrine

Samuel F. Bemis, *John Quincy Adams and the Foundations of American Foreign Policy* (1949); Walter LaFeber, ed., *John Quincy Adams and American Continental Empire* (1965); Ernest R. May, *The Making of the Monroe Doctrine* (1976).

CHAPTER

10

Rails, Markets, and Mills:
The North and West
1800–1860

The Hutchinson family—Abby, Asa, Jesse, John, and Judson—also known as the Tribe of Jesse, was the most popular singing group in nineteenth-century America. They performed throughout the United States and across the Atlantic, singing the patriotic, religious, and sentimental songs that had dominated popular music since the Revolution. Unlike most groups that just sang, the Tribe of Jesse presented well-rehearsed and elaborately produced performances. They used traditional airs but wrote political lyrics advocating such reforms as abolitionism and temperance.

The Hutchinson Family was part of a new phenomenon: singers, songwriters, musicians, publishers, and managers who made a business of music and entertainment. Drawing their largest audiences in the growing cities, they entered the commercial world and made a living from writing and performing music. Each performance was planned and choreographed, and the group had an entourage of managers, agents, publishers, and concert-hall representatives. Hawkers sold sheet music, portraits, and songbooks at their concerts. A traditional rural pastime had become a big business.

The Hutchinsons were able to tour the nation in concert because of advances in transportation and communications that linked the growing national economy between 1800 and 1860. The canal boat, steamboat, locomotive, and telegraph made possible a Hutchinson Family concert tour. But more enduringly, these technological advances opened up the frontier and helped expand farm production for markets at home and abroad. Equally significant to improved transportation was increased specialization in agriculture, manufacturing, and finance, which fostered a nationwide, capitalist, market-oriented economy.

This dramatic transformation began early in the century and spread nearly everywhere. In 1800 most of the 5.3 million Americans earned their living working the land or serving those who did. Settlements clustered on the East Coast, along the Ohio and Mississippi river valleys, along the Gulf Coast, across present-day Texas, and on the West Coast. By 1860, 31.4 million Americans had spread across the continent. Meanwhile, the economy, though still primarily agricultural, was being transformed by enormous commercial and manufacturing expansion.

Promotion of economic growth became the hallmark of the federal government, which encouraged individual enterprise by promoting an environment in which farming and industry could flourish. New financial institutions amassed the capital for large-scale enterprises like factories and railroads. Mechanization took hold; factories and precision-made machinery competed successfully with home workshops and handmade goods, and reapers and sowers revolutionized farming.

Not everyone profited from economic growth. The experience of a journeyman tailor displaced by retailers and cheaper labor was far different from that of the new merchant princes. New England farm daughters who became wage workers found their world changing no less radically. Moreover, boom-and-bust cycles became part of the fabric of ordinary life. And canals, railroads, and urban and industrial growth brought with them destruction of the environment.

Transportation and Regionalization

The North, South, and West followed distinct economic paths between 1800 and 1860. Everywhere, agriculture remained the foundation of the American economy. Nevertheless, the North increasingly

invested its resources in industry, commerce, and finance; the South in plantations and subsistence farms; and the West in commercialized family farms, agricultural processing, and implement manufacturing. This tendency toward regional specialization made the various sections of the country at once less alike and more interdependent.

The revolution in transportation and communications was probably the single overriding cause of these changes. Heavy investment in canals and railroads made the North the center of American commerce. The South, with most of its capital invested in slave labor, built fewer canals, railroads, and factories and remained mostly rural and undeveloped.

Before the 1820s and 1830s, it was by no means certain that New England and the Middle Atlantic states would dominate American finance and commerce. Indeed, the

Change in Trade Routes

southward-flowing Mississippi and Ohio Rivers oriented the frontier of 1800—Tennessee, Kentucky, and Ohio—toward the South. Flatboats transported western grain and hogs southward for consumption or transfer to oceangoing vessels at New Orleans. Steamboats, successfully introduced in 1807 when Robert Fulton's *Clermont* paddled up the Hudson River from New York City, began in 1815 to carry cargo upstream on the Mississippi and Ohio Rivers, further reinforcing ties between the South and the West.

But this pattern changed in the 1820s when new arteries opened up east-west travel. The National Road—a stone-based, gravel-topped highway originating in Cumberland, Maryland—reached Wheeling, Virginia (now West Virginia), in 1818 and Columbus, Ohio, in 1833. More important, the Erie Canal, completed in 1825, linked the Great Lakes with New York City and the Atlantic Ocean. Railroads and later the telegraph would solidify these east-west links. By contrast, at only one place—Bowling Green, Kentucky—did northern and southern railroads connect with one another. Although trade still moved southward along the Ohio and Mississippi, the bulk of western trade flowed eastward by 1850. Thus by the

• *Important Events* •

1790	First American textile mill, using water-powered spinning machines, opens in Pawtucket, Rhode Island	**1825**	Erie Canal completed
1807	Robert Fulton's steamboat, *Clermont*, makes its debut	**1834**	Women workers strike at Lowell textile mills
1812–15	War of 1812 stimulates domestic manufactures War of 1812 is fought	**1836**	Second Bank of the United States closes
		1837	*Charles River Bridge* v. *Warren Bridge* encourages new enterprises
1813	New England capitalists found the Boston Manufacturing Company and build the first large-scale American factory	**1839–43**	Hard times strike again
		1844	A government grant develops telegraph line between Baltimore and Washington
1816	Congress charters the Second Bank of the United States	**1848**	Regularly scheduled steamship passage begins between Liverpool and New York City
1818	National Road reaches Wheeling, Virginia, opening the West	**1849**	California gold rush transforms the West Coast
1819–23	Hard times bring unemployment and business bankruptcies	**1853**	British study of American system of manufacturing
1820s	New England textile mills expand	**1857**	Hard times mark end of third boom-or-bust cycle
1824	*Gibbons* v. *Ogden* affirms federal over state authority in interstate commerce		

eve of the Civil War, the northern and Middle Atlantic states were closely linked to the former frontier of the Old Northwest.

Construction of the 363-mile-long Erie Canal (completed in 1825) was a visionary enterprise. When the state of New York authorized it in 1817, the longest American canal was only 28 miles long. Vigorously promoted by Governor DeWitt Clinton, the Erie Canal shortened the journey between Buffalo and New York City from twenty to six days and reduced freight charges from $100 to $5 a ton. By 1835, traffic was so heavy that the canal had to be widened from forty to seventy feet and deepened from four to seven feet.

Sensing the advantage New York had gained, other states and cities rushed to follow suit. By 1840, canals crisscrossed the Northeast and Midwest, and total canal mileage reached 3,300—an increase of more than 2,000 miles in a single decade. Unfortunately for investors, none of these canals enjoyed the financial success achieved by the Erie. As the high cost of construction combined with an economic contraction, investment in canals began to slump in the 1830s. By 1850 more miles were being abandoned than built, and the canal era had unmistakably ended.

Meanwhile, railroad construction boomed. The railroad era in the United States began in 1830 when Peter Cooper's locomotive Tom Thumb first steamed along 13 miles of track constructed by the Baltimore and Ohio Railroad. In 1833 the nation's second railroad ran 136 miles from Charleston to

Canals

Railroads

Hamburg in South Carolina. By 1850 the United States had nearly 9,000 miles of railroad; by 1860, roughly 31,000 (see figure). Canal fever stimulated this early railroad construction. Promoters of the Baltimore and Ohio believed that railroads would compete successfully with canals. Similarly, the line between Boston and Worcester in Massachusetts was intended as the first link in a rail line to Albany, at the eastern end of the Erie Canal.

The earliest railroads connected nearby cities; not until the 1850s did railroads offer long-distance service at reasonable rates. But in the 1850s technological improvements, competition, economic recovery, and a desire for national unity prompted development of regional and, eventually, national rail networks. By 1853 rail lines linked Chicago to eastern cities. By 1860 rails stretched as far west as St. Joseph, Missouri. Short lines merged to create two unified systems, the New York Central and the Pennsylvania Railroad. Most lines, however, were still independently run.

Railroad Mileage, 1830–1860

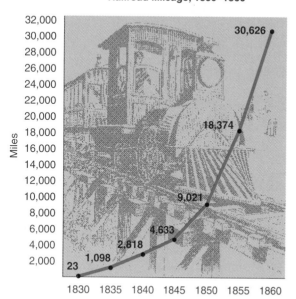

Railroad Mileage, 1830–1860 In the 1850s, railroads developed a natural rail network east of the Mississippi River. Source: U.S. Bureau of the Census, *Historical Statistics of the United States, Colonial Times to 1970*, 2 parts (Washington, D.C., 1975), Part 2, p. 731.

Differences in gauge, scheduling, car design, and a commitment to serve their hometowns first and foremost prevented cooperation and mergers.

Railroads did not completely replace water transportation. The federal government assisted water transportation by improving ports and clearing rivers for navigation. Ship-

Steamboats

ping routes linked newer areas, like Texas and California, to the rest of the United States. At midcentury, steamships still carried bulk cargo more cheaply than railroads did, except during freezing weather. The sealike Great Lakes accommodated giant ships with propellers in place of paddlewheels; these leviathans carried heavy bulk cargoes like lumber, grain, and ore. On the high seas, steamships gradually replaced sailing vessels, which were dependent on prevailing winds and thus usually could not meet regular schedules. The biggest breakthrough occurred in 1848, when Samuel Cunard introduced regularly scheduled steamships between Liverpool and New York, reducing travel time across the Atlantic from twenty-five days eastbound and forty-nine days westbound to between ten and fourteen days each way.

By far the fastest-spreading technological advance of the era was the magnetic telegraph. Invented by Samuel F. B. Morse, the telegraph made instantaneous communication, even over long distances, pos-

Telegraph

sible. By 1853, only nine years after construction of the first experimental telegraph line, 23,000 miles of telegraph wire had spread across the United States; by 1860, 50,000 miles were in use. In 1861 the telegraph bridged the continent, literally joining the nation together and ending the isolation of Texans and Californians. Rarely has an innovation had so great an impact so quickly: it revolutionized newsgathering, provided advance information for railroads, and altered patterns of business and finance.

Time was key to the revolutionary changes in transportation and communications that took place from 1800 to 1860. In 1800 it took four days to travel by coach from New York City to Baltimore and nearly four weeks to reach Detroit. By 1830 Baltimore was only a day-and-a-half away, and by 1857, Detroit was an overnight train ride from New York City. Reduced travel time not only saved money and facilitated commerce but also brought frontier areas under the control of Chicago and eastern businesses. During the first two decades of the century, wagon transportation cost 30 to 70 cents per ton per mile. By 1860, railroads moved wheat from Chicago to New York for 1.2 cents per ton-mile. In sum, the transportation revolution transformed the economy.

 ## The Market Economy

Before the transportation revolution, most farmers had geared production to family needs and to local and foreign markets. They lived in interdependent communities and kept detailed accounts of labor and goods exchanged with their neighbors. Farm families produced much of what they needed and traded for or purchased items they could not produce. By the Civil War, however, the United States was industrializing. Increasing numbers of men and women worked for wages, and most people outside the South—farmers and workers alike—purchased increasing amounts of store-bought goods produced in workshops and factories.

In the market economy, men and women grew crops and produced goods for sale at home or abroad. The money that individuals received from market transactions—from the sale of goods or from the sale of a person's labor—purchased items produced by other people. Such a system encouraged specialization. Farmers began to grow only one or two crops or to raise only livestock for market. Farm women gave up spinning and weaving and purchased fabric produced by wage-earning farm girls in Massachusetts textile mills.

Definition of a Market Economy

Improvements in transportation and technology, the division of labor, and new methods of financing all fueled the expansion of the economy. Goods and services multiplied. This growth, in turn, prompted new improvements and greater opportunities for wage labor. The effect was cumulative; by the 1840s the economy was growing at a faster rate than in the previous four decades. While per capita income doubled between 1800 and 1860, the price of manufactured goods and food fell.

The pace of economic growth, however, was uneven. Prosperity reigned during two long periods, from 1823 to 1835 and from 1843 to 1857.

Boom-and-Bust Cycles

But there were long stretches of economic contraction as well. Between Jefferson's 1807 embargo and the end of the War of 1812, the growth rate was negative—that is, fewer goods and services were produced. Contraction and deflation (decline in the general price level) occurred again during the hard times of 1819–1823, 1839–1843, and 1857. During these periods banks collapsed, businesses went under, wages and prices declined, and jobs were hard to find or to keep.

Hard times were devastating for workers. In 1857, the Mercantile Agency—the forerunner of Dun and Bradstreet—recorded 5,123 bankruptcies, nearly double the number of the previous year. Contemporary reports estimated twenty to thirty thousand unemployed people in Philadelphia, and thirty to forty thousand in New York City. Female benevolent societies expanded their soup kitchens and distributed free firewood to the needy. In New York, the city hired the unemployed to repair streets and develop Central Park; in Fall River, Massachusetts, a citizens' committee disbursed public funds on a weekly basis to nine hundred families. The soup kitchen, the bread line, and public aid had become fixtures in urban America.

Cause of Boom-and-Bust Cycles

What caused the boom-and-bust cycles? Generally speaking, they were a direct result of the market economy. Prosperity stimulated demand for staples and for finished goods such as clothing and furniture. Increased demand in turn led not only to higher prices and still higher production but also, because of business confidence and expectation of higher prices, to speculation in land and to the flow of foreign currency into the country. Eventually production surpassed demand, causing prices and wages to fall; in response, inflated land and stock values collapsed. The inflow of foreign money led first to easy credit and then to collapse when unhappy investors withdrew their funds.

Some contemporary economists considered this process beneficial—a self-adjusting cycle in which unprofitable economic ventures were eliminated. In theory, people concentrated on the activities they did best, and the economy as a whole became more efficient. Advocates of the system also argued that it enhanced individual freedom, since theoretically each seller, whether of goods or labor, was free to determine the conditions of the sale. But in fact the system tied workers to a perpetual roller coaster; they became dependent on wages—and on the availability of jobs—for their very existence.

The market economy also ushered in another type of boom-and-bust cycle: harvest and destruction. Canals and railroads stimulated demand for distant resources, then accelerated the destruction of forests, natural waterways, and any landscape features that represented obstacles. Railroads made possible large-scale lumbering of pinewood forests in northern Michigan, Wisconsin, and Minnesota. During the 1850s, 40 million acres were cleared of lumber, leaving most of that land unfit even for agriculture. Similarly, the extension of railroads to Kansas and Nebraska brought hunters who slaughtered the great herds of bison for sport. The process of harvest and destruction eventually would change the ecology of the United States.

 ## Government Promotes Economic Growth

The eighteenth-century political ideas that had captured the imagination of the Revolutionary War generation and found expression in the ideal of republican virtue had economic counterparts in the writings of Adam Smith, a Scottish political economist. Smith's *The Wealth of Nations* first appeared in 1776, the year of the Declaration of Independence. Both works emphasized individual liberty, and both were reactions against active government: Thomas Jefferson denounced monarchy and distant government; Smith rejected mercan-

tilism, or government regulation of the economy to benefit the state. Both declared that virtue resided in individual freedom and that the community would benefit most from individuals' pursuit of their own self-interest.

Jefferson believed that freedom thrived where individuals were unfettered by government, monopoly, or economic dependence. Limited government was not an end, according to Jefferson, but a means to greater freedom. Committed to the idea that republican democracy would flourish best in a nation of independent farmers and artisans and in an atmosphere of widespread political participation, Jefferson recognized that government was needed to promote individual freedom. Beginning with the purchase of Louisiana in 1803, Republican policy, no less than that of the Federalists, endorsed using the federal government to promote economic growth.

After acquiring Louisiana, the federal government facilitated economic growth and geographic expansion by encouraging westward exploration and settlement, by promoting agriculture, and by developing transportation. The Lewis and Clark expedition (see page 160) began ongoing federal interest in geographic and geologic surveying and opened western lands to exploitation and settlement. In subsequent decades, Henry Rowe Schoolcraft explored the Missouri and Arkansas region (1817–1818), Major Stephen Long the Great Plains (1819–1820), and John C. Frémont the areas along the Oregon Trail and then south to California (1843–1844). Frémont dispelled a long-standing myth that the center of the continent was a desert.

To encourage settlement and cultivation of western lands, the federal government evicted Indians from their traditional lands and offered the land at reasonable prices. The government also first financed roads and canals and later subsidized railroad construction by means of land grants. Even the State Department aided agriculture: its consular offices overseas collected horticultural information, seeds, and cuttings, and it published technical reports in an effort to improve American farming.

The federal government also played an active role in technological and industrial growth. Federal arsenals pioneered new manufacturing techniques and helped to develop the machine-tool industry. The United States Post Office provided a communications link that stimulated interregional trade and briefly played a crucial role in the development of the telegraph. The federal government financed the first telegraph line, from Washington to Baltimore, in 1844; it was briefly managed by the Post Office. To create an atmosphere conducive to economic growth and individual creativity, the government protected inventions and domestic industries. Patent laws gave inventors a seventeen-year monopoly on their inventions, and tariffs protected American industry from foreign competition.

Legal Foundations of Commerce

The federal judiciary validated government promotion of the economy and encouraged business enterprise. In *Gibbons* v. *Ogden* (1824), the Supreme Court overturned the New York State law that had given Robert Fulton and Robert Livingston a monopoly on the New York–New Jersey steamboat trade. Aaron Ogden, their successor, lost the monopoly when Chief Justice of the United States John Marshall ruled that the congressional prerogative of licensing new enterprises took precedence over New York's grant of monopoly rights to Fulton and Livingston. Marshall declared that Congress's power under the commerce clause of the Constitution extended to "every species of commercial intercourse," including transportation systems. In defining interstate commerce broadly, the Marshall Court expanded federal powers over the economy while restricting the ability of states to control economic activity within their borders.

Federal and state courts, in conjunction with state legislatures, also encouraged the proliferation of corporations—organizations entitled to hold property and transact business as if they were a person. Corporation owners, called shareholders, were granted *limited liability*, or freedom from responsibility for the company's debts. In 1800 the United States had about three hundred incorporated firms; in 1817 there were about two thousand. By 1830 the New England states alone had issued nineteen hundred charters. At first each firm needed a special legislative act to incorporate,

but after the 1830s, applications became so numerous that states established routine procedures allowing firms to incorporate.

Another encouragement to corporate development and free enterprise was the Supreme Court's ruling in *Charles River Bridge* v. *Warren Bridge* (1837) that new enterprises could not be restrained by implied privileges under old charters. The case involved issues of great importance: should a new interest be allowed to compete against existing enterprises, and should the state protect existing privilege or encourage innovation and the growth of commerce through competition?

The Massachusetts legislature had chartered the Charles River Bridge Company in 1785 and six years later extended its charter for seventy years. In return for assuming the risk of building a bridge between Charlestown and Boston, the owners were granted the privilege of collecting tolls. In 1828 the legislature chartered another company to build the Warren Bridge across the Charles nearby; the owner would have the right to collect tolls for six years, after which the bridge would be turned over to the state and be free of tolls. The Charles River Bridge Company sued in 1829, claiming that the new bridge breached the earlier charter.

Speaking for the Court majority, Marshall's successor Roger Taney declared that the original charter did not confer the privilege of monopoly and that exclusivity could not therefore be implied. Taney further ruled that charter grants should be interpreted narrowly and that ambiguities would be decided in favor of the public interest. New enterprises should not be restricted by old charters.

State Promotion of the Economy

In promoting the economy, state governments far surpassed the federal government. From 1815 through 1860, for example, 73 percent of the $135 million invested in canals was government money, most of it from the states. In the 1830s the states started to invest in rail construction. Though the federal government played a larger role in constructing railroads than in building canals, state and local governments provided more than half the capital for southern rail lines.

State governments also invested in corporate and bank stocks, providing corporations and banks with much-needed capital.

Largely as a result of government efforts, the United States experienced uneven but sustained economic growth from the end of the War of 1812 until 1860. Political controversy raged over questions of state versus federal activity, but all parties agreed on the general goal of economic expansion. Indeed, during these years the major restraint on government action was not philosophical but financial: the public purse was small.

The Rise of Manufacturing and Commerce

In 1851, hundreds of American products made their international debut at the 1851 London Crystal Palace Exhibition, the first modern world's fair. There the design and quality of American machines and wares astonished observers, and American manufacturers returned home with dozens of medals. Most impressive to the Europeans were three simple machines: Alfred C. Hobb's unpickable padlocks, Samuel Colt's revolvers, and Robbins and Lawrence's rifles with completely interchangeable parts. All were machine-tooled rather than handmade, products of what the British called the American system of manufacturing. So impressed were the British—whose nation was the leading industrial power of the time—that in 1853 they sent a parliamentary commission to study the American system. Other nations quickly followed Great Britain's lead, sending delegations across the Atlantic to bring back American machines.

The American system of manufacturing used precision machinery to produce interchangeable parts that did not require individual adjustment to fit. Eli Whitney had promoted the idea of interchangeable parts in 1798 when he contracted with the federal government to make ten thousand rifles in twenty-eight months. By the 1820s the United States Ordnance Department had contracted with private firms to introduce machine-made interchangeable parts for

American System of Manufacturing

firearms. The American system quickly spread beyond the arsenals, giving birth to the machine-tool industry—the manufacture of machines for the purposes of mass production. One outcome was an explosion in consumer goods of uniformly high quality.

Interchangeable parts and the machine-tool industry were uniquely American contributions to the industrial revolution. Both paved the way for the swift industrialization the nation experienced after the Civil War. In 1800, however, manufacturing was a relatively unimportant component of the American economy. Most took place in small workshops and homes, where master craftsmen supervised journeymen and taught apprentices, and women worked alone spinning thread and weaving cloth. Tailors, shoemakers, and blacksmiths made articles by hand, to order for specific customers.

The rise of textile mills illustrates the changes in manufacturing wrought by the market economy. Although some farm families continued to make their own cloth, the nineteenth-century machine-tool industry made textile and clothing production a function of mills and factories rather than kitchens and home workshops. The first American textile mill—Almy and Brown's 1790 Pawtucket, Rhode Island, factory—used water-powered spinning machines constructed from British models by the English immigrant Samuel Slater. Soon other mills sprang up, stimulated by the embargo on British imports from 1807 through 1815.

Production of Cloth

These early mills, dependent on waterpower, were located in rural areas. By erecting dams and watercourses, mill owners diverted water from farmers and destroyed fishing, an important source of income and protein in rural and village America. To protect their customary rights, fishermen and farmers fought the manufacturers in New England state legislatures, but petitions from hopeful job seekers in the mill environs supported the manufacturers. The ensuing compromises promoted mill development.

Construction of the first American power loom and the chartering of the Boston Manufacturing Company in 1813 radically transformed textile manufacturing. The corporation was capitalized at $400,000—ten times the amount behind the Rhode Island mills—by Francis Cabot Lowell and other Boston merchants. Its goal was to eliminate the problems of coordination, quality control, and shipping inherent in the subcontracting of work in the putting-out system. The owners erected their factories in Waltham, Massachusetts, bringing all the manufacturing processes to a single location. They employed a resident manager to run the mill, thus separating ownership from management. Workers were paid by the piece or by the hour, and the cloth was sold throughout the United States.

Waltham (Lowell) System

When managers could not find enough hands in rural Waltham to staff the mill, they recruited New England farm daughters, accepting responsibility for their living conditions. As inducements, they offered cash wages, company-run boarding houses, and cultural events such as evening lectures—none of which was available on the farm. This paternalistic approach, called the Waltham (or Lowell) system, was adopted in other mills erected alongside New England rivers.

By 1860 a cotton mill resembled a modern factory. The work force consisted mainly of immigrant Irish women who lived at home, not in mill-subsidized housing. New England farm women continued to live in the few remaining boarding houses. Technological improvements in the looms and other machinery had made the work less skilled and more routine. The mills could thus pay lower wages, drawing from a reservoir of unskilled labor.

Textile Mills

Textiles became the most important industry in the nation before the Civil War, employing 115,000 workers in 1860, more than half of them women and immigrants. The key to the success of the textile industry was that the machines, not the women, spun the yarn and wove the cloth. Workers watched the machines and intervened to maintain smooth operation. When a thread broke, the machine stopped automatically; a worker found the break, pieced the ends together, and restarted the machine. New England textile mills used increasingly specialized machines, relying heavily on advances in the machine-tool industry. Their application of the American system of manufacturing enabled American firms to compete successfully with British cotton mills.

The appearance of ready-made clothing was a major change in the textile industry. Before the 1820s, most clothing was sewn at home by women. Tailors and seamstresses made wealthy men's and women's clothing to order. By the 1820s and 1830s, ready-made clothing became common. Manufacturers produced it by one of two methods: production within a factory, or by the putting-out system. This time, however, a journeyman tailor typically cut the fabric panels in the factory, and the sewing was put out at piece rates to unskilled or semiskilled labor, often women working at home.

Ready-made Clothing

Most of the first mass-produced clothes, crudely made and limited to a few loose-fitting sizes, were produced for men, and they were purchased by men who lived in city boarding houses and rooming houses. Improvements in fit and changes in men's fashion eventually made ready-to-wear apparel more acceptable to white-collar and professional men. By the 1850s many were wearing the short sack coat. A forerunner of the modern suit jacket, it fit loosely and needed little custom tailoring. Now even upper-class men were willing to consider ready-made apparel. In 1818 Henry Sands Brooks (later Brooks Brothers), offered tailoring services and ready-made apparel to the carriage trade.

Retail clothing stores well stocked with ready-made clothes appeared in the 1820s. Their owners often bought goods wholesale, though many manufactured garments in their own factories. Lewis and Hanford of New York City boasted of cutting more than one hundred thousand garments in the winter of 1848–1849. The New York firm sold most of its clothing in the South and owned its own retail outlet in New Orleans. In the West, Cincinnati became the center of the new men's clothing industry. By midcentury, Cincinnati's ready-to-wear apparel industry employed fifteen hundred men and ten thousand women.

Though cotton-textile mills and factories were in the vanguard, large-scale manufacturing also transformed woolen textiles, farm implements, machine tools, iron, steel, glass, and finished consumer goods. "White coal"—waterpower—was widely used to run the machines. By 1860, manufacturing accounted for one-third of the nation's total production, an increase of 200 percent in twenty years.

To a striking extent, large-scale manufacturing in this period was an outcome rather than an agent of change in American life. For example, in the early republic, greater profits could be made by transporting British products to the United States than by producing them at home. Surplus capital thus flowed into the merchant marine, but the embargo and the War of 1812 reversed this situation and merchants began to shift their capital from shipping to manufacturing. Industry was also stimulated by population growth, government policy (protective tariffs, for example), the rise of commercial agriculture, and the transportation revolution.

Stimulants to Industry

Commerce expanded hand in hand with manufacturing. Cotton, for instance, had once been traded by plantation agents, who sold the raw cotton and bought manufactured goods that they then sold to plantation owners, extending them credit when necessary. As cotton became a great staple export after the invention of the cotton gin in 1793, cotton exports rose from half a million pounds in that year to 83 million pounds in 1815. Gradually, some agents came to specialize in finance alone: they were cotton brokers, who for a commission brought together buyers and sellers. Similarly, wheat and hog brokers sprang up in the West—in Cincinnati, Louisville, and St. Louis. The distribution of finished goods also became more specialized as wholesalers bought large quantities of particular items from manufacturers, and jobbers broke down the wholesale lots for retail stores and country merchants.

Specialization of Commerce

Commercial specialization transformed some traders in big cities, especially New York, into virtual merchant princes. After the Erie Canal opened, New York City became a standard stop on every major trade route from Europe, the southern ports, and the West. New York traders were the middlemen for southern cotton and western grain trading. Merchants in other cities played a similar role within their own regions. Newly rich traders in turn invested their profits in processing enterprises and then in manufacturing. Some cities specialized: Rochester became a milling center, and Cincinnati—"Porkopolis"—became the first meatpacking center.

Banks and other financial institutions, which played a significant role in the expansion of commerce and manufacturing, also became a leading industry themselves. Financial institutions (banks, insurance companies, and corporations) linked savers—those who deposited money in banks—with producers and speculators who wished to borrow money. The expiration of the first Bank of the United States in 1811 acted as a stimulus to state-chartered banks, and over the next five years, the number of such banks more than doubled. When state banks proved inadequate to spur national growth, Congress chartered the Second Bank of the United States in 1816.

Banking and Credit Systems

The closing of the Second Bank in 1836 (see Chapter 13) caused a nationwide credit shortage, which, in conjunction with the Panic of 1837, stimulated fundamental reforms in banking. Michigan and New York introduced charter laws promoting what was called *free banking*. Previously, every new bank needed a special legislative charter before it could open for business; thus each bank incorporation was in effect a political decision. Under the new laws, any proposed bank that met certain minimum conditions—amount of capital invested, number of notes issued, and types of loans to be made—would receive a state charter automatically. Banks in Michigan, New York, and soon, other states were thus freer to incorporate, although the legislatures placed some restrictions on their operation to reduce the risk of bank failure.

Free banking proved to be a significant stimulus to the economy in the late 1840s and 1850s.

New banks sprang up everywhere, providing merchants and manufacturers with the credit they needed. The free-banking laws also served as a precedent for general incorporation statutes that allowed manufacturing firms to receive state charters without special acts of the state legislature.

In the 1850s, with both credit and capital easily obtainable, manufacturing spread. In the North, industry began to rival agriculture and commerce in dollar volume. Meanwhile, commercial farming, financed by the credit boom, was integrating the early frontier into the northern economy. By 1860 Massachusetts, New York, Pennsylvania, Connecticut, Rhode Island, and Ohio were highly industrialized. Their clothing, textile, and shoe industries employed more than one hundred thousand workers each; lumber, seventy-five thousand; iron, sixty-five thousand; and woolens and leather, fifty thousand. Although agriculture still predominated even in these states, industrial employment would soon surpass it.

 ## Workers and the Workplace

> Oh, sing me the song of the Factory Girl!
> So merry and glad and free!
> The bloom in her cheeks, of health how it speaks,
> Oh! a happy creature is she!
> She tends the loom, she watches the spindle,
> And cheerfully toileth away,
> Amid the din of wheels, how her bright eyes kindle,
> And her bosom is ever gay.

This idyllic portrait of factory work appeared in the Chicopee, Massachusetts, *Telegraph* in 1850. It was a fitting anthem for the teenage single women who first left the villages and farms of New England to work in the mills. New England mill owners, convinced that the degradation of English factory workers arose from their living conditions and not from the work itself, designed boarding-house communities offering airy courtyards and river views, prepared meals, and cultural activities.

The promise of steady work, good pay, and kinship ties at first lured eager rural young women to the mills. Many pairs of sisters and cousins worked in the same mill and helped each other adjust; their letters home drew other kin to the mills.

Young women then had few opportunities for work outside their own homes, and the commercial production of yarn and cloth had reduced their workload in New England farm households. Averaging sixteen and one-half years of age when they entered the mills, the girls usually stayed only about five years. Most left the mills to marry and were replaced by other women interested in earning a wage.

Between 1837 and 1842, most mills ran only part-time because of a decline in demand for cloth. Subsequently managers applied still greater pressures on workers by means of the speed-up, the stretch-out, and the premium system. The speed-up increased the speed of the machines; the stretch-out increased the number of machines each worker had to operate; and premiums paid to the overseers whose departments produced the most cloth encouraged them to pressure workers for greater output. Thus the concern for workers' living conditions gave way to the corporate quest to maximize profits by cutting wages, lengthening the workday, and tightening discipline.

New England millworkers responded to their deteriorating working conditions by organizing and striking. In 1834, in reaction to a 25 percent wage cut, they unsuccessfully "turned out" (struck) against the Lowell mills. Two years later, when boarding-house rates increased, they turned out again. In the 1840s, Massachusetts mill women adopted another method of resistance: they joined forces with other workers to press for state legislation mandating a ten-hour day.

Protests by Mill Women

The women's labor organizations were weakened by the short tenure of most workers. Few of the militant native-born millworkers stayed on to fight the managers and owners, and gradually there were fewer New England daughters to enter the mills. By the end of the 1850s the women who constituted the majority of millworkers were mostly Irish immigrants, driven to the mills by the need to support their families and unable to afford to complain about their working conditions.

A growing gender division in the workplace, especially in the textile, clothing, and shoemaking industries, was one important outcome of large-scale manufacturing. Although women and men in traditional agricultural and artisan households tended to perform different tasks, they worked as a family unit. As wage work spread, however, men's and women's work cultures became increasingly separate. The women and girls who left home to work in textile mills worked and lived in a mostly female world. In the clothing and shoemaking industries, whose male artisans had once worked at home assisted by unpaid family labor, men began working outside the home while women continued to work at home through the putting-out system. Tasks and wages, too, became rigidly differentiated: women sewed, whereas men shaped materials and finished products, receiving higher wages in shops employing men only.

Gender Divisions in Work

The market system, wage labor, and the specialization of labor had an impact on unpaid household labor as well. As home and workplace became separate and labor came to be defined in terms of wages (what could be sold in the marketplace) rather than production, the unpaid labor of women was devalued. But the family depended on women's work within the household, and as the family became more dependent on wage labor, more family members sought outside employment and had less time to do their share of household labor. Thus gender defined household labor and placed a low value on it.

The new textile mills, shoe factories, iron mills, wholesale stores, and railroads were the antithesis of traditional workshop and household production. Factories created a workplace in which authority was hierarchically organized. Factory workers lost their sense of autonomy as impersonal market forces seemed to dominate their lives. Competition among mills in the growing textile industry of the 1820s and 1830s led to layoffs and the replacement of operatives with cheaper, less-skilled workers or children. The formal rules of the factory contrasted sharply with the more relaxed pace and atmosphere of artisan shops and farm households. Supervisors represented owners whom workers never saw. The division of labor and the use of machines narrowed the skills required of workers. And the flow of work was governed by the bell, the steam whistle, or the clock. The factory bell controlled when the workers awoke, ate, began and ended work, and went to sleep. The central problem, of course, was the quickening pace of the work between the bells. Moreover, millworkers had to tolerate the roar of the looms, and all workers on power machines risked accidents that could kill or maim. Perhaps most demoralizing, opportunities for advancement in the new system were virtually nil.

Changes in the Workplace

Changes in the workplace in turn transformed the workers. Initially, mill women drew on kinship, village, and gender ties to build supportive networks in factories. In the 1840s and after, as recently arrived Irish immigrant women came to predominate, more workers were strangers to each other before they entered the mills. Once employed, their only bases for friendship and mutual support were their work experiences. As a sense of distance from their employers took hold, so did deep-seated differences among workers.

Nationality, religion, education, and future prospects separated Irish and Yankee millworkers. Many New England women resented the immigrants, and management set one group against the other through selective hiring and promotions. Mill work was not a stage in the life of most Irish women; it was permanent employment. Unlike their Yankee sisters, they could not risk striking and losing their jobs; they and their families were dependent on their earnings.

While some female textile workers and shoemakers organized and protested, many male workers became active in reform politics. Organized labor's greatest achievement during this period was to gain relief from the threat of conspiracy laws. When journeyman shoemakers organized during the first decade of the century, their employers turned to the courts, charging criminal conspiracy. The cordwainers' (shoemakers') cases, which resulted in six trials be-

Emergence of a Labor Movement

How do historians know what working conditions New England millworkers experienced? This 1853 timetable from the Lowell Mills is among the rich sources historians consult to reconstruct workers' experiences in the mills. Textile factories were the first corporations to impose rigid work rules. The size of the labor force, the management structure, and the organization of the work made it necessary to publish work rules. Exact times were established for beginning and ending work and for meals. Few workers carried their own timepieces, so a system of bells regulated the lives of the factory community. From March 20 to September 19, when work began at 6:30 A.M., bells alerted the workers at 4:30 and 5:50 A.M. and again at 6:20 A.M., ten minutes before they had to be at the factory. For their main meal at midday, they had forty-five minutes away from work; the 12:35 P.M. bell warned that they had ten minutes to return. For young mill women from the New England countryside, and later for Irish women, such regimentation must have seemed a world apart from the rhythms of rural life. Photo: Museum of American Textile History.

TIME TABLE OF THE LOWELL MILLS,

Arranged to make the working time throughout the year average 11 hours per day,

TO TAKE EFFECT SEPTEMBER 21st., 1853,

The Standard time being that of the meridian of Lowell, as shown by the Regulator Clock of AMOS SANBORN, Post Office Corner, Central Street.

From March 20th to September 19th, inclusive.

COMMENCE WORK, at 6.30 A. M. LEAVE OFF WORK, at 6.30 P. M., except on Saturday Evenings.
BREAKFAST at 6 A. M. DINNER, at 12 M. Commence Work, after dinner, 12.45 P. M.

From September 20th to March 19th, inclusive.

COMMENCE WORK, at 7.00 A. M. LEAVE OFF WORK, at 7.00 P. M., except on Saturday Evenings.
BREAKFAST at 6.30 A. M. DINNER, at 12.30 P. M. Commence Work, after dinner, 1.15 P. M.

BELLS.

From March 20th to September 19th, inclusive.

Morning Bells.	Dinner Bells.	Evening Bells.
First bell...........4.30 A. M.	Ring out,.............12.00 M.	Ring out,...........6.30 P. M.
Second, 5.30 A. M. ; Third, 6.20.	Ring in,...........12.35 P. M.	Except on Saturday Evenings.

From September 20th to March 19th, inclusive.

Morning Bells.	Dinner Bells.	Evening Bells.
First bell,...........5.00 A. M.	Ring out,...........12.30 P. M.	Ring out at...........7.00 P. M.
Second, 6.00 A. M. ; Third, 6.50.	Ring in,............1.05 P. M.	Except on Saturday Evenings.

SATURDAY EVENING BELLS.

During APRIL, MAY, JUNE, JULY, and AUGUST, Ring Out, at 6.00 P. M.
The remaining Saturday Evenings in the year, ring out as follows :

SEPTEMBER.	NOVEMBER.	JANUARY.
First Saturday, ring out 6.00 P. M.	Third Saturday ring out 4.00 P. M.	Third Saturday, ring out 4.25 P. M.
Second " " 5.45 "	Fourth " " 3.55 "	Fourth " " 4.35 "
Third " " 5.30 "		
Fourth " " 5.20 "	DECEMBER.	FEBRUARY.
OCTOBER.	First Saturday, ring out 3.50 P. M.	First Saturday, ring out 4.45 P. M.
First Saturday, ring out 5.05 P. M.	Second " " 3.55 "	Second " " 4.55 "
Second " " 4.55 "	Third " " 3.55 "	Third " " 5.00 "
Third " " 4.45 "	Fourth " " 4.00 "	Fourth " " 5.10 "
Fourth " " 4.35 "	Fifth " " 4.00 "	
Fifth " " 4.25 "		MARCH.
	JANUARY.	First Saturday, ring out 5.25 P. M.
NOVEMBER.	First Saturday, ring out 4.10 P. M.	Second " " 5.30 "
First Saturday, ring out 4.15 P. M.	Second " " 4.15 "	Third " " 5.35 "
Second "· 4.05 "		Fourth " " 5.45 "

YARD GATES will be opened at the first stroke of the bells for entering or leaving the Mills.

∴ *SPEED GATES commence hoisting three minutes before commencing work.*

Penhallow, Printer, Wyman's Exchange, 28 Merrimack St.

---

tween 1806 and 1815, left labor organizations in a tenuous position. Although the journeymen's right to organize was acknowledged, the courts ruled unlawful any coercive action by them that would harm other businesses or the public. In other words, strikes were ruled illegal. Eventually a Massachusetts case, *Commonwealth* v. *Hunt* (1842),

effectively reversed this decision when Chief Justice Lemuel Shaw ruled that Boston journeyman bootmakers could strike "in such manner as best to subserve their own interests." Conspiracy laws no longer thwarted unionization.

Yet permanent labor organizations were difficult to maintain. Most workers outside the crafts were unskilled or semiskilled at best. Moreover, religion, race, ethnicity, and gender divided workers. The first unions arose among urban journeymen in printing, woodworking, shoemaking, and tailoring. These early labor unions tended to be local; the strongest resembled medieval guilds in that members sought to protect themselves against the competition of inferior workmen by regulating apprenticeship and establishing minimum wages. They also excluded women and African-Americans.

Umbrella organizations composed of individual craft unions, like the National Trades Union (1834), arose in several cities in the 1820s and 1830s. But the movement fell apart amid wage reductions and unemployment in the hard times of 1839–1843. In the 1850s the deterioration of working conditions strengthened the labor movement again, and affiliated craft unions began to organize into national unions. Workers won a reduction in hours, and the ten-hour day became standard. Though the Panic of 1857 wiped out the umbrella organizations, some of the new national unions in specific trades survived.

Economic and technological change inevitably affected individual workers more heavily than it affected their organizations. As a group, workers' share of the national wealth declined after the 1830s. Individual producers—craftsmen, factory workers, and farmers—had less economic power than they had had a generation or two earlier. And workers were increasingly losing control over their own work.

 ## Commercial Farming

Although manufacturing increased steadily, agriculture remained the backbone of the economy. In 1800 New England and Middle Atlantic farmers worked as their fathers and mothers had. Life centered around a household economy in which the needs of the family and the labor at its disposal determined what was produced and in what amounts. Most implements—wooden plows, rakes, shovels, and yokes—were homemade, with iron parts obtained from the local blacksmith.

When canals and railroads began transporting grain, especially wheat, eastward from the fertile

Old Northwest, northeastern agriculture could not compete. Eastern farmers had already cultivated all the land available to them; expansion was impossible. Moreover, small New England farms with their uneven terrain did not lend themselves to the new labor-saving farm implements introduced in the 1830s—mechanical sowers, reapers, threshers, and balers.

Northeastern Agriculture

In response to these problems and to competition from the West, many northern farmers either moved west or gave up farming for jobs in the merchant houses and factories. Between 1820 and 1860 the percentage of the population of the North living on farms declined from 71 to 40 percent. The farmers who remained proved as adaptable on the farm as were their children working at copy desks and waterpowered looms. By the 1850s many New England and Middle Atlantic farm families had abandoned the commercial production of wheat and corn and stopped tilling poor land. Instead, they were improving their livestock, especially cattle, and specializing in vegetable and fruit production and dairy farming, financing these initiatives through land sales and borrowing. In fact, their greatest potential profit was from increasing land values, not from farming itself.

Farm families everywhere gradually adjusted to market conditions. In 1820 about one-third of all food produced was intended for market. By 1860 the amount had increased to about two-thirds. Middlemen specializing in the grain and food trades replaced the country storekeepers who had handled all transactions for local farmers, acting both as retailers and as marketing and purchasing agents.

Women's Paid Labor

Women's earning power from wages or market sales was an important factor in the market economy. With increasing commercialization and dependency on cash, women's earnings became essential to the survival of the family farm. The put-out work that women did in New England had its parallel in the Middle Atlantic states and in Ohio—especially near towns and cities—in women's dairy production, which was crucial to family income. Butter and cheese making for local and regional markets replaced spinning and weaving as farm women's major activity. The work was physically demanding and did not replace regular home and farm chores but was added to them. Yet women took pride in their work; it gave many a sense of independence.

Most farm families seemed to welcome the opportunities offered by the market economy. While continuing to take pride in self-sufficiency and to value rural culture, they shifted toward specialization and market-oriented production. The rewards for such flexibility were great. Produce sold at market financed land and equipment purchases and made credit arrangements possible. Many farm families flourished.

Others—hired hands and farm tenants—were less fortunate. The rising cost of land and farming meant that by the 1850s it took from ten to twenty years for a rural laborer to save enough money to farm for himself. Thus the number of tenant farmers increased.

Individually and collectively, Americans still valued agrarian life. State governments energetically promoted commercial agriculture to spur economic growth and sustain the values of an agrarian-based republic. Massachusetts in 1817 and New York in 1819 subsidized agricultural prizes and county fairs. New York required contestants to submit written descriptions of how they grew their prize crops; the state then published the best essays to encourage the use of new methods and promote specialization. Farm journals also helped familiarize farmers with developments in agriculture.

Even so, the Old Northwest gradually and inevitably replaced the northeastern states as the center of American family agriculture. Farms in the Old Northwest were much larger and better suited to

Mechanization of Agriculture

the new mechanized farming implements than were their northeastern counterparts. The farmers of the region bought machines such as the McCormick reaper on credit and paid for them with the profits from their high yields. By 1847 Cyrus McCormick was selling a thousand reapers a year. By introducing interchangeable parts, he

expanded production to five thousand a year, but demand still outstripped supply. Similarly, John Deere's steel plow, invented in 1837, replaced the inadequate iron plow; steel blades kept the soil from sticking and were tough enough to break the roots of prairie grass. By 1856, Deere's sixty-five employees were making 13,500 plows a year.

Mechanized farming was the basis of expanded production. In the 1850s alone wheat production surged 70 percent. By that time the area that had been the western wilderness in 1800 had become one of the world's leading agricultural regions. Midwestern farm families fed an entire nation and still had enough food to export.

 ## Settling and Conquering the West

Integral to the development of the market economy was the steady expansion of the United States. In 1800 the edge of settlement extended in an arc from western New York State through the new states of Kentucky and Tennessee and south to Georgia. By 1820, it had shifted westward to Ohio, Indiana, and Illinois in the North, and Louisiana, Alabama, and Mississippi in the South. By 1860, Texas and California were states, and settlement had reached its twentieth-century continental limits. Unsettled and sporadically settled land remained—mostly the plains and mountain territory between the Mississippi River and the Sierra Nevada—but elsewhere the land and its Indian inhabitants had given way to white settlement (see maps).

Most Americans saw western settlers as civilizers; a minority, including Indians, viewed them as conquerors. In myth, literature, and song Americans glorified the explorers, fur trappers and scouts,

Conquerors and Civilizers

and pioneers. James Fenimore Cooper's Leatherstocking tales, a series of novels that began appearing in 1823, introduced Hawkeye (Natty Bumppo), America's first popular fictional hero. At heart a romantic, Hawkeye preferred the freedom of the virgin forest to domesticated society. Yet

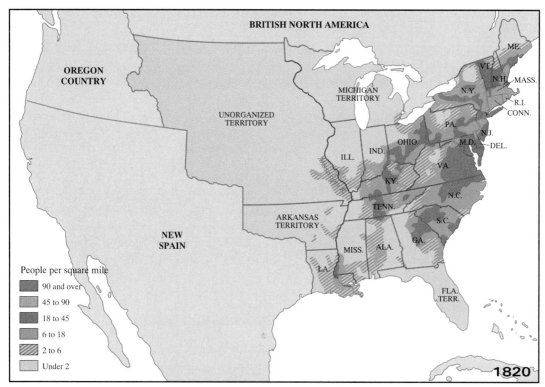

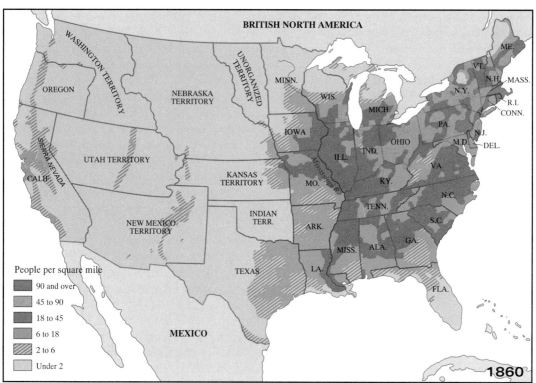

United States Population, 1820 and 1860 *Between 1820 and 1860, the population of the United States grew from 9.6 million to 31.4 million, and the density increased significantly in the North, the Old Northwest, and California. Settlement, too, spread farther away from the eastern seaboard.*

SIR JOS JEBB.

The fur trade was part of a market system that extended from the Far West through St. Louis, Montréal, and New York to the hat merchants of Europe. These Ottawa fur traders, painted at Fort Michilimackinac in Upper Michigan, most likely traded with fur merchants based in Montréal.   National Archives of Canada.

whatever noble Eden the wilderness offered, it inevitably gave way, as Cooper described in *The Last of the Mohicans* (1826), to civilization.

The frontier represented not only the peaceful settlement of the West and the extension of farming and republican virtue but also the conquering of the native inhabitants and the environment. The history of the West was often violent and intolerant. The Mormons who sought a new Jerusalem near the Great Salt Lake were fleeing the gehenna (hell) imposed on them by frontier folk farther east (see page 216). Those who sought to farm the land, dig the gold, trap the furs, and cut the lumber destroyed the natural landscape

and ecological balance in the name of progress and development.

The market economy provided a great impetus for expansion. Early on, the fur trapper system brought the Far West—way beyond settlement—into a market system that extended through St. Louis, Montréal, and New York to the hat merchants of Europe. Then, in the late 1840s, settlement jumped over the trapping areas to the West Coast of the American continent, when the promise of instant wealth in the form of gold sparked a gold rush.

Gold stimulated a mass migration to the West Coast. The United States had acquired Alta

California from Mexico in the Treaty of Guadalupe Hidalgo (see page 259),

California Gold Rush

and the province was inhabited mostly by native peoples, some Mexicans living on large estates, and a chain of small settlements around military forts (presidios) and missions. That changed almost overnight after James Marshall, a carpenter, spotted gold particles in the millrace at Sutter's Mill (now Coloma, California, northwest of Sacramento) in January 1848. Word of the discovery spread, and other Californians rushed to scrabble for instant fortunes.

By 1849 the news had spread around the world, and hundreds of thousands of fortune seekers streamed into California. The newcomers came for one reason: instant wealth. Success in the market economy required capital, hard labor, and time; by contrast, gold mining seemed to promise instant riches. Most "forty-niners," however, never found enough gold to pay their expenses. "The stories you hear frequently in the States," one gold seeker wrote home, "are the most extravagant lies imaginable—the mines are a humbug. . . . The almost universal feeling is to get home." But many stayed, either unable to afford the passage home or tempted by the growing labor shortage in California's cities and agricultural districts.

The forty-niners had their eyes on gold nuggets, but they had to be fed. Thus began the great California agricultural boom. Wheat was the preferred staple; it required minimal investment, was easily planted, and offered a quick return at the end of a relatively short growing season. By the mid-1850s, California was exporting wheat. Meanwhile, enterprising merchants rushed to supply, feed, and clothe the new settlers. One such merchant was Levi Strauss, a German Jewish immigrant, whose tough mining pants found an enduring and eventually worldwide market as blue jeans.

In the Midwest, family farms were the basic unit of production. In California, by contrast, mining, grazing, and large-scale wheat farming

Women Settlers

were overwhelmingly male occupations. The experiences of women, who constituted about one-seventh of the travelers on

the overland trails, differed from those of men moving westward. Most men came alone. Women who accompanied their husbands found their lives uprooted. Moving was a traumatic experience for many; they left behind networks of friends and kin to journey, often with children, along an unknown path to a strange environment. Yet in the West their domestic skills were in great demand. They received high fees for cooking, laundering, and sewing, and they ran boarding houses and hotels (men shunned domestic work). Not all women, however, were entrepreneurs. Some wives, at their spouses' behest, cooked for and served their husbands' friends, enabling their husbands to build reputations as hosts.

Gold altered the pattern of settlement along the entire Pacific coast. Before 1848 most overland traffic flowed north over the Oregon Trail; few pioneers turned south to California. By 1849 a pioneer observed that the Oregon Trail "bore no evidence of having been much traveled this year." Traffic was flowing south instead, and California was becoming the new population center of the Pacific Slope. One measure of this shift was the overland mail routes. In the 1840s the Oregon Trail had been the main communications link between the Midwest and the Pacific. But the post office officials who organized mail routes in the 1850s terminated them in California, not Oregon; there was no route north of Sacramento.

By 1860 farmers in California, as in the Great Plains and prairies farther east, had become firmly linked to the market economy. They cleared the

Western Farming

land of trees or prairie grass, hoed corn and wheat, fenced in animals, and constructed cabins of logs or sod. Success often depended on their access to water, and they sought to divert the streams and rivers of the West to irrigate their land. As settled areas expanded, farmers built roads to carry their stock and produce to market and bring back supplies they could not produce for themselves. Growth brought specialization; as western farmers shifted from self-sufficiency to commercial farming, they too tended to concentrate on one crop.

What made farm settlements possible was the availability of land and credit. Some public lands were granted as a reward for military service: veterans of the War of 1812 received 160 acres; veterans of the Mexican War could purchase land at reduced prices. And until 1820, civilians could buy government land at $2 an acre (a relatively high price) on a liberal four-year payment plan. From 1800 to 1817 the government successively reduced the minimum purchase from 640 to 80 acres, bringing the land within the reach of more Americans. But when the availability of land prompted the flurry of land speculation that ended in the Panic of 1819, the government discontinued credit sales. Instead, it reduced the price further, to $1.25 an acre.

Land Grants and Sales

Some eager pioneers settled land before it had been surveyed and offered for sale. Such illegal settlers, or squatters, then had to buy the land at auction and faced the risk of being unable to purchase it. In 1841, to facilitate settlement and end property disputes, Congress passed the Pre-emption Act, which legalized settlement prior to surveying.

Since most settlers needed to borrow money, private credit systems arose: banks, private investors, country storekeepers, and speculators all extended credit to farmers. Railroads also sold land on credit—land they had received from the government as construction subsidies. (The Illinois Central, for example, received 2.6 million acres in 1850.) Indeed, nearly all economic activity in the West involved credit, from land sales to the shipping of produce to railroad construction.

From the start, the agricultural West was dependent on its links with towns and cities. Cities along the Ohio River—Louisville and Cincinnati—and the old French settlements—Detroit on the Great Lakes, St. Louis on the Mississippi River—predated and promoted the earliest settlement of much of the West. New population centers, however, bypassed such old French towns as Vincennes and Kaskaskia. Chicago spearheaded settlement farther west. Steamboats connected the

Frontier Cities

river cities with eastern markets and ports, carrying grain east and returning with finished goods. As the center of a rail network, Chicago exercised sway over the settling and development of most of the middle United States. As in the Northeast, western cities eventually developed into manufacturing centers as merchants shifted their investments from commerce to industry.

Urban growth in the West was so spectacular that by 1860 Cincinnati, St. Louis, and Chicago each had populations exceeding one hundred thousand, and Buffalo, Louisville, San Francisco, Pittsburgh, Detroit, and Milwaukee had surpassed forty thousand. Thus commerce, urban growth, and industrialization overtook the farmers' frontier, wedding the West to the Northeast.

 Conclusion

For the North and the West the period from 1800 through 1860 was one of explosive growth. Population increased sixfold. The United States now extended from sea to sea, incorporating new peoples—Indians, Mexicans, Californians—sending out settlers to plow the land and inhabit the cities, and recruiting immigrants from around the world. Agriculture, which had completely dominated the nation at the turn of the century, was by midcentury being challenged by a booming manufacturing sector. And agriculture itself was becoming market-oriented and mechanized.

Economic development changed the way people lived. Canals, railroads, steamboats, and telegraph lines linked economic activities hundreds and even thousands of miles apart. The market economy brought sustained growth; it also ushered in cycles of boom and bust. Hard times and unemployment became frequent occurrences. The growing economy meant larger-scale destruction of the environment.

Large-scale manufacturing also altered traditional patterns of production and consumption. Farmers began to purchase goods formerly made by their wives and daughters, and farm families geared production to faraway markets. Farm women increasingly contributed income from market sales to the family farm. In New England many young women left the family farm to become the first factory workers in the new textile industry. As the master-journeyman-apprentice system faded away, workplace relations became more impersonal and working conditions harsher, and men's and women's work became increasingly dissimilar. Industrial jobs began to attract large numbers of immigrants, and some workers organized labor unions.

The American people, too, were changing. Immigration and western expansion were making the population more diverse. Urbanization, commerce, and industry were creating significant divisions among Americans, reaching deeply into the home as well as the workshop. The South was not totally insulated from these changes, but its dependence on slave rather than free labor set it apart. Above all else, slavery defined the South.

Suggestions for Further Reading

General

David Klingaman and Richard Vedder, eds., *Essays in Nineteenth-Century History* (1975); Jack Larkin, *The Reshaping of Everyday Life, 1790–1840* (1988); Otto Mayr and Robert C. Post, eds., *Yankee Enterprise: The Rise of the American System of Manufactures* (1981); Douglass C. North, *Economic Growth of the United States, 1790–1860* (1966); Nathan Rosenberg, *Technology and American Economic Growth* (1972); Melvyn Stokes and Stephen Conway (eds.), *The Market Revolution in America: Social, Political, and Religious Expressions, 1800–1860* (1996).

Transportation

Carter Goodrich, *Government Promotion of American Canals and Railroads, 1800–1890* (1960); Louis C. Hunter, *Steamboats on the Western Rivers* (1949); Ronald E. Shaw, *Canals for a Nation: The Canal Era in the United States, 1790–1860* (1990); George R. Taylor, *The Transportation Revolution, 1815–1860* (1951); James A. Ward, *Railroads and the Character of America, 1820–1887* (1986).

Commerce and Manufacturing

Alfred D. Chandler, Jr., *The Visible Hand: Managerial Revolution in American Business* (1977); Robert F. Dalzell, Jr., *Enterprising Elite: The Boston Associates and the World They Made* (1987); Louis Hartz, *Economic Policy and Democratic Thought: Pennsylvania, 1776–1860* (1954); Stanley I. Kutler, *Privilege and Creative Destruction: The Charles River Bridge Case* (1971); Walter Licht, *Industrializing America: The Nineteenth Century* (1995); Merritt Roe Smith, *Harpers Ferry Armory and the New Technology* (1977); Theodore Steinberg, *Nature Incorporated: Industrialization and the Waters of New England* (1991); Anthony F. C. Wallace, *Rockdale: The Growth of an American Village in the Early Industrial Revolution* (1978).

Agriculture

Jeremy Atack and Fred Bateman, *To Their Own Soil: Agriculture in the Antebellum North* (1987); Allen G. Bogue, *From Prairie to Corn Belt: Farming on the Illinois and Iowa Prairies in the Nineteenth Century* (1963); Christopher Clark, *The Roots of Rural Capitalism: Western Massachusetts, 1780–1860* (1990); John Mack Faragher, *Sugar Creek: Life on the Illinois Prairie* (1986); Paul W. Gates, *The Farmer's Age: Agriculture, 1815–1860* (1962); Joan M. Jensen, *Loosening the Bonds: Mid-Atlantic Farm Women, 1750–1850* (1986); Robert Leslie Jones, *History of Agriculture in Ohio to 1880* (1983); Sally McMurry, *Transforming Rural Life: Dairying Families and Agricultural Change, 1820–1885* (1995).

Conquerors and Civilizers

William Cronon, *Nature's Metropolis: Chicago and the Great West* (1991); John Mack Faragher, *Women and Men on the Overland Trail* (1979); William H. Goetzmann, *Exploration and Empire: The Explorer and the Scientist in the Winning of the American West* (1966); Theodore J. Karamanski, *Fur Trade and Exploration: Opening the Far Northwest, 1821–1852* (1983); Lillian Schlissel, *Women's Diaries of the Westward Journey* (1982); David J. Weber, *The Spanish Frontier in North America* (1992).

Workers

Jeanne Boydston, *Home and Work: Housework, Wages, and the Ideology of Labor in the Early Republic* (1990); Alan Dawley, *Class and Community: The Industrial Revolution in Lynn* (1977); Thomas Dublin, *Transforming Women's Work: New England Lives in the Industrial Revolution* (1994); Thomas Dublin, *Women at Work: The Transformation of Work and Community in Lowell, Massachusetts, 1826–1860* (1979); Bruce Laurie, *Artisans into Workers: Labor in Nineteenth-Century America* (1989); Howard B. Rock, Paul A. Gilje, and Robert Asher, eds., *American Artisans: Crafting Social Identity, 1750–1850* (1995); Sean Wilentz, *Chants Democratic: New York City and the Rise of the American Working Class, 1788–1850* (1984).

11

Slavery and the Growth of the South

1800–1860

Dressed in silk and adorned in jewelry, Eliza seemed bewildered as she clung to the hands of her children, a little boy and a girl. That morning in 1841 Eliza had been told that she was going into Washington, D.C., to receive her long-promised freedom. Now she found herself in "a slave pen within the very shadow of the Capitol."

Eliza had been her owner's concubine, but a division of his property had placed her under the control of his resentful daughter. The daughter, deciding to remove all evidence of her father's illicit relationship, arranged for a slave trader to move Eliza and her children by ship to New Orleans. At the New Orleans slave market a man offered to purchase her son. To no avail, Eliza pleaded with him to buy the family group. Later, when her daughter was sold away, Eliza had to be physically torn apart from the last person she loved.

Sent to work in the fields of a plantation on Bayou Boeuf, Eliza grew "feeble and emaciated." Within two years she was dead. Eliza's fate was one of many human tragedies accompanying the vast expansion of plantation slavery that took place between 1800 and 1860. Tens of thousands of African-Americans suffered as slavery spread westward; across the Mississippi River and into Texas.

Many northerners remained undisturbed by slavery, but a growing number came to see it as shocking and backward. In the years after the Revolution, northerners—possessing few slaves and influenced by the revolutionary concept of natural rights—had adopted gradual emancipation laws. At the same time, the North's emerging industrial society rendered forced labor obsolete.

Meanwhile, the South witnessed a different kind of growth and prosperity. New lands were settled and new states peopled, but growth in the South only reinforced existing economic patterns. Steadily the South emerged as the world's most extensive and vigorous slave economy. Its people were slaves, slaveholders, and nonslaveholders rather than farmers, merchants, mechanics, mill girls, and manufacturers. Southern wealth came from export crops; its population thus remained almost wholly rural rather than both rural and urban.

Migration, Growth, and the Cotton Boom

Between 1800 and 1860, a vastly larger slaveholding society emerged. Attracted by rich new lands, thousands of southerners moved across the Appalachian Mountains. Small farmers and ambitious slaveowners poured across the mountains, pushing the Indians off their lands in the Gulf region. The floodtide of westward migration reached Alabama and Mississippi in the 1830s, then spilled into Texas in the 1850s.

The earliest settlers in the swelling stream of migration were often yeomen—small farmers, most of whom owned no slaves. Yeomen pioneered

Yeoman Farmers

the southern wilderness, moving into undeveloped regions and building log cabins. After the War of 1812, they moved in successive waves down the southern Appalachians into new Gulf lands, first as herders of livestock and then as farmers.

Migration became almost a way of life for some yeoman families. Lured by stories of good land beyond the horizon, many men uprooted their wives and children repeatedly. Their wives, often dreading the loneliness of the frontier, seldom shared the men's excitement about moving. Once in the new environment, women labored in

the household economy and patiently re-created the social ties—to relatives, neighbors, fellow churchgoers—that enriched everyone's experience.

Some yeomen acquired large tracts of level land, purchased slaves, and became wealthy. Others clung to the beautiful mountainous areas they loved or kept moving as independent subsistence farmers. Those who moved tended to stick to the climate and soils they knew best. Yeomen could not afford the richest bottomlands, which were swampy and required expensive draining, but they acquired land almost everywhere else.

For slaveholding southerners another powerful motive impelled westward movement: the chance to profit from a spectacular cotton boom. Southern planters were not sentimentalists, holding onto slavery while

Rise of the Cotton South

northerners grew rich from commerce and manufacturing. Like other Americans, slaveholding southerners were profit oriented, and the cotton boom caused nonmechanized, slave-based agriculture to remain highly profitable in the South.

This outcome had not always seemed likely. At the time of the Revolution, slave-based agriculture was not very profitable in the Upper South, where most southerners then lived. Persistent debt plagued Virginia's extravagant and aristocratic tobacco growers. Farther south, along the coast of the Carolinas and Georgia, slaves grew rice and some indigo. Cotton was a profitable crop only for the Sea-Island planters of South Carolina and Georgia, who grew the luxurious long-staple variety. Short-staple cotton, which grew readily in the interior, was unmarketable because its sticky seeds lay tangled in the fibers.

Then England's burgeoning textile industry demanded more and more cotton. Sea Island cotton became so profitable between 1785 and 1795 that thousands of farmers in the interior tried growing the short-staple variety, most with the hope that some innovation would make the crop salable to the English. Eli Whitney, an inventor from Connecticut, responded in 1793 with a simple machine that removed the seeds from the fibers. By 1800 cotton was spreading rapidly westward from the seaboard states.

• *Important Events* •

1793	Eli Whitney invents the cotton gin Production of short-staple cotton begins to expand	1832	Virginia holds last serious debate in South about the future of slavery
1800	Gabriel's conspiracy is discovered in Virginia	1832 and after	Legislators in several states increase restrictions on slaves
1808	Congress bans further importation of slaves	1830s	Class tensions lead to electoral reforms in much of the South
1810–20	137,000 slaves are forced to move from North Carolina and the Chesapeake to Alabama, Mississippi, and other western regions	1836	Arkansas gains admission to the Union
		1839	Mississippi's Married Women's Property Act gives married women some property rights
1812	Louisiana gains admission to the Union		
1817	Mississippi gains admission to the Union	1845	Florida and Texas gain admission to the Union
1819	Alabama gains admission to the Union		
1822	Denmark Vesey's plot is discovered in South Carolina	1857	North Carolina slaveholder Hinton R. Helper denounces the slave system in *The Impending Crisis*
1831	Nat Turner leads a violent rebellion in Virginia		

The voracious appetite of English mills caused a meteoric rise in cotton production (see maps). Despite occasional periods of low prices, the demand for cotton surged ahead every decade. Southerners with capital bought more land and more slaves and planted ever more cotton. By 1825 the South was the world's dominant supplier of cotton; by the 1850s the South was the source of over 70 percent of all the cotton that Britain imported.

Thus the antebellum South—the Old South before the Civil War—became primarily a cotton South. Large amounts of tobacco and hemp continued to be grown in the Upper South, and rice and sugar were important crops in certain coastal areas. But cotton was the largest and most widespread cash crop, and the wealth it generated shaped the society.

Small slaveowners and wealthier planters (those who owned twenty or more slaves) sought out alluvial bottomland and other fertile soils, eager to grasp the opportunity for wealth the cotton boom offered. The desire to plant more cotton and buy more slaves often caused men with new wealth to postpone the enjoyment of luxuries. Yet the planters' wealth put ease and refinement within their grasp, and riches and high social status arrived quickly for some.

Slavery's expansion across the Appalachians meant another kind of migration—involuntary— for black southerners. Since Congress had closed the international slave trade in 1808, slaves for new cotton regions had to come from the Upper South, where the slave population was growing through natural increase while tobacco prices fell. Worried by soil exhaustion and low prices, planters in Virginia and North Carolina were shifting toward less labor-intensive crops and were glad to sell excess slaves to fertile regions in the cotton South.

Between 1810 and 1820 alone, 137,000 slaves were forced to move from North Carolina and the

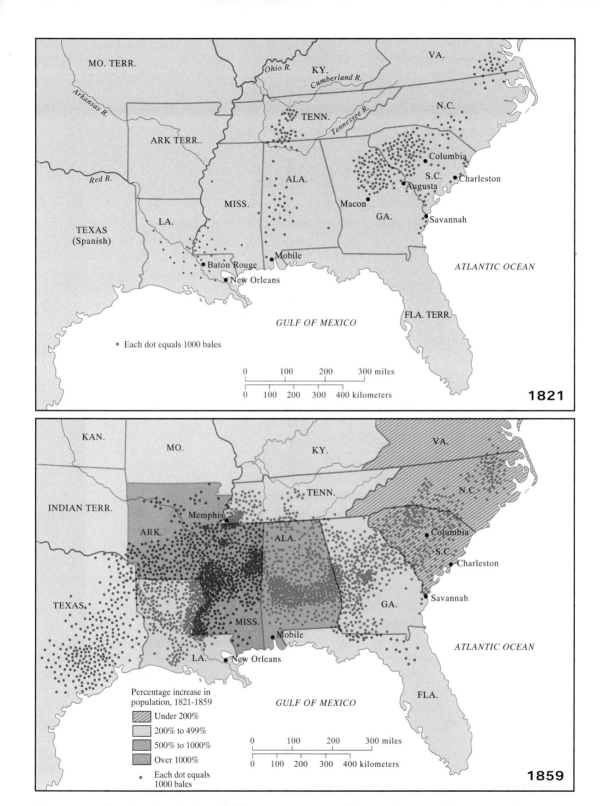

Cotton Production in the South *These two maps reveal the rapid westward expansion of cotton production and its importance to antebellum South.*

Chesapeake states to Alabama, Mississippi, and other western regions. Interregional sales and transfers continued thereafter: an estimated 2 million people were sold between 1820 and 1860 to satisfy the need for slave labor. Thousands of black families like Eliza's were disrupted every year to serve the needs of the cotton economy.

To white southerners the period from 1800 to 1860 was a time of great change and progress. The South was growing and expanding, but its growth was different from the North's: its distinguishing features were those of an agricultural and a slave society.

 ## An Agrarian Society

The South did exhibit some of the diversity of the North. There were merchants, artisans, and craftsmen in the larger cities, as well as men who promoted railways and transportation improvements. Immigrants from Ireland and other parts of Europe arrived in southern ports in increasing numbers during the 1840s and 1850s. But these developments were only faint shadows of their northern counterparts and had little impact. Southern development was dominated by agriculture and slavery and by the prominence of rural slaves, slaveholders, and yeoman farmers in the population.

Population distribution remained thin. Cotton growers spread out over as large an area as possible to maximize production and income. Farms were set far apart, rather than clustered around villages, and southern society remained predominantly rural. Because most immigrants to the United States sought urban locations, population growth fell behind the North's. Population density was low in the older plantation states and extremely low in the frontier areas. In 1860 there were only 2.3 people per square mile in largely unsettled Texas and 15.6 in Louisiana. By contrast, population density in the nonslaveholding states east of the Mississippi River was almost three times higher. The Northeast had an average of 65.4 people per square mile.

Population Distribution

Even in the 1850s, much of the South seemed a virtual wilderness. Frederick Law Olmsted, a northerner later renowned as a landscape architect, made several trips through the South in the 1850s as a journalist. Olmsted found that the few trains and stagecoaches available to travelers offered crude accommodations and kept their schedules poorly. Indeed, he had to do most of his traveling on horseback along primitive trails. Between Columbus, Georgia, and Montgomery, Alabama, Olmsted found "a hilly wilderness, with a few dreary villages, and many isolated cotton farms."

Society in such rural areas was characterized by relatively weak institutions, for it takes a concentration of people to create and support organized activity. Where people were scarce, it was difficult to finance and operate schools, churches, libraries, or even inns. Southerners were strongly committed to their churches, and some believed in the importance of universities, but all such institutions were far less developed than those in the North.

The South's cities were likewise smaller and less developed. Confined to the region's perimeter, the largest urban areas functioned as ports rather than centers of a vigorous internal commerce. They exported mainly staple crops, such as cotton or tobacco, and imported only a few necessary manufactured goods and luxuries. Factories were rare because planters invested most of their capital in slaves. A few southerners did invest in iron or textiles on a small scale. But the largest southern "industry" was lumbering, and the largest factories used slave labor to make cigars.

Weak Urban Sector

More decisively, the South was slower than the North to develop a unified market economy and a regional transportation network. Because planters could use waterways for transportation, far less money was spent on canals, turnpikes, or railroads. The South had only 26 percent of the nation's railroad mileage in 1850. As a result, urban growth after 1820 was far less vigorous than in the North, and metropolitan centers were almost nonexistent. In 1860 less than 3 percent of Mississippi's population and 7 percent of South Carolina's lived in towns with at least 2,500 residents. In the same year, the population of Richmond, Virginia, was only 38,000. New Orleans, by far the largest southern city, had only 169,000 residents and was being left behind because it was not linked to the national railroad network.

Thus although the South sold huge amounts of cotton on the international market, its economy at home was semideveloped relative to other sections of the country. Its white people were prospering, but not as rapidly as most residents of the North. There, changes in commerce and industry brought unprecedented advances in productivity, raising the average person's standard of living. In the South, change was quantitative rather than qualitative: the region grew but remained rural and its internal market undeveloped.

Free Southerners: Farmers, Planters, and Free Blacks

A large majority of white southern families (three-quarters in 1860) owned no slaves. Some lived in towns, but most were yeoman farmers who owned their own land and grew their own food. They were the typical whites, but the social distance between different groups of whites was great. Still greater was the distance between whites and blacks.

The yeomen were independent, individualistic, and given to hard work. Though they were a numerical majority, their status did not mean that they set the direction of the slave society. Absorbed in the work of their farms, they normally occupied a relatively autonomous position within the slavery-based staple-crop economy expanding around them. By slowly improving their acreage or settling new and better land, yeoman families improved their lot and made steady progress.

Because few railroads penetrated the southern interior, yeomen generally had little contact with the market or the type of progress it could introduce. Families might raise a small surplus to sell for cash or to trade for needed items, but they were remote from large market networks and therefore not particularly concerned about increasing their cash income. Yeomen constituted an important, though often silent, part of southern society. If their rights were threatened, however, they could react strongly.

The yeomen were mostly from Scottish and Irish backgrounds, and they enjoyed a folk culture based on family, church, and neighborhood.

Folk Culture of the Yeomen

Once a year they flocked to religious revivals called protracted meetings or camp meetings, and in between they enjoyed house-raisings, log-rollings, quilting bees, and corn-shuckings. Such occasions combined work with fun, offered food in abundance, and provided fellowship that was especially welcome to isolated rural dwellers.

Social conventions imposed uniform roles on yeoman women. At harvest they frequently helped in the fields, and throughout the year the drying, preserving, and preparing of food consumed much of their time. Household tasks continued during frequent pregnancies and the care of small children. Primary nursing and medical care also fell to the mother, who might have a book of remedies but often relied on family and folk wisdom. In some evangelical churches women played respected roles on certain committees, but overwhelmingly the busy life of the yeoman woman was tied to the home.

Among the men there were many who aspired to wealth, eager to join the race for slaves, land, and profits from cotton. Others were content with their independence, recreation, family life, and religion. But whether they strove to become rich or were satisfied with their status, they worked hard.

Ferdinand L. Steel, a North Carolinian who moved to Tennessee and later to Mississippi, was a typical yeoman. He rose every day at five and worked until sundown. With the help of his family he raised corn, wheat, pork, and vegetables for the family table. Cotton was his cash crop: he sold five or six bales (about 2,000 pounds) a year to obtain money for sugar, coffee, salt, calico, gunpowder, and a few other store-bought goods.

Steel's life in Mississippi in the 1840s retained much of the flavor of the frontier. He made all the family's shoes; his wife and sister sewed dresses, shirts, and "pantiloons." The Steel women also rendered their own soap and spun and wove cotton into cloth; the men hunted game. For Steel, God and family—not work and entertainment—were the focal points of life. Eventually he became

How do historians know about the values and ways of life of nonslaveholders in the South? Letters, diaries, and family papers of these people, who generally were not rich or famous, have not been preserved as frequently as the records of the slaveholding elite. Thus historians have turned to various other sources—including travelers' accounts, folklore, and United States census records—to learn more about them. This page from the manuscript "Population Schedules" of the census of 1860 supplies information on family structure and a variety of personal characteristics. The "Census of Agriculture" contains much additional information about the size of each family's farm and the crops grown there.   Photo: North Carolina Division of Archives and History.

a traveling Methodist minister. "My life is one of toil," he reflected, "but blessed be God that it is as well with me as it is."

Toil was also the lot of two other groups of free southerners: landless whites and free blacks. A sizable minority of white southern workers—from 25 to 40 percent—were unskilled laborers who owned no land and worked for others in the countryside and towns. Their property consisted of a few household items and some animals—usually pigs—that could feed themselves on the open range. The landless included some immigrants, especially Irish, who did heavy and dangerous work such as building railroads and digging ditches.

Landless Whites

In the countryside, white farm laborers struggled to become yeomen in the face of low wages or, if they rented, unpredictable market prices for their crops. Thus when James and Nancy Bennitt of North Carolina succeeded in their ten-year struggle to buy land, they decided to avoid the unstable market in cotton; thereafter they raised extra corn and wheat as sources of cash.

For the nearly quarter-million free blacks in the South in 1860, conditions were often little better than the slave's. The free blacks of the Upper South were usually descendants of men and women emancipated by their owners in the 1780s and 1790s. They usually did not own land and had to labor in someone else's fields, often beside slaves. By law free blacks could not own a gun, buy liquor, violate curfew, assemble (except in church), testify in court, or (throughout the South after 1835) vote. Still, a minority bought land, and others found jobs as artisans, draymen, boatmen, and fishermen. A few prospered and bought slave laborers, but most who owned slaves had purchased their own wives and children (whom they could not free, since laws required newly emancipated blacks to leave their state).

Free Blacks

Farther south, in the cotton and Gulf regions, a large proportion of free blacks were mulattos, the offspring of wealthy planters. Not all planters freed their mixed-race offspring, but those who did often recognized a moral obligation and gave their children good educations and financial backing. In a few cities like New Orleans and Mobile, extensive interracial sex had produced a mulatto population that was recognized as a distinct class. These people formed a society of their own and sought a status above slaves and other freedmen, if not equal to that of planters. But outside New Orleans, Mobile, and Charleston, such groups were rare.

At the opposite end of the social spectrum from free blacks were slaveholders. As a group they lived well, on incomes that enabled them to enjoy superior housing, food, clothing, and luxuries. But most lived in comfortable farmhouses, not on the opulent scale that legend suggests. A few statistics tell the story: 50 percent of southern slaveholders had fewer than five slaves; 72 percent had fewer than ten; 88 percent had fewer than twenty. Thus the average slaveholder was not a wealthy aristocrat but an aspiring farmer, usually a person of humble origins, with little formal education and many rough edges to his manner.

Planters

Slaveholding men dominated society and, especially among the wealthiest and oldest families, justified their dominance through a paternalistic ideology. Instead of stressing the profitable aspects of commercial agriculture, they focused on noblesse oblige, seeing themselves as custodians of the welfare of society as a whole and of the black families who depended on them in particular. The paternalistic planter viewed himself not as an oppressor but as the benevolent guardian of an inferior race. He developed affectionate feelings toward his slaves (as long as they knew their place) and was genuinely shocked at criticism of his behavior.

Southern Paternalism

The letters of Paul Carrington Cameron, North Carolina's largest slaveholder, illustrate this mentality. After a period of sickness among his one thousand North Carolina slaves, Cameron wrote, "I fear the Negroes have suffered much from the want of proper attention and kindness under this

Most slaveowners lived in comfortable country homes rather than in stately mansions. This rare daguerreotype, dating from about 1853, shows a family in front of their home. Notice the presence of a male slave in the left background.   The J. Paul Getty Museum, Los Angeles, California.

late distemper . . . no love of lucre shall ever induce me to be cruel, or even to make or permit to be made any great exposure of their persons at inclement seasons."

It was comforting to the richest southern planters to see themselves in this way, and slaves—accommodating to the realities of power—encouraged their masters to think their benevolence was appreciated. Paternalism also served as a defense against abolitionist criticism. Still, paternalism affected the manner and not the substance of most planters' behavior. Its softness and warmth were a matter of style, covering harsher assumptions: blacks were inferior, and planters should make money.

Relations between men and women in the planter class were similarly paternalistic. The life of an upper-class southern woman was bound by the household, and she was raised and educated to be a wife, mother, and subordinate companion to men. South Carolina's Mary Boykin Chesnut wrote of her husband, "He is master of the house. To hear is to obey. . . . All the comfort of my life depends upon his being in a good humor." In a social system based on the coercion of an entire race, women were not allowed to challenge society's rules on sexual or racial relations.

After spending her early years within the family circle, a planter's daughter usually attended one of the South's rapidly multiplying academies or boarding schools. There she received an education that emphasized grammar, composition,

Elite Women's Role

penmanship, geography, literature, and languages, but little science and mathematics. Typically the young woman maintained dutiful and affectionate ties with her parents and entertained suitors whom they approved.

Upon marriage, she ceded to her husband most of her legal rights, became part of his family, and was expected to get along with numerous in-laws during extended visits. Most of the year she was isolated on a large plantation, where she had to oversee the cooking and preserving of food, manage the house, supervise care of the children, and attend sick slaves. It is not surprising that an intelligent and perceptive young woman some-times approached marriage with anxiety, for her future depended on the man she chose.

Childbearing brought grief and sickness, as well as joy, to southern women. In 1840 the birth rate for white southern women in their child-bearing years was almost 30 percent higher than the national average. The average southern white woman could expect to bear eight children in 1800; by 1860 the figure had decreased only to six, with one or more miscarriages likely. For those women who wanted to plan their families, meth-ods of contraception were uncertain. Complica-tions of childbirth were a major cause of death, oc-curring twice as often in the hot, moist South as in the Northeast. Moreover, a mother had to endure the loss of many of the children she bore. In the South in 1860 almost five out of ten children died before age five.

Slavery was another source of problems that white women had to endure but were not supposed to notice. "Violations of the moral law . . . made mulattoes as common as blackberries," protested a woman in Georgia, but wives had to play "the ostrich game."

In the early 1800s, some southern women, es-pecially Quakers, had spoken out against slavery. Although most white women did not criticize the "peculiar institution," they often viewed it less as a system and more as a series of relationships among individuals. Perhaps sensing this, southern men tolerated no discussion by women of the slavery is-sue. In the 1840s and 1850s, as northern and inter-national criticism of slavery increased, southern

men published a barrage of articles stressing that women should restrict their concerns to the home.

But some southern women were beginning to seek a larger role. A study of women in Peters-burg, Virginia, has revealed behavior that valued financial autonomy. Over several decades before 1860, the proportion of women who never mar-ried, or did not remarry after the death of a spouse, grew to exceed 33 percent. Likewise the number of women who worked for wages, con-trolled their own property, and ran businesses in-creased. In managing property, women benefited from legal changes—beginning with Mississippi's Married Women's Property Act of 1839—that had been intended to protect families from the hus-band's indebtedness during business panics and re-cessions. The legal reforms gave married women some property rights.

For a large category of southern men and women, rights were nil, freedom was wholly de-nied, and education in any form was not allowed. Male and female slaves were expected to accept bondage and ignorance as their condition.

 ## Slaves and Their Status in Bondage

For African-Americans, slavery was a curse that brought no blessings other than the strengths they developed to survive it. Slaves knew a life of poverty, coercion, toil, heartbreak, and resent-ment. They had to bear separation from their loved ones and were despised as an inferior race. That they endured and found loyalty and strength among themselves is a tribute to their courage.

Southern slaves enjoyed few material comforts beyond the bare necessities. Although they gen-erally had enough to eat, their diet was plain and monotonous. The basic ra-tion was cornmeal, fat pork, molasses, and occasionally cof-fee. Many masters allowed slaves to tend gardens, which provided the variety and extra nutrition of greens and sweet potatoes, and some could fish and hunt. Slaves' diets were often nutri-

Slaves' Diet, Clothing, and Housing

tionally deficient, with the result that many slaves suffered from such diseases as beriberi and pellagra.

Clothing too was plain, coarse, and inexpensive. Few slaves received more than one or two changes of clothing for hot and cold seasons and one blanket each winter. When big enough to go to the fields, boys received a work shirt and a pair of breeches, and girls a simple dress. On many plantations slave women made their own clothing of osnaburg, a coarse cotton fabric. Many slaves had to go without shoes until December. The shoes they received were uncomfortable brass-toed brogans or stiff wraparounds made from leather tanned on the plantation.

Slaves typically lived in small one-room cabins. Logs chinked with mud formed the walls; dirt was the only floor; and a wattle-and-daub or stone chimney vented the fireplace, which provided both heat and light. Bedding consisted of heaps of straw, straw mattresses, or wooden bedframes lashed to the walls with rope. A few crude pieces of furniture and cooking utensils completed the furnishings. The gravest drawback of slave cabins was their unhealthfulness. Each small cabin housed one or two entire families. Crowding and lack of sanitation fostered the spread of infection and contagious diseases.

Hard work was the central fact of slaves' existence. The long hours and large work gangs that characterized Gulf Coast cotton districts seemed like factories in the field compared to the small clusters of slaves who had worked in the eighteenth-century Chesapeake. Overseers rang the morning bell before dawn, thus ensuring that slaves would be in the fields by first light. Except in urban settings and on some rice plantations, where slaves were assigned daily tasks to complete at their own pace, working "from sun to sun" became universal in the South. Long hours and hard work were at the heart of the advantage that slave labor gave slaveowners.

Slaves' Work Routines

Profit also took precedence over paternalistic "protection" of women: slave women did heavy fieldwork, often as much as the men and even during pregnancy. Old people—of whom there were few—were kept busy caring for young children,

doing light chores, or carding, ginning, and spinning cotton. Children had to gather kindling, carry water to the fields, or sweep the yard. But slaves had a variety of ways to keep from being worked to death. It was impossible to supervise every slave every minute, and slaves slacked off when they were not being watched.

Slaves could not slow their pace too much, of course, because the owner enjoyed a monopoly on force and violence. Whites throughout the South believed that slaves "can't be governed except with the whip." Evidence suggests that whippings were less frequent on small farms than on large plantations, but even most small farmers plied the lash. These beatings symbolized authority to the master and tyranny to the slaves, who made them a benchmark for evaluating a master. In the words of former slaves, a good owner was one who did not "whip too much," whereas a bad owner "whipped till he's bloodied you and blistered you."*

Physical and Mental Abuse of Slaves

As these reports suggest, terrible abuses could and did occur. The master wielded virtually absolute authority on his plantation, and courts did not recognize the word of chattel. Pregnant women were whipped, and there were burnings, mutilations, tortures, and murders. Yet physical cruelty may have been less prevalent in the United States than in other slaveholding parts of the New World. In sugar-growing and mining regions of the Western Hemisphere in the 1800s, slaves were regarded as an expendable resource to be replaced after seven years. Treatment was so poor that death rates were high and the heavily male slave population rapidly shrank in size. In the United States, by contrast, the slave population experienced a steady natural increase as births exceeded deaths and each generation grew larger.

---

*Accounts by ex-slaves are quoted from *The American Slave: A Composite Autobiography*, edited by George P. Rawick (Westport, Conn.: Greenwood Press, First Reprint Edition 1972, Second Reprint Edition 1974), from materials gathered by the Federal Writers' Project and originally published in 1941. The spelling in these accounts has been standardized.

The worst evil of American slavery was not its physical cruelty but the nature of slavery itself: coercion, lack of freedom, belonging to another person, virtually no hope for change. A woman named Delia Garlic made the essential point when she said, "It's bad to belong to folks that own you soul an' body." American slaves hated their oppression and, contrary to whites' stereotype of slaves as docile Sambos, were not grateful to their oppressors. They had to be subservient and speak honeyed words to their masters, but they talked quite differently among themselves. The evidence of their resistant attitudes comes from their actions and their own life stories.

Former slaves reported some warm feelings between masters and slaves, but the prevailing picture was one of antagonism and resistance.

**Slaves'
Attitudes
Toward Whites**
Slaves mistrusted kindness from whites and saw the self-interest in it. A man recalled that his owners took good care of their slaves, "and Grandma Maria say, 'Why shouldn't they—it was their money.'" Christmas presents of clothing from the master did not mean anything, observed another, "'cause he was going to [buy] that anyhow."

Slaves were alert to the signs of their degraded status. One man recalled his master eyeing the slave children and saying, "'That one will be worth a thousand dollars.' . . . You see, it was just like raisin' young mules." Another recollected, "Us catch lots of 'possums," but "the white folks ate 'em. Our mouths would water for some of that 'possum, but it wasn't often they let us have none." If the owner took his slaves' garden produce to town and sold it for them, the slaves suspected him of pocketing part of the profits.

Suspicion and resentment often grew into hatred. According to a former slave from Virginia, white people treated blacks "so mean that all the slaves prayed God to punish their cruel masters." As late as the 1930s an elderly ex-slave named Minnie Fulkes cherished the conviction that God was going to punish white people for their cruelty to blacks. She described the whippings that her mother had had to endure, and then she ex-

claimed, "Lord, Lord, I hate white people and the flood waters goin' to drown some more."

 ## Slave Culture and Everyday Life

The resource that enabled slaves to maintain such defiance was their culture: a body of beliefs and values born of their past and their present and of fellowship in their own community. It was not possible for slaves to change their world, but by drawing strength from their culture they could resist their condition and struggle on against it.

Slave culture changed significantly after the turn of the century. For a few years South Carolina reopened the international slave trade. After 1808, however, when Congress banned further importations, the proportion of native-born blacks rose steadily, reaching 96 percent in 1840 and almost 100 percent in 1860. Meanwhile, more and more slaves adopted Christianity as African culture gave way to a maturing African-American culture.

African influences remained strong, for African practices and beliefs reminded slaves that they were and ought to be different from their op-

**Influence of
African Culture**
pressors. The most visible features of African culture were slaves' appearance and forms of recreation. Some slave men plaited their hair into rows and fancy designs; slave women often wore their hair "in string"—tied in small bunches secured by a string or piece of cloth. A few men and many women wrapped their heads in kerchiefs of the styles and colors of West Africa.

For entertainment slaves made musical instruments with carved motifs that resembled African stringed instruments. Their drumming and dancing clearly followed African patterns; whites marveled at them. One visitor to Georgia in the 1860s described a ritual dance of African origin: "A ring of singers is formed. . . . They then utter a kind of melodious chant, which gradually increases in strength, and in noise, until it fairly shakes the house."

Many slaves continued to believe in spirits. Their belief resembled the African concept of the living dead—the idea that deceased relatives visit the earth for many years until the process of dying is complete. Slaves also practiced conjuration, voodoo, and quasi-magical root medicine. By 1860 the most notable conjurers and root doctors were reputed to live in South Carolina, Georgia, Louisiana, and other isolated coastal areas of heavy slave importation.

These cultural survivals provided slaves with a sense of their separate past. Conjuration and folklore also directly fed resistance; slaves could cast a spell or direct the power of a hand (a bag of articles belonging to the person to be conjured) against the master. Not all masters felt confident enough to dismiss such a threat.

Slaves fashioned Christianity into an instrument of support and resistance. Theirs was a religion of justice, quite unlike the religious propaganda their masters pushed at them. "You ought to have heard that preachin'," said one man. "'Obey your master and mistress, don't steal chickens and eggs and meat,' but nary a word about havin' a soul to save." Slaves believed that Jesus cared about their souls and their plight and that slaveholders would be "broilin' in hell for their sin" when God's justice came.

Slaves' Religion

For slaves, Christianity was a religion of personal and group salvation. Beyond seeking personal guidance, slaves prayed for deliverance. Many nurtured an unshakable belief that God would end their bondage. This faith—and the joy and emotional release that accompanied worship—sustained blacks.

Enslaved African-Americans also developed a sense of racial identity. They naturally drew together, helping each other in danger, need, and resistance. "We never told on each other," one woman declared. Although some slaves did betray others, former slaves were virtually unanimous in denouncing those who were disloyal to the group or sought personal gain through allegiance to whites.

Of course, different jobs, talents, and circumstances created variations in status among slaves. But most slaves did not encounter a class system within the black community. Only one-quarter of all slaves lived on plantations of fifty or more

blacks, so few sensed a wide chasm separating house servants and lowly field hands.

The main source of support for individuals was the family. Slave families faced severe dangers. At any moment the master could sell a husband or wife, give a slave child away as a wedding present, or die in debt, forcing a division of his property. Many families were broken up in such ways. Others were separated in the trans-Appalachian expansion of the South. When the Union Army registered thousands of black marriages in Mississippi and Louisiana in 1864 and 1865, fully 25 percent of the men over forty reported that they had been forcibly separated from a previous wife.

Slaves' Family Life

But this did not mean that slave families could not exist. American slaves clung tenaciously to the personal relationships that gave meaning to life. Although American law did not protect slave families, masters permitted them; in fact, slaveowners expected slaves to form families and have children. As a result, there was a normal ratio of men to women, young to old, even on the frontier.

Following African kinship taboos, African-Americans avoided marriage between cousins. Adapting the West African custom of polygyny to American circumstances, they did not condemn unwed mothers but did expect a young woman to enter a monogamous relationship after one pregnancy, if not before. By naming their children after relatives of past generations, African-Americans emphasized their family histories. If they chose to bear the surname of a slaveowner, it was often the name of the owner under whom their family had begun in America.

Slaves abhorred interference in their family lives. Some of their strongest protests sought to prevent the breakup of a family. Rape was a horror for both men and women. Some husbands faced death rather than permit their wives to be sexually abused, and the women sometimes fought back. In other cases slaves seethed with anger at the injustice but could do nothing except soothe each other and condemn the guilty party.

Slave men and women followed gender roles similar to West African customs. After work in the fields was done, men's activities focused on

This photograph of five generations of a slave family, taken in Beaufort, South Carolina, in 1862, is silent but powerful testimony to the importance that enslaved African-Americans placed on their ever-threatened family ties.   Library of Congress.

Gender Roles in Slavery

"outdoor" tasks and women did "indoor" work. Men hunted and fished, made furniture, and repaired implements; women cooked, mended, and cleaned house. Slave families resembled white families in that African-American men held a respected place in their homes. The men did not dominate their wives in a manner similar to that of free husbands, but it would be misleading to say that slave women enjoyed equality in gender roles and family life. Under the pressures of bondage men and women had to share parental and household responsibilities. At any time, each might have to stand in for the other and assume extra duties. Similarly, uncles, aunts, and grandparents sometimes raised the children of those who had been sold away.

Work routines frequently promoted among slave women close associations that heightened their sense of sisterhood. On plantations young girls worked together as house servants. Nursing mothers got together to feed and care for their children, and adults worked together at tasks like soap making and stitching quilts. Female slaves thus spent significant portions of their lives as participants in a group of women, an experience that strengthened their ties to each other.

American slavery produced some fearless and implacable revolutionaries. Gabriel's conspiracy apparently was known to more than a thousand slaves when it was discovered in 1800, just before it was put into action (see page 153). A similar conspiracy in Charleston in 1822, led by a

Resistance to Slavery

free black named Denmark Vesey, involved many of the prominent whites' most trusted slaves. And the most famous rebel of all, Nat Turner, rose in violence in Southampton County, Virginia, in 1831.

The son of an African woman who passionately hated her enslavement, Nat Turner was a precocious child who learned to read when he was very young. Encouraged by his first owner to study the Bible, he enjoyed certain privileges but also endured hard work and changes of masters. Eventually young Nat became a preacher; he also developed a tendency toward mysticism and became increasingly withdrawn. After nurturing his plan for several years, Turner led a band of rebels from farm to farm in the predawn darkness of August 22, 1831. The group severed limbs and crushed skulls with axes or killed their victims with guns. Before they were stopped, Turner and his followers had slaughtered sixty whites of both sexes and all ages. The rebellion was crushed, Turner was hanged, and an estimated two hundred African-Americans, including many innocent individuals, were killed by retaliating whites.

Nat Turner Rebellion

Most slave resistance, however, was not violent, for the odds against revolution were especially poor in North America. Consequently slaves directed their energies toward creating the means of survival and resistance within slavery. Many individual slaves attempted to run away to the North, and some received assistance from a loose network of sympathetic citizens, known collectively as the Underground Railroad. But it was more common for slaves to run off temporarily to hide in the woods. Every day that a slave "lay out" in this way, the master lost a day's labor. Most owners chose not to mount an exhaustive search and instead sent word through other slaves that the grievances would be redressed. The runaway would then return to bargain with the master, who often was glad to have his property back.

Other modes of resistance had the same object: to resist but survive under bondage. Appropriating food (stealing, in the master's eyes) was common. Blacks also learned to ingratiate themselves and play off one white person against another. Field hands frequently tested a new overseer to intimidate him or win more favorable working conditions.

 ## Harmony and Tension in a Slave Society

As the 1800s advanced, slavery impinged on laws and customs, individual values, and—increasingly—every aspect of southern politics. Legal restrictions on slaves, in effect since the seventeenth century, steadily increased. In all things, slaves fell under the supervision of whites. State courts held that a slave "has no civil right" and could not even hold property "except at the will and pleasure of his master." In response to revolts, legislators tightened the legal straitjacket: after the Nat Turner insurrection of 1831, for example, they prohibited owners from teaching their slaves to read. As political conflicts between North and South deepened, fears of slave revolt grew, and restrictions on slaves increased accordingly.

State and federal laws aided the capture of fugitive slaves and required nonslaveholders to support the slave system. All white male citizens had a legal duty to ride in patrols to discourage slave movements at night. Ship captains and harbor masters were required to scrutinize the papers of African-Americans who might be attempting to escape bondage. Urban residents who did not supervise their domestic slaves as closely as planters did were subject to criticism for endangering the community. And the South's few manufacturers often felt pressure to substitute slave labor for free labor.

Slavery had a deep effect on southern values precisely because it was the main determinant of wealth in the South. Ownership of slaves guaranteed the labor to produce cotton and other crops on a large scale. Slaves were therefore vital to the acquisition of a fortune. In fact, throughout southern society, slaveholding indicated overall wealth with

Slavery as the Basis of Wealth and Social Standing

remarkable precision. Variations in wealth from county to county corresponded very closely to variations in slaveholding; important economic enterprises not based on slavery were too rare to affect this pattern.

Wealth in slaves also translated into political power: a solid majority of political officeholders were slaveholders, and the most powerful were usually large-scale slaveholders. Lawyers and newspaper editors were sometimes influential, but they did not hold independent positions in the economy or society. Dependent on planters for business and support, they served planters' interests and reflected their outlook.

Slavery also left its imprint on the values of nonslaveholders. Its existence tended to debase free labor; thus nonslaveholders often refused jobs they considered demeaning. Such thinking engendered an aristocratic value system ill-suited to a newly established democracy.

The values of the aristocrat—lineage, privilege, pride, and refinement of person and manner—gained considerable respect among the masses.

Aristocratic Values and Frontier Individualism

Many of those qualities were in short supply, however, in the recently settled portions of the cotton kingdom, where frontier values of courage and self-reliance modified the aristocratic ideal. Independence and defense of one's honor became highly valued traits for planter and frontier farmer alike. Thus, instead of gradually disappearing as it did in the North, the code duello, which required men to defend their honor through violence, hung on in the South and gained acceptance throughout the society.

Other aristocratic values of the planter class were less acceptable to the average voter. Planters believed they were better than other people. In their pride, planters expected not only to wield power but to receive special treatment. By the 1850s, some openly rejected the democratic creed, vilifying Thomas Jefferson for his statement that all men were equal.

Such beliefs were never acceptable to the individualistic members of the yeoman class. Independent and proud, yeomen resisted any infringement of their rights. They believed they were as good as anyone, and many belonged to evangelical faiths that exalted values of simplicity and other-worldliness that were alien to the planters' love of wealth. They were conscious, too, that they lived in a nation in which democratic ideals were gaining strength. Thus occasional conflicts erupted between aristocratic pretensions and democratic zeal.

Yeoman farmers and other citizens resented their underrepresentation in state legislatures, the corruption in government, and the undemocratic control over local government.

Movements for Electoral Reform

In the 1820s and 1830s, the reformers won most of their battles. Voters in more recently settled areas—Alabama, Mississippi, Tennessee, Arkansas, and Texas—adopted white manhood suffrage and other electoral reforms, including popular election of governors, legislative apportionment based on white population only, and locally chosen county government. Only South Carolina and Virginia effectively defended property qualifications for office, legislative malapportionment, appointment of county officials, and selection of the governor by lawmakers. The formal structure of government thus became more democratic than many planters wished.

Slaveowners knew that a more open government structure could permit troubling issues to arise. In Virginia, nonslaveholding westerners raised a basic challenge to the slave system in 1832, a year after the Nat Turner Rebellion. Advocates of gradual abolition forced a two-week legislative debate on slavery, arguing that it was injurious to the state and inherently dangerous. When the House of Delegates finally voted, the motion favoring abolition lost by just 73 to 58. This was the last public debate on slavery in the antebellum South.

Given such tensions, it was perhaps remarkable that slaveholders and nonslaveholders did not experience more overt conflict. Why were class confrontations among whites so infrequent? One of the most important factors was race. The South's racial ideology stressed the superiority of all whites to blacks. Moreover,

Relations Between the Classes

family ties linked some nonslaveholders to wealthy planters. The experience of frontier living, in which all were starting out together, also created a relatively informal, egalitarian atmosphere. And the cotton boom itself relieved tension by bringing opportunity to thousands of whites. The "Old South" was a new and mobile society in which many people rose in status by acquiring land or slaves and far more moved about geographically.

Most important, in their daily lives yeomen and slaveholders were seldom in conflict. Before the Civil War most yeomen were able to pursue unhindered their independent lifestyle. Marginally involved in the market economy, they worked their farms, avoided debt, and lived their lives with little reference to, or interference from, slaveholders. Likewise, slaveholders pursued their goals quite independently of yeomen.

Suppression of dissent also played a significant and increasing role. After 1830 white southerners who criticized the slave system were intimidated, attacked, or legally prosecuted. Intellectuals developed elaborate justifications for slavery, and by the 1850s, the defense of the South's "peculiar institution" had become the top priority of southern politicians.

Still, there were disquieting signs between slaveholders and nonslaveholders. As cotton lands filled up, nonslaveholders saw their opportunities beginning to narrow. The risks of entering cotton production were becoming too great and the cost of slaves too high for many yeomen to rise in society. From 1830 to 1860 the percentage of white southern families holding slaves declined steadily from 36 to 25 percent. At the same time, the monetary gap between the classes was widening. By 1860, the average slaveholder was almost fourteen times as rich as the average nonslaveholder.

Hardening of Class Lines

Urban artisans and mechanics felt the pinch acutely. Their numbers were few and their place in society was hardly recognized. Moreover, they faced stiff competition from urban slaves, whose masters wanted to hire them out to practice trades. White workers demanded that economic competition from slaves be forbidden, but slaveowners would not tolerate interference with their property and their income. The angry protests of white workers, however, resulted in harsh restrictions on *free* African-American workers and craftsmen.

Pre–Civil War politics reflected these tensions. Anticipating the prospect of a war to defend slavery, slaveowners expressed growing fear about the loyalty of nonslaveholders. Schemes to widen the ownership of slaves were discussed, including reopening the African slave trade. In North Carolina, a prolonged and increasingly bitter controversy erupted over the combination of high taxes on land and low taxes on slaves, and a class-conscious nonslaveholder named Hinton R. Helper denounced the slave system in *The Impending Crisis*, published in New York in 1857. Discerning planters knew that such fiery controversies could easily erupt in every southern state.

But for the moment slaveowners stood secure. They occupied from 50 to 85 percent of the seats in state legislatures and a similarly high percentage of the South's congressional seats. They had established their point of view in all the other major social institutions, too. Professors who criticized slavery had been dismissed from colleges and universities; schoolbooks that contained "unsound" ideas had been replaced. And almost all the Methodist and Baptist clergy had given up preaching against slavery. In fact, except for a few obscure persons of conscience, southern clergy had become slavery's most vocal defenders.

 Conclusion

The South of the early to mid-1800s was a diverse society that embraced a variety of elements and differing viewpoints, but the coercive influence of slavery was increasingly pressing the region into a single mold. Powerful groups dependent on slavery worked tirelessly to promote unity and eradicate dissent. The potential for conflict persisted, but few southerners saw it. Instead, they saw a system that seemed to be stable, with threats to the status quo under control. The static appearance of the slave South contrasted sharply with the dynamic market forces in the North, where industrialism was rapidly changing society.

Suggestions for Further Reading

Southern Society

Bradley G. Bond, *Political Culture in the Nineteenth-Century South* (1995); William J. Cooper, *The South and the Politics of Slavery, 1828–1856* (1978); Clement Eaton, *Freedom of Thought in the Old South* (1940); William W. Freehling, *Prelude to Civil War* (1965); Eugene D. Genovese, *The Political Economy of Slavery* (1965); Peter Kolchin, *Unfree Labor: American Slavery and Russian Serfdom* (1987); Donald G. Mathews, *Religion in the Old South* (1977); James Hebron Moore, *The Emergence of the Cotton Kingdom in the Old Southwest: Mississippi, 1770–1860* (1987); Frederick Law Olmsted, *The Slave States*, ed. Harvey Wish (1959); Charles S. Sydnor, *The Development of Southern Sectionalism, 1819–1848* (1948); Larry E. Tise, *Proslavery* (1987); Ralph A. Wooster, *The People in Power* (1969); Gavin Wright, *The Political Economy of the Cotton South* (1978); Bertram Wyatt-Brown, *Southern Honor* (1982).

Slaveholders and Nonslaveholders

Bennet H. Barrow, *Plantation Life in the Florida Parishes of Louisiana, as Reflected in the Diary of Bennet H. Barrow*, ed. Edwin Adams Davis (1943); Ira Berlin, *Slaves Without Masters* (1974); Joan E. Cashin, *A Family Venture* (1991); Bill Cecil-Fronsman, *The Common Whites* (1992); Everett Dick, *The Dixie Frontier* (1948); Paul D. Escott, ed., *North Carolina Yeoman* (1996); Drew Faust, *James Henry Hammond and the Old South* (1982); John Inscoe, *Mountain Masters* (1989); Michael P. Johnson and James L. Roark, *Black Masters* (1984); Robert E. May, *John A. Quitman* (1985); Stephanie McCurry, *Masters of Small Worlds* (1995); Robert Manson Myers, ed., *The Children of Pride* (1972); James Oakes, *The Ruling Race* (1982); Frank L. Owsley, *Plain Folk of the Old South* (1949); Loren Schweninger, *Black Property Owners in the South, 1790–1915* (1990).

Southern Women

Carol Bleser, ed., *Tokens of Affection* (1995); Victoria Bynum, *Unruly Women* (1992); Jane Turner Censer, *North Carolina Planters and Their Children, 1800–1860* (1984); Elizabeth Fox-Genovese, *Within the Plantation Household* (1988); Jean E. Friedman, *The Enclosed Garden* (1985); Harriet Jacobs, *Incidents in the Life of a Slave Girl*, ed. Jean Fagan Yellin (1987); Frances Anne Kemble, *Journal of a Residence on a Georgia Plantation in 1838–1839* (1863); Suzanne Lebsock, *Free Women of Petersburg* (1984); Sally McMillen, *Motherhood in the Old South* (1990); Patricia Morton, ed., *Discovering the Women in Slavery* (1995); Mary D. Robertson, ed., *Lucy Breckinridge of Grove Hill* (1979); Deborah G. White, *Ar'n't I a Woman?* (1985).

Conditions of Slavery

Kenneth F. Kiple and Virginia H. Kiple, "Black Tongue and Black Men," *Journal of Southern History* 43 (August 1977): 411–428; Peter Kolcin, *American Slavery, 1619–1877* (1993); Richard G. Lowe and Randolph B. Campbell, "The Slave Breeding Hypothesis," *Journal of Southern History* 42 (August 1976): 400–412; Todd L. Savitt, *Medicine and Slavery* (1978); Kenneth M. Stampp, *The Peculiar Institution* (1956); Robert S. Starobin, *Industrial Slavery in the Old South* (1970).

Slave Culture and Resistance

John W. Blassingame, *The Slave Community* (1979); Judith Wragg Chase, *Afro-American Art and Craft* (1971); Douglas Egerton, *Gabriel's Rebellion* (1993); Dena J. Epstein, *Sinful Tunes and Spirituals* (1977); Paul D. Escott, *Slavery Remembered: A Record of Twentieth-Century Slave Narratives* (1979); Eric Foner, ed., *Nat Turner* (1971); Eugene D. Genovese, *Roll, Jordan, Roll* (1974); Herbert G. Gutman, *The Black Family in Slavery and Freedom, 1750–1925* (1976); Lawrence W. Levine, *Black Culture and Black Consciousness* (1977); Robert S. Starobin, *Denmark Vesey* (1970); Sterling Stuckey, *Slave Culture* (1987).

CHAPTER

12

The American Social Landscape

1800 – 1860

"I hope that things will get better," Anna Maria Klinger wrote from New York to her family in Germany in March 1849. "For it's always like that, no one really likes it at first, and especially if you are so lonely and forlorn in a foreign land like I am, no friends or relatives around." Twenty-eight-year-old Anna Maria had crossed the Atlantic among strangers. Her religious faith kept her going. "The dear Lord is my shield and refuge," she wrote home.

Anna Maria was the first in her immediate family to emigrate. Soon after arriving in New York, she found work as a domestic servant at $4 a month, and she also met her future husband, Franz Schano, a deserter from the Bavarian army. Over the next decade she and Schano brought five of her siblings to New York: Babett, Gottlieb, Katharina, Daniel, and Rosina.

Finding work could be difficult—Franz, a stonecutter, was unemployed for a time—but teenagers like Babett and Katharina could always get jobs as servants. Babett, who now called herself Barbara, found work and repaid her sister for her fare to America. But within a year of Barbara's arrival, she became pregnant. She gave birth to a son, but the father refused to marry her. He did, however, provide a cash settlement of $80.

Anna Maria, assisted by Franz, guided the family, keeping them together by sheer force of will. But the siblings' lives eventually diverged. In 1855 Anna Maria and Franz moved to Albany, New York, where Franz died of consumption five years later. Within thirteen months, Anna Maria married Adam Plantz, a Prussian-born blacksmith; he too died of consumption, only five weeks after the wedding. Anna Maria now had a son and a stepson to support. She feared losing her home, but she had been left enough money to prosper. As Anna Maria became more preoccupied with providing for her son and stepson, her brother Gottlieb took over the role of head of the family.

Through Gottlieb, the Klinger siblings stayed in touch for most of their lives. Gottlieb and his brother, Daniel, settled in Albany near Anna Maria and rode the roller coaster of the economy, prospering in good times, unemployed in hard times. Barbara moved to Indiana where she married, became a widow, remarried, and raised seven "Christian children" on her farm. Eventually, the family lost touch with two of their sisters. After Katharina, a widow, married a prosperous New York grocer, they no longer heard from her. They also lost contact with Rosina, who had moved to Canada. Years later they heard she was living again in New York and had "a whole brood of children" with her tinsmith husband.

The Klingers represented both the old values of traditional culture and the new values of the market system. Anna Maria worked hard, saved money, and found success in Albany. Barbara lived a hard-scrabble life and was an unwed mother before eventually finding peace in a German-American rural community 700 miles from New York. Katharina worked hard but spent most of her income on herself; her siblings complained of her selfishness. Even after years in the United States, the Klinger siblings were only partially Americanized. They always lived in German neighborhoods, and they socialized almost exclusively with family and fellow immigrants.

The Klinger family's experiences were similar to those of millions of other Americans. From the 1830s through the 1850s, millions of immigrants arrived on America's shores, and hundreds of thousands of native-born Americans moved from farm to town and from town to city. The populations of the largest cities numbered in the hundreds of thousands and were highly diverse ethnically, religiously, and racially. Within large cities and in the countryside, whole districts became enclaves of ethnic groups.

What it meant to be an American had changed. European immigrants, slaves, free people of color, and Native Americans had cultural traditions different from those of the American colonial past. New cultural patterns flourished. Economic opportunity, the market economy, and expansionism energized Americans. In the nation's cities, both wealth and poverty reached extremes unknown in agrarian America. As in the past, Americans sought community in their neighborhoods, not in the nation, but ethnic, racial, and religious differences were greater than ever before. Farm families attempted to maintain cohesive, rural villages while utopians and groups like the Mormons sought to create self-governing communal havens.

Family life was changing too. With the growth of commerce and industry, the home began to lose its function as a workplace and center of leisure. Cities took over some of the traditional family's educational role, and consumer items and leisure became commodities to be purchased. Families shrank in size, and more people lived outside family units.

Many Americans were uncomfortable with the new direction of American life. Antipathy toward immigrants was common among native-born Americans, who feared competition for jobs. Riots and violence became commonplace in cities. Free African-Americans fought their second-class status, and Indians tried unsuccessfully to prevent their forced removal to lands west of the Mississippi River. In a society growing ever more diverse and complex, conflict became common.

The United States remained a predominantly agricultural country, but economic and social traditions were yielding to the influence of the market economy, urban growth, and immigration. Clearly, an industrializing, urbanizing, and pluralist society was emerging before the Civil War.

 Country Life

Rural life changed significantly in the first half of the nineteenth century. Within a generation many western settlements became sources rather than

• *Important Events* •

1821	Horseracing legalized in New York State	**1835**	Arkansas passes first women's property law
1823	Catharine and Mary Beecher establish Hartford Female Seminary	**1835–42**	Seminoles resist removal in Second Seminole War
1824	President Monroe proposes removal of Indians west of the Mississippi	**1837**	Boston employs paid policemen
1830	Joseph Smith founds Mormon Church Congress passes Indian Removal Act	**1837–48**	Horace Mann heads the Massachusetts Board of Education
1830s–50s	Urban riots commonplace	**1841–47**	Brook Farm combines spirituality, work, and play in a utopian rural community
1831	Cherokees turn to courts to defend treaty rights in *Cherokee Nation* v. *Georgia*	**1842**	Knickerbocker baseball club formed
1831–32	Alexis de Tocqueville travels across America: his observations form the basis for *Democracy in America*	**1845**	Start of the Irish potato famine
		1846–47	Mormon trek to the Great Salt Lake
1831–38	Indian tribes resettled in the West	**1847–57**	Peak period of immigration before the Civil War
1832	Chief Justice Marshall declares the Cherokee nation to be a distinct political community in *Worcester* v. *Georgia*, but the ruling is never enforced	**1848**	Abortive revolutions in German states
		1868	Louisa May Alcott publishes *Little Women*

destinations of migrants. The villages of western New York State had lured the sons and daughters of New England in the first two decades of the century; after the mid-1820s, New York sent its young people to new lands in the Midwest. Later, Ohio and Michigan towns and farms would watch their young people move farther west. Their counterparts in the Upper South went to Illinois and Ohio, and those farther south settled the Gulf states.

Government policy fostered farm life. The acquisition of Louisiana in 1803 and later annexations of Florida, Texas, and Oregon all increased available agricultural land. The internal improvements—harbors, roads, canals, and railroads—following the War of 1812 were a boost to agriculture. Indian removal opened additional land for farmers, and the inexpensive sale of public lands facilitated new farm settlements. State governments promoted agricultural education through schools and county and state fairs.

The farm village, with its churches, post office, general store, and tavern, was the center of rural life. But rural social life was not limited to trips to the village; families gathered on one another's farms to ac-

Farm Communities

complish as a community what they could not manage individually. Barn-raisings regularly brought people together. A farmer and an itinerant carpenter prepared the site before the neighbors arrived to help on the appointed day. After the walls were put together and raised into position, they attached a roof. Then everyone celebrated with a communal meal and sang, danced, and played games. Similar gatherings took place at harvest time and on special occasions.

People had active social lives. Men met frequently at general stores, weekly markets, and taverns, and they hunted and fished together. Some women also attended market. More typically, they met at after-church dinners, prayer and Bible-study groups, sewing and corn-husking bees, and quilting parties. These were occasions to exchange experiences, thoughts, and spiritual support, and to swap letters, books, and news.

Traditional country bees had their town counterparts. Fredrika Bremer, a Swedish visitor to the United States, described a sewing bee in Cambridge, Massachusetts, in 1849, at which neighborhood women made clothes for "a family who had lost all their clothing by fire." Yet town bees were not the all-day family affairs of the countryside, and those who moved from farm to town often missed the country gatherings.

Americans were increasingly conscious of such changes. Some turned to rural utopian experiments in an effort to find an antidote to the market economy and the untamed growth of large urban communities and an opportunity to restore tradition and social cohesion. In the religious ferment of the Second Great Awakening (see pages 150, 152), many people reacted favorably to new religious communities, whatever their philosophy. Virtually all of the utopian experiments offered a cooperative rather than a competitive environment; communal living; and nontraditional work, family, and gender roles.

The Shakers, named for the way they danced at worship services, undertook one of the earliest utopian experiments. Founder Ann Lee imported

Shakers

this offshoot of the Quakers to America in 1774. While living in England, she had experienced a vision foretelling Jesus's second coming in America and urging her to go there. The Shakers believed that the end of the world was near and that sin entered the world through sexual intercourse. They considered existing churches too worldly and viewed the Shaker community as the instrument of salvation.

In 1787 the Shakers "gathered in" at New Lebanon, New York, to live and work communally. At its peak, between 1820 and 1860, the sect had about six thousand members in twenty settlements in eight states; it was the largest and most permanent of the utopian experiments. Though economically conservative, the Shakers were social radicals. They abolished individual families, practiced celibacy, and gave women new prospects for spiritual leadership. During its period of greatest growth, the Shaker ministry was headed by a woman, Lucy Wright. The sect's practice of celibacy, however, led inevitably to its demise.

The most successful communitarian group was the Church of Jesus Christ of Latter-day Saints, known as the Mormons. Joseph Smith, a young farmer in western New York, reported in

Mormon Community of Saints

1827 that he had been visited by the angel Moroni, who gave him a set of gold plates engraved with divine revelation. Smith published his revelations as the *Book of Mormon* and organized a church in western New York in 1830. Violence stalked the Mormons; angry mobs drove them from Ohio, Illinois, and Missouri. People objected most to the Mormon belief in continuous revelation and the practice of allowing men to have several wives at once. Finally in 1846 and 1847 the Mormons found a home in the Great Salt Lake valley. There, under Brigham Young, they established a patriarchal community of Saints based on communal republicanism. They achieved not only religious freedom but political self-government.

In Utah the Mormons distributed agricultural land according to family size. An extensive irrigation system, constructed by men who contributed their labor in proportion to the quantity of land they received and the amount of water they expected to use, transformed the arid valley into a rich oasis. As the colony developed, the church elders gained control of water, trade, industry, and even the territorial government of Utah.

Not all utopian communities were founded by religious sects. In 1825 Robert Owen, a wealthy Scottish industrialist, attempted to establish a socialist utopia in New Harmony, Indiana. According to his plan, its nine hundred members were to exchange their labor for goods at a communal store. Handicrafts (hat and boot making) flourished at New Harmony, but a textile mill—which was to have been the economic base of the community—failed after Owen gave it to the community to run. By 1827 Owen's experiment had ended.

The impact of the Brook Farm cooperative in West Roxbury, Massachusetts, was longer lasting. Inspired by transcendentalism—the belief that the physical world is secondary to the spiritual realm—Brook **Brook Farm** Farm's members rejected materialism in favor of rural communalism, combining spirituality, manual labor, intellectual life, and play.

Though short-lived (1841–1847), Brook Farm played a significant role in the flowering of a national literature. During these years Nathaniel Hawthorne, Ralph Waldo Emerson, and Margaret Fuller, editor of the *Dial* (the leading transcendentalist journal), joined Henry David Thoreau, James Fenimore Cooper, Herman Melville, and others in creating what is known today as the American Renaissance. In its philosophical intensity and moral idealism, their work was both distinctively American and an outgrowth of the European romantic movement. Their themes were universal, their settings and character American.

The essayist Ralph Waldo Emerson was the prime mover of the American Renaissance and a pillar of the transcendental movement. "We live in succession, in division, in parts, in particles," Emerson wrote. "We see the world piece by piece, as the sun, the moon, the animal, the tree; but the whole, of which these are the shining parts, is the soul." Intuitive experience of God is attainable, insisted Emerson, because "the Highest dwells" within every individual in the form of the "Over-soul."

Utopian communities can be seen as attempts to recapture the cohesiveness of traditional agricultural and artisan life in reaction to the competitive pressures of the market economy and urbanization. Utopians, like the Separatists of seventeenth-century New England (see page 37), sought to begin anew in their own colonies.

 # City Life

The transportation revolution and the expansion of commerce and manufacturing enabled the urban population to grow geometrically between 1800 and 1860, especially in the North. The nation's population increased during this period from 5 million to 31 million. Meanwhile, settlement spread westward, and small rural settlements became towns. In 1800 the nation had only 33 towns with 2,500 or more people and only 3 with more than 25,000. By 1860, 392 towns exceeded 2,500 residents, 35 had more than 25,000, and 9 exceeded 100,000 (see maps, page 218).

New York City became the nation's foremost metropolis, growing from 60,500 in 1800 to over 800,000 in 1860. Although contemporary depictions of New York appear almost pastoral, the city's energy **New York City** and aromas of sweat, horse dung, and garbage would make twentieth-century cities seem sanitized in comparison. An immigrant port city, mostly Irish and German by the 1850s, New York City teemed with people.

New York City literally had burst its boundaries in the 1820s. Up to that time New Yorkers regarded the city as a village because they could walk from one end to the other in an hour. Until the 1820s nearly all New Yorkers lived within two miles of City Hall. Mass transit, however, made it possible for cities to expand. Horse-drawn buses appeared in New York in 1827, and the Harlem Railroad, completed in 1832, ran the length of Manhattan. By the 1850s all big cities had horse-drawn streetcars.

By modern standards early-nineteenth-century cities were disorderly, unsafe, and unhealthy. Expansion occurred so rapidly that few cities could handle the problems it brought. For example, migrants from rural areas were accustomed to relieving themselves outside and throwing refuse in any vacant area. In the city, such waste smelled, spread disease, and polluted water. New York City partially solved the problem in the 1840s by abandoning wells in favor of reservoir water piped into

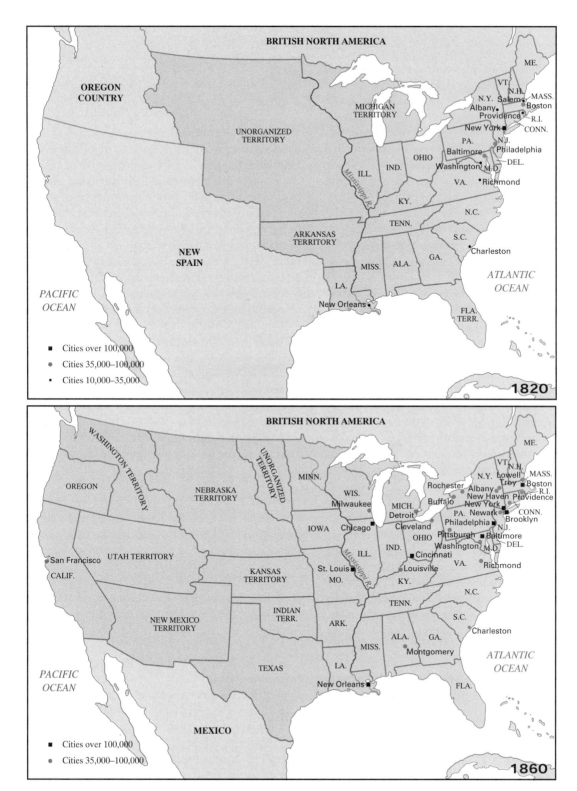

Major American Cities in 1820 and 1860 *Between 1820 and 1860 many Americans moved to cities with the result that the number of communities with populations exceeding 100,000 increased from one to nine.*

buildings and outdoor fountains. In some districts, scavengers and refuse collectors carted away garbage and human waste, but in much of the city it just rotted on the ground. Only one-quarter of New York City's streets had sewers by 1857.

New York and other cities lacked adequate taxing power to provide services for all. The best the city could do was to assess the adjoining property for the cost of sewers, street paving, and water mains. Thus the spread of new services and basic sanitation depended on residents' ability to pay. As a result, those most in need of services typically got them last. Another solution was to charter private companies to sell basic services. This plan worked well with gas service. Baltimore first chartered a private gas company in 1816. By midcentury every major city was lit by a private gas supplier. The private sector, however, failed to supply the water the cities needed. Private firms lacked the capital to build adequate systems, and they laid pipe only in commercial and well-to-do residential areas, ignoring the poor. As population grew, city governments had to take over.

A singular urban innovation was the creation of public education. In 1800 there were no public schools outside New England; by 1860 every state offered some public education.

Horace Mann and Public Schools

Massachusetts led in expansion of schooling under Horace Mann, secretary of the state board of education from 1837 to 1848. Massachusetts established a minimum school term of six months, formalized the training of teachers, and emphasized secular subjects and applied skills rather than religious training. In the process, schoolteaching became a woman's profession.

Mann's preaching on behalf of free, state-sponsored education changed schooling throughout the nation. "If we do not prepare children to become good citizens," he argued, "if we do not develop their capacities, . . . then our republic must go down to destruction." The abolition of ignorance, according to Mann, would end misery, crime, and suffering. He advocated educating all children. Mann and others were responding to the changes wrought by the market economy, urbanization, and immigration. The typical city dweller

was a newcomer, whether from abroad or from the country. Public schools would take the children of strangers and give them shared values.

Free public schools altered the scope of education. Schooling previously had focused on literacy, religious training, and discipline. Under Mann's leadership, the school curriculum became more secular and appropriate for the future clerks, farmers, and workers of America. Students studied geography, American history, arithmetic, and science. Moral education was retained, but direct religious indoctrination was dropped.

The basic texts—*McGuffey's Eclectic Readers*—used Protestant Scripture to teach children to accept their position in society. A good child, McGuffey taught, does not envy the rich: "It is God who makes some poor and others rich." Although Catholics, immigrants, blacks, and working-class people sought to have local control over their own schools, the state legislatures established secular statewide standards under Protestant educators. Catholics in New York responded by building their own educational system over the next half-century.

Urban population concentration, growth in commerce, and shifts in work altered patterns of leisure. In rural society, both leisure and work activities often took place at home. But in cities, new dedicated spaces—streets, theaters, sports fields—constituted a social sphere where people could come together away from home. Through the sale of admission tickets or membership in various types of associations, leisure became a commodity to be purchased. Even in cities, some traditional activities continued as they had since colonial times. Fishing remained popular, men played games of skill and strength in taverns, and churches continued to serve as centers for leisure.

Leisure

But Americans also read more. Thanks to the expansion of public education, the vast majority of native-born white Americans were literate by the 1850s. For the reading public, fiction and autobiographies competed with religious tracts as popular literature. Susanna Rowson's 1794 novel *Charlotte Temple*, which offered a critique of women's dependence on men, and the powerful attack on slavery in the *Narrative of the Life of Frederick Douglass*, *an American Slave, Written by Himself* (1845) were widely read. Many popular novels, written by women, often for women, were set in the home and upheld Christian values. Some might also be read as a challenge to prevailing values. Rowson's *Charlotte Temple*, for instance, never depicts the heroine performing domestic chores. And, although Susan Warners' *The Wide, Wide, Wide World* (1850), Nathaniel Hawthorne's *The House of the Seven Gables* (1851), and Fanny Fern's *Ruth Hall* (1855) did not challenge women's traditional domestic roles, they gave women a special moral bearing. In describing in positive terms community and republican virtue, they implicitly criticized the growing market economy.

Theater was a central institution in American life. A theater was often the second public building constructed in a town—after a church. Large cities boasted two or more theaters catering to different classes. Some plays, however, cut across class lines. Shakespeare was performed so often and appreciated so widely that even illiterate theatergoers knew passages of his blank verse well. In the 1840s, musical and dramatic presentations took on a more professional tone; newly popular minstrel shows and traveling circuses offered carefully rehearsed routines.

Sports, like theater, increasingly involved city dwellers as spectators. Horseracing, boxing, walking races, and, in the 1850s, baseball began to attract large urban male crowds.

Sports

After New York State legalized horseracing in 1821, a track opened in Queens County across the East River from New York City. Two years later a single race drew fifty thousand people. By 1849 boxing was so popular that a round-by-round account of a Maryland boxing match was telegraphed throughout the East.

Increasingly, urban sports and recreation became more formal and a commodity to be purchased. A group of Wall Street office workers formed the Knickerbocker Club in 1842, and in 1845 they drew up rules for the game of baseball. Their rules continue to serve as the basis for the game. Entertainment became a commodity: one had to buy a ticket to go to the theater, the circus, the racetrack, or the ballpark.

Ironically, public leisure soon developed a private dimension. Exclusive private associations arose to provide space and occasions for leisure. Some represented class divisions, as the growing middle and upper classes distanced themselves from the crowds and rowdiness of public events. Others were created by ethnic, racial, or religious groups seeking to socialize and share and preserve similar traditions. Thus the Irish had their Hibernian Society; African-Americans, their chapters of the Prince Hall Masons; and Jewish men, B'nai B'rith. Women, too, organized their own associations, ranging from social organizations to benevolent societies.

As cities grew, their populations seemed increasingly fragmented. Finding people similar to oneself required more of a conscious effort. The new associations served as a bulwark against the cultures of other groups— immigrants, migrants, blacks, and artisans. Middle- and upper-class New Yorkers who felt alienated in the city of their birth founded exclusive clubs. Some joined the Masonic order, which offered everything the bustling city did not: an elaborate hierarchy, an orderly code of deference between ranks, harmony, and shared values. Members knew each other. Americans of all sorts—native- and foreign-born, black and white—also formed churches and church-associated clubs. Associations brought together like people, but they also formalized divisions between different groups.

City Culture

Cities offered not only diversity but also anonymity. People interested in same-sex liaisons, though often publicly ostracized, could find each other in the city and live together in urban boarding houses.

Even a youth culture developed on the Bowery in the 1840s. Older New Yorkers feared the "Bowery boys and gals," whose ostentatious dress and behavior seemed threatening to them. A Bowery Boy's swaggering gait, especially when he had a girlfriend on his arm, frightened many in the middle class. Equally disturbing to old New Yorkers were the young working women who promenaded on the Bowery. Unlike more genteel ladies who wore modest veils or bonnets, Bowery "gals" drew attention to themselves with bright, outlandish clothes and ornate hats.

Most working people spent much of their lives outdoors; they worked in the streets as laborers, shopped in open markets, and paraded on special occasions. Young people courted, neighbors argued, and ethnic groups defended their turf on the streets. Increasingly, urban streets served as a political arena as crowds formed to listen to speakers, to parade, and sometimes to form mobs.

In the 1830s, riots became commonplace as professionals and merchants, craftsmen and laborers vented their rage against political and economic rivals. "Gentlemen of property and standing," un-

Urban Riots nerved by antislavery proponents, sacked abolitionist and antislavery organizations, even murdering newspaper editor Elijah Lovejoy in Alton, Illinois, in 1837. In the 1840s, "respectable" citizens drove the Mormons out of Illinois and Missouri. In Philadelphia native-born workers attacked Irish weavers in 1828, and whites and blacks fought on the docks in 1834 and 1835. Philadelphia's riots came to a head in 1844 when mostly Protestant skilled workers attacked Irish Catholics. Smaller cities, too, became battlegrounds as nativist riots peaked in the 1850s. By 1840 more than 125 people had died in urban riots, and by 1860 fatalities exceeded 1,000.

As public disorder spread, Boston hired uniformed policemen in 1837 to supplement its part-time watchmen and constables, and New York in 1845 established an entirely uniformed force. Nonetheless, middle-class men and women did not venture out alone at night, and even during the day they avoided certain districts. Ironically, in the midst of so much noise, crime, and conflict, the rich built lavish residences.

 ## Extremes of Wealth

The French nobleman Alexis de Tocqueville (in 1831 and 1832) and other observers characterized the United States before the Civil War as primarily a place of equality and opportunity. Tocqueville attributed American equality—the relative fluidity of the social order—to Americans' mobility and restlessness. Geographic mobility offered people a chance to start anew, regardless of where they came from or who they were. Wealth and family mattered little; a person could be known by deeds alone. According to the conventional wisdom, anyone could advance by working hard and saving money.

Others disagreed with this egalitarian view of American life. Among those who traced the rise of a new aristocracy based on wealth and power was *New York Sun* publisher Moses

"If Not an Aristocracy" Yale Beach. Author of twelve editions of *Wealth and Biography of the Wealthy Citizens of New York City*, Beach listed 750 New Yorkers with assets of $100,000 or more in 1845. John Jacob Astor led the list of nineteen millionaires with a fortune of $25 million. Ten years later, Beach reported more than a thousand New Yorkers worth $100,000, among them twenty-eight millionaires. Tocqueville himself, sensitive to conflicting trends in American life, had described the new industrial wealth. The rich and well educated "come forward to exploit industries," Tocqueville wrote, and become "more and more like the administrators of a huge empire. . . . What is this if not an aristocracy?"

Wealth throughout the United States was becoming concentrated in the hands of a relatively small number of people. In New York City between 1828 and 1845, the richest 4 percent of the city's population increased their holdings from an estimated 63 percent to 80 percent of all individual wealth. By 1860 the top 5 percent of American families owned more than half of the nation's wealth.

Meanwhile, a cloud of uncertainty hovered over working men and women. Many feared hard times and resented the competition of immigrant and slave labor. They dreaded the insecurities and indignities

Urban Poverty of poverty, chronic illness, disability, old age, widowhood, and desertion. Women feared having to raise a family without a spouse. And they had good reason: few women could find a job that paid sufficient money to support a family.

Poverty dogged the urban working class. Newly arrived immigrants, indigent free blacks, the working poor, and thieves, beggars, and prostitutes eked out a living in urban slums. New York City's Five Points exemplified the worst of urban life. The predominantly Irish and black neighborhood lacked running water and sewers. More than a thousand people crowded into the Old Brewery there, which had been converted to housing. Throughout the city, houses built for two families often held four; tenements built for six families held twelve.

In a world apart from Five Points lived the upper-class elite society of Philip Hone, one-time mayor of New York. Hone's diary, meticulously kept from 1826 until his death in 1851, records the activities of an American aristocrat. On February 28, 1840, for instance, Hone attended a masked ball at the Fifth Avenue mansion of Henry Breevoort, Jr., and Laura Carson Breevoort. The ball began at the fashionable hour of 10 P.M., and the five hundred ladies and gentlemen who filled the mansion wore costumes adorned with ermine and gold. At one time or another similar parties were held in Boston, Philadelphia, Baltimore, and Charleston.

The Urban Elite

Much of this new wealth was inherited. For every John Jacob Astor who made millions in the western fur trade, ten others used money they had inherited or married as a steppingstone to additional wealth. Many of the wealthiest New Yorkers bore the names of the colonial commercial elite: Beekman, Breevoort, Roosevelt, Van Rensselaer, and Whitney. These rich New Yorkers were not idle; they worked at increasing their fortunes and power by investing in the transportation, commercial, and manufacturing revolutions. Wealth begat wealth, and marriage cemented family ties.

Meanwhile, a distinct middle class became part of the urban scene, and the growth and specialization of trade rapidly increased its numbers. Middle-class families enjoyed the new consumer items: wool carpeting, fine wallpaper, rooms full of furniture, and indoor toilets. They filled the family pews in

The Middle Class

church on Sunday, and their children pursued the available educational opportunities. They were as distant from Philip Hone's world as they were from the working class and the poor.

Women, Families, and the Domestic Ideal

Marriage and family life were the central adult experiences of most women. Families were dominated by husbands and fathers who by English common law had control over the family. Men owned their wives' personal property and all wealth produced by family members. They also were the legal guardians of the children. Married women, however, began to make modest gains in property and spousal rights from the 1830s on. Arkansas in 1835 passed the first women's property law, and by 1860 sixteen more states had followed suit. In those states, women, including wives, could own and convey property: when a wife inherited, earned, or acquired property, it was hers, not her husband's; and she could write a will. In the 1830s states began to liberalize divorce, adding cruelty and desertion as grounds for divorce. Women who had the financial means could leave unhappy marriages.

As the urban workplace and home became separate, men worked for wages outside the home. Rural sons worked on their family farms, worked for hire on other people's farms, or sought wage work in towns. New England daughters left farms to work in textile mills. In the 1840s the new urban department stores hired young women as clerks and cash runners. Many women worked for a time as teachers. Paid employment typically represented a brief stage in women's lives before they left their parental households and entered their marital households.

Supporting Families

Working-class women—the poor, widows, and free blacks—worked to support themselves and their families. Leaving their parental homes as early as age twelve, they earned wages most of their lives, with only short respites for bearing and rearing children. But unlike men and New England farm daughters, most of these women did not work in the new shops and factories. Instead, they worked as domestic servants and as laundresses, seamstresses, and cooks. Few of these occupations enabled them to support themselves or a family at a respectable level.

Most women's work continued to be unpaid labor in the home. As the urban family lost its role in the production of goods, household upkeep and child rearing claimed women's full-time attention. Religion, morality, domestic arts, and music and literature filled the void left by the decline in the economic functions of the family; these realms came to be known as woman's sphere. A woman who achieved mastery in these areas lived up to the middle-class ideal of the cult of domesticity.

Middle-class Americans idealized the family as a moral institution characterized by selflessness and cooperation. Women were idealized in turn as the embodiment of self-sacrificing republicanism. The role of the mother was to strengthen the nation by rearing her children in a spiritual and virtuous environment unlike the world outside the home. The world of work—the market economy—was seen as an arena of conflict increasingly identified with men and dominated by base self-interest. In a rapidly changing world, the family represented stability and traditional values.

The domestic ideal restricted the range of paying jobs available to middle-class women. Most paid work was viewed with disapproval, but one occupation was considered consonant with the genteel female role: teaching. In 1823 the Beecher sisters, Catharine and Mary, established the Hartford Female Seminary and offered history and science in addition to the traditional women's curriculum of domestic arts and religion. A decade later Catharine Beecher successfully campaigned for teacher-training schools for women. By the 1850s teaching was regarded as a woman's vocation, and most urban teachers were unmarried women who were paid about half the salary of male teachers.

Meanwhile, family size was shrinking. In 1800 American women bore an average of six to seven children; by 1860 the figure had dropped to five.

Decline in Family Size

A number of factors reduced family size. Small families were viewed as increasingly desirable in an economy in which the family was a unit of consumption rather than production. Children in smaller families would have greater opportunities: parents could give them more attention, better education, and more financial help. Also, contemporary marriage manuals stressed that too many births had a harmful effect on a woman's health. Thus, evidence suggests, many wives and husbands made deliberate decisions to limit the size of families.

How did men and women limit their families in the early nineteenth century? Average age at marriage rose, thus shortening the period of potential childbearing. Women also bore their last child at a younger age, suggesting that family planning was becoming more common.

Limiting Families

Many couples used traditional forms of birth control, such as coitus interruptus (withdrawal of the male before completion of the sexual act) and breast-feeding, which makes some women temporarily infertile. Some couples used the rhythm method—attempting to confine intercourse to a woman's infertile periods—but awareness of the "safe period" was uncertain. Others used cheap rubber condoms, which became available in the 1850s. For those desiring to terminate a pregnancy, surgical abortions became common after 1830. By 1860, however, twenty states restricted or outlawed abortions.

Significantly, the birth-control methods that women themselves controlled—the rhythm method, abstinence, and abortion—became increasingly common. The new emphasis on domesticity encouraged women's autonomy in the home and by extension gave them greater control over their own bodies. Women ruled the household, including the bedroom, with refinement and purity.

Urban life and the market economy offered independence and new roles for women. Single women departed from the centuries-old pattern in

Single Men and Women

which a woman moved from her father's household to the household of her husband. Louisa May Alcott (1832–1888), the author of *Little Women* (1868), sought independence and financial security for herself. Alcott worked as a seamstress, governess, teacher, and housemaid before her writing brought her success. "I think I shall come out right, and prove that . . . I *can* support myself," she wrote her father in 1856. "I like the independent feeling; and though not an easy life, it is a free one, and I enjoy it."

Louisa May Alcott foreswore marriage. She and other single women pursued careers and a life defined by female relationships. Given the difficulty women had finding work that would allow them to be self-supporting, they undertook independence at great risk. Nonetheless, the proportion of single women in the population increased significantly in the first three quarters of the nineteenth century. Independent white women, in sum, were taking advantage of new opportunities offered by the market economy and urban expansion.

 Immigrant Lives in America

The 5 million immigrants who came to the United States between 1820 and 1860 outnumbered the entire population of the country recorded in the first census in 1790. They came from every continent, though the vast majority were European (see figure). During the peak period of pre–Civil War immigration, from 1847 through 1857, 3.3 million immigrants entered the United States; 1.3 million were from Ireland and 1.1 million from the German states. By 1860, 15 percent of the white population was foreign-born.

This massive migration had been set in motion decades earlier. At the turn of the nineteenth century, the Napoleonic wars had given rise to one of the greatest population shifts in history; it was ultimately to last more than a century. War, revolution, famine, religious persecution, and the lure of industrialization led many Europeans to leave home. Most Asian immigrants came from southern China to work in heavy construction. The United States beckoned, offering economic opportunity and religious freedom.

Both private firms and governments recruited European immigrants. Midwestern and western states lured potential settlers to promote economic growth. In the 1850s, for instance, Wisconsin appointed a commissioner of emigration, who advertised the state's advantages in European newspapers. Wisconsin also opened an office in New York and hired European agents to compete with other states and with firms like the Illinois Central Railroad in recruiting immigrants.

Promotion of Immigration

Large construction projects and mines needed strong young laborers. Textile mills and cities attracted young women workers. Europeans' awareness of the United States grew as employers, states, and shipping companies advertised opportunities across the Atlantic. The price of a ticket on the regularly scheduled sailing ships crossing the ocean after 1848 was within easy reach of millions of Europeans.

So they came, enduring the hardships of travel and of living in a strange land. The average transatlantic crossing took six weeks; in bad weather it could take three months. Disease spread unchecked among people packed together like cattle in steerage. More than seventeen thousand immigrants, mostly Irish, died from "ship fever" in 1847. On arrival, immigrants became fair game for the con artists and swindlers who worked the docks. Boarding-house and employment agents tried to lure them from their chosen destinations. In response, New York State established Castle Garden as an immigrant center in 1855. There, at the tip of Manhattan Island, the major port for European entry, immigrants were somewhat sheltered from fraud. Authorized transportation companies maintained offices in the large rotunda and assisted new arrivals with their travel plans.

Most immigrants gravitated toward cities. Many stayed in New York City itself; of its 623,000 inhabitants, 52 percent were immigrants in 1855. Boston also took on a European tone; throughout

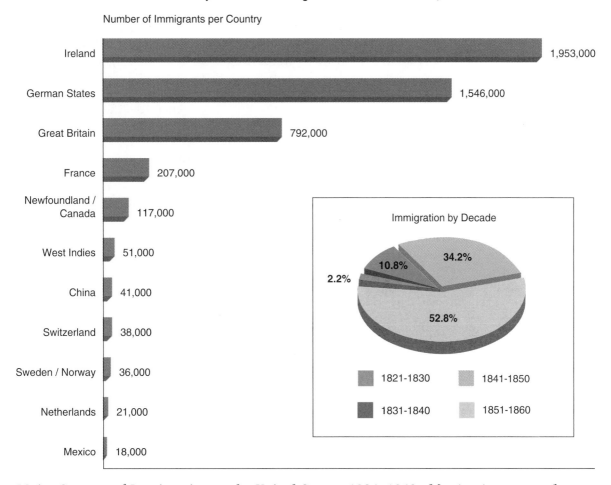

Major Sources of Immigration to the United States, 1821–1860

Number of Immigrants per Country

Country	Number
Ireland	1,953,000
German States	1,546,000
Great Britain	792,000
France	207,000
Newfoundland / Canada	117,000
West Indies	51,000
China	41,000
Switzerland	38,000
Sweden / Norway	36,000
Netherlands	21,000
Mexico	18,000

Immigration by Decade

- 2.2%
- 10.8%
- 34.2%
- 52.8%

1821-1830   1841-1850
1831-1840   1851-1860

Major Sources of Immigration to the United States, 1821–1860 *Most immigrants came from two areas: Great Britain, of which Ireland was a part, and the German states. These two areas sent more immigrants between 1820 and 1860 than the inhabitants of the United States enumerated at the first census in 1790. By 1860, 15 percent of the white population was of foreign birth.* Source: U.S. Bureau of the Census, *Historical Statistics of the United States, Colonial Times to 1970,* 2 parts (Washington, D.C., 1975), Part 1, pp. 206, 208.

the 1850s the city was about 35 percent foreign-born, of whom more than two-thirds were Irish. Southern cities also had sizable immigrant populations. In 1860 New Orleans was 44 percent foreign-born, Savannah 33 percent, and the western city of St. Louis 61 percent. On the West Coast, San Francisco had a foreign-born majority.

Some immigrants settled in rural areas. German, Dutch, and Scandinavian farmers, in particular, gravitated toward the Midwest. Greater percentages of Scandinavians and Netherlanders took up farming than did other nationalities; both groups came mostly as religious dissenters and migrated in family units. The Dutch who founded colonies in Michigan and Wisconsin, for instance, had seceded from the official Reformed Church of the Netherlands, fleeing persecution in their native land to establish new and more pious communities such as Holland and Zeeland in Michigan.

Not all immigrants found success in the United States; hundreds of thousands returned to their homelands disappointed. Before the potato blight hit Ireland, American recruiters had lured many Irish to swing picks and shovels on American canals and railroads and to work in construction. Among them was Michael Gaugin, who for thirteen years had been an assistant engineer in the construction of a Dublin canal. Gaugin was attracted to the United States by the promise that "he should soon become a wealthy man." The Dublin agent for a New York firm convinced him to quit his job, which included a house and an acre of ground, and emigrate. Gaugin had the misfortune to land in New York City during the financial panic of 1837, and within two months of arriving he was a pauper.

Immigrant Disenchantment

Such experiences did not deter other Irish men and women from coming to the United States. Ireland was the most densely populated place in Europe and among the most impoverished. From 1815 on, small harvests prompted a steady stream of Irish to emigrate to America. Then in 1845 and 1846 potatoes—Ireland's staple food—rotted in the fields. From 1845 to 1849, death from starvation, malnutrition, and typhus spread. In all, 1 million died and about 1.5 million fled, two-thirds of them to the United States. Ireland's major export was its people. Indeed, with only two exceptions, the Irish constituted the largest group of immigrants annually between 1820 and 1854.

Irish Immigrants

The new Irish immigrants differed greatly from those who had left Ireland to settle in the American colonies. The Protestant Scots-Irish who predominated in the eighteenth century (see page 68) had journeyed from one part of the British Empire to another. The nineteenth-century Irish immigrants to America, however, were mostly Roman Catholic, and they moved from a British colony to an independent republic. Moreover, most of the new immigrants from Ireland were young, female, and from rural counties.

In American cities Irish immigrants met anti-Catholic sentiment. "No Irish Need Apply" signs were common. During the colonial period, white Protestants had feared "popery" as a system of tyranny and had discriminated against the few Catholics in America. After the Revolution anti-Catholicism receded, but in the 1830s it reappeared wherever the Irish did.

Anti-Catholicism

The native-born who embraced anti-Catholicism were motivated largely by anxiety. They feared the Roman Catholic Church, unskilled Irish workers, and the urban slums inhabited by the Irish (among others). They blamed every social problem—from immorality and alcoholism to poverty and economic upheaval—on immigrant Irish Catholics. And the new public schools, with their Protestant bias, represented another form of attack on Irish Catholics. Friction increased as Irish-American men fought back by entering politics.

In 1854, Germans replaced the Irish as the largest group of new arrivals. Potato blight also had prompted emigration from the German states in the 1840s; other hardships added to the steady stream. Many people came from regions where small landholdings made it hard to eke out a living. Others were craftsmen displaced by the industrial revolution. These refugees were joined by middle-class Germans—a whole generation of liberals and freethinkers who emigrated to the United States after the abortive revolutions of 1848.

German Immigrants

It is not easy to characterize German-Americans. Germans settled everywhere in the United States. In the South they were peddlers and merchants; in the North and West they worked as farmers, urban laborers, and businessmen. Their tendency to migrate as families and groups helped them maintain German culture and institutions. Many settled in small towns and rural areas where they could preserve their local and regional identities. In larger cities immigrants from the same German states tended to cluster together. Their presence transformed the tone and culture of cities like Cincinnati and Milwaukee.

Native-born Americans accepted German immigrants more readily than they accepted the Irish, stereotyping Germans as hard working, self-reliant, and intelligent. Many believed that Germans would "harmonize" better with American culture. Nevertheless, Germans, too, encountered hostility. A significant number of German immigrants were Jewish, and they experienced anti-Semitism. Many German immigrants were Catholic, and their Sabbath traditions differed from those of Protestants. On Sundays urban German families customarily gathered at beer gardens to eat and drink beer, to dance, sing, and listen to band music, and sometimes to play cards. Protestants were outraged by this behavior, which they believed to be a violation of the Lord's day.

Some Hispanic groups became "immigrants" to the United States without actually moving. Mexican inhabitants of northern Mexico—present-day New Mexico and California—

Hispanics

were unhappy because under the Mexican constitution of 1824 they lived in Mexican territory, not states. Similarly Texas was part of the Mexican state of Coahuila. Lack of political autonomy made Mexicans in these areas unhappy, and many welcomed the events that brought them into the United States: the independence and later annexation of Texas, the Mexican War, and the Gadsden Purchase (see pages 254, 258).

In Texas, Anglos and European immigrants seized economic and political power. For instance, in Nueces County, Texas, at the time of the Texas Revolution (1836), Mexicans held all the land; twenty years later, they had lost it all. Moreover, although many Tejanos had fought for Texas's independence, arriving Anglo settlers tended to treat them as inferiors. They became second-class citizens on land where they had lived for generations.

Nonetheless, Tejanos retained their culture. They held fast to Roman Catholic and Hispanic traditions. San Antonio illustrates the persistence of Hispanic culture. The church, free public schools (established in 1827), life-cycle events from baptism to marriage to funerals, and public holidays and celebrations all supported Hispanic Roman Catholic traditions. Thus during the period of Texas independence, from 1836 to 1845, and after Texas statehood in 1845, Hispanic identity continued even in the face of a loss of political power.

In California—unlike Texas, New Mexico, and Arizona—Hispanic culture quickly gave way to American and European culture. Californios, the Mexican population, numbered 10,000 in 1848, or two-thirds of the non-Indian population. By the end of the century the Hispanic population was 15,000 out of 1.5 million, and Hispanic culture was only a remnant, though it would be reestablished by Mexican immigrants in the twentieth century.

For immigrants, becoming part of American society involved conflict, but once in the United States they claimed their right to a fair economic and political share. Native Americans, however, like the Hispanics in the Southwest, had to defend what they regarded as prior rights. Their lands, their religions, and their ways of life came under constant attack.

Indian Resistance and Removal

The Constitution gave the United States government responsibility for dealing with Indians. For better or worse, there had to be a federal Indian policy. From the Indians' point of view, it usually was for the worse. United States territorial expansion took place at the Indians' expense. The result was removal of the great Native American nations to lands west of the Mississippi. While the population of other groups was increasing by leaps and bounds, the Indian population was shrinking. In the 1830s alone, more than half of the Pawnees, Omahas, Otoes, Missouris, and Kansas died.

Like the colonial powers in North America, the United States government treated Native American groups as sovereign nations, until Congress ended the practice in 1871. Agreements between a given Indian nation and the United States were signed, sealed, and ratified like any other international pact. In practice, however, Native American sovereignty was a fiction. Treaty making was essentially a tactic that the American government used to acquire Indian land. Instead of bargains struck by two equal nations, treaties often were agreements imposed by the victor on the vanquished. Old treaties gave way to new ones requiring Native Americans to cede their traditional holdings in return for different lands in the West.

The War of 1812 snuffed out whatever realistic hopes eastern Indian leaders had of resisting American expansion by warfare. After the war, Indian armed resistance persisted, but it only delayed the inevitable. The Shawnee chiefs Prophet and Tecumseh led the most significant movement against the United States (see page 165), but Prophet failed to sustain the movement after Tecumseh's death.

The experiences of Prophet and other Shawnees were typical of the wanderings of an uprooted people. After giving up 17 million acres in Ohio in the 1795 Treaty of Greenville (see page 131), the Shawnees scattered to Indiana and eastern Missouri. After the War of 1812, Prophet's Indiana group withdrew to Canada. In 1822 other Shawnees sought Mexican protection and moved from Missouri to present-day eastern Texas. As the United States government began promoting removal to Kansas, Prophet returned from Canada to lead a group to the new Shawnee lands in eastern Kansas in 1825. When Missouri achieved statehood in 1821, Shawnees living there were also forced to move to Kansas, where they were joined in the 1830s by Shawnees removed from Ohio and others expelled from Texas. By 1854 Kansas was open to white settlement, and the Shawnees had to cede back seven-eighths of their land there—1.4 million acres.

Shawnees

Removal had a profound impact on all Shawnees. The men had to give up their traditional role as providers; their methods of hunting and their knowledge of woodland animals were useless on the prairies of Kansas. As grain became the tribe's dietary staple, Shawnee women played a greater role as providers, supplemented by government aid under treaty provisions. Remarkably, the Shawnees preserved their language and culture in the face of these drastic changes.

In the 1820s Indians in Ohio, southern Indiana and Illinois, southwestern Michigan, most of Missouri, central Alabama, and southern Mississippi were pressured to cede their lands. They gave up nearly 200 million acres for pennies an acre. The federal Indian agency system, which monopolized trade with Indians and paid out the rations, supplies, and annuities they received in exchange for abandoning their land, made Indians dependent on government payments. Dependency made them pliant in treaty negotiations and furthered assimilation by bringing them into the market system.

Federal Indian Policy

Ever since the early days of European colonization, the assimilation of Native Americans through education and Christianity had been an explicit goal of whites. It took on renewed urgency as the United States expanded westward. In 1819, in response to missionary lobbying, Congress appropriated $10,000 annually for "civilization of the tribes adjoining the frontier settlements." Protestant missionaries administered the "civilizing fund" and established mission schools. These new boarding schools substituted English for native languages and taught agriculture alongside the Christian Gospel. To settlers eyeing Indian land, assimilation through education seemed too slow a process. At any given time there were never more than fifteen hundred students in all the schools; at that rate it would take centuries to assimilate all the Indians. Thus wherever Indians lived, illegal settlers disrupted their lives. Though obligated to protect the integrity of treaty lands, the federal government did so only halfheartedly. With government supporting westward expansion, legitimate Indian claims had to give way to the advance of white civilization.

In the 1820s it became apparent that not economic dependency, education, or Christianity could persuade Indians to cede more land to meet the demands of expansionists. Attention focused on southeastern tribes—Cherokees, Creeks, Choctaws, Chickasaws, and Seminoles—because much of their land remained intact after the War of 1812 and because they aggressively resisted white encroachment.

In his last annual message to Congress in late 1824, President James Monroe suggested that all

Indians be moved beyond the Mississippi River. Three days later he sent a special message to Congress proposing removal. The proposal was aimed at the Cherokees, Creeks, Choctaws, and Chickasaws, and they unanimously rejected it.

Indian Removal to the West

Pressure from Georgia had prompted Monroe's policy. Cherokees and Creeks lived in northwestern Georgia, and in the 1820s the state accused the federal government of not fulfilling its 1802 promise to remove the Indians in return for the state's renunciation of its claim to western lands. Georgia was satisfied neither by Monroe's removal messages nor by further cessions by the Creeks. In 1826, under federal pressure, the Creek nation ceded all but a small strip of its Georgia acreage. But Georgia still was not satisfied. Only the removal of the Georgia Creeks to the West could resolve the conflict between Georgia and the federal government.

If civilizing Indians was the American goal, no tribe met that test better than the Cherokees. Between 1819 and 1829 the tribe became economically self-sufficient and politically self-governing: during this Cherokee renaissance the twelve to fifteen thousand adult Cherokees came to think of themselves as a nation, not a collection of villages. Between 1820 and 1823 the Cherokees created a formal government with a bicameral legislature, a court system, and a salaried bureaucracy. In 1827 they adopted a written constitution, modeled after that of the United States. Cherokee land laws, however, differed from United States law. The tribe as a whole owned all Cherokee land, and complex provisions covered land sales (forbidden to outsiders). Nonetheless, the Cherokees assimilated American cultural patterns. By 1833 they held fifteen hundred black slaves whose legal status was the same as that of slaves held by southern whites. Moreover, missionaries had been so successful that the Cherokees could be considered a Christian community.

Cherokees

Although the Cherokees developed a political system similar to that of an American state, they failed to win respect or acceptance from southerners. Georgia pressed them to sell the 7,200 square miles of land they held in the state. Most Cherokees, however, preferred to stay where they were. Impatient with their refusals to negotiate cession, Georgia annulled the Cherokee's constitution, extended the state's sovereignty over them, and ordered their lands seized.

Backed by sympathetic whites but not by the new president, Andrew Jackson, the Cherokees under Chief John Ross turned to the federal courts to defend their treaty with the United States and prevent Georgia's seizure of their land. In *Cherokee Nation* v. *Georgia* (1831), Chief Justice John Marshall ruled that under the federal Constitution an Indian tribe was neither a foreign nation nor a state and therefore had no standing in federal courts. Nonetheless, said Marshall, the Indians had an unquestionable right to their lands; they could lose title only by voluntarily giving it up. A year later, in *Worcester* v. *Georgia*, Marshall defined the Cherokee position more clearly. The Indian nation was, he declared, a distinct political community in which "the laws of Georgia can have no force" and into which Georgians could not enter without permission or treaty privilege. Georgia refused to comply.

Cherokee Nation v. Georgia

President Andrew Jackson refused to interfere because the case involved a state action. Keen to open up new lands for settlement, Jackson was determined to remove the Cherokees. In the Removal Act of 1830 Congress provided Jackson with the funds he needed to negotiate new treaties and resettle the resistant tribes west of the Mississippi (see map).

The Choctaws were the first to go; they made the forced journey from Mississippi and Alabama to the West in the winter of 1831 and 1832. Other tribes soon joined the forced march. The Creeks in Alabama resisted removal until 1836, when the army pushed them westward. A year later the Chickasaws followed.

Trail of Tears

Having fought removal in the courts, the Cherokees were divided. Some believed that further resistance was hopeless and accepted removal as the only chance to preserve their civilization. The leaders of this minority agreed in 1835 to

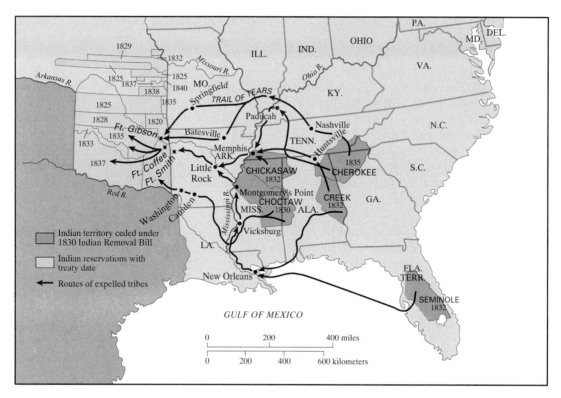

Removal of Indians from the South, 1820–1840 *Over a twenty-year period, the federal government and southern states forced Indians to exchange their traditional homes for western land. Some tribal groups remained in the South, but most settled in the alien western environment.* Source: Acknowledgment is due to Martin Gilbert and George Weidenfeld and Nicholson Limited for permission to reproduce this map taken from* American History Atlas.*

exchange their southern home for western land. But when the time for evacuation came in 1838, most Cherokees refused to move. President Martin Van Buren sent federal troops to round them up. About twenty thousand Cherokees were evicted, held in detention camps, and marched to Indian Territory in present-day Oklahoma under military escort. Nearly one-quarter of them died of disease and exhaustion on what came to be known as the Trail of Tears.

When the forced march to the West ended, the Indians had traded about 100 million acres east of the Mississippi for 32 million acres west of the river plus $68 million. Only a few scattered remnants, among them the Seminoles in Florida and the Cherokees in the southern Appalachian Mountains, remained in the East and South.

The impact of the forced removal on Indian life was disastrous. In the West they encountered an alien environment, and, lacking traditional ties with the new land, few felt at peace with it. The animals and plants they found were unfamiliar. No longer able to live off the land, many Native Americans became dependent on government payments for survival. Removal also brought new internal conflicts. The Cherokees in particular struggled over their tribal government. Moreover, conflicts arose among migrating Indian groups from the South and East and Indians already living in the West, as they were forced to share land and scarce resources.

Some waged war to avoid removal. In the Southeast a small band of Seminoles successfully resisted and remained in Florida. Some Seminole

The Trail of Tears *by contemporary Cherokee artist Brummet Echohawk. About twenty thousand Cherokees were evicted in 1838–1839, and about one quarter of them died on the forced march to present-day Oklahoma.*   Thomas G. Krease Institute

Second Seminole War

leaders agreed in the 1832 Treaty of Payne's Landing to relocate to the West within three years. A minority under Osceola, a charismatic leader, refused to vacate their homes and fought the pro-treaty group. When federal troops were sent to impose removal in 1835, Osceola waged a fierce guerrilla war against them. Though Osceola—who was captured under a white flag of truce—died in an army prison in 1838, the Seminoles continued the war. Finally, in 1842 the United States abandoned the removal effort. Most of Osceola's followers agreed to move west to Indian Territory in 1858, but many Seminoles remained in the Florida Everglades, proud of having resisted conquest.

A complex set of attitudes drove whites to re-move Indians forcibly. Most wanted land and had little or no respect for the Indians' rights or culture. Others were aware of the injustice but believed that Indians inevitably had to give way to white settlement. Some, like John Quincy Adams, believed the only way to preserve Indian civilization was to separate Indians and white settlers physically. Others hoped to "civilize" Indians and

assimilate them gradually into American culture. Whatever the source of white attitudes, it resulted in the devastation of Native American cultures.

Free People of Color

Free people of color also struggled for recognition and legal rights. Like Indians, they were involuntary participants in American society. Unlike Indians, however, they wished to partake fully in American life.

On the surface, the Bill of Rights seemed to protect free African-Americans. The Fifth Amendment specified that "no person shall . . . be deprived of life, liberty, or property, without due process of law." But eighteenth-century political theory had defined the republic as being for whites only (see page 126), and early federal legislation reflected this exclusionist thinking: naturalization, for example, was limited to white aliens in 1790. After the admission of Missouri in 1821, every new state admitted until the Civil War banned blacks from voting. When the Oregon and New Mexico Territories were organized, public land grants were reserved for whites.

African-Americans in the North were second-class citizens. Newly admitted states barred free blacks or required them to post bonds ranging from $500 to $1,000 to guarantee their good conduct. Only in Massachusetts, New Hampshire, Vermont, and Maine could blacks vote on an equal basis with whites throughout the pre–Civil War period. In 1842 African-Americans gained the right to vote in Rhode Island, but they had lost it earlier in Pennsylvania and Connecticut. Only Massachusetts permitted blacks to serve on juries. Four midwestern states and California did not allow African-Americans to testify against whites. In Oregon, blacks could not own real estate, make contracts, or sue in court. Throughout the North white social custom excluded or segregated free people of color. Hotels and restaurants barred them, as did most theaters and white churches. Discrimination in hiring existed everywhere. Countinghouses, retail stores, and factories refused to hire black men except as janitors and handymen. New England mills hired only whites.

Exclusion and Segregation of African-Americans

Free people of color faced severe legal and social barriers in the southern slave states. Whites viewed their presence as subversive. Fearing free African-Americans, southern states restricted their presence. After the Nat Turner Rebellion in 1831, the position of free blacks deteriorated throughout the South. Within five years nearly every southern state prohibited the freeing of slaves without legislative or court approval, and by the 1850s Texas, Mississippi, and Georgia had banned manumission altogether.

Southern Free Blacks

In essence, the legal status of southern free people of color was somewhere between slave and free. Southern states adopted elaborate "black codes" to curtail the activities and opportunities of African-Americans, who provided most of the South's skilled labor. Virginia and Georgia denied work to black riverboat captains and pilots. Some states forbade blacks to assemble without a license. Some prohibited them from learning to read and write. In the late 1830s, the codes were tightened,

and free people of color moved northward even though northern states discouraged the migration.

In spite of these obstacles, the free African-American population rose from 108,000 in 1800 to almost 500,000 in 1860. Nearly half lived in the North, some in rural settlements but far more in cities like Philadelphia, New York, and Cincinnati. Baltimore had the largest community, but sizable free black populations formed in New Orleans, Charleston, and Mobile.

The ranks of free people of color were constantly increased by ex-slaves. Some, like Frederick Douglass and Harriet Tubman, were fugitives. Tubman, a slave in Maryland, escaped to Philadelphia in 1849 when it was rumored that she would be sold out of the state. Within the next two years she returned twice to free her two children, her sister, her mother, and her brother and his family. Some slaves received freedom in owners' wills when masters sought, at death, to rid themselves of the stain of owning slaves. Other owners freed elderly slaves after a lifetime of service rather than support them in old age.

Free people of color forged cohesive communities and created autonomous institutions within them. Churches became the center of community life, and pastors became political leaders. Church buildings functioned as town halls, and they housed schools, political forums and conventions, protest meetings, and benevolent and self-help associations.

African-American Communities

Like European immigrants, free people of color sought to assist members of their own community. But they had a greater burden. Although their taxes supported white schools, for instance, they had to raise additional funds to establish African-American schools because their children were excluded from the new public schools. A network of voluntary associations—self-help societies, female benevolent societies, and literary and social clubs—became the hallmark of their communities. Most of these organizations were political as well as social.

In the majority of states where free blacks were excluded from the ballot, they formed

How do historians know about African-American political thought and activity in the early nineteenth century? One important source is the published minutes of black conventions, first held in 1830. Free people of color held at least eleven national conventions and about forty state conventions prior to the Civil War. The first national convention, a special meeting in Philadelphia in September 1830, was presided over by Bishop Richard Allen, founder of the African Methodist Episcopal Church. The delegates agreed to explore a settlement in Canada as a haven for free people of color and fugitive slaves. They also called for pursuing "all legal means for the speedy elevation of ourselves and brethren to the scale and standing of men." Less than a year later, delegates to the "First Annual Meeting of the People of Colour" condemned the persecution of African-Americans, appealed for funds to support their work, called for the establishment of a college for poor blacks, and stressed the importance of education. They also were consciously building a movement of annual conventions. The report of this convention, and subsequent convention minutes and addresses, demonstrate the involvement of African-Americans in the reforms of the times and the importance they placed on education and equality of opportunity. At conventions held in the 1850s nationalism took hold among African-Americans.

The convention movement was democratic. Most communities elected their delegates to the national conventions at public meetings or at local and state conventions. Although the minutes reveal a wide range of opinion within black communities, there was agreement about the abolition of slavery, immediate emancipation, and equal rights for free people of color.   Minutes of the Proceedings of the Natural Negro Convention, 1831.

CONSTITUTION

OF THE

AMERICAN SOCIETY

OF

FREE PERSONS OF COLOUR,

FOR IMPROVING THEIR CONDITION IN THE UNITED STATES; FOR PURCHASING LANDS; AND FOR THE ESTABLISHMENT OF A SETTLEMENT IN UPPER CANADA.

ALSO

THE PROCEEDINGS OF THE CONVENTION,

WITH THEIR

ADDRESS

TO

THE FREE PERSONS OF COLOUR

IN THE

UNITED STATES.

PHILADELPHIA:
PRINTED BY J. W. ALLEN, NO 26, STRAWBERRY-ST.
1831.

protest organizations to fight for equal rights. Among the early efforts to organize for self-defense was the Negro Convention movement. From 1830 to 1835, and irregularly thereafter, free blacks held national conventions with delegates drawn from city and state organizations. Under the leadership of the small black middle class, which included the Philadelphia sail manufacturer James Forten and the orator Reverend Henry Highland Garnet, the convention movement served as a forum to attack slavery and agitate for equal rights. Militant new black newspapers joined the struggle.

The mood of free blacks began to shift in the late 1840s and 1850s. Many were frustrated by the failure of the abolitionist movement and angered

Black Nationalism

by the passage of the Fugitive Slave Act of 1850 (see page 263). Some were swept up in a wave of black nationalism that stressed racial solidarity, self-help, and a growing interest in Africa. Before this time, efforts to send African-Americans "back to Africa" had originated with whites seeking to rid the United States of blacks. But in the 1850s blacks held emigrationist conventions of their own under the leadership of abolitionists Henry Bibb and Martin Delany. With the coming of the Civil War, the status of blacks would move onto the national political agenda, and African-Americans would focus on their position at home.

 Conclusion

The American people and communities were far more diverse and turbulent in 1860 than they had been in 1800. The market economy, immigration, and the growth of cities had altered the way people lived and worked. Inequality increased everywhere, and competition and insecurity produced resentment and conflict. Cities housed both ostentatious wealth and abject poverty, and disorder became commonplace. Many Americans felt as if they were strangers to each other.

In the midst of these changes, middle-class families sought to insulate their homes from the competition of the market economy. Many women found fulfillment in the domestic ideal: others found it confining. Middle-class urban women became associated with nurturing roles, first in homes and schools, then in churches and reform societies. Working-class women had more modest goals: escaping poverty and winning respect. Most Americans found some comfort in religion.

Famine and religious and political oppression in Europe propelled millions of people across the Atlantic. They were drawn to the United States by the promise of jobs and tolerance. Most found the going rough. In the process of adapting, immigrants changed the profile of the American people. Competition and diversity in turn bred intolerance. Native Americans, free African-Americans, and Hispanics were made to feel like aliens in their own land.

Conflict became increasingly commonplace in the public arena. The manifestations of division in America were many: utopian communities, conflicts over public space, backlash against immigrants, urban riots, black protest, and Indian resistance. Conflict also took the form of reform movements, which came to characterize American life from the 1820s through the 1850s. Through reform and political action, many Americans sought to harness and control the forces of change. Spurred on by religious revival and individualism, they turned to politics as a collective means of restoring harmony and order. In the process, divisions became even sharper.

Suggestions For Further Reading

Rural and Utopian Communities

Priscilla J. Brewer, *Shaker Communities, Shaker Lives* (1986); David B. Danbom, *Born in the Country: A History of Rural America* (1995); John Mack Faragher, *Sugar Creek: Life on the Illinois Prairie* (1986); Steven Hahn and Jonathan Prude, eds., *The Countryside in the Age of Capitalist Transformation* (1985); Joan M. Jensen, *Loosening the Bonds: Mid-Atlantic Farm Women, 1750–1850* (1986); Sally McMurry, *Families and Farmhouses in Nineteenth Century America: Vernacular Design and Social Change* (1988); Anthony F. C. Wallace, *Rockdale: The Growth of an American Village in the Early Industrial Revolution* (1978); Kenneth H. Winn, *Exiles in a Land of Liberty: Mormons in America, 1830–1846* (1989).

Urban Communities

Stuart M. Blumin, *The Emergence of the Middle Class: Social Experience in the American City, 1760–1900* (1989); Susan G. Davis, *Parades and Power: Street Theater in Nineteenth-Century Philadelphia* (1986); Timothy J. Gilfoyle, *City of Eros: New York City, Prostitution, and the Commercialization of Sex, 1790–1920* (1992); Karen V. Hansen, *A Very Social Time: Crafting Community in Antebellum New England* (1994); Jack Larkin, *The Reshaping of Everyday Life, 1790–1840* (1988); Edward Pessen, *Riches, Class and Power Before the Civil War* (1973); Christine Stansell, *City of Women: Sex and Class in New York, 1789–1860* (1986); Richard B. Stott, *Workers in the Metropolis: Class, Ethnicity, and Youth in Antebellum New York City* (1990); Alexis de Tocqueville, *Democracy in America*, 2 vols. (1835, 1840).

American Families

Virginia K. Bartlett, *Keeping House: Women's Lives in Western Pennsylvania, 1790–1850* (1994); Janet Farrell Brodie, *Contraception and Abortion in Nineteenth-Century America* (1994); Lee Virginia Chambers-Schiller, *Liberty, A Better Husband: Single Women in America: The Generations of 1780–1840* (1984); Nancy F. Cott, *The Bonds of Womanhood: "Woman's Sphere" in New England, 1780–1835* (1977); Joan Hoff, *Law, Gender and Injustice: A Legal History of U.S. Women* (1991); Suzanne Lebsock, *The Free Women of Petersburg: Status and Culture in a Southern Town, 1784–1860* (1984); Mary P. Ryan, *Women in Public: Between Banners and Ballots, 1825–1880* (1990); Mary P. Ryan, *Cradle of the Middle Class: The Family in Oneida County, New York, 1790–1865* (1981); Kathryn Kish Sklar, *Catharine Beecher: A Study in American Domesticity* (1973); Robert V. Wells, *Revolutions in Americans' Lives* (1982); Barbara Welter, "The Cult of True Womanhood, 1820–1860," *American Quarterly* 18 (Summer 1966): 151–174.

Immigrants and Hispanics

Gunther Barth, *Bitter Strength: A History of Chinese in the United States, 1850–1870* (1964); Kathleen Neils Conzen, *Immigrant Milwaukee: 1836–1860* (1976); Hasia R. Diner, *Erin's Daughters in America: Irish Immigrant Women in the Nineteenth Century* (1983); Jay P. Dolan, *The Immigrant Church: New York's Irish and German Catholics, 1815–1865* (1975); David A. Gerber, *The Making of an American Pluralism: Buffalo, New York, 1825–60* (1989); Walter D. Kamphoefner, *The Westfalians: From Germany to Missouri* (1987); Walter D. Kamphoefner et al., eds., *News from the Land of Freedom: German Immigrants Write Home* (1991); Timothy M. Matovina, *Tejano Religion and Ethnicity: San Antonio, 1821–1860* (1995); Kerby A. Miller, *Emigrants and Exiles: Ireland and the Irish Exodus to North America* (1985); Philip Taylor, *The Distant Magnet: European Emigration to the United States of America* (1971).

Native Americans

Robert F. Berkhofer, Jr., *The White Man's Indian* (1978); James W. Covington, *The Seminoles of Florida* (1993); Michael D. Green, *The Politics of Indian Removal: Creek Government and Society in Crisis* (1982); William G. McLoughlin, *Cherokee Renascence in the New Republic* (1986); Francis P. Prucha, *American Indian Policy in the Formative Years* (1967); Ronald N. Satz, *American Indian Policy in the Jacksonian Era* (1975); Anthony F. C. Wallace, *The Long, Bitter Trail: Andrew Jackson and the Indians* (1993); Richard White, *The Roots of Dependency: Subsistence, Environment, and Social Change Among the Choctaws, Pawnees, and Navajos* (1983).

Free People of Color

Ira Berlin, *Slaves Without Masters: The Free Negro in the Antebellum South* (1974); James O. Horton and Lois E. Horton, *In Hope of Liberty: Culture, Community and Protest Among Northern Free Blacks, 1700–1860* (1996); Luther Porter Jackson, *Free Negro Labor and Property Holding in Virginia, 1830–1860* (1942); David M. Katzman, *Before the Ghetto: Black Detroit in the Nineteenth Century* (1973); Rudolph M. Lapp, *Blacks in Gold Rush California* (1977); Leon Litwack, *North of Slavery: The Negro in the Free States, 1790–1860* (1961); Floyd J. Miller, *The Search for a Black Nationality: Black Colonization and Emigration, 1787–1863* (1975).

CHAPTER

13

Reform, Politics, and Expansion
1824–1844

"I proceed, Gentlemen, briefly to call your attention to the *present* state of Insane persons confined within this Commonwealth," Dorothea Dix petitioned the Massachusetts legislature in 1843, "in *cages, closets, stalls, pens! Chained, naked, beaten with rods and lashed into obedience.*"

A year earlier, in a surprise visit to a Newburyport almshouse, Dix had discovered one man residing in a shed whose door opened to the local "dead room" or morgue; the man's only campanions were corpses. Shocked, she heard from an attendant about another insane inmate whom no one spoke of: "a woman in a *cellar.*"

She asked to see the woman. The superintendent tried to dissuade her, but Dix pressed on: "If you will not go with me," she said, "give me the keys and I will go alone." They unlocked the doors and entered an underground cell. In the shadows Dix saw "a female apparently wasted to a skeleton, partially wrapped in blankets." When the inmate saw the visitors, she wailed with despair: "Why am I consigned to hell? I have done no crime in my heart; I had friends, why have all forsaken me!—my God! my God! why hast *those* forsaken me?"

What drove Dix in her obsession to explore the ill treatment of the insane was not only her sense of outrage but also a belief in human perfectibility and in the corollary idea that the insane could be treated and cured. Proper humane treatment, Dix argued, could bring them back to the community; they could be healed if they were treated as ill rather than as criminal.

Dix epitomized so much of early- to mid-nineteenth-century reform. She started with a belief in individual self-improvement that led her to advocate collective responsibility, especially on behalf of those dependent on the kindness of others. She was single-minded, expressing little concern for abolition or women's rights. Unlike Susan B. Anthony, Lucretia Mott, or Elizabeth Cady Stanton, Dix never joined the early feminists in agitating for women's political equality. Nonetheless, her obsession with reform took her into politics. In investigating asylums, in petitioning the Massachusetts General Court in 1843, and in lobbying other state legislatures and Congress, she joined other women in moving from reform to politics, and she helped create a new public role for women.

The reform fervor of the 1820s to the 1850s arose in part as a response to the enormous transformation that the United States experienced after the War of 1812. Immigration, internal migration, urbanization, the spread of a market economy, growing inequality, loosening family and community ties, the westward advance of settlement, and territorial expansion all contributed to the remaking of the United States. Many Americans felt they were no longer masters of their own fate and that the changes in society were undermining traditional values.

Religious reformers sought to reimpose order on a society in which economic change and discord had reached a crescendo. Prompted by the evangelical spirit of the Second Great Awakening and convinced of their moral rectitude, they crusaded for individual self-improvement. Many renounced alcohol and gambling. Gradually the personal impulse to reform oneself led to the creation of benevolent and reform societies. Religious ardor drew men and women to reform, in time broadening the political base. Reform soon eclipsed benevolent work and became an instrument for restoring discipline and order in a changing society. Women became prominent in reform, first to improve life for others, then to secure rights and freedom for themselves.

Members of reform organizations eventually turned to politics, viewing it as an instrument of change. The line between social reform and politics was not always clear, however. Temperance, institutional reform, and, most notably, Antimasonry and abolition lured new voters into politics. But opponents of reform were just as concerned with social problems and just as interested in political solutions. What distinguished them from reformers was their skepticism about human perfectibility and their distrust of institutions and the exercise of power, both public and private. To them, government coercion was the greater evil. They sought to reverse, not shape, change.

Two issues in particular served as bridges between reform and politics: the short-lived Antimasonry frenzy and the intense, uncompromising crusade for immediate emancipation. Though Antimasons organized the first third-party movement, abolition eventually overrode all other concerns. No single issue evoked the passion that slavery did. Moreover, territorial expansion in the 1840s and 1850s made slavery politically explosive.

Opponents of religious reform found a champion in Andrew Jackson and a home in the Democratic Party in the late 1820s. Yet the Jacksonians, too, saw themselves as reformers; they sought to foster individualism and restore restraint in the federal government. They opposed special privileges and the Second Bank of the United States. President Jackson believed that a strong federal government restricted individual freedom by favoring one group over another. In response, social reformers rallied around the new Whig Party, which became the vehicle of humanitarian reform. Democrats and Whigs constituted a new party system, characterized by strong organizations, intensely loyal followings, and energetic religious and ethnic competition.

Both parties eagerly promoted expansionism during the prosperous 1840s. Democrats saw the agrarian West as an antidote to urbanization and industrialization; Whigs focused on the new commercial opportunities it offered. Expansion from coast to coast seemed to Americans to be the manifest destiny of the United States.

From Revival to Reform

Religion was probably the prime motivating force behind organized benevolence and reform. Religious revival stimulated by the Second Great Awakening galvanized Protestants, especially women, from the late 1790s to the 1840s. Under its influence, the role of churches and ministers in community life began to change, and Christians in all parts of the country tried to right the wrongs of the world.

Revivals—the lifeblood of evangelical Christianity—won converts to a religion of the heart rather than the head. In 1821 New York lawyer Charles G. Finney, the father of modern revivalism, experienced a soul-shaking conversion that he interpreted as "a retainer from the Lord Jesus Christ to plead his cause." Finney then began taking revival services and three- to four-day camp meetings to towns in western New York. Using everyday language, he preached that "God has made man a moral free agent." In other words, evil was avoidable: Christians were not doomed by original sin, and anyone could achieve salvation.

Second Great Awakening

The Second Great Awakening raised people's hopes for the Second Coming of the Christian messiah and establishment of the Kingdom of God on earth. Revivalists resolved to speed the Second Coming by creating a heaven on earth, marshaling the forces of good and light—reform—to combat the forces of evil and darkness.

Regardless of theology, all revivalists shared a belief in individual self-improvement. Thus the Second Great Awakening bred reform. Evangelical Protestants became missionaries for both religious and secular salvation and helped organize associations to address pressing issues: temperance, education, Sabbath observance, dueling, and (later) antislavery. Collectively these groups constituted a national web of benevolent and moral-reform societies.

Women were the earliest converts to evangelism, and they tended to sustain the Second Great Awakening. Pious middle-class women in Roches-

Role of Women

ter, New York, for instance, responded to Finney's prayer meetings by spreading the word to other women during the day while their husbands were at work. Gradually they brought their families and husbands into church and reform. Women more than men tended to feel personally responsible for counteracting the increasingly secular orientation of the expanding market economy. Many felt guilty for neglecting their religious duties, and the emotionally charged conversion experience returned them to what they believed was the right path.

Religion and Reform

Beyond conversion, the great influence of the Second Great Awakening was the spread of women's participation in benevolent societies to ameliorate social ills. In cities women responded to the growing inequality, turbulence, and wretched conditions around them. The poverty and vice that accompanied urbanization touched the hearts of women. By 1800 most cities had women's benevolent societies to help needy women and orphans.

Both female and male reformers sometimes opposed traditional political leaders. An exposé of prostitution in New York City illustrates the gulf between reform-minded men and women and the political establishment. In response to an 1830 report documenting the prevalence of prostitution in New York City, New York businessmen and politicians united to defend the city's good name against "those base slanders." Reform-minded women, however, moved by the plight of "fallen women" organized to fight prostitution. While male reformers made the prostitutes the target of their zeal, the newly organized Female Moral Reform Society focused on the men who victimized young women, publicizing the names of men who entered brothels in New York City.

The New York–based Female Moral Reform Society led the crusade against prostitution. During the 1830s, the organization expanded its activities, calling itself the American Female Moral Reform Society. By 1840 it had 555 affiliated female societies across the nation. They combated prostitution by focusing on men and by assisting poor women whose economic desperation might lead them to

• *Important Events* •

1790s–1840s	Second Great Awakening spreads religious fervor
1820s	Reformers in New York and Pennsylvania establish model penitentiaries
1824	No presidential candidate wins a majority in the electoral college
1825	House of Representatives elects John Quincy Adams president
1826	American Society for the Promotion of Temperance founded Morgan affair is catalyst for Antimasonry movement
1828	Protectionist Tariff stirs nullification Andrew Jackson elected president
1830	Webster-Hayne debate explores the nature of the Union
1830s–40s	Democratic-Whig competition gels in second party system
1831	Abolitionist newspaper *The Liberator* begins publication First national Antimason convention
1832	Jackson vetoes rechartering of the Second Bank of the United States Jackson reelected president
1832–33	South Carolina nullifies the Tariff of 1832, prompting nullification crisis
1836	Republic of Texas established after breaking from Mexico Specie Circular ends credit purchase of public lands Martin Van Buren elected president
1837	Financial panic ends boom of the 1830s
1838–39	United States and Canada mobilize their militias over Maine–New Brunswick border dispute
1839–43	Hard times spread unemployment and deflation
1840	Whigs win presidency under William Henry Harrison
1841	John Tyler assumes the presidency after Harrison's death "Oregon fever" attracts settlers to the Northwest and intensifies expansionism
1843	Dorothea Dix petitions Massachusetts legislature regarding deplorable condition of insane asylums
1844	James K. Polk elected president
1848	Woman's Rights Convention at Seneca Falls, New York, calls for women's suffrage

turn to prostitution. They also entered the political sphere. In New York State in the 1840s the movement successfully crusaded for criminal sanctions against the men who seduced women into prostitution and against the prostitutes themselves.

As the pace of social change quickened in the 1830s and 1840s, so did religious fervor and reform. In western New York and Ohio, Finney's preaching acted as a catalyst to reform. Western New York experienced such continuous and heated waves of revivalism that it became known as "the burned-over district." The westward movement of people carried the religious ferment into Ohio where revivalist institutions—notably Ohio's Lane Seminary and Oberlin College—sent committed graduates out into the world to spread the gospel of reform. The efforts of those early reformers stirred nonevangelical Protestants, Catholics, and Jews, as well as evangelical Christians, and they became involved in new grassroots political movements. In the late 1830s and 1840s they rallied around the Whig Party in hopes of using government as an instrument of reform.

One of the most successful reform efforts was the campaign against alcohol. American men gathered in public houses, saloons, and rural inns to gossip, talk politics, play cards, escape work and home, and drink. Respectable women did not drink in public, but many regularly tippled alcohol-based patent medicines promoted as cure-alls. Why then did temperance become such a vital issue? And why were women especially active in the movement? Like all nineteenth-century reform, temperance had a strong religious foundation.

Temperance

Evangelicals considered drinking a sin, and forsaking alcohol was part of conversion. The sale of whiskey often involved a Sabbath violation, for workers commonly labored six days a week and spent Sunday at the public house drinking and socializing. Equally important, alcoholism destroyed families. In the early 1840s thousands of ordinary women formed Martha Washington societies to protect families by reforming alcoholics, raising children as teetotalers, and spreading temperance.

As the temperance movement gained momentum, its goal shifted from moderate use of alcohol to voluntary abstinence and finally to prohibition. The American Society for the Promotion of Temperance, organized in 1826 to sign drinkers to a pledge of abstinence, became a pressure group for state prohibition legislation. By the mid-1830s there were five thousand state and local temperance societies, and more than a million people had taken the pledge. As the movement spread, the per capita consumption of alcohol fell from five gallons to less than two gallons in the 1840s. Moreover, a number of northern states followed Maine's lead and outlawed the sale of alcohol except for medicinal purposes.

Temperance Societies

Another aspect of the temperance movement was opposition to gambling. People gambled in taverns, and reformers believed that both drinking and gambling undermined independence and self-reliance. Of special concern in the nineteenth century was the spread of lotteries.

Lotteries were common in colonial times. The Continental Congress tried to raise $1.5 million from a lottery to wage revolutionary war against England. In the early nineteenth century, state and local governments seeking to ease the tax burden used lotteries to raise money for capital improvements. Lotteries, however, became a target of reform, and between 1830 and 1860 every state banned them.

Lotteries

Reformers compared lotteries to slavery and alcohol. Others objected to the abuses inherent in the states' practice of delegating their lottery powers to private sponsors. An 1831 Pennsylvania investigation, for instance, revealed that a state-authorized lottery to raise $27,000 a year for internal improvements had generated enormous profits for the lottery company. From annual sales of $5 million, the state received its $27,000, and the sponsors received $800,000.

The age of reform also brought about the construction of asylums and other institutions to house prisoners, the mentally ill, orphans, delinquent children, and the poor. Such institutions were needed, reformers believed, to shelter victims of society's instability and turbulence. In an environment of order, stability, and discipline, inmates would have an opportunity to become self-reliant and responsible.

Penitentiaries and Asylums

The penitentiary movement exemplified this outlook. In the 1820s New York and Pennsylvania rejected incarceration simply to punish criminals or remove them from society. Believing instead that rehabilitation was possible, the two systems sought to separate criminals from evil societal and individual influences and to expose them to a regimen of order and discipline. Because idleness was believed to be both a symptom and a cause of individual corruption and crime, the clock governed a prisoner's day, and idleness was banished.

Similar approaches were employed in insane asylums, hospitals, and orphanages. By exposing the inhumane treatment of the mentally ill, Dorothea Dix built a national movement. Through her efforts and those of reform societies, twenty-eight of the thirty-three states had public institutions for the mentally ill by 1860.

 # Antimasonry

More intense though of shorter duration than the asylum movement was the crusade against Freemasonry, a secret middle- and upper-class fraternity that had come to the United States from England in the eighteenth century. Sons of the Enlightenment such as Benjamin Franklin and George Washington were attracted to Masonry, with its emphasis on individual belief in a deity (as opposed to organized religion) and on brotherhood (as opposed to one church). In the early nineteenth century Freemasonry attracted men prominent in commerce and civic affairs.

Opponents of Masonry charged that the order's secrecy was antidemocratic and antirepublican. Evangelicals labeled the order satanic. Antimasons argued that Masonry threatened the family because it excluded women and encouraged men to neglect their families for alcohol and ribald entertainments at Masonic lodges.

The Antimasonry movement arose overnight in the burned-over district of western New York in 1826 and virtually disappeared in the 1830s. Foreshadowing abolitionism, it quickly became a political movement. Antimasonry created the first third-party movement and drew new white voters into politics at a time when male suffrage was being extended. Antimasons sought to liberate society from the grip of what they considered a powerful and antirepublican secret fraternity. The political arena quickly absorbed Antimasonry, and its short life illustrates the close association of politics and reform between the 1820s and the 1840s.

The catalyst for Antimasonry as an organized movement was the Morgan affair. In 1826 William Morgan, a disillusioned Mason, published an exposé of Masonry to which his printer, David Miller, added a scathing attack on the order. Just prior to the book's appearance, a group of Masons abducted Morgan in

Morgan Affair

Canandaigua, New York. It was widely believed that they murdered him.

Events seemed to confirm the Antimasonry crusade's depiction of Masonry as a secret conspiracy. Many officeholders in western New York, especially prosecutors, were Masons, and they appeared to obstruct the investigation of Morgan's abduction. The public pressed for justice, and the series of notorious trials that ensued from 1827 through 1831 led many to suspect a conspiracy. The cover-up became as much of an issue as distrust of Masonry itself, and the

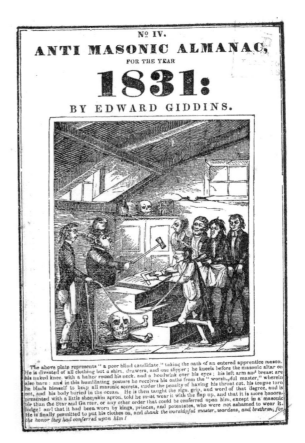

Antimasonic publications, such as this 1831 almanac, made much of the allegedly sinister initiation rites that bound a new member "to keep all Masonic secrets, under the penalty of having his throat cut, his tongue torn out, and his body buried in the ocean." Print collection, Miriam and Ira D. Wallach Division of Art, Prints, and Photographs, New York Public Library.

movement spread from the burned-over district to other states.

As a moral crusade, Antimasonry spilled over into the political arena almost immediately. The issue itself was political, because of the perceived obstruction of justice. Furthermore, Antimasonry attracted the lower and middle classes, pitting them against higher-status Masons and exploiting the general public's distrust and envy of local political leaders.

Unwittingly, the Masons stoked the fires of Antimasonry. By their silence they seemed to condone the murder of Morgan, and by their construction of monumental lodges in Boston and elsewhere they called attention to their affluence and prominence. The conflict aroused a high level of public interest in politics. Wherever religious fervor flared and wherever families were entering the market economy for the first time, Antimasonry flourished.

As Antimasonry won a popular following, it introduced the convention system in place of caucuses for choosing political candidates. In-

Convention System

voking public morality and republican principles, the Antimasons held conventions in 1827 to select candidates to oppose Masons. The next year the conventions supported the National Republican candidate, John Quincy Adams, and opposed Andrew Jackson because he was a Mason. The Antimasons held the first national political convention in Baltimore in 1831, and a year later nominated William Wirt as their presidential candidate. Thus the Antimasons became a rallying point for those opposed to President Andrew Jackson.

By the mid-1830s, Antimasonry had lost momentum as a moral and political movement. A single-issue party, the Antimasons declined along with Freemasonry. Yet the movement left its mark on the politics of the era. As a moral crusade focused on public officeholders, it inspired broad participation in the political process. The Antimasons also changed party organization by pioneering the convention system and stimulating grassroots involvement.

 ## Abolitionism and the Women's Movement

The issue of slavery eventually became so compelling that it consumed all other reforms. Passions became so heated that they threatened the nation itself. Those who advocated immediate emancipation saw slavery as, above all, a moral issue—evidence of the sinfulness of the American nation.

Before the 1830s few whites advocated the abolition of slavery. Some, most notably the Quakers, hoped that moral suasion would convince slaveholders to free their chattels. Others favored gradual abolition coupled with the resettling of former slaves in Africa. In 1816 the American Colonization Society had been founded with this in mind.

African-Americans rejected this gradual approach and demanded an immediate end to slavery. By 1830 more than fifty black abolitionist societies assisted fugitive slaves, lobbied for emancipation, exposed the evils of slavery, and reminded the nation that its mission as defined in the Declaration of Independence remained unfulfilled. A free black press helped to spread the word. Black abolitionists Frederick Douglass, Sojourner Truth, and Harriet Tubman joined forces in the 1840s with white reformers in the American Anti-Slavery Society.

Black Abolitionists

In the 1830s a small minority of white reformers, driven by moral urgency, also crusaded for immediate emancipation. The most prominent and uncompromising immediatist was William Lloyd Garrison, who demanded "immediate and complete emancipation."

William Lloyd Garrison

In 1831 Garrison broke with moderate abolitionists and began publishing *The Liberator*, which was to be his major weapon against slavery for thirty-five years. As he declared in the first issue, "I am in earnest—I will not equivocate—I will not excuse—I will not retreat a single inch—*and I will be heard.*" Garrison's staunch refusal to work with anyone who tolerated the delay of emancipation isolated him from other opponents of slavery.

Still, through sheer rhetorical power, Garrison helped to make antislavery a national issue.

It is difficult to differentiate between those who became immediatists and those who did not.

Immediatists

Immediatists were often young evangelicals active in benevolent societies in the 1820s; many became ordained ministers or flirted with the ministry as a career; and they had personal contact with free blacks and were sympathetic to African-American rights. They were convinced that slaveholding was a sin. They also shared great moral intensity and were unwilling to compromise their beliefs.

Most benevolent workers and reformers kept their distance from the immediatists. Many regarded the intensity of the immediatist approach as unchristian. They shared with immediatists the view that slavery was a sin but believed in gradual emancipation.

Immediatists' greatest recruitment successes resulted from their defense of their own constitutional and natural rights, not the rights of slaves.

Opposition to Abolitionists

Wherever they went, immediatists found their civil rights, especially free speech at risk. Hostile crowds threatened abolitionist speakers and presses. Abolitionist conventions provoked hostility by welcoming blacks and women. Fear and hatred moved proslavery proponents to take to the streets. In 1837 a mob in Alton, Illinois, murdered abolitionist editor Elijah P. Lovejoy. Public outrage at Lovejoy's murder broadened the base of antislavery support in the North. Southern mobs blocked the distribution of abolitionist literature, much of which was printed by the immediatists and their main organizational vehicle, the American Anti-Slavery Society (1831). South Carolina seized such materials from the United States mails and burned it.

The opposition saw danger in abolitionism. At a rally in Boston's Faneuil Hall in 1835 former Federalist Harrison Gray Otis portrayed abolitionists as subversives. The abolitionists, he predicted, would soon turn to politics, causing unforeseeable calamity. "What will become of the union?" Otis asked. Others believed that the immediatists' opposition to sending black people back to Africa undermined the best solution.

Another confrontation focused on the House of Representatives. Abolitionists, exercising their constitutional right to petition Congress, campaigned to abolish slavery and the slave trade in the District of Columbia. The House responded in 1836 by adopting the "gag rule," which automatically tabled abolitionist petitions, effectively preventing debate on them. In a dramatic defense of the right of petition, former president John Quincy Adams, a Massachusetts representative, took to the floor repeatedly to defy the gag rule and in 1844 succeeded in getting it repealed.

Gag Rule

Frustration with the federal government also fed northern support for antislavery. Generally speaking, politicians and government officials sought to avoid the question of slavery. The Missouri Compromise of 1820 had been an effort to make debate on the slave or free status of new states unnecessary (see map, page 253). Censorship of the mails and the gag rule also represented attempts to keep the issue out of the political arena. Yet the more intensely the national leaders, especially Democrats, worked to avoid the matter, the more they hardened the resolve of the antislavery forces.

The unlawful and violent tactics used by opponents of abolition unified the movement by forcing the various factions to work together for mutual defense. Antislavery was not at the outset a unified movement. Its adherents divided over Garrison's emphasis on "moral suasion" versus the more practical political approach of James G. Birney, the Liberty Party's candidate for president in 1844. They also split over support for other reforms, especially the rights of women. And they disagreed about the place of free people of color in American society.

Many women joined local female antislavery societies through churches as part of the network of reform societies. Though some opposed extending benevolent work into the political arena, issues related to abolition and women's rights had that result. Moreover, in abolitionists' circles

Women Abolitionists

How do historians know how the abolitionists, especially women and African-Americans, built their movement? Abolitionists lived open lives. They used newspapers, pamphlets, speeches, and sermons to expose the evils of slavery, to mount a crusade for emancipation, and to build a network of like-minded people. Much of their correspondence and most of their speeches were printed in abolitionist newspapers, such as The Liberator, *published by William Lloyd Garrison.*

Here, twentieth-century African-American artist Jacob Lawrence depicts abolitionist Frederick Douglass lecturing in eastern Massachusetts, describing his life as a slave and telling of the cruelty of the system. In 1841

Douglass became a supporter of Garrison and a contributor to The Liberator, *which appeared from 1831 to 1866. The newspaper printed passionate attacks on slavery, reported on meetings of antislavery societies, and published letters, especially from women and African-American abolitionists. Under the banners "No Union with Slaveholders" and "The United States Constitution is a 'convenant with death, and an agreement with hell,'"* The Liberator *circulated to abolitionists advocating immediate emancipation. The subscription lists that have survived indicate that a majority of its subscribers probably were African-Americans.*   Hampton University Museum, Hampton Virginia.

women took an equal role with men. Lydia Maria Child, Maria Chapman, and Lucretia Mott all joined the American Anti-Slavery Society's executive committee. Child edited its official organ, the *National Anti-Slavery Standard*, from 1841 to 1843, and Chapman coedited it from 1844 until 1848. Garrison's *moral* suasion attracted many women be-

cause it gave them a platform from which to oppose slavery. Where *political* power was stressed, women were often excluded because they could not vote.

Opposition to women's prominent public roles in reform movements led some women to reexamine their position in society. In the 1830s Angelina and Sarah Grimké challenged slavery and women's right to speak out. Born into a slaveholding family in South Carolina, both sisters experienced conversion and became Quakers. Concerned about slavery, they found in Garrison's immediatism a home. Yet they were soon attacked for speaking before mixed groups of men and women. This reaction turned the Grimkés' attention from slavery to the women's condition. The two attacked the concept of "subordination to man," insisting that men and women had the "same rights and same duties." Sarah Grimké's *Letters on the Condition of Women and the Equality of the Sexes* (1838) and her sister's *Letters to Catharine E. Beecher* (1838) were the opening volleys in the long war over the legal and social inequality of women.

Women's Rights

In July 1848 three hundred women and men reformers gathered at the Woman's Rights Convention at Seneca Falls, New York, to demand political, social, and economic equality for women. Led by Elizabeth Cady Stanton, Lucretia Mott, and Lucy Stone, they protested women's legal disabilities—inability to vote, limited property rights—and their social restrictions—exclusion from advanced schooling and from most occupations. Their Declaration of Sentiments was an indictment of the injustices suffered by women, and it launched the women's rights movement. "All men and women are created equal," the declaration proclaimed. If women had the vote, participants argued, they could protect themselves and realize their full potential as moral and spiritual leaders.

Advocates of women's rights were slow to garner support, especially from men. Even within the antislavery movement, a majority declared themselves opposed to women's rights. Still, some men joined the ranks, notably Garrison and Frederick Douglass.

Jacksonianism and Party Politics

In the 1820s the distinction between reform and politics began to erode as reform pushed its way into politics. No less than reformers, politicians sought to control the direction of change in the expanding nation. After a brief flirtation with single-party politics after the War of 1812, the United States entered a period of intense political competition.

The election of 1824, in which John Quincy Adams and Andrew Jackson faced off for the first time, heralded a new, more open political system.

End of the Caucus System

From 1800 through 1820 the system in which a congressional caucus chose Jefferson, Madison, and Monroe as the Republican nominees had worked well. Such a system limited voter involvement in choosing candidates but at first was not an anomaly because in 1800 only five of the sixteen states selected presidential electors by popular vote. (In most cases, state legislatures selected the electors who voted for president.) By 1824, however, eighteen of the twenty-four states chose electors by popular vote.

The Republican caucus in 1824 chose William H. Crawford, secretary of the treasury, as its presidential candidate. But other Republicans, emboldened by the chance to appeal directly to voters, put themselves forward as sectional candidates. Secretary of State John Quincy Adams drew support from New England, and westerners backed Speaker of the House Henry Clay of Kentucky. Secretary of War John C. Calhoun looked to the South for support and hoped to win Pennsylvania as well. The Tennessee legislature nominated Andrew Jackson, a popular military hero whose political views were unknown. Jackson had the most widespread support. By boycotting the caucus and by attacking it as undemocratic, these men and their supporters ended the role of Congress in nominating presidential candidates.

Election of 1824

In the four-way presidential election of 1824, Andrew Jackson led in both electoral and popular votes, but no candidate received a majority in the electoral college. Adams finished second, and Crawford and Clay trailed far behind. (Calhoun had dropped out of the race before the election.) As required by the Constitution, the House of Representatives, voting by state delegation, one vote to a state, in 1825 selected the next president from among the leaders in electoral votes. Clay, who had received the fewest votes, was dropped. Crawford, a stroke victim, never received serious consideration. The influential Clay—Speaker of the House and leader of the Ohio valley states—backed Adams, who received the votes of thirteen of twenty-four state delegations. Clay then became secretary of state in the Adams administration, the traditional steppingstone to the presidency. With angry Jacksonians denouncing the election's outcome as a "corrupt bargain" that had stolen the office from the front-runner, the Republican Party split. The Adams wing emerged as the National Republicans, and the Jacksonians became the Democratic-Republicans (shortened to Democrats). The Jacksonians immediately began planning for 1828.

After taking the oath of office, Adams proposed a strong nationalist policy incorporating Henry Clay's program of protective tariffs, a national bank, and internal improvements. Adams believed the federal government should take an activist role not only in the economy but also in education, science, and the arts. Brilliant as a secretary of state, Adams was an inept president. He underestimated the lingering effects of the Panic of 1819 and the resulting bitter opposition to a national bank and protective tariffs. Meanwhile, supporters of Andrew Jackson sabotaged Adams's administration at every opportunity.

The 1828 campaign pitted Adams against Jackson in an intensely personal conflict. Principles gave way to mudslinging by both sides. When

Election of 1828

Rachel Jackson died a month after the election, the president-elect attributed his wife's death to the abuse heaped on him in the campaign. Jackson had swamped Adams at the polls, with 56 percent of the popular vote, and he won in the electoral college by 178 to 83 votes. He and his supporters believed that the will of the people had finally been served. Through a lavishly financed coalition of state parties, political leaders, and newspaper editors, a popular movement had elected the president, and an era had ended. The Democratic Party became the first well-organized national political party in the United States. Tightly organized parties would become the hallmark of nineteenth-century American politics.

Nicknamed "Old Hickory" after the toughest of the American hardwoods, Andrew Jackson was a rough-and-tumble, ambitious man. He rose from humble beginnings to become a wealthy planter and slaveholder and the first American president from the West.

Andrew Jackson

Though given to violent displays of temper, he could charm away the suspicions of those opposed to him. He had an instinct for politics and picked both issues and supporters shrewdly.

Jackson and his Democratic supporters offered a distinct alternative to the strong federal government advocated by John Quincy Adams. The Democrats represented a wide range of views but shared a fundamental commitment to the Jeffersonian concept of an agrarian society. They harkened back to the belief that a strong central government is the enemy of individual liberty, a tyranny to be feared.

Jacksonians feared the concentration of economic and political power. They believed that government intervention in the economy benefited special-interest groups and favored the rich. They sought to restore the independence of the individual—the artisan and the yeoman farmer—by ending federal support of banks and corporations and restricting the use of paper currency, which they distrusted.

Jackson and his supporters also opposed reform as a movement. Reformers eager to turn their programs into legislation were calling for a more activist and interventionist government. But Democrats tended to oppose programs like educational reform and the establishment of public education. They believed, for instance, that public schools restricted individual liberty by interfering with parental responsibility and undermined freedom of religion by replacing church schools. Nor did Jackson share reformers' humanitarian concerns.

Jackson and the Jacksonians considered themselves reformers in a different way. By restraining government and emphasizing individualism, they

President Andrew Jackson is portrayed here on a snuff box, an example of the campaign paraphernalia that were widely sold to partisan Jackson supporters.   David R. and Janice L. Frent.

Jacksonians as Reformers

sought to restore old republican virtues, such as prudence and economy. Jackson sought to encourage self-reliance and to restore the harmony and unity that he saw disrupted by economic and social change.

Like Jefferson, Jackson strengthened the executive branch of government even as he weakened the federal role. Given his popularity and the strength of his personality, this concentration of power in the presidency was perhaps inevitable, but in combining the roles of party leader and chief of state, he increased the centralization of power in the White House. Invoking the principle that rotating officeholders would make government more responsive to the public will, Jackson used the spoils system to appoint loyal Democrats to office. Patronage thus became a means to strengthen party organization and loyalty.

Jackson stressed rejection of elitism and special favors, rotation of officeholders, and belief in popular government. Time and again he declared that sovereignty resided with the people, not with the states or the courts. In this respect Jackson was

a reformer; he returned government to majority rule. Yet it is hard to distinguish between Jackson's belief in himself as the instrument of the people and demagogic arrogance.

Animosity grew year by year among President Jackson's supporters and opponents. Massachusetts senator Daniel Webster feared the men around Jackson; Henry Clay most feared Jackson himself. Rotation in office, they contended, corrupted government. Opponents mocked Jackson as "King Andrew I," charging him with abusing his presidential powers by ignoring the Supreme Court's ruling on Cherokee rights, by his use of the spoils system, and by his dependence on the "Kitchen Cabinet"—political friends—for advice. Critics rejected his claim of restoring republican virtue. They charged him with recklessly and impulsively destroying the economy.

Jackson injected new vigor into the philosophy of limited government. In 1830 he vetoed the Maysville Road bill—which would have funded construction of a 60-mile turnpike from Maysville to Lexington, Kentucky. A federally subsidized internal improvement confined to one state was unconstitutional, he charged; such projects were properly a state responsibility. The veto undermined Henry Clay's nationalist program and personally embarrassed Clay because the project was in his home district.

Federalism at Issue: The Nullification and Bank Controversies

Soon Jackson had to face more directly the question of the proper division of sovereignty between state and central government. The slave South feared federal power, no state more so than South Carolina, where the planter class was strongest.

To protect their interests, South Carolinian political leaders articulated the doctrine of *nullification*, according to which a state had the right to overrule, or nullify, federal legislation. Nullification was based on the idea expressed in the Virginia and Kentucky Resolutions of 1798 (see page 149)—that the states, representing the people, have a right to judge the constitutionality of federal actions. Jackson's vice president, John C. Calhoun of South Carolina, argued in his unsigned *Exposition and Protest* that, in any disagreement between the federal government and a state, a special state convention—like the conventions called to ratify the Constitution—should decide the conflict by either nullifying or affirming the federal law. Only the power of nullification, Calhoun asserted, could protect the minority against the tyranny of the majority.

In public, Calhoun let others take the lead in advancing nullification. He hoped to avoid embarrassing the Democratic ticket and to gain Jackson's support as the Democratic presidential heir-apparent. Thus Calhoun presided silently over the Senate and its packed galleries when Senator Daniel Webster of Massachusetts and Senator Robert Y. Hayne of South Carolina debated nullification in early 1830. The debate explored North-South frictions and the nature of the Union. At the climax of the debate, Webster, whose remarks were aimed at Calhoun, invoked two powerful images. One was the outcome of nullification: "States dissevered, discordant, belligerent; on a land rent with civil feuds, or drenched . . . in fraternal blood!" The other was a patriotic vision of a great nation flourishing under the motto "Liberty *and* Union, now and forever, one and inseparable."

Webster-Hayne Debate

Though sympathetic to states' rights and distrustful of the federal government, Jackson rejected the idea of state sovereignty. He strongly believed that sovereignty rested with the people, and he shared Webster's dread of nullification. Soon after the Webster-Hayne debate, the president made his position clear at a Jefferson Day dinner with the toast "Our Federal Union, it *must* and *shall be* preserved." Vice President Calhoun, when his turn came, toasted: "The Federal Union—next to our liberty the most dear." Calhoun had revealed his preference for states' rights.

South Carolina invoked the theory of nullification against the Tariff of 1832, which reduced some duties but retained high taxes on imported iron, cottons, and woolens. Though a majority of southern representatives supported the new tariff, South Carolinians refused to go along. In their eyes, the constitutional right to control their own destiny had been sacrificed to the demands of northern industrialists. More than the tariff, they feared the consequences of accepting such an act, because it could set a precedent for congressional legislation on slavery. In November 1832 a South Carolina state convention nullified the tariff, making it unlawful for Federal officials to collect duties in the state.

Nullification Crisis

Old Hickory responded with toughness. In December he issued a presidential proclamation nullifying nullification. He moved troops to federal forts in South Carolina and prepared United States marshals to collect the required duties. At Jackson's request, Congress passed the Force Act, which gave the president renewed authority to call up troops but also offered a way to avoid using force by collecting duties before foreign ships reached South Carolina. At the same time, Jackson extended an olive branch by recommending tariff reductions.

Calhoun, disturbed by South Carolina's drift toward separatism, resigned as vice president and soon won election to represent South Carolina in the United States Senate. There he worked with Henry Clay to draw up the compromise Tariff of 1833. Quickly passed by Congress and signed by the president, the new tariff lengthened the list of duty-free items and reduced duties over nine years. Satisfied, South Carolina's convention repealed its nullification law. In a final salvo, it also nullified Jackson's Force Act. Jackson ignored the gesture.

Nullification offered a genuine debate on the nature and principles of the republic. Each side believed it was upholding the Constitution. Neither side won a clear victory, though both claimed to have done so. It took another crisis, over a central bank, to define the powers of the federal government more clearly.

At stake was survival of the Second Bank of the United States, whose twenty-year charter was scheduled to expire in 1836. One of the bank's func-

Second Bank of the United States

tions was to act as a clearing-house for state banks, keeping them honest by refusing to accept in transactions state bank notes from any state bank that had insufficient gold in reserve. Most state banks resented the central bank's police role: by presenting a state bank's notes for redemption all at once, the Second Bank could easily ruin a state bank. Moreover, with less money in reserve, state banks found themselves unable to compete on an equal footing with the Second Bank.

Many state governments also regarded the national bank, with its headquarters in Philadelphia, as unresponsive to local needs. Westerners and urban workers remembered with bitterness the bank's conservative credit policies during the Panic of 1819. As a private, profit-making institution, the bank's policies reflected the interest of its owners. Its president, Nicholas Biddle, was an eastern patrician who symbolized all that westerners found wrong with the bank.

Rechartering was a volatile issue in the 1832 presidential campaign. The bank's charter was valid until 1836, but Henry Clay, the National Republican presidential candidate, persuaded Biddle to ask Congress to approve an early rechartering. This strategy was designed to marshal public pressure to force Jackson to sign the rechartering bill or to override his veto of it. The plan backfired when the Senate failed to override the president's veto. Jackson's veto message was an emotional attack on the undemocratic nature of the bank. The bank thus became the prime issue in the presidential campaign of 1832, and Jackson used it to denounce special privilege and economic power.

After his sweeping victory and second inauguration, Jackson moved in 1833 to permanently destroy the Second Bank of the United States.

Jackson's Second Term

He deposited federal funds in state-chartered banks (critics called them his "pet banks"). Without federal money, the Second Bank shriveled. When its federal charter expired in 1836, it became just another Pennsylvania-chartered private bank. Five years later it closed its doors.

In conjunction with this coup de grâce to the Bank of the United States, Congress passed the Deposit Act of 1836. The act authorized the secretary of the treasury to designate one bank in each state and territory to provide the services formerly performed by the Bank of the United States. The act provided that the federal surplus in excess of $5 million be distributed to the states as interest-free loans beginning in 1837.

The surplus had derived from wholesale speculation in public lands: speculators bought public land on credit, used the land as collateral to borrow more money to buy additional acreage, and repeated the cycle. The state banks providing the loans issued bank notes. Jackson, an opponent of paper money, feared that the speculative craze threatened the stability of state banks and undermined the interests of settlers, who could not compete with speculators in bidding for the best land.

Specie Circular

In keeping with his hard-money instincts and opposition to paper currency, the president ordered Treasury Secretary Levi Woodbury to issue the Specie Circular. It provided that after August 1836 only specie—gold or silver—or Virginia scrip would be accepted as payment for federal lands. By ending credit sales, the circular significantly reduced purchases of public land and the federal budget surplus. As a result the government suspended its loan payments to the states soon after they began.

The policy was a disaster. Although federal land sales were sharply reduced, speculation continued as available land for sale became scarce. The ensuing increased demand for specie squeezed banks, and many suspended the redemption of bank notes for specie. Credit contracted further as banks issued fewer notes and gave less credit. In the waning days of Jackson's administration, Congress voted to repeal the circular, but the president pocket-vetoed the bill. Finally in mid-1838, a joint resolution of Congress overturned the circular. Restrictions on land sales ended, but the speculative fervor was over. The federal government did not revive loans to states.

From George Washington to John Quincy Adams, presidents had vetoed nine bills; Jackson vetoed twelve. Previous presidents believed that vetoes were justified only on constitutional grounds, but Jackson considered policy disagreement legitimate grounds as well. He made the veto an effective weapon for controlling Congress, since representatives and senators had to consider the possibility of a presidential veto in their deliberations on any bill. In effect, Jackson made the executive for the first time a rival branch of government, equal in power to Congress.

Use of the Veto

The Whig Challenge and the Second Party System

Most modern historians view the 1830s and 1840s as an age of reform and popularly based political parties. Only when the passionate concerns of reformers and abolitionists spilled over into politics did party differences become paramount and party loyalties solidify. For the first time in American history, grassroots political groups, organized from the bottom up, set the tone of political life.

Opponents of the Democrats found shelter under a common umbrella, the Whig Party, in the 1830s. Resentful of Jackson's domination of Congress, the Whigs borrowed the name of the British party that had opposed the tyranny of Hanoverian monarchs in the eighteenth century. From 1834 through the 1840s, the Whigs and the Democrats competed on a nearly equal footing. They fought at the city, county, state, and national levels and achieved a stability previously unknown in American politics. The political competition of this period—known as the second party system—was more intense and well organized than that of the first party system of Republicans and Federalists.

The two parties adopted different approaches to the basic issues of the 1830s and the 1840s. Whigs favored economic expansion through an activist government; Democrats, through limited central government. Whigs supported corporate charters, a national bank, and paper currency; Democrats were opposed. Whigs also favored more humanitarian reforms than did Democrats, including public schools, abolition of capital punishment, prison and asylum reform, and temperance.

Whigs

Whigs were more optimistic than Democrats, generally speaking, and more enterprising. They did not object to helping a specific group if doing so would promote the general welfare. The chartering of corporations, they argued, expanded economic opportunity for everyone, including laborers and farmers. Democrats, distrustful of concentrated economic power and of moral and economic coercion, held fast to the Jeffersonian principle of limited government.

Religion and ethnicity rather than economics and class most influenced party membership. The Whigs won the favor of evangelical Protestants in the North, as well as the small number of free black voters. Democrats, by contrast, tended to be foreign-born Catholics and nonevangelical Protestants, both of whom preferred to keep religious and secular affairs separate.

The Whig Party was the vehicle of revivalist Protestantism. The membership rolls of reform societies overlapped those of the party. Indeed, Whigs practiced a kind of political revivalism. Their rallies resembled camp meetings; their speeches employed evangelical rhetoric; their programs embodied the perfectionist beliefs of reformers.

Whigs and Reformers

In their appeal to evangelicals, Whigs alienated members of other faiths. The evangelicals' ideal Christian state had no room for Catholics, Mormons, Unitarians, Universalists, or religious freethinkers. Those groups opposed Sabbath laws and temperance legislation in particular and state interference in moral and religious questions in general. As a result, more than 95 percent of Irish Catholics, 90 percent of Reformed Dutch, and 80 percent of German Catholics voted Democratic.

Vice President Martin Van Buren, handpicked by Jackson, headed the Democratic ticket in the presidential election of 1836. The Whigs, who in 1836 had not yet coalesced into a national party, entered three sectional candidates: Daniel Webster of New England, Hugh White of the

Election of 1836

South, and William Henry Harrison of the West. By splintering the vote, they hoped to throw the election into the House. Van Buren, however, comfortably captured the electoral college even though he had only a 25,000-vote edge out of a total of 1.5 million votes cast.

Van Buren took office just weeks before the American credit system collapsed. In response to the impact of the Specie Circular, New York banks stopped redeeming paper currency with gold in mid-1837. Soon all banks suspended payments in hard coin. Thus began a cycle that led to curtailment of bank loans and reduced business confidence. Hard times persisted until 1843.

President Martin Van Buren and Hard Times

Ill advisedly, Van Buren followed Jackson's hard-money policies. He cut federal spending, which caused prices to drop further, and he opposed a national bank, which would have expanded credit. Even worse, the president proposed a new regional treasury system for government deposits. The proposed treasury branches would accept and pay out only gold and silver coin; they would not accept paper currency or checks drawn on state banks. Van Buren's independent treasury bill became law in 1840. By creating a constant demand for hard coin, it deprived banks of gold and further accelerated the deflation of prices.

With the nation in the grip of hard times, the Whigs prepared confidently for the election of 1840. The Democrats renominated President Van

Using techniques that look familiar to twentieth-century politicians, General William Henry Harrison in 1840 ran a "log cabin and hard cider" campaign against Jackson's heir, President Martin Van Buren. The campaign handkerchief shows Harrison welcoming two of his comrades to his log cabin, with a barrel of cider outside. The Log Cabin, *a newspaper edited by Horace Greeley, was the voice of the Harrison campaign, and it reached eighty thousand partisans.* Handkerchief: New-York Historical Society. Newspaper: Division of Political History, Smithsonian Institution, Washington, D.C.

Buren at a somber convention. The Whigs rallied behind a military hero, General William Henry Harrison, conqueror of the Shawnees at Tippecanoe Creek in 1811. Harrison, or "Old Tippecanoe," and his running mate, John Tyler of Virginia, ran a people's crusade against the aristocratic incumbent in "the palace." In a huge turnout, 80 percent of eligible voters cast ballots. Harrison won the popular vote by a narrow margin but swept the electoral college by 234 to 60.

Unfortunately for the Whigs, the sixty-eight-year-old Harrison died within a month of his inauguration. His successor, John Tyler, was a former Democrat who had left the party to protest Jackson's nullification proclamation. In office, Tyler turned out to be more of a Democrat than a Whig. He consistently opposed the Whig congressional program. He repeatedly vetoed Henry Clay's protective tariffs, internal improvements, and bills aimed at reviving the Bank of the United States. The only important measures that became law during his term were repeal of the independent treasury system and passage of a higher tariff. Two days after Tyler's second veto of a bank bill, the entire cabinet except Secretary of State Daniel Webster resigned; Webster, busy negotiating a new treaty with Great Britain, left shortly thereafter. Tyler thus became a president without a party, and the Whigs lost the presidency without losing an election.

Hard times in the late 1830s and early 1840s deflected attention from a renewal of Anglo-American tensions that had multiple sources: northern commercial rivalry with Britain, the default of state governments and corporations on British-held debts during the Panic of 1837, rebellion in Canada, boundary disputes, southern alarm over West Indian emancipation, and American expansionism.

A major crisis with Great Britain erupted over an unresolved border dispute between Maine and New Brunswick. The area was wooded, and in the winter of 1838–1839 Canadian lumbermen moved into the region to cut trees. Maine residents then attempted to expel them. The lumbermen captured the Maine land agent and posse, both sides mobilized their militias, and Congress authorized a call-up of fifty thousand men. Ultimately, no blood was spilled. General Winfield Scott was dispatched to Aroostook, Maine, where he arranged a truce. The two sides compromised on their conflicting claims in the Webster-Ashburton Treaty (1842).

The border dispute with Great Britain prefigured the conflicts that were to erupt in the 1840s over the expansion of the United States. With Tyler's succession to power in 1841 and a Democratic victory in the presidential election of 1844, federal activism in the domestic sphere ended for the rest of the decade, and attention turned to the debate over territorial expansion.

 ## Manifest Destiny and Expansionism

The belief that American expansion westward and southward was inevitable, just, and divinely ordained was first labeled *manifest destiny* by John L. O'Sullivan, editor of the *United States Magazine and Domestic Review*. The annexation of Texas, O'Sullivan wrote in 1845, was "the fulfillment of our manifest destiny to overspread the continent allotted by Providence for the free development of our yearly multiplying millions." In the 1840s expansionism reached a new fervor.

Since colonial days Americans had hungered for more land. As the proportion of Americans living west of the Appalachians grew (see map), both national parties joined the popular clamor for expansion. Agrarian Democrats saw the West as an antidote to urbanization and industrialization. Enterprising Whigs looked to the new commercial opportunities the West offered. Southerners envisioned the extension of slavery and more slave states.

Fierce national pride spurred the quest for land. Americans were convinced that theirs was the greatest country on earth, with a special role to play in the world. The acquisition of new territory, many Americans reasoned, would extend the ben-

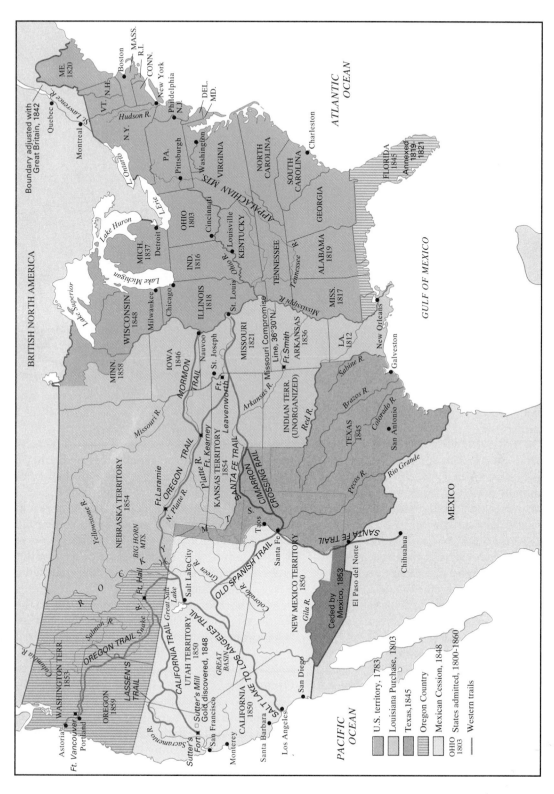

Westward Expansion, 1800–1860 Through exploration, purchase, war, and treaty, the United States became a continental nation, stretching from the Atlantic to the Pacific.

efits of America's republican system of government to the less fortunate and the inferior.

In part, racism drove the belief in manifest destiny. Native Americans were perceived as savages best confined to small areas in the West. Hispanics were seen as inferior peoples, best controlled or conquered. Thus the same racism that justified slavery in the South and discrimination in the North supported expansion in the West. But racism also could limit expansion, for Americans did not look on Mexicans—whether Indian, European, African, or mestizo—with favor.

Among the long-standing objectives of expansionists was the Republic of Texas, which in addition to Texas included parts of present-day Oklahoma, Kansas, Colorado, Wyoming, and New Mexico.

Republic of Texas

After winning its independence from Spain in 1821, Mexico encouraged the development of its rich but remote northern province, offering large tracts of land virtually free to settlers called *empresarios*. The settlers in turn agreed to become Mexican citizens, adopt the Catholic religion, and bring two hundred or more families into the area.

By 1835, thirty-five thousand Americans, including many slaveholders, lived in Texas. The new settlers' power grew. The dictatorship of General Antonio López de Santa Anna tightened control over the region. In response, Anglos and Tejanos rebelled. At the Alamo mission in San Antonio in 1836, fewer than two hundred Texans made a heroic but unsuccessful stand against three thousand Mexicans under General Santa Anna. "Remember the Alamo" became the Texans' rallying cry. A few months later, Sam Houston's victory over Santa Anna in the Battle of San Jacinto gained Texas its independence.

Texas established the independent Lone Star Republic but soon sought annexation to the United States. The issue, however, quickly became politically explosive. Southerners favored annexing proslavery Texas; abolitionists, many northerners, and most Whigs opposed annexation. In recognition of the political dangers, President Jackson reneged on his promise to recognize

Texans believed that their war for independence paralleled the Revolutionary War. The lady of liberty on this banner, carried by Texans in 1836, brings to mind similar images that stirred patriots during the American Revolution. Archives Division, Texas State Library.

Texas, and President Van Buren ignored annexation. Texans then talked about closer ties with the British and extending their republic all the way to the Pacific coast. President Tyler feared that a Texas alliance with the British might threaten American independence. He was also committed to expansion and hoped to build political support in the South by extending the area of slavery. But in a sectional vote, the Senate in 1844 rejected a treaty of annexation.

Like southerners who sought expansion to the Southwest, northerners looked to the Northwest. "Oregon fever" struck thousands in 1841. Lured by the glowing reports, migrants in wagon trains took to the Oregon Trail. The 2,000-mile journey took six months or more, but within a few years five thousand settlers had arrived in the fertile Willamette valley.

Oregon Fever

Britain and the United States had jointly occupied the disputed Oregon Territory since the

Anglo-American Convention of 1818 (see page 170). Beginning with the administration of President John Quincy Adams, the United States had tried to fix the boundary at the 49th parallel, but Britain refused. Time only increased the American appetite. In 1843 a Cincinnati convention of expansionists demanded the entire Oregon Country for the United States, up to its northernmost border at latitude 54°40'. Soon "Fifty-four Forty or Fight" became the rallying cry of American expansionists.

Expansion into Oregon and rejection of the annexation of Texas, both favored by antislavery forces, worried southern leaders. Anxious about their diminishing ability to control the debate over slavery, they persuaded the 1844 Democratic convention to adopt a rule requiring the presidential nominee to receive two-thirds of the convention votes. In effect, the southern states acquired a veto, and they blocked Van Buren as the nominee; most southerners objected to his antislavery stance and opposition to Texas annexation. Instead, the party chose House Speaker James K. Polk, a hard-money Jacksonian, avid expansionist, and slave-holding cotton planter from Tennessee. Henry Clay, the Whig nominee, who believed that the Democrats' belligerent nationalism would lead to war with Great Britain, Mexico, or both, favored expansion through negotiations.

James K. Polk Wins Election of 1844

With a well-organized campaign, Polk and the Democrats won the election by 170 electoral votes to 105. (They won the popular vote by just 38,000 out of 2.7 million votes cast.) Polk won New York's 36 electoral votes by just 6,000 popular votes. Abolitionist James G. Birney, the Liberty party candidate, had drawn almost 16,000 votes away from Clay, handing New York and the election to Polk.

Interpreting Polk's victory as a mandate for annexation, President Tyler proposed in his final days in office that Texas be admitted by joint resolution of Congress. Congress approved the resolution, Tyler signed it, and Mexico immediately broke relations with the United States. War was inevitable.

 ## Conclusion

Religion, reform, and expansionism colored politics in the 1830s and 1840s. As the Second Great Awakening spread through villages and towns, the converts, especially women, changed American religion and organized to reform a rapidly changing society. Religion imbued men and women with zeal to right the wrongs of American society and the world. Reformers pursued perfectionism and republican virtue by doing battle with the evils of the growing cities, seeking to ban alcohol and gambling, and expanding education.

Once reform forced itself into politics, it generated a broader-based interest in politics that would remake the political system. The ensuing conflicts, and the highly organized parties that arose during the era, stimulated even greater interest in campaigns and political issues. The Democrats, who rallied around Andrew Jackson, and Jackson's opponents, who found shelter under the Whig tent, competed almost equally for the loyalty of voters.

Territorial expansion would provide the kindling for the firestorm that would overtake the United States in 1861. Manifest destiny, the admission of Texas, and debates over territorial expansion awaited a spark. Ultimately, one issue would rivet the attention of nearly all Americans and ignite the fire that would threaten to sever the Union: slavery.

Suggestions for Further Reading

Religion, Revivalism, and Reform

Robert H. Abzug, *Cosmos Crumbling: American Reform and the Religious Imagination* (1994); Michael Barkun, *Crucible of the Millennium: The Burned-over District of New York in the 1840s* (1986); Terry Bilhartz, *Urban Religion and the Second Great Awakening: Church and Society in Early National Baltimore* (1986); Clifford S. Griffen, *Their Brother's Keepers: Moral Stewardship in the United States, 1800–1865* (1960); Keith J. Hardman, *Charles Grandison Finney, 1792–1875: Revivalist and Reformer* (1987); Nathan O. Hatch, *The Democratization of American Christianity* (1989); Curtis D. Johnson, *Islands of Holiness: Rural Religion in Upstate New York, 1790–1860* (1989); Paul E. Johnson, *A Shopkeeper's Millennium: Society and Revivals* in Rochester, New York, 1815–1837 (1978); Steven Mintz, *Moralists and Modernizers: America's Pre–Civil War Reformers* (1995); Richard D. Shiels, "The Scope of the Second Great Awakening: Andover, Massachusetts, as a Case Study," *Journal of the Early Republic* 5 (Summer 1985): 223–246; Timothy L. Smith, *Revivalism and Social Reform in Mid–Nineteenth Century America* (1957); Alice Felt Tyler, *Freedom's Ferment* (1944); Ronald G. Walters, *American Reformers, 1815–1860* (1978).

Temperance, Asylums, and Antimasonry

David Gollaher, *Voice for the Mad: The Life of Dorothea Dix* (1995); Paul Goodman, *Towards a Christian Republic: Antimasonry and the Great Transition in New England, 1826–1836* (1988); Gerald N. Grob, *Mental Institutions in America: Social Policy to 1875* (1973); Kathleen Smith Kutolowski, "Antimasonry Reexamined: Social Bases of the Grass-Roots Party," *Journal of American History* 71 (September 1984): 269–293; W. J. Rorabaugh, *The Alcoholic Republic: An American Tradition* (1979); David J. Rothman, *The Discovery of the Asylum: Social Order and Disorder in the New Republic* (1971); Ian R. Tyrrell, *Sobering Up: From Temperance to Prohibition in Antebellum America, 1800–1860* (1979); William Preston Vaughn, *The Antimasonic Party in the United States, 1826–1843* (1983).

Women and Reform

Barbara J. Berg, *The Remembered Gate: Origins of American Feminism: The Woman and the City, 1800–1860* (1977); Ellen C. Du Bois, *Feminism and Suffrage: The Emergence of an Independent Woman's Movement in America, 1848–1869* (1978); Barbara Leslie Epstein, *The Politics of Domesticity: Women, Evangelism, and Temperance in Nineteenth-Century America* (1981); Lori D. Ginzberg, *Women and the Work of Benevolence: Morality, Politics, and Class in the Nineteenth-Century United States* (1990); Debra Gold Hansen, *Strained Sisterhood: Gender and Class in the Boston Female Anti-Slavery Society* (1993); Nancy A. Hewitt, *Women's Activism and Social Change: Rochester, New York, 1822–1872* (1984); Sylvia D. Hoffert, *When Hens Crow: The Woman's Rights Movement in Antebellum America* (1995); Gerda Lerner, *The Grimké Sisters of South Carolina* (1967); Mary P. Ryan, *Cradle of the Middle Class: The Family in Oneida County, New York, 1790–1865* (1981); Shirley J. Yee, *Black Women Abolitionists: A Study in Activism, 1828–1860* (1992); Jean Fagan Yellin, *Women & Sisters: The Antislavery Feminists in American Culture* (1989).

Antislavery and Abolitionism

David Brion Davis, *Slavery and Human Progress* (1984); Frederick Douglass, *Life and Times of Frederick Douglass* (1881);

George M. Fredrickson, *The Black Image in the White Mind: The Debate on Afro-American Character and Destiny, 1817–1914* (1971); Lawrence J. Friedman, *Gregarious Saints: Self and Community in American Abolitionism, 1830–1870* (1982); Aileen S. Kraditor, *Means and Ends in American Abolitionism: Garrison and His Critics on Strategy and Tactics* (1967); William Lee Miller, *Arguing About Slavery: The Great Battle in the United States Congress* (1995); William H. Pease and Jane H. Pease, *They Who Would Be Free: Blacks' Search for Freedom, 1830–1861* (1974); Benjamin Quarles, *Black Abolitionists* (1969); John L. Thomas, *The Liberator: William Lloyd Garrison* (1963); Ronald G. Walters, *The Antislavery Appeal: American Abolitionism After 1830* (1976).

Andrew Jackson and the Jacksonians

Donald B. Cole, *Martin Van Buren and the American Political System* (1984); Daniel Feller, *The Jacksonian Promise: America, 1815–1840* (1995); Marvin Meyers, *The Jacksonian Persuasion* (1960); John Niven, *Martin Van Buren* (1983); Edward Pessen, *Jacksonian America: Society, Personality, and Politics*, rev. ed. (1979); Robert V. Remini, *The Legacy of Andrew Jackson: Essays on Democracy, Indian Removal, and Slavery* (1988); Robert V. Remini, *The Life of Andrew Jackson* (1988); Charles Sellers, *The Market Revolution: Jacksonian America, 1815–1846* (1991); Harry L. Watson, *Liberty and Power: The Politics of Jacksonian America* (1990).

Democrats and Whigs

William J. Cooper, *The South and the Politics of Slavery, 1828–1856* (1978); Ronald P. Formisano, *The Transformation of Political Culture: Massachusetts Parties, 1790s–1840s* (1983); William W. Freehling, *Prelude to Civil War: The Nullification Controversy in South Carolina* (1966); Daniel Walker Howe, *The Political Culture of the American Whigs* (1979); Richard P. McCormick, *The Second American Party System: Party Formation in the Jacksonian Era* (1966); Robert V. Remini, *Henry Clay: Statesman for the Union* (1991); James Roger Sharp, *The Jacksonians Versus the Banks: Politics in the States After the Panic of 1837* (1970).

Manifest Destiny and Foreign Policy

John M. Belohlavek, *"Let the Eagle Soar!" The Foreign Policy of Andrew Jackson* (1985); Thomas R. Hietala, *Manifest Destiny: Anxious Aggrandizement in Late Jacksonian America* (1985); Reginald Horsman, *Race and Manifest Destiny* (1981); Michael Hunt, *Ideology and U.S. Foreign Policy* (1987); Bradford Perkins, *The Creation of a Republican Empire, 1776–1865* (1993); Charles G. Sellers, Jr., *James K. Polk: Continentalist, 1843–1846* (1966); Anders Stephanson, *Manifest Destiny: American Expansionism and the Empire of Right* (1995).

CHAPTER
14

Slavery and America's Future:
The Road to War
1845–1861

Almost sixty and a widower, Robert Newsom lived with his two adult daughters and four of his grandchildren. In Missouri in 1850 he purchased Celia, a fourteen-year-old slave. She probably assumed that Newsom wanted her to cook and clean for the family, but he had more in mind for Celia. Almost immediately he raped her and made it clear that he would continue to demand her sexual services. Newsom's adult daughters and his neighbors knew what he was doing to Celia but said nothing. They respected him and knew that slavery spawned such arrangements.

In 1855, Celia began a relationship with George, another of the Newsom slaves, and resolved to end the relationship with her master. Neither pleas to Newsom's daughters nor appeals to him stopped the assaults, however. One night after Newsom brushed aside her objections to sex, Celia grabbed a club and struck him on the skull. As he sank to the floor, she struck him again. He never arose. Panicked at having killed her master, Celia proceeded to burn his body all through the night in her large fireplace.

Physical evidence of Newsom's murder soon came to light, and Celia was arrested. Celia's attorneys sympathized with her plight enough to argue, unsuccessfully, that laws against rape entitled her to defend herself. After a jury of twelve white men convicted her, Celia went to the gallows four days before Christmas.

By the time Celia was hanged, her drama had been overshadowed by a larger drama of violence in the territory of Kansas. Open warfare had broken out there between advocates and foes of slavery. Proslavery men, intent on spreading the peculiar institution and preserving a balance of free and slave states in the United States Senate, rode across the border from Missouri, stole elections by voting illegally, and physically attacked those who wanted Kansas to be free soil. Antislavery activists organized the New England Emigrant Aid Company to send opponents of slavery to Kansas. As new territories were opened, the passions over slavery intensified. Thus in the 1850s, slavery pulled Americans deeper and deeper into a maelstrom of conflict and violence.

Between 1845 and 1853 the United States added Texas, the West Coast, and the Southwest to its domain and launched the settlement of the Great Plains. Each time the nation expanded, it confronted a thorny issue: should new territories and states be slave or free? This question stirred disagreements too extreme for compromise. A host of political leaders, including Henry Clay, Lewis Cass, Stephen A. Douglas, and Presidents Jackson and Van Buren, tried to postpone or resolve disagreements about slavery in the territories. Repeatedly, though, these disputes injected into national politics the bitterness surrounding slavery.

The United States had always been a diverse society. Now, however, diverse interests that used to balance each other became linked to a divisive issue. The second party system disintegrated, and a realigned system with sectional parties that emphasized conflict emerged. The new Republican Party charged that southerners were taking over the federal government and planning to make slavery legal throughout the Union. Republicans believed that America's future depended on the free labor of free men, whose rights were protected by a government devoted to liberty. Southern leaders defended slavery and charged the North with lawless behavior in violation of the Constitution. To these southerners enslavement of blacks was the foundation of equality and republicanism among whites, and a government that failed to protect slavery was un-American.

Not all citizens were obsessed with these conflicts. In fact, the results of the 1860 presidential election indicated that most voters wanted neither disunion nor civil war. Within six months, however, they had both.

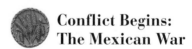 ## Conflict Begins: The Mexican War

Territorial expansion surged forward under the leadership of President James K. Polk. The annexation of Texas just before his inauguration did not weaken Polk's determination to acquire California and the Southwest, and he desired Oregon as well. Polk achieved his goals but was unaware of the price in domestic harmony that expansion would exact. Territorial conquest divided the Whig Party, drove southern Whigs into a full embrace of slavery, and brought into the open an aggressive new southern theory about slavery's position in the territories. Expansion also sparked protests and proposals from the North that angered southerners.

During the 1844 campaign, Polk's supporters had threatened war with Great Britain to gain all of Oregon. As president, however, Polk turned first to diplomacy. Not wanting to fight Mexico and Great Britain at the same time, he tried to avoid bloodshed in the Northwest, where America and Britain had jointly occupied disputed territory since 1818. Dropping the demand for a boundary at latitude 54°40', he pressured the British to accept the 49th parallel. In 1846 Great Britain agreed. The Oregon Treaty gave the United States all of present-day Oregon, Washington, and Idaho and parts of Wyoming and Montana.

Toward Mexico, Polk was more aggressive. He ordered American troops to defend the border claimed by Texas but contested by Mexico (see map, page 260), and he attempted to buy from the angry Mexicans a huge tract of land in the Southwest. When that effort failed, Polk resolved to ask Congress for a declaration of war. As he was drawing up a list of grievances, word arrived that Mexican forces had engaged American troops on disputed territory and American blood had been shed. Eagerly, Polk declared that "war exists by the act of Mexico itself."

• *Important Events* •

1846	War with Mexico begins Oregon Treaty negotiated Wilmot Proviso inflames sectional divisions	1856	"Bleeding Kansas" troubles nation Preston Brooks attacks Charles Sumner in Senate chamber James Buchanan elected president
1847	Lewis Cass proposes idea of popular sovereignty	1857	*Dred Scott* v. *Sanford* endorses southern views on race and territories Lecompton Constitution proposed; President Buchanan supports it
1848	Treaty of Guadalupe Hidalgo gives United States new territory in the Southwest Free-Soil Party formed Zachary Taylor elected president	1858	Kansas voters reject Lecompton Constitution Lincoln-Douglas debates attract attention Stephan A. Douglas proposes Freeport Doctrine
1849	California applies for admission to Union as free state	1859	John Brown raids Harpers Ferry
1850	Compromise of 1850 passed in separate bills	1860	Democratic party splits in two Abraham Lincoln elected president Crittenden Compromise fails South Carolina secedes from Union
1852	Publication of *Uncle Tom's Cabin*, by Harriet Beecher Stowe Franklin Pierce elected president	1861	Six more Deep South states secede Confederacy established at Montgomery, Alabama Attack on Fort Sumter begins Civil War Four states in the Upper South join the Confederacy
1854	Kansas-Nebraska Act wins approval and ignites controversy Republican Party formed Democrats lose ground in congressional elections		

Congress recognized a state of war between Mexico and the United States in May 1846, and soon American forces made significant gains. Despite the quarreling of politically ambitious officers, progress was steady. General Zachary Taylor's forces attacked and occupied Monterrey, securing northeastern Mexico (see map, page 260). Polk then ordered Colonel Stephen Kearny and a small detachment to invade the remote and thinly populated provinces of New Mexico and California. Taking Santa Fe without opposition, Kearny pushed into California, where he joined forces with rebellious American settlers led by Captain John C. Frémont and with a couple of United States naval units. A quick victory was followed by reverses, but American soldiers soon reestablished their dominance in distant California.

Because losses on the periphery had not broken Mexican resistance, General Winfield Scott carried the war to the enemy's heartland. From Veracruz on the Gulf of Mexico, he led fourteen thousand men toward Mexico City. After a series of hard-fought battles, United States troops captured the Mexican capital and brought the war to an end.

Representatives of both countries signed the Treaty of Guadalupe Hidalgo in February 1848. The United States gained California and New

Treaty of Guadalupe Hidalgo

Mexico (including present-day Nevada, Utah, and Arizona) and recognition of the Rio Grande as the southern boundary of Texas. In return, the American government agreed to settle the claims of its citizens against Mexico and to pay Mexico a mere $15 million.

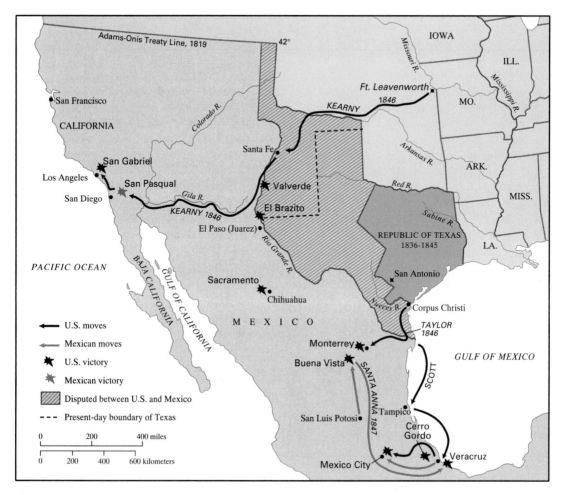

The Mexican War *This map shows the territory disputed between the United States and Mexico. After United States gains in northeastern Mexico and in New Mexico and California, General Winfield Scott captured Mexico City in the decisive campaign of the war.*

The war led to the deaths of thirteen thousand Americans and fifty thousand Mexicans. It also sharply divided public opinion in the United States. Southwesterners were enthusiastic about the war; New Englanders strenuously opposed it. Whigs in Congress charged that Polk, a Democrat, had "literally provoked" an unnecessary war (which they called "Mr. Polk's war") and "usurped the power of Congress." The aged John Quincy Adams denounced the war; and a tall, young, Illinois Whig named Abraham Lincoln questioned its justification. Abolitionists and a small minority of antislavery Whigs charged that the war was no less than a plot to extend slavery.

These charges fed northern fear of the so-called Slave Power. Abolitionists had long warned of a Slave Power—a slaveholding oligarchy that controlled the South and intended to dominate the nation.

Idea of a Slave Power

The Slave Power's assault on northern liberties, abolitionists argued, had begun in 1836, when Congress passed the gag rule (see page 243). Many white northerners, even those who saw nothing wrong with slavery, had opposed restrictions on free speech and the right of petition. It was the battle over free speech that first made the idea of a Slave Power credible. The Mexican War deepened fears about this sinister power. Why, asked antislavery northerners, had claims to part of Oregon been abandoned and a questionable war begun for slave territory?

Northern opinion began to shift, but the impact of events on southern opinion and southern leaders was even more dramatic. At first many southern leaders criticized the war with Mexico. Southern Whigs attacked the Democratic president for causing the war. Once slavery became the central issue, however, no Southern Whig could oppose it. That happened in August 1846, when David Wilmot, a Pennsylvania Democrat, proposed an amendment, or proviso, to a military appropriations bill: that "neither slavery nor involuntary servitude shall ever exist" in any territory gained from Mexico. His proviso did not pass both houses of Congress, but it immediately transformed the debate.

John C. Calhoun responded to the proviso with a radical new southern position. The territories, Calhoun insisted, belonged to all the states, and the federal government could do nothing to limit the spread of slavery there. Southern slaveholders had a constitutional *right*, Calhoun claimed, to take their slaves anywhere in the territories. This position was a radical reversal of history. In 1787 the Confederation Congress had excluded slavery from the Northwest Territory (see pages 130–131); Article IV of the federal Constitution had authorized Congress to make "all needful rules and regulations" for the territories; and the Missouri Compromise had barred slavery from most of the Louisiana Purchase. Now, however, southern leaders demanded protection for slavery.

Wilmot Proviso

In the North, the Wilmot Proviso became a rallying cry for abolitionists. Eventually the legislatures of fourteen northern states endorsed it—and not because all its supporters were abolitionists. David Wilmot, like most white northerners, was neither an abolitionist nor an antislavery Whig. His

goal, for instance, was to defend "the rights of white freemen" and to obtain California "for free white labor."

Fear of the Slave Power, however, was building a potent antislavery movement that united abolitionists *and* antiblack voters. The latter's concern was to protect themselves, not southern blacks, from the Slave Power.

The slavery question divided northerners and southerners in both parties and could not be kept out of national politics. After Polk renounced a second term as president, the Democrats nominated Senator Lewis Cass of Michigan for president. In 1847 Cass had devised the idea of "popular sovereignty" for the territories—letting residents in the territories decide the question of slavery for themselves. His party's platform declared that Congress lacked the power to interfere with slavery and criticized those who pressed the question. The Whigs nominated General Zachary Taylor, a southern slaveholder and the conqueror of Monterrey; Congressman Millard Fillmore of New York was his running mate. The Whig convention similarly refused to assert that Congress had power over slavery in the territories.

Election of 1848 and Popular Sovereignty

Among northerners, concern over slavery led to the formation of a new party. New York Democrats committed to the Wilmot Proviso rebelled against Cass and nominated former president Van Buren. Antislavery Whigs and former supporters of the Liberty Party then joined them to organize the Free-Soil Party, with Van Buren as its candidate (see table). This party, whose slogan was "Free Soil, Free Speech, Free Labor, and Free Men," won almost 300,000 northern votes. Taylor polled 1.4 million votes to Cass's 1.2 million and won the White House, but the results were more ominous than decisive. In both public opinion and the political parties, a North-South division was deepening.

The conflicts of 1848 would dominate politics throughout the 1850s, as slavery in the territories colored every other national issue. Debate over slavery pushed other issues aside, raised questions

New Political Parties

Party	Period of Influence	Area of Influence	Outcome
Liberty Party	1839–1848	North	Merged with other antislavery groups to form Free-Soil Party
Free-Soil Party	1848–1854	North	Merged with Republican Party
Know-Nothings (American Party)	1853–1856	Nationwide	Disappeared, freeing some northern voters to join Republican Party
Republican Party	1854–present	North (later nationwide)	Became rival of Democratic Party in third party system

about the nature of the Union, and led to the demise of the second party system.

Territorial Problems Are Compromised but Reemerge

The first sectional battle of the decade involved California. More than eighty thousand Americans flooded into California during the gold rush of 1849. With Congress unable to agree on a formula to govern the territories, President Taylor urged these settlers to apply directly for admission to the Union. They promptly did so, proposing a state constitution that prohibited slavery. Southern politicians, who at a minimum wanted to extend the Missouri Compromise line west to the Pacific, objected.

Henry Clay sensed that the Union was in peril. Twice before—in 1820 and 1833—Clay, the "Great Pacificator," had taken the lead in shaping sectional compromise; now he struggled one last time to preserve the nation. In a problem-laded compromise package, Clay sought to resolve several basic questions. Should all or part of California be free? How should the lands gained from Mexico be governed? What was the solution to Texas's land claims? Could the slave trade be abolished in the nation's capital? What should be done about fugitive slaves who escaped to free areas and were neither arrested nor returned to their owners? Of all the questions, the most

troublesome dealt with the status of slavery in the territories.

Clay and Senator Stephen A. Douglas of Illinois, his partner in steering the compromise through debate, hoped to avoid a specific formula, for Lewis Cass's idea of popular sovereignty possessed a vagueness that appealed to practical politicians. Like many others, Cass wanted Congress to stay out of the territorial wrangle. Ultimately Congress would have to approve statehood for a territory, but "in the meantime," he said, it should allow the people living there "to regulate their own concerns in their own way."

Those simple words proved highly ambiguous. When could settlers prohibit slavery? To avoid dissension within their party, northern and southern Democrats explained Cass's statement to their constituents in two incompatible ways. Southerners claimed that neither Congress nor a territorial legislature could bar slavery. Only when settlers assumed sovereignty under a state constitution could they take that step. Northerners insisted that Americans living in a territory could outlaw slavery at any time.

The cause of compromise gained a powerful supporter when Senator Daniel Webster committed his prestige and eloquence to Clay's bill. Yet even Webster's influence was not enough. After months of labor, Clay and Douglas finally brought their legislative package to a vote, and lost. Then, with Clay sick and absent from Washington, Douglas reintroduced the compromise measures one at a time. He shrewdly realized that different majorities might be created for the separate measures. The strategy worked, and the Compromise of 1850 became law.

Under its various measures, California became a free state, and the Texas boundary was set at its present limits. The United States paid Texas $10 million in consideration of the boundary agreement.

Compromise of 1850

The territories of New Mexico and Utah were organized with power to legislate on "all rightful subjects . . . consistent with the Constitution." A stronger fugitive slave law and an act to suppress the slave trade in the District of Columbia completed the compromise.

Jubilation greeted passage of the compromise; crowds in Washington celebrated the happy news, but there was less cause for celebration than people hoped. Fundamentally, the Compromise of 1850 was not a settlement of sectional disputes. At best, it was an artful evasion that bought time for the nation without setting guidelines for solving future territorial questions. Furthermore, the compromise had two basic flaws. The first concerned the ambiguity of territorial legislation: what were "rightful subjects of legislation, consistent with the Constitution"? During debate, southerners said these words meant that there would be no prohibition of slavery during the territorial stage, and northerners declared that settlers could bar slavery whenever they wished.

The second flaw lay in the Fugitive Slave Act, which empowered slaveowners to go into court in their own states to present evidence that a slave who owed them service had escaped. The resulting transcript and a description of the fugitive would then serve as legal proof of a person's slave status, even in free states and territories. Court officials would decide only whether the person brought before them was the person described, not whether he or she was indeed a slave. Penalties discouraged citizens from harboring fugitives, and the fees paid to United States marshals seemed to favor slaveholders. (Authorities were paid $10 if the alleged fugitive was turned over to the slave-

Fugitive Slave Act

owner, $5 if not.) Because of the law's provisions, especially the denial of an alleged fugitive's right to a jury trial, northerners staged protests in several states.

At this point a novel portrayed the humanity and suffering of slaves in a way that touched millions of northerners. Harriet Beecher Stowe, whose New England family had produced many prominent ministers, wrote *Uncle Tom's Cabin* out of deep moral conviction. Her story, serialized in 1851 and published as a book in 1852, conveyed the agonies faced by slave families. Stowe also portrayed slavery's evil effects on slaveholders, indicting the institution itself more harshly than she indicted the southerners caught in its web. By mid-1853 the book had sold over a million copies and led many who had ignored slavery to now see its evil.

Uncle Tom's Cabin

The popularity of *Uncle Tom's Cabin* alarmed southern whites. In the territorial controversies and now in popular literature they saw threats to their way of life. Behind the South's aggressive claims about territorial rights lay the fear that nearby free soil areas would be used as bases from which to spread abolitionism into the slave states. To defend slavery against political threats, southern leaders relied on Calhoun's territorial theories and the dogmas of states' rights and strict construction.

To protect slavery in the arena of ideas, southerners needed to counter indictments of the institution as a moral wrong. Accordingly, proslavery theorists elaborated numerous arguments based on partially scientific or pseudoscientific data. They discussed anthropological evidence suggesting separate origins of the races and physicians' views on the physical infirmities of blacks. Other proslavery spokesmen expounded the new "science" of phrenology, citing measurements of skulls to "prove" that blacks were an inferior race. Yet in private and in their hearts, most southern leaders fell back on two rationales for slavery: their belief that blacks were inferior and biblical accounts of slaveholding. Some, like Jefferson Davis, reverted to the eighteenth-century argument that southerners

Proslavery Theories

were doing the best they could with a situation they had inherited.

The 1852 election gave Davis and other southerners hope that slavery would be secure under the administration of a new president. Franklin Pierce, a Democrat from New Hampshire, won an easy victory over the Whig presidential nominee, General Winfield Scott. Pierce believed that the defense of each section's rights was essential to the nation's unity. And the victory of a proponent of the Compromise of 1850 suggested its popular support.

Election of 1852

That interpretation of the election, however, was erroneous. Pierce's victory derived less from his strengths than from the Whig Party's weakness. The Whigs were a congressional and state-based party that never had achieved much success in presidential politics. Sectional discord was splitting the party in two, and the deaths of President Taylor, Daniel Webster, and Henry Clay had deprived Whigs of the few dominant personalities they had. In 1852 the Whig Party ran on little but its past reputation.

In 1854, upon learning that a runaway slave named Anthony Burns was in custody in Boston, President Pierce moved decisively to enforce the Fugitive Slave Act. He telegraphed local officials to "incur any expense to insure the execution of the law" and sent marines, cavalry, and artillery to Boston. When Burns's owner seemed willing to sell his property, the United States attorney blocked the sale and won a decision that Anthony Burns must return to slavery. United States troops marched Burns to Boston harbor through streets draped in black and hung with American flags at half mast. At a cost of $100,000, equivalent to roughly $2 million today, a single black man was returned to slavery through the power of federal law.

This demonstration of federal support for slavery radicalized opinion. Textile manufacturer Amos A. Lawrence observed that "we went to bed one night old fashioned, conservative, Compromise Union Whigs & waked up stark mad Abolitionists." In New England, states passed personal-liberty laws designed to impede or block federal enforcement. But where northerners saw evidence that the Slave Power was dominating American government, outraged slaveholders saw northern "faithlessness" to the law.

Pierce seemed unable to avoid sectional conflict in other arenas as well. His proposal for a transcontinental railroad derailed when congressmen fought over its location, North or South. His attempts to acquire foreign territory stirred more trouble. An annexation treaty with Hawai'i failed because southern senators would not vote for another free state, and efforts to acquire slaveholding Cuba angered antislavery northerners. Then another territorial bill threw Congress and the nation into a bitter conflict that was to have significant results.

 ## Territorial Problems Shatter the Party System

In 1854, Stephen A. Douglas introduced a bill to establish the Kansas and Nebraska Territories. As a senator from Illinois, Douglas hoped for a midwestern transcontinental railroad to boost Chicago's economy and encourage settlement of the Great Plains. No company, however, would build such a railroad before Congress organized the territories it would cross. Thus it was probably for the sake of promoting the construction of a railroad that Douglas introduced a bill that inflamed sectional passions, finished off the Whig Party, damaged the northern Democrats, and gave birth to a new Republican Party.

The Kansas-Nebraska bill exposed the first flaw of the Compromise of 1850—the conflicting interpretations of popular sovereignty. Douglas's bill left "all questions pertaining to slavery in the Territories . . . to the people residing therein." Northerners and southerners, however, still disagreed violently over what territorial settlers could constitutionally do. Moreover, the Kansas and Nebraska Territories lay within the Louisiana Purchase, and the Missouri Compromise prohibited slavery in all that land from latitude 36°30' north to the Canadian border. If popular sovereignty were to mean anything in Kansas and Nebraska, it had to mean that the Missouri Com-

Kansas-Nebraska Bill

promise was no longer in effect and that settlers could establish slavery there.

After a titanic struggle in Congress, lasting more than three months, the bill became law in May 1854 (see map below). Northern reaction to the bill was immediate, widespread, and enduring. Abolitionists charged sinister aggression by the Slave Power, and northern fears of slavery's influence deepened. Opposition to the Fugitive Slave Act grew dramatically; between 1855 and 1859 Connecticut, Rhode Island, Massachusetts, Michigan, Maine, Ohio, and Wisconsin passed personal-liberty laws. These laws interfered with the Fugitive Slave Act—and enraged southern leaders—by providing counsel for alleged fugitives and requiring trial by jury. More important was the devastating impact of the Kansas-Nebraska Act on political parties. The weakened Whig Party broke apart into northern and southern wings that could no longer cooperate nationally. One of the two foundations of the second party system was now gone. The Democrats survived, but their support in the North fell drastically in the 1854 elections.

The beneficiary of northern voters' wrath was a new political party. During the summer and fall of 1854, antislavery Whigs and Democrats, Free-Soilers, and other reformers throughout the Old Northwest met to form the new Republican Party, dedicated to keeping slavery out of the territories. The influence of the Republicans rapidly spread to the East, and they won a stunning victory in the 1854 elections by capturing a majority of northern House seats.

For the first time, too, a sectional party had gained significant power in the political system.

The New Republican Party

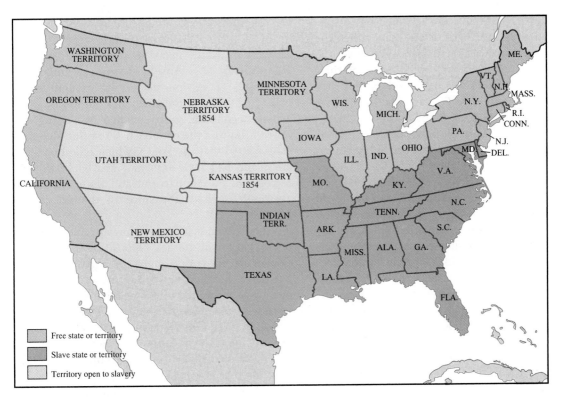

The Kansas-Nebraska Act, 1854 *Stephen Douglas's bill raised a storm of opposition in the North because it repealed the Missouri Compromise's limitation on slavery. In Kansas and Nebraska, land was opened to slavery where it had been prohibited before.*

Previously, every major party was a national organization whose leaders patched up sectional differences to achieve partisan goals. Now the Whigs were gone, and only the Democrats struggled to maintain a national following. The sectional Republican Party, which absorbed the Free-Soil Party, grew rapidly in the North by raising moral issues that angered many southerners.

Nor were Republicans the only new party. For a brief period, an anti-immigrant organization, the American Party, seemed likely to replace the Whigs. This party, popularly known as the Know-Nothings (because its first members kept their purposes secret, answering "I know nothing" to all questions), exploited nativist fear of foreigners. Between 1848 and 1860, nearly 3.5 million immigrants entered the United States—proportionally the heaviest inflow of foreigners ever in American history (see pages 224–227). In 1854 anti-immigrant fears gave the Know-Nothings more supporters in some northern states than either the Republicans or the Free-Soilers. But like the Whigs, the Know-Nothings could not keep their northern and southern wings together, and they melted away after 1856. That left the field to the Republicans (see table, page 262).

Know-Nothings

Republicans, Know-Nothings, and Democrats were all scrambling to attract former Whig voters. The demise of that party ensured a major realignment of the political system, with nearly half of the old electorate up for grabs. To woo these homeless Whigs, the remaining parties made appeals to various segments of the electorate. Immigration, temperance, homestead bills, the tariff, internal improvements—all played important roles in attracting voters during the 1850s.

Realignment of the Political System

The Republicans appealed strongly to those interested in the economic development of the West. Commercial agriculture was booming in the Ohio–Mississippi–Great Lakes area, but residents of that region desired more canals, roads, and river and harbor improvements to reap

Republican Appeals

the full benefit of their labors. There was also widespread interest in a program that would provide homesteaders with western public land at no cost. Whigs had favored and Democrats opposed all these things. Seizing their opportunity, the Republicans added internal improvements and land-grant planks to their platform. They also backed higher tariffs as an enticement to industrialists and businessmen.

Partisan ideological appeals, which had a significant impact on the sectional crisis, were another major feature of the realigned political system. In the North, Republicans attracted many voters through effective use of ideology. When they preached "Free Soil, Free Labor, Free Men," they captured an image that northerners had of themselves and their future. These phrases resonated with traditional ideals of equality, liberty, and opportunity.

"Free Soil, Free Labor, Free Men" seemed an appropriate motto for a northern economy that was energetic, expanding, and prosperous. The key to progress appeared, to many people, to be free labor. Any hard-working and virtuous man, it was thought, could improve his condition and achieve economic independence by seizing opportunities that the country had to offer. Republicans argued that the South, which relied on slave labor and had little industry, was backward and retrograde by comparison, and their arguments captured much of the spirit of the age in the North.

Republican Ideology

The Republican Party thus attracted support from a variety of sources. Opposition to the extension of slavery had brought the party into being, but party members carefully broadened their appeal by adopting the causes of other groups. They were wise to do so. As the New York newspaper editor Horace Greeley wrote in 1860, "an Anti-Slavery man *per se* cannot be elected." But, he added, "a Tariff, River-and-Harbor, Pacific Railroad, Free Homestead man, *may* succeed *although* he is Anti-Slavery." As these elements joined the Republican Party, they also learned more about the dangers of slavery. Thus the process of party building deepened the sectional conflict.

A similar process was under way in the South. In the increasingly tense atmosphere of sectional crisis, homeless southern Whigs were highly susceptible to strong states' rights positions and defense of slavery. Democratic leaders emphasized such appeals and managed to convert most of the formerly Whig slaveholders, who responded to their class interests. South of the Mason-Dixon line, however, yeomen—not planters—constituted the Democratic Party's heart. Thus Democratic politicians, though often slaveowners themselves, lauded the common man and argued that their policies advanced his interests. According to the southern version of republicanism, white citizens in a slave society enjoyed liberty and social equality *because* black people were enslaved. As Jefferson Davis put it in 1851, slavery elevated every white person's status and allowed the nonslaveholder to "*stand upon the broad level of equality with the rich man.*" Slave-holding Democrats warned that the issue was "shall negroes govern white men, or white men govern negroes?" Southern leaders also portrayed the well-ordered South as the true defender of constitutional principles.

Southern Democrats

The arguments had their effect. Racial fears and traditional political loyalties helped keep the political alliance between yeoman farmers and planters intact through the 1850s. No viable party emerged to replace the Whigs. The result was a one-party system that emphasized sectional issues. In the South as in the North, political realignment sharpened sectional divisions.

Political leaders of both sections argued that racial change threatened opportunity. The *Montgomery* (Alabama) *Mail* warned southern whites in 1860 that the Republicans intended "to free the negroes and force amalgamation between them and the children of the poor men of the South." Republicans warned northern workers that if slavery entered the territories, the great reservoir of opportunity for ordinary citizens would be poisoned. Such charges aroused fear and anxiety, but events in the territory of Kansas did more to deepen the conflict. When implemented, the Kansas-Nebraska Act spawned hatred and violence. Abolitionists and religious groups sent in armed Free-Soil settlers; southerners sent in their reinforcements to establish slavery and prevent "northern hordes" from stealing Kansas away. Soon the whole nation was talking about "Bleeding Kansas."

Politics in the territory resembled war more than democracy. During elections for a territorial legislature in 1855, thousands of proslavery Missourians invaded the polls and ran up a large but fraudulent majority for slavery candidates. The resulting legislature legalized slavery, and in response Free-Soilers held an unauthorized convention at which they created their own government and constitution. A proslavery posse sent to arrest the Free-Soil leaders sacked the town of Lawrence. In revenge John Brown, an antislavery zealot who saw himself as God's instrument to destroy slavery, murdered five proslavery settlers. Soon, armed bands of guerrillas roamed the state.

Bleeding Kansas

These passions brought violence to the United States Senate in May 1856, when Charles Sumner of Massachusetts denounced "the Crime against Kansas." Radical in his antislavery views, Sumner bitterly assailed the president, the South, and Senator Andrew P. Butler of South Carolina. Soon thereafter Butler's cousin, Representative Preston Brooks, approached Sumner at the latter's Senate desk, raised his cane, and began to beat Sumner on the head. Shocked northerners recoiled from what they saw as another southern assault on free speech and the South's readiness to use violence to have its way. South Carolina voters reelected Brooks and sent him dozens of new canes. The country was becoming polarized.

The election of 1856 showed how extreme that polarization had become. The Democrats bypassed prominent figures and nominated James Buchanan of Pennsylvania, whose chief virtue was that for the past four years he had been ambassador to Britain and thus uninvolved in territorial controversies. This anonymity and superior party organization helped Buchanan win the election, but he owed his victory to southern support. The Republican candidate, John C. Frémont, won eleven of the sixteen free states; Republicans had become the dominant party in the North. The

Know-Nothing candidate won almost 1 million votes, but this election was to be his party's last hurrah. Only a sectional Republican Party and divided Democratic Party remained.

 ## Slavery and the Nation's Future

For years the issue of slavery in the territories had convulsed Congress, and for years Congress had tried to settle the issue with vague formulas. In 1857 the Supreme Court took up this emotionally charged subject and attempted to silence controversy with a definitive verdict.

A Missouri slave named Dred Scott had sued his owner for his freedom. Scott based his claim on the fact that his former owner, an army surgeon, had taken him for several years into Illinois, a free state, and into the Wisconsin Territory, from which slavery had been barred by the Missouri Compromise. Scott first won and then lost his case as it moved on appeal through the state courts, into the federal system, and finally to the Supreme Court.

Dred Scott **Case**

Was a black person like Dred Scott a citizen of the United States and thus eligible to sue in federal court? Had residence in a free state or free territory made him free? Did Congress have the power to prohibit slavery in a territory or to delegate that power to a territorial legislature?

In March 1857, Chief Justice Roger B. Taney of Maryland answered each of the questions when he delivered the majority opinion of a divided Court in *Dred Scott* v. *Sanford*. Taney declared that Scott was not a citizen of either the United States or Missouri; that residence in free territory did not make Scott free; and that Congress had no power to bar slavery from a territory, as it had done in the Missouri Compromise. The decision not only overturned a sectional compromise that had been honored for years; it also invalidated the basic ideas of the Wilmot Proviso and probably popular sovereignty as well.

The Slave Power seemed to have won a major constitutional victory. African-Americans were especially dismayed, for Taney's decision asserted that the founders had never intended for black people to be citizens. Taney was mistaken, however. African-Americans had been citizens in several of the original states. Nevertheless, the *Dred Scott* decision seemed to shut the door permanently on their hopes for justice and equal rights.

A storm of angry reaction broke in the North. The decision alarmed a wide variety of northerners and seemed to confirm every charge against the aggressive Slave Power.

Abraham Lincoln on the Slave Power

"There is such a thing as the slave power," warned the *Cincinnati Daily Commercial.* "It has marched over and annihilated the boundaries of the states. We are now one great homogenous slaveholding community." "Where will it end?" asked the *Atlantic Monthly.* To Abraham Lincoln, the territorial question affected every citizen. "The whole nation," he declared as early as 1854, "is interested that the best use shall be made of these Territories. We want them for homes of free white people. This they cannot be, to any considerable extent, if slavery shall be planted within them." After the *Dred Scott* decision, he charged, it was clear that slavery's advocates, including highly placed government officials, were trying to "push it forward, till it shall become lawful in *all* the states . . . *North* as well as *South.*" The next step in the unfolding Slave Power conspiracy, Lincoln alleged, would be a Supreme Court decision "declaring that the Constitution does not permit a State to exclude slavery from its limits. . . ." This charge was not pure hyperbole, for lawsuits soon challenged state laws that freed slaves brought within their borders.

Lincoln's most eloquent statement against the Slave Power was his famous "House Divided" speech, in which he declared:

> I do not expect the Union to be dissolved—I do not expect the House to fall—but I do expect it to cease to be divided. It will become all one thing or all the other. Either the opponents of slavery will arrest the further spread of it, and place it where the public mind shall rest in the belief that it is in the course of ultimate extinction; or its advocates will push it forward, till it shall become alike lawful in all the States, old as well as new, North as well as South.

How do historians know what motivated Abraham Lincoln to oppose the extension of slavery? Lincoln, of course, was a public man who made many addresses and public statements. His words as a politician and leader of the Republican Party show his reverence for the Declaration of Independence and America's heritage of freedom. But Lincoln also produced many private writings. The page reproduced below comes from a notebook in which he recorded his reactions to a proslavery book, *Slavery Ordained of God*, by Rev. Fred A. Ross. Criticizing Ross, Lincoln revealed his dislike of privilege and exposed the self-interest of those who would exploit others: "Dr. Ross sits in the shade, with gloves on his hands, and subsists on the bread that Sambo is earning in the burning sun" rather than "delv[ing] for his own bread." Illinois State Historical Society and Library.

Events convinced countless northerners that slave-holders were nearing their goal of making slavery a national institution.

Politically, these forceful Republican arguments offset the difficulties that the *Dred Scott* decision posed. By endorsing Calhoun's theories, the Court had in effect declared that the central position of the Republican Party—no extension of slavery—was unconstitutional. Republicans could only repudiate the decision, appealing to a "higher law," or hope to change the personnel of the Court. They did both.

Stephen A. Douglas, however, as a northern Democrat with presidential aspirations, faced an awful dilemma. He could not afford to offend the southern wing of the party; yet he had to ease the fears of the northern wing. Douglas chose to stand by his principle of popular sovereignty. In 1857 Kansans voted on a proslavery constitution that had been drafted at Lecompton. It was defeated by more than ten thousand votes. The evidence was overwhelming that Kansans did not want slavery, but President Buchanan tried to force the Lecompton Constitution through Congress. Breaking with the administration, Douglas threw his weight against the Lecompton Constitution. He gauged opinion in Kansas correctly; in 1858, voters there rejected the constitution again. But his action infuriated southern Democrats.

Douglas further alienated the South in his debates with Abraham Lincoln, who challenged him for the Illinois Senate seat in 1858. Speaking at Freeport, Illinois, Douglas attempted to revive the concept of popular sovereignty with some tortured arguments. Asserting that the Supreme Court had ruled only on the powers of Congress, not on the powers of a *territorial* legislature, Douglas claimed that the latter could bar slavery either by passing a law against it or by doing nothing. Without the patrol laws and police regulations that supported slavery, he reasoned, the institution could not exist. This argument, called the Freeport Doctrine, temporarily shored up Douglas's crumbling position in the North. But it gave southern Democrats further evidence that

Stephen Douglas Proposes the Freeport Doctrine

Douglas was unreliable. Some, like Representative William L. Yancey of Alabama, concluded that southern rights and slavery would be safe only in a separate nation.

The immediate consequence for politics, however, was the likelihood of a split in the Democratic Party. Northern Democrats could not support the territorial protection for slavery that southern Democrats insisted was theirs as a constitutional right. Thus the issue of slavery in the territories continued to generate wider conflict, even though it had little immediate, practical significance. In territories outside Kansas the number of settlers was small, and in all territories the number of African-Americans was negligible—less than 1 percent of the populations of Kansas and New Mexico. Nevertheless, the situation had become explosive.

 Breakup of the Union

One year before the 1860 presidential election, John Brown led a small band in an attack on the federal arsenal at Harpers Ferry, Virginia. Hoping to trigger a slave rebellion, Brown failed miserably and was quickly captured, tried, and executed. Yet his attempted insurrection struck fear into the South. Then it became known that Brown had received financial backing from several prominent abolitionists. When northern intellectuals such as Emerson and Thoreau praised Brown as a hero and a martyr, white southerners' fears and anger multiplied many times over.

Many believed that the election of 1860 would decide the fate of the Union. Only the Democratic Party remained as an organization that was truly national in scope. Even religious denominations had split into northern and southern wings during the 1840s and 1850s. "One after another," wrote a Mississippi newspaper editor, "the links which have bound the North and South together, have been severed . . . [but] the Democratic party looms gradually up, its nationality intact, and waves the olive branch over the troubled waters of politics." At its 1860 convention, however, the Democratic Party broke in two.

Stephen A. Douglas wanted his party's presidential nomination, but he could not afford to alienate northern voters by accepting the southern position on the territories.

Splintering of the Democratic Party

Southern Democrats, however, insisted on recognition of their rights and they moved to block Douglas's nomination. When Douglas obtained a majority for his version of the platform, delegates from eight slave states walked out of the party convention in Charleston. After efforts at compromise failed, the Democrats presented two nominees: Douglas for the northern wing, and Vice President John C. Breckinridge of Kentucky for the southern. The Republicans nominated Abraham Lincoln. A Constitutional Union Party, formed to preserve the nation but strong only in the Upper South, nominated John Bell of Tennessee.

The results of the balloting were sectional in character. Lincoln won, but Douglas, Breckinridge, and Bell together received most of the votes. Douglas had broad-based support but won few states. Breckinridge carried nine southern states. Bell won pluralities in Virginia, Kentucky, and Tennessee. Lincoln prevailed in the North, but in the states that ultimately remained loyal to the Union he gained only a plurality, not a majority. Lincoln's victory was won in the electoral college.

Election of 1860

Given the heterogeneous nature of Republican voters, it is likely that many of them did not view the issue of slavery in the territories as paramount. But opposition to slavery's extension was the core issue of the Republican Party, and abolitionists and supporters of free soil in the North worked to keep the Republicans from compromising on their territorial stand. Meanwhile in the South, proslavery advocates and secessionists demanded that state conventions assemble to consider secession.

Lincoln made the crucial decision not to soften his party's position on the territories. His refusal to compromise probably derived both from conviction and from concern for the unity of the Republican Party. Although many conservative Republicans—eastern businessmen and former Whigs who did not feel strongly about slavery—hoped for a compromise, the original and most committed Republicans—antislavery voters and "conscience Whigs"—were adamant for free soil. Lincoln chose to preserve party unity by standing firm against slavery's extension.

Southern leaders in the Senate were willing, conditionally, to accept a compromise drawn up by Senator John J. Crittenden of Kentucky. Crittenden proposed that the two sections divide the territories between them at latitude 36°30'. But the southerners would agree to this *only* if the Republicans did, too. When Lincoln ruled out concessions on the territorial issue, Crittenden's peacemaking effort collapsed. Virginians called for a special convention in Washington, but this gathering, too, failed to find a solution.

Misjudgment also played a role in the coming of war. Lincoln and other prominent Republicans believed that southerners were bluffing when they threatened secession; Republicans expected a pro-Union majority in the South to assert itself. On their side, southern leaders had become convinced that northern leaders were not taking them seriously and that a posture of strength was necessary to win respect for their demands. Confrontation was more likely than compromise.

Meanwhile, the Union was being destroyed. On December 20, 1860, South Carolina passed an ordinance of secession. This step marked the inauguration of the strategy of separate-state secession. Recognizing the difficulty of persuading all the southern states to challenge the federal government simultaneously, secessionists concentrated their efforts on the most extreme proslavery state. They hoped South Carolina's secession would induce other states to follow, with each decision building momentum for disunion.

Secession of South Carolina

Southern extremists soon got their way in the Deep South. They called separate state conventions and passed secession ordinances in

Confederate States of America

Mississippi, Florida, Alabama, Georgia, Louisiana, and Texas. By February 1861 these states had joined South Carolina to form a new government in Montgomery, Alabama: the Confederate States of America. The delegates at Montgomery chose Jefferson Davis as their president.

This apparent unanimity of action was deceiving. Many southerners who in 1860 had voted in the United States presidential election stayed home a few months later rather than vote for delegates who would decide upon secession. Even so, in some state conventions the vote to secede was close, with secession decided by overrepresentation of plantation districts. Furthermore, the conventions were noticeably unwilling to let voters ratify their acts. Four states in the Upper South—Virginia, North Carolina, Tennessee, and Arkansas—flatly rejected secession and did not join the Confederacy until after fighting had begun. In the border states, popular sentiment was deeply divided; minorities in Kentucky and Missouri tried to secede, but these slave states ultimately came under Union control, along with Maryland and Delaware (see map, page 273).

Such misgivings were not surprising. Secession posed the possibility of war and the question of who would die. Analysis of election returns from 1860 and 1861 indicates that heavily slaveholding counties strongly supported secession and that most counties with few slaves took an antisecession position or were staunchly Unionist (see figure, page 274). Thus, with war on the horizon, nonslaveholders were beginning to consider their class interests and to ask how far they would go to support slavery and slaveowners.

The dilemma facing President Lincoln on inauguration day in March 1861 was how to maintain the authority of the federal government

Attack on Fort Sumter

without provoking war. Proceeding cautiously, he sought only to hold on to forts in the states that had left the Union, reasoning that in this way he

On February 18, 1861, in Montgomery, Alabama, Jefferson Davis took an oath as president of the Confederate States of America. Davis later recalled that he foresaw "troubles innumerable" but was committed to seek independence as his paramount goal.   Boston Athenaeum.

could assert federal sovereignty while waiting for a restoration of relations. But Jefferson Davis, who could not claim to lead a sovereign nation if the Confederate forts were under foreign (that is, United States) control, was unwilling to be so patient. A collision was inevitable.

It arrived in the early morning hours of April 12, 1861, at Fort Sumter in Charleston harbor. A federal garrison there ran low on food, and Lincoln notified the South Carolinians that he was sending a ship to resupply the fort. For the Montgomery government, the alternatives were to attack the fort or to acquiesce to Lincoln's authority. After the Confederate cabinet met, the Secretary of War ordered local commanders to obtain a sur-

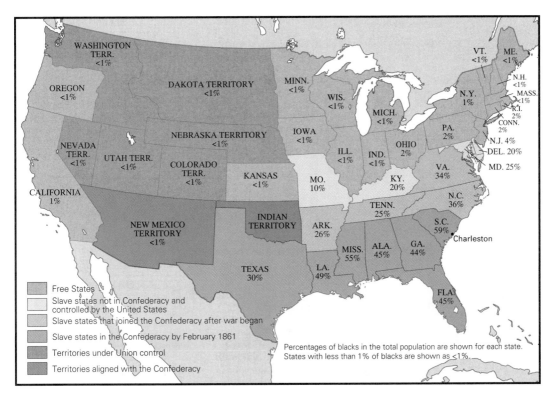

The Divided Nation—Slave and Free Areas, 1861 *After fighting began, the Upper South joined the Deep South in the Confederacy.*

render or attack the fort. After two days of heavy bombardment, the federal garrison finally surrendered. Confederates permitted the United States troops to sail away on unarmed vessels while Charlestonians celebrated wildly. Thus began the bloodiest war in America's history.

 ## Conclusion

Throughout the 1840s and 1850s many able leaders had worked diligently to avert this outcome. Most people, North and South, had hoped to keep the nation together. As late as 1858 even Jefferson Davis had declared, "This great country will continue united," saying that "to the innermost fibers of my heart I love it all, and every part." Why, then, had war broken out?

Slavery was an issue on which compromise was impossible. The emotions bound up in attacking and defending it were too powerful, and the motives it affected too vital, for compromise. Because it was deeply entwined with major policy questions of the present and the foreseeable future, each section ultimately regarded slavery as too important to be put aside.

North and South had fundamentally different attitudes toward the institution. The logic of Republican ideology tended in the direction of abolishing slavery, even though Republicans denied any such intention. The logic of southern leaders' arguments led toward establishing slavery everywhere, though southern leaders denied that they sought to do any such thing. Lincoln put these facts succinctly. In a postelection letter to his old friend Alexander Stephens of Georgia, Lincoln wrote, "You think slavery is *right* and ought to be

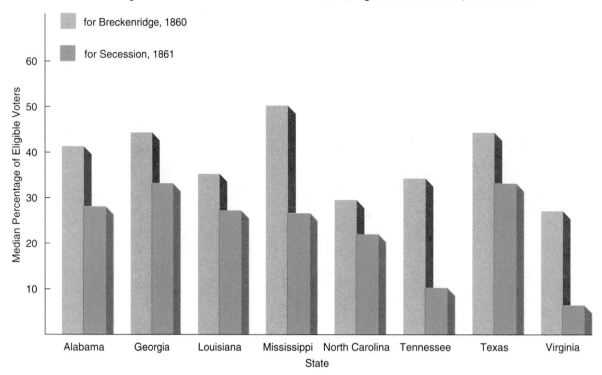

Voting Returns of Counties with Few Slaveholders, Eight Southern States, 1860 and 1861

Voting Returns of Counties with Few Slaveholders, Eight Southern States, 1860 and 1861 *This graph depicts voting in counties whose percentage of slaveholders ranked them among the lower half of the counties in their state. How does voters' support for secession in 1861 compare with support for John Breckinridge, the southern Democratic candidate in 1860? Why was their support for secession so weak? At this time counties with many slaveholders were giving increased support to secession.*

expanded; while we think it is *wrong* and ought to be restricted. That I suppose is the rub."

The issue of slavery in the territories made conflict impossible to avoid. Territorial expansion generated disputes so frequently that the nation never enjoyed a breathing space. As the conflict recurred, its influence on policy and effect on the government deepened. Every southern victory increased fear of the Slave Power, and each new expression of Free-Soil sentiment made alarmed slaveholders more insistent in their demands. Concern over slavery had driven all the other conflicts. But as the fighting began, this, the war's central issue, was shrouded in confusion. How would the Civil War affect slavery, its place in the law, and African-Americans' place in society?

Suggestions for Further Reading

Politics: General

Thomas B. Alexander, *Sectional Stress and Party Strength* (1967); Tyler Anbinder, *Nativism and Slavery* (1992); Paul Bergeron, *The Presidency of James K. Polk* (1987); Frederick J. Blue, *The Free Soilers: Third Party Politics, 1848–1854* (1973); Stanley W. Campbell, *The Slave Catchers* (1968); Don E. Fehrenbacher, *The Dred Scott Case* (1978); George M. Fredrickson, *The Black Image in the White Mind* (1971); Holman Hamilton, *Prologue to Conflict: The Crisis and Compromise of 1850* (1964); Michael F. Holt, *The Political Crisis of the 1850s* (1978); William Lee Miller, *Arguing About Slavery* (1996); Russell B. Nye, *Fettered Freedom* (1949); Merrill D. Peterson, *The Great Triumvirate: Webster, Clay, and Calhoun* (1987); David M. Potter, *The Impending Crisis, 1848–1861* (1976); Joel H. Silbey, *The Transformation of American Politics, 1840–1960* (1967); Kenneth M. Stampp,

America in 1857 (1991); Gerald W. Wolff, *The Kansas-Nebraska Bill* (1977).

The South and Slavery

William L. Barney, *The Secessionist Impulse* (1974); Steven A. Channing, *A Crisis of Fear: Secession in South Carolina* (1970); William J. Cooper, Jr., *The South and the Politics of Slavery, 1828–1856* (1978); Daniel W. Crofts, *Reluctant Confederates: Upper South Unionists in the Secession Crisis* (1989); Lacy K. Ford, Jr., *Origins of Southern Radicalism* (1988); William W. Freehling, *The Road to Disunion* (1990); Eugene D. Genovese, *The Political Economy of Slavery* (1967); Michael P. Johnson, *Toward a Patriarchal Republic: The Secession of Georgia* (1977); John Niven, *John C. Calhoun and the Price of Union* (1988); Thomas E. Schott, *Alexander H. Stephens of Georgia* (1988); William R. Stanton, *The Leopard's Spots* (1960); J. Mills Thornton III, *Politics and Power in a Slave Society* (1978); Ralph Wooster, *The Secession Conventions of the South* (1962).

The North and Antislavery

Dale Baum, *The Civil War Party System* (1984); Eugene H. Berwanger, *The Frontier Against Slavery* (1967); David Donald, *Charles Sumner and the Coming of the Civil War* (1960); Louis Filler, *The Crusade Against Slavery, 1830–1860* (1960); Eric Foner, *Free Soil, Free Labor, Free Men* (1970); Louis S. Gerteis, *Morality and Utility in American Antislavery Reform* (1987); William E. Gienapp, *The Origins of the Republican Party, 1852–1856* (1986); Robert W. Johannsen, *Stephen A. Douglas* (1973); Aileen S. Kraditor, *Means and Ends in American Abolitionism* (1969); Lewis Perry and Michael Fellman, eds., *Antislavery Reconsidered* (1979).

The Mexican War and Foreign Policy

K. Jack Bauer, *Zachary Taylor* (1985); Gene M. Brack, *Mexico Views Manifest Destiny, 1821–1846* (1976); Richard Griswold del Castillo, *The Treaty of Guadalupe Hidalgo* (1990); Neal Harlow, *California Conquered* (1982); Reginald Horsman, *Race and Manifest Destiny* (1981); Robert W. Johannsen, *To the Halls of the Montezumas: The Mexican War and the American Imagination* (1985); Ernest M. Lander, Jr., *Reluctant Imperialists: Calhoun, the South Carolinians, and the Mexican War* (1980); Robert E. May, *The Southern Dream of a Caribbean Empire, 1854–1861* (1973); Frederick Merk, *Manifest Destiny and Mission in American History* (1963); David M. Pletcher, *The Diplomacy of Annexation: Texas, Oregon, and the Mexican War* (1973); Dirk Raat, *Mexico and the United States* (1992); Anders Stephanson, *Manifest Destiny* (1995); David J. Weber, *The Mexican Frontier, 1821–1846* (1982).

CHAPTER

15

Transforming Fire: The Civil War

1861–1865

He was a living legend—a frontiersman who had a distinguished career as lawyer, congressman, and governor of Tennessee. But in 1829 he abruptly resigned his governorship and spent the next three years living among the Cherokees. In 1836 he reemerged as commander-in-chief of the armies winning Texan independence. He then served two terms as president of the Republic of Texas and later was a United States senator. After being elected governor of Texas in 1859, Sam Houston was deposed in March 1861. Why? Houston opposed secession, refused to take an oath of allegiance to the Confederacy, and challenged the authority of the secession convention. Its members ended his career by declaring his office vacant.

The Civil war brought astonishing, unexpected changes everywhere in the nation. For some, wealth changed to poverty and hope to despair; for others, the suffering of war spelled opportunity. Contrasts abounded between noble and crass motives. Even slaves, who hoped they were witnessing God's "Holy War for liberation," encountered unsympathetic liberators. When a Yankee soldier ransacked a slave woman's cabin, she denounced him for betraying his cause of freedom. Angrily the soldier contradicted her, saying, "I'm fightin' for $14 a month and the Union."

Northern troops were not the only ones to feel anger over their sacrifice. Impoverished by the war, one southern farmer had endured inflation, taxes, and shortages to support the Confederacy. Then an impressment agent arrived to take still more from him—grain and meat, horses and mules, and wagons. In return, the agent offered only a certificate promising repayment sometime in the future. Bitter and disgusted, the farmer declared, "The sooner this damned Government falls to pieces, the better it will be for us."

For these people and millions of others, the Civil War was a life-changing event. It obliterated the normal patterns and circumstances of life. Millions of men were swept away into training camps and battle units. Families struggled to survive without their men; businesses tried to cope with the loss of workers. Women in both North and South took on extra responsibilities in the home and moved into new jobs in the work force. No sphere of life was untouched.

Change was most drastic in the South, where the leaders of the secession movement had launched a revolution for the purpose of keeping things unchanged. Their actions, however, led to a war that turned southern life upside down, imperiled the very existence of slavery, and resulted in policies more objectionable to the elite than any proposed by President-elect Lincoln. Life in the Confederacy proved to be a shockingly unsouthern experience.

War altered the North as well, but less deeply. Because most of the fighting took place on southern soil, northern farms and factories remained virtually unscathed. The drafting of workers and the changing need for products slowed the pace of industrialization somewhat, but factories and businesses remained busy. Workers lost ground to inflation, but the economy hummed. A new probusiness atmosphere dominated Congress. To the alarm of many, the powers of the federal government and of the president increased during the war.

Ultimately, the Civil War forced on the nation new social and racial arrangements. Its greatest effect was to compel leaders and citizens to deal directly with the issue they had debated and argued over but had been unable to resolve: slavery.

 ## "Fighting Means Killing": The War in 1861 and 1862

Few Americans understood what they were getting into when the war began. The onset of hostilities sparked patriotic sentiments and joyous ceremonies in both North and South. Northern communities raised companies of volunteers eager to save the Union. In the South, confident recruits boasted of whipping the Yankees and returning home in time for dinner.

Through the spring of 1861 both sides scrambled to organize and train their armies. On July 21, 1861, the first battle took place outside Manassas Junction, Virginia, near a stream called Bull Run. General Irvin McDowell and 30,000 Union troops attacked General P. G. T. Beauregard's 22,000 southerners (see map, page 278). As raw recruits struggled amid the confusion of their first battle, federal forces began to gain ground. Then they ran into a line of Virginia troops under General Thomas Jackson. "There is Jackson standing like a stone wall," shouted one Confederate. "Stonewall" Jackson's line held, and the arrival of 9,000 Confederate reinforcements won the day for the South. Union troops fled back to Washington and shocked northerners, who feared their capital would be taken.

Battle of Bull Run

The unexpected rout at Bull Run gave northerners their first hint of the nature of the war to come. Victory would not be easy, even though the United States enjoyed an enormous advantage in resources. Pro-Union feeling was growing in western Virginia, and loyalties were divided in the four border slave states—Missouri, Kentucky, Maryland, and Delaware. But the rest of the Upper South had joined the Confederacy. Moved by an outpouring of regional loyalty, half a million southerners volunteered to fight.

Lincoln gave command of the army to General George B. McClellan, an officer who proved to be better at organization and training than at fighting. McClellan devoted the fall and winter of 1861 to readying a formidable force of a quarter-million men. The Union also began to implement other parts of its overall strategy, which called for a blockade of southern ports and eventual capture of the Mississippi River. Like a constricting snake, this "Anaconda plan" would strangle the Confederacy (see map, page 280). At first the Union Navy had too few ships to patrol 3,550 miles of coastline. Gradually, however, the navy increased the

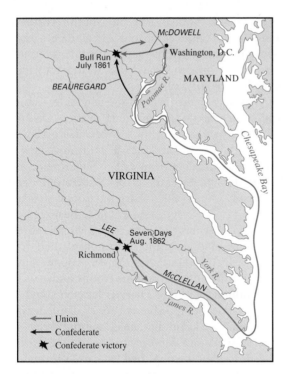

McClellan's Campaign   *The water route chosen by McClellan to threaten Richmond during the peninsular campaign.*

blockade's effectiveness, though it never bottled up southern commerce completely.

Confederate strategy was essentially defensive. A defensive posture not only was consistent with the South's claim that it merely wanted to be left alone, but also took into account the North's advantage in resources (see figure, page 281). Jefferson Davis, however, rejected a wholly defensive strategy. The South would pursue an "offensive defensive," taking advantage of opportunities to attack and using its interior lines of transportation to concentrate troops at crucial points.

Strategic thinking on both sides slighted the importance of "the West," that vast expanse of territory between Virginia and the Mississippi River. When the war began, both sides were unprepared for large-scale and sustained operations in the West, but before the end of the war it would prove to be a crucial theater.

The last half of 1861 brought no major land battles, but the North made gains by sea. Late in the summer Union naval forces captured Cape Hatteras and then seized Hilton Head, one of the Sea Islands off Port Royal, South Carolina (see map, page 280).

Union Naval Campaign

A few months later, similar operations secured vital coastal points in North Carolina, as well as Fort Pulaski, which defended Savannah. The coastal victories off South Carolina frightened planters, who abandoned their lands and fled. Their slaves greeted what they hoped to be freedom with rejoicing and broke the hated cotton gins. The Lincoln administration, however, was initially unwilling to wage a war against slavery and did not recognize their freedom.

The coastal incursions worried southerners, but the spring of 1862 brought even stronger evidence of the war's seriousness. In April Union ships commanded by Admiral David Farragut smashed through log booms blocking the Mississippi River and fought their way upstream to capture New Orleans. Farther west a Union victory at Elkhorn Tavern, Arkansas, shattered Confederate control of Indian Territory.

In February 1862 Union land and river forces in northern Tennessee won significant victories. There, General Ulysses S. Grant secured two prime routes to the Confederacy's heartland by capturing Forts Henry and Donelson. A path into Tennessee, Alabama, and Mississippi now lay open before the Union Army.

Grant's Campaign in Tennessee

Grant moved on into southern Tennessee and the first of the war's shockingly bloody encounters, the Battle of Shiloh. On April 6, Confederate General Albert Sidney Johnston caught Grant's troops with their backs to the Tennessee River. The Union forces took heavy casualties, but Johnson was killed. The next day federal reinforcements arrived and the Confederates withdrew. Neither side won a victory, yet the losses were staggering. Northern troops lost 13,000 men (killed, wounded, or cap-

Battle of Shiloh

• *Important Events* •

1861 Battle of Bull Run takes place
General George McClellan organizes
    Union Army
Union blockade begins
United States Congress passes first
    confiscation act
Trent affair
 	
1862 Union captures Fort Henry and Fort
    Donelson
United States Navy captures New Orleans
Battle of Shiloh shows the war's
    destructiveness
Confederacy enacts conscription
General Robert E. Lee thwarts McClellan's
    offensive on Richmond
United States Congress passes second
    confiscation act
Confederacy mounts offensive in Maryland
    and Kentucky
Battle of Antietam ends Lee's drive into
    Maryland
 	
1863 Emancipation Proclamation takes effect
United States Congress passes National
    Banking Act
Union enacts conscription
African-American soldiers join Union Army
Food riots occur in southern cities
	Battle of Chancellorsville ends in
	    Confederate victory but General
	    "Stonewall" Jackson's death
	Union wins key victories at Gettysburg and
	    Vicksburg
	Draft riots take place in New York City
	Battle of Chattanooga leaves South
	    vulnerable to General William T.
	    Sherman's march
	
	1864 Battles of the Wilderness and Spotsylvania
	    produce heavy casualties on both sides in
	    the effort to capture and defend Richmond
	Battle of Cold Harbor continues carnage
	    in Virginia
	Abraham Lincoln requests Republican Party
	    plank abolishing slavery
	General Sherman captures Atlanta
	Lincoln wins reelection
	Jefferson Davis proposes emancipation
	    within the Confederacy
	Sherman marches through Georgia
	
	1865 United States Congress approves Thirteenth
	    Amendment
	Hampton Roads Conference
	Lee abandons Richmond and Petersburg
	Lee surrenders at Appomattox Courthouse
	Lincoln assassinated

tured) out of 63,000; southerners sacrificed 11,000 out of 40,000.

Meanwhile, on the Virginia front, President Lincoln had a different problem. Conquest was impossible without battles, but General McClellan seemed unwilling to fight. Habitually overestimating the size of enemy forces, McClellan called repeatedly for reinforcements and ignored Lincoln's directions to advance. Finally McClellan chose to move by a roundabout water route, sailing his troops around the York peninsula and advancing on Richmond from the east (see map, page 278). By June the sheer size of the federal armies outside the Confederacy's capital was highly threatening. But southern leaders foiled McClellan's legions. First, Stonewall Jackson moved north into the Shenandoah valley behind Union forces and threatened Washington, D.C., drawing some of the federal troops away from Richmond to protect their own capital. Then, in a series of engagements known as the Seven Days Battles, General Robert E. Lee struck at McClellan's army and on August 3 McClellan withdrew to the Potomac. Richmond remained safe for almost two more years.

Buoyed by these results, Jefferson Davis conceived an ambitious plan to turn the tide of the war and gain recognition of the Confederacy by

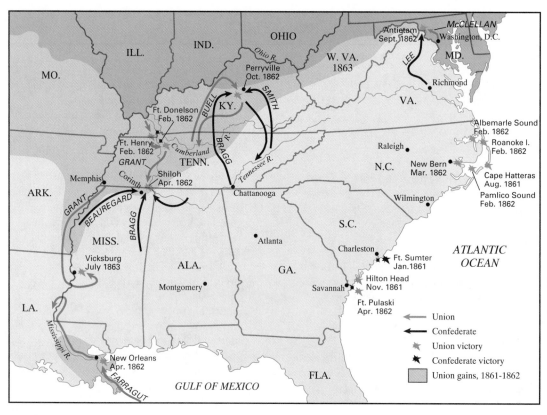

The Civil War, 1861–1863   *An overview of the Union's "Anaconda Plan" and key battles on the coast and in the West, 1861–1863.*

**Confederate
Offensive
in Maryland
and Kentucky**

European nations. He ordered a general offensive, sending Lee north into Maryland and Generals Kirby Smith and Braxton Bragg into Kentucky, calling on residents of Maryland and Kentucky to make a separate peace with his government.

The plan was promising, but every part of the offensive failed. In the bloodiest day of the entire war, September 17, 1862, McClellan turned Lee back in the Battle of Antietam near Sharpsburg, Maryland. In Kentucky Generals Smith and Bragg were also forced to withdraw. Outnumbered and disadvantaged in resources (see figure, page 281) and having failed in its general offensive, the South's only long-range hope seemed to be a tenacious defense and stoic endurance.

But 1862 also brought painful lessons to the North. Confederate General James E. B. (Jeb) Stuart executed a daring cavalry raid into Pennsylvania in October. Then on December 13 Union general Ambrose Burnside unwisely ordered his soldiers to attack Lee's army, which held fortified positions on high ground at Fredericksburg, Virginia. Lee's men controlled the engagement so thoroughly that Lee was moved to say, "It is well that war is so terrible. We should grow too fond of it."

 War Transforms the South

Even more than the fighting itself, disruptions in civilian life robbed southerners of their gaiety and nonchalance. The war altered southern society

Comparative Resources, Union and Confederate States, 1861

■ Union States   ■ Confederate States

Total Population, 2.5 to 1

Naval Ship Tonnage, 25 to 1

Farm Acreage, 3 to 1

Free Men 18–60 Yrs., 4.4 to 1

Factory Production Value, 10 to 1

Draft Animals, 1.8 to 1

44%   90%

Free Men in Military Service, 1864

Textile Goods Production, 14 to 1

Livestock, 1.5 to 1

Wealth Production, 3 to 1

Iron Production, 15 to 1

Wheat Production, 4.2 to 1

Railroad Mileage, 2.4 to 1

Coal Production, 38 to 1

Corn Production, 2 to 1

Merchant Ship Tonnage, 9 to 1

Firearms Production, 32 to 1

Cotton Production, 1 to 24

Comparative Resources, Union and Confederate States, 1861 *The North had vastly superior re-sources. Although the North's advantages in manpower and industrial capacity proved very important, the South could not really be conquered until it chose to give up the fight.* Source: From *The Times Atlas of World History.* Time Books, London, 1978. Used with permission.

beyond all expectations. One of the first traditions to fall was the southern preference for local government. The South had been characterized by limited government. States' rights had been its motto, but by modern standards even the state governments were weak. To withstand the massive power of the North, the South needed to centralize, and no one saw the necessity of centralization more clearly than Jefferson Davis.

Although Davis moved promptly to bring all arms, supplies, and troops under his control, by early 1862 the scope and duration of the conflict required something more. When the states failed to provide sufficient numbers of troops, Davis secured passage in April 1862 of the first national conscription (draft) law in American history. He also adopted a firm leadership role toward the

Confederate congress, which raised taxes and later passed a tax-in-kind—a tax paid in farm products. Where opposition arose, the government suspended the writ of habeas corpus (which prevented individuals from being held without trial) and imposed martial law. In the face of political opposition that cherished states' rights, Davis proved unyielding.

Soon the Confederate administration in Richmond was exercising virtually complete control over the southern economy. Because it controlled the supply of labor through conscription, the administration could compel industry to work on government contracts and supply the military's needs. The Confederate Congress also gave the central

Centralization of Power

In October 1862 in New York City, photographer Matthew Brady opened an exhibition of photographs from the Battle of Antietam. The camera, whose modern form had been invented only in 1826, made war's carnage hideously real. Although few knew it, Brady's vision was very poor, and this photograph of Confederate dead was actually made by his assistants, Alexander Gardner and James F. Gibson.   Confederate dead: Library of Congress; camera: George Eastman House Collection.

government almost complete control of the railroads; in 1864 shipping, too, came under extensive regulation. New statutes even limited corporate profits and dividends. A large bureaucracy sprang up to administer these operations. By the war's end, the southern bureaucracy was larger in proportion to population than its northern counterpart.

Clerks and subordinate officials crowded the towns and cities where Confederate departments had their offices. The sudden population booms

Effects of War on Southern Cities and Industry

that resulted overwhelmed the housing supply and stimulated new construction. The pressure was especially great in Richmond, whose population increased 250 percent. But there was another prime cause of urban growth in the South: industrialization. The Union blockade caused the traditionally agricultural South to become interested in industry. Davis exulted that manufacturing was making the

South "more and more independent of the rest of the world." Indeed, beginning almost from scratch, the Confederacy achieved tremendous feats of industrial development.

Southerners adopted new ways in response to these changes. Women, restricted to narrow roles in antebellum society, gained substantial new responsibilities. The wives and mothers of soldiers now headed households and performed men's work, adding to their traditional chores the tasks of raising crops and tending animals. Women in non-slaveowning families cultivated fields themselves, while wealthier women suddenly had to manage field hands. In cities, white women—who had been virtually excluded from the labor force—found a limited number of respectable new paying jobs. "Government girls" staffed the Confederate bureaucracy, and female schoolteachers became commonplace in the South for the first time. Some women gained confidence from their new responsibilities. Others, especially some wealthy women, found their changed situation and new tasks both difficult and distasteful.

Change in the Role of Southern Women

For millions of ordinary southerners the war brought privation and suffering. Mass poverty descended for the first time on a large minority of the white population. Many yeoman families had lost their breadwinners to the army. As a South Carolina newspaper put it, "The duties of war have called away from home the sole supports of many, many families. . . . Help must be given, or the poor will suffer." The poor sought help from relatives, neighbors, friends, anyone. Sometimes they pleaded their cases to the Confederate government.

Human Suffering

Other factors aggravated the effect of the labor shortage. The South was in many places so sparsely populated that the conscription of one skilled craftsman could work a hardship on the people of an entire county. Often they begged in unison for the exemption or discharge of a local miller, a neighborhood tanner, or—especially—a blacksmith needed to repair farm implements.

Inflation raged out of control, fueled by the Confederate government's heavy borrowing and inadequate taxes, until prices had increased almost 7,000 percent. Inflation particularly imperiled urban dwellers and the many who could no longer provide for themselves. As early as 1861 and 1862, newspapers reported that "want and starvation are staring thousands in the face." Some concerned citizens tried to help. "Free markets," which disbursed goods as charity, sprang up in various cities, and some families came to the aid of their neighbors. But other people were less generous. The need was so vast that it overwhelmed private charity. A rudimentary relief program organized by the Confederacy offered hope but was soon curtailed to supply the armies. Thus southern yeomen sank into poverty and suffering.

As their fortunes declined, people of once-modest means looked around and found abundant evidence that all classes were not sacrificing equally. They saw that the wealthy gave up only their luxuries, while many poor families went without necessities. And they noted that the Confederate government contributed to these inequities through policies that favored the upper class. Until the last year of the war, for example, prosperous southerners could avoid military service by hiring substitutes. Anger at such discrimination exploded in October 1862 when the Confederate Congress exempted from military duty anyone who was supervising at least twenty slaves. Protests poured in from every corner of the Confederacy, and North Carolina's legislators formally condemned the law. Its defenders argued, however, that the exemption preserved order and aided food production, and the statute remained on the books.

Inequities of the Confederate Draft

Dissension spread as growing numbers of citizens concluded that the struggle was "a rich man's war and a poor man's fight." Alert politicians and newspaper editors warned that class resentment was building to a dangerous level. The bitterness of letters to Confederate officials during this period suggests the depth of the people's anger. "If I and my little children suffer [and] die while there Father is in service," threatened one woman, "I invoke God Almighty that our blood rest upon the South." War was magnifying social tensions in the Confederacy.

 ## The Northern Economy Copes with War

With the onset of war, a tidal wave of change rolled over the North as well. Factories and citizens' associations geared up to support the war, and the federal government and its executive branch gained new powers. The energies of an industrializing, capitalist society were harnessed to serve the cause of the Union. Idealism and greed flourished together, and the northern economy proved its awesome productivity.

At first the war was a shock to business. Northern firms lost their southern markets, and many companies had to change their products and find new customers in order to remain open. Southern debts became uncollectible, jeopardizing not only northern merchants but also many western banks. In farming regions, families struggled with an aggravated shortage of labor.

Initial Slump in Northern Business

Overall the war slowed the pace of industrialization in the North, but its economic impact was not all negative. Certain entrepreneurs, such as wool producers, benefited from shortages of competing products. As demand for war-related goods soared, the federal government pumped unprecedented sums into the economy to feed the hungry war machine. Companies producing weapons, munitions, uniforms, boots, saddles, ships, and other war necessities soon prospered.

War production promoted the development of heavy industry in the North. Coal output rose substantially. Iron makers improved the quality of their product while boosting the production of pig iron. Foundries developed new and less expensive ways to make steel. Although new railroad construction slowed, repairs helped the manufacture of

Effects of War on Northern Industry and Agriculture

rails to increase. Of considerable significance for the future was the railroad industry's adoption of a standard gauge (width) for track, which eliminated the unloading and reloading of boxcars and created a unified transportation system.

Another strength of the northern economy was the complementary relationship between agriculture and industry. Mechanization of agriculture had begun before the war. Wartime recruitment and conscription, however, gave western farmers an added incentive to purchase labor-saving machinery. The shift from human labor to machines created new markets for industry and expanded the food supply for the urban industrial work force. Mechanization also meant that northern farm families whose breadwinners went to war did not suffer as their counterparts did in the South. "We have seen," one magazine observed, "a stout matron whose sons are in the army, cutting hay with her team . . . and she cut seven acres with ease in a day, riding leisurely upon her cutter."

Compared with farmers, northern industrial and urban workers did not fare so well. After the initial slump, jobs became plentiful, but inflation ate up much of a worker's paycheck. Between 1860 and 1864 consumer prices rose at least 76 percent, while daily wages rose only 42 percent. Workers' families consequently suffered a substantial decline in their standard of living.

As their real wages shrank, industrial workers lost job security. To increase production, some employers were replacing workers with labor-saving machines. Other employers urged the government to promote immigration so they could import cheap labor. Workers responded by forming unions and sometimes by striking. Skilled craftsmen organized to combat the loss of their jobs and status to machines; women and unskilled workers, excluded by the craftsmen, formed their own unions. In recognition of the increasingly national scope of business activity, thirteen occupational groups—including tailors, coal miners, and railway engineers—formed national unions during the Civil War.

New Militancy Among Northern Workers

Employers reacted with hostility to this new spirit among workers. Manufacturers viewed labor activism as a threat to their property rights and freedom of action, and accordingly formed statewide or craft-based associations to cooperate and pool information. These employers shared blacklists of union members and required new workers to sign "yellow dog" contracts (promises not to join a union). To put down strikes, they hired strikebreakers from the ranks of the poor and desperate—blacks, immigrants, and women— and sometimes received additional help from federal troops.

Troublesome as unions were, they did not prevent many employers from making a profit. The highest profits were made from profiteering on government contracts. Unscrupulous businessmen took advantage of the suddenly immense demand for army supplies by selling clothing and blankets made of "shoddy"—wool fibers reclaimed from rags or worn cloth. Shoddy goods often came apart in the rain; most of the shoes purchased in the early months of the war were worthless, too. Contractors sold inferior guns for double the usual price and passed off tainted meat as good.

Legitimate enterprises also made healthy profits. The output of woolen mills increased so dramatically that dividends in the industry nearly tripled. Some cotton mills made record profits on what they sold, even though they reduced their output. Railroads carried immense quantities of freight and passengers, increasing their business to the point that railroad stocks doubled or even tripled in value.

Wartime Benefits to Northern Business

Railroads also were a leading beneficiary of government largesse. Congress had failed in the 1850s to resolve the question of a northern versus a southern route for the first transcontinental railroad. With the South absent from Congress, the northern route quickly prevailed. In 1862 and 1864 Congress chartered two corporations, the Union Pacific Railroad and the Central Pacific Railroad, and assisted them financially in connecting Omaha, Nebraska, with Sacramento, California. Overall, the two corporations gained approximately 20 million acres of public land and nearly $60 million in loans.

Morrill Land Grant Act

Other businessmen benefited handsomely from the Morrill Land Grant Act (1862). To promote public education in agriculture, engineering, and military science, Congress granted each state 30,000 acres of federal land for each of its congressional districts. Hard-pressed to meet wartime expenses, some states sold their land cheaply to wealthy entrepreneurs. Still, the intent of the land grant act was fulfilled in that the law eventually fostered sixty-nine colleges and universities.

Higher tariffs also pleased many businessmen. Northern businesses did not uniformly favor high import duties; some manufacturers desired cheap imported raw materials more than they feared foreign competition. But northeastern congressmen traditionally supported higher tariffs, and after southern lawmakers left Washington, they had their way: the Tariff Act of 1864 raised tariffs generously. Some healthy industries earned artificially high profits by raising their prices to a level just below that of the foreign competition. By 1865, tariff rates were more than double those of 1857.

 ## Wartime Society in the North

The outbreak of war stimulated patriotism in the North just as it initially had done in the South. Northern society, which had suffered the stresses associated with industrialization, immigration, and widespread social change, found a unifying cause in the preservation of the nation. In thousands of self-governing towns and communities, northern citizens felt a personal connection to representative government. Secession threatened to destroy their system, and northerners rallied to its defense.

Such enthusiasm proved useful as northerners encountered a multitude of wartime changes. The powers of the federal government and the

Expanded Powers of the United States President

president grew steadily during the crisis. At the beginning of the conflict, President Lincoln launched a major shipbuilding program without waiting for Congress to assemble. The lawmakers later approved his decision, and Lincoln continued to act in advance of Congress when he deemed such action necessary. In one striking exercise of executive power, Lincoln, acting to ensure the loyalty of Maryland, suspended the writ of habeas corpus for everyone living between Washington, D.C. and Philadelphia. On occasion Lincoln used his wartime authority to bolster his own political fortunes. He and his generals proved adept at furloughing soldiers so they could vote in close elections; those whom Lincoln furloughed, of course, usually voted Republican.

Among the clearest examples of the wartime expansion of federal authority were the National Banking Acts of 1863, 1864, and 1865. Before the Civil War, the nation lacked a uniform currency. Banks operating under state charters issued no fewer than seven thousand different kinds of notes, which were difficult to distinguish from a variety of forgeries. On the recommendation of Secretary of the Treasury Salmon Chase, Congress established a national banking system empowered to issue national bank notes. At the close of the war in 1865, Congress imposed a prohibitive tax on state bank notes and forced most state institutions to join the national system.

War also bred changes in social attitudes on the home front, and some of the lavish displays would have shocked the soldiers in the field. In

Extravagance Amid War

the largest cities, an eagerness to display one's wealth flourished. *Harper's Monthly* reported that "the suddenly enriched contractors, speculators, and stock-jobbers . . . are spending money with a profusion never before witnessed in our country. . . . The men button their waistcoats with diamonds . . . and the women powder their hair with gold and silver dust." And a writer for the *New York Herald* observed that the "individual who makes the most money—no matter how—and spends the most—no matter for what—is considered the greatest man."

Yet idealism coexisted with ostentation. Abolitionists, after initial uncertainty over whether to let the South go, campaigned to turn the war into a crusade against slavery. Free black communities and churches both black and white responded to the needs of slaves who flocked to the Union lines, sending clothing, ministers, and teachers to aid the runaways.

Northern women, like their southern counterparts, took on new roles. Those who stayed home organized over ten thousand soldiers' aid societies, rolled innumerable bandages, and raised $3 million to aid injured troops. Thousands served as nurses in front-line hospitals, where they pressed for better care of the wounded. Women, however, had to fight for a chance to serve at all. The professionalization of medicine since the Revolution had created a medical system dominated by men, and many male physicians did not want women's aid. Female nurses proved their worth, but only the wounded welcomed them. Even Clara Barton, the most famous female nurse, was ousted from her post in 1863.

Thus northern society embraced strangely contradictory tendencies. Materialism and greed flourished alongside idealism, religious conviction, and self-sacrifice. While some risked their lives willingly out of a desire to preserve the Union or extend freedom, others avoided military service by providing a substitute or paying a $300 commutation fee. In all, 118,000 substitutes were provided and 87,000 commutations paid before Congress ended the commutation system in 1864.

 ## The Strange Advent of Emancipation

At the highest levels of government in the United States and in the Confederacy there was a similar lack of clarity about the purpose of the war. Both Davis and Lincoln studiously avoided references to slavery. Davis, realizing that emphasis on the issue could increase class conflict in the South, told southerners they were fighting for constitutional liberty. Lincoln avoided the issue because he did not want to anger the border slave states. He also hoped that a pro-Union majority would assert itself in the South. It might be possible, he thought, to coax the South back into the Union and stop the fighting. Moreover, not all Republicans burned with moral outrage over slavery. A forthright stand by Lincoln on the subject of slavery could split the party, gratifying some groups and alienating others.

Lincoln first broached the subject of slavery in a substantive way in March 1862, when he proposed that the states consider emancipation on

Lincoln's Plan for Gradual Emancipation

their own. He asked Congress to promise aid to any state that decided to emancipate, and he appealed to border-state representatives to consider this course seriously. What Lincoln proposed was gradual emancipation, with compensation for slaveholders and colonization of the freed slaves outside the United States, in some region like Central America. To a delegation of free blacks he explained that "it is better for us both . . . to be separated." Thus his was a conservative scheme, and since the states would make the decision voluntarily, no responsibility for it would attach to Lincoln.

Others wanted to go much further. A group of Republicans in Congress, known as the Radicals, had from the early days of the war concerned themselves with slavery. In

Confiscation Acts

August 1861, at the Radicals' instigation, Congress passed its first confiscation act. Designed to punish the Confederate rebels, the law confiscated all property used for "insurrectionary purposes." Thus if the South used slaves in a hostile action, those slaves were declared seized and liberated. A second confiscation act (July 1862) was much more drastic: it confiscated the property of all those who supported the rebellion, even those who merely resided in the South and paid Confederate taxes. Their slaves were declared "forever free of their servitude, and not again [to be] held as slaves." Let the government use its full powers, free the slaves, and crush the revolution, urged the Radicals.

Lincoln refused to adopt that view. He stood by his proposal of voluntary gradual emancipation by the states and made no effort to enforce the second confiscation act. His stance provoked a public protest from Horace Greeley, editor of the powerful *New York Tribune*. In an open letter to the president, Greeley pleaded with Lincoln to "execute the laws" and declared, "On the face of this wide earth, Mr. President, there is not one disinterested, determined, intelligent champion of the Union cause who does not feel that all attempts to put down the Rebellion and at the same time uphold its inciting cause are preposterous and futile."

Lincoln's reply was an explicit statement of his complex and calculated approach to the question: "I would save the Union. If I could save the Union without freeing *any* slave I would do it, and if I could save it by freeing *all* the slaves I would do it; and if I could save it by freeing some and leaving others alone I would also do that. What I do about slavery, and the colored race, I do because I believe it helps to save the Union."

When he wrote those words, Lincoln had already decided on a new step: issuance of the Emancipation Proclamation. On the advice of the cabinet, however, he was waiting for a Union victory before announcing the proclamation.

Emancipation Proclamations

On September 22, 1862, shortly after the Battle of Antietam, Lincoln issued the first part of his two-part proclamation. Invoking his powers as commander-in-chief of the armed forces, he announced that on January 1, 1863, he would emancipate the slaves in states whose people "shall then be in rebellion against the United States." Thus his September proclamation was less a declaration of the right of slaves to be free than a threat to southerners to end the war. Lincoln may not actually have expected southerners to give up their effort, but he was careful to offer them the option, thus putting the onus of emancipation on them.

When Lincoln designated the areas in rebellion on January 1, his proclamation excepted every Confederate county or city that had fallen under Union control. Those areas, he declared, "are, for the present, left precisely as if this proclamation were not issued." Nor did Lincoln liberate slaves in the border slave states that remained in the Union. "The President has purposely made the proclamation inoperative in all places where . . . the slaves [are] accessible," charged the anti-administration *New York World*. "He has proclaimed emancipation only where he has notoriously no power to execute it."

As a moral and legal document, the Emancipation Proclamation, which in reality freed no slaves, was inadequate. As a political document it was nearly flawless. Because the proclamation defined the war as a war against slavery, radicals could applaud it, even if the president had not gone as far as Congress. Yet at the same time it protected Lincoln's position with conservatives, leaving him room to retreat if he chose and forcing no immediate changes on the border slave states.

The need for men soon convinced the administration to recruit northern and southern blacks for the Union Army. By the spring of 1863, African-American troops were proving their value. Lincoln came to see them as "the great *available* and yet *unavailed of* force for restoring the Union." African-American leaders hoped that military service would secure equal rights for their people. Once the black soldier had fought for the Union, wrote Frederick Douglass, "there is no power on earth which can deny that he has earned the right of citizenship in the United States."

In June 1864, Lincoln gave his support to a constitutional ban on slavery. On the eve of the Republican national convention, Lincoln called the party's chairman to the White House and instructed him to have the party "put into the platform as the keystone, the amendment of the Constitution abolishing and prohibiting slavery forever." The party promptly called for a new amendment, the Thirteenth. Lincoln demonstrated his commitment by lobbying Congress for quick approval of the measure. The proposed amendment passed in 1865 and was sent to the states for ratification or rejection. Lincoln's strong support for the Thirteenth Amendment—an unequivocal prohibition of slavery—constitutes his best claim to the title "Great Emancipator."

Yet Lincoln soon clouded that clear stand, for in 1865 the newly reelected president considered allowing the defeated southern states to reenter the Union and delay or defeat the amendment. In February he and Secretary of State Seward met with three Confederate commissioners at Hampton Roads, Virginia. With the end of the war in sight, Lincoln was apparently contemplating the creation of a new national party based on a postwar alliance with southern Whigs and moderate and conservative Republicans. The cement for the coalition would be concessions to planter interests.

Hampton Roads Conference

Pointing out that the Emancipation Proclamation was only a war measure, Lincoln predicted that the courts would decide whether it had granted all, some, or none of the slaves their freedom. Seward observed that the Thirteenth Amendment, which would be definitive, was not yet ratified and that reentry into the Union would allow the southern states to defeat it. Lincoln did not contradict Seward but spoke in favor of "prospective" ratification: approval with the effective date postponed for five years. He also promised to seek $400 million in compensation for slaveholders. The financial aid would provide an economic incentive for planters to rejoin the Union and capital to cushion the economic blow of emancipation. Most northerners opposed such proposals. In the South, Jefferson Davis, who rejected anything short of independence, prevented them from being discussed.

Before the war was over, the Confederacy, too, addressed the issue of emancipation. Jefferson Davis offered a strong proposal in favor of liberation. He was dedicated to independence, and he was willing to sacrifice slavery to achieve that goal. After considering the alternatives for some time, Davis concluded late in 1864 that the military status of the Confederacy was desperate and that independence with emancipation was preferable to defeat with emancipation. He proposed that the Confederate government purchase forty thousand

Davis's Plan for Emancipation

slaves to work for the army as laborers, with a promise of freedom at the end of their service. Soon Davis upgraded his proposal, calling for the recruitment and arming of slaves as soldiers, who likewise would gain their freedom at the end of the war. The wives and children of these soldiers, he made plain, must also receive freedom from the states.

Confederate emancipation began too late to revive southern armies or win diplomatic advantages with antislavery Europeans. By contrast, Lincoln's Emancipation Proclamation stimulated a vital infusion of forces into the Union armies. Beginning in 1863, slaves shouldered arms for the North. Before the war was over, 134,000 slaves (and 52,000 free African-Americans) had fought for freedom and the Union. Their participation aided northern victory while it discouraged recognition of the Confederacy by foreign governments.

The Soldier's War

The intricacies of policymaking were far from the minds of ordinary soldiers. Military service completely altered their lives. Army life meant tedium, physical hardship, and separation from loved ones even in the best of times. Soldiers in battle confronted fear and danger, and the risk of death from wounds or disease was very high. For many soldiers, however, wartime experiences led to bonds with their comrades and a connection to a noble purpose that they cherished for years afterward.

Soldiers benefited from certain new products, such as canned condensed milk, but blankets, clothing, and arms were often of poor quality. Vermin abounded. Hospitals were badly managed at first. Rules of hygiene in large camps were badly written or unenforced; latrines were poorly made or carelessly used. Water supplies were unsafe and typhoid epidemics common. About 57,000 army men died from dysentery and diarrhea. Overall, the Union death toll of 224,000 from disease or accidents vastly exceeded the 140,000 who died as a result of battle.

On both sides troops quickly learned that soldiering was far from glorious. Beyond sleeping on the ground in all types of weather, being unable to wash one's clothes, and dealing with body lice, there was carnage. "Any one who goes over a battlefield after a battle," wrote one Confederate, "never cares to go over another. . . . It is a sad sight to see the dead and if possible more sad to see the wounded—shot in every possible way you can imagine."

Realities of a Soldier's Life

Advances in technology made the Civil War particularly deadly. By far the most important were the rifle and the "minie ball." Bullets fired from a smooth-bore musket tumbled and wobbled as they flew through the air and thus were not accurate at distances over eighty yards. Cutting spiraled grooves inside the barrel gave the projectile a spin and much greater accuracy, but rifles remained difficult to load and use until the Frenchman Claude Minie and the American James Burton developed a new kind of bullet. Civil War bullets were sizable lead slugs with a cavity at the bottom that expanded upon firing so that the bullet "took" the rifling and flew accurately. With these bullets, rifles were accurate at four hundred yards and useful up to one thousand yards.

This meant, of course, that soldiers assaulting a position defended by riflemen were in greater peril than ever before, and the toll from Civil War battles was very high. Never before in Europe or America had such massive forces pummeled each other with weapons of such destructive power. Yet even in the bloodiest engagements, in which thousands of men died, the losing army was never destroyed.

Impact of the Rifle

Civil War soldiers nonetheless developed deep commitments to each other and to their task. The bonding may have been most dramatic among officers and men in the northern black regiments, for there white and black troops took their first steps toward bridging a deep racial divide. Racism in the Union Army was strong. Most white soldiers wanted nothing to do

Black Soldiers Fight for Acceptance

How do historians know what the average soldier thought and felt? A vast number of diaries and letters written by soldiers have been preserved in archives and libraries and reveal a wide range of experiences. Many soldiers acted on noble ideals, but others did not. Papers at the University of Michigan document one Union soldier's worry that *"If this experiment in self-government by the people shall fail, where are the oppressed and the downtrodden millions of the earth to look for hope of better days?"* They also contain letters from Private Robert Sherry of New York, shown here. Sherry cared little for the Republican Party. The enlisted men and officers in his regiment rarely got along, and after twenty soldiers were sent to Dry Tortugas, in the Gulf of Mexico, as punishment for a mutiny, Sherry wrote bitterly that he hoped *"to see the day when we will get into some battle that will be the means of getting a great portion of our Officers killed or wounded."* A rough man in a rough regiment, Sherry enjoyed looting and fighting. William I. Clements Library University of Michigan.

with black people and regarded them as inferior. "I never came out here for to free the black devils," wrote one soldier. For many, acceptance of black troops grew only because they could do heavy labor and "stop Bullets as well as white people."

But some changed their initial views. White officers who volunteered for black units only to gain promotion found that experience altered their opinions. One general reported that his "colored regiments" possessed "remarkable aptitude for military training," and another observer said, "They fight like fiends." Black troops created this change through their dedication. They had a mission to destroy slavery and demonstrate their equality. Corporal James Henry Gooding of Massachusetts's black 54th Regiment explained that his unit intended "to live down all prejudice against its color, by a determination to do well in any position it is put." After an engagement he was proud that "a regiment of white men gave us three cheers as we were passing them," because "it shows that we did our duty as men should."

African-Americans demonstrated valor in battle despite blatant discrimination. The Union government, for instance, paid white privates $13 per month plus a $3.50 clothing allowance. Black privates received $10 a month, less $3 for clothing.

The Tide of Battle Begins to Turn

The fighting in the spring and summer of 1863 did not settle the war, but it began to place clear limits on the outcome. The campaigns began in a deceptively positive way for Confederates, as their Army of Northern Virginia performed brilliantly in the Battle of Chancellorsville. On May 2 and 3, some 130,000 members of the Union Army of the Potomac bore down on fewer than 60,000 Confederates. Boldly, as if they enjoyed being outnumbered, Lee and Stonewall Jackson divided their forces, ordering 30,000 men under Jackson on a day-long march westward to gain position for a flank attack. Jackson's seasoned "foot cavalry"

Battle of Chancellorsville

found unprepared Union troops laughing, smoking, and playing cards. The Confederate attack drove the entire right side of the Union Army back in confusion. The next day Union forces left in defeat. Chancellorsville was a remarkable southern victory but costly because Jackson's own men had inadvertently killed him.

July brought crushing defeats for the Confederacy in two critical battles—Vicksburg and Gettysburg—that effectively circumscribed Confederate hopes for independence. Vicksburg was the last major fortification on the Mississippi River in southern hands. With the intent of cutting the Confederacy in half and securing a path to its interior, General Grant laid siege to the city in May. Meanwhile, General Robert E. Lee proposed a Confederate invasion of the North.

Battle of Vicksburg

Lee's troops streamed through western Maryland and into Pennsylvania, threatening both Washington and Baltimore. The possibility of a major victory near the Union capital became more and more likely. Confederate prospects along the Mississippi, however, darkened. Davis repeatedly wired General Joseph E. Johnston, urging him to concentrate his forces and attack Grant's army. Johnston, however, did nothing effective. Grant's men, meanwhile, were supplying themselves from the abundant crops of the Mississippi River valley and could continue their siege indefinitely.

In such circumstances the fall of Vicksburg was inevitable, and on July 4, 1863, its commander surrendered. The same day a battle that had been raging for three days concluded at Gettysburg, Pennsylvania. On July 1 Confederate forces collided with part of the Union Army. Heavy fighting on the second day left federal forces in possession of high ground along Cemetery Ridge. There they enjoyed the protection of a stone wall and a clear view of their foe across almost a mile of open field. Undaunted, Lee believed his splendid troops could break the Union line, and on July 3 he ordered a direct assault. Brave troops under General George E. Pickett marched up the slope

Battle of Gettysburg

in a doomed assault later known as Pickett's Charge. For a moment a hundred Confederates breached the enemy's line, but most fell in heavy slaughter. On July 4 Lee withdrew, having suffered almost 4,000 dead and about 24,000 missing and wounded.

Southern troops displayed unforgettable courage and dedication at Gettysburg, but the results there and at Vicksburg were disastrous. The Confederacy was split in two, with its heartland exposed to invasion. Moreover, Lee's defeat spelled the end of major southern offensive actions. Too weak to prevail in attack, the Confederacy henceforth would have to conserve its limited resources and rely on a prolonged defense.

The Disintegration of Confederate Unity

Both northern and southern governments waged the final two years of the war in the face of increasing opposition at home. Dissatisfactions that had surfaced earlier grew more intense and sometimes violent. The gigantic costs of a war that neither side seemed able to win fed the unrest. But protest also arose from fundamental stresses in the social structures of North and South.

One ominous development was the planters' increasing opposition to their own government, whose actions often had a negative effect on them. Not only did the Richmond government impose new taxes and the tax-in-kind, but Confederate military authorities also impressed slaves to build fortifications. And when Union forces advanced on plantation areas, Confederate commanders burned stores of cotton that lay in the enemy's path. Such interference with plantation routines and financial interests was not what planters had expected of their government, and they complained bitterly.

Nor were the centralizing policies and the increasing size and power of the Richmond administration popular. In fact, the Confederate constitution had granted substantial powers to the central government. But many planters assumed with R. B. Rhett, editor of the *Charleston Mercury*, that the Confederate constitution "leaves the

States untouched in their Sovereignty, and commits to the Confederate Government only a few simple objects, and a few simple powers to enforce them."

Years of opposition to the federal government within the Union had frozen southerners in a defensive posture. Now they erected the barrier of states' rights as a defense against change. Planters sought, above all, a guarantee that their plantations and their lives would remain untouched; they were not deeply committed either to building a southern nation or to winning independence. If the Confederacy had been allowed to depart from the Union in peace and continue as a semideveloped cotton-growing region, they would have been content. When secession revolutionized their world, they could not or would not adjust.

Meanwhile, for ordinary southerners, the dire predictions of hunger and suffering were becoming a reality. Food riots occurred in the spring of 1863 in Atlanta, Macon, Columbus, and Augusta, Georgia, and in Salisbury and High Point, North Carolina. On April 2, a crowd assembled in Richmond, the Confederate capital, to demand relief. A passerby, noticing the excitement, asked a young girl, "Is there some celebration?" "We celebrate our right to live," replied the girl. "We are starving. As soon as enough of us get together we are going to the bakeries and each of us will take a loaf of bread." Soon they did just that, sparking a riot that Davis himself had to quell at gunpoint.

Food Riots in Southern Cities

Throughout the rural South, ordinary people resisted more quietly—by refusing to cooperate with conscription, tax collection, and impressments of food. "In all the States impressments are evaded by every means which ingenuity can suggest, and in some openly resisted," wrote a high-ranking commissary officer. Farmers who did provide food for the army refused to accept payment in certificates of credit or government bonds, as required by law. Conscription officers increasingly found no one to draft—men of draft age were hiding out in the forests.

Such discontent was certain to affect the Confederate armies. Worried about their loved ones and resentful of what they saw as a rich man's war,

Desertions from the Confederate Army

large numbers of men did indeed leave the armies. The problem of desertion became so acute by late 1863 that Secretary of War James Seddon admitted that one-third of the army could not be accounted for. The situation was to worsen.

The defeats at Gettysburg and Vicksburg dealt a body blow to Confederate morale. In desperation President Davis and several state governors resorted to threats and racial scare tactics to drive southern whites to further sacrifice. Instead of greater sacrifices, the pace of internal disintegration quickened. Support from the common people waned, and a few newspapers began openly to call for peace.

Southern Peace Movements

In North Carolina a peace movement grew under the leadership of William W. Holden, a popular Democratic politician and editor. Over one hundred public meetings took place there in the summer of 1863 in support of peace negotiations. Early in 1864, Governor Joseph E. Brown and Alexander H. Stephens, vice president of the Confederacy, led a similar effort in Georgia. Although these movements ultimately came to naught, the fact that they existed at all demonstrates deep disaffection.

By 1864 much of the opposition to the war had moved entirely outside the political sphere. Southerners were simply giving up the struggle and withdrawing their cooperation from the government. Deserters dominated whole towns and counties. Secret societies favoring reunion sprang up. Active dissent spread everywhere and was particularly common in upland and mountain regions. The government was losing the support of its citizens.

Antiwar Sentiment in the North

In the North opposition to the war was similar but less severe. Alarm intensified over the growing centralization of government, and war-weariness was widespread. Resentment of the draft sparked protest, especially among poor citizens, and the

Union Army struggled with a desertion rate as high as the Confederates'. But the Union was so much richer than the South in human resources that fresh recruits were always available and its people never faced food shortages.

Also, Lincoln possessed a talent Davis lacked: he knew how to stay in touch with the ordinary citizen. Through letters to newspapers and to soldiers' families, he reached the common people and demonstrated that he had not forgotten them. The daily carnage, the tortuous political problems, and the ceaseless criticism weighed heavily on him. But this self-educated man of humble origins was able to communicate his suffering with words that helped to contain northern discontent.

Peace Democrats

Much of the wartime protest in the North was political in origin. The Democratic Party fought to regain power by blaming Lincoln for the war's carnage, the expansion of federal powers, inflation and the high tariff, and the emancipation of blacks. Appealing to tradition, its leaders called for an end to the war and reunion on the basis of "the Constitution as it is and the Union as it was." The Democrats denounced conscription and martial law and defended states' rights and the interests of agriculture. In the 1862 congressional elections, the Democrats made a strong comeback, and peace Democrats had influence in New York State and majorities in the legislatures of Illinois and Indiana.

Led by outspoken men like Representative Clement L. Vallandigham of Ohio, the peace Democrats made themselves highly visible. Vallandigham criticized Lincoln as a dictator who had suspended the writ of habeas corpus without congressional authority and had arrested thousands of innocent citizens. Like other Democrats, Vallandigham condemned both conscription and emancipation. He stayed carefully within legal bounds, but his attacks seemed so damaging to the war effort that military authorities arrested him for treason after Lincoln suspended habeas corpus. Lincoln wisely decided against punishment—and martyr's status—for the senator and exiled him to the Confederacy.

Lincoln believed that antiwar Democrats were linked to secret organizations that harbored traitorous ideas. Likening such groups to a poisonous snake, Republicans sometimes branded them— and by extension the peace Democrats—as Copperheads. Though Democrats were connected with these organizations, most engaged in politics rather than treason.

More violent opposition to the government arose from ordinary citizens facing the draft enacted in 1863. The urban poor and immigrants in strongly Democratic areas were especially hostile to conscription. Many men managed to avoid the army by hiring a substitute or paying commutation, but the poor viewed the commutation fee as discriminatory. Many immigrants suspected (wrongly, on the whole) that they were called in disproportionate numbers.

As a result, enrolling officers received rough treatment in many parts of the North, and riots occurred in New Jersey, Ohio, Indiana, Pennsylvania, Illinois, and Wisconsin.

New York City Draft Riot

By far the most serious outbreak of violence occurred in New York City in July 1863, where three days of rioting left seventy-four people dead. The riots had racist and class overtones. Working-class New Yorkers feared an inflow of black labor from the South, and Irish immigrants resented being forced to serve in the place of others who could afford to avoid the draft.

Discouragement and war-weariness reached a peak in the summer of 1864, when the Democratic Party nominated the popular General George B. McClellan for president and inserted a peace plank into its platform. Lincoln, running with Tennessee's Andrew Johnson on a "National Union" ticket, concluded that it was "exceedingly probable that this Administration will not be re-elected." The fortunes of war, however, soon changed the electoral situation.

Northern Pressure and Southern Will

The North's long-term diplomatic goal was to prevent recognition of the Confederacy by European nations and the financial and military aid it would bring. The British

Northern Diplomatic Strategy

elite, however, felt considerable sympathy for southern planters, whose aristocratic values were similar to their own. And both England and France stood to benefit from a divided and weakened America. Thus to achieve their goal, Lincoln and Secretary of State Seward needed to avoid both serious military defeats and unnecessary controversies with the European powers.

Aware that the textile industry employed one-fifth of the British population directly or indirectly, southerners assumed that British leaders would have to recognize the Confederacy. But at the beginning of the war, British mills had a 50 percent surplus of cotton on hand; later, new sources of supply helped to meet Britain's needs. Refusing to be stampeded into recognition of the Confederacy, the British government kept its eye on the battlefield. France, though sympathetic to the South, was unwilling to act independently of Britain.

More than once the Union strategy nearly broke down. In one crisis in 1861, the commander of an American frigate stopped the British steamer *Trent* and removed two Confederate ambassadors. The British protested this violation of freedom of the seas and demanded the prisoners' release. Lincoln and Seward waited until northern public opinion cooled and then released the two southerners. Another incident that sparked vigorous protest from the North was the sale to the Confederacy of warships constructed in England. A few English-built ships, notably the *Alabama*, reached open water to serve the South. Over a period of twenty-two months, the *Alabama* destroyed or captured more than sixty northern ships. But the British government, as a neutral power, soon barred delivery of warships such as the Laird rams, formidable vessels whose pointed prows were designed to end the blockade by battering the Union ships.

Despite such diplomatic victories, the northern victory on the battlefield was far from won in 1864. Military authorities had long agreed that deep invasion is extremely risky: the farther an army penetrates enemy territory, the more vulnerable its own communications and support become. General Grant, by now in command of all the federal armies, decided to test these conditions—and southern will—with a strategic innovation of his own: raids on a massive scale. Grant proposed to use whole armies, not just cavalry, to destroy Confederate railroads, thus ruining the enemy's transportation and damaging the South's economy. Abandoning their lines of support, Union troops would live off the land while laying to waste all resources useful to the military and to the civilian population of the Confederacy. After General George H. Thomas's troops won the Battle of Chattanooga in November 1863 by ignoring orders and charging up Missionary Ridge, the heartland of the South lay open. Moving to Virginia, Grant entrusted General Sherman with 100,000 men for a raid deep into the South, toward Atlanta.

Jefferson Davis countered by positioning the army of General Joseph E. Johnston in Sherman's path. Davis's entire political strategy for 1864 was based on demonstrating Confederate military strength and successfully defending Atlanta. The United States presidential election of 1864 was approaching, and Davis hoped that southern resolve would lead to the defeat of Lincoln and the election of a president who would sue for peace. When General Johnston slowly but steadily fell back toward Atlanta, Davis grew anxious and sought assurances that Atlanta would be held. From a purely military point of view, Johnston maneuvered skillfully, but Davis replaced him with the one-legged General John Hood, who knew his job was to fight. Hood attacked but was beaten, and Sherman's army occupied Atlanta on September 2, 1864. The victory buoyed northern spirits, ensured Lincoln's reelection, and cleared the way for Sherman's march from Atlanta to the sea (see map below).

Sherman's army was an unusually formidable force, composed almost entirely of battle-tested

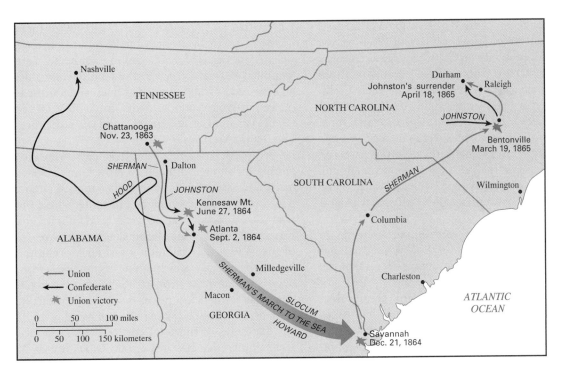

Sherman's March to the Sea   *The West proved a decisive theater at the end of the war. From Chattanooga, Union forces drove into Georgia, capturing Atlanta. Then General Sherman embarked on his march of destruction through Georgia to the coast and then northward through the Carolinas.*

The March to the Sea

veterans and officers who had risen through the ranks. Tanned, bearded, tough, and unkempt, they were determined, as one put it, "to Conquer this Rebelien or Die." As the army marched across Georgia, it cut a path 50 to 60 miles wide and more than 200 miles long. The totality of the destruction they caused was awesome. A Georgia woman described the "Burnt Country" this way: "The fields were trampled down and the road was lined with carcasses of horses, hogs, and cattle that the invaders, unable either to consume or to carry with them, had wantonly shot down to starve our people and prevent them from making their crops. The stench in some places was unbearable." Such devastation diminished the South's material resources and sapped its will to resist.

In Virginia the preliminaries to victory proved protracted and ghastly. Throughout the spring and summer of 1864, intent on capturing Richmond, Grant hurled his troops at Lee's army in Virginia and suffered appalling losses: almost 18,000 casualties in the Battle of the Wilderness; more than 8,000 at Spotsylvania; and 12,000 in the space of a few hours at Cold Harbor. Before the last battle, Union troops pinned scraps of paper bearing their names and addresses to their backs, certain they would be mowed down as they rushed Lee's trenches. In four weeks in May and June, Grant lost as many men as were enrolled in Lee's entire army. Though costly, these battles prepared the way for eventual victory: Lee's army shrank until offensive action was no longer possible, while Grant's army kept replenishing its forces with new recruits.

The end finally came in the spring of 1865. Grant kept battering Lee, who tried but failed to break through the Union line. With the numerical superiority of Grant's army now greater than two to one, Confederate defeat was inevitable. On April 2 Lee abandoned Richmond and Petersburg. On April 9, hemmed in by Union troops, short of rations, and having fewer than thirty thousand men left, Lee surrendered at Appomattox Courthouse. Grant

Heavy Losses Force Lee's Surrender

treated his rival with respect and paroled the defeated troops. Within weeks, Davis was captured in Georgia, and the remaining Confederate forces laid down their arms and surrendered. The war was over at last.

Lincoln did not live to see the war's end. On the evening of Good Friday, April 14, he went to Ford's Theater in Washington, D.C., where the assassin John Wilkes Booth shot him in the head at point-blank range. The Union had lost its wartime leader, and millions publicly mourned the martyred chief. Relief at the war's end mingled uncomfortably with a renewed sense of loss and uncertainty about the future.

 Costs and Effects

The human costs of the Civil War were enormous. The total number of military casualties on both sides exceeded 1 million—a frightful toll for a nation of 31 million people. Approximately 364,000 Union soldiers died, 140,000 of them from wounds suffered in battle. Another 275,175 Union soldiers were wounded but survived. On the Confederate side, an estimated 258,000 lost their lives, and almost as many suffered wounds. More men died in the Civil War than in all other American wars combined until Vietnam.

Casualties

Property damage and financial costs were also enormous, though difficult to tally. United States loans and taxes during the conflict totaled almost $3 billion, and interest on the war debt was $2.8 billion. The Confederacy borrowed over $2 billion but lost far more in the destruction of homes, crops, livestock, and other property. Scholars have noted that small farmers lost just as much, proportionally, as planters whose slaves were emancipated.

Financial Cost of the War

Estimates of the total cost of the war exceed $20 billion—five times the total expenditures of the federal government from its creation to 1861. The northern government increased its spending by 700 percent in the first full year of the war; by the last year its spending had soared to twenty times the prewar level. By 1865 the federal government accounted for over 26 percent of the gross national product.

Many of these changes were more or less permanent. In the 1880s, interest on the war debt still accounted for approximately 40 percent of the federal budget and Union soldiers' pensions for as much as 20 percent. Thus although many southerners had hoped to remove government from the economy, the war made such separation an impossibility. After the war, federal expenditures shrank but stabilized at twice the prewar level, or at 4 percent of the gross national product.

 ## Conclusion

The Civil War altered American society in many ways. During the war, in both North and South, women had taken on new roles, which could grow or stagnate. Industrialization and large economic enterprises played a larger role than ever before. Politically, the defense of national unity brought far-reaching changes in government and policy. Under Republican leadership, the federal government had expanded its power. Extreme forms of states' rights dogma clearly were dead, but would Americans continue to favor a state-centered federalism? How would white southerners respond to efforts to reconstruct the nation?

Closely related to these issues was a question of central importance: what would be the place of black men and women in American life? The Union victory provided a partial answer: slavery as it had existed before the war could not persist. But whether full citizenship and equal rights would take slavery's place remained unclear.

Suggestions for Further Reading

The War and the South

Thomas B. Alexander and Richard E. Beringer, *The Anatomy of the Confederate Congress* (1972); Stephen Ash, *When the Yankees Came* (1995); Richard E. Beringer et al., *Why the South Lost the Civil War* (1986); Richard N. Current, *Lincoln's Loyalists* (1992) Robert F. Durden, *The Gray and the Black: The Confederate Debate on Emancipation* (1972); Paul D. Escott, *After Secession: Jefferson Davis and the Failure of Confederate Nationalism* (1978);

Ella Lonn, *Desertion During the Civil War* (1928); Mary Elizabeth Massey, *Refugee Life in the Confederacy* (1964); Harry P. Owens and James J. Cooke, eds., *The Old South in the Crucible of War* (1983); James L. Roark, *Masters Without Slaves* (1977); Georgia Lee Tatum, *Disloyalty in the Confederacy* (1934); Emory M. Thomas, *The Confederate Nation* (1979); William A. Tidwell, *April '65* (1995); Bell Irvin Wiley, *The Plain People of the Confederacy* (1943); W. Buck Yearns, ed., *The Confederate Governors* (1985).

The War and the North

Ralph Andreano, ed., *The Economic Impact of the American Civil War* (1962); David Donald, ed., *Why the North Won the Civil War* (1960); James W. Geary, *We Need Men* (1991); Wood Gray, *The Hidden Civil War* (1942); Frank L. Klement, *The Copperheads in the Middle West* (1960); James M. McPherson, *Battle Cry of Freedom* (1988); Phillip S. Paludan, *"A People's Contest": The Union and the Civil War, 1861–1865* (1989); George Winston Smith and Charles Burnet Judah, *Life in the North During the Civil War* (1966); George Templeton Strong, *Diary*, 4 vols., ed. Allan Nevins and Milton Hasley Thomas (1952); Paul Studenski, *Financial History of the United States* (1952).

Women

John R. Brumgardt, ed., *Civil War Nurse: The Diary and Letters of Hannah Ropes* (1980); Beth Gilbert Crabtree and James W. Patton, eds., *"Journal of a Secesh Lady": The Diary of Catherine Ann Devereux Edmondston, 1860–1866* (1979); George C. Rable, *Civil Wars: Women and the Crisis of Southern Nationalism* (1989); C. Vann Woodward and Elisabeth Muhlenfeld, eds., *Mary Chesnut's Civil War* (1981); Agatha Young, *Women and the Crisis* (1959).

African-Americans

Virginia M. Adams, ed., *On the Altar of Freedom: A Black Soldier's Civil War Letters from the Front* (1991); Ira Berlin, ed., *Freedom: A Documentary History of Emancipation, 1861–1867*, Series I, *The Destruction of Slavery* (1979), and Series II, *The Black Military Experience* (1982); Dudley Cornish, *The Sable Arm* (1956); Joseph T. Glatthaar, *Forged in Battle* (1990); Leon Litwack, *Been in the Storm So Long* (1979); James M. McPherson, *The Negro's Civil War* (1965); James M. McPherson, *The Struggle for Equality* (1964); Clarence L. Mohr, *On the Threshold of Freedom* (1986).

Military History

Albert Castel, *Decision in the West* (1992); Benjamin Franklin Cooling, *Forts Henry and Donelson* (1988); Peter Cozzens, *This Terrible Sound* (1992); Michael Fellman, *Citizen Sherman* (1995); Shelby Foote, *The Civil War, a Narrative*, 3 vols. (1958–1974); Douglas Southall Freeman, *R. E. Lee*, 4 vols. (1934–1935); Joseph T. Glatthaar, *The March to the Sea and Beyond* (1985); Herman Hattaway and Archer Jones, *How the North Won* (1983); Laurence M. Hauptman, *Between Two Fires:*

American Indians in the Civil War (1995); Archer Jones, *Civil War Command and Strategy* (1992); Alvin M. Josephy, Jr., *The Civil War in the American West* (1991); Thomas L. Livermore, *Numbers and Losses in the Civil War in America* (1957); Grady McWhiney and Perry D. Jamieson, *Attack and Die* (1982); J. B. Mitchell, *Decisive Battles of the Civil War* (1955); Reid Mitchell, *Civil War Soldiers* (1988); Roy Morris, Jr., *Sheridan* (1992); Stephen W. Sears, *To the Gates of Richmond* (1992); Emory M. Thomas, *Robert E. Lee* (1995); Steven E. Woodworth, *Jefferson Davis and His Generals* (1990).

Foreign Relations

Kinley J. Brauer, "The Slavery Problem in the Diplomacy of the American Civil War," *Pacific Historical Review* 46, no. 3 (1977): 439–469; David P. Crook, *The North, the South, and the Powers, 1861–1865* (1974); Howard Jones, *Union in Peril* (1992); Frank J. Merli, *Great Britain and the Confederate Navy* (1970); Frank L. Owsley and Harriet Owsley, *King Cotton Diplomacy* (1959); Gordon H. Warren, *Fountain of Discontent: The Trent Affair and Freedom of the Seas* (1981).

Abraham Lincoln and the Union Government

Allan G. Bogue, *The Earnest Men: Republicans of the Civil War Senate* (1981); Richard N. Current, *The Lincoln Nobody Knows* (1958); Leonard P. Curry, *Blueprint for Modern America: Non-Military Legislation of the First Civil War Congress* (1968); Christopher Dell, *Lincoln and the War Democrats* (1975); David Donald, *Charles Sumner and the Rights of Man* (1970); Ludwell H. Johnson, "Lincoln's Solution to the Problem of Peace Terms, 1864–1865," *Journal of Southern History* 34 (November 1968): 441–447; Peyton McCrary, *Abraham Lincoln and Reconstruction: The Louisiana Experiment* (1978); James M. McPherson, *Abraham Lincoln and the Second American Revolution* (1990); Mark Neely, *The Fate of Liberty* (1991); Joel Silbey, *A Respectable Minority: The Democratic Party in the Civil War Era* (1977).

CHAPTER

16

Reconstruction: A Partial Revolution
1865–1877

For both men, war and Reconstruction brought stunning changes and swift reversals of fortune. In 1861 Robert Smalls was a slave in South Carolina, while Wade Hampton was a South Carolina legislator and one of the richest planters in the South. The events of the next fifteen years turned each man's world upside down more than once.

Robert Smalls became a Union hero when he stole a Confederate ship from Charleston harbor and piloted it to the blockading federal fleet. Thereafter, he guided Union gunboats and toured the North recruiting black troops. After the war, Smalls entered politics and served in both the state legislature and Congress. There he worked for educational and economic opportunity for African-Americans.

Wade Hampton joined the Confederate Army in 1861 and soon became a lieutenant-general. The South's defeat profoundly shocked him. The postwar years brought further painful and unexpected changes, including forced bankruptcy. By 1876 Hampton's fortunes were again on the rise: Democrats nominated him for governor, promising that he would "redeem" South Carolina from Republican misrule. While Hampton spoke misleadingly of respect for blacks' rights, each member of the paramilitary Red Shirts who supported him pledged to "control the vote of at least one Negro, by intimidation, purchase," or other means. Hampton won the governor's chair and then a seat in the United States Senate.

As the careers of Smalls and Hampton suggest, Reconstruction's change was extensive but not lasting. Smalls rose from bondage to experience glory, emancipation, political power, and, ultimately, disappointment. Hampton fell from privilege to endure failure, bankruptcy, powerlessness, and, eventually, a return to power. Similarly, American society experienced both extraordinary change and fundamental continuity. Unprecedented social, political, and constitutional changes took place, but the underlying realities of economic power, racial prejudice, and judicial conservatism limited Reconstruction's revolutionary potential.

Nowhere was the turmoil of Reconstruction more evident than in national politics. Lincoln's successor, Andrew Johnson, and Congress fought bitterly over the shaping of a plan for Reconstruction. Though a southerner, Johnson had always been a foe of the South's wealthy planters, and his first acts as president suggested that he would be tough on traitors. Before the end of 1865, however, Johnson's policies changed direction. Although Jefferson Davis stayed in prison for two years, Johnson pardoned other rebel leaders and allowed them to occupy high offices. He also ordered tax officials to return plantations to their original owners, including abandoned coastal lands on which forty thousand freed men and women had settled by order of General William Tecumseh Sherman early in 1865.

This turn of events alarmed northern voters. Republican congressmen began to discuss plans to keep rebels from regaining control of the South or of Congress. Northern legislators produced a new Reconstruction program, embodied in the Fourteenth Amendment. But southern intransigence blocked that plan and forced a more radical step, the Reconstruction Act of 1867. When Congress put the act into effect, Johnson tried to subvert it, and by 1868 the president and Congress were bitterly antagonistic.

Before these struggles were over, Congress had impeached the president, enfranchised the freed men, and given them a role in reconstructing the South. The nation also adopted the Fourteenth and Fifteenth Amendments. Yet little was done to open the doors of economic opportunity to black southerners. Moreover, by 1869 the Ku Klux Klan was employing extensive violence to thwart Reconstruction and undermine black freedom.

As the 1870s advanced, northerners grew weary of Reconstruction and began to focus on other issues. Industrial growth accelerated, interest in territorial expansion revived, and political corruption became a nationwide scandal. Eventually these other forces triumphed. As politics moved on to new concerns, the courts turned their attention away from civil rights, and even northern Republicans abandoned racial reforms in 1877.

Only limited change emerged from this period of tremendous upheaval. Congress asserted the principle of equality before the law for African-Americans and gave black men the right to vote. But few whites saw equal rights for African-Americans as the central aim of Reconstruction, and thus more far-reaching measures to advance black freedom never had much support in Congress. And Supreme Court interpretations soon crippled the Fourteenth and Fifteenth Amendments. Reconstruction proclaimed anew the American principle of human equality but failed to secure it in reality.

 ## Equal Rights: The Unresolved Issue

For America's former slaves, Reconstruction had one paramount meaning: a chance to explore freedom. A southern white woman admitted in her diary that the black people "showed a natural and exultant joy at being free." Former slaves remembered singing far into the night after federal troops reached their plantations. The slaves on a Texas plantation jumped up and down and clapped their hands as one man shouted, "We is free—no more whippings and beatings." Another man recalled that he and others "started on the move," either to search for family members or just to exercise their new-found freedom of movement.

• *Important* **Events** •

1865	President Andrew Johnson begins Reconstruction	**1871**	Congress passes second Enforcement Act and Ku Klux Klan Act
	Confederate leaders regain power	**1872**	Amnesty Act frees almost all remaining Confederates from restrictions on holding office
	White southern governments pass restrictive black codes		Liberal Republicans organize
	Congress refuses to seat southern representatives		Debtors urge government to keep greenbacks in circulation
	Thirteenth Amendment ratified		Grant reelected
1866	Congress passes Civil Rights Act and renewal of Freedmen's Bureau over Johnson's veto	**1873**	*Slaughter-House* cases limit power of Fourteenth Amendment
	Congress approves Fourteenth Amendment		Panic of 1873 damages economy
	Most southern states reject Fourteenth Amendment	**1874**	Grant vetoes increase in supply of paper money
	In *Ex parte Milligan* the Supreme Court reasserts its influence		Democrats win majority in House of Representatives
1867	Congress passes Reconstruction Act and Tenure of Office Act	**1875**	Several Grant appointees indicted for corruption
	Constitutional conventions called in southern states		Congress passes weak Civil Rights Act
1868	House impeaches Johnson; Senate acquits him		Congress requires that after 1878 greenbacks be convertible into gold
	Most southern states gain readmission to the Union	**1876**	*U.S.* v. *Cruikshank* and *U.S.* v. *Reese* further weaken Fourteenth Amendment
	Fourteenth Amendment ratified		Presidential election disputed
	Ulysses S. Grant elected president	**1877**	Congress elects Rutherford B. Hayes president
1869	Congress approves Fifteenth Amendment (ratified in 1870)		Exodusters migrate to Kansas
1870	Congress passes first Enforcement Act		

Most freed men and women reacted cautiously and shrewdly, taking care to test the boundaries of their new condition. As slaves they had learned to expect hostility from white people, and they did not presume it would instantly disappear. Life in freedom might still be a matter of what was allowed, not what was right. One sign of this shrewd caution was the way freed people evaluated potential employers. If a white person had been relatively considerate to blacks in bondage, they stayed on the plantation, reasoning that he might prove a desirable employer in freedom. Others left their plantations all at once, for, as one

put it, "that master am sure mean and if we doesn't have to stay we shouldn't, not with that master."

In addition to a fair employer, freed men and women wanted opportunity through education and, especially, through landownership. Land ownership represented their chance to enjoy the independence that generations of American farmers valued. A northern observer noted that slaves freed in the Sea Islands of South Carolina and Georgia made "plain, straight-forward" inquiries as they settled the land

African-Americans' Desire for Land

set aside for them by Sherman. They wanted to be sure the land "would be theirs after they had improved it."

But how much of a chance would whites give to blacks? There were some victories for civil rights. In 1864 the federal courts accepted black testimony, and the next year the Thirteenth Amendment became law. One state, Massachusetts, enacted a comprehensive public accommodations law. But there were defeats, too. The Democratic Party fought hard against equality, charging that Republicans favored race-mixing and were undermining the status of white workers. Voters in three states—Connecticut, Minnesota, and Wisconsin—rejected black suffrage in 1865.

Even northern reformers showed little sympathy for black aspirations. In the Sea Islands, for instance, the former slaves wanted to establish small, self-sufficient farms. Northern officials and missionaries, however, emphasized profit and insisted that the freedmen grow more cotton. And when tax officials sold Sea Island land that had been seized for nonpayment of taxes, 90 percent of it went to wealthy northern investors. The tracts, as one African-American complained, were made "too big, and cut we out." Thus, with only partial support from their strongest advocates, former slaves awaited the answer to one vital question. How much opportunity would freedom bring?

 ## Johnson's Reconstruction Plan

When Reconstruction began under President Andrew Johnson, many expected his policies to be harsh. Throughout his career in Tennessee he had criticized the wealthy planters and championed the small farmers. Southern aristocrats and northern Radicals thus had reason to believe that Johnson would deal sternly with the South.

Through 1865 Johnson alone controlled Reconstruction policy, for Congress recessed shortly before he became president and did not reconvene until December. In the following eight months,

Johnson devised and put into operation his own plan, forming new state governments in the South by using his power to grant pardons.

Wartime proposals for Reconstruction had produced much controversy but no consensus. In December 1863 Lincoln had proposed a "10 percent" plan for a government being organized in captured parts of Louisiana. Under this plan, a state government could be established as soon as 10 percent of those who had voted in 1860 took an oath of future loyalty to the Union. Only high-ranking Confederate officials would be denied a chance to take the oath, and Lincoln urged that at least a few well-qualified blacks be given the ballot. Radicals bristled, however, at such a mild plan, and Congress backed the much stiffer Wade-Davis bill, which required 50 percent of the voters to swear an "iron-clad" oath that they had never voluntarily supported the rebellion. Lincoln pocket-vetoed this measure. At the time of his death, he had given tentative approval to a plan, drafted by Secretary of War Edwin Stanton, to impose military authority and appoint provisional governors as steps toward the creation of new state governments.

Lincoln's Reconstruction Plan

Johnson began with Stanton's plan, but his advisers split evenly on the question of giving voting rights to black men in the South. Johnson claimed that he favored black suffrage, but *only* if the southern states adopted it voluntarily. A champion of states' rights and no friend of African-Americans, he regarded this decision as too important to be taken out of the hands of the states.

This racial conservatism had an enduring effect on Johnson's policies. Where whites were concerned, however, Johnson seemed to be pursuing radical changes in class relations. He proposed rules that would keep the wealthy planter class out of power. Southerners were required to swear an oath of loyalty as a condition of gaining amnesty or pardon, but Johnson barred several categories of people from taking the oath. Former federal

Oaths of Amnesty and New State Governments

Combative and inflexible, President Andrew Johnson contributed greatly to the failure of his own reconstruction program.   Library of Congress.

officials who had violated their oaths to support the United States and had aided the Confederacy could not take the oath. Nor could high-ranking Confederate officers and political leaders or graduates of West Point or Annapolis who had resigned their commissions to fight for the South. To this list Johnson added another important group: all southerners who aided the rebellion and whose taxable property was worth more than $20,000. All such individuals had to apply personally to the president for pardon and restoration of their political rights; otherwise, they risked legal penalties, which included confiscation of their land. Thus it appeared that the leadership class of the Old South would be re-

moved from power and replaced by deserving yeomen.

Johnson appointed provisional governors who began the Reconstruction process by calling constitutional conventions. The delegates chosen had to draft new constitutions that eliminated slavery and invalidated secession. After ratification of these constitutions, new governments could be elected, and the states would be restored to the Union with full congressional representation. Only southerners who had taken the oath of amnesty and been eligible to vote on the day the state seceded could participate in this process. Thus unpardoned whites and former slaves were not eligible.

If Johnson intended to strip the old elite of its power, his plan did not work as he hoped. Surprisingly, Johnson helped to subvert his own plan by pardoning aristocrats and leading rebels. These pardons, plus the return of planters' abandoned lands, restored the old elite to power. After the states drafted new constitutions, Johnson endorsed their governments and proclaimed Reconstruction complete. In the elections held under these constitutions, many former Confederate leaders, including the vice president of the Confederacy, were elected to serve in Congress.

The election of such prominent rebels troubled many northerners. So did other results of Johnson's program. Some of the state conventions were slow to repudiate secession; others admitted only grudgingly that slavery was dead. Furthermore, to define the status of freed men and women and control their labor, some legislatures merely revised large sections of the slave codes by substituting the word *freedmen* for *slave*. The new black codes compelled the former slaves, now supposedly free, to carry passes, observe a curfew, live in housing provided by a landowner, and give up hope of entering many desirable occupations. Stiff vagrancy laws and restrictive labor contracts bound supposedly free laborers to plantations. State-supported institutions in the South, such as schools and orphanages, excluded blacks entirely.

It seemed to northerners that the South was intent on returning African-Americans to a position

Black Codes

of servility. Thus the Republican majority in Congress decided to take a closer look at the results of Johnson's plan. On reconvening, the House and Senate considered the credentials of the newly elected southern representatives and decided not to admit them. Instead, they established a joint committee to study Reconstruction and consider new policies. Reconstruction thus entered a second phase, one in which Congress would play the decisive role.

The Congressional Reconstruction Plan

Northern congressmen disagreed about what to do, but they did not doubt their right to shape Reconstruction policy. The Constitution mentioned neither secession nor reunion, but it declared that the United States shall guarantee to each state a republican government. This provision, legislators believed, gave them the right to devise policies for Reconstruction.

They soon found that other constitutional questions affected their policies. What, for example, had rebellion done to the relationship between southern states and the Union? Lincoln had always insisted that states could not secede and that the Union remained intact. In contrast, congressmen who favored vigorous Reconstruction measures argued that the war *had* broken the Union. They maintained that the southern states had committed legal suicide and reverted to the status of territories, or that the South was a conquered nation subject to the victor's will. Moderate congressmen held that the states had forfeited their rights through rebellion and thus had come under congressional supervision.

These diverse theories mirrored the diversity of Congress itself. Northern Democrats denounced any idea of racial equality and supported Johnson's policies. Conservative Republicans, despite their party loyalty, favored a limited federal role in Reconstruction. The Radical Republicans wanted to transform the South. Although a minority within their

The Radicals

party, they had the advantage of a clearly defined goal. They believed it was essential to democratize the South, establish public education, and ensure the rights of freed people. They favored black suffrage, often supported land confiscation and redistribution, and were willing to exclude the South from the Union for several years if necessary to achieve their goals. A large group of moderate Republicans did not want to go as far as the Radicals but believed some change in Johnson's policies was necessary.

Ironically, Johnson and the Democrats forced the diverse Republican factions to coalesce by refusing to cooperate with moderate and conservative Republicans and insisting that Reconstruction was over and that southern representatives should be seated in Congress. Moreover, Johnson rejected an apparent compromise on Reconstruction. Under its terms Johnson would agree to two modifications of his program: extension of the life of the Freedmen's Bureau—which Congress had established in 1865 to feed the hungry, negotiate labor contracts, and start schools—and passage of a civil rights bill to counteract the black codes. This bill would force southern courts to practice equality before the law by allowing federal judges to remove from state courts cases in which blacks were treated unfairly. Its provisions applied to discrimination by private individuals as well as by government officials. This was the first major bill to enforce the Thirteenth Amendment's abolition of slavery.

Congress Struggles for a Compromise

Johnson destroyed the compromise by vetoing both bills. (They later became law when Congress overrode the president's veto.) Denouncing any change in his program, the president condemned Congress's action and questioned its right to make policy. All hope of working with the president was now dead. Instead of a compromise program, the various Republican factions drew up a new plan. It took the form of a proposed amendment to the Constitution, and it represented a compromise between radical and conservative elements of the party. The Fourteenth Amendment was Congress's alternative to Johnson's program of Reconstruction.

Of the four points in the amendment, there was near-universal agreement on one: the Confederate debt was declared null and void, and the war debt of the United States was guaranteed. There was also general support for prohibiting prominent Confederates from holding political office. The amendment therefore barred Confederate leaders from state and federal office. Only Congress, by a two-thirds vote of each house, could remove the penalty.

Fourteenth Amendment

The first section of the Fourteenth Amendment, which would have the greatest legal significance in later years, conferred citizenship on freedmen and prohibited states from abridging their constitutional "privileges and immunities." It also barred any state from taking a person's life, liberty, or property "without due process of law" and from denying "equal protection of the laws." These broad phrases became powerful guarantees of African-Americans' civil rights—indeed, of the rights of all citizens—in the twentieth century.

The second section of the amendment dealt with representation. Under the Constitution, each slave had counted as three-fifths of a person. Emancipation made every former slave five-fifths of a person, a fact that would increase southern representation. Thus the postwar South stood to *gain* power in Congress, and if white southerners did not allow blacks to vote, former secessionists would derive all the political benefit from emancipation. To prevent this result, the Fourteenth Amendment stipulated that states denying black men the vote would have their representation reduced accordingly. States enfranchising black men would have their representation increased proportionally—but, of course, Republicans could seek the support of the new black voters.

The Fourteenth Amendment raised the possibility of suffrage for black men but ignored female citizens, black and white. When legislators defined women as nonvoting citizens, prominent leaders such as Elizabeth Cady Stanton and Susan B. Anthony decided that it was time to end their alliance with abolitionists and fight more deter-

minedly for themselves. Thus the amendment infused new determination into the independent women's rights movement.

In 1866, however, the major question in Reconstruction politics was how the public would respond to the amendment. Johnson did his best to block the Fourteenth Amendment in both North and South.

Southern Rejection of the Fourteenth Amendment

Condemning Congress for its refusal to seat southern representatives, the president urged state legislatures in the South to vote against ratification. Every southern legislature except Tennessee's rejected the amendment by a wide margin.

To present his case to northerners, Johnson organized a National Union Convention and took to the stump himself. He boarded a special train for a "swing around the circle" that carried his message deep into the Midwest and then back to Washington, D.C. Increasingly, however, audiences rejected his views and hooted and jeered at him.

The elections of 1866 were a resounding victory for Republicans in Congress. Radical and moderate Republicans whom Johnson had denounced won reelection by large margins, and the Republican majority grew. The North had spoken clearly: Johnson's policies were giving the advantage to rebels and traitors. Thus Republican congressional leaders won a mandate to pursue their Reconstruction plan.

Recognizing that nothing could be accomplished under the existing southern governments and with blacks excluded from the electorate, Congress passed the Reconstruction Act of 1867. The act incorporated only a small part of the Radical program. Until new state governments could be set up, Union generals assumed control in five military districts in the South. Confederate leaders designated in the Fourteenth Amendment were barred from voting until new state constitutions were ratified. The law guaranteed freedmen the right to vote in elections for state constitutional conventions and in subsequent elections under the

Reconstruction Act of 1867

Plans for Reconstruction Compared

	Johnson's Plan	Radicals' Plan	Fourteenth Amendment	Reconstruction Act of 1867
Voting	Whites only; Confederate leaders must seek pardons	Give vote to black males	Southern whites may decide but can lose representation	Black men gain vote; whites barred from office by Fourteenth Amendment cannot vote while new state governments are being formed
Officeholding	Many prominent Confederates regain power	Only loyal white and black males eligible	Confederate leaders barred until Congress votes amnesty	Fourteenth Amendment in effect
Time out of Union	Brief	Years; until South is thoroughly democratized	Brief	Brief
Other change in southern society	Little; gain of power by yeomen not realized	Expand public education; confiscate land and provide farms for freedmen	Probably slight	Depends on action of new state governments

new constitutions. In addition, each southern state was required to ratify the Fourteenth Amendment and to ratify its new constitution and submit it to Congress for approval. Thus African-Americans gained an opportunity to fight for a better life through the political process.

Congress's role as the architect of Reconstruction was not quite over. To restrict Johnson's influence and safeguard its plan, Congress passed a number of controversial laws. First, it set the date for its own reconvening—an unprecedented act, for the president traditionally summoned legislators to Washington. Then it limited Johnson's power over the army by requiring the president to issue military orders through the General of the Army, Ulysses S. Grant, who could not be sent from Washington without the Senate's consent. Finally, Congress passed the Tenure of Office Act, which gave the Senate power to interfere with changes in the president's cabinet. Designed to protect Secretary of War Stanton, who sympa-

thized with the Radicals, this law violated the tradition that a president controlled his own cabinet.

Johnson took several belligerent steps of his own. He issued orders to military commanders in the South limiting their powers and increasing the powers of the civil governments he had created in 1865. Then he removed officers who were conscientiously enforcing Congress's new law. Finally, he tried to remove Secretary of War Stanton. With that attempt the confrontation reached its climax.

In 1868, the House Judiciary Committee initiated impeachment proceedings against the president. The indictment concentrated on his violation of the Tenure of Office Act, though modern scholars regard his efforts to impede enforcement of the Reconstruction Act of 1867 as a far more serious offense. Johnson's trial in the Senate began promptly and lasted more than three months. The prosecution at-

Impeachment of President Johnson

tempted to prove that Johnson was guilty of "high crimes and misdemeanors." But they also argued that the trial was a means to judge Johnson's performance, not a judicial determination of guilt or innocence. The Senate ultimately rejected such reasoning, which could have made removal from office a political weapon against any chief executive who disagreed with Congress. Although a majority of senators voted to convict Johnson, the prosecution fell one vote short of the necessary two-thirds majority. Johnson remained in office, politically weakened and with only a few months left in his term. His acquittal established a precedent that only serious misdeeds merited removal from office.

In 1869, in an effort to write democratic principles and colorblindness into the Constitution, the Radicals succeeded in presenting the Fifteenth Amendment for ratification. This measure forbade states to deny the right to vote "on account of race, color, or previous condition of servitude."

Fifteenth Amendment

Such wording did not guarantee the right to vote. It deliberately left states free to restrict suffrage on other grounds so that northern states could continue to deny suffrage to women and certain groups of men. Ironically, the votes of four uncooperative southern states—compelled by Congress to approve the amendment as an added condition to rejoining the Union—proved necessary to impose even this language on parts of the North. Although several states outside the South refused to ratify, the Fifteenth Amendment became law in 1870.

Reconstruction Politics in the South

From the start, Reconstruction encountered the resistance of white southerners. In the black codes and in private attitudes, many whites stubbornly opposed emancipation, and the former planter class proved especially unbending. In 1866 a Georgia newspaper frankly observed that "most of the white

White Resistance

citizens believe that the institution of slavery was right, and . . . they will believe that the condition, which comes nearest to slavery, that can now be established will be the best."

Fearing loss of control over their slaves, some planters attempted to postpone freedom by denying or misrepresenting events. Former slaves reported that their owners "didn't tell them it was freedom" or "wouldn't let [them] go." To hold onto their workers, some landowners claimed control over black children and used guardianship and apprentice laws to bind black families to the plantation. Whites also blocked blacks from acquiring land and used force to keep them submissive.

After President Johnson encouraged the South to resist congressional Reconstruction, white conservatives worked hard to capture the new state governments. Many whites also boycotted the polls in an attempt to defeat Congress's plans; by sitting out the elections, whites might block the new constitutions, which had to be approved by a majority of registered voters. This tactic was tried in North Carolina and succeeded in Alabama, forcing Congress to base ratification on a majority of those voting.

Very few black men stayed away from the polls. Enthusiastically and hopefully, they voted Republican. Illiteracy did not prohibit blacks from making intelligent choices. One Mississippi black testified that he and his friends had no difficulty selecting the Republican ballot. "We stood around and watched," he explained. "We saw D. Sledge vote; he owned half the county. We knowed he voted Democratic so we voted the other ticket so it would be Republican."

Thanks to a large black turnout and the restrictions on prominent Confederates, a new southern Republican Party came to power in the constitutional conventions. Republican delegates consisted of a sizable contingent of blacks (265 out of the total of just over 1,000 delegates throughout the South), some northerners who had moved to the South, and native southern whites who favored change. Together these Republicans brought the South into line with progressive reforms that had been adopted in the rest of the nation. The new constitutions were more democratic. They eliminated property qualifications for voting and holding office, and they

How do historians know *about the relationships between former slaves and former slaveholders during Reconstruction? The records of the Federal Bureau of Refugees, Freedmen, and Abandoned Lands contain a wealth of information on daily conflicts and confrontations. They reveal that one strategy used by planters to retain the labor of their former slaves was to control the slaves' children. The entry shown here, from a Bureau record book in Texas, recounts the complaint of Amanda Hayes. In 1866, her former owner, Captain William Hayes, took her son "to help him drive his cattle." In July 1867, "Mr. Hayes has not returned the boy yet," and Amanda Hayes "wishes the Bureau to compel" his return, with pay.* National Archives.

6 Bureau R, F, and A, L.
Boston July 16 1867

Philip Howard Esqr.
S.A. Commissioner
48th District,

Copy

Dear Sir

Amanda Hayes - freedwoman living in this County complains that captain Wm Hayes took her son Henry in the year 1866, away with him to Johnson County Texas saying that he wanted the boy Henry to help him drive his cattle from Bowie Co, to Johnson County, and that he would return him to her, Mr Hayes has not returned the boy yet - She wishes the Bureau to compel Mr Hayes to return the boy to her, and have Mr Hayes pay her for his time -

Kate Featherston freedwoman living in Bowie County Complains that Mr Robert Pool, took her daughter Chissy to Johnson Co Texas, in Company with Mr Hayes in 1866. She is about fourteen (14) years of age. Kate Featherston wishes to have her daughter returned to her.

Please get the particulars of the above cases of amelia H- & Kate F. and return the boy & Girl if possible acknowledge this immediately with statement of the particulars in the case, Very Respy Your Obt Servt

W.G. Kirkman, S.A. Commissioner

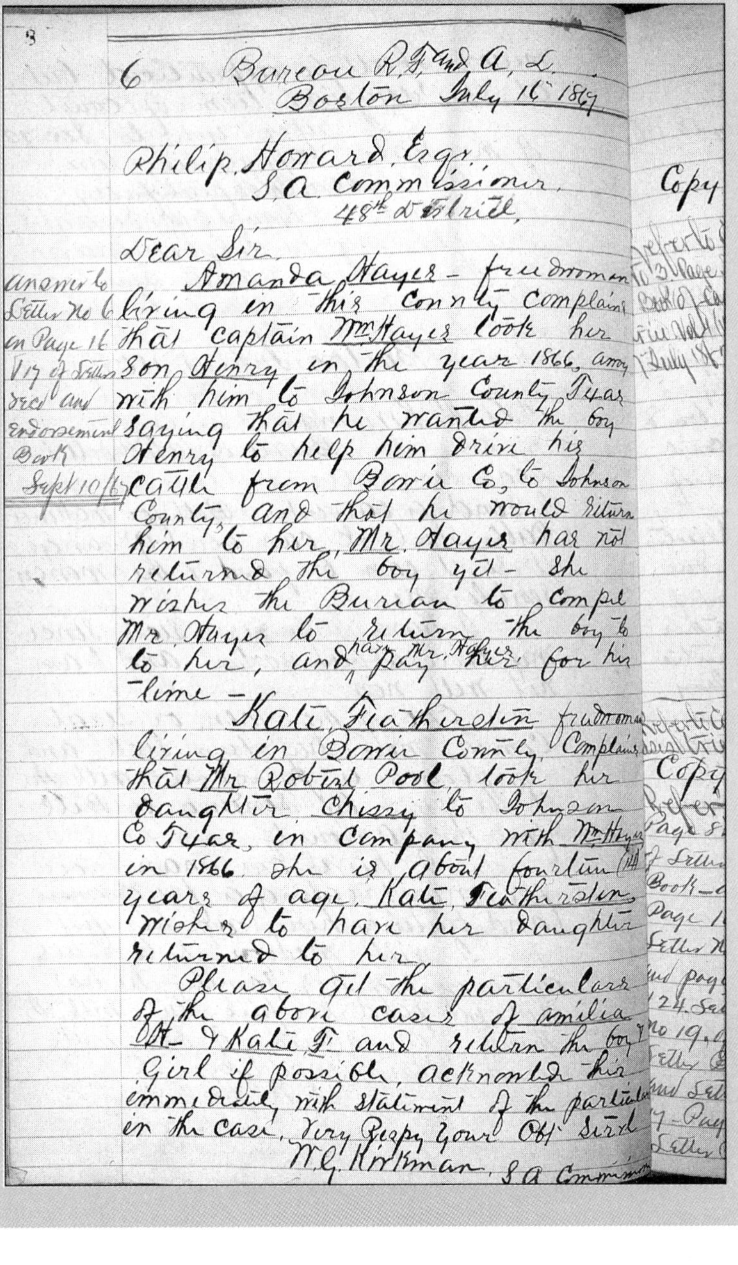

turned many appointed offices into elective posts. They provided for public schools and institutions to care for the mentally ill, the blind, the deaf, the destitute, and the orphaned. They also put an end to imprisonment for debt and to punishments such as branding.

The conventions broadened women's rights in property holding and divorce. Usually, the goal was not to make women equal with men but to provide relief to thousands of suffering debtors. In families left poverty-stricken by the war and weighed down by debt, it was usually the husband who had contracted the debts. Thus giving women legal control over their own property provided some protection to their families. The goal of some delegates, however, was to elevate women. Blacks in particular called for laws to provide for women's suffrage, but they were ignored by their white colleagues.

Under these new constitutions the southern states elected new governments. Again the Republican Party triumphed, putting new men in positions of power. For the first

Triumph of Republican Governments

time, the ranks of state legislators in 1868 included some black southerners. Congress's second plan for Reconstruction was well under way. It remained to be seen what these new governments would do and how much social change they would bring about.

One way to achieve radical change would have been to disfranchise substantial numbers of Confederate leaders. Barring many whites from politics as punishment for rebellion would have given the Republicans a solid electoral majority based on black voters and their white allies. Land reform and the assurance of racial equality would have been possible. No Republican government ever seriously considered this course of action, for two reasons.

First, they appreciated the realities of power and the depth of racial enmity. In most states, whites were in the majority and former slaveowners controlled the best land and other sources of economic power. James Lynch, a leading black politician from Mississippi, explained why African-Americans shunned the "folly" of disfranchisement. Unlike northerners who "can leave when it becomes too

uncomfortable," landless former slaves "must be in friendly relations with the great body of the whites in the state." Second, blacks believed in the principle of universal suffrage and the Christian goal of reconciliation. Far from being vindictive, they treated leading rebels with generosity.

The South's Republican Party therefore committed itself to a strategy of winning white support. To put the matter another way, the Republican Party condemned itself to defeat if white voters would not cooperate. But for a time both Republicans and their opponents, who called themselves Conservatives or Democrats, moved to the center and appealed for a broad range of support. Some propertied whites accepted congressional Reconstruction as a reality and declared themselves willing to compete under the new rules. While these Democrats angled for some black votes, Republicans sought to attract more white voters. Both parties found an area of agreement in economic policies.

The Reconstruction governments enthusiastically promoted industry. This policy reflected northern ideals, but it also sprang from a grow-

Industrialization

ling southern eagerness to build up the region. Accordingly, Reconstruction legislatures encouraged investment with loans, subsidies, and exemptions from taxation for periods up to ten years. The southern railroad system was rebuilt and expanded, and coal and iron mining made possible Birmingham's steel plants. Between 1860 and 1880, the number of manufacturing establishments in the South nearly doubled. This emphasis on big business, however, produced higher state debts and taxes, drew money away from schools and other programs, and multiplied possibilities for corruption.

Policies appealing to African-American voters never went beyond equality before the law. In fact, the whites who controlled the southern Repub-

Other Republican Policies

lican Party were reluctant to allow blacks a share of offices proportionate to their electoral strength. Aware of their weakness, black leaders did not push for revolutionary economic or social change. Though land was important to African-Americans, few promoted confiscation. Instead, they led efforts to establish public schools but usually did not press for integrated facilities. Having a school to attend was the most important thing at the time. As a result, virtually every public school organized during Reconstruction was racially segregated, and these separate schools established a precedent for segregated theaters, trains, and other public accommodations in the South.

Within a few years, as centrists in both parties met with failure, white hostility to congressional Reconstruction began to dominate. Some conservatives had always desired to fight Reconstruction through pressure and racist propaganda. Charging that the South had been turned over to ignorant blacks, conservatives deplored "black domination" and "Negro rule."

Such attacks were inflammatory but inaccurate. African-Americans participated in politics but did not dominate or control events. They were a majority in only two out of ten state conventions (transplanted northerners were a majority in one). In the state legislatures, only in the lower house in South Carolina did blacks ever constitute a majority; among officeholders, their numbers generally were far inferior to their proportion in the population. Sixteen blacks won seats in Congress before Reconstruction was over, but none was ever elected governor. Only eighteen served in a high state office such as lieutenant governor, treasurer, superintendent of education, or secretary of state.

Conservatives also assailed the allies of black Republicans. Their propaganda denounced whites from the North as "carpetbaggers," greedy crooks planning to pour stolen tax revenues into their sturdy luggage made of carpet material. In fact, most northerners who settled in the South had come seeking business opportunities or a warmer climate and never entered politics. Those who did enter politics generally wanted to democratize the South and to introduce northern ways, such as industry, public education, and the spirit of enterprise.

Carpetbaggers and Scalawags

Conservatives invented the term *scalawag* to discredit any native white southerner who cooperated with the Republicans. A substantial number of southerners did so. Most scalawags were yeoman farmers, men from mountain areas and nonslaveholding districts who saw that they could benefit from the education and opportunities promoted by Republicans. Banding together with freedmen, they pursued common class interests and hoped to make headway against the power of long-dominant planters. Most scalawags, however, shied away from support for racial equality.

Taxation was a major problem for the Reconstruction governments. Republicans wanted to maintain prewar services, repair the war's destruction, stimulate industry, and support important new ventures such as public schools. But the Civil War had destroyed much of the South's tax base. Thus an increase in taxes was necessary even to maintain traditional services, and new ventures required still higher taxes.

Corruption was another serious charge levied against the Republicans. Unfortunately, it often was true. Many carpetbaggers and black politicians engaged in fraudulent schemes, sold their votes, or padded expenses. Many white Democrats shared in corruption, and some Republicans fought it, but the Democrats successfully pinned the blame on unqualified blacks and greedy carpetbaggers.

All these problems hurt the Republicans, but in many southern states the deathblow came through violence. The Ku Klux Klan, a secret veterans' club that began in Tennessee, spread through the South and rapidly evolved into a terrorist organization. Violence against African-Americans occurred from the first days of Reconstruction but became far more organized and purposeful after 1867. Klansmen rode to frustrate Reconstruction and keep the freedmen in subjection. Nighttime harassment, whippings, beatings, and murder became common, and terrorism dominated some areas.

Ku Klux Klan

The Klan's main purpose was political. Lawless nightriders made active Republicans the target of their attacks. Leading white and black Republi-

Members of the Ku Klux Klan devised ghoulish costumes to heighten the terror inspired by their acts. This photograph shows the costume of a Mississippi Klansman from 1871. Courtesy, Herbert Peck, Jr.

cans were killed in several states. After freedmen who worked for a South Carolina scalawag started voting, terrorists visited the plantation and, in the words of one victim, "whipped every nigger man they could lay their hands on." Klansmen also attacked Union League Clubs—Republican organizations that mobilized the black vote—and schoolteachers who were aiding the freedmen.

Klan violence was not a spontaneous outburst of racism; very specific social forces shaped and di-

rected it. In North Carolina, for example, Alamance and Caswell Counties were the sites of the worst Klan violence. Slim Republican majorities there rested on cooperation between black voters and white yeomen. Together, these black and white Republicans had ousted officials long entrenched in power. In a successful effort to restore Democratic control, wealthy and powerful men served as Klan leaders. Through a campaign of terror, the Ku Klux Klan weakened the Republican coalition and restored a Democratic majority.

Klan violence injured Republicans across the South. No fewer than one-tenth of the black leaders who had been delegates to the 1867–1868 state constitutional conventions were attacked, seven fatally. In Eutaw, Alabama, a single Klan attack left four blacks dead and fifty-four wounded. In South Carolina five hundred masked Klansmen lynched eight black prisoners at the Union County jail. According to historian Eric Foner, the Klan "made it virtually impossible for Republicans to campaign or vote in large parts of Georgia."

Thus a combination of difficult fiscal problems, Republican mistakes, racial hostility, and terror brought down the Republican regimes. In most

Failure of Reconstruction

southern states so-called Radical Reconstruction lasted only a few years. The most enduring failure of Reconstruction, however, was not political; it was social and economic. Reconstruction failed to alter the South's social structure or its distribution of wealth and power. Without land of their own, blacks were dependent on white landowners who could and did use their economic power to compromise blacks' political freedom. Armed only with the ballot, freed men in the South had little chance to effect major changes.

 ## The Social and Economic Meaning of Freedom

Black southerners entered into life after slavery hopefully but not naively. They had had too much experience with white people to assume that all would be easy. Expecting hostility, freed men and women tried to gain as much as they could from their new circumstances. Often the changes they valued the most were personal.

One of the first decisions was whether to leave the old plantation. This choice meant making a judgment about where opportunities for liberty and progress were likely to be greatest. Many cruel slaveholders saw their former property walk off en masse, as former slaves used their experience in bondage to assess the whites with whom they had to deal.

After choosing an employer, ex-slaves reached out for valuable things in life that had been denied them. One of these was education. They

Education for African-Americans

started schools and filled classrooms both day and night. On log seats and dirt floors, freed men and women of all ages studied their letters in old almanacs, discarded dictionaries, or whatever was available. Young children brought infants to school with them, and adults attended at night or after "the crops were laid by." The federal government and northern reformers of both races assisted this pursuit of education. In its brief life the Freedmen's Bureau founded over four thousand schools, and idealistic northerners established and staffed others.

Blacks and their white allies also saw the need for colleges and universities to train teachers, ministers, and professionals for leadership. The American Missionary Association founded seven colleges, including Fisk and Atlanta Universities, between 1866 and 1869. The Freedmen's Bureau helped to establish Howard University in Washington, D.C., and northern religious groups supported dozens of seminaries, colleges, and teachers' colleges. By the late 1870s black churches had joined in the effort, founding numerous colleges despite limited resources.

Even during Reconstruction, African-American leaders often were highly educated individuals; many of them came from the prewar elite of free people of color. This group had benefited from its association with wealthy whites, many of whom were blood relatives; some planters had given their mulatto children outstanding educations. The two

black senators from Mississippi, Blanche K. Bruce and Hiram Revels, for instance, had had privileged educations. Bruce was the son of a planter who had provided tutoring at home; Revels was the son of free North Carolina mulattos who had sent him to Knox College in Illinois. These men and many self-educated former slaves brought to political office their experience as artisans, businessmen, lawyers, teachers, and preachers.

Meanwhile, millions of former slaves concentrated on improving life on their farms and in their neighborhoods. Surrounded by an unfriendly white population, black men and women sought to insulate themselves from white interference and to strengthen the bonds of their own community. Throughout the South they devoted themselves to reuniting their families, moving away from the slave quarters, and founding black churches. Given the eventual failure of Reconstruction, the gains African-Americans made in their daily lives often proved the most enduring.

The search for family members who had been sold away during slavery was awe inspiring. With only shreds of information to guide them,

Reunification of African-American Families

thousands of freed people embarked on odysseys in search of a husband, wife, child, or parent. By relying on the black community for help and information, many succeeded. Others walked through several states and never found loved ones.

Husbands and wives who had belonged to different masters established homes together for the first time, and parents asserted the right to raise their own children. A mother bristled when her old master claimed a right to whip her children. She informed him that "he warn't goin' to brush none of her chilluns no more." The freed men and women were too much at risk to act recklessly, but, as one man put it, they were tired of punishment and "sure didn't take no more foolishness off of white folks."

Many black people wanted to minimize contact with whites. To avoid overbearing whites who were used to supervising and controlling them, blacks abandoned the slave quarters and fanned out to distant corners of the land they worked. Others established small all-black settlements that still exist today.

The other side of movement away from whites was closer communion within the black community. Freed from slavery, blacks could build their own institutions as they saw fit, and the secret churches of slavery came out into the open. Within a few years independent branches of the Methodist and Baptist denominations had attracted the great majority of black Christians in the South.

Founding of Black Churches

The desire to gain as much independence as possible also shaped the former slaves' economic arrangements. Since most of them lacked money to buy land, they preferred the next best thing: renting the land they worked. But few whites would consider renting land to blacks, and most blacks had no means to get cash before the harvest. Thus other alternatives had to be tried.

Northerners and officials of the Freedmen's Bureau favored contracts between owners and laborers. To northerners who believed in "Free Soil, Free Labor, Free Men," contracts and wages seemed the key to progress. For a few years the Freedmen's Bureau helped draw up and enforce such contracts, but they proved unpopular with both races. Owners often filled the contracts with detailed requirements that led to close supervision and reminded blacks of their circumscribed lives under slavery. Besides, cash for wages was not readily available in the early years of Reconstruction. Times were hard, and the failure of Confederate banks had left the South with a shortage of credit facilities.

Black farmers and white landowners therefore turned to sharecropping, a system in which farmers kept part of their crop and gave the rest to the landowner while living on his property. The landlord or a merchant "furnished" food and supplies needed before the harvest, and he received payment from the crop.

Rise of the Sharecropping System

Although landowners tried to set the laborers' share at a low level, black farmers had some bargaining power.

The sharecropping system originated as a desirable compromise. It eased landowners' problems with cash and credit; blacks accepted it because it gave them more freedom from daily supervision. Instead of working under a white overseer, as in slavery, they farmed a plot of land on their own in family groups. But sharecropping later proved to be a disaster for all concerned. Because African-Americans lived in a discriminatory society, the system placed them at the mercy of unscrupulous white landowners and merchants. The South suffered because the region became increasingly dependent upon cotton at the very time the growth rate in world demand for that crop began to drop, compared with the prewar years.

Reconstruction's Decline and Fall

Northerners had always been far more interested in suppressing rebellion than in aiding southern blacks, and by the early 1870s the North's partial commitment to bringing about change in the South was weakening. Criticism of the southern governments grew, new issues captured people's attention, and soon voters began to look favorably on reconciliation with southern whites. In one southern state after another, Democrats regained control, and soon the situation had returned to "normal" in the eyes of southern whites.

Antagonism between Unionists and rebels was still very strong in 1868. That year Ulysses S. Grant, running as a Republican, defeated Horatio Seymour, a New York Democrat, for president. Grant was not a Radical, but his platform supported congressional Reconstruction and endorsed black suffrage in the South. (Significantly, Republicans stopped short of endorsing it in the North.)

Election of 1868

In office Grant acted as an administrator of Reconstruction but not as its enthusiastic advocate. He vacillated in his dealings with the southern states, sometimes defending Republican regimes and sometimes currying favor with Democrats. On occasion Grant called out federal troops to stop violence or enforce acts of Congress, but neither he nor Andrew Johnson imposed anything approaching a military occupation on the South.

In 1870 and 1871 the violent campaigns of the Ku Klux Klan forced Congress to pass two Enforcement Acts and an anti-Klan law. These laws made actions by *individuals* against the civil and political rights of others a federal criminal offense for the first time. They also provided for election supervisors and permitted martial law and suspension of the writ of habeas corpus to combat murders, beatings, and threats by the Klan. Federal prosecutors used the laws rather selectively. In 1872 and 1873 Mississippi and the Carolinas saw many prosecutions; but in other states where violence flourished, the laws were virtually ignored. Southern juries sometimes refused to convict Klansmen.

Some conservative but influential Republicans opposed the anti-Klan laws. Rejecting other Republicans' arguments that the Thirteenth, Fourteenth, and Fifteenth Amendments had made the federal government the protector of the rights of citizens, these dissenters echoed an old Democratic charge that Congress was infringing on states' rights. This opposition foreshadowed a more general revolt within Republican ranks in 1872.

Disenchanted with Reconstruction, a group calling itself the Liberal Republicans bolted the party in 1872 and nominated Horace Greeley, the well-known editor of the

Liberal Republicans Revolt

New York Tribune, for president. The Liberal Republicans were a varied group, including civil service reformers, foes of corruption, and advocates of a lower tariff. They were united by two popular attitudes: distaste for federal intervention in the South and a desire to let market forces and the "best men" determine events there. The Dem-

ocrats also gave their nomination to Greeley in 1872. The combination was not enough to defeat Grant, who won reelection, but it reinforced Grant's desire to avoid confrontation with white southerners.

Dissatisfaction with Grant's administration grew during his second term. Corruption within the administration had become widespread, and Grant defended some of the culprits. In 1874, as Grant's popularity and his party's prestige declined, the Democrats recaptured the House of Representatives.

The effect of Democratic gains in Congress was to weaken the legislature's resolve on southern issues. Congress had already lifted the political disabilities of the Fourteenth Amendment from many former

Amnesty Act

Confederates. In 1872 it had adopted a sweeping Amnesty Act, which pardoned most of the remaining rebels and left only five hundred barred from political officeholding. In 1875 Congress passed a Civil Rights Act purporting to guarantee black people equal accommodations in public places, but the bill was watered down and contained no effective provisions for enforcement. Moreover, by 1876 the Democrats had regained control in all but three southern states.

Meanwhile, new concerns were capturing the public's attention. Industrialization and immigration were surging, hastening the pace of change in national life. Within only eight years, postwar industrial production increased by an impressive 75 percent. For the first time, non-agricultural workers outnumbered farmers, and only Britain's industrial output was greater than that of the United States.

Then the Panic of 1873 ushered in over five years of economic contraction. Three million people lost their jobs, and the clash between labor and capital became the major issue of the day. Class attitudes diverged, especially in large cities. Debtors and the unemployed sought easy money policies to spur economic expansion. Businessmen, disturbed by the strikes and industrial violence that accompanied the panic, became increasingly concerned about the defense of property.

Class conflict fueled a monetary issue: whether paper money—the Civil War greenbacks—should be kept in circulation. In 1872, Democratic farmers and debtors urged this policy to expand the money supply and raise prices, but businessmen, bankers, and creditors overruled them. Now hard times swelled the ranks of the "greenbackers"—voters who favored greenbacks and easy money. Congress voted in 1874 to increase the number of greenbacks in circulation, but Grant vetoed the bill in deference to the opinions of financial leaders. The next year, "sound money" interests prevailed in Congress, winning passage of a law requiring that greenbacks be convertible into gold after 1878. This law limited the inflationary impact of the greenbacks and aided creditors rather than debtors (such as the hard-pressed and angry farmers).

Greenbacks Versus Sound Money

The Supreme Court also participated in the northern retreat from Reconstruction. During the Civil War, the Court, had been cautious and reluctant to assert itself. Reaction to the *Dred Scott* decision (1857) had been so violent, and the Union's wartime emergency so great, that the Court avoided interference with government actions. In 1866, however, a case, *Ex parte Milligan*, reached the Court. Lambdin P. Milligan of Indiana had plotted to free Confederate prisoners of war and overthrow state governments. For these acts a military court sentenced Milligan, a civilian, to death. Milligan challenged the authority of the military tribunal, claiming that he had a right to a civil trial. The Supreme Court declared that military trials were illegal when civil courts were open and functioning, and its language indicated that the Court intended to reassert itself as a major force in national affairs.

In the 1870s the Court successfully renewed its challenge to Congress's actions when it narrowed the meaning and effectiveness of the Fourteenth Amendment. The *Slaughter-House* cases (1873) began in 1869, when the Louisiana legislature granted one company a monopoly on the slaughtering of livestock in

Supreme Court Decisions on Reconstruction

New Orleans. Rival butchers in the city promptly sued. Their attorney, former Supreme Court justice John A. Campbell, argued that the Fourteenth Amendment had revolutionized the constitutional system by bringing individual rights under federal protection.

The Court rejected Campbell's argument and thereby dealt a stunning blow to the scope and vitality of the Fourteenth Amendment. Indeed, it interpreted the "privileges and immunities" of citizens so narrowly that it reduced them almost to trivialities. State citizenship and national citizenship were separate, the Court declared. National citizenship involved only matters such as the right to travel freely from state to state and to use the navigable waters of the nation, and only these narrow rights were protected by the Fourteenth Amendment. With this interpretation, the words "No state shall make or enforce any law which shall abridge the privileges or immunities of citizens of the United States" disappeared, from that day until now, as a meaningful and effective part of the Constitution.

The Supreme Court also concluded that the butchers who sued had not been deprived of their rights or property in violation of the due-process clause of the amendment. The Court's majority declared that the framers of the recent amendments had not intended to "destroy" the federal system, in which the states exercised "powers for domestic and local government, including the regulation of civil rights." Thus the justices severely limited the amendment's potential for securing and protecting the rights of black citizens.

The next day the Court decided *Bradwell* v. *Illinois*, a case in which Myra Bradwell, a female attorney, had been denied the right to practice law in Illinois on account of her gender. Pointing to the Fourteenth Amendment, Bradwell's attorneys contended that the state had unconstitutionally abridged her "privileges and immunities" as a citizen. The Supreme Court rejected her claim, alluding to women's traditional role in the home.

In 1876 the Court weakened the Reconstruction-era amendments even further by emasculating the enforcement clause of the Fourteenth Amendment and revealing deficiencies inherent in the Fifteenth Amendment. In *U.S.* v. *Cruikshank* the Court overruled the conviction under the 1870 Enforcement Act of Louisiana of whites who had attacked a meeting of blacks and conspired to deprive them of their rights. The justices ruled that the Fourteenth Amendment did not give the federal government power to act against these whites. The duty of protecting citizens' equal rights "was originally assumed by the States; and it still remains there." As for the protection of "unalienable rights," the Court said that "Sovereignty, for this purpose, rests alone with the States." In *U.S.* v. *Reese* the Court noted that the Fifteenth Amendment did not guarantee a citizen's right to vote but merely listed certain impermissible grounds for denying suffrage. Thus a path lay open for southern states to disfranchise blacks for supposedly nonracial reasons—lack of education or property or descent from a grandfather qualified to vote before the Reconstruction Act of 1867. These "grandfather clauses" became a means to give the vote to illiterate whites while excluding blacks.

As the 1876 elections approached, most political observers saw that the North was no longer willing to pursue the goals of Reconstruction. The

Election of 1876

results of a disputed presidential election confirmed this fact. Samuel J. Tilden, the Democratic governor of New York, ran strongly in the South and needed only one more electoral vote to triumph over Rutherford B. Hayes, the Republican nominee. Nineteen votes from Louisiana, South Carolina, and Florida were disputed; both Democrats and Republicans claimed to have won in those states despite fraud committed by their opponents. One vote from Oregon was undecided because of a technicality.

To resolve this unprecedented situation, Congress established a fifteen-member electoral commission. In the interest of impartiality, membership on the commission was to be balanced between Democrats and Republicans. But one independent Republican, Supreme Court Justice

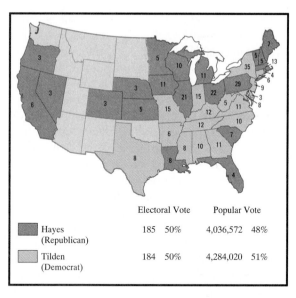

	Electoral Vote		Popular Vote	
Hayes (Republican)	185	50%	4,036,572	48%
Tilden (Democrat)	184	50%	4,284,020	51%

Presidential Election, 1876   *In 1876 a combination of solid southern support and Democratic gains in the North gave Samuel Tilden the majority of popular votes, but Rutherford B. Hayes won the disputed election in the electoral college.*

David Davis, refused appointment in order to accept his election as a senator. A regular Republican took his place, and the Republican Party prevailed 8 to 7 on every decision, along strict party lines. Hayes would become president if Congress accepted the commission's findings.

Congressional acceptance was not certain, and many citizens worried that the nation had entered a major constitutional crisis and would slip once again into civil war. The crisis was resolved when Democrats acquiesced in the election of Hayes (see map above). Scholars have found evidence of negotiations between Hayes's supporters and southerners who wanted federal aid to railroads, internal improvements, federal patronage, and removal of troops from southern states. But studies of Congress conclude that these negotiations did not have a deciding effect on the outcome: neither party was well enough organized to implement and enforce a bargain between the sections. Northern and southern

Democrats simply decided they could not win and did not contest the election. Thus Hayes became president, and Reconstruction was unmistakably over.

Southern Democrats rejoiced, but African-Americans grieved over the betrayal of their hopes for equality. For many African-Americans, the

Exodusters Move West

only hope was to leave the South, where real freedom was no longer a possibility. In South Carolina, Louisiana, Mississippi, and other southern states, thousands gathered up their possessions and migrated to Kansas. They were known as Exodusters, disappointed people still searching for their share in the American dream.

 ## Conclusion

The nation ended over fifteen years of bloody Civil War and controversial Reconstruction without establishing full freedom for African-Americans. This contradictory record typified the results of Reconstruction in many other ways. A tumultuous period brought tremendous change, yet many things remained the same. Because extraordinary situations required revolutionary changes, the North had acted. The Union victory brought about an increase in federal power, stronger nationalism, unprecedented federal intervention in the southern states, and landmark amendments to the Constitution. But there was no commitment to make these changes endure, so the revolution remained partial. The nation turned away from the needs of its African-American citizens and began to focus on issues related to industrialism and an increasingly interrelated national economy.

Suggestions for Further Reading

National Policy, Politics, and Constitutional Law

Richard H. Abbott, *The Republican Party and the South, 1855–1877* (1986); Herman Belz, *Emancipation and Equal Rights* (1978); Michael Les Benedict, *A Compromise of Principle:*

Congressional Republicans and Reconstruction, 1863–1869 (1974); Michael Les Benedict, *The Impeachment and Trial of Andrew Johnson* (1973); Michael Kent Curtis, *No State Shall Abridge* (1987); Harold M. Hyman, *A More Perfect Union* (1973); Ronald J. Jensen, *The Alaska Purchase and Russian-American Relations* (1975); William S. McFeely, *Grant* (1981); Brooks D. Simpson, *Let Us Have Peace* (1991); Kenneth M. Stampp, *The Era of Reconstruction* (1965); Hans L. Trefousse, *Andrew Johnson* (1989).

The Freed Slaves

Ira Berlin, ed., *Freedom: A Documentary History of Emancipation, 1861–1867* (1984); Orville Vernon Burton, *In My Father's House Are Many Mansions* (1985); Edmund L. Drago, *Black Politicians and Reconstruction in Georgia* (1982); Gerald Jaynes, *Branches Without Roots: The Genesis of the Black Working Class in the American South, 1862–1882* (1986); Leon Litwack, *Been in the Storm So Long* (1979); Edward Magdol, *A Right to the Land* (1977); Robert Morris, *Reading, 'Riting and Reconstruction* (1981); Howard Rabinowitz, ed., *Southern Black Leaders in Reconstruction* (1982); Clarence Walker, *A Rock in a Weary Land* (1982).

Politics and Reconstruction in the South

Richard N. Current, *Those Terrible Carpetbaggers* (1988); Jonathan Daniels, *Prince of Carpetbaggers* (1958); W. E. B. Du Bois, *Black Reconstruction* (1935); Paul D. Escott, *Many Excellent People: Power and Privilege in North Carolina, 1850–1900* (1985); W. McKee Evans, *Ballots and Fence Rails: Reconstruction on the Lower Cape Fear* (1966); Michael W. Fitzgerald, *The Union League Movement in the Deep South* (1989); Eric Foner, *Reconstruction: America's Unfinished Revolution, 1863–1877* (1988); William C. Harris, *The Day of the Carpetbagger* (1979); Thomas Holt, *Black over White: Negro Political Leadership in South Carolina During Reconstruction* (1977); Michael Perman, *The Road to Redemption* (1984); Michael Perman, *Reunion Without Compromise* (1973); Lawrence N. Powell, *New Masters* (1980); George C. Rable, *But There Was No Peace* (1984); James Roark, *Masters Without Slaves* (1977); James Sefton, *The United States Army and Reconstruction, 1865–1877* (1967); Mark W. Summers, *Railroads, Reconstruction, and the Gospel of Prosperity* (1984); Allen Trelease, *White Terror* (1967); Michael Wayne, *The Reshaping of Plantation Society* (1983); Sarah Woolfolk Wiggins, *The Scalawag in Alabama Politics, 1865–1881* (1977).

Women, Family, and Social History

Ellen Carol Dubois, *Feminism and Suffrage* (1978); Herbert G. Gutman, *The Black Family in Slavery and Freedom, 1750–1925* (1976); Elizabeth Jacoway, *Yankee Missionaries in the South* (1979); Jacqueline Jones, *Labor of Love, Labor of Sorrow* (1985); Jacqueline Jones, *Soldiers of Light and Love* (1980); Mary P. Ryan, *Women in Public* (1990).

The End of Reconstruction

William Gillette, *Retreat from Reconstruction, 1869–1879* (1980); William Gillette, *The Right to Vote* (1969); Keith Ian Polakoff, *The Politics of Inertia* (1973); C. Vann Woodward, *Reunion and Reaction* (1951).

Reconstruction's Legacy for the South

Robert G. Athearn, *In Search of Canaan* (1978); Jay R. Mandle, *The Roots of Black Poverty* (1978); Nell Irvin Painter, *Exodusters* (1976); Howard Rabinowitz, *Race Relations in the Urban South, 1865–1890* (1978); Roger L. Ransom and Richard Sutch, *One Kind of Freedom* (1977); Jonathan M. Wiener, *Social Origins of the New South* (1978); C. Vann Woodward, *Origins of the New South* (1951).

Historical Reference Books by Subject:
Encyclopedias, Dictionaries, Atlases, Chronologies, and Statistics

American History: General

Gorton Carruth, ed., *The Encyclopedia of American Facts and Dates* (1993); *Dictionary of American History* (1976) and Joan Hoff and Robert H. Ferrell, eds., *Supplement* (1996); Eric Foner and John A. Garraty, eds., *The Reader's Companion to American History* (1991); Bernard Grun, *The Timetables of History* (1991); *International Encyclopedia of the Social Sciences* (1968–); Richard B. Morris and Jeffrey B. Morris, eds., *Encyclopedia of American History* (1996); Harry Ritter, *Dictionary of Concepts in History* (1986); Arthur M. Schlesinger, Jr., ed., *The Almanac of American History* (1983); Lawrence Urdang, ed., *The Timetables of American History* (1996); U.S. Bureau of the Census, *Historical Statistics of the United States* (1975).

American History: General, Twentieth Century

John D. Buenker and Edward R. Kantowicz, eds., *Historical Dictionary of the Progressive Era, 1890–1920* (1988); Robert H. Ferrell and John S. Bowman, eds., *The Twentieth Century: An Almanac* (1984); George H. Gallup, *The Gallup Poll: Public Opinion, 1935–1971* (1972), *1972–1977* (1978), and annual reports (1979–); Stanley Hochman and Eleanor Hochman, *A Dictionary of Contemporary American History* (1993); Stanley I. Kutler, ed., *Encyclopedia of the United States in the Twentieth Century* (1995); Peter B. Levy, *Encyclopedia of the Reagan-Bush Years* (1996); James S. Olson, *Historical Dictionary of the 1920s* (1988); Thomas Parker and Douglas Nelson, *Day by Day: The Sixties* (1983).

American History: General Atlases and Gazetteers

Geoffrey Barraclough, ed., *The Times Atlas of World History* (1994); Rodger Doyle, *Atlas of Contemporary America* (1994); Robert H. Ferrell and Richard Natkiel, *Atlas of American History* (1987); Edward W. Fox, *Atlas of American History* (1964); Archie Hobson, *The Cambridge Gazetteer of the United States and Canada* (1996); Eric Homberger, *The Penguin Historical Atlas of North America* (1995); Kenneth T. Jackson and James T. Adams, *Atlas of American History* (1978); Catherine M. Mattson and Mark T. Mattson, *Contemporary Atlas of the United States* (1990); National Geographic Society, *Historical Atlas of the United States* (1994); U.S. Department of the Interior, *National Atlas of the United States* (1970). Other atlases are listed under specific categories.

American History: General Biographies

Lucian Boia, ed., *Great Historians of the Modern Age* (1991); John S. Bowman, *The Cambridge Dictionary of American Biography* (1995); *Current Biography* (1940–); *Dictionary of American Biography* (1928–); John Garraty and Jerome L. Sternstein, eds., *The Encyclopedia of American Biography* (1996); *National Cyclopedia of American Biography* (1898–). Other biographical works appear under specific categories.

African Americans

Molefi Asante and Mark T. Mattson, *Historical and Cultural Atlas of African-Americans* (1991); John N. Ingham, *African-American Business Leaders* (1993); Bruce Kellner, *The Harlem Renaissance* (1984); Rayford W. Logan and Michael R. Winston, eds., *The Dictionary of American Negro Biography* (1983); W. A. Low and Virgil A. Clift, eds., *Encyclopedia of Black America* (1981); Sharon Harley, *The Timetables of African-American History* (1995); Darlene C. Hine et al., eds., *Black Women in White America* (1994); Charles D. Lowery and John F. Marszalek, eds., *Encyclopedia of African-American Civil Rights* (1992); Randall M. Miller and John D. Smith, eds., *Dictionary of Afro-American Slavery* (1997); Larry G. Murphy et al., eds., *Encyclopedia of African American*

Religions (1993); Harry A. Ploski and James Williams, eds., *The Negro Almanac* (1989); Dorothy C. Salem, ed., *African American Women* (1993).

American Revolution and Colonies

Richard Blanco and Paul Sanborn, eds., *The American Revolution* (1993); Lester J. Cappon, ed., *Atlas of Early American History: The Revolutionary Era, 1760–1790* (1976); Jacob E. Cooke, ed., *Encyclopedia of the American Colonies* (1993); John M. Faragher, ed., *The Encyclopedia of Colonial and Revolutionary America* (1990); Jack P. Greene and J. R. Pole, eds., *The Blackwell Encyclopedia of the American Revolution* (1991); Douglas W. Marshall and Howard H. Peckham, *Campaigns of the American Revolution* (1976); Gregory Palmer, ed., *Biographical Sketches of Loyalists of the American Revolution* (1984); John W. Raimo, ed., *Biographical Directory of American Colonial and Revolutionary Governors, 1607–1789* (1980); *Rand-McNally Atlas of the American Revolution* (1974); Seymour I. Schwartz, *The French and Indian War, 1754–1763* (1995).

Architecture

William D. Hunt, Jr., ed., *Encyclopedia of American Architecture* (1980).

Asian Americans

Hyung-Chan Kim, ed., *Dictionary of Asian American History* (1986); Brian Niiya, ed., *Japanese American History* (1993). See also "Immigration and Ethnic Groups."

Business and the Economy

Christine Ammer and Dean S. Ammer, *Dictionary of Business and Economics* (1983); Douglas Auld and Graham Bannock, *The American Dictionary of Economics* (1983); Michael J. Freeman, *Atlas of World Economy* (1991); Douglas Greenwald, *Encyclopedia of Economics* (1982); John N. Ingham, *Biographical Dictionary of American Business Leaders* (1983); John N. Ingham and Lynne B. Feldman, *Contemporary American Business Leaders* (1990); William H. Mulligan, Jr., ed., *A Historical Dictionary of American Industrial Language* (1988); Glenn G. Munn, *Encyclopedia of Banking and Finance* (1973); Paul Paskoff, ed., *Encyclopedia of American Business History and Biography* (1989); Glenn Porter, *Encyclopedia of American Economic History* (1980); Richard Robinson, *United States Business History, 1602–1988* (1990); Malcolm Warner, ed., *International Encyclopedia of Business and Management* (1996). See also "African Americans" and "Transportation."

Cities and Towns

Charles Abrams, *The Language of Cities: A Glossary of Terms* (1971); John L. Androit, ed., *Township Atlas of the United States* (1979); David J. Bodenhamer and Robert J. Barrows, eds., *The Encyclopedia of Indianapolis* (1994); Melvin G. Holli and Peter d'A. Jones, eds., *Biographical Dictionary of American Mayors, 1820–1980: Big City Mayors* (1981); Kenneth T. Jackson, ed., *Encyclopedia of New York City* (1995); Ory M. Nergal, ed., *The Encyclopedia of American Cities* (1980); David D. Van Tassel and John J. Grabowski, eds., *The Dictionary of Cleveland Biography* (1996); David D. Van Tassel and John J. Grabowski, eds., *The Encyclopedia of Cleveland History* (1987). See also "Politics and Government."

Civil War and Reconstruction

Mark M. Boatner III, *The Civil War Dictionary* (1988); Richard N. Current, ed., *Encyclopedia of the Confederacy* (1993); John T. Hubbell and James W. Geary, eds., *Biographical Dictionary of the Union* (1995); Kenneth C. Martis, *The Historical Atlas of the Congresses of the Confederate States of America: 1861–1865* (1994); James M. McPherson, ed., *The Atlas of the Civil War* (1994); Mark E. Neely, Jr., *The Abraham Lincoln Encyclopedia* (1982); Craig L. Symonds, *A Battlefield Atlas of the Civil War* (1983); Hans L. Trefousse, *Historical Dictionary of Reconstruction* (1991); U.S. War Department, *The Official Atlas of the Civil War* (1958); Jon L. Wakelyn, ed., *Biographical Dictionary of the Confederacy* (1977); Ezra J. Warner and W. Buck Yearns, *Biographical Register of the Confederate Congress* (1975); Steven E. Woodworth, ed., *The American Civil War* (1996). See also "South" and "Politics and Government."

Constitution, Supreme Court, and Judiciary

David Bradley and Shelly F. Fishkin, eds., *The Encyclopedia of Civil Rights* (1997); Congressional Quarterly, *The Supreme Court A to Z* (1994); Kermit L. Hall, ed., *The Oxford Companion to the Supreme Court of the United States* (1992); Richard F. Hixson, *Mass Media and the Constitution* (1989); Robert J. Janosik, ed., *Encyclopedia of the American Judicial System* (1987); John W. Johnson, ed., *Historic U.S. Court Cases, 1690–1990* (1992); Arthur S. Leonard, ed., *Sexuality and the Law* (1993); Leonard W. Levy et al., eds., *Encyclopedia of the American Constitution* (1986); Fred R. Shapiro, *The Oxford Dictionary of American Legal Quotations* (1993); Melvin I. Urofsky, ed., *The Supreme Court Justices* (1994). See also "Politics and Government."

Crime, Violence, Police, and Prisons

William G. Bailey, *Encyclopedia of Police Science* (1994); Sanford H. Kadish, ed., *Encyclopedia of Crime and Justice* (1983); Marilyn D. McShane and Frank P. Williams III, eds., *Encyclopedia of American Prisons* (1995); Michael Newton and Judy Ann Newton, *Racial and Religious Violence in America* (1991); Michael Newton and Judy Newton, *The Ku Klux Klan* (1990); Carl Sifakis, *Encyclopedia of Assassinations* (1990); Carl Sifakis, *The Encyclopedia of American Crime* (1982).

Culture and Folklore

Hennig Cohen and Tristam Potter Coffin, eds., *The Folklore of American Holidays* (1987); Richard M. Dorson, ed., *Handbook of American Folklore* (1983); Robert L. Gale, *A Cultural Encyclopedia of the 1850s in America* (1993); Robert L. Gale, *The Gay Nineties in America* (1992); M. Thomas Inge, ed., *Handbook of American Popular Culture* (1979–1981); Wolfgang Mieder et al., eds., *A Dictionary of American Proverbs* (1992); J. F. Rooney, Jr., et al., eds., *This Remarkable Continent: An Atlas of United States and Canadian Society and Cultures* (1982); Jane Stern and Michael Stern, *Encyclopedia of Pop Culture* (1992); Justin Wintle, ed., *Makers of Nineteenth Century Culture, 1800–1914* (1982). See also "Entertainment," "Mass Media and Journalism," "Music," and "Sports."

Education and Libraries

Lee C. Deighton, ed., *The Encyclopedia of Education* (1971); Joseph C. Kiger, ed., *Research Institutions and Learned Societies* (1982); John F. Ohles, ed., *Biographical Dictionary of American Educators* (1978); Wayne A. Wiegard and Donald E. Davis, Jr., eds., *Encyclopedia of Library History* (1994).

Entertainment

Tim Brooks and Earle Marsh, *The Complete Directory to Prime Time Network and Cable TV Shows, 1946–Present* (1995); Barbara N. Cohen-Stratyner, *Biographical Dictionary of Dance* (1982); John Dunning, *Tune in Yesterday* (radio) (1967); Larry Langman and Edgar Borg, *Encyclopedia of American War Films* (1989); Larry Langman and David Ebner, *Encyclopedia of American Spy Films* (1990); *Notable Names in the American Theater* (1976); Andrew Sarris, *The American Cinema: Directors and Directions, 1929–1968* (1968); Anthony Slide, *The American Film Industry* (1986); Anthony Slide, *The Encyclopedia of Vaudeville* (1994); Evelyn M. Truitt, *Who Was Who on Screen* (1977); Don B. Wilmeth and Tice L. Miller, eds., *The Cambridge Guide to American Theatre* (1993). See also "Culture and Folklore," "Mass Media and Journalism," "Music," and "Sports."

Environment and Conservation

André R. Cooper, ed., *Cooper's Comprehensive Environmental Desk Reference* (1996); Forest History Society, *Encyclopedia of American Forest and Conservation History* (1983); Irene Franck and David Brownstone, *The Green Encyclopedia* (1992); Robert J. Mason and Mark T. Mattson, *Atlas of United States Environmental Issues* (1990); Robert Paehlke, ed., *Conservation and Environmentalism* (1995); World Resources Institute, *Environmental Almanac* (1992).

Exploration: From Columbus to Space

Silvio A. Bedini, ed., *The Christopher Columbus Encyclopedia* (1992); Michael Cassutt, *Who's Who in Space* (1987); W. P. Cumming et al., *The Discovery of North America* (1972); William Goetzmann and Glyndwr Williams, *The Atlas of North American Exploration* (1992); Clive Holland, *Arctic Exploration and Development* (1993); Adrian Johnson, *America Explored* (1974); Kenneth Nebenzahl, *Atlas of Columbus and the Great Discoveries* (1990). See also "Science and Technology."

Foreign Relations

Thomas S. Arms, *Encyclopedia of the Cold War* (1994); Gerard Chaliand and Jean-Pierre Rageau, *Strategic Atlas* (1990); Alexander DeConde, ed., *Encyclopedia of American Foreign Policy* (1978); Margaret B. Denning and J. K. Sweeney, *Handbook of American Diplomacy* (1992); Graham Evans and Jeffrey Newnham, eds., *The Dictionary of World Politics* (1990); John E. Findling, *Dictionary of American Diplomatic History* (1989); Chas. W. Freeman, Jr., *The Diplomat's Dictionary* (1997); Michael Kidron and Ronald Segal, *The State of the World Atlas* (1995); Bruce W. Jentleson and Thomas G. Paterson, eds., *Encyclopedia of U.S. Foreign Relations* (1997); Warren F. Kuehl, ed., *Biographical Dictionary of Internationalists* (1983); Edward Lawson, *Encyclopedia of Human Rights* (1991); Jack C. Plano and Roy Olton, eds., *The International Relations Dictionary* (1988). See also "Peace Movements and Pacifism," "Politics and Government," "Military and Wars," and specific wars.

Immigration and Ethnic Groups

James P. Allen and Eugene J. Turner, *We the People: An Atlas of America's Ethnic Diversity* (1988); Gerald

Chaliand and Jean-Pierre Rageau, *The Penguin Atlas of Diasporas* (1995); Francesco Cordasco, ed., *Dictionary of American Immigration History* (1990); Judy B. Litoff and Judith McDonnell, eds., *European Immigrant Women in the United States* (1994); Sally M. Miller, ed., *The Ethnic Press in the United States* (1987); Stephan Thernstrom, ed., *Harvard Encyclopedia of American Ethnic Groups* (1980). See also "Asian Americans," "Jewish Americans," and "Latinos."

Jewish Americans

American Jewish Yearbook (1899–); Jack Fischel and Sanford Pinsker, eds., *Jewish-American History and Culture* (1992); Geoffrey Wigoder, *Dictionary of Jewish Biography* (1991). See also "Immigration and Ethnic Groups."

Labor

Ronald L. Filippelli, *Labor Conflict in the United States* (1990); Gary M. Fink, ed., *Biographical Dictionary of American Labor* (1984); Gary M. Fink, ed., *Labor Unions* (1977); Philip S. Foner, *First Facts of American Labor* (1984).

Latinos

Nicolás Kanellos, ed., *The Hispanic-American Almanac* (1993); Nicolás Kanellos, ed., *Reference Library of Hispanic America* (1993); Matt S. Meier, *Mexican-American Biographies* (1988); Matt S. Meier, *Notable Latino Americans* (1997); Matt S. Meier and Feliciano Rivera, *Dictionary of Mexican American History* (1981); Joseph C. Tardiff and L. Mpho Mabunda, eds., *Dictionary of Hispanic Biography* (1996). See also "Immigration and Ethnic Groups."

Literature

James T. Callow and Robert J. Reilly, *Guide to American Literature* (1976–1977); *Dictionary of Literary Biography* (1978–); Eugene Ehrlich and Gorton Carruth, *The Oxford Illustrated Literary Guide to the United States* (1982); Jon Tuska and Vicki Piekarski, *Encyclopedia of Frontier and Western Fiction* (1983). See also "Culture and Folklore," "The South," and "Women."

Mass Media and Journalism

Robert V. Hudson, *Mass Media* (1987); Joseph P. McKerns, ed., *Biographical Dictionary of American Journalism* (1989); William H. Taft, ed., *Encyclopedia of Twentieth-Century Journalists* (1986). See also "Constitution, Supreme Court, and Judiciary," "Entertainment," and "Immigration and Ethnic Groups."

Medicine and Nursing

Rima D. Apple, ed., *Women, Health, and Medicine in America* (1990); Vern L. Bullough et al., eds., *American Nursing: A Biographical Dictionary* (1988); Martin Kaufman et al., eds., *Dictionary of American Nursing Biography* (1988); Martin Kaufman et al., eds., *Dictionary of American Medical Biography* (1984); George L. Maddox, ed., *The Encyclopedia of Aging* (1987).

Military and Wars

William M. Arkin et al., *Encyclopedia of the U.S. Military* (1990); Charles D. Bright, ed., *Historical Dictionary of the U.S. Air Force* (1992); Andre Corvisier, ed., *A Dictionary of Military History* (1994); R. Ernest Dupuy and Trevor N. Dupuy, *The Harper Encyclopedia of Military History* (1993); John E. Jessup, ed., *Encyclopedia of the American Military* (1994); Kenneth Macksey and William Woodhouse, *The Penguin Encyclopedia of Modern Warfare* (1992); Franklin D. Margiotta, ed., *Brassey's Encyclopedia of Naval Forces and Warfare* (1996); James I. Matray, ed., *Historical Dictionary of the Korean War* (1991); Stanley Sandler, ed., *The Korean War* (1995); Roger J. Spiller and Joseph G. Dawson III, eds., *Dictionary of American Military Biography* (1984); Jerry K. Sweeney, ed., *A Handbook of American Military History* (1996); Peter G. Tsouras et al., *The United States Army* (1991); U.S. Military Academy, *The West Point Atlas of American Wars, 1689–1953* (1959); Bruce W. Watson et al., eds., *United States Intelligence* (1990); *Webster's American Military Biographies* (1978); Bruce W. Watson and Susan M. Watson, *The United States Air Force* (1992); Bruce W. Watson and Susan M. Watson, *The United States Navy* (1991). See also "American Revolution and Colonies," "Civil War and Reconstruction," "Vietnam War," and "World War II."

Music

John Chilton, *Who's Who of Jazz* (1972); Donald Clarke, ed., *The Penguin Encyclopedia of Popular Music* (1989); Edward Jablonski, *The Encyclopedia of American Music* (1981); Roger Lax and Frederick Smith, *The Great Song Thesaurus* (1984); Philip D. Morehead, *The New International Dictionary of Music* (1993); Austin Sonnier, Jr., *A Guide to the Blues* (1994). See also "Culture and Folklore" and "Entertainment."

Native Americans and Indian Affairs

Gretchen M. Bataille, ed., *Native American Women* (1992); Michael Coe et al., *Atlas of Ancient America* (1986); Mary B. Davis, ed., *Native America in the Twentieth Century* (1994); Frederick J. Dockstader, *Great*

North American Indians (1977); *Handbook of North American Indians* (1978–); Sam D. Gill and Irene F. Sullivan, *Dictionary of Native American Mythology* (1992); J. Norman Heard et al., *Handbook of the American Frontier: Four Centuries of Indian-White Relationships* (1987–); Bruce E. Johnson and Donald A. Grinde, *The Encyclopedia of Native American Biography* (1997); Barry Klein, ed., *Reference Encyclopedia of the American Indian* (1993); Francis P. Prucha, *Atlas of American Indian Affairs* (1990); Paul Stuart, *Nation Within a Nation: Historical Statistics of American Indians* (1987); Helen H. Tanner, ed., *Atlas of Great Lakes Indian History* (1987); Carl Waldman, *Encyclopedia of Native American Tribes* (1988); Carl Waldman, *Atlas of the North American Indian* (1985).

The New Deal and Franklin D. Roosevelt

Otis L. Graham, Jr., and Meghan R. Wander, eds., *Franklin D. Roosevelt: His Life and Times* (1985); James S. Olson, ed., *Historical Dictionary of the New Deal* (1985). See also "Politics and Government."

Peace Movements and Pacifism

Harold Josephson et al., eds., *Biographical Dictionary of Modern Peace Leaders* (1985); Ervin Laszlo and Jong Y. Yoo, eds., *World Encyclopedia of Peace* (1986); Robert S. Meyer, *Peace Organizations Past and Present* (1988); Nancy L. Roberts, *American Peace Writers, Editors, and Periodicals* (1991). See also "Military and Wars" and specific wars.

Politics and Government: General

Erik W. Austin and Jerome M. Clubb, *Political Facts of the United States Since 1789* (1986); *The Columbia Dictionary of Political Biography* (1991); Jack P. Greene, ed., *Encyclopedia of American Political History* (1984); Leon Hurwitz, *Historical Dictionary of Censorship in the United States* (1985); Edwin V. Mitchell, *An Encyclopedia of American Politics* (1968); Philip Rees, *Biographical Dictionary of the Extreme Right Since 1890* (1991); Charles R. Ritter et al., *American Legislative Leaders, 1850–1910* (1989); William Safire, *Safire's Political Dictionary* (1978); Robert Scruton, *A Dictionary of Political Thought* (1982); Jay M. Shafritz, *The HarperCollins Dictionary of American Government and Politics* (1992). See also "Cities and Towns," "Constitution, Supreme Court, and Judiciary," "States," and the following sections.

Politics and Government: Congress

Donald C. Brown et al., eds., *The Encyclopedia of the United States Congress* (1995); Stephen G. Christianson, *Facts About the Congress* (1996); Congressional Quarterly, *Biographical Directory of the American Congress, 1774–1996* (1997); Congressional Quarterly, *Congress and the Nation, 1945–1984* (1965–1985); Kenneth C. Martis, *Historical Atlas of Political Parties in the United States Congress, 1789–1989* (1989); Kenneth C. Martis, *Historical Atlas of United States Congressional Districts, 1789–1983* (1982); Joel H. Silbey, ed., *Encyclopedia of the American Legislative System* (1994).

Politics and Government: Election Statistics

Congressional Quarterly, *Guide to U.S. Elections* (1975); L. Sandy Maisel, ed., *Political Parties and Elections in the United States* (1991); Richard M. Scammon et al., eds., *America Votes* (1956–); Harold W. Stanley and Richard G. Niemi, *Vital Statistics on American Politics* (1990); G. Scott Thomas, *The Pursuit of the White House* (1987).

Politics and Government: Parties

Earl R. Kruschke, *Encyclopedia of Third Parties in the United States* (1991); George T. Kurian, ed., *The Encyclopedia of the Republican Party and The Encyclopedia of the Democratic Party* (1996); Edward L. Schapsmeier and Frederick H. Schapsmeier, eds., *Political Parties and Civic Action Groups* (1981). See also other listings for "Politics and Government."

Politics and Government: Presidency and Executive Branch

Henry F. Graff, *The Presidents* (1996); Bernard S. Katz and C. Daniel Vencill, eds., *Biographical Dictionary of the United States Secretaries of the Treasury, 1789–1995* (1996); Richard S. Kirkendall, ed., *The Harry S Truman Encyclopedia* (1989); Leonard W. Levy and Louis Fisher, eds., *Encyclopedia of the American Presidency* (1993); Merrill D. Peterson, ed., *Thomas Jefferson: A Reference Biography* (1986); Lyn Ragsdale, *Vital Statistics on the Presidency* (1995); Robert A. Rutland, ed., *James Madison and the American Nation* (1994); Robert Sobel, ed., *Biographical Directory of the United States Executive Branch, 1774–1977* (1977). See other categories for various presidents.

Politics and Government: Radicalism and the Left

Mari Jo Buhle et al., eds., *The American Radical* (1994); Mari Jo Buhle et al., eds., *Encyclopedia of the American Left* (1998); David DeLeon, ed., *Leaders of the 1960s* (1994); Bernard K. Johnpoll and Harvey Klehr, eds., *Biographical Dictionary of the American Left* (1986).

Religion and Cults

Henry Bowden, *Dictionary of American Religious Biography* (1993); S. Kent Brown et al., eds., *Historical Atlas of Mormonism* (1995); John T. Ellis and Robert Trisco, *A Guide to American Catholic History* (1982); Edwin Gaustad and Philip L. Barlow, *New Historical Atlas of Religion in America* (1998); Samuel S. Hill, Jr., ed., *Encyclopedia of Religion in the South* (1984); Bill J. Leonard, *Dictionary of Baptists in America* (1994); Donald Lewis, ed., *A Dictionary of Evangelical Biography* (1995); Charles H. Lippy and Peter W. Williams, eds., *Encyclopedia of the American Religious Experience* (1988); J. Gordon Melton, *The Encyclopedia of American Religions* (1987); J. Gordon Melton, *Biographical Dictionary of American Cult and Sect Leaders* (1986); J. Gordon Melton, *The Encyclopedic Handbook of Cults in America* (1992); Mark A. Noll and Nathan O. Hatch, eds., *Eerdmans Handbook to Christianity in America* (1983); Arthur C. Piepkorn, *Profiles in Belief: The Religious Bodies of the United States and Canada* (1977–1979); Paul J. Weber and W. Landis Jones, *U.S. Religious Interest Groups* (1994). See also "African Americans."

Science and Technology

James W. Cortada, *Historical Dictionary of Data Processing* (1987); Clark A. Elliott, *Biographical Index to American Science: The Seventeenth Century to 1920* (1990); Charles C. Gillispie, ed., *Dictionary of Scientific Biography* (1970–); National Academy of Sciences, *Biographical Memoirs* (1877–); Roy Porter, ed., *The Biographical Dictionary of Scientists* (1994). See also "Exploration."

Social History and Reform

Mary K. Cayton et al., eds., *Encyclopedia of American Social History* (1993); Wayne R. Dynes, ed., *Encyclopedia of Homosexuality* (1990); Louis Filler, *Dictionary of American Social Change* (1982); Louis Filler, *A Dictionary of American Social Reform* (1963); Robert S. Fogarty, *Dictionary of American Communal and Utopian History* (1980); Joseph M. Hawes and Elizabeth I. Nybakken, eds., *American Families* (1991); David Hey, ed., *The Oxford Companion to Local and Family History* (1996); Harold M. Keele and Joseph C. Kiger, eds., *Foundations* (1984); Mark E. Lender, *Dictionary of American Temperance Biography* (1984); Patricia M. Melvin, ed., *American Community Organizations* (1986); Randall M. Miller and Paul A. Cimbala, eds., *American Reform and Reformers* (1996); Roger S. Powers and William B. Vogele, eds., *Protest, Power, and Change* (1996); Alvin J. Schmidt, *Fraternal Organizations* (1980); Peter N. Stearns, ed., *Encyclopedia of Social History* (1993); Walter I. Trattner, *Biographical Dictionary of Social Welfare in America* (1986); Alden Whitman, ed., *American Reformers* (1985). See also "Crime, Violence, Police, and Prisons."

South

Edward L. Ayers and Brad Mittendorf, eds., *The Oxford Book of the American South* (1997); Robert Bain et al., eds., *Southern Writers* (1979); Kenneth Coleman and Charles S. Gurr, eds., *Dictionary of Georgia Biography* (1983); William S. Powell, ed., *Dictionary of North Carolina Biography* (1979–1996); David C. Roller and Robert W. Twyman, eds., *The Encyclopedia of Southern History* (1979); Walter P. Webb et al., eds., *The Handbook of Texas* (1952, 1976); Charles R. Wilson and William Ferris, eds., *Encyclopedia of Southern Culture* (1986). See also "Civil War and Reconstruction," "Politics and Government," and "States."

Sports

Peter C. Bjarkman, ed., *Encyclopedia of Major League Baseball Team Histories* (1991); Ralph Hickok, *The Encyclopedia of North American Sports History* (1991); Zander Hollander, *The NBA's Official Encyclopedia of Pro Basketball* (1981); Frank G. Menke and Suzanne Treat, *The Encyclopedia of Sports* (1977); *The NFL's Official Encyclopedic History of Professional Football* (1977); David L. Porter, *Biographical Dictionary of American Sports: Baseball* (1987), *Basketball and Other Indoor Sports* (1989), *Football* (1987), and *Outdoor Sports* (1988); David L. Porter, ed., *Biographical Dictionary of American Sports: 1989–1992 Supplement* (1992) and *1992–1995 Supplement* (1995); Paul Soderberg et al., *The Big Book of Halls of Fame in the United States and Canada* (1977); David Wallechinsky, *The Complete Book of the Summer Olympics* (1996); David Wallechinsky, *The Complete Book of the Winter Olympics* (1993). See also "Culture and Folklore."

States

Gary Alampi, ed., *Gale State Rankings Reporter* (1994); Roy R. Glashan, comp., *American Governors and Gubernatorial Elections, 1775–1978* (1979); John Hoffmann, ed., *A Guide to the History of Illinois* (1991); Edith R. Hornor, *Almanac of the Fifty States* (1993); Joseph E. Kallenback and Jessamine S. Kallenback, *American State Governors, 1776–1976* (1977); Joseph N. Kane et al., eds., *Facts About the States* (1994); John E. Kleber et al., eds., *The Kentucky Encyclopedia* (1992); Thomas A. McMullin and Marie Mullaney, *Biographical Directory of the Governors of the United States, 1983–1987* (1988) and

1988–1993 (1994); Marie Mullaney, *Biographical Directory of the Governors of the United States 1988–1994* (1994); Thomas J. Noel, *Historical Atlas of Colorado* (1994); John W. Raimo, ed., *Biographical Directory of the Governors of the United States, 1978–1983* (1985); James W. Scott and Ronald L. De Lorme, *Historical Atlas of Washington* (1988); Benjamin F. Shearer and Barbara S. Shearer, *State Names, Seals, Flags, and Symbols* (1994); Robert Sobel and John W. Raimo, eds., *Biographical Directory of the Governors of the United States, 1789–1978* (1978); Richard W. Wilkie and Jack Tager, eds., *Historical Atlas of Massachusetts* (1991). See also "Politics and Government," "South," and "West and Frontier."

Transportation

Keith L. Bryant, ed., *Railroads in the Age of Regulation, 1900–1980* (1988); Rene De La Pedraja, *A Historical Dictionary of the U.S. Merchant Marine and Shipping Industry* (1994); Robert L. Frey, ed., *Railroads in the Nineteenth Century* (1988). See also "Business and the Economy."

Vietnam War

John S. Bowman, ed., *The Vietnam War: An Almanac* (1986); Stanley I. Kutler, ed., *Encyclopedia of the Vietnam War* (1996); James S. Olson, ed., *Dictionary of the Vietnam War* (1988); Harry G. Summers, Jr., *Vietnam War Almanac* (1985). Also see "Peace Movements and Pacifism" and "Military and Wars."

West and Frontier

William A. Beck and Ynez D. Haase, *Historical Atlas of the American West* (1989); Doris O. Dawdy, *Artists of the American West* (1974–1984); J. Norman Heard, *Handbook of the American Frontier* (1987); Howard R. Lamar, ed., *The Reader's Encyclopedia of the American West* (1977); Clyde A. Milner III et al., eds., *The Oxford History of the American West* (1994); Jay Robert Nash, *Encyclopedia of Western Lawmen and Outlaws* (1992); Doyce B. Nunis, Jr., and Gloria R. Lothrop, eds., *A Guide to the History of California* (1989); Charles Phillips and Alan Axelrod, eds., *Encyclopedia of the American West* (1996); Dan L. Thrapp, *The Encyclopedia of Frontier Biography* (1988–1994); David Walker, *Biographical Directory of American Territorial Governors* (1984). See also "Literature" and "Native Americans and Indian Affairs."

Women

Anne Gibson and Timothy Fast, *The Women's Atlas of the United States* (1986); Karen Greenspan, *The Timetables of Women's History* (1996); Maggie Humm, *The Dictionary of Feminist Theory* (1990); Edward T. James et al., *Notable American Women, 1607–1950* (1971); Lina Mainiero, ed., *American Women Writers* (1979–1982); Wilma Mankiller et al., *The Reader's Companion to U.S. Women's History* (1998); Kirstin Olsen, *Chronology of Women's History* (1994); Barbara G. Shortridge, *Atlas of American Women* (1987); Barbara Sicherman and Carol H. Green, eds., *Notable American Women, The Modern Period* (1980); Helen Tierney, ed., *Women's Studies Encyclopedia* (1991); Angela H. Zophy and Frances M. Kavenik, eds., *Handbook of American Women's History* (1990). See also "African Americans," "Immigration and Ethnic Groups," "Medicine and Nursing," and "Native Americans and Indian Affairs."

World War I

Arthur Banks, *A Military History Atlas of the First World War* (1975); Martin Gilbert, *Atlas of World War I* (1994); Holger H. Herwig and Neil M. Heyman, *Biographical Dictionary of World War I* (1982); George T. Kurian, *Encyclopedia of the First World War* (1990); Stephen Pope and Elizabeth-Anne Wheal, *The Dictionary of the First World War* (1995); Anne C. Venzon, *The United States in the First World War* (1995). See also "Military and Wars."

World War II

Marcel Baudot et al., eds., *The Historical Encyclopedia of World War II* (1980); David G. Chandler and James Lawton Collins, Jr., eds., *The D-Day Encyclopedia* (1993); I. C. B. Dear and M. R. D. Foot, eds., *The Oxford Companion to World War II* (1995); Simon Goodenough, *War Maps: Great Land Battles of World War II* (1988); Robert Goralski, *World War II Almanac* (1981); John Keegan, ed., *The Times Atlas of the Second World War* (1989); George T. Kurian, *Encyclopedia of the Second World War* (1991); Norman Polmer and Thomas B. Allen, *World War II: America at War* (1991); Louis L. Snyder, *Louis L. Snyder's Historical Guide to World War II* (1982); U.S. Military Academy, *Campaign Atlas to the Second World War: Europe and the Mediterranean* (1980); Peter Young, ed., *The World Almanac Book of World War II* (1981). See also "Military and Wars."

Documents

DECLARATION OF INDEPENDENCE IN CONGRESS, JULY 4, 1776

When, in the course of human events, it becomes necessary for one people to dissolve the political bonds which have connected them with another, and to assume, among the powers of the earth, the separate and equal station to which the laws of nature and of nature's God entitle them, a decent respect to the opinions of mankind requires that they should declare the causes which impel them to the separation.

We hold these truths to be self-evident: That all men are created equal; that they are endowed by their Creator with certain unalienable rights; that among these are life, liberty, and the pursuit of happiness; that, to secure these rights, governments are instituted among men, deriving their just powers from the consent of the governed; that whenever any form of government becomes destructive of these ends, it is the right of the people to alter or to abolish it, and to institute new government, laying its foundation on such principles, and organizing its powers in such form, as to them shall seem most likely to effect their safety and happiness. Prudence, indeed, will dictate that governments long established should not be changed for light and transient causes; and accordingly all experience hath shown that mankind are more disposed to suffer, while evils are sufferable, than to right themselves by abolishing the forms to which they are accustomed. But when a long train of abuses and usurpations, pursuing invariably the same object, evinces a design to reduce them under absolute despotism, it is their right, it is their duty, to throw off such government, and to provide new guards for their future security. Such has been the patient sufferance of these colonies; and such is now the necessity which constrains them to alter their former systems of government. The history of the present King of Great Britain is a history of repeated injuries and usurpations, all having in direct object the establishment of an absolute tyranny over these states. To prove this, let facts be submitted to a candid world.

He has refused his assent to laws, the most wholesome and necessary for the public good.

He has forbidden his governors to pass laws of immediate and pressing importance, unless suspended in their operation till his assent should be obtained; and, when so suspended, he has utterly neglected to attend to them.

He has refused to pass other laws for the accommodation of large districts of people, unless those people would relinquish the right of representation in the legislature, a right inestimable to them, and formidable to tyrants only.

He has called together legislative bodies at places unusual, uncomfortable, and distant from the depository of their public records, for the sole purpose of fatiguing them into compliance with his measures.

He has dissolved representative houses repeatedly, for opposing, with manly firmness, his invasions on the rights of the people.

He has refused for a long time, after such dissolutions, to cause others to be elected; whereby the legislative powers, incapable of annihilation, have returned to the people at large for their exercise; the state remaining, in the mean time, exposed to all the dangers of invasions from without and convulsions within.

He has endeavored to prevent the population of these states; for that purpose obstructing the laws for naturalization of foreigners; refusing to pass others to encourage their migration hither, and raising the conditions of new appropriations of lands.

He has obstructed the administration of justice, by refusing his assent to laws for establishing judiciary powers.

He has made judges dependent on his will alone, for the tenure of their offices, and the amount and payment of their salaries.

He has erected a multitude of new offices, and sent hither swarms of officers to harass our people and eat out their substance.

He has kept among us, in times of peace, standing armies, without the consent of our legislatures.

He has affected to render the military independent of, and superior to, the civil power.

He has combined with others to subject us to a jurisdiction foreign to our constitution, and unacknowledged by our laws, giving his assent to their acts of pretended legislation:

For quartering large bodies of armed troops among us;

For protecting them, by a mock trial, from punishment for any murders which they should commit on the inhabitants of these states;

For cutting off our trade with all parts of the world;

For imposing taxes on us without our consent;

For depriving us, in many cases, of the benefits of trial by jury;

For transporting us beyond seas, to be tried for pretended offenses;

For abolishing the free system of English laws in a neighboring province, establishing therein an arbitrary government, and enlarging its boundaries, so as to render it at once an example and fit instrument for introducing the same absolute rule into these colonies;

For taking away our charters, abolishing our most valuable laws, and altering fundamentally the forms of our governments;

For suspending our own legislatures, and declaring themselves invested with power to legislate for us in all cases whatsoever.

He has abdicated government here, by declaring us out of his protection and waging war against us.

He has plundered our seas, ravaged our coasts, burned our towns, and destroyed the lives of our people.

He is at this time transporting large armies of foreign mercenaries to complete the works of death, desolation, and tyranny already begun with circumstances of cruelty and perfidy scarcely paralleled in the most barbarous ages, and totally unworthy the head of a civilized nation.

He has constrained our fellow-citizens, taken captive on the high seas, to bear arms against their country, to become the executioners of their friends and brethren, or to fall themselves by their hands.

He has excited domestic insurrection among us, and has endeavored to bring on the inhabitants of our frontiers the merciless Indian savages, whose known rule of warfare is an undistinguished destruction of all ages, sexes, and conditions.

In every stage of these oppressions we have petitioned for redress in the most humble terms; our repeated petitions have been answered only by repeated injury. A prince, whose character is thus marked by every act which may define a tyrant, is unfit to be the ruler of a free people.

Nor have we been wanting in our attentions to our British brethren. We have warned them, from time to time, of attempts by their legislature to extend an unwarrantable jurisdiction over us. We have reminded them of the circumstances of our emigration and settlement here. We have appealed to their native justice and magnanimity; and we have conjured them, by the ties of our common kindred, to disavow these usurpations, which would inevitably interrupt our connections and correspondence. They, too, have been deaf to the voice of justice and of consanguinity. We must, therefore, acquiesce in the necessity which denounces our separation, and hold them, as we hold the rest of mankind, enemies in war, in peace friends.

We, therefore, the representatives of the United States of America, in General Congress assembled, appealing to the Supreme Judge of the world for the rectitude of our intentions, do, in the name and by the authority of the good people of these colonies, solemnly publish and declare, that these United Colonies are, and of right ought to be, FREE AND INDEPENDENT STATES; that they are absolved from all allegiance to the British crown, and that all political connection between them and the state of Great Britain is, and ought to be, totally dissolved; and that, as free and independent states, they have full power to levy war, conclude peace, contract alliances, establish commerce, and do all other acts and things which independent states may of right do. And for the support of this declaration, with a firm reliance on the protection of Divine Providence, we mutually pledge to each other our lives, our fortunes, and our sacred honor.

JOHN HANCOCK
and fifty-five others

CONSTITUTION OF THE UNITED STATES OF AMERICA AND AMENDMENTS*

Preamble

We the people of the United States, in order to form a more perfect union, establish justice, insure domestic tranquillity, provide for the common defense, promote the general welfare, and secure the blessings of liberty to ourselves and our posterity, do ordain and establish this Constitution for the United States of America.

Article I

Section 1 All legislative powers herein granted shall be vested in a Congress of the United States, which shall consist of a Senate and a House of Representatives.

---

*Passages no longer in effect are printed in italic type.

Section 2 The House of Representatives shall be composed of members chosen every second year by the people of the several States, and the electors in each State shall have the qualifications requisite for electors of the most numerous branch of the State Legislature.

No person shall be a Representative who shall not have attained to the age of twenty-five years, and been seven years a citizen of the United States, and who shall not, when elected, be an inhabitant of that State in which he shall be chosen.

Representatives and direct taxes shall be apportioned among the several States which may be included within this Union, according to their respective numbers, *which shall be determined by adding to the whole number of free persons, including those bound to service for a term of years and excluding Indians not taxed, three-fifths of all other persons.* The actual enumeration shall be made within three years after the first meeting of the Congress of the United States, and within every subsequent term of ten years, in such manner as they shall by law direct. The number of Representatives shall not exceed one for every thirty thousand, but each State shall have at least one Representative; *and until such enumeration shall be made, the State of New Hampshire shall be entitled to choose three, Massachusetts eight, Rhode Island and Providence Plantations one, Connecticut five, New York six, New Jersey four, Pennsylvania eight, Delaware one, Maryland six, Virginia ten, North Carolina five, South Carolina five, and Georgia three.*

When vacancies happen in the representation from any State, the Executive authority thereof shall issue writs of election to fill such vacancies.

The House of Representatives shall choose their Speaker and other officers; and shall have the sole power of impeachment.

Section 3 The Senate of the United States shall be composed of two Senators from each State, *chosen by the legislature thereof,* for six years; and each Senator shall have one vote.

Immediately after they shall be assembled in consequence of the first election, they shall be divided as equally as may be into three classes. The seats of the Senators of the first class shall be vacated at the expiration of the second year, of the second class at the expiration of the fourth year, and of the third class at the expiration of the sixth year, so that one-third may be chosen every second year; *and if vacancies happen by resignation or otherwise, during the recess of the legislature of any State, the Executive thereof may make temporary appointments until the next meeting of the legislature, which shall then fill such vacancies.*

No person shall be a Senator who shall not have attained to the age of thirty years, and been nine years a citizen of the United States, and who shall not, when elected, be an inhabitant of that State for which he shall be chosen.

The Vice-President of the United States shall be President of the Senate, but shall have no vote, unless they be equally divided.

The Senate shall choose their other officers, and also a President *pro tempore,* in the absence of the Vice-President, or when he shall exercise the office of President of the United States.

The Senate shall have the sole power to try all impeachments. When sitting for that purpose, they shall be on oath or affirmation. When the President of the United States is tried, the Chief Justice shall preside: and no person shall be convicted without the concurrence of two-thirds of the members present.

Judgment in cases of impeachment shall not extend further than to removal from the office, and disqualification to hold and enjoy any office of honor, trust or profit under the United States: but the party convicted shall nevertheless be liable and subject to indictment, trial, judgment and punishment, according to law.

Section 4 The times, places and manner of holding elections for Senators and Representatives shall be prescribed in each State by the legislature thereof; but the Congress may at any time by law make or alter such regulations, except as to the places of choosing Senators.

The Congress shall assemble at least once in every year, and such meeting *shall be on the first Monday in December, unless they shall by law appoint a different day.*

Section 5 Each house shall be the judge of the elections, returns and qualifications of its own members, and a majority of each shall constitute a quorum to do business; but a smaller number may adjourn from day to day, and may be authorized to compel the attendance of absent members, in such manner, and under such penalties, as each house may provide.

Each house may determine the rules of its proceedings, punish its members for disorderly behavior, and with the concurrence of two-thirds, expel a member.

Each house shall keep a journal of its proceedings, and from time to time publish the same, excepting such parts as may in their judgment require secrecy; and the yeas and nays of the members of either house on any question shall, at the desire of one-fifth of those present, be entered on the journal.

Neither house, during the session of Congress, shall, without the consent of the other, adjourn for more than three days, nor to any other place than that in which the two houses shall be sitting.

Section 6   The Senators and Representatives shall receive a compensation for their services, to be ascertained by law and paid out of the treasury of the United States. They shall in all cases except treason, felony and breach of the peace, be privileged from arrest during their attendance at the session of their respective houses, and in going to and returning from the same; and for any speech or debate in either house, they shall not be questioned in any other place.

No Senator or Representative shall, during the time for which he was elected, be appointed to any civil office under the authority of the United States, which shall have been created, or the emoluments whereof shall have been increased, during such time; and no person holding any office under the United States shall be a member of either house during his continuance in office.

Section 7   All bills for raising revenue shall originate in the House of Representatives; but the Senate may propose or concur with amendments as on other bills.

Every bill which shall have passed the House of Representatives and the Senate, shall, before it become a law, be presented to the President of the United States; if he approve he shall sign it, but if not he shall return it with objections to that house in which it originated, who shall enter the objections at large on their journal, and proceed to reconsider it. If after such reconsideration two-thirds of that house shall agree to pass the bill, it shall be sent, together with the objections, to the other house, by which it shall likewise be reconsidered, and, if approved by two-thirds of that house, it shall become a law. But in all such cases the votes of both houses shall be determined by yeas and nays, and the names of the persons voting for and against the bill shall be entered on the journal of each house respectively. If any bill shall not be returned by the President within ten days (Sundays excepted) after it shall have been presented to him, the same shall be a law, in like manner as if he had signed it, unless the Congress by their adjournment prevent its return, in which case it shall not be a law.

Every order, resolution, or vote to which the concurrence of the Senate and House of Representatives may be necessary (except on a question of adjournment) shall be presented to the President of the United States; and before the same shall take effect, shall be approved by him, or being disapproved by him, shall be repassed by two-thirds of the Senate and House of Representa-

tives, according to the rules and limitations prescribed in the case of a bill.

Section 8   The Congress shall have power

To lay and collect taxes, duties, imposts, and excises, to pay the debts and provide for the common defense and general welfare of the United States; but all duties, imposts and excises shall be uniform throughout the United States;

To borrow money on the credit of the United States;

To regulate commerce with foreign nations, and among the several States, and with the Indian tribes;

To establish an uniform rule of naturalization, and uniform laws on the subject of bankruptcies throughout the United States;

To coin money, regulate the value thereof, and of foreign coin, and fix the standard of weights and measures;

To provide for the punishment of counterfeiting the securities and current coin of the United States;

To establish post offices and post roads;

To promote the progress of science and useful arts by securing for limited times to authors and inventors the exclusive right to their respective writings and discoveries;

To constitute tribunals inferior to the Supreme Court;

To define and punish piracies and felonies committed on the high seas and offenses against the law of nations;

To declare war, grant letters of marque and reprisal, and make rules concerning captures on land and water;

To raise and support armies, but no appropriation of money to that use shall be for a longer term than two years;

To provide and maintain a navy;

To make rules for the government and regulation of the land and naval forces;

To provide for calling forth the militia to execute the laws of the Union, suppress insurrections, and repel invasions;

To provide for organizing, arming, and disciplining the militia, and for governing such part of them as may be employed in the service of the United States, reserving to the States respectively the appointment of the officers, and the authority of training the militia according to the discipline prescribed by Congress;

To exercise exclusive legislation in all cases whatsoever, over such district (not exceeding ten miles square) as may, by cession of particular States, and the acceptance of Congress, become the seat of government of the

United States, and to exercise like authority over all places purchased by the consent of the legislature of the State, in which the same shall be, for erection of forts, magazines, arsenals, dockyards, and other needful buildings; — and

To make all laws which shall be necessary and proper for carrying into execution the foregoing powers, and all other powers vested by this Constitution in the government of the United States, or in any department or officer thereof.

Section 9   The migration or importation of such persons as any of the States now existing shall think proper to admit shall not be prohibited by the Congress prior to the year 1808; but a tax or duty may be imposed on such importation, not exceeding $10 for each person.

The privilege of the writ of habeas corpus shall not be suspended, unless when in cases of rebellion or invasion the public safety may require it.

No bill of attainder or ex post facto law shall be passed.

No capitation, or other direct, tax shall be laid, unless in proportion to the census or enumeration herein before directed to be taken.

No tax or duty shall be laid on articles exported from any State.

No preference shall be given by any regulation of commerce or revenue to the ports of one State over those of another; nor shall vessels bound to, or from, one State, be obliged to enter, clear, or pay duties in another.

No money shall be drawn from the treasury, but in consequence of appropriations made by law; and a regular statement and account of the receipts and expenditures of all public money shall be published from time to time.

No title of nobility shall be granted by the United States: and no person holding any office of profit or trust under them, shall, without the consent of the Congress, accept of any present, emolument, office, or title, of any kind whatever, from any king, prince, or foreign state.

Section 10   No State shall enter into any treaty, alliance, or confederation; grant letters of marque and reprisal; coin money; emit bills of credit; make anything but gold and silver coin a tender in payment of debts; pass any bill of attainder, ex post facto law, or law impairing the obligation of contracts, or grant any title of nobility.

No State shall, without the consent of Congress, lay any imposts or duties on imports or exports, except what may be absolutely necessary for executing its inspection laws: and the net produce of all duties and imposts, laid by any State on imports or exports, shall be for the use of the treasury of the United States; and all such laws shall be subject to the revision and control of the Congress.

No State shall, without the consent of Congress, lay any duty of tonnage, keep troops or ships of war in time of peace, enter into any agreement or compact with another State, or with a foreign power, or engage in war, unless actually invaded, or in such imminent danger as will not admit of delay.

Article II

Section 1   The executive power shall be vested in a President of the United States of America. He shall hold his office during the term of four years, and, together with the Vice-President, chosen for the same term, be elected as follows:

Each State shall appoint, in such manner as the legislature thereof may direct, a number of electors, equal to the whole number of Senators and Representatives to which the State may be entitled in the Congress; but no Senator or Representative, or person holding an office of trust or profit under the United States, shall be appointed an elector.

The electors shall meet in their respective States, and vote by ballot for two persons, of whom one at least shall not be an inhabitant of the same State with themselves. And they shall make a list of all the persons voted for, and of the number of votes for each; which list they shall sign and certify, and transmit sealed to the seat of government of the United States, directed to the President of the Senate. The President of the Senate shall, in the presence of the Senate and House of Representatives, open all the certificates, and the votes shall then be counted. The person having the greatest number of votes shall be the President, if such number be a majority of the whole number of electors appointed; and if there be more than one who have such majority, and have an equal number of votes, then the House of Representatives shall immediately choose by ballot one of them for President; and if no person have a majority, then from the five highest on the list said house shall in like manner choose the President. But in choosing the President the votes shall be taken by States, the representation from each State having one vote; a quorum for this purpose shall consist of a member or members from two-thirds of the States, and a majority of all the States shall be necessary to a choice. In every case, after the choice of the President, the person having the greatest number of votes of the electors shall be the Vice-President. But if there should remain two or more who have equal votes, the Senate shall choose from them by ballot the Vice-President.

The Congress may determine the time of choosing the electors and the day on which they shall give their votes; which day shall be the same throughout the United States.

No person except a natural-born citizen, *or a citizen of the United States at the time of the adoption of this Constitution*, shall be eligible to the office of President; neither shall any person be eligible to that office who shall not have attained to the age of thirty-five years, and been fourteen years a resident within the United States.

In cases of the removal of the President from office or of his death, resignation, or inability to discharge the powers and duties of the said office, the same shall devolve on the Vice-President, and the Congress may by law provide for the case of removal, death, resignation, or inability, both of the President and Vice-President, declaring what officer shall then act as President, and such officer shall act accordingly, until the disability be removed, or a President shall be elected.

The President shall, at stated times, receive for his services a compensation, which shall neither be increased nor diminished during the period for which he shall have been elected, and he shall not receive within that period any other emolument from the United States, or any of them.

Before he enter on the execution of his office, he shall take the following oath or affirmation:—"I do solemnly swear (or affirm) that I will faithfully execute the office of the President of the United States, and will to the best of my ability preserve, protect and defend the Constitution of the United States."

Section 2   The President shall be commander in chief of the army and navy of the United States, and of the militia of the several States, when called into the actual service of the United States; he may require the opinion, in writing, of the principal officer in each of the executive departments, upon any subject relating to the duties of their respective offices, and he shall have power to grant reprieves and pardons for offenses against the United States, except in cases of impeachment.

He shall have power, by and with the advice and consent of the Senate, to make treaties, provided two-thirds of the Senators present concur; and he shall nominate, and by and with the advice and consent of the Senate, shall appoint ambassadors, other public ministers and consuls, judges of the Supreme Court, and all other officers of the United States, whose appointments are not herein otherwise provided for, and which shall be established by law: but Congress may by law vest the appointment of such inferior officers, as they think proper, in the President alone, in the courts of law, or in the heads of departments.

The President shall have power to fill up all vacancies that may happen during the recess of the Senate, by granting commissions which shall expire at the end of their next session.

Section 3   He shall from time to time give to the Congress information of the state of the Union, and recommend to their consideration such measures as he shall judge necessary and expedient; he may, on extraordinary occasions, convene both houses, or either of them, and in case of disagreement between them, with respect to the time of adjournment, he may adjourn them to such time as he shall think proper; he shall receive ambassadors and other public ministers; he shall take care that the laws be faithfully executed, and shall commission all the officers of the United States.

Section 4   The President, Vice-President and all civil officers of the United States shall be removed from office on impeachment for, and on conviction of, treason, bribery, or other high crimes and misdemeanors.

Article III

Section 1   The judicial power of the United States shall be vested in one Supreme Court, and in such inferior courts as the Congress may from time to time ordain and establish. The judges, both of the Supreme and inferior courts, shall hold their offices during good behavior, and shall, at stated times, receive for their services a compensation which shall not be diminished during their continuance in office.

Section 2   The judicial power shall extend to all cases, in law and equity, arising under this Constitution, the laws of the United States, and treaties made, or which shall be made, under their authority;—to all cases affecting ambassadors, other public ministers and consuls;—to all cases of admiralty and maritime jurisdiction;—to controversies to which the United States shall be a party;—to controversies between two or more States;—*between a State and citizens of another State;*—between citizens of different States;—between citizens of the same State claiming lands under grants of different States, and between a State, or the citizens thereof, and foreign states, citizens or subjects.

In all cases affecting ambassadors, other public ministers and consuls, and those in which a State shall be party, the Supreme Court shall have original jurisdiction. In all the other cases before mentioned, the Supreme Court shall have appellate jurisdiction, both as to law and fact, with such exceptions, and under such regulations, as the Congress shall make.

The trial of all crimes, except in cases of impeachment, shall be by jury; and such trial shall be held in the State where said crimes shall have been committed; but when not committed within any State, the trial shall be at such place or places as the Congress may by law have directed.

Section 3   Treason against the United States shall consist only in levying war against them, or in adhering to their enemies, giving them aid and comfort. No person shall be convicted of treason unless on the testimony of two witnesses to the same overt act, or on confession in open court.

The Congress shall have power to declare the punishment of treason, but no attainder of treason shall work corruption of blood, or forfeiture except during the life of the person attainted.

Article IV

Section 1   Full faith and credit shall be given in each State to the public acts, records, and judicial proceedings of every other State. And the Congress may by general laws prescribe the manner in which such acts, records, and proceedings shall be proved, and the effect thereof.

Section 2   The citizens of each State shall be entitled to all privileges and immunities of citizens in the several States.

A person charged in any State with treason, felony, or other crime, who shall flee from justice, and be found in another State, shall on demand of the executive authority of the State from which he fled, be delivered up, to be removed to the State having jurisdiction of the crime.

No person held to service or labor in one State, under the laws thereof, escaping into another, shall, in consequence of any law or regulation therein, be discharged from such service or labor, but shall be delivered up on claim of the party to whom such service or labor may be due.

Section 3   New States may be admitted by the Congress into this Union; but no new State shall be formed or erected within the jurisdiction of any other State; nor any State be formed by the junction of two or more States, or parts of States, without the consent of the legislatures of the States concerned as well as of the Congress.

The Congress shall have power to dispose of and make all needful rules and regulations respecting the territory or other property belonging to the United States; and nothing in this Constitution shall be so construed as to prejudice any claims of the United States, or of any particular State.

Section 4   The United States shall guarantee to every State in this Union a republican form of government, and shall protect each of them against invasion; and on application of the legislature, or of the executive (when the legislature cannot be convened), against domestic violence.

Article V

The Congress, whenever two-thirds of both houses shall deem it necessary, shall propose amendments to this Constitution, or, on the application of the legislatures of two-thirds of the several States, shall call a convention for proposing amendments, which, in either case, shall be valid to all intents and purposes, as part of this Constitution, when ratified by the legislatures of three-fourths of the several States, or by conventions in three-fourths thereof, as the one or the other mode of ratification may be proposed by the Congress; provided *that no amendments which may be made prior to the year one thousand eight hundred and eight shall in any manner affect the first and fourth clauses in the ninth section of the first article;* and that no State, without its consent, shall be deprived of its equal suffrage in the Senate.

Article VI

All debts contracted and engagements entered into, before the adoption of this Constitution, shall be as valid against the United States under this Constitution, as under the Confederation.

This Constitution, and the laws of the United States which shall be made in pursuance thereof; and all treaties made, or which shall be made, under the authority of the United States, shall be the supreme law of the land; and the judges in every State shall be bound thereby, anything in the Constitution or laws of any State to the contrary notwithstanding.

The Senators and Representatives before mentioned, and the members of the several State legislatures, and all executive and judicial officers, both of the United States and of the several States, shall be bound by oath or affirmation to support this Constitution; but no religious test shall ever be required as a qualification to any office or public trust under the United States.

Article VII

The ratification of the conventions of nine States shall be sufficient for the establishment of this Constitution between the States so ratifying the same.

Done in Convention by the unanimous consent of the States present, the seventeenth day of September in the year of our Lord one thousand seven hundred and eighty-seven and of the Independence of the United States of America the twelfth. In witness whereof we have hereunto subscribed our names.

GEORGE WASHINGTON
and thirty-seven others

Amendments to the Constitution*

Amendment I

Congress shall make no law respecting an establishment of religion, or prohibiting the free exercise thereof; or abridging the freedom of speech, or of the press; or the right of the people peaceably to assemble, and to petition the government for a redress of grievances.

Amendment II

A well-regulated militia being necessary to the security of a free State, the right of the people to keep and bear arms shall not be infringed.

Amendment III

No soldier shall, in time of peace, be quartered in any house without the consent of the owner, nor in time of war, but in a manner to be prescribed by law.

Amendment IV

The right of the people to be secure in their persons, houses, papers, and effects, against unreasonable searches and seizures, shall not be violated, and no warrants shall issue but upon probable cause, supported by oath or affirmation, and particularly describing the place to be searched, and the persons or things to be seized.

Amendment V

No person shall be held to answer for a capital, or otherwise infamous crime, unless on a presentment or indictment of a grand jury, except in cases arising in the land or naval forces, or in the militia, when in actual service in time of war or public danger; nor shall any person be subject for the same offense to be twice put in jeopardy of life or limb; nor shall be compelled in any criminal case to be a witness against himself, nor be deprived of life, liberty, or property, without due process of law; nor shall private property be taken for public use without just compensation.

Amendment VI

In all criminal prosecutions, the accused shall enjoy the right to a speedy and public trial, by an impartial jury of the State and district wherein the crime shall have been committed, which district shall have been previously ascertained by law, and to be informed of the nature and cause of the accusation; to be confronted with the witnesses against him; to have compulsory process for obtaining witnesses in his favor, and to have the assistance of counsel for his defense.

Amendment VII

In suits at common law, where the value in controversy shall exceed twenty dollars, the right of trial by jury shall be preserved, and no fact tried by a jury shall be otherwise reexamined in any court of the United States, than according to the rules of the common law.

Amendment VIII

Excessive bail shall not be required, nor excessive fines imposed, nor cruel and unusual punishments inflicted.

Amendment IX

The enumeration in the Constitution, of certain rights, shall not be construed to deny or disparage others retained by the people.

Amendment X

The powers not delegated to the United States by the Constitution, nor prohibited by it to the States, are reserved to the States respectively, or to the people.

Amendment XI

[Adopted 1798]

The judicial power of the United States shall not be construed to extend to any suit in law or equity, commenced or prosecuted against one of the United States by citizens of another State, or by citizens or subjects of any foreign state.

Amendment XII

[Adopted 1804]

The electors shall meet in their respective States, and vote by ballot for President and Vice-President, one of whom, at least, shall not be an inhabitant of the same State with themselves; they shall name in their ballots the person voted for as President, and in distinct ballots the person voted for as Vice-President, and they shall make distinct lists of all persons voted for as President, and of all persons voted for as Vice-President, and of the num-

---

*The first ten Amendments (the Bill of Rights) were adopted in 1791.

ber of votes for each, which lists they shall sign and certify, and transmit sealed to the seat of government of the United States, directed to the President of the Senate;—the President of the Senate shall, in the presence of the Senate and House of Representatives, open all the certificates and the votes shall then be counted;—the person having the greatest number of votes for President shall be the President, if such number be a majority of the whole number of electors appointed; and if no person have such majority, then from the persons having the highest numbers not exceeding three on the list of those voted for as President, the House of Representatives shall choose immediately, by ballot, the President. But in choosing the President, the votes shall be taken by States, the representation from each State having one vote; a quorum for this purpose shall consist of a member or members from two-thirds of the States, and a majority of all the States shall be necessary to a choice. And if the House of Representatives shall not choose a President whenever the right of choice shall devolve upon them, before *the fourth day of March* next following, then the Vice-President shall act as President, as in the case of the death or other constitutional disability of the President.

The person having the greatest number of votes as Vice-President shall be the Vice-President, if such number be a majority of the whole number of electors appointed; and if no person have a majority, then from the two highest numbers on the list the Senate shall choose the Vice-President; a quorum for the purpose shall consist of two-thirds of the whole number of Senators, and a majority of the whole number shall be necessary to a choice. But no person constitutionally ineligible to the office of President shall be eligible to that of Vice-President of the United States.

Amendment XIII

[Adopted 1865]

Section 1   Neither slavery nor involuntary servitude, except as a punishment for crime whereof the party shall have been duly convicted, shall exist within the United States, or any place subject to their jurisdiction.

Section 2   Congress shall have power to enforce this article by appropriate legislation.

Amendment XIV

[Adopted 1868]

Section 1   All persons born or naturalized in the United States, and subject to the jurisdiction thereof, are citizens of the United States and of the State wherein they reside. No State shall make or enforce any law which shall abridge the privileges or immunities of citizens of the United States; nor shall any State deprive any person of life, liberty, or property, without due process of law; nor deny to any person within its jurisdiction the equal protection of the laws.

Section 2   Representatives shall be apportioned among the several States according to their respective numbers, counting the whole number of persons in each State, excluding Indians not taxed. But when the right to vote at any election for the choice of Electors for President and Vice-President of the United States, Representatives in Congress, the executive and judicial officers of a State, or the members of the legislature thereof, is denied to any of the male inhabitants of such State, being twenty-one years of age and citizens of the United States, or in any way abridged, except for participation in rebellion, or other crime, the basis of representation therein shall be reduced in the proportion which the number of such male citizens shall bear to the whole number of male citizens twenty-one years of age in such State.

Section 3   No person shall be a Senator or Representative in Congress, or Elector of President and Vice-President, or hold any office, civil or military, under the United States, or under any State, who, having previously taken an oath, as a member of Congress, or as an officer of the United States, or as a member of any State legislature, or as an executive or judicial officer of any State, to support the Constitution of the United States, shall have engaged in insurrection or rebellion against the same, or given aid or comfort to the enemies thereof. Congress may, by a vote of two-thirds of each house, remove such disability.

Section 4   The validity of the public debt of the United States, authorized by law, including debts incurred for payment of pensions and bounties for services in suppressing insurrection or rebellion, shall not be questioned. But neither the United States nor any State shall assume or pay any debt or obligation incurred in aid of insurrection or rebellion against the United States, or any claim for the loss of emancipation of any slave; but all such debts, obligations, and claims shall be held illegal and void.

Section 5   The Congress shall have power to enforce, by appropriate legislation, the provisions of this article.

Amendment XV

[Adopted 1870]

Section 1   The right of citizens of the United States to vote shall not be denied or abridged by the United

States or by any State on account of race, color, or previous condition of servitude.

Section 2 The Congress shall have power to enforce this article by appropriate legislation.

Amendment XVI

[Adopted 1913]

The Congress shall have power to lay and collect taxes on incomes, from whatever source derived, without apportionment among the several States, and without regard to any census or enumeration.

Amendment XVII

[Adopted 1913]

Section 1 The Senate of the United States shall be composed of two Senators from each State, elected by the people thereof, for six years; and each Senator shall have one vote. The electors in each State shall have the qualifications requisite for electors of [voters for] the most numerous branch of the State legislatures.

Section 2 When vacancies happen in the representation of any State in the Senate, the executive authority of such State shall issue writs of election to fill such vacancies: Provided, that the Legislature of any State may empower the executive thereof to make temporary appointments until the people fill the vacancies by election as the Legislature may direct.

Section 3 This amendment shall not be so construed as to affect the election or term of any Senator chosen before it becomes valid as part of the Constitution.

Amendment XVIII

[Adopted 1919; Repealed 1933]

Section 1 After one year from the ratification of this article the manufacture, sale, or transportation of intoxicating liquors within, the importation thereof into, or the exportation thereof from the United States and all territory subject to the jurisdiction thereof, for beverage purposes, is hereby prohibited.

Section 2 The Congress and the several States shall have concurrent power to enforce this article by appropriate legislation.

Section 3 This article shall be inoperative unless it shall have been ratified as an amendment to the Constitution by the legislatures of the several States, as provided by the Constitution, within seven years from the date of the submission thereof to the States by the Congress.

Amendment XIX

[Adopted 1920]

Section 1 The right of citizens of the United States to vote shall not be denied or abridged by the United States or by any State on account of sex.

Section 2 The Congress shall have power to enforce this article by appropriate legislation.

Amendment XX

[Adopted 1933]

Section 1 The terms of the President and Vice-President shall end at noon on the 20th day of January, and the terms of Senators and Representatives at noon on the 3rd day of January, of the years in which such terms would have ended if this article had not been ratified; and the terms of their successors shall then begin.

Section 2 The Congress shall assemble at least once in every year, and such meeting shall begin at noon on the 3d day of January, unless they shall by law appoint a different day.

Section 3 If, at the time fixed for the beginning of the term of the President, the President-elect shall have died, the Vice-President-elect shall become President. If a President shall not have been chosen before the time fixed for the beginning of his term, or if the President-elect shall have failed to qualify, then the Vice-President-elect shall act as President until a President shall have qualified; and the Congress may by law provide for the case wherein neither a President-elect nor a Vice-President-elect shall have qualified, declaring who shall then act as President, or the manner in which one who is to act shall be selected, and such persons shall act accordingly until a President or Vice-President shall have qualified.

Section 4 The Congress may by law provide for the case of the death of any of the persons from whom the House of Representatives may choose a President whenever the right of choice shall have devolved upon them, and for the case of the death of any of the persons from whom the Senate may choose a Vice-President whenever the right of choice shall have devolved upon them.

Section 5 Sections 1 and 2 shall take effect on the 15th day of October following the ratification of this article.

Section 6 This article shall be inoperative unless it shall have been ratified as an amendment to the Constitution by the Legislatures of three-fourths of the several States within seven years from the date of its submission.

Amendment XXI

[Adopted 1933]

Section 1   The eighteenth article of amendment to the Constitution of the United States is hereby repealed.

Section 2   The transportation or importation into any State, Territory, or Possession of the United States for delivery or use therein of intoxicating liquors, in violation of the laws thereof, is hereby prohibited.

Section 3   This article shall be inoperative unless it shall have been ratified as an amendment to the Constitution by conventions in the several States, as provided in the Constitution, within seven years from the date of submission thereof to the States by the Congress.

Amendment XXII

[Adopted 1951]

Section 1   No person shall be elected to the office of President more than twice, and no person who has held the office of President, or acted as President, for more than two years of a term to which some other person was elected President shall be elected to the office of President more than once. But this article shall not apply to any person holding the office of President when this article was proposed by the Congress, and shall not prevent any person who may be holding the office of President, or acting as President, during the term within which this article becomes operative from holding the office of President or acting as President during the remainder of such term.

Section 2   This article shall be inoperative unless it shall have been ratified as an amendment to the Constitution by the legislatures of three-fourths of the several States within seven years from the date of its submission to the States by the Congress.

Amendment XXIII

[Adopted 1961]

Section 1   The District constituting the seat of Government of the United States shall appoint in such manner as the Congress may direct:

A number of electors of President and Vice-President equal to the whole number of Senators and Representatives in Congress to which the District would be entitled if it were a State, but in no event more than the least populous State; they shall be in addition to those appointed by the States, but they shall be considered for the purposes of the election of President and Vice-President, to be electors appointed by a State; and they shall

meet in the District and perform such duties as provided by the twelfth article of amendment.

Section 2   The Congress shall have the power to enforce this article by appropriate legislation.

Amendment XXIV

[Adopted 1964]

Section 1   The right of citizens of the United States to vote in any primary or other election for President or Vice-President, for electors for President or Vice-President, or for Senator or Representative in Congress, shall not be denied or abridged by the United States or any State by reason of failure to pay any poll tax or other tax.

Section 2   The Congress shall have the power to enforce this article by appropriate legislation.

Amendment XXV

[Adopted 1967]

Section 1   In case of the removal of the President from office or of his death or resignation, the Vice-President shall become President.

Section 2   Whenever there is a vacancy in the office of the Vice-President, the President shall nominate a Vice-President who shall take office upon confirmation by a majority vote of both Houses of Congress.

Section 3   Whenever the President transmits to the President pro tempore of the Senate and the Speaker of the House of Representatives his written declaration that he is unable to discharge the powers and duties of his office, and until he transmits to them a written declaration to the contrary, such powers and duties shall be discharged by the Vice-President as Acting President.

Section 4   Whenever the Vice-President and a majority of either the principal officers of the executive departments or of such other body as Congress may by law provide, transmit to the President pro tempore of the Senate and the Speaker of the House of Representatives their written declaration that the President is unable to discharge the powers and duties of his office, the Vice-President shall immediately assume the powers and duties of the office as Acting President.

Thereafter, when the President transmits to the President pro tempore of the Senate and the Speaker of the House of Representatives his written declaration that no inability exists, he shall resume the powers and duties of his office unless the Vice-President and a majority of either the principal officers of the executive department[s] or of such other body as Congress may by law provide, transmit within four days to the President pro tempore of the Senate and the Speaker of the House of Representatives their written declaration that the President is unable to discharge the powers and duties of his office. Thereupon Congress shall decide the issue, assembling within forty-eight hours for that purpose if not in session. If the Congress, within twenty-one days after receipt of the latter written declaration, or, if Congress is not in session, within twenty-one days after Congress is required to assemble, determines by two-thirds vote of both Houses that the President is unable to discharge the powers and duties of his office, the Vice-President shall continue to discharge the same as Acting President; otherwise, the President shall resume the powers and duties of his office.

Amendment XXVI

[Adopted 1971]

Section 1   The right of citizens of the United States, who are eighteen years of age or older, to vote shall not be denied or abridged by the United States or by any State on account of age.

Section 2   The Congress shall have power to enforce this article by appropriate legislation.

Amendment XXVII

[Adopted 1992]

No law, varying the compensation for the services of the Senators and Representatives, shall take effect, until an election of Representatives shall have intervened.

The American People and Nation: A Statistical Profile

Population of the United States

Year	Number of States	Population	Percent Increase	Population Per Square Mile	Percent Urban/ Rural	Percent Male/ Female	Percent White/ Non-white	Persons Per House-hold	Median Age
1790	13	3,929,214		4.5	5.1/94.9	NA/NA	80.7/19.3	5.79	NA
1800	16	5,308,483	35.1	6.1	6.1/93.9	NA/NA	81.1/18.9	NA	NA
1810	17	7,239,881	36.4	4.3	7.3/92.7	NA/NA	81.0/19.0	NA	NA
1820	23	9,638,453	33.1	5.5	7.2/92.8	50.8/49.2	81.6/18.4	NA	16.7
1830	24	12,866,020	33.5	7.4	8.8/91.2	50.8/49.2	81.9/18.1	NA	17.2
1840	26	17,069,453	32.7	9.8	10.8/89.2	50.9/49.1	83.2/16.8	NA	17.8
1850	31	23,191,876	35.9	7.9	15.3/84.7	51.0/49.0	84.3/15.7	5.55	18.9
1860	33	31,443,321	35.6	10.6	19.8/80.2	51.2/48.8	85.6/14.4	5.28	19.4
1870	37	39,818,449	26.6	13.4	25.7/74.3	50.6/49.4	86.2/13.8	5.09	20.2
1880	38	50,155,783	26.0	16.9	28.2/71.8	50.9/49.1	86.5/13.5	5.04	20.9
1890	44	62,947,714	25.5	21.2	35.1/64.9	51.2/48.8	87.5/12.5	4.93	22.0
1900	45	75,994,575	20.7	25.6	39.6/60.4	51.1/48.9	87.9/12.1	4.76	22.9
1910	46	91,972,266	21.0	31.0	45.6/54.4	51.5/48.5	88.9/11.1	4.54	24.1
1920	48	105,710,620	14.9	35.6	51.2/48.8	51.0/49.0	89.7/10.3	4.34	25.3
1930	48	122,775,046	16.1	41.2	56.1/43.9	50.6/49.4	89.8/10.2	4.11	26.4
1940	48	131,669,275	7.2	44.2	56.5/43.5	50.2/49.8	89.8/10.2	3.67	29.0
1950	48	150,697,361	14.5	50.7	64.0/36.0	49.7/50.3	89.5/10.5	3.37	30.2
1960	50	179,323,175	18.5	50.6	69.9/30.1	49.3/50.7	88.6/11.4	3.33	29.5
1970	50	203,302,031	13.4	57.4	73.6/26.4	48.7/51.3	87.6/12.4	3.14	28.0
1980	50	226,542,199	11.4	64.0	73.7/26.3	48.6/51.4	85.9/14.1	2.75	30.0
1990	50	248,718,301	9.8	70.3	75.2/24.8	48.7/51.3	83.9/16.1	2.63	32.8
1995*	50	263,034,000*	5.1	70.7	NA	48.8/51.2	83.0/17.0	2.65	34.3

NA = Not available.
*Population in 1997 = 268, 921, 733.

Vital Statistics

| Year | Birth Rate* | Death Rate* | Life Expectancy in Years | | | | | Marriage Rate | Divorce Rate |
			Total Population	White Females	Nonwhite Females	White Males	Nonwhite Males		
1790	NA	NA	NA	NA	NA	NA	NA	NA	NA
1800	55.0	NA	NA	NA	NA	NA	NA	NA	NA
1810	54.3	NA	NA	NA	NA	NA	NA	NA	NA
1820	55.2	NA	NA	NA	NA	NA	NA	NA	NA
1830	51.4	NA	NA	NA	NA	NA	NA	NA	NA
1840	51.8	NA	NA	NA	NA	NA	NA	NA	NA
1850	43.3	NA	NA	NA	NA	NA	NA	NA	NA
1860	44.3	NA	NA	NA	NA	NA	NA	NA	NA
1870	38.3	NA	NA	NA	NA	NA	NA	NA	NA
1880	39.8	NA	NA	NA	NA	NA	NA	NA	NA
1890	31.5	NA	NA	NA	NA	NA	NA	NA	NA
1900	32.3	17.2	47.3	48.7	33.5	46.6	32.5	NA	NA
1910	30.1	14.7	50.0	52.0	37.5	48.6	33.8	NA	NA
1920	27.7	13.0	54.1	55.6	45.2	54.4	45.5	12.0	1.6
1930	21.3	11.3	59.7	63.5	49.2	59.7	47.3	9.2	1.6
1940	19.4	10.8	62.9	66.6	54.9	62.1	51.5	12.1	2.0
1950	24.1	9.6	68.2	72.2	62.9	66.5	59.1	11.1	2.6
1960	23.7	9.5	69.7	74.1	66.3	67.4	61.1	8.5	2.2
1970	18.4	9.5	70.8	75.6	69.4	68.0	61.3	10.6	3.5
1980	15.9	8.8	73.7	78.1	73.6	70.7	65.3	10.6	5.2
1990	16.6	8.6	75.4	79.4	75.2	72.7	67.0	9.8	4.7
1994	15.3	8.8	75.7	79.6	75.8	73.2	67.5	9.1	4.6

Data per one thousand for Birth, Death, Marriage, and Divorce rates.

NA = Not available. *Data for 1800, 1810, 1830, 1850, 1870, and 1890 for whites only.

Immigrants to the United States

Immigration Totals by Decade			
Years	Number	Years	Number
1820–1830	151,824	1911–1920	5,735,811
1831–1840	599,125	1921–1930	4,107,209
1841–1850	1,713,251	1931–1940	528,431
1851–1860	2,598,214	1941–1950	1,035,039
1861–1870	2,314,824	1951–1960	2,515,479
1871–1880	2,812,191	1961–1970	3,321,677
1881–1890	5,246,613	1971–1980	4,493,314
1891–1900	3,687,546	1981–1990	7,338,062
1901–1910	8,795,386	1991–1994	4,509,852
		Total	61,503,866

Major Sources of Immigrants by Country or Region (in thousands)

Period	Asia[a]	Germany	Mexico	Italy	Great Britain (UK)[b]	Ireland	Canada	Austria and Hungary	Soviet Union (Russia)	Caribbean	Central America and South America	Norway and Sweden
1820–1830	—	8	5	—	27	54	2	—	—	4	—	—
1831–1840	—	152	7	2	76	207	14	—	—	12	—	1
1841–1850	—	435	3	2	267	781	42	—	—	14	4	14
1851–1860	42	952	3	9	424	914	59	—	—	11	2	21
1861–1870	65	787	2	12	607	436	154	8	3	9	1	109
1871–1880	124	718	5	56	548	437	384	73	39	14	1	211
1881–1890	70	1,453	2[c]	307	807	655	393	354	213	29	3	568
1891–1900	75	505	1[c]	652	272	388	3	593	505	33	2	321
1901–1910	324	341	50	2,046	526	339	179	2,145	1,597	108	25	440
1911–1920	247	144	219	1,110	341	146	742	896	921	123	59	161
1921–1930	112	412	459	455	340	211	925	64	62	75	58	166
1931–1940	17	114	22	68	32	11	109	11	1	16	14	9
1941–1950	37	227	61	58	139	20	172	28	—	50	43	21
1951–1960	153	478	300	185	203	48	378	104	—	123	136	45
1961–1970	428	191	454	214	214	33	413	26	2	470	359	33
1971–1980	1,588	74	640	129	137	11	170	16	39	741	430	10
1981–1990	2,738	92	2,336	67	160	32	182	25	58	872	930	15
1991–1994	1,315	43	1,400	49	77	47	88	13	193	333	505	8
Total	7,334	7,126	5,970	5,422	5,196	4,772	4,408	4,356	3,637	3,036	2,575	2,154

Notes: Numbers for periods are rounded. Dash indicates less than one thousand; [a]Includes Middle East; [b]Since 1925, includes England, Scotland, Wales, and Northern Ireland data; [c]No data available for 1886–1894.

The American Worker

Year	Total Number of Workers	Males as Percent of Total Workers	Females as Percent of Total Workers	Married Women as Percent of Female Workers	Female Workers as Percent of Female Population	Percent of Labor Force Unemployed	Percent of Workers in Labor Unions
1870	12,506,000	85	15	NA	NA	NA	NA
1880	17,392,000	85	15	NA	NA	NA	NA
1890	23,318,000	83	17	14	19	4 (1894 = 18)	NA
1900	29,073,000	82	18	15	21	5	3
1910	38,167,000	79	21	25	25	6	6
1920	41,614,000	79	21	23	24	5 (1921 = 12)	12
1930	48,830,000	78	22	29	25	9 (1933 = 25)	11.6
1940	53,011,000	76	24	36	27	15 (1944 = 1)	26.9
1950	62,208,000	72	28	52	31	5.3	31.5
1960	69,628,000	67	33	55	38	5.5	31.4
1970	82,771,000	62	38	59	43	4.9	27.3
1980	106,940,000	58	42	55	52	7.1	21.9
1990	125,840,000	55	45	54	58	5.6	16.1
1995	132,304,000	54	46	55	59	5.6	15.5

NA = Not available.

The American Economy

Year	Gross National Product (GNP) (in $ billions)	Steel Production (in tons)	Automobiles Registered	New Housing Starts	Foreign Trade (in millions of dollars)	
					Exports	Imports
1790	NA	NA	NA	NA	20	23
1800	NA	NA	NA	NA	71	91
1810	NA	NA	NA	NA	67	85
1820	NA	NA	NA	NA	70	74
1830	NA	NA	NA	NA	74	71
1840	NA	NA	NA	NA	132	107
1850	NA	NA	NA	NA	152	178
1860	NA	13,000	NA	NA	400	362
1870	7.4[a]	77,000	NA	NA	451	462
1880	11.2[b]	1,397,000	NA	NA	853	761
1890	13.1	4,779,000	NA	328,000	910	823
1900	18.7	11,227,000	8,000	189,000	1,499	930
1910	35.3	28,330,000	458,300	387,000 (1918 = 118,000)	1,919	1,646
1920	91.5	46,183,000	8,131,500	247,000 (1925 = 937,000)	8,664	5,784
1930	90.7	44,591,000	23,034,700	330,000 (1933 = 93,000)	4,013	3,500
1940	100.0	66,983,000	27,465,800	603,000 (1944 = 142,000)	4,030	7,433
1950	286.5	96,836,000	40,339,000	1,952,000	9,997	8,954
1960	506.5	99,282,000	61,682,300	1,365,000	19,659	15,093
1970	1,016.0	131,514,000	89,279,800	1,434,000	42,681	40,356
1980	2,819.5	111,835,000	121,601,000	1,292,000	220,626	244,871
1990	5,764.9	98,906,000	143,550,000	1,193,000	394,030	485,453
1995	7,237.5	104,930,000	133,930,000[c]	1,354,000	584,742	743,445

[a]Figure is average for 1869–1878.

[b]Figure is average for 1879–1888.

[c]Figure for 1994.

NA = Not available.

Federal Budget Outlays and Debt

Year	Defense[a]	Veterans Benefits[a]	Income Security[a]	Social Security[a]	Health and Medicare[a]	Education[a][d]	Net Interest Payments[a]	Federal Debt (dollars)
1790	14.9	4.1[b]	NA	NA	NA	NA	55.0	75,463,000[c]
1800	55.7	.6	NA	NA	NA	NA	31.3	82,976,000
1810	48.4 (1814: 79.7)	1.0	NA	NA	NA	NA	34.9	53,173,000
1820	38.4	17.6	NA	NA	NA	NA	28.1	91,016,000
1830	52.9	9.0	NA	NA	NA	NA	12.6	48,565,000
1840	54.3 (1847: 80.7)	10.7	NA	NA	NA	NA	.7	3,573,000
1850	43.8	4.7	NA	NA	NA	NA	1.0	63,453,000
1860	44.2 (1865: 88.9)	1.7	NA	NA	NA	NA	5.0	64,844,000
1870	25.7	9.2	NA	NA	NA	NA	41.7	2,436,453,000
1880	19.3	21.2	NA	NA	NA	NA	35.8	2,090,909,000
1890	20.9 (1899: 48.6)	33.6	NA	NA	NA	NA	11.4	1,222,397,000
1900	36.6	27.0	NA	NA	NA	NA	7.7	1,263,417,000
1910	45.1 (1919: 59.5)	23.2	NA	NA	NA	NA	3.1	1,146,940,000
1920	37.1	3.4	NA	NA	NA	NA	16.0	24,299,321,000
1930	25.3	6.6	NA	NA	NA	NA	19.9	16,185,310,000
1940	17.5 (1945: 89.4)	6.0	16.0	.3	.5	20.8	9.4	42,967,531,000
1950	32.2	20.3	9.6	1.8	.6	.6	11.3	256,853,000,000
1960	52.2	5.9	8.0	12.6	.9	1.0	7.5	290,525,000,000
1970	41.8	4.4	8.0	15.5	6.2	4.4	7.3	308,921,000,000
1980	22.7	3.6	14.6	20.1	9.4	5.4	8.9	909,050,000,000
1990	23.9	2.3	11.7	19.8	12.4	3.1	14.7	3,206,564,000,000
1995	17.9	2.5	14.5	22.1	18.1	3.6	15.3	5,207,298,000,000[e]

[a]Figures represent percentage of total federal spending for each category. Not included are categories of transportation, commerce, and housing.

[b]1789–1791 figure.

[c]1791 figure.

[d]Includes training, employment, and social services.

[e]1996 figure.

NA = Not available.

The Fifty States, District of Columbia, and Puerto Rico

State	Date of Admission (with Rank)	Capital City	Population (1995) (with Rank)	Racial/Ethnic Distribution (1995)	Per Capita Personal Income (1995) (with Rank)	Total Area in Square Miles (with Rank)
Alabama (AL)	Dec. 14, 1819 (22)	Montgomery	4,253,000 (22)	White: 3,140,000; Black: 1,083,000; Hispanic: 29,000; Asian: 33,000	$18,781 (41)	52,423 (30)
Alaska (AK)	Jan. 3, 1959 (49)	Juneau	604,000 (48)	White: 477,000; Black: 26,000; Hispanic: 22,000; Asian: 29,000; Native American: 102,000	$24,182 (10)	656,424 (1)
Arizona (AZ)	Feb. 14, 1912 (48)	Phoenix	4,218,000 (23)	White: 3,606,000; Black: 123,000; Hispanic: 853,000; Asian: 91,000; Native American: 251,000	$20,421 (35)	114,006 (6)
Arkansas (AR)	June 15, 1836 (25)	Little Rock	2,484,000 (33)	White: 2,047,000; Black: 386,000; Hispanic: 27,000; Asian: 26,000	$17,429 (49)	53,182 (29)
California (CA)	Sept. 9, 1850 (31)	Sacramento	31,589,000 (1)	White: 25,701,000; Black: 2,512,000; Hispanic: 9,143,000; Asian: 3,908,000; Native American: 277,000	$23,699 (12)	163,707 (3)
Colorado (CO)	Aug. 1, 1876 (38)	Denver	3,747,000 (25)	White: 3,431,000; Black: 156,000; Hispanic: 511,000; Asian: 89,000; Native American: 34,000	$23,449 (16)	104,100 (8)
Connecticut (CT)	Jan. 9, 1788 (5)	Hartford	3,275,000 (28)	White: 2,915,000; Black: 293,000; Hispanic: 258,000; Asian: 60,000	$30,303 (1)	5,544 (48)
Delaware (DE)	Dec. 7, 1787 (1)	Dover	717,000 (46)	White: 570,000; Black: 132,000; Hispanic: 22,000; Asian: 14,000	$24,124 (11)	2,489 (49)
District of Columbia (DC)	U.S. Capital, Dec. 1, 1800*	Washington (coextensive with DC)	554,000 (not ranked)	White: 185,000; Black: 384,000; Hispanic: 35,000; Asian: 16,000	$32,274*	68*
Florida (FL)	Mar. 3, 1845 (27)	Tallahassee	14,166,000 (4)	White: 11,867,000; Black: 2,073,000; Hispanic: 1,948,000; Asian: 231,000	$22,916 (20)	65,756 (22)
Georgia (GA)	Jan. 2, 1788 (4)	Atlanta	7,201,000 (10)	White: 5,025,000; Black: 1,955,000; Hispanic: 144,000; Asian: 109,000	$21,278 (28)	59,441 (24)
Hawai'i (HI)	Aug. 21, 1959 (50)	Honolulu	1,187,000 (40)	White: 499,000; Black: 36,000; Hispanic: 106,000; Asian: 679,000	$24,738 (9)	10,932 (43)
Idaho (ID)	July 3, 1890 (43)	Boise	1,163,000 (41)	White: 1,118,000; Black: 5,000; Hispanic: 74,000; Asian: 15,000; Native American: 18,000	$19,264 (38)	83,574 (14)
Illinois (IL)	Dec. 3, 1818 (21)	Springfield	11,830,000 (6)	White: 9,603,000; Black: 1,843,000; Hispanic: 1,086,000; Asian: 383,000	$24,763 (8)	57,918 (25)
Indiana (IN)	Dec. 11, 1816 (19)	Indianapolis	5,803,000 (14)	White: 5,275,000; Black: 476,000; Hispanic: 122,000; Asian: 55,000	$21,273 (29)	36,420 (38)
Iowa (IA)	Dec. 28, 1846 (29)	Des Moines	2,842,000 (30)	White: 2,763,000; Black: 57,000; Hispanic: 45,000; Asian: 33,000	$21,012 (30)	56,276 (26)
Kansas (KS)	Jan. 29, 1861 (34)	Topeka	2,565,000 (32)	White: 2,365,000; Black: 159,000; Hispanic: 116,000; Asian: 50,000	$21,825 (23)	82,282 (15)
Kentucky (KY)	June 1, 1792 (15)	Frankfort	3,860,000 (24)	White: 3,535,000; Black: 286,000; Hispanic: 23,000; Asian: 24,000	$18,612 (43)	40,411 (37)

The Fifty States, District of Columbia, and Puerto Rico (continued)

State	Date of Admission (with Rank)	Capital City	Population (1995) (with Rank)	Racial/Ethnic Distribution (1995)	Per Capita Personal Income (1995) (with Rank)	Total Area in Square Miles (with Rank)
Louisiana (LA)	Apr. 30, 1812 (18)	Baton Rouge	4,342,000 (21)	White: 2,909,000; Black: 1,371,000; Hispanic: 109,000; Asian: 60,000	$18,827 (39)	51,843 (31)
Maine (ME)	Mar. 15, 1820 (23)	Augusta	1,241,000 (39)	White: 1,217,000; Black: 5,000; Hispanic: 9,000; Asian: 8,000; Native American: 6,000	$20,527 (34)	35,387 (39)
Maryland (MD)	Apr. 28, 1788 (7)	Annapolis	5,042,000 (19)	White: 3,500,000; Black: 1,368,000; Hispanic: 158,000; Asian: 196,000	$25,927 (5)	12,407 (42)
Massachusetts (MA)	Feb. 6, 1788 (6)	Boston	6,074,000 (13)	White: 5,445,000; Black: 340,000; Hispanic: 342,000; Asian: 180,000	$26,994 (3)	10,555 (44)
Michigan (MI)	Jan. 26, 1837 (26)	Lansing	9,549,000 (8)	White: 7,958,000; Black: 1,417,000; Hispanic: 242,000; Asian: 140,000; Native American: 61,000	$23,551 (15)	96,705 (11)
Minnesota (MN)	May 11, 1858 (32)	Saint Paul	4,610,000 (20)	White: 4,344,000; Black: 104,000; Hispanic: 68,000; Asian: 113,000; Native American: 58,000	$23,118 (19)	86,943 (12)
Mississippi (MS)	Dec. 10, 1817 (20)	Jackson	2,697,000 (31)	White: 1,688,000; Black: 952,000; Hispanic: 18,000; Asian: 17,000	$16,531 (50)	48,434 (32)
Missouri (MO)	Aug. 10, 1821 (24)	Jefferson City	5,324,000 (16)	White: 4,629,000; Black: 581,000; Hispanic: 71,000; Asian: 56,000	$21,627 (26)	69,709 (21)
Montana (MT)	Nov. 8, 1889 (41)	Helena	870,000 (44)	White: 798,000; Black: 2,000; Hispanic: 15,000; Asian: 6,000; Native American: 55,000	$18,482 (44)	147,046 (4)
Nebraska (NE)	Mar. 1, 1867 (37)	Lincoln	1,637,000 (37)	White: 1,550,000; Black: 64,000; Hispanic: 53,000; Asian: 17,000; Native American: 14,000	$21,703 (25)	77,358 (16)
Nevada (NV)	Oct. 3, 1864 (36)	Carson City	1,530,000 (38)	White: 1,281,000; Black: 100,000; Hispanic: 195,000; Asian: 70,000; Native American: 27,000	$25,013 (7)	110,567 (7)
New Hampshire (NH)	June 21, 1788 (9)	Concord	1,148,000 (42)	White: 1,109,000; Black: 7,000; Hispanic: 13,000; Asian: 14,000	$25,151 (6)	9,351 (46)
New Jersey (NJ)	Dec. 18, 1787 (3)	Trenton	7,945,000 (9)	White: 6,405,000; Black: 1,156,000; Hispanic: 898,000; Asian: 356,000	$28,858 (2)	8,722 (47)
New Mexico (NM)	Jan. 6, 1912 (47)	Santa Fe	1,685,000 (36)	White: 1,460,000; Black: 32,000; Hispanic: 686,000; Asian: 25,000; Native American: 159,000	$18,055 (47)	121,598 (5)
New York (NY)	July 26, 1788 (11)	Albany	18,136,000 (3)	White: 14,025,000; Black: 3,249,000; Hispanic: 2,372,000; Asian: 846,000; Native American: 57,000	$26,782 (4)	54,471 (27)
North Carolina (NC)	Nov. 21, 1789 (12)	Raleigh	7,195,000 (11)	White: 5,378,000; Black: 1,594,000; Hispanic: 100,000; Asian: 88,000; Native American: 90,000	$20,604 (33)	53,821 (28)
North Dakota (ND)	Nov. 2, 1889 (39)	Bismarck	641,000 (47)	White: 600,000; Black: 4,000; Hispanic: 5,000; Asian: 5,000; Native American: 28,000	$18,663 (42)	70,704 (19)
Ohio (OH)	Mar. 1, 1803 (17)	Columbus	11,151,000 (7)	White: 9,806,000; Black: 1,253,000; Hispanic: 170,000; Asian: 122,000	$22,021 (21)	44,828 (34)

The Fifty States, District of Columbia, and Puerto Rico (continued)

State	Date of Admission (with Rank)	Capital City	Population (1995) (with Rank)	Racial/Ethnic Distribution (1995)	Per Capita Personal Income (1995) (with Rank)	Total Area in Square Miles (with Rank)
Oklahoma (OK)	Nov. 16, 1907 (46)	Oklahoma City	3,278,000 (27)	White: 2,699,000; Black: 244,000; Hispanic: 106,000; Asian: 52,000; Native American: 276,000	$18,152 (46)	69,903 (20)
Oregon (OR)	Feb. 14, 1859 (33)	Salem	3,141,000 (29)	White: 2,929,000; Black: 54,000; Hispanic: 151,000; Asian: 111,000; Native American: 47,000	$21,736 (24)	98,386 (9)
Pennsylvania (PA)	Dec. 12, 1787 (2)	Harrisburg	12,072,000 (5)	White: 10,768,000; Black: 1,167,000; Hispanic: 297,000; Asian: 185,000	$23,279 (18)	46,058 (33)
Puerto Rico (PR)	Ascession 1898; Commonwealth Status 1952	San Juan	3,720,000*	White: >1,000; Black: >1,000; Hispanic: 3,621,000; Asian: >1,000	$6,360*	3,427*
Rhode Island (RI)	May 29, 1790 (13)	Providence	990,000 (43)	White: 927,000; Black: 44,000; Hispanic: 58,000; Asian: 25,000	$23,310 (17)	1,545 (50)
South Carolina (SC)	May 23, 1788 (8)	Columbia	3,673,000 (26)	White: 2,561,000; Black: 1,131,000; Hispanic: 40,000; Asian: 31,000	$18,788 (40)	32,008 (40)
South Dakota (SD)	Nov. 2, 1889 (40)	Pierre	729,000 (45)	White: 663,000; Black: 3,000; Hispanic: 7,000; Asian: 5,000; Native American: 62,000	$19,506 (37)	77,121 (17)
Tennessee (TN)	June 1, 1796 (16)	Nashville	5,256,000 (17)	White: 4,327,000; Black: 845,000; Hispanic: 42,000; Asian: 46,000	$20,376 (36)	42,149 (36)
Texas (TX)	Dec. 29, 1845 (28)	Austin	18,724,000 (2)	White: 15,814,000; Black: 2,251,000; Hispanic: 5,260,000; Asian: 461,000	$20,654 (32)	268,601 (2)
Utah (UT)	Jan. 4, 1896 (45)	Salt Lake City	1,951,000 (34)	White: 1,843,000; Black: 14,000; Hispanic: 106,000; Asian: 54,000; Native American: 33,000	$18,223 (45)	84,904 (13)
Vermont (VT)	Mar. 4, 1791 (14)	Montpelier	585,000 (49)	White: 570,000; Black: 2,000; Hispanic: 4,000; Asian: 4,000; Native American: 2,000	$20,927 (31)	9,615 (45)
Virginia (VA)	June 25, 1788 (10)	Richmond	6,618,000 (12)	White: 5,127,000; Black: 1,284,000; Hispanic: 193,000; Asian: 220,000	$25,597 (14)	42,777 (35)
Washington (WA)	Nov. 11, 1889 (42)	Olympia	5,431,000 (15)	White: 4,915,000; Black: 164,000; Hispanic: 291,000; Asian: 318,000; Native American: 101,000	$23,639 (13)	71,302 (18)
West Virginia (WV)	June 20, 1863 (35)	Charleston	1,828,000; (35)	White: 1,756,000; Black: 54,000; Hispanic: 10,000; Asian: 11,000	$17,915 (48)	24,231 (41)
Wisconsin (WI)	May 29, 1848 (30)	Madison	5,123,000 (18)	White: 4,750,000; Black: 288,000; Hispanic: 118,000; Asian: 76,000; Native American: 45,000	$21,839 (22)	65,499 (23)
Wyoming (WY)	July 10, 1890 (44)	Cheyenne	480,000 (50)	White: 467,000; Black: 4,000; Hispanic: 31,000; Asian: 4,000; Native American: 12,000	$21,321 (27)	97,818 (10)

*Not ranked.

Presidential Elections

Year	Number of States	Candidates	Parties	Popular Vote	% of Popular Vote	Electoral Vote	% Voter Participation[b]
1789	11	**George Washington**	No party			69	
		John Adams	designations			34	
		Other candidates				35	
1792	15	**George Washington**	No party			132	
		John Adams	designations			77	
		George Clinton				50	
		Other candidates				5	
1796	16	**John Adams**	Federalist			71	
		Thomas Jefferson	Democratic-Republican			68	
		Thomas Pinckney	Federalist			59	
		Aaron Burr	Democratic-Republican			30	
		Other candidates				48	
1800	16	**Thomas Jefferson**	Democratic-Republican			73	
		Aaron Burr	Democratic-Republican			73	
		John Adams	Federalist			65	
		Charles C. Pinckney	Federalist			64	
		John Jay	Federalist			1	
1804	17	**Thomas Jefferson**	Democratic-Republican			162	
		Charles C. Pinckney	Federalist			14	
1808	17	**James Madison**	Democratic-Republican			122	
		Charles C. Pinckney	Federalist			47	
		George Clinton	Democratic-Republican			6	
1812	18	**James Madison**	Democratic-Republican			128	
		DeWitt Clinton	Federalist			89	
1816	19	**James Monroe**	Democratic-Republican			183	
		Rufus King	Federalist			34	
1820	24	**James Monroe**	Democratic-Republican			231	
		John Quincy Adams	Independent Republican			1	

Presidential Elections (continued)

Year	Number of States	Candidates	Parties	Popular Vote	% of Popular Vote	Electoral Vote	% Voter Participation[b]
1824	24	**John Quincy Adams**	Democratic-Republican	108,740	30.5	84	26.9
		Andrew Jackson	Democratic-Republican	153,544	43.1	99	
		Henry Clay	Democratic-Republican	47,136	13.2	37	
		William H. Crawford	Democratic-Republican	46,618	13.1	41	
1828	24	**Andrew Jackson**	Democratic	647,286	56.0	178	57.6
		John Quincy Adams	National Republican	508,064	44.0	83	
1832	24	**Andrew Jackson**	Democratic	688,242	54.5	219	55.4
		Henry Clay	National Republican	473,462	37.5	49	
		William Wirt	Anti-Masonic	101,051	8.0	7	
		John Floyd	Democratic			11	
1836	26	**Martin Van Buren**	Democratic	765,483	50.9	170	57.8
		William H. Harrison	Whig			73	
		Hugh L. White	Whig	739,795	49.1	26	
		Daniel Webster	Whig			14	
		W. P. Mangum	Whig			11	
1840	26	**William H. Harrison**	Whig	1,274,624	53.1	234	80.2
		Martin Van Buren	Democratic	1,127,781	46.9	60	
1844	26	**James K. Polk**	Democratic	1,338,464	49.6	170	78.9
		Henry Clay	Whig	1,300,097	48.1	105	
		James G. Birney	Liberty	62,300	2.3		
1848	30	**Zachary Taylor**	Whig	1,360,967	47.4	163	72.7
		Lewis Cass	Democratic	1,222,342	42.5	127	
		Martin Van Buren	Free Soil	291,263	10.1		
1852	31	**Franklin Pierce**	Democratic	1,601,117	50.9	254	69.6
		Winfield Scott	Whig	1,385,453	44.1	42	
		John P. Hale	Free Soil	155,825	5.0		
1856	31	**James Buchanan**	Democratic	1,832,955	45.3	174	78.9
		John C. Frémont	Republican	1,339,932	33.1	114	
		Millard Fillmore	American	871,731	21.6	8	
1860	33	**Abraham Lincoln**	Republican	1,865,593	39.8	180	81.2
		Stephen A. Douglas	Democratic	1,382,713	29.5	12	
		John C. Breckinridge	Democratic	848,356	18.1	72	
		John Bell	Constitutional Union	592,906	12.6	39	
1864	36	**Abraham Lincoln**	Republican	2,206,938	55.0	212	73.8
		George B. McClellan	Democratic	1,803,787	45.0	21	

Presidential Elections (continued)

Year	Number of States	Candidates	Parties	Popular Vote	% of Popular Vote	Electoral Vote	% Voter Participation[b]
1868	37	**Ulysses S. Grant**	Republican	3,013,421	52.7	214	78.1
		Horatio Seymour	Democratic	2,706,829	47.3	80	
1872	37	**Ulysses S. Grant**	Republican	3,596,745	55.6	286	71.3
		Horace Greeley	Democratic	2,843,446	43.9	a	
1876	38	**Rutherford B. Hayes**	Republican	4,036,572	48.0	185	81.8
		Samuel J. Tilden	Democratic	4,284,020	51.0	184	
1880	38	**James A. Garfield**	Republican	4,453,295	48.5	214	79.4
		Winfield S. Hancock	Democratic	4,414,082	48.1	155	
		James B. Weaver	Greenback-Labor	308,578	3.4		
1884	38	**Grover Cleveland**	Democratic	4,879,507	48.5	219	77.5
		James G. Blaine	Republican	4,850,293	48.2	182	
		Benjamin F. Butler	Greenback-Labor	175,370	1.8		
		John P. St. John	Prohibition	150,369	1.5		
1888	38	**Benjamin Harrison**	Republican	5,477,129	47.9	233	79.3
		Grover Cleveland	Democratic	5,537,857	48.6	168	
		Clinton B. Fisk	Prohibition	249,506	2.2		
		Anson J. Streeter	Union Labor	146,935	1.3		
1892	44	**Grover Cleveland**	Democratic	5,555,426	46.1	277	74.7
		Benjamin Harrison	Republican	5,182,690	43.0	145	
		James B. Weaver	People's	1,029,846	8.5	22	
		John Bidwell	Prohibition	264,133	2.2		
1896	45	**William McKinley**	Republican	7,102,246	51.1	271	79.3
		William J. Bryan	Democratic	6,492,559	47.7	176	
1900	45	**William McKinley**	Republican	7,218,491	51.7	292	73.2
		William J. Bryan	Democratic; Populist	6,356,734	45.5	155	
		John C. Wooley	Prohibition	208,914	1.5		
1904	45	**Theodore Roosevelt**	Republican	7,628,461	57.4	336	65.2
		Alton B. Parker	Democratic	5,084,223	37.6	140	
		Eugene V. Debs	Socialist	402,283	3.0		
		Silas C. Swallow	Prohibition	258,536	1.9		
1908	46	**William H. Taft**	Republican	7,675,320	51.6	321	65.4
		William J. Bryan	Democratic	6,412,294	43.1	162	
		Eugene V. Debs	Socialist	420,793	2.8		
		Eugene W. Chafin	Prohibition	253,840	1.7		
1912	48	**Woodrow Wilson**	Democratic	6,296,547	41.9	435	58.8
		Theodore Roosevelt	Progressive	4,118,571	27.4	88	
		William H. Taft	Republican	3,486,720	23.2	8	
		Eugene V. Debs	Socialist	900,672	6.0		
		Eugene W. Chafin	Prohibition	206,275	1.4		

Presidential Elections (continued)

Year	Number of States	Candidates	Parties	Popular Vote	% of Popular Vote	Electoral Vote	% Voter Participation[b]
1916	48	**Woodrow Wilson**	Democratic	9,127,695	49.4	277	61.6
		Charles E. Hughes	Republican	8,533,507	46.2	254	
		A. L. Benson	Socialist	585,113	3.2		
		J. Frank Hanly	Prohibition	220,506	1.2		
1920	48	**Warren G. Harding**	Republican	16,143,407	60.4	404	49.2
		James M. Cox	Democratic	9,130,328	34.2	127	
		Eugene V. Debs	Socialist	919,799	3.4		
		P. P. Christensen	Farmer-Labor	265,411	1.0		
1924	48	**Calvin Coolidge**	Republican	15,718,211	54.0	382	48.9
		John W. Davis	Democratic	8,385,283	28.8	136	
		Robert M. La Follette	Progressive	4,831,289	16.6	13	
1928	48	**Herbert C. Hoover**	Republican	21,391,993	58.2	444	56.9
		Alfred E. Smith	Democratic	15,016,169	40.9	87	
1932	48	**Franklin D. Roosevelt**	Democratic	22,809,638	57.4	472	56.9
		Herbert C. Hoover	Republican	15,758,901	39.7	59	
		Norman Thomas	Socialist	881,951	2.2		
1936	48	**Franklin D. Roosevelt**	Democratic	27,752,869	60.8	523	61.0
		Alfred M. Landon	Republican	16,674,665	36.5	8	
		William Lemke	Union	882,479	1.9		
1940	48	**Franklin D. Roosevelt**	Democratic	27,307,819	54.8	449	62.5
		Wendell L. Wilkie	Republican	22,321,018	44.8	82	
1944	48	**Franklin D. Roosevelt**	Democratic	25,606,585	53.5	432	55.9
		Thomas E. Dewey	Republican	22,014,745	46.0	99	
1948	48	**Harry S Truman**	Democratic	24,179,345	49.6	303	53.0
		Thomas E. Dewey	Republican	21,991,291	45.1	189	
		J. Strom Thurmond	States' Rights	1,176,125	2.4	39	
		Henry A. Wallace	Progressive	1,157,326	2.4		
1952	48	**Dwight D. Eisenhower**	Republican	33,936,234	55.1	442	63.3
		Adlai E. Stevenson	Democratic	27,314,992	44.4	89	
1956	48	**Dwight D. Eisenhower**	Republican	35,590,472	57.6	457	60.6
		Adlai E. Stevenson	Democratic	26,022,752	42.1	73	
1960	50	**John F. Kennedy**	Democratic	34,226,731	49.7	303	62.8
		Richard M. Nixon	Republican	34,108,157	49.5	219	
1964	50	**Lyndon B. Johnson**	Democratic	43,129,566	61.1	486	61.7
		Barry M. Goldwater	Republican	27,178,188	38.5	52	
1968	50	**Richard M. Nixon**	Republican	31,785,480	43.4	301	60.6
		Hubert H. Humphrey	Democratic	31,275,166	42.7	191	
		George C. Wallace	American Independent	9,906,473	13.5	46	

Presidential Elections (continued)

Year	Number of States	Candidates	Parties	Popular Vote	% of Popular Vote	Electoral Vote	% Voter Participation[b]
1972	50	**Richard M. Nixon**	Republican	47,169,911	60.7	520	55.2
		George S. McGovern	Democratic	29,170,383	37.5	17	
		John G. Schmitz	American	1,099,482	1.4		
1976	50	**James E. Carter**	Democratic	40,830,763	50.1	297	53.5
		Gerald R. Ford	Republican	39,147,793	48.0	240	
1980	50	**Ronald W. Reagan**	Republican	43,899,248	50.8	489	52.6
		James E. Carter	Democratic	35,481,432	41.0	49	
		John B. Anderson	Independent	5,719,437	6.6	0	
		Ed Clark	Libertarian	920,859	1.1	0	
1984	50	**Ronald W. Reagan**	Republican	54,455,075	58.8	525	53.1
		Walter F. Mondale	Democratic	37,577,185	40.6	13	
1988	50	**George H. W. Bush**	Republican	48,901,046	53.4	426	50.2
		Michael S. Dukakis	Democratic	41,809,030	45.6	111[c]	
1992	50	**William J. Clinton**	Democratic	44,908,233	43.0	370	55.0
		George H. W. Bush	Republican	39,102,282	37.4	168	
		H. Ross Perot	Independent	19,741,048	18.9	0	
1996	50	**William J. Clinton**	Democratic	47,401,054	49.2	379	49.0
		Robert J. Dole	Republican	39,197,350	40.7	159	
		H. Ross Perot	Reform	8,085,285	8.4	0	
		Ralph Nader	Green	684,871	0.7	0	

Candidates receiving less than 1 percent of the popular vote have been omitted. Thus the percentage of popular vote given for any election year may not total 100 percent.

Before the passage of the Twelfth Amendment in 1804, the Electoral College voted for two presidential candidates; the runner-up became vice president.

Before 1824, most presidential electors were chosen by state legislatures, not by popular vote.

[a]Greeley died shortly after the election; the electors supporting him then divided their votes among minor candidates.

[b]Percent of voting-age population casting ballots.

[c]One elector from West Virginia cast her Electoral College presidential ballot for Lloyd Bentsen, the Democratic party's vice-presidential candidate.

Presidents and Vice Presidents

1. President	**George Washington**	1789–1797
Vice President	John Adams	1789–1797
2. President	**John Adams**	1797–1801
Vice President	Thomas Jefferson	1797–1801
3. President	**Thomas Jefferson**	1801–1809
Vice President	Aaron Burr	1801–1805
Vice President	George Clinton	1805–1809
4. President	**James Madison**	1809–1817
Vice President	George Clinton	1809–1813
Vice President	Elbridge Gerry	1813–1817
5. President	**James Monroe**	1817–1825
Vice President	Daniel Tompkins	1817–1825
6. President	**John Quincy Adams**	1825–1829
Vice President	John C. Calhoun	1825–1829
7. President	**Andrew Jackson**	1829–1837
Vice President	John C. Calhoun	1829–1833
Vice President	Martin Van Buren	1833–1837
8. President	**Martin Van Buren**	1837–1841
Vice President	Richard M. Johnson	1837–1841
9. President	**William H. Harrison**	1841
Vice President	John Tyler	1841
10. President	**John Tyler**	1841–1845
Vice President	None	
11. President	**James K. Polk**	1845–1849
Vice President	George M. Dallas	1845–1849
12. President	**Zachary Taylor**	1849–1850
Vice President	Millard Fillmore	1849–1850
13. President	**Millard Fillmore**	1850–1853
Vice President	None	
14. President	**Franklin Pierce**	1853–1857
Vice President	William R. King	1853–1857
15. President	**James Buchanan**	1857–1861
Vice President	John C. Breckinridge	1857–1861
16. President	**Abraham Lincoln**	1861–1865
Vice President	Hannibal Hamlin	1861–1865
Vice President	Andrew Johnson	1865
17. President	**Andrew Johnson**	1865–1869
Vice President	None	
18. President	**Ulysses S. Grant**	1869–1877
Vice President	Schuyler Colfax	1869–1873
Vice President	Henry Wilson	1873–1877
19. President	**Rutherford B. Hayes**	1877–1881
Vice President	William A. Wheeler	1877–1881

20. President	**James A. Garfield**	1881
Vice President	Chester A. Arthur	1881
21. President	**Chester A. Arthur**	1881–1885
Vice President	None	
22. President	**Grover Cleveland**	1885–1889
Vice President	Thomas A. Hendricks	1885–1889
23. President	**Benjamin Harrison**	1889–1893
Vice President	Levi P. Morton	1889–1893
24. President	**Grover Cleveland**	1893–1897
Vice President	Adlai E. Stevenson	1893–1897
25. President	**William McKinley**	1897–1901
Vice President	Garret A. Hobart	1897–1901
Vice President	Theodore Roosevelt	1901
26. President	**Theodore Roosevelt**	1901–1909
Vice President	Charles Fairbanks	1905–1909
27. President	**William H. Taft**	1909–1913
Vice President	James S. Sherman	1909–1913
28. President	**Woodrow Wilson**	1913–1921
Vice President	Thomas R. Marshall	1913–1921
29. President	**Warren G. Harding**	1921–1923
Vice President	Calvin Coolidge	1921–1923
30. President	**Calvin Coolidge**	1923–1929
Vice President	Charles G. Dawes	1925–1929
31. President	**Herbert C. Hoover**	1929–1933
Vice President	Charles Curtis	1929–1933
32. President	**Franklin D. Roosevelt**	1933–1945
Vice President	John N. Garner	1933–1941
Vice President	Henry A. Wallace	1941–1945
Vice President	Harry S Truman	1945
33. President	**Harry S Truman**	1945–1953
Vice President	Alben W. Barkley	1949–1953
34. President	**Dwight D. Eisenhower**	1953–1961
Vice President	Richard M. Nixon	1953–1961
35. President	**John F. Kennedy**	1961–1963
Vice President	Lyndon B. Johnson	1961–1963
36. President	**Lyndon B. Johnson**	1963–1969
Vice President	Hubert H. Humphrey	1965–1969
37. President	**Richard M. Nixon**	1969–1974
Vice President	Spiro T. Agnew	1969–1973
Vice President	Gerald R. Ford	1973–1974
38. President	**Gerald R. Ford**	1974–1977
Vice President	Nelson A. Rockefeller	1974–1977

Presidents and Vice Presidents (continued)

39. President	**James E. Carter**	1977–1981		41. President	**George H. W. Bush**	1989–1993
Vice President	Walter F. Mondale	1977–1981		Vice President	J. Danforth Quayle	1989–1993
40. President	**Ronald W. Reagan**	1981–1989		42. President	**William J. Clinton**	1993–
Vice President	George H. W. Bush	1981–1989		Vice President	Albert Gore	1993–

Party Strength in Congress

Period	Congress	House Majority Party		House Minority Party		Others	Senate Majority Party		Senate Minority Party		Others	Party of President	
1789–91	1st	Ad	38	Op	26		Ad	17	Op	9		F	Washington
1791–93	2nd	F	37	DR	33		F	16	DR	13		F	Washington
1793–95	3rd	DR	57	F	48		F	17	DR	13		F	Washington
1795–97	4th	F	54	DR	52		F	19	DR	13		F	Washington
1797–99	5th	F	58	DR	48		F	20	DR	12		F	J. Adams
1799–1801	6th	F	64	DR	42		F	19	DR	13		F	J. Adams
1801–03	7th	DR	69	F	36		DR	18	F	13		DR	Jefferson
1803–05	8th	DR	102	F	39		DR	25	F	9		DR	Jefferson
1805–07	9th	DR	116	F	25		DR	27	F	7		DR	Jefferson
1807–09	10th	DR	118	F	24		DR	28	F	6		DR	Jefferson
1809–11	11th	DR	94	F	48		DR	28	F	6		DR	Madison
1811–13	12th	DR	108	F	36		DR	30	F	6		DR	Madison
1813–15	13th	DR	112	F	68		DR	27	F	9		DR	Madison
1815–17	14th	DR	117	F	65		DR	25	F	11		DR	Madison
1817–19	15th	DR	141	F	42		DR	34	F	10		DR	Monroe
1819–21	16th	DR	156	F	27		DR	35	F	7		DR	Monroe
1821–23	17th	DR	158	F	25		DR	44	F	4		DR	Monroe
1823–25	18th	DR	187	F	26		DR	44	F	4		DR	Monroe
1825–27	19th	Ad	105	J	97		Ad	26	J	20		C	J. Q. Adams
1827–29	20th	J	119	Ad	94		J	28	Ad	20		C	J. Q. Adams
1829–31	21st	D	139	NR	74		D	26	NR	22		D	Jackson
1831–33	22nd	D	141	NR	58	14	D	25	NR	21	2	D	Jackson
1833–35	23rd	D	147	AM	53	60	D	20	NR	20	8	D	Jackson
1835–37	24th	D	145	W	98		D	27	W	25		D	Jackson
1837–39	25th	D	108	W	107	24	D	30	W	18	4	D	Van Buren
1839–41	26th	D	124	W	118		D	28	W	22		D	Van Buren
1841–43	27th	W	133	D	102	6	W	28	D	22	2	W	W. Harrison
												W	Tyler
1843–45	28th	D	142	W	79	1	W	28	D	25	1	W	Tyler
1845–47	29th	D	143	W	77	6	D	31	W	25		D	Polk
1847–49	30th	W	115	D	108	4	D	36	W	21	1	D	Polk
1849–51	31st	D	112	W	109	9	D	35	W	25	2	W	Taylor
												W	Fillmore
1851–53	32nd	D	140	W	88	5	D	35	W	24	3	W	Fillmore
1853–55	33rd	D	159	W	71	4	D	38	W	22	2	D	Pierce
1855–57	34th	R	108	D	83	43	D	40	R	15	5	D	Pierce
1857–59	35th	D	118	R	92	26	D	36	R	20	8	D	Buchanan
1859–61	36th	R	114	D	92	31	D	36	R	26	4	D	Buchanan
1861–63	37th	R	105	D	43	30	R	31	D	10	8	R	Lincoln
1863–65	38th	R	102	D	75	9	R	36	D	9	5	R	Lincoln

Party Strength in Congress (continued)

Period	Congress	House Majority Party		House Minority Party		Others	Senate Majority Party		Senate Minority Party		Others	Party of President	
1865–67	39th	U	149	D	42		U	42	D	10		R	Lincoln
												R	A. Johnson
1867–69	40th	R	143	D	49		R	42	D	11		R	A. Johnson
1869–71	41st	R	149	D	63		R	56	D	11		R	Grant
1871–73	42nd	R	134	D	104	5	R	52	D	17	5	R	Grant
1873–75	43rd	R	194	D	92	14	R	49	D	19	5	R	Grant
1875–77	44th	D	169	R	109	14	R	45	D	29	2	R	Grant
1877–79	45th	D	153	R	140		R	39	D	36	1	R	Hayes
1879–81	46th	D	149	R	130	14	D	42	R	33	1	R	Hayes
1881–83	47th	D	147	R	135	11	R	37	D	37	1	R	Garfield
												R	Arthur
1883–85	48th	D	197	R	118	10	R	38	D	36	2	R	Arthur
1885–87	49th	D	183	R	140	2	R	43	D	34		D	Cleveland
1887–89	50th	D	169	R	152	4	R	39	D	37		D	Cleveland
1889–91	51st	R	166	D	159		R	39	D	37		R	B. Harrison
1891–93	52nd	D	235	R	88	9	R	47	D	39	2	R	B. Harrison
1893–95	53rd	D	218	R	127	11	D	44	R	38	3	D	Cleveland
1895–97	54th	R	244	D	105	7	R	43	D	39	6	D	Cleveland
1897–99	55th	R	204	D	113	40	R	47	D	34	7	R	McKinley
1899–1901	56th	R	185	D	163	9	R	53	D	26	8	R	McKinley
1901–03	57th	R	197	D	151	9	R	55	D	31	4	R	McKinley
												R	T. Roosevelt
1903–05	58th	R	208	D	178		R	57	D	33		R	T. Roosevelt
1905–07	59th	R	250	D	136		R	57	D	33		R	T. Roosevelt
1907–09	60th	R	222	D	164		R	61	D	31		R	T. Roosevelt
1909–11	61st	R	219	D	172		R	61	D	32		R	Taft
1911–13	62nd	D	228	R	161	1	R	51	D	41		R	Taft
1913–15	63rd	D	291	R	127	17	D	51	R	44	1	D	Wilson
1915–17	64th	D	230	R	196	9	D	56	R	40		D	Wilson
1917–19	65th	D	216	R	210	6	D	53	R	42		D	Wilson
1919–21	66th	R	240	D	190	3	R	49	D	47		D	Wilson
1921–23	67th	R	301	D	131	1	R	59	D	37		R	Harding
1923–25	68th	R	225	D	205	5	R	51	D	43	2	R	Coolidge
1925–27	69th	R	247	D	183	4	R	56	D	39	1	R	Coolidge
1927–29	70th	R	237	D	195	3	R	49	D	46	1	R	Coolidge
1929–31	71st	R	267	D	167	1	R	56	D	39	1	R	Hoover
1931–33	72nd	D	220	R	214	1	R	48	D	47	1	R	Hoover
1933–35	73rd	D	310	R	117	5	D	60	R	35	1	D	F. Roosevelt
1935–37	74th	D	319	R	103	10	D	69	R	25	2	D	F. Roosevelt
1937–39	75th	D	331	R	89	13	D	76	R	16	4	D	F. Roosevelt
1939–41	76th	D	261	R	164	4	D	69	R	23	4	D	F. Roosevelt
1941–43	77th	D	268	R	162	5	D	66	R	28	2	D	F. Roosevelt
1943–45	78th	D	218	R	208	4	D	58	R	37	1	D	F. Roosevelt

Party Strength in Congress (continued)

Period	Congress	House Majority Party		House Minority Party		Others	Senate Majority Party		Senate Minority Party		Others	Party of President	
1945–47	79th	D	242	R	190	2	D	56	R	38	1	D	Truman
1947–49	80th	R	245	D	188	1	R	51	D	45		D	Truman
1949–51	81st	D	263	R	171	1	D	54	R	42		D	Truman
1951–53	82nd	D	234	R	199	1	D	49	R	47		D	Truman
1953–55	83rd	R	221	D	211	1	R	48	D	47	1	R	Eisenhower
1955–57	84th	D	232	R	203		D	48	R	47	1	R	Eisenhower
1957–59	85th	D	233	R	200		D	49	R	47		R	Eisenhower
1959–61	86th	D	284	R	153		D	65	R	35		R	Eisenhower
1961–63	87th	D	263	R	174		D	65	R	35		D	Kennedy
1963–65	88th	D	258	R	117		D	67	R	33		D	Kennedy
												D	L. Johnson
1965–67	89th	D	295	R	140		D	68	R	32		D	L. Johnson
1967–69	90th	D	246	R	187		D	64	R	36		D	L. Johnson
1969–71	91st	D	245	R	189		D	57	R	43		R	Nixon
1971–73	92nd	D	254	R	180		D	54	R	44	2	R	Nixon
1973–75	93rd	D	239	R	192	1	D	56	R	42	2	R	Nixon
1975–77	94th	D	291	R	144		D	60	R	37	3	R	Ford
1977–79	95th	D	292	R	143		D	61	R	38	1	D	Carter
1979–81	96th	D	276	R	157		D	58	R	41	1	D	Carter
1981–83	97th	D	243	R	192		R	53	D	46	1	R	Reagan
1983–85	98th	D	267	R	168		R	55	D	45		R	Reagan
1985–87	99th	D	253	R	182		R	53	D	47		R	Reagan
1987–89	100th	D	258	R	177		D	55	R	45		R	Reagan
1989–91	101st	D	259	R	174		D	54	R	46		R	Bush
1991–93	102nd	D	267	R	167	1	D	56	R	44		R	Bush
1993–95	103rd	D	258	R	176	1	D	56	R	44		D	Clinton
1995–97	104th	R	230	D	204	1	R	52	D	48		D	Clinton
1997–99	105th	R	227	D	207	1	R	55	D	45		D	Clinton

AD = Administration; AM = Anti-Masonic; C = Coalition; D = Democratic; DR = Democratic-Republican; F = Federalist; J = Jacksonian; NR = National Republican; Op = Opposition; R = Republican; U = Unionist; W = Whig. Figures are for the beginning of first session of each Congress, except the 93rd, which are for the beginning of the second session.

Justices of the Supreme Court

	Term of Service	Years of Service	Life Span		Term of Service	Years of Service	Life Span
John Jay	1789–1795	5	1745–1829	Ward Hunt	1873–1882	9	1810–1886
John Rutledge	1789–1791	1	1739–1800	*Morrison R. Waite*	1874–1888	14	1816–1888
William Cushing	1789–1810	20	1732–1810	John M. Harlan	1877–1911	34	1833–1911
James Wilson	1789–1798	8	1742–1798	William B. Woods	1880–1887	7	1824–1887
John Blair	1789–1796	6	1732–1800	Stanley Mathews	1881–1889	7	1824–1889
Robert H. Harrison	1789–1790	—	1745–1790	Horace Gray	1882–1902	20	1828–1902
James Iredell	1790–1799	9	1951–1799	Samuel Blatchford	1882–1893	11	1820–1893
Thomas Johnson	1791–1793	1	1732–1819	Lucius Q. C. Lamar	1888–1893	5	1825–1893
William Paterson	1793–1806	13	1745–1806	*Melville W. Fuller*	1888–1910	21	1833–1910
John Rutledge*	1795	—	1739–1800	David J. Brewer	1890–1910	20	1837–1910
Samuel Chase	1796–1811	15	1741–1811	Henry B. Brown	1890–1906	16	1836–1913
Oliver Ellsworth	1796–1800	4	1745–1807	George Shiras, Jr.	1892–1903	10	1832–1924
Bushrod Washington	1798–1829	31	1762–1829	Howell E. Jackson	1893–1895	2	1832–1895
Alfred Moore	1799–1804	4	1755–1810	Edward D. White	1894–1910	16	1845–1921
John Marshall	1801–1835	34	1755–1835	Rufus W. Peckham	1895–1909	14	1838–1909
William Johnson	1804–1834	30	1771–1834	Joseph McKenna	1898–1925	26	1843–1926
H. Brockholst Livingston	1806–1823	16	1757–1823	Oliver W. Holmes	1902–1932	30	1841–1935
Thomas Todd	1807–1826	18	1765–1826	William D. Day	1903–1922	19	1849–1923
Joseph Story	1811–1845	33	1779–1845	William H. Moody	1906–1910	3	1853–1917
Gabriel Duval	1811–1835	24	1752–1844	Horace H. Lurton	1910–1914	4	1844–1914
Smith Thompson	1823–1843	20	1768–1843	Charles E. Hughes	1910–1916	5	1862–1948
Robert Trimble	1826–1828	2	1777–1828	Willis Van Devanter	1911–1937	26	1859–1941
John McLean	1829–1861	32	1785–1861	Joseph R. Lamar	1911–1916	5	1857–1916
Henry Baldwin	1830–1844	14	1780–1844	*Edward D. White*	1910–1921	11	1845–1921
James M. Wayne	1835–1867	32	1790–1867	Mahlon Pitney	1912–1922	10	1858–1924
Roger B. Taney	1836–1864	28	1777–1864	James C. McReynolds	1914–1941	26	1862–1946
Philip P. Barbour	1836–1841	4	1783–1841	Louis D. Brandeis	1916–1939	22	1856–1941
John Catron	1837–1865	28	1786–1865	John H. Clarke	1916–1922	6	1857–1945
John McKinley	1837–1852	15	1780–1852	*William H. Taft*	1921–1930	8	1857–1930
Peter V. Daniel	1841–1860	19	1784–1860	George Sutherland	1922–1938	15	1862–1942
Samuel Nelson	1845–1872	27	1792–1873	Pierce Butler	1922–1939	16	1866–1939
Levi Woodbury	1845–1851	5	1789–1851	Edward T. Sanford	1923–1930	7	1865–1930
Robert C. Grier	1846–1870	23	1794–1870	Harlan F. Stone	1925–1941	16	1872–1946
Benjamin R. Curtis	1851–1857	6	1809–1874	*Charles E. Hughes*	1930–1941	11	1862–1948
John A. Campbell	1853–1861	8	1811–1889	Owen J. Roberts	1930–1945	15	1875–1955
Nathan Clifford	1858–1881	23	1803–1881	Benjamin N. Cardozo	1932–1938	6	1870–1938
Noah H. Swayne	1862–1881	18	1804–1884	Hugo L. Black	1937–1971	34	1886–1971
Samuel F. Miller	1862–1890	28	1816–1890	Stanley F. Reed	1938–1957	19	1884–1980
David Davis	1862–1877	14	1815–1886	Felix Frankfurter	1939–1962	23	1882–1965
Stephen J. Field	1863–1897	34	1816–1899	William O. Douglas	1939–1975	36	1898–1980
Salmon P. Chase	1864–1873	8	1808–1873	Frank Murphy	1940–1949	9	1890–1949
William Strong	1870–1880	10	1808–1895	*Harlan F. Stone*	1941–1946	5	1872–1946
Joseph P. Bradley	1870–1892	22	1813–1892	James F. Byrnes	1941–1942	1	1879–1972

Justices of the Supreme Court (continued)

	Term of Service	Years of Service	Life Span		Term of Service	Years of Service	Life Span
Robert H. Jackson	1941–1954	13	1892–1954	Thurgood Marshall	1967–1991	24	1908–1993
Wiley B. Rutledge	1943–1949	6	1894–1949	*Warren C. Burger*	1969–1986	17	1907–1995
Harold H. Burton	1945–1958	13	1888–1964	Harry A. Blackmun	1970–1994	24	1908–1998
Fred M. Vinson	1946–1953	7	1890–1953	Lewis F. Powell, Jr.	1972–1987	15	1907–1998
Tom C. Clark	1949–1967	18	1899–1977	*William H. Rehnquist*	1972–	—	1924–
Sherman Minton	1949–1956	7	1890–1965	John P. Stevens III	1975–	—	1920–
Earl Warren	1953–1969	16	1891–1974	Sandra Day O'Connor	1981–	—	1930–
John Marshall Harlan	1955–1971	16	1899–1971	Antonin Scalia	1986–	—	1936–
William J. Brennan, Jr.	1956–1990	34	1906–1977	Anthony M. Kennedy	1988–	—	1936–
Charles E. Whittaker	1957–1962	5	1901–1973	David H. Souter	1990–	—	1939–
Potter Stewart	1958–1981	23	1915–1985	Clarence Thomas	1991–	—	1948–
Byron R. White	1962–1993	31	1917–	Ruth Bader Ginsburg	1993–	—	1933–
Arthur J. Goldberg	1962–1965	3	1908–1990	Stephen Breyer	1994–	—	1938–
Abe Fortas	1965–1969	4	1910–1982				

*Appointed and served one term, but not confirmed by the Senate.

Note: Chief justices are in italics.

Index